D1372690

Belize

Mara Vorhees
Joshua Samuel Brown

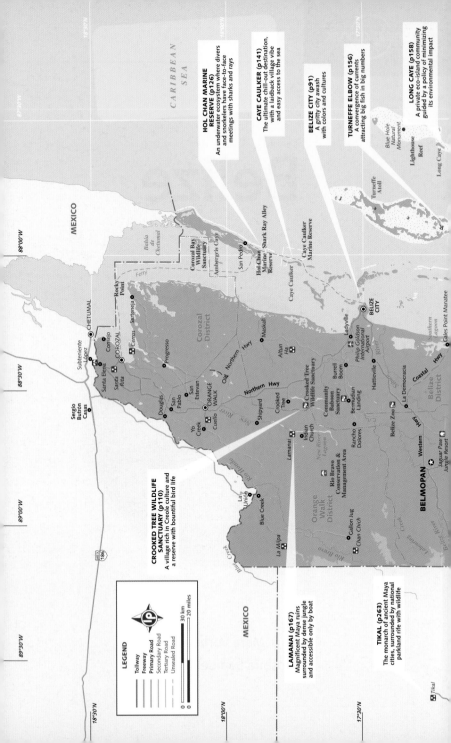

HOL CHAN MARINE RESERVE (p126)
An underwater ecosystem where divers and snorkelers have face-to-face meetings with sharks and rays

CAYE CAULKER (p141)
The ultimate chill-out destination, with a laidback village vibe and easy access to the sea

BELIZE CITY (p91)
A gritty city awash with colors and cultures

TURNEFFE ELBOW (p156)
A convergence of currents attracting big fish in big numbers

LONG CAYE (p158)
A private eco-island community guided by a policy of minimizing its environmental impact

CROOKED TREE WILDLIFE SANCTUARY (p110)
A village rich in Creole culture and a reserve with bountiful bird life

LAMANAI (p167)
Magnificent Maya ruins surrounded by dense jungle and accessible only by boat

TIKAL (p263)
The monarch of ancient Maya cities, surrounded by national parkland rife with wildlife

CARIBBEAN SEA

MEXICO

LEGEND

Tollway
Freeway
Primary Road
Secondary Road
Tertiary Road
Unsealed Road

0   30 km
0   20 miles

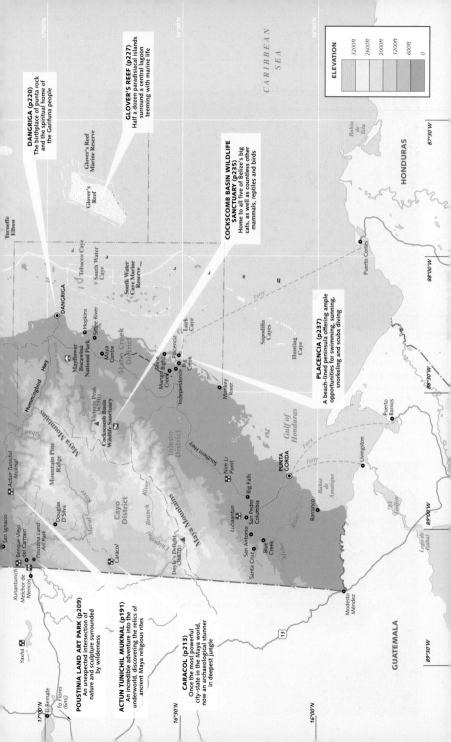

DANGRIGA (p220)
The birthplace of punta rock and the spiritual home of the Garifuna people

GLOVER'S REEF (p227)
Half a dozen paradisiacal islands surround a central lagoon teeming with marine life

COCKSCOMB BASIN WILDLIFE SANCTUARY (p235)
Home to all five of Belize's big cats, as well as countless other mammals, reptiles and birds

PLACENCIA (p237)
A beach-lined peninsula offering ample opportunities for swimming, sunning, snorkeling and scuba diving

POUSTINIA LAND ART PARK (p209)
An unexpected intersection of nature and sculpture surrounded by wilderness

ACTUN TUNICHIL MUKNAL (p191)
An incredible adventure into the underworld, discovering the relics of ancient Maya religious rites

CARACOL (p213)
Once the most powerful city-state in the Maya world, now an archaeological stunner in deepest jungle

ELEVATION

3200ft
2600ft
2000ft
1200ft
600ft
0

CARIBBEAN SEA

HONDURAS

GUATEMALA

On the Road

MARA VORHEES Coordinating Author

Polly-O is the resident parrot at the Leeside Rooms (p150) on Caye Caulker. He is the most talkative parrot I have ever met. During my stint as Polly-O's downstairs neighbor, I would often hear him imitating the cat, imitating the telephone and calling out 'Tom?' for his absent owner. Polly-O always seemed ecstatic when perched on my shoulder, especially if I was trying to have a conversation. As soon as I opened my mouth, he would start jabbering away (loudly, in my ear). This never ceased to crack me up, but it usually ended the conversation pretty quickly.

JOSHUA SAMUEL BROWN It took seven seconds to descend from the platform into Fresh Water Creek via zip-line, seven seconds of wondering if the creek was indeed as '100% crocodile free' as I'd been promised. I was, after all, in a park called Crocodile Isle (p228), a crocodile sanctuary run by an Australian crocodile wrangler named 'Croc.' With all this crocodile mojo floating around, was it irrational of me to find myself concerned about what might live in the river? Would I be the first Lonely Planet author eaten on assignment? And would I taste like chicken?

For full author biographies see p306

BOUNDLESS BELIZE

Come to Belize for action and adventure, to mount seemingly insurmountable temples and to dive to the ocean's darkest depths, to feel the sticky heat of the jungle and the salty air of the sea. Come to Belize to discover the enigmatic Maya, to unravel the mysteries of a past civilization and to meet – in person – its modern-day successors. Come for the country's vibrancy and diversity, to witness the patchwork of cultures and colors that comprise modern Belize.

Under the Sea

Just off the coast of Belize, 80 miles of nearly unbroken barrier reef make the country one of the world's superlative spots for diving and snorkeling. Life under the sea is dramatic and diverse, from the fantastical coral formations and the kaleidoscopic fish that feed there, to the massive (and sometimes menacing) creatures that lurk in deeper waters.

① True Blue

The sheer walls of the Blue Hole National Monument (p157) drop more than 400 feet into the ocean depths. The wall is decorated with a dense forest of stalactites and stalagmites from times past.

② Schools Rule

The convergence of currents at Turneffe Elbow (p156) attracts huge congregations of cubera snappers, horse eye jacks, Atlantic spadefish, reef sharks and king mackerel. Peer into deeper cracks and canyons to catch a glimpse of some gigantic grouper.

③ Shark Park

Fishers always came to Shark Ray Alley (p126) to clean their catch. Their discards would attract hungry nurse sharks and stingrays. These predators have long become accustomed to boats, so they don't swim away from snorkelers.

④ Coral Arrangements

Half Moon Caye Wall (p157) is adorned with a fantastic variety of coral formations along the wall, within its canyons and inside the swimthroughs. Keep a lookout for a field of garden eels found on the sand flats near the wall.

⑤ See a Manatee

As many as 30 West Indian manatees inhabit the shallow waters around Swallow Caye (p144), now designated a marine wildlife sanctuary. Patient observers watching from the boat will see these gentle giants surfacing for air, then diving back down to their seagrass feast.

Skimming the Surface

With 240 miles of coastline and a network of inland waterways, Belize beckons travelers who are into water sports. Inland rivers flow through tropical forests and captivating caves, providing an irresistible environment for river-tubing, cave-tubing, canoeing and kayaking.

❶ River-tubing

Cool your body and relax your mind as you float down the lazy Mopan River from San José Succotz in an inner tube (p206). Watch for birds and other animals while the current carries you through the jungle to your final destination at Clarissa Falls.

❷ Fishing

San Pedro is fast becoming the base for anglers drawn to the flats off the Northern Cayes (p128), a prime spot to pull off a 'Grand Slam' – reeling in a permit, tarpon and bonefish in one outing.

❸ Windsurfing & Kitesurfing

A brisk breeze is almost always blowing (especially between January and June), but the waters off of Caye Caulker (p147) are protected by the reef, creating optimal conditions to cruise across the water while powered by the wind.

❹ Kayaking

The isles of Glover's Reef Atoll (p227) are ideal for island-hopping, which you can do powered only by paddle. Kayak across crystal clear waters, admiring the prolific marine life from above.

❺ Sailing

Key Largo, Montego, Baby why don't we go…to Placencia (p237), where sailing activities await the adventurous. Many operators offer combination snorkeling/sailing expeditions, which are a great way to experience the waves over and under.

❻ Cave-tubing

A distinctly Belizean activity, cave-tubing at Cave's Branch (p219) combines the mystery of spelunking with the cool (in temperature and fun) adventure of river-rafting. As a lengthy walk is involved (how do you think you get to the top of the river?), go with a guide who knows the jungle.

A Cultural Tapestry

Originally inhabited by indigenous Maya, Belize was harassed by Spanish conquistadors, settled by British pirates and built by African slaves. Latterly, Belize has become a safe haven for Mestizos, Mennonites, Chinese and not a few North Americans seeking a better way of life.

6

1 Mennonite Markets
Spanish Lookout (p192) is a thriving community of Mennonites that is small but disproportionately productive.

2 Maya Handicrafts
On the outskirts of San Antonio village, the five García Sisters (p194) originated the art of slate carving, depicting local wildlife and Maya deities.

3 Maya Medicine
The Maya have long used the richness of the rainforest to cure their ills. The Chaa Creek Rainforest Medicine Trail (p207) identifies 100 endemic plants that are used in traditional Maya and modern medicine.

4 Garifuna Cooking
You'll find Belize's tastiest, most stick-to-your-ribs Garifuna cooking in Dangriga (p220). Though definitely good for the soul, Garifuna cuisine may not be quite so beneficial for the old cholesterol level.

5 Drumming
Craft your own drum with one of Belize's renowned Creole drummers (p116) in Gales Point Manatee, or learn the beats of Garifuna drumming (p230) at Hopkins.

6 Colonial Architecture
Two of the best places in Belize to see beautiful examples of Belize's colonial past are Belize City (p91) and Corozal Town (p172). If you like your walking tours laid back, go for the latter; if you don't mind some urban grit, the former might be for you.

7 Contemporary Crafts
Small in size, the village of Hopkins (p229) has a number of skilled artisans and an abundance of shops opened by locals selling paintings, carvings, and crafts of all sorts.

5

Into the Wild

More than 40% of Belizean territory is protected in the form of national parks, forest reserves and wildlife sanctuaries. That's a lot of room for animals to run wild and birds to fly free. Wildlife-watchers, bird nerds and floral freaks will be amazed by the biodiversity found in little Belize.

① Poustinia Land Art Park

At once nature preserve and art museum, Poustinia (p209) breaks down all barriers between manmade and natural creations. Set in the wilds of the jungle, the sculpture garden is a place where art and nature are allowed interact.

② Mountain Pine Ridge Forest Reserve

In the remote west, the highlands of Maya Mountains are covered with pine forest, an unexpected aberration in the landscape. Big Rock Falls are the impressive waterfalls at Privassion Creek (p212), which rush down the mountainside.

③ Half Moon Caye Bird Sanctuary

Part of the Lighthouse Reef atoll, Half Moon Caye (p158) provides a nesting ground for the rare red-footed booby. Thousands of this otherwise rare water fowl make their homes in the treetops, alongside the magnificent frigate bird and the 98 other species.

④ Belize Botanic Gardens

It's not the wildest place in Belize, but it may be the most verdant. The Belize Botanic Gardens (p207) cover 45 acres, with four different ecosystems, two ponds and an infinite number of plant and bird species.

⑤ Belize Zoo

Humane, earthy and educational, even people philosophically opposed to the very concept of zoos will approve of this combination halfway house and rehabilitation center for injured, orphaned and rescued Belizean jungle animals (p113).

⑥ Cockscomb Basin Wildlife Sanctuary

Coatimundis and kinkajous, otters and peccaries, birds and snakes of all sorts and yes, jaguar as well: Cockscomb Basin Wildlife Sanctuary (p235) is a must-visit for those looking to spend time in Belize's truly wild side.

Maya Mysteries

For almost 3000 years, the ancient Maya civilization flourished in Belize, building towering temples as tributes to their god-like rulers. The remains of these once-mighty city-states are scattered throughout the country. The region's most extensive and thoroughly excavated site, Tikal, lies just across the Guatemalan border.

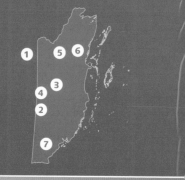

1 Tikal

Historically powerfully and geographically huge, Tikal (p263) is the region's most significant Maya archaeological site. The towering Temple of the Grand Jaguar dominates the expansive Gran Plaza, the centerpiece of the site.

2 Caracol

Once the most powerful kingdom of the Maya world, Caracol (p213) covers a vast, jungle-clad area atop the Vaca Plateau. The centerpiece is the 141ft Caana, or 'Sky Place,' which is still the tallest structure in Belize.

3 Actun Tunichil Muknal

Among the most curious and chilling aspects of ancient Maya culture, the rituals of food offerings, blood-letting and human sacrifice are little understood. But evidence of these sacred rites still remains in situ in caves such as Actun Tunichil Muknal (p191).

4 Xunantunich

Relatively small but easily accessible, Xunantunich (p205) shows off the artistic eye of the ancient Maya. The top of El Castillo is adorned with elaborately carved friezes, which circle the entire structure.

5 Lamanai

Spanning all phases of ancient Maya civilization, the ruins at Lamanai (p167) are known for their stone reliefs, impressive architecture and for their marvelous setting overlooking the New River Lagoon and surrounded by some of Northern Belize's densest jungle.

6 Altun Ha

You've drunk the beer; now visit the ruins that inspired the label that adorns every Belikin bottle from Barranco to Consejo. The most accessible of Belize's ancient ruins, Altun Ha (p106) is also the home to some of the nation's most recognizable icons.

7 Deep South

Not many travelers make it as far as Toledo District, but those who make the trek into the villages and ruins of Belize's Deep South (p250) find the most vibrant corner of modern Maya society living side by side with some of the most ancient and mysterious ruins.

Celebrate Good Times

Local festivals celebrate historic events and contemporary culture with food, music and dancing in the street. Many such celebrations are rooted in specific ethnic enclaves, but these days everybody gets in on the fun.

❶ International Costa Maya Festival

On the streets of San Pedro, participants come from El Salvador, Guatemala, Honduras, Mexico, Costa Rica and Nicaragua to join Belize in celebrating their shared heritage (p131). Traditional food, music and dancing are complemented by nontraditional activities including a bodybuilding competition and a beauty pageant.

❷ Lobsterfest

Normally a bastion of peace and quiet, Caye Caulker celebrates the opening of lobster season with an old-fashioned beach party. The streets are filled with punta drumming, Belikin beer and grilled lobster (p149).

❸ Garifuna Settlement Day

Remembering and celebrating the Garifuna Diaspora, November 19 is the best time to feast on great Garifuna cuisine while listening to amazing drumming lasting day and night. Dangriga is a fantastic place to spend the day (p222), but if you can make it to Barranco (p254) you'll be in for a rare treat indeed.

❹ The Feast of San Luis

From about August 15 to the 25th, the Mopan Maya village of San Antonio (p253) celebrates the beautiful Feast of San Luis, a 10-day harvest festival. Here you'll see the famous Deer Dance of the Mopan people.

Contents

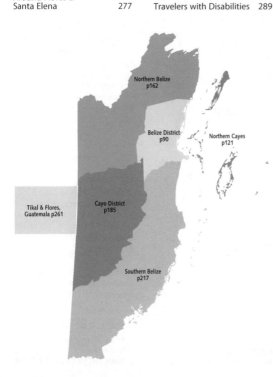

Destination Belize

With one foot planted in the Central American jungles and the other dipped in the Caribbean Sea, Belize blends the best of both worlds.

Offshore, kayakers glide from one sandy, palm-dotted islet to another, while snorkelers swim through translucent seas, gazing at a kaleidoscope of coral, fish, dolphins and turtles. Inland, explorers investigate ruins of ancient civilizations, and birders aim their binoculars at some 570 species. Between national parks, wildlife sanctuaries and marine reserves, more than 40% of the country's area is protected in one form or another, creating a haven for countless creatures of land, sea and sky.

The value of these natural resources is unquantifiable, but Belize attracts more than 850,000 annual visitors eager to climb a Maya temple, spot a toucan, snorkel the reef and otherwise partake of paradise. Tourism is the country's top source of employment and investment. The irony is that it is also the country's biggest environmental threat.

Belize does not yet have the infrastructure to support the massive numbers of tourists that arrive, especially by way of cruise ships. It does not have the resources to truly protect its sanctuaries and reserves and their inhabitants. And it does not have the political will to stop the rampant coastal development, which would mean turning down millions in investment dollars. According to sources such as Tropical Conservation Science, as much as 80% of coastal land has already been sold to foreign interests with the intention of building condos and resorts.

Fortunately, Belizeans are environmentally aware and indefatigably active. Thanks to a progressive populace, Belize offers myriad ways for travelers to tread lightly, from beach resorts powered by solar energy to jungle lodges built from reclaimed hardwoods. Licensed guides not only direct, but also educate their clients – about the fragility of the reef, the medicinal uses of flora and the threats to the jaguar's habitat.

It's never easy to maintain the delicate balance between preserving natural resources and cashing in on economic opportunity. But most Belizeans are proud of their natural heritage and they recognize that the goals of environmental conservation and economic prosperity are not mutually exclusive. This is the enlightened approach that has earned Belize its reputation as a paradigm of ecotourism.

Sub Umbra Florero reads the motto on the Belizean flag. It refers to the mighty mahogany tree, and it means 'Under the shade, I flourish.' The mahogany may not be as prevalent as it once was, but with its loss has come an understanding of its value. Belizeans recognize that their country's greatest asset must be respected and protected, and that tourists have an important role to play.

It's no wonder that Belizeans extend such a warm welcome to travelers. These easy-going people are eager to share – the staggering scenery, the bountiful biodiversity, all that exists in the shade of the mahogany tree.

FAST FACTS

Population: 294,400

Population density:
34 people per sq mile

GDP per person:
BZ$15,600

Inflation: 2.8%

Unemployment rate:
9.4%

Literacy: 77%

HIV prevalence rate: 2.4%

Cruise-ship tourists per annum: 624,530

Other tourists per annum:
251,650

Resident & migratory bird species: 570

Species of hard & soft coral: 110

Native orchid species: 304

Getting Started

Belize has something for everyone. If you are an impulsive adventurer seeking an adrenaline rush, you will find it in Belize. If you prefer to spend quality time with a good book on a sunswept beach, there are a few of those, too.

Despite its variety, Belize is a tiny place; it's relatively easy to get anywhere, even the deepest jungle or the most isolated island. Transport around the country is easy enough, but it can be expensive. Local buses and water taxis travel frequently along the main routes, but as soon as you venture off these primary highways and waterways, you'll have to rent a car, hire a taxi or book a tour. Domestic flights and charters are also useful for reaching the more remote corners.

Accommodations range from bargain-basement cabins, campsites and hammock hotels, all the way up to first-class resorts loaded with luxury. Lodging is abundant and it's usually easy to find someplace to stay when you arrive in town. However, if you have your heart set on staying somewhere in particular, it is wise to book in advance. Plan ahead for the weeks between Christmas and New Year's Day, and before and during Santa Semana (the week preceding Easter Sunday). It is also a good idea to book accommodations ahead of time during the school vacation in January and February.

For more information, see Climate Charts (p281).

Note that because Belize has a high standard of living, prices here tend to be a good deal higher than those of other Central American nations.

WHEN TO GO

In Belize the high season for tourists corresponds roughly with the dry season: December to May. The shoulder months – especially December – receive a fair amount of rain, but not enough to scare away the multitudes of travelers who want to spend their holidays in the tropics. Most hotels and resorts are more expensive during this period (high-season rates are quoted throughout this book).

The biggest influx of tourists comes between December 15 and January 15, and during the weeks around Easter. Some hotels and resorts, especially top-end accommodations, charge extra-high prices during these peak periods. If you're using top-end or some midrange accommodations, you'll certainly save money by avoiding these seasons. See p279 for more on accommodations in Belize.

The rainy season runs from June to November. The early months, especially May and June, are actually a wonderful time to travel to Belize: you can avoid the tourist bustle and lodging is slightly cheaper. The only ownside is

---

DON'T LEAVE HOME WITHOUT...

- Checking the latest visa situation (p289) and government travel advisories (p283)
- Any necessary immunizations or medications (see p299)
- Insect repellent containing DEET
- Pepto-Bismol or an anti-diarrheal, in case you get a bad dose of the trots
- A flashlight for those dark Belizean streets, stairs and caves.
- Waterproof sunscreen and sun hat, so you don't cook in the tropical sun
- Pocket binoculars
- An underwater camera

SUPERLATIVES

If you want to...

- See the biggest and best selection of wildlife – visit the **Belize Zoo** (p113)
- Watch the fieriest sunset – sit on the back dock on **Caye Caulker** (p141)
- Dive the deepest (and darkest) wall – take on the **Blue Hole** (p157)
- Explore the deepest (and darkest) cave – descend into **Actun Tunichil Muknal** (p191) in Cayo District
- Admire the wildest sculpture and art – don't miss **Poustinia Land Art Park** (p209) near Benque Viejo del Carmen
- Sleep in the sweetest camping spot – pitch your tent at **Backpacker's Paradise** (p180) in Sarteneja, Corozal District
- Eat the tangiest ceviche – dine at **Cerros Beach Inn** (p179) in Corozal District
- Stay at the chillest budget guesthouse – relax at the **Sea Breeze Hotel** (p175) in Corozal
- Lay your head at the quirkiest resort – make a reservation at **Singing Sands** (p243) on Placencia Peninsula
- Leave the lightest environmental footprint – visit the **Maya Mountain Research Farm** (p253) in Toledo
- Climb the highest temple – tackle Templo IV at **Tikal** (p267)

---

that it's outside the lobster season, so you'll have to forego at least one local specialty. Rivers start to swell and dirt roads get muddy. Some more remote roads may not be accessible to public transportation. With too much rain, some of the caves such as Actun Tunichil Muknal (p191) are dangerous and therefore closed to the public. Southern Belize is especially precarious during the rainy season; this relatively remote region receives two to three times as much rain as the rest of the country.

COSTS & MONEY

Travel costs are significantly higher here than in most Central American countries, but cheaper than in the USA or Europe. If you're arriving from inexpensive Central American nations such as Honduras or Guatemala, get ready to bust that wallet wide open. High taxes, many imports and the fact that much of its tourism industry is geared to North Americans on fairly short vacations are the factors that keep prices high.

Prices in Belize are frequently listed in US dollars, especially at upmarket hotels, where you can expect to pay international prices. Most types of tours are charged in US dollars. In fact, US dollars are widely accepted, but the standard unit of currency is still the Belizean dollar (BZ$). The exchange rate has hovered around US$1=BZ$2 for years. Prices in this book are quoted in BZ$ and include all taxes and service charges. See p286 for more on Belizean money matters.

Shoestring travelers can survive on BZ$60 to BZ$80 a day, covering just the basics of food, lodging and public transportation. The cheapest hotels start at about BZ$20 per person for a bed, four walls and shared bathroom. Better rooms with private bathrooms start at roughly BZ$40, depending on the area. It is possible to eat cheaply at the stand-up snack bars and markets and fill up for BZ$20 or less.

Midrange budgeters can travel comfortably on BZ$200 to BZ$300 per person per day. Hotels in this category offer very good value, and double rooms come with comfortable beds, private bathroom, hot water (most of the

HOW MUCH?

Papaya smoothie: BZ$6

Water taxi to San Pedro: BZ$20

Grilled spinytail lobster: BZ$30

Hardwood cutting board: BZ$45

Half-day snorkel trip: BZ$45

time) and – usually – some stylish details. Expect to pay anywhere between BZ$150 and BZ$200 per night. Some hotels in this price range also have shared or private kitchenettes, which is a great option for families. A good two- or three-course meal with a couple of drinks in a pleasant restaurant will average BZ$30 to BZ$50 (more if you have lobster).

Top-end visitors will find a good selection of restaurants and hotels in the touristy towns and within some of the major resorts. Luxurious beachside lodges and boutique hotels cost anywhere from BZ$300 – and all the way up – and offer meals that begin at BZ$50.

Traveling by public bus is dirt cheap, but car hire, taxis, boats and hotel transfers are not. Expect a day's auto rental to cost between BZ$150 and BZ$200. Tours and excursions mostly run from BZ$100 to BZ$200 per person for a day (more for diving trips).

Lodging prices are generally higher in the dry season (December to May), and highest during holiday periods (between Christmas and New Year and during Semana Santa). During slower seasons, most hotels are eager for your business, so you can try to negotiate a lower rate.

Ambergris Caye is definitely the most expensive place in the country. Budget travelers can make their money last longer by hanging out in places like Caye Caulker and San Ignacio.

'To date, the single biggest environment-related issue of the 21st century for Belize is cruise-ship tourism'

TRAVELING RESPONSIBLY

Belize has one of the most eco-conscious populaces you'll find anywhere on the planet. Here you'll meet some of the pioneers of the sustainable tourism movement. Today more than 40% of the national territory is under official protection.

The conservation fee of BZ$7.50 that every visitor pays when leaving Belize goes to the **Protected Areas Conservation Trust** (PACT; www.pactbelize.org), which helps provide funding for protected areas. Besides paying the obligatory fee, there are other simple steps that travelers can take to minimize their impact:

- Don't remove coral or shells from the sea, and avoid purchasing items made from turtle shell or coral.
- Don't swim with manatees or attempt to piggyback sea turtles.
- Use air-con judiciously. It's expensive and a strain on local energy reserves.
- In the jungle, stay on trails to avoid trampling fragile plants. Never feed wild animals, including those in the sea.
- Do not order lobster, crab or fresh shrimp in their closed seasons (lobster February 15 to June 14; conch July 1 to September 30; shrimp April 15 to August 14).
- Don't fish in protected areas and always check the seasons and other regulations concerning the place and species that you're planning to fish. Catch-and-release is obligatory for some species.
- Dispose of trash properly, even if it means carrying it with you until you find a trash bin.
- For tips on responsible diving and snorkeling, see p73.

Getting There & Away

To date, the single biggest environment-related issue of the 21st century for Belize is cruise-ship tourism. Every year, cruise liners anchoring off Belize City bring more than 600,000 passengers into the country (that's two times the population of the country itself). Although the excursions made by these visitors are highly lucrative, many small-scale tour operators and officials fear that the cruisers could potentially be a threat to Belizean tourism.

Most cruise-ship passengers are in the country for less than a day, making it next to impossible for them to experience the country in any substantive way. Furthermore, such massive numbers are likely to inflict environmental damage, whether it's by harming the reef, trampling through the rainforest or simply overtaxing the infrastructure. Finally, many ecologically aware travelers – who would normally spend lots of time (and money) in Belize – may not want to come if they know they will be sharing space with a shipload of day-trippers. So not only do the cruise ship tourists have the potential to damage the archaeological and natural sites of Belize; they could also seriously impair Belize's image as an environmentally responsible country.

When planning your trip to Belize, keep in mind that you will see more, do more and learn more if you spend some time actually exploring beautiful Belize; as a bonus, the country will also benefit more from your visit. If you really want to investigate the concept of slow travel, consider overland (or water) travel via Mexico, Honduras or Guatemala. See p292 for details.

Sleeping & Eating

Many resorts and restaurants throughout Belize are taking steps to minimize their environmental impact, by recycling and composting, managing wastewater, utilizing alternative power sources, growing their own organic ingredients and working with local community and environmental organizations. Unfortunately, Belize does not have any sort of eco-certification program to give a stamp of approval to businesses that are fulfilling these goals. We have done some on-the-ground research, creating a 'GreenDex' of Belizean businesses that are taking steps to implement environmentally sound practices (see p316). You can help by patronizing these businesses, as well as doing your own research and providing feedback. For more suggestions, see the 'Green World' itinerary, p29.

Cultural Awareness

Traveling responsibly means being culturally aware as well as minimizing environmental impact; in short, showing respect for the country and cultures you are visiting. See the boxed text (p40) for some tips.

Giving Back to Belize

One of the best ways to travel responsibly is to be proactive about it, spending some time doing volunteer work. See p68 for a list of NGOs that are active in Belize and p289 for other ideas about volunteering in Belize.

'The Last Flight of the Scarlet Macaw recounts the story of Sharon Matola and her fight against the construction of the Chalillo Dam'

TRAVEL LITERATURE

Belizean character Emory King wrote *Hey Dad, This is Belize* and *I Spent it All in Belize*. They are not exactly travel books, but more collections of amusing and insightful articles on the many quirks of a country that King has been chronicling since he bumped into it (after being shipwrecked) one night in 1953.

Bruce Barcott is a contributing editor for *Outside* magazine and an author. His latest book, *The Last Flight of the Scarlet Macaw: One Woman's Fight to Save the World's Most Beautiful Bird*, is a compelling story of Belizean culture, society and politics. He recounts with unflinching honesty the story of Sharon Matola (local celebrity and founder of the Belize Zoo) and her fight against the construction of the Chalillo Dam on the Macal River.

If your inner adventurer dreams of packing up and moving to paradise, take along *Belize Survivor,* by Nancy Koerner. The jungle and the sea are the backdrop for the author's harrowing tale of betrayal, courage and survival.

Richard Timothy Conroy's *Our Man in Belize* is a fun, engaging memoir of his stint as US vice-consul to the impoverished British Honduras of the early 1960s, a period marked by the devastating Hurricane Hattie.

In *Following Mateo,* Jesuit Service Corp Volunteer Tom Molanphy writes of his two years in Southern Belize and his deepening friendship with a wise village elder.

Thor Janson's *Belize: Land of the Free by the Carib Sea* captures Belize in pictures – all the color of its forests, islands, wildlife, festivals and ruins, and the smiles of its people.

Ronald Wright's *Time Among the Maya* is an acutely observed account of travels through Belize, Guatemala and Mexico in the troubled 1980s, delving into the past and present of the Maya and the profound importance they attach to their calendar and the passing of time. Peter Canby also focuses on Maya culture in his insightful 1990s book *The Heart of the Sky: Travels Among the Maya,* which has one chapter on Belize.

INTERNET RESOURCES

Belize (www.travelbelize.org) The Belize Tourism Board's site is a fine place to start for almost any Belize-related travel topic.

Belize by Naturalight (www.belizenet.com) This Belize portal has hosts of travel and business links.

Belize Forums (www.belizeforum.com) Great message board and forum discussing just about everything under the Belizean sun.

BelizeNews.com (www.belizenews.com) Links to all 18 of the country's media outlets, including newspapers, magazines and TV stations.

Government of Belize (www.governmentofbelize.gov.bz) Official site of the Belizean government. Includes political information, press releases and a general country overview.

Lonely Planet (www.lonelyplanet.com) Succinct summaries on Belize travel, the popular Thorn Tree travel forum and travel news.

Toucan Trail (www.toucantrail.com) A network of small hotels that offer rooms for budget travelers.

Itineraries
CLASSIC ROUTES

NORTHERN LIGHTS   One Week/Northern Cayes to Lamanai

If you only have a week to spare, there is no sense moving around too much. From your base on one of the **Northern Cayes** (p120), you have access to an impressive array of activities on land and sea.

Choose **Caye Caulker** (p141) or **San Pedro** (p123), as they are closest to the mainland. (We prefer Caye Caulker – not only for its easy-going vibe, but also for its easy access to Belize City, which is only 45 minutes away by water taxi.) From here, you can take snorkel or dive trips to **Turneffe Atoll** (p156) and **Lighthouse Reef** (p157), the latter home to no sense the amazing **Blue Hole** (p157).

But you can also use either of these islands as a base for day trips to the mainland. Spend a day in the Belize District to spy on birds at **Crooked Tree Wildlife Sanctuary** (p110) or to see the Maya ruins at **Altun Ha** (p106).

It's also an easy trip to eastern Cayo District, where you can go cave-tubing in the **Nohoch Che'en Caves Branch Archaeological Reserve** (p186), **zip-lining** (p187) through the forest canopy or **horseback riding** (p187) along groomed trails. With an early departure, you can go north to **Lamanai** (p167), enjoying a peaceful boat ride on the New River along the way.

You'll cover about 350 miles if you stay on Caye Caulker and take two trips to the mainland and two trips to the outer atolls. Add an extra day and 200 miles if you want to make the long trip to Lamanai.

SURF & TURF
Two Weeks/San Pedro to San Ignacio

This traditional Belize sampler gives you the best of both worlds – a taste of the jungle and a glimpse of the sea – all within your two weeks of vacation time.

Start your trip at holiday central: **San Pedro** (p123) on Ambergris Caye. Soak up the sun on the beaches, swim from the docks, snorkel or dive among coral gardens, get up close and personal with the sharks and stingrays of **Shark Ray Alley** (p131), indulge in gourmet meals and dance the night away. Use San Pedro as your launching pad for dives at **Blue Hole** (p157) and other atoll sites.

After a week of sun and fun, make your way to dry land. Take the water taxi or fly to **Belize City** (p91), where you can visit the Museum of Belize and Government House if you are curious about the country's history. Then head out along the Western Hwy, stopping to visit the recovering and rescued animals at the **Belize Zoo** (p113).

Continue on to the Wild West of Belize, the **Cayo District** (p183). Base yourself at a luxurious lodge on **Chial Road** (p207) or **Crysto Rey Road** (p194). Or, for slimmer budgets, pick a hotel in **San Ignacio** (p199). From here, you can explore caves loaded with ancient remains, such as **Actun Tunichil Muknal** (p191), travel by canoe or river-tube along jungle rivers, dip beneath the waterfalls of the **Mountain Pine Ridge** (p211) and explore Belize's greatest Maya site, **Caracol** (p213).

If you have the time and inclination, venture for a day or more over the border into Guatemala, where you can visit the region's most significant Maya archaeological site at **Tikal** (p263).

You'll travel around 500 miles on water and land on this great 'surf-and-turf' trip, the best recipe for introducing yourself to Belize's multifarious attractions. You'll need your swimsuit, sunglasses and sun hat for the islands, your binoculars and insect repellent for the jungle.

SOUTHERN SENSATIONS   Three Weeks/Belize City to Punta Gorda

Southern Belize – including Stan Creek and Toledo Districts – covers a vast expanse. With miles of coastline and massive swathes of protected land – not to mention thriving enclaves of Garifuna and Maya culture – the region could easily absorb your entire vacation.

From **Belize City** (p91) head westward just as far as the start of the beautiful Hummingbird Hwy, which carries you across the thickly forested northern foothills of the Maya Mountains. Stop at **Ian Anderson's Jungle Lodge** (p219) for some cave exploration, jungle expeditions and abseiling down bottomless sinkholes.

Hang out in the Garifuna capital **Dangriga** (p220) or the nearby coastal village of **Hopkins** (p229) to absorb some Garifuna rhythms. From here, you can make trips out to watch manatees at **Gales Point Manatee** (p115) and hike the beautiful jungle trails at **Mayflower Bocawina National Park** (p229) or **Cockscomb Basin Wildlife Sanctuary** (p235).

Head seaward to indulge your tropical-island fantasies at **Tobacco Caye** (p226) or **South Water Caye** (p226). From nearby **Sittee River** (p234) you can journey to **Glover's Reef** (p227), the most southerly and most complete of Belize's three offshore atolls.

Continue south to **Placencia** (p237) to enjoy lovely sandy beaches, lively bars, wide-ranging accommodation options and whatever water sports you like.

The southernmost town in Belize, **Punta Gorda** (p245) has yet to see tourism on a serious scale, which is part of its appeal. From here, head out for a day or two on the equally unspoiled **Sapodilla Cayes** (p247). Punta Gorda is also a good base to explore the lagoons, caves, waterfalls, forests, ancient Maya archaeological sites and modern Maya villages of the **Deep South** (p250).

Your trip through the Belizean south will carry you 600 or 700 miles on land and water. Give yourself more time to truly soak up the culture, the climate and the complexity of this region that is little known and less traveled.

ISLAND HOPPING

A COCKTAIL OF CAYES   Three Weeks/Ambergris Caye to Sapodilla Cayes

Saltwater junkies need hardly set foot on mainland soil as they roam from one idyllic sandy island to another. Out on Belize's cayes and atolls you can truly devote yourself to the sun and sea in whatever form takes your fancy – swimming, snorkeling, diving, kayaking, sailing, fishing… Though regular island-to-island transportation is rare, you can (at a price) charter small launches for most hops (see p294 for information on boat services).

Ease your way into island life on **Ambergris Caye** (p123), where comfortable to luxurious lodgings and fine restaurants will pamper you between water activities. Smooth away any lingering symptoms of stress with a few days on **Caye Caulker** (p141). Then head to **Lighthouse Reef** (p157) or **Turneffe Atoll** (p156) for a spell of more remote island life, with as much top-class diving, snorkeling and fishing as you can take. Accommodations range from the eco-retreats on **Long Caye** (p158) to the luxurious lodges of **Blackbird Caye** (p157).

South of Turneffe Atoll, the Central Cayes pop their heads up off the barrier reef. **Tobacco Caye** (p226) houses a cluster of midrange accommodations, while **South Water Caye** (p226) has just three lodges. The most idyllic of Belize's three atolls is even further out. **Glover's Reef** (p227) is home to the only true budget resort on Belize's outer islands, as well as a couple of more expensive places.

Continue by visiting beautiful reef islands such as the **Silk Cayes** (p228). Round off your peregrinations on Belize's southernmost offshore gems, the unspoiled **Sapodilla Cayes** (p247).

If you charter boats and hop directly from island to island, you'll cover around 220 miles in this ramble of Belize's most idyllic offshore spots from north to south. Using more traditional routes – back and forth from Belize City, Dangriga and Placencia – might double your distance and add a couple of days to your time.

TAILORED TRIPS

GREEN WORLD

Ecotourism was practically invented in the Cayo District. Many lodges manage to combine sound environmental policy with sumptuous elements of luxury, including **Pook's Hill Lodge** (p191), **Table Rock Camp & Cabanas** (p195) and all three lodges on **Chial Road** (p207).

In Corozal District, travelers can stay at the artsy, organic **Maya World Guest House** (p175) or at the solar-powered, rainwater-fed **Cerros Beach Inn** (p179).

On the Guatemalan border in the northwestern part of the country, **Chan Chich Lodge** (p171) is one of Belize's original ecolodges. Its 200 sq miles are adjacent to the **Rio Bravo Conservation & Management Area** (p169), and the combined area is one of the country's largest tracts of pristine forest.

Long Caye (p158) – a small privately owned island – has been designated as a sort of eco-village, setting strict standards for anyone who wants to buy property or build on it.

Another eco-island paradise is **Thatch Caye Resort** (p228) on Thatch Caye. Precariously perched on a mangrove island, the place is powered almost exclusively by sun and wind.

Besides the well-known wildlife sanctuary at **Cockscomb Basin** (p235), Stann Creek is home to the equally enticing (though smaller) **Mayflower Bocawina National Park** (p229). Access its miles of hiking trails and prolific wildlife by staying at **Mama Noots Jungle Resort** (p229).

Not many tourists make it to Toledo District. But if you do, you can enjoy hospitality and a clean conscience at **Hickatee Cottages** (p248) in Punta Gorda, or live in the lap of eco-luxury at **Cotton Tree Lodge** (p257), 10 miles south.

Inspired to run a permaculture farm or build a solar energy system yourself? Stop by the **Maya Mountain Research Farm** (p253) to find out how.

KIDS' WORLD

Most kids love the brightly colored tropical fish they'll see while snorkeling at places such as **Laughing Bird Caye** (p228), **Tobacco Caye** (p226) and **Glover's Reef** (p227). Older kids can kayak or even learn to dive in **Placencia** (p237).

If your children tire of sun and surf, head to **KSV Playland** (p132), San Pedro, and let them loose on go-carts, trampolines and table games.

Back on solid ground, head to **Old Belize** (p112) for an introduction to Belizean history and culture in one handy, entertaining package, and to **Belize Zoo** (p113) to see the requisite colorful and furry beasties.

All kids get a charge out of venturing into the dark coolness of an unknown cave. Canoe into **Barton Creek Cave** (p193) or float through in a river-tube at **Nohoch Che'en Caves Branch Archaeological Reserve** (p186).

Ian Anderson's Jungle Lodge (p219) on the Hummingbird Hwy delivers many of Belize's most exciting land adventures in one handy package. It is particularly popular among families with children who are 11 years and over. You can also take children horseback riding at **Banana Bank** (p187), near Belmopan.

MAYA WORLD

Arguably the most spectacular, if not quite the most important, of Belize's many ancient Maya sites is **Lamanai** (p167), for its superb jungle setting beside New River Lagoon and the river trip by which most people approach it. Also in the north of the country, the important Classic Period trading town of **Altun Ha** (p106) is probably one of the most famous sites, as it is featured on Belizean beer labels. Archaeology enthusiasts can hit **Cerros** (p178), once a seaside dependency of Lamanai, and **La Milpa** (p169), a large site in the remote jungles of the Rio Bravo Conservation & Management Area.

Way out west in the jungles near the Guatemalan border, **Caracol** (p213) was the biggest and most powerful ancient city in Belize (bigger than Belize City is today). Also out west, don't miss **Xunantunich** (p205), an impressive hilltop site that once commanded the Belize River valley. Cayo also provides plenty of opportunities to visit the Maya underworld – caves such as **Actun Tunichil Muknal** (p191), **Barton Creek Cave** (p193) or **Che Chem Ha** (p210), where the relics of offerings, sometimes human sacrifices, to the ancient gods have lain undisturbed for centuries.

While you're out west, you might as well pop over the Guatemalan border to visit **Tikal** (p263), the most extensive and most thoroughly excavated site in the region.

Southern Belize was out of the ancient Maya mainstream but still left us **Nim Li Punit** (p253) and **Lubaantun** (p252), two medium-sized centers on fine hilltop sites.

ANIMAL WORLD

The waters of Belize's barrier reef and offshore atolls teem with marine life. Ambergris Caye's **Shark Ray Alley** (p131) and Caye Caulker's **Shark Ray Village** (p145) guarantee close encounters with nurse sharks and stingrays. Awesome whale sharks up to 60ft long frequent **Gladden Spit** (p228) for up to 10 days after the full moon, from March through June.

On the mainland, head to **Crooked Tree Wildlife Sanctuary** (p110) for some of the best birding in the country. Giant jabiru storks congregate here in April and May. Move on to the **Community Baboon Sanctuary** (p108) for surefire encounters with black howler monkeys. Try to get out to **Chan Chich Lodge** (p171) or the **Rio Bravo Conservation & Management Area** (p169), where your chances of seeing coatimundis, peccaries, kinkajous and spider or howler monkeys are among the highest in Belize. Even jaguars are regularly sighted around Chan Chich.

Watch for manatees at **Gales Point Manatee** (p115) and don't miss the **Cockscomb Basin Wildlife Sanctuary** (p235), the world's first jaguar reserve. You're unlikely to see any of the sanctuary's 40 or 50 jaguars or other large mammals in the flesh, but you'll learn a lot about them and probably see jaguar footprints, and their environment is spectacular.

Even if you spend all week in the wilds, make sure you don't leave Belize without visiting the **Belize Zoo** (p113), the only place you are guaranteed to spot a jaguar!

History

FROM LORDLY REALM TO LOST WORLD: ANCIENT MAYA

Belize hosted one of the great Mesoamerican civilizations of ancient times, the Maya. The Maya created vibrant commercial centers, monumental religious temples and exquisite art works. They possessed sophisticated knowledge about their earthly and cosmological environments, much of which they wrote down. The Maya thrived from roughly 2000 BC to AD 1500, before succumbing to domestic decline and alien assault. The stone foundations of their lordly realm became a lost world submerged beneath dense jungle.

The Maya ranged across Central America, from the Yucatán to Honduras, from the Pacific to the Caribbean. They were not ethnically homogenous, but only loosely related, divided by kinship, region and dialect. The different communities sometimes cooperated and often competed with one another, building alliances for trade and warfare.

The name Belize is derived from the Mayan word *'Belix'* which means 'muddy water' and refers to the mouth of the Belize River.

Archaeological findings indicate that Maya settlements in Belize were among the oldest. In the west, Cahal Pech, an important commercial center between the coast and interior, was dated to at least 1200 BC. In the north, majestic Lamanai, a major religious site for over 2000 years, was founded as early as 900 BC. In Belize today, three distinct Maya tribes still exist: the indigenous Mopan in the north; the Yucatec, who migrated from Mexico, also in the north; and, the Kekchi, who migrated from Guatemala, in the west and south.

The Maya were organized into kingdoms, in which social and economic life was an extension of a rigid political hierarchy. At the top were the king – or high lord – and his royal family, followed by an elite stratum of priests, warriors and scribes; next came economically valued artisans and traders; and finally, holding it all up were subsistence farmers and servant workers. The system rested on a cultural belief that the high lord had some influence with the powerful and dark gods of the underworld, who sometimes took the form of a jaguar when intervening in human affairs. This view was reinforced through the ruling elite's elaborately staged power displays, a temple theater of awe.

Joyce Kelly's *An Archaeological Guide to Northern Central America* offers the best descriptions of the Maya sites of Belize, along with those in Guatemala and Mexico.

Even before the germ-ridden Europeans arrived, the cultural underpinnings of Maya society were already coming undone. A prolonged drought had caused severe economic hardship, leaving the impression that the kings and priests had somehow lost their supernatural touch. It was left to the Spanish, however, to officially cancel the show.

Possibly the most impressive of the Maya kingdoms in Belize was at Caracol (p213), in the western Pine Ridge Mountains. At its height, in the 6th and 7th centuries, Caracol was a major urban metropolis, with over

TIMELINE

2000 BC–AD 250	AD 250–1000	562
The earliest sedentary Maya communities are formed during the Preclassic Period. The earliest settlements in Belize are at Cuello in Orange Walk and Cahal Pech in Cayo.	The Classic Period of the Maya civilization is characterized by construction of cities and temples, inscriptions recording historic events and other artistic and intellectual achievements. The population reaches around 400,000.	Water Lord of Caracol defeats King Double Bird of Tikal. The latter is sacrificed and Caracol becomes the dominant city in the Maya world.

100,000 residents. It boasted first-rate jewelers and skilled craftsmen, an intricately terraced agriculture system, a prosperous trading market, and 40 miles of paved roads (considerably more than it has today). According to the story carved by Maya artists into commemorative stone, the king of Caracol, Water Lord, defeated his chief rival, Double Bird, king of Tikal, in a decisive battle in AD 562, ushering in a long period of Caracol supremacy in the central highlands. The pictographic stone inscriptions also suggest that Water Lord personally sacrificed Double Bird to further emphasize the Caracol triumph. Perhaps this had something to do with the still-simmering feud between Belize and Guatemala.

Emory King's *The Great Story of Belize* is a fun read, and quite detailed, even though it has come under criticism for glamorizing the swashbuckling ways of the early British settlers.

In the 1500s, the jaguar kings were forced to take cover in the rainforest, when the sword-wielding Spanish arrived in Belize with the aim of plundering Maya gold and spreading the word of God. The Maya population of Belize at this time numbered about a quarter of a million, but their ranks were quickly decimated by as much as 90 percent, from the lethal combination of the diseases and greed of the Spanish. In the 1540s, a conquistador force based in the Yucatán set out on an expedition through much of present-day Belize, down the coast and across to the central highlands. Disappointed by the lack of riches uncovered, they left a bloody trail of slaughtered victims and abandoned villages in their wake. Religious sites, such as Lamanai, were forcibly converted to Catholicism.

In the early 1600s, the Maya finally staged a counter offensive that successfully drove out the few Spanish settlers and missionaries that had decided to stay. Weakened and fearful, the Maya did not return to the now desolate old cities, choosing instead to stay huddled in the remote interior.

BAYMEN OF THE CARIBBEAN: BRITISH SETTLEMENT

The virtually unexplored Glover's Atoll is named for the pirate John Glover, who hung out there in the 1750s; there are supposed to be pirate graves on Northeastern Caye.

When Columbus accidentally bumped into the continental landmass soon to be known as the Americas, his Spanish royal patrons had it made. Soon, Aztec gold and Incan silver overflowed in the king's coffers, making Spain a transatlantic superpower. In 1494, the Treaty of Tordesillas established an exclusive Iberian claim on the region, declaring New World riches off-limits to old-world rivals. But the temptations were too great, and the hiding places too many. Spain's spoils were set upon by British buccaneers, French corsairs and Dutch freebooters. In times of war, they were put into the service of their Crown as privateers; at other times, they were simply pirates.

Belize emerged as one of several Caribbean outposts for Britain's maritime marauders. In the early 17th century, English sea dogs first began using the Bay of Honduras as a staging point for raids on Spanish commerce; henceforth the Brits in the region came to be known as Baymen.

The Belizean coast had several strategic advantages from a pirate's perspective. The land was both bountiful and uninhabited as the Spanish had already driven the Maya out but never bothered to settle in themselves. It

900–1000	1100–1600	1540s
The great Maya civilization declines, possibly as a result of drought, disease or environmental disaster. Large urban centers come under stress and their populations disperse throughout the region.	During the Postclassic Period, the Maya civilization continues to persist and develop, although populations are not as concentrated. Political and cultural centers migrate from the lowlands to sites in northern Belize and the Yucatán.	Spanish conquistadors sweep through northern and western Belize, attempting to establish strongholds in Chetumal in Corozal, Lamanai in Orange Walk, and Tipu in Cayo.

THE FIRST MESTIZO

In 1511, the Spanish ship *Valdivia* was wrecked at sea, when a reef ripped through its hull. About 15 survivors drifted for several days before making it to shore in northern Belize, where they were promptly apprehended by anxious Maya. Just to be on the safe side, the locals sent 10 to the gods and kept five for themselves.

One of the captives was conquistador Gonzalo Guerrero, a skilled warrior and apparently not a bad diplomat either. Guerrero managed to win his freedom and a position of status with the Maya chief at Chetumal. He became a tribal consultant on military matters and married the chief's daughter; their three children are considered to be the first Mestizos (mixed race Spanish and Amerindian) in the New World.

Eight years later, Hernán Cortés arrived in the Yucatán and summoned Guerrero to serve him in his campaign of conquest. But Guerrero had gone native, with facial tattoos and body piercings. He turned down the offer, saying instead that he was a captain of the Maya. Cortés moved on in his search for gold and glory. Guerrero, meanwhile, organized Maya defenses in the wars that followed. It would take the Spanish more than 20 years to finally defeat the Maya of Yucatán and Belize.

was just a short sail away from the heavily trafficked Yucatán Straits, where – if luck be with ye – the Treasure Fleet might be gathering in Havana or the Silver Train passing through on its way from Panama. And, the shoreline, concealed behind thick mangroves and littoral islands, offered protective cover, while the long barrier reef was a treacherous underwater trap that kept Spanish war galleons at a distance.

For the sake of historical record, the year 1638 was made the official founding date of a British settlement at the mouth of the Belize River. It was sometime around then that a Scottish pirate captain, Peter Wallace, decided to organize the building of a new port town. Legend has it that he laid the first foundations of what became Belize City with woodchips and rum bottles, presumably empty.

Meanwhile, the Baymen found yet another activity to annoy the Spanish king – poaching his rainforest. The settlement became a rich source of hardwoods, especially mahogany, much valued by carpenters, furniture-makers and shipbuilders back in Britain. In addition, the lowland forest was abundant in logwood trees, which provided a valuable dye extract used to make woolen textiles.

By the 18th century, Britain's monarch finally had a navy and merchant fleet to match Spain's. Privateers were no longer needed, and pirates were a nuisance. In 1765 Jamaican-based British naval commander Admiral Burnaby paid a visit to the rough-hewn Baymen and delivered a code of laws on proper imperial etiquette: thieving, smuggling and cursing were out; paying taxes and obeying the sovereign were in.

A History of Belize (www.belizenet.com/history/toc.html) is an online version of a Belizean school textbook – quite a good read, with some excellent illustrations.

1638–40	1638	1724
Maya rebellion finally drives out the Spanish once and for all, although they never give up their claim on the territory. The Maya population drops dramatically in number due to war, drought and disease.	The British Baymen 'settle' Belize when former pirate Peter Wallace lays the foundations for a new port at the mouth of the Belize River, on the site of today's Belize City.	The first African slaves are recorded in Belize. Slaves are put to work cutting logwood and mahogany, as well as doing domestic work and farming.

BELIZEAN STARS & BARS

At the end of the US Civil War, several thousand Confederate soldiers chose not to return to their defeated and occupied homeland. The rebels instead accepted an invitation to resettle under the British flag in Belize.

The white colonial elite of Belize sympathized with the Southern cause during the conflict. During the war, they supplied the Confederacy with raw materials and guns. After the war, colonial officials enticed the war veterans with promises of land grants and other economic incentives. It was hoped that these expatriate Americans could help rejuvenate the Belizean economy, which suffered from a decline in timber exports, by sharing their expertise of the plantation system.

As many as 7000 American Southerners made it to Belize in the 1860s, mostly arriving from Mississippi and Louisiana, with the dream of re-creating the Old South in tropical climes. Their initial attempts to cultivate cotton, however, were dashed by the inhospitable steamy jungle climate. They had better luck with sugarcane. The Confederate contribution to the colonial economy was notable, as Belizean sugar exports between 1862 and 1868 increased four-fold, from 400,000lb to 1,700,000lb.

But the move did not go smoothly. The American newcomers had run-ins with the local white landowners, who resented their presence and privileges, and with the local black workforce, who refused to submit and serve. All but a couple of hundred of the Confederate contingent eventually cashed out and returned home. Maybe they should have bought time-shares instead.

As the British settlement became more profitable, the Spanish king became more irritable. His armed forces made several unsuccessful attempts to dislodge the well-ensconced and feisty squatters. With the Treaty of Paris, in 1763, Spain instead tried diplomacy, negotiating a deal in which the Brits could stay and harvest wood as long as they paid rent to the Spanish Crown and promised not to expand the settlement. The Baymen did neither.

September is the holiday season in Belize, including National Day on September 10 and Independence Day on September 21. See www .septembercelebrations .com for information on celebrations around the country.

Spain finally got the better of the Baymen in 1779, burning down Belize City in a surprise attack and consigning the prisoners to slavery in Cuba. The conflict reached a decisive conclusion in 1798 at the Battle of St George's Caye when a squadron of 30 Spanish warships was met and turned back by the alerted Baymen operating in smaller but faster craft. From this point, Spain gave up trying to boot the Brits from Belize. And the battle made such a good story that it eventually inspired a national holiday (see National Day, p285).

IN LIVING COLOR: BRITISH HONDURAS

In the 19th century, modern Belize began to take form, largely shaped by its economic role and political status in the Empire, where it was officially dubbed British Honduras. At first it was administered from Jamaica, but later was made a Crown Colony with its own appointed royal governor. Belizean society was an overlapping patchwork of British, African, Maya and

1717–63	1779–98	1832
Spanish attacks attempt to end British extraction of hardwoods. Finally, the Treaty of Paris gives Britain the right to cut and export logwood, but the Spanish still claim the land as their own.	The Spanish capture St George's Caye. Despite attempts to reach a compromise, Spain and Britain are unable to reach an agreement. Spain launches another attack but is defeated at the Battle of St George's Caye.	A group of Garifuna settle in present-day Dangriga, after migrating from Honduras. This ethnic enclave was previously deported from the British-ruled island of St Vincent, after being defeated in the Carib Wars.

Spanish influences. It was a haven for refugees and a labor camp for slaves, a multicultural but hierarchical Crown Colony in living color.

At the top of the colonial social order were the descendants of the Baymen. In earlier times, their outlaw ancestors comprised an ethnically mixed and relatively democratic community. But as the colony grew larger and ties with the Empire stronger, an oligarchy of leading families emerged. They may have descended from antiestablishment renegades, but now they were all about aristocratic manners. They touted their white, cultured British lineage, and used the Crown's authority to reinforce their status. By order of His Majesty's Superintendent for British Honduras, they alone were given political rights in colonial affairs and private entitlement to the forest and land. This elite colonial cohort managed to hold sway until the early 20th century.

As the economy was centered on timber exports, strong bodies were needed to perform the arduous labor of harvesting hardwoods from the dense rainforest. Like elsewhere in the Americas, African slaves provided the muscle, along with much sweat and pain. By 1800 the settlement numbered about 4000 in total: 3000 black slaves, 900 mixed-race coloreds and free blacks, and 100 white colonists. Slave masters could count, and acted shrewdly to stay on top. Male slaves were kept divided into small work teams based on tribal origins. They were forced to do long tours of duty in remote jungle camps, separated from other teams and from their families. Slave women performed domestic chores and farm work. Intraracial separation, however, did not mean interracial segregation, as mixed-race Creoles (descendents of African slaves) would eventually make up nearly 75% of the population.

In 1838 slavery was abolished in the British Empire. The plight of Afro-Belizeans, however, did not much improve. They were forbidden from owning land, which would have enabled them to be self-sufficient, and thus remained dependent on the white-controlled export economy. Instead of slaves, they were called 'apprentices' and worked for subsistence wages.

When the timber market declined in the 1860s, landowners diversified their holdings by introducing fruit and sugarcane. One persistent historical narrative has it that slave life in Belizean logging camps was more benign than the harsh conditions that existed on Caribbean sugar plantations. While this may be so, the facts remain that Belize experienced four major slave revolts between 1760 and 1820, and recorded high annual incidences of runaways, suggesting instead that repressive inhumanity may come in different packages.

Toward the mid-19th century, British colonists finally came into contact – and conflict – with the indigenous Maya. As loggers penetrated deeper into the interior, they encountered the elusive natives, who responded with hit-and-run assaults on the encroaching axmen.

At this time in the neighboring Yucatán Peninsula, an armed conflict broke out among the lowly Maya, second-class Mestizos and privileged

Most slaves came to Belize via the West Indies from Niger and Nigeria in West Africa and from Congo and Angola further south. Around the year 1800, slaves comprised more than 75% of the population.

Assad Shoman's *13 Chapters of a History of Belize* is a detailed, readable, anticolonialist account up to the 1990s; the author himself has helped make modern history as a pro-independence activist and People's United Party cabinet minister.

In 1872 the Crown Lands Ordinance established 'Carib Reserves' and 'Maya Reserves,' which prevented the Garifuna and Maya from owning private property.

1838	**1847**	**1862**
According to the Abolition Act, slavery is outlawed throughout the British Empire, including Belize. However, former slaves are unable to own property and they are dependent on their ex-masters for employment.	Spanish, Mestizo and Maya peoples engage in the War of the Castes in the neighboring Yucatán Peninsula. The violence sends streams of refugees into Belize.	The settlement in Belize is declared a Crown Colony and is named British Honduras. Initially it is administered from Jamaica, but a separate royal governor is appointed soon thereafter.

Spanish-descended landlords. The bloody War of the Castes raged for over a decade and forced families to flee. Caste War refugees more than doubled the Belize population, from less than 10,000 in 1845 to 25,000 in 1861.

The movement of peoples redefined the ethnic character of northern Belize. Mestizo refugees, of mixed Spanish-Indian stock, brought their Hispanic tongue, corn tortillas and Catholic churches to scattered small town settlements. Yucatecan Maya refugees, meanwhile, moved into the northwestern Belizean forest, where they quickly clashed with the logging industry. In 1872 the desperate Maya launched a quixotic attack on British colonists at Orange Walk, in what was a fierce but futile last stand. Diminished and dispirited, the remaining Maya survived on the territorial and social fringes of the colony.

The Caste War of the Yucatán by Nelson Reed is a dramatic account of that event and a detailed analysis of the causes and outcomes, both in Mexico and Belize.

PATIENCE & RESISTANCE: BELIZEAN INDEPENDENCE

Belize remained a British colony until 1981; rather late for the West Indies. Spain and France lost most Caribbean possessions in the early 19th century, while Her Majesty's island colonies were liberated in the 1960s. With its deep ethnic divisions, a unifying national identity formed slowly, and the Belizean independence movement displayed more patience than resistance.

As the 19th century closed, the orderly ways of colonial life in British Honduras showed signs of breakdown. The old elite was becoming more isolated and less feared. Its cozy connections to the mother country were unraveling. By 1900 the United States surpassed Britain as the main destination of the mahogany harvest; by 1930 the US was taking in 80% of all Belizean exports.

Belize: A Concise History by PAB Thomson, a former British high commissioner to Belize, tells the country's story right up to the 21st century in a comprehensive but not overly lengthy form.

The colonial elite's economic position was further undercut by the rise of a London-based conglomerate, the British Estate and Produce Company, which bought out local landowners and took over the commodity trade. Declining timber fortunes caused colonial capitalists to impose a 50% wage cut on mahogany workers in Belize City, which provoked both riotous protests and the first stirrings of social movement.

During the first half of the 20th century, Belizean nationalism developed in explosive fits and starts. During WWI, a regiment of local Creoles was recruited for the Allied cause. The experience proved both disheartening and enlightening. Ill-treated because of their dark skin, they were not even allowed to go to the front line and fight alongside white troops. They may have enlisted as patriotic Brits, but they were discharged as resentful Belizeans. Upon their return, in 1919, they coaxed several thousand into the streets of Belize City in an angry demonstration against the existing order.

It was not until the 1930s that a more sustained anticolonial movement arose. It began as the motley 'Unemployed Brigade,' staging weekend ral-

1866–72	1919	1950
Loggers conflict with the Maya, who launch attacks on the British settlements in an attempt to extract payment for the use and destruction of the land. The Maya are defeated and forced off the land.	After returning from WWI, demobilized Creole soldiers protest against the discrimination they experience at the hands of the colonial administration. The protest is violently crushed by police.	A severe economic crisis sparks anti-British protests, and the pro-independence movement is launched under the leadership of George Price and the People's United Party (PUP).

WHEN ROYALTY MEETS

In the 1980s, big-cat specialists determined that the Cockscomb Basin, in the Maya Mountain foothills of southern Belize, was a vital habitat for the long-term survival of the jaguar – not only in Belize, but in Central America as a whole. They successfully persuaded the government to protect the region from loggers and ranchers. In 1988 the Duke of Edinburgh and World Wildlife Fund head, Prince Philip, was on hand to celebrate the creation of the Cockscomb Basin Wildlife Sanctuary (p235), the world's first wildlife sanctuary for the jaguar. The protected realm of the Belizean jungle's king eventually reached more than half a million acres. The reserve soon attracted a steady stream of visitors, eager to catch a glimpse of the ferocious feline. The ecotourism boom was on.

lies in Battlefield Park in Belize City (p91). The movement fed on the daily discontents of impoverished black workers, and spewed its wrath at prosperous white merchants. It soon was organizing boycotts and strikes, and shortly thereafter its leaders were thrown into jail.

Finally, in the early 1950s, a national independence party, the People's United Party (PUP), became politically active. When WWII caused the sudden closing of export markets, the colony experienced a severe economic crisis that lasted until well after the war's end. Anti-British demonstrations spread all across Belize, becoming more militant and occasionally violent. Colonial authorities declared a state of emergency, forbidding public meetings and intimidating independence advocates.

In response, the PUP organized a successful general strike that finally forced Britain to make political concessions. Universal suffrage was extended to all adults and limited home rule was permitted in the colony. The imperial foundations of the old ruling elite crumbled, as the colony's ethnically divided peoples now danced to a common Belizean drum beat.

The Belizean government tells its side of the story about the Belizean-Guatemalan territorial dispute at www.belize -guatemala.gov.bz.

Full independence for Belize was put off until a nagging security matter was resolved. Spain never formally renounced her territorial claim to Belize, which was later appropriated by Mexico and Guatemala. In the 19th century, Britain signed agreements with both claimants to recognize the existing colonial borders, but the one with Guatemala did not stick.

Guatemala's caudillo rulers – mostly inept at managing their own affairs – remained obsessed with the perceived wealth of British Honduras. The 1945 Guatemalan constitution explicitly included Belize as part of its territorial reach. Britain, in turn, stationed a large number of troops in the west. Guatemala barked, but did not bite. By the 1960s, the border threat was stabilized and the demand for independence was renewed.

Belizeans waited patiently. In 1964 the colony became fully self-governing, installing a Westminster-style parliamentary system. In 1971 the capital

1958	1961	1972
After being driven out of Mexico, the first wave of Mennonites settles in Belize and begins to farm the land, producing much of the fruit, vegetables, poultry and dairy consumed in the country.	Hurricane Hattie devastates Belize, killing hundreds of people and destroying Belize City. In response to this catastrophe, a new inland capital is established at Belmopan 10 years later.	Jacques Cousteau takes his research ship *Calypso* to the Blue Hole, bringing unprecedented publicity to the amazing natural resources of this tiny country and kicking off its popularity as a destination for divers and snorkelers.

In 1984, 18-year-old David Stuart became the youngest person to receive a McArthur Genius Award for his work in cracking the Mayan hieroglyphic code, which he had been working on since the age of 10.

was relocated to Belmopan (p188), a geographic center symbolically uniting all regions and peoples. In 1973 the name was officially changed from the colonial sounding British Honduras to the more popular Belize. And in September 1981 Belize was at last declared an independent nation-state within the British Commonwealth. Even Guatemala recognized Belize as a sovereign nation in 1991, although to this day it maintains its territorial claim, whatever that means.

RETURN OF THE JAGUAR KING: CONTEMPORARY BELIZE

Independence did not turn out to be a cure-all. The angry nationalists that led Belize to independence turned into accommodating capitalists. The country had a small economy whose fortunes were determined beyond its control in global commodity markets. Belizeans eventually discovered that rather than remain vulnerable to exports, they had something valuable to import: tourists. The rise of ecotourism and revival of Maya culture has reshaped contemporary Belize, and cleared the jungle overgrowth for a return of the jaguar king.

Timber, Tourists and Temples: Conservation and Development in the Maya Forest of Belize, Guatemala & Mexico is an academic assessment of the pros and cons of ecotourism.

Belizean politics was long dominated by the founder of the nationalist People's United Party, George Price. His party won nearly every parliamentary election, consolidating political independence and promoting a new middle class. In 1996, at age 75 years, Price finally stepped down with his national hero status intact; the PUP, however, looked vulnerable.

The party was tainted by corruption scandals: missing pension funds, selling off of public lands. According to critics, the PUP never met a greased palm it wouldn't shake. Supporters argue that other parties' politicians are guilty of similar crimes. Once a haven for pirates, Belize became a new kind of haven – for tax-avoiding North Americans. In a hotly contested 2008 election, the PUP was sent packing.

Long the opposition party, the United Democratic Party (UDP) won a landslide victory in the 2008 elections, promising to clean up corruption and stick up for the little guy. Follow their progress at www.udp.org.bz.

The frail economy inherited at the time of independence was slow to recover. Many Creoles began to look for work outside the country, forming sizable diaspora communities in New York and London. As much as one third of the Belizean people now live abroad. Meanwhile, civil war and rural poverty in neighboring Guatemala and Honduras sent more refugees into Belize, whose demographic profile changed accordingly, with Spanish-speaking Mestizos becoming the majority ethnic group. From the time of independence, the Belize nation has doubled in size, from 150,000 in 1981 to 321,000 in 2008.

Belize was an ideal candidate for a green revolution. Wide swaths of lowland rainforest were unspoiled by loggers, while sections of the interior highland had never even been explored by Europeans. The jungle hosted a rich stock of exotic flora and fauna, feathered and furry; while just offshore was the magnificent coral reef and mysterious Blue Hole (p157), which Jacques Cousteau had already made famous.

1973	1981	1981–2008
In response to an increase in nationalist sentiment, the country officially changes its name from the colonial 'British Honduras' to the more popular moniker 'Belize.'	After years of anticolonial and pro-independence political movements, Belize receives formal international recognition of independent statehood. George Price (PUP) is the first prime minister of independent Belize.	In the years following independence, the population of Belize more than doubles, reaching 321,000 in 2008. The increase is attributed to high birth rates and a steady stream of immigration from neighboring countries.

A Tourist Ministry was created in 1984, but it was not until the 1990s that the government began to recognize ecotourism as a viable revenue source and invested in its promotion and development. Infrastructure associated with various sites improved, small business loans became available, training programs were organized for guides, and a Bachelor's degree in tourism was created at Belize University.

Over the next decade, more than 20 sites from the western mountains to the eastern cayes were designated as national parks, wildlife sanctuaries, forest reserves and marine preserves (see p64). More than 40% of Belizean territory received some form of protective status, including 80% of its pristine rainforest. The number of visitors rose steadily, from 140,000 in 1988 to 250,000 in 2006. By the end of the 1990s, tourism was Belize's fastest growing economic sector, surpassing commodity exports.

For lots on Ambergris Caye and some great stuff on the rest of Belize, including a hugely detailed Maya Sites in Belize section, go to www .belizehistory.com.

The ecocraze coincided with archaeological advances to spur a revival of Maya culture. In the 1980s, significant progress was made in cracking the Mayan hieroglyphic code, enabling researchers to gain deeper insight into this once-shrouded world, while NASA satellite technology revealed over 600 previously unknown sites and hidden temples beneath the Belizean rainforest. In 2000 the government allocated nearly $30 million to support excavation projects. A lost culture became a live commodity. Maya descendants re-engaged with traditional ceremonies, craft-making, food preparation and healing techniques, often in response to touristy curiosity.

The commercial aspects of cultural revival are controversial. Maya human-rights activist and Nobel Prize winner Rigoberta Menchú spoke out against the outside world's desire to mystify the Maya experience, stating 'we are not the myths of the past, or ruins in the jungle; we are people, and we want to be respected.'

In contemporary Belize, the new understanding of the Maya past fostered a changed attitude in the Maya present. The Maya culture is no longer disparaged at the fringe of society, but now is a source of pride and a defining feature of Belizean identity, just as is the jaguar king, who has reclaimed his ancient throne.

1991	2006	2008
Guatemala finally recognizes Belize as a sovereign, independent state. Tensions continue, however, as the neighbor to the west refuses to relinquish its territorial claim over parts of Belize.	Black gold. After more than four years of exploration around the country, oil is discovered in commercially viable quantities in the Mennonite village of Spanish Lookout.	Led by Dean Barrow, the United Democratic Party (UDP) overwhelmingly defeats the PUP in countrywide elections, capturing 25 out of 31 seats in the House of Representatives.

The Culture

THE NATIONAL PSYCHE

Belizeans have elevated 'taking it easy' to an art form. (Where else will you be told that checkout time is 'Whatever time you like'?) Shopkeepers will close early if they feel they've made enough money for the day, and hammock swinging is pretty much a national pastime. Most people live life at a sane pace. The idea is that taking time to communicate with fellow human beings is more important than stressing out for the sake of an extra bit of profit. Not that they don't work, of course – but they know when they have done enough. As a visitor, you too will find yourself slowing down to the Belizean pace and relearning some of the forgotten art of human communication.

Most Belizeans look around at other Central American countries and find their own country measures up favorably. Its peaceful history and high standard of living are indisputable factors; socialized medicine, mandatory and free education and a relatively clean record on human rights are also positives.

Not that the picture is completely rosy. Poverty is still widespread, with an estimated one-third of the population living below the poverty line. Crime is almost a way of life in some sectors of Belize City and some rural areas. (Even the Belize City Council reports that 'the crime rate...is escalating at an appalling rate.') Corruption in the government was the thorniest issue in the 2008 election. Each party came up with its own strategy to combat the corruption that it claimed other parties were perpetrating. All of this has left most Belizeans with a deep cynicism about the country's possibilities for progress.

Because of the mix of ethnicities and cultures in Belize, its residents are very open, tolerant and accepting of other people's differences. The cultural influence of the United States is significant; indeed, most educated Belizeans have spent time studying or working in the US. But Belizeans are proud of their cultural heritage, whether it is Maya, Garifuna, Mestizo or Creole. Tourism is playing a role in preserving some cultural practices, as visitors to Belize are keen to purchase Maya handicrafts, to hear Garifuna drumming or to attend a local food festival. Tourism has also made Belizeans more

Belizean Journeys (www
.belizeanjourneys.com)
is an on-line magazine
of culture and nature,
showcasing articles,
photographs and
multimedia art from
contemporary Belize.

RESPONSIBLE TRAVEL

We hear a lot about the environmental impact of tourism, but what about the cultural impact? Traveling responsibly means being aware of cultural norms and showing respect for the people in your host country, as well as for their customs and beliefs. Here are some tips for traveling responsibly in Belize:

- Follow local laws. Foreigners are not exempt!

- Do not take photos of people without asking permission.

- Do not sunbathe topless unless your beach is completely deserted.

- Feel free to haggle in markets and souvenir stalls. Vendors will likely start the process by offering a 'discount' off the bat.

- Be patient and enjoy the slower pace. Belizeans have a relatively loose interpretation of time. Tours may not leave precisely when indicated, buses may not arrive on schedule and stores may close at random.

- Support the preservation of local cultures: purchase handicrafts straight from the source, go to hear local bands and drummers and attend festivals.

BELIZEANS BUILD HOUSES ON STILTS BECAUSE...

- They avoid floods
- They get more breeze
- They get less ground heat
- It's easier to control termites
- It keeps other bugs and rodents out
- It provides shelter for dogs, cats etc
- It permits infilling if the family gets bigger
- It's tradition!

---

aware of the value of their ecological and archaeological heritage, and its preservation has become a high priority for most.

LIFESTYLE

According to the most basic benchmarks, Belize is flourishing, with compulsory education, a relatively stable democracy, a thriving tourism industry and an economy that is plugging along. Unfortunately, many people have not seen the benefits of these positive developments. A few entrepreneurs have made big money from arcane financial dealings, and a small middle class survives from business, tourism and other professions. But many more Belizeans live on subsistence incomes in rudimentary circumstances. You can admire lovely, large, breezy, two-story, old, Caribbean-style wooden houses in parts of Belize City, but these are not typical dwellings. New houses are usually small, cinder-block boxes, while old wooden ones are often warped and rotting.

Labor – whether washing dirty hotel sheets, cutting sugarcane or packing bananas – is poorly paid, especially compared with the high cost of living. (The average income in Belize is less than BZ$600 per month.) Unemployment hovers just under 10% and it is estimated that one third of the population lives below the poverty line. That's why tens of thousands of Belizeans live in the USA these days.

Among the blessings of Belize are its tiny population and tiny area. It's said that everyone here knows everyone else. It is true that many people have supportive networks of family and friends, not only in their local neighborhood, but also in other parts of the country. Belize's different ethnic groups socialize primarily among themselves, but there is little animosity between them.

Education in Belize is free and compulsory up to the age of 14. After that, instruction is free, but students are required to buy their own books, which is a deterrent against higher education. Most schools are state-subsidized church schools, mainly run by Catholics, Methodists and Anglicans; recently evangelical religions such as the Seventh Day Adventists have opened schools.

Belize doesn't have much of a gay scene, but this does not imply that in this tolerant land people are secretive, just that they are low-key.

MULTICULTURALISM

Belize is a tiny country (population around 321,000), but it enjoys a diversity of ethnicities that is undeniably stimulating and improbably serene.

Creoles are descendants of British loggers, colonists and African slaves. They now form only about 25% of Belize's population, but theirs remains a sort of paradigm culture. Racially mixed and proud of it, Creoles speak a fascinating and unique version of English: it sounds familiar at first, but it

Experts estimate that the number of Belizeans living overseas is roughly equal to the number of Belizeans living at home.

Belize Kriol (www.kriol .org.bz), the website of the National Kriol Council of Belize, has interesting information on Creole history, culture, language and more.

BILEEZ KRIOL

While English is the official language of Belize, when speaking among themselves most locals use Creole, or Kriol. According to one local journalist, Kriol is *'di stiki stiki paat,'* or 'the glue that holds Belize together.' While this patois sounds like English, most Anglophones will have a hard time understanding it. It is a language that 'teases but just escapes the comprehension of a native English speaker,' as one frustrated American traveler so aptly stated.

Kriol derives mainly from English, with influences from Mayan and West African languages, as well as Spanish. Linguists claim that it has its own grammatical rules and a small body of literature, as well as speaking populations in different countries – criteria that determine the difference between a dialect and a language.

In 1995 the **National Kriol Council** (www.kriol.org.bz) was established to promote Kriol language in Belize. The council believes that the use and recognition of the language can solidify national identity and promote interaction and cooperation among different ethnic groups. Kriol is used by more than 70% of the population; not only by Creoles, but also many Garifuna, Mestizos and Maya who speak Kriol as their second language. The council believes that a better understanding of Kriol will actually improve local English. As people recognize that Kriol is a different language – and not just improper English – both children and adults will make the effort to learn the differences in grammatical construction.

---

is not easily intelligible to a speaker of standard English (see the boxed text, above). Most of the people you'll encounter in Belize City and the center of the country will be Creole.

Mestizos are people of mixed Spanish and Amerindian descent. Over the last couple of decades, Mestizos have become Belize's largest ethnic group, now making up about 49% of the population. The first Mestizos arrived in the mid-19th century, when refugees from the Yucatán flooded into northern and western Belize. Their modern successors have been thousands of political refugees from troubled neighboring Central American countries. While English remains Belize's official language, Spanish is spoken by over half of the population; this has caused some resentment among Creoles, who are fiercely proud of their country's Anglo roots.

Garifuna History, Language & Culture of Belize, Central America & the Caribbean, by Sebastian Cayetano, gives an easily understood overview of the Garifuna people and their culture.

The Maya of Belize make up almost 11% of the population and are divided into three linguistic groups. The Yucatec Maya live mainly in the north, the Mopan Maya in the southern Toledo District and in western Belize, and the Kekchi Maya, who also live in the Toledo District. Use of both Spanish and English is becoming more widespread among the Maya. Traditional Maya culture is strongest among the Maya of the south.

Southern Belize is also the main home of the Garifuna (see opposite), who account for 6% of the population. The remaining 9% of the population is composed of several groups: East Indians (people of Indian subcontinent origins), Chinese, Arabs (generally known as Lebanese), the small but influential group of Mennonites (see p44), and North Americans and Europeans who have settled here in the last couple of decades.

MEDIA

Belizean newspapers are small in size and circulation, and present news by party line. The twice-weekly, left-wing *Amandala* (www.amandala.com.bz) has the largest circulation. Its Sunday edition comes out on Thursday or Friday and its Tuesday edition comes out on Tuesday but is datelined Wednesday. Other papers are Sunday only: the *Belize Times* (www.belizetimes.bz) represents the People's United Party (PUP) perspective, while the *Guardian* (www.guardian.bz) is the voice of the United Democratic Party (UDP). The *Reporter* (www.reporter.bz) presents the most independent coverage.

Most TV you'll see in Belize will be international cable channels, but there are a few local stations: Channel 5 ('Great Belize TV'; www.channel5belize .com), Channel 7 ('Where News Comes First'; www.7newsbelize.com) and CTV ('We bring the world into your home'; www.ctv3belizenews.com). This is a country where the national news can contain items such as 'There will be a fireworks display on the football field in Hattieville at 7pm tonight.'

Love FM (www.lovefm.com) is the most widely broadcast radio station in Belize, with spots at 95.1MHz and 98.1MHz. It's a charming mix of local news, public-service announcements and the world's best love songs. KREM FM, at 96.5MHz, plays a more modern selection of music.

For links to most of Belize's main media, including on-line radio, visit www.belizenews .com.

RELIGION

Ethnicity is a big determinant of religion in Belize, with most Mestizos, Maya and Garifuna espousing Catholicism as a result of their ethnic origins in Spanish- or French-ruled countries or colonies. Catholicism among Creoles increased with the work of North American missionaries in the late 19th and early 20th centuries. Approximately a quarter of Belizeans are Protestants,

THE GARIFUNA

In the 17th century, shipwrecked African slaves washed ashore on the Caribbean island of St Vincent. They hooked up with the indigenous population of Caribs and Arawaks and formed a whole new ethnicity, now known as the Garifuna (plural Garinagu, also called Black Caribs).

France claimed possession of St Vincent in the early 18th century, but eventually ceded it to Britain according to the Treaty of Paris. After prolonged resistance and a series of wars, the Garifuna finally surrendered in 1796, and Britain decided to deport them. Over the course of several years, the Garifuna were shuffled around various spots in the Caribbean, with many dying of malnutrition or disease. Finally, 1465 of the original 4338 deportees arrived at the Honduran coastal town of Trujillo. From here, this people of mixed Native American and African heritage began to spread along the Caribbean coast of Central America.

The first Garifuna arrived in Belize around the turn of the 19th century. But the biggest migration took place in 1832, when, on November 19, some 200 Garifuna reached Belize in dugout canoes from Honduras.

Most Garifuna in Belize still live in the south of the country, from Dangriga to Punta Gorda. The Garifuna excelled at growing food and made a significant contribution to the colonial economy. By the 1850s they numbered over 2000. Today the Belize Garifuna are around 16,000 people, about 6% of Belize's population.

The Garifuna language is a combination of Arawak and African languages with bits of English and French thrown in. The Garifuna maintain a unique culture with a strong sense of community and ritual, in which drumming and dancing play important roles. The *dügü* ('feasting of the ancestors' ceremony) involves several nights and days of dancing, drumming and singing by an extended family. Its immediate purpose is to heal a sick individual, but it also serves to reaffirm community solidarity. Some participants may become 'possessed' by the spirits of dead ancestors. Other noted Garifuna ceremonials include the *beluria* (ninth-night festivity), for the departure of a dead person's soul, attended by entire communities with copious drumming, dancing and drinking; and the *wanaragua* or *jonkonu* dance, performed in some places during the Christmas-to-early-January festive season (see p222).

Garifuna culture has been enjoying a revival since the 1980s, with no small part played by the punta rock phenomenon (see p45). The anniversary of the Garifuna arrival on November 19, 1832 is celebrated as Garifuna Settlement Day, a national holiday. In southern towns – especially Dangriga – a festival takes place with traditional Garifuna food, punta music and a re-enactment of the first landing (see p222). In 2001 Unesco declared Garifuna language, dance and music in Belize to be a 'Masterpiece of the Oral and Intangible Heritage of Humanity' – one of the initial selections for what is intended to become the cultural equivalent of the World Heritage list.

THE MENNONITES

It almost seems like an aberration, an odd sight inspired by the hot sun, or maybe just a blurry result of too much sweat dripping in your eyes. But the vision of women in bonnets and wintry frocks, and blond men with blue eyes, denim overalls and straw cowboy hats is not something your imagination has conjured up: you're looking at Belizean Mennonites.

The Mennonites originate from an enigmatic Anabaptist group that dates back to 16th-century Netherlands. Like the Amish of Pennsylvania, the Mennonites have strict religion-based values that keep them isolated in agricultural communities. Speaking mostly Low German, they run their own schools, banks and churches. Traditional groups reject any form of mechanization or technology, which is why they're often seen riding along in horse-drawn buggies.

Mennonites are devout pacifists and reject most of the political ideologies (including paying taxes) that societies down the centuries have tried to thrust upon them, so they have a long history of moving about the world trying to find a place where they could be left in peace. They left the Netherlands for Prussia and Russia in the late 17th century. In the 1870s, when Russia insisted on military conscription, the Mennonites there upped and moved to Canada. They built communities in isolated parts of Saskatchewan, Alberta and British Columbia. But after WWI the Canadian government demanded that English be taught in Mennonite schools, and the Mennonites' exemption from conscription was reconsidered. Again, the most devout Mennonites moved, this time to northern Mexico and South America. By the 1950s Mexico wanted the Mennonites to join its social security program, so once again the Mennonites packed up.

The first wave of about 3500 Mennonites settled in Belize (then called British Honduras) in 1958. Belize was happy to have their industriousness and farming expertise.

Today, Belize has both progressive and traditional Mennonite communities. The progressives, many of whom came from Canada, speak English and have no qualms about using tractors to clear their land, or pickup trucks to shuttle their families about. These well-off groups are found in Blue Creek, west of Orange Walk, or at Spanish Lookout in Cayo District. Strongly conservative groups, such as the ones at Shipyard near Orange Walk or Barton Creek in Cayo District, still ride in horse-drawn buggies and shun electricity.

Belize has been good to the Mennonites and in turn the Mennonites have been good to Belize. Mennonite farms now supply most of the country's dairy products, eggs and poultry. Furniture-making is another Mennonite specialty and you'll often see them selling their goods at markets.

Some Mennonites are open to the rest of the world and don't mind a good chat. Others don't want contact, so treat them with respect and ask permission if you want to take a photo.

chiefly Anglicans and Methodists. Today, the number of Pentecostalists and Adventists is growing due to the strength of their evangelical movements. Mennonites also constitute a small minority (see above).

Among the Garifuna, and to a lesser extent the Maya and Creoles, Christianity coexists with other beliefs. Maya Catholicism has long been syncretized with traditional beliefs and rites that go back to pre-Hispanic times, while some Creoles (especially older people) have a belief in obeah, a form of witchcraft.

Belize's tradition of tolerance also encompasses Hindus, Muslims, Baha'i, Jehovah's Witnesses and a small (but eye-catching) number of Rastafarians.

WOMEN IN BELIZE

On the surface, women in Belize enjoy a fair degree of freedom. Laws protect women from discrimination with regards to education, ownership and inheritance of property, management of business or participation in politics. Girls outnumber boys in classrooms and, in recent years, boast higher rates of graduation.

In reality, however, women are a long way from achieving equality. Traditionally, women have devoted their lives to raising families and managing households. Birth control and family planning are not widely practiced, thanks in part to the religious influence in schools. The average family in Belize has four or five children, which leaves little time for mum to find a job. As a result, women are often financially dependent on their husbands and fathers.

Women who work outside the home are generally concentrated in female-dominated occupations with low status and low wages, including the service sector and agricultural jobs. Unemployment is twice as high for women as it is for men. Women often find it harder than men to obtain business or agricultural financing. Women are not active in politics at a national level (at the time of research, there were no women in the House of Representatives). Furthermore, research shows that women consistently receive less pay than their male counterparts.

In contrast, Belizean women are widely employed in the world's oldest profession, as are women from neighboring countries. The British military presence and the growth of tourism have both contributed to the rise in prostitution, which is not explicitly illegal in Belize. On a related note, Belize has the highest rate of HIV/AIDS infection in Central America, estimated at 2.4%.

Domestic violence is another issue that affects far too many women. Country-specific numbers are hard to come by, but the Pan-American Health Organization reports that approximately one in three women in Latin America and the Caribbean are victims of domestic violence. Unfortunately, most women are too scared to report crimes for fear (justifiably) they will not receive the support they need. In recent years, this subject has started to receive the attention it deserves, including the implementation of public awareness campaigns, and of the zero-tolerance Domestic Violence Act in 2007.

Author Zee Edgell shocked the country when she wrote about the realities of domestic violence and discrimination in *The Festival of San Joaquin* (1997).

ARTS
Music
Belize knows how to get its groove on. You'll hear a variety of pan-Caribbean musical styles, including calypso (of which Belize has its own star in Gerald 'Lord' Rhaburn), *soca* (an up-tempo fusion of calypso with Indian rhythms) and, of course, reggae.

But much of the music you'll hear is specifically Belizean – especially the phenomenon known as punta rock, which has attained the status of Belize's national music. Punta rock is a combination of punta – a traditional Garifuna drumming style – and the electrified instruments of rock. Punta rock was invented in 1981 by Dangriga's Pen Cayetano after travels in other Central American countries made him aware that Garifuna traditions were in danger of withering away. Punta rock can be frenetic or it can be mellow, but at its base are always fast rhythms designed to get the hips swiveling. The dance is strongly sexually suggestive, with men and women gyrating their pelvises in close proximity to each other. Cayetano's Turtle Shell Band spread the word, and the rhythm, to neighboring Guatemala, Honduras (both with their own Garifuna populations), Mexico and even the USA (where there are sizable Belizean and Garifuna communities). They have been followed by a host of other performers.

Andy Palacio was a leading ambassador of punta rock until his untimely death in 2008. As his last project, he collaborated with other musicians, known as the Garifuna Collective, to create *Wattina*. Each track on the album is based on a traditional Garifuna rhythm, and all of the songs are in the Garifuna language.

After musician Andy Palacio's untimely death, an estimated 2500 people descended on his home village of Barranco, where he was laid to rest following a Catholic mass, a Garifuna ceremony and an official state funeral.

TOP PICKS – ALBUMS

▪ **Wattina** (Andy Palacio & the Garifuna Collective) The last masterpiece by the late great one.

▪ **Cult Cargo: Belize City Boil Up** (Various artists) Check out the funky blend of reggae and jazz that was coming out of Belize in the 1960s.

▪ **Bumari** (Lugua Centeno) Raw passionate vocals accompanied by traditional Garifuna drumming.

▪ **Garifuna Soul** (Aurelio Martínez) The quintessential *paranda* piece.

Another recent sensation is Supa G, who provides a fusion of punta rock, techno and even a spot of Mexican balladeering. Also look out for Mohobub, Myme Martinez (both members of the Turtle Shell Band and still going strong), Aziatic (who has blended punta with R&B, jazz and pop), Lloyd and Reckless, and the Coolie Rebels, a popular East Indian punta rock group from Punta Gorda. For more traditional Garifuna drumming, keep an eye open for Lugua Centeno.

Another great Garifuna style is *paranda,* which grew out of the melding of African percussion and chanting with Spanish-style acoustic guitar and Latin rhythms that occurred when the Garifuna reached Spanish-dominated parts of Central America. *Paranda's* Belizean master is Paul Nabor from Punta Gorda, born in the 1920s, and its bright young light is Aurelio Martínez, a Honduran who is often in Belize. The title of Martínez' album *Garifuna Soul* gives a good idea of what *paranda* is about. Its rhythms are fairly fast, but it has a lyrical tone, too.

The Creoles have given us *brukdown,* traditionally played by an ensemble of accordion, banjo, harmonica and a percussion instrument – usually the jawbone of a pig, its teeth rattled with a stick. Nowadays a drum and/or electric guitar or two might be added. Deeply African-rooted with its layered rhythms and call-and-response vocals, *brukdown* developed in the logging camps during the 18th and 19th centuries and its heartland is the Belize River valley. Wilfred Peters, with his band Mr Peters' Boom & Chime, is still the preeminent *brukdown* artist after many years, but watch out for singer Leela Vernon from Punta Gorda.

Bredda David & Tribal Vibes are the creators of *kungo* music, a fast-paced fusion of Creole styles with other African rhythms.

The Maya of Belize have their own favored instruments. Top artists include flautist Pablo Collado and harpist Florencio Mess. In the north you'll hear plenty of Mexican styles popular with the Mestizo people.

Hearing live music in Belize is a matter of keeping your eyes open for posters and press announcements of coming events. Gig organizers make sure the public knows what's cooking.

You can take classes in Garifuna drumming in Hopkins (p230), and in Creole drumming at Gales Point Manatee (p117).

Listen to a great sampling of Belizean music at the website of Stonetree Records (www .stonetreerecords.com), which produces many of the best artists.

Literature

Belizean writer Zee Edgell has won international attention with three novels treating different aspects of Belizean society and history. *Beka Lamb* (1982) tells of adolescence at a Belize City girls' school amid the political upheavals of the mid-20th century, with detailed pictures of life in the city during that time. *In Times Like These* (1991) delves into the independence-era political and social landscapes through the experience of a woman returned from studies in London, and *The Festival of San Joaquin* (1997) focuses on a Mestizo woman's painful clashes with machismo, poverty and class discrimination.

Another talented writer is Zoila Ellis, whose *On Heroes, Lizards and Passion* brings together seven short stories that demonstrate an acute perception of Belize and Belizeans.

Carlos Ledson Miller's *Belize* is the closest you'll get to a Belizean bodice-ripper. The story begins in 1961 with Hurricane Hattie, and tells the tale of a Belizean-American man and his two sons, with a realistic portrayal of Belize's recent history, including the mahogany industry, drug smuggling, hurricanes, the move to independence and the development of ecotourism. It's fun to walk through neighborhoods in Belize City and Ambergris Caye that are described in the book.

While you're in Belize, look for titles in the Belizean Writers Series, which includes anthologies of poetry, plays and short fiction.

Cinema & Television

Belize doesn't have a film industry but it does stage the admirable **Belize International Film Festival** (www.belizefilmfestival.com) in Belize City. The festival started in 2003, thanks to the efforts of the Film Commissioner (and well-known American expat) Emory King (www.emoryking.com). After a few successful runs, the film festival took a break for a few years, but was expected to re-launch in the summer of 2008.

The 1986 film *The Mosquito Coast,* with Harrison Ford and River Phoenix, was filmed in Belize, even though the story is set in Nicaragua. Likewise, Belize substituted for Africa in the 1993 version of *The Heart of Darkness,* with John Malkovich, as well as the 1980 film *The Dogs of War,* with Christopher Walken.

There are two major TV channels in Belize: Channel 5 and Channel 7. Most programming is from the United States and other Caribbean countries, although both channels show some local programming that is not particularly innovative. One of the most popular shows on Belizean TV is the ubiquitous *Karaoke TV.* Its main competition is the local soap opera, *Noh Matta Wat!,* which follows the members of the Diego family while they struggle with relationships, finances and other life obstacles. Other locally produced shows are documentary-style programs about Belizean history, geography, nature and culture, including a music show that was hosted by Andy Palacio.

Painting & Sculpture

Belizean art started to develop in the 1970s. Today, a distinct Belizean style has emerged, focusing on flora and fauna, landscapes, seascapes and ethnic groups. Pen Cayetano (www.cayetano.de) is a polymathic figure who started the punta rock musical phenomenon, but he also does oil paintings in a realist style. A native of Dangriga, he now lives in Germany but usually returns to Belize each year.

Benjamin Nicholas has a primitivist style, with flat perspective, bright colors and stylized figures. Also look out for the street scenes of Terryl Godoy. Beach areas such as Caye Caulker, Placencia and Corozal have attracted communities of expat artists who love to depict local village life, cultural festivals and wildlife.

In western Belize, art lovers should make an effort to visit the avant-garde rainforest sculpture park, Poustinia (p209).

Belizean wood-carvers work chiefly with the hardwoods zericote and mahogany. Ignatius Peyrefitte Jr has developed a distinctive personal style with Madonnas, abstracts and family scenes. The García sisters, of San Antonio, Cayo (see p194), carve some finely worked figures from Maya mythology and Belizean wildlife out of local black slate – a craft that has spawned a host of imitators.

The annual Sidewalk Art Festival in Placencia, held on the weekend nearest to Valentine's Day, provides an excellent window on Belizean art.

SPORTS

Like any Central American country worth its stripes, Belize is a soccer-playing nation and has national tournaments contested by a number of semi-pro clubs. The Regent Insurance Cup competition runs from about January to June, and the Prime Minister's Cup starts in August. Leading clubs include Kulture Yabra of Belize City, Juventus of Orange Walk, Sagitún of Independence and San Pedro Seahawks. Games are played on Saturday and Sunday. The stadiums are easy enough to find in each town: you'll be in a crowd of a few hundred at most.

Softball, basketball and cricket are also popular (cricket mainly in Belize District, from February to June); horse races and long-distance cycling races occur at times such as New Year's Day and the Easter weekend. Burrell Boom, 18 miles west of Belize City, is the main horse-racing venue. Belize's most unique sporting event is La Ruta Maya Belize River Challenge, a four-day canoe race down the Belize River from San Ignacio to Belize City, which takes place in March (see p195).

The Ancient Maya World Dr Allen J Christenson

The ancient Maya patterned their lives according to precedents set by their first ancestors. Nearly all aspects of Maya faith begin with their view of the creation, when the gods and divine forebears established the world at the beginning of time. From their hieroglyphic texts (see p53) and art carved on stone monuments and buildings, or painted on pottery, we can now piece together much of the Maya view of the creation. We can even read the precise date when the creation took place.

In AD 775, a Maya lord with the high-sounding name of K'ak' Tiliw Chan Yoat (Fire Burning Sky Lightning God) set up an immense stone monument in the center of his city, Quirigua, in Guatemala. The unimaginative archaeologists who discovered the stone called it Stela C. This monument bears the longest single hieroglyphic description of the creation, noting that it took place on the day 13.0.0.0.0, 4 Ahaw, 8 Kumk'u, a date corresponding to August 13, 3114 BC on our calendar. This date appears over and over in other inscriptions throughout the Maya world. On that day the creator gods set three stones or mountains in the dark waters that once covered the primordial world. These three stones formed a cosmic hearth at the center of the universe. The gods then struck divine new fire by means of lightning, which charged the world with new life.

This account of the creation is echoed in the first chapters of the *Popol Vuh*, a book compiled by members of the Maya nobility soon after the Spanish conquest in 1524, many centuries after the erection of Quirigua Stela C. Although this book was written in their native Mayan language, its authors used European letters rather than the more terse hieroglyphic script. Thus the book gives a fuller account of how they conceived the first creation:

> This is the account of when all is still, silent and placid. All is silent and calm. Hushed and empty is the womb of the sky. These then are the first words, the first speech. There is not yet one person, one animal, bird, fish, crab, tree, rock, hollow, canyon, meadow or forest. All alone the sky exists. The face of the earth has not yet appeared. Alone lies the expanse of the sea, along with the womb of all the sky. There is not yet anything gathered together. All is at rest. Nothing stirs. All is languid, at rest in the sky. Only the expanse of the water, only the tranquil sea lies alone. All lies placid and silent in the darkness, in the night.

> All alone are the Framer and the Shaper, Sovereign and Quetzal Serpent, They Who Have Borne Children and They Who Have Begotten Sons. Luminous they are in the water, wrapped in feathers…They are great sages, great possessors of knowledge…
> Then they called forth the mountains from the water. Straightaway the great mountains came to be. It was merely their spirit essence, their miraculous power, that brought about the conception of the mountains.

The Maya saw this pattern all around them. In the night sky, the three brightest stars in the constellation of Orion's Belt were

Dr Allen J Christenson has an MA and a PhD in Pre-Columbian Maya Art History, and works as an associate professor in the Humanities, Classics and Comparative Literature department of Brigham Young University in Provo, Utah. His works include a critical translation of the *Popol Vuh* from the original Maya text, *Popol Vuh: The Sacred Book of the Maya* (2003).

The oldest known copy of the *Popol Vuh* was made around 1701–03 by a Roman Catholic priest named Francisco Ximénez in Guatemala. The location of the original *Popol Vuh* from which Ximénez made his copy, if it still survives, is unknown.

conceived as the cosmic hearth at the center of the universe. On a clear night in the crisp mountain air of the Maya highlands, one can even see what looks like a wisp of smoke within these stars, although it is really only a far-distant string of stars within the M4 Nebula.

Popol Vuh: The Sacred Book of the Maya

MAYA CITIES AS THE CENTER OF CREATION

Perhaps because the ancient Maya of northern Belize didn't have real mountains as symbols of the creation, they built them instead in the form of plaza-temple complexes. In hieroglyphic inscriptions, the large open-air plazas at the center of Maya cities are often called *nab'* (sea) or *lakam ja'* (great water). Rising above these plastered stone spaces are massive pyramid temples, often oriented in groups of three, representing the first mountains to emerge out of the 'waters' of the plaza. The tiny elevated sanctuaries of these temples served as portals into the abodes of gods that lived within. Offerings were burned on altars in the plazas, as if the flames were struck in the midst of immense three-stone hearths. Only a few elite persons were allowed to enter the small interior spaces atop the temples, while the majority of the populace observed their actions from the plaza below. The architecture of ancient Maya centers thus replicated sacred geography to form an elaborate stage on which rituals that charged their world with regenerative power could be carried out.

Many of the earliest-known Maya cities were built in Belize, including Cuello (p164), Lamanai (p167), Cerros (p178), Caracol (p213) and Altun Ha (p106), all of which were founded at some point during the Middle and late Preclassic Periods (in the first millennium BC). The earliest temples at these sites are often constructed in this three-temple arrangement, grouped together on a single platform, as an echo of the first three mountains of creation. The ancient name for the site known today as Caracol was Oxwitza' (Three Hills Place), symbolically linking this community with the three mountains of creation and thus the center of life. The Caana (Sky Place) is the largest structure at Caracol and consists of a massive pyramid-shaped platform topped by three temples that represent these three sacred mountains.

The Belizean site of Lamanai is one of the oldest and largest Maya cities known. It is also one of the few Maya sites that still bears its ancient name (which means Submerged Crocodile). While other sites were abandoned well before the Spanish Conquest in the 16th century, Lamanai continued to be occupied by the Maya centuries afterward. For the ancient Maya the crocodile symbolized the rough surface of the earth, newly emerged from the primordial sea that once covered the world. The name of the city reveals that its inhabitants saw themselves as living at the center of creation, rising from the waters of creation. Its massive pyramid temples include Structure N10-43,

A good introduction to the art of the Maya world is Mary Ellen Miller's *Maya Art and Architecture*. For a more complete overview of Maya cities and culture from the point of view of an eminent archaeologist, try *The Ancient Maya* by Robert J Sharer.

For up-to-date articles on archaeological discoveries as well as essays on Maya theology and ritual practices, visit www.mesoweb.com.

GUIDE TO THE GODS *Mara Vorhees*

The Maya worshipped a host of heavenly beings. It's practically impossible to remember them all (especially since some of them have multiple names), but here's a primer for the most powerful Maya gods.

Ah Puch – God of Death

Chaac – God of Rain and Thunder

Izamma – God of Priestly Knowledge and Writing

Hun Hunahpu – Father of the Hero Twins, sometimes considered the Maize God

Hunahpu & Ixbalanque – The Hero Twins (see p53)

Ixchel – Goddess of Fertility and Birth

which is the second-largest pyramid known from the Maya Preclassic Period and represents the first mountain and dwelling place of the gods.

THE MAYA CREATION OF MANKIND

According to the *Popol Vuh,* the purpose of the creation was to give form and shape to beings who would 'remember' the gods through ritual. The Maya take their role in life very seriously. They believe that people exist as mediators between this world and that of the gods. If they fail to carry out the proper prayers and ceremonies at just the right time and place, the universe will come to an abrupt end.

The gods created the first people out of maize (corn) dough, literally from the flesh of the Maize God, the principal deity of creation. Because of their divine origin, they were able to see with miraculous vision:

> Perfect was their sight, and perfect was their knowledge of everything beneath the sky. If they gazed about them, looking intently, they beheld that which was in the sky and that which was upon the earth. Instantly they were able to behold everything…Thus their knowledge became full. Their vision passed beyond the trees and the rocks, beyond the lakes and the seas, beyond the mountains and the valleys. Truly they were very esteemed people.
>
> *Popol Vuh: The Sacred Book of the Maya*

In nearly all of their languages, the Maya refer to themselves as 'true people' and consider that they are literally of a different flesh than those who do not eat maize. They are maize people, and foreigners who eat bread are wheat people. This mythic connection between maize and human flesh influenced birth rituals in the Maya world for centuries.

No self-respecting Maya, raised in the traditional way, would consider eating a meal that didn't include maize. They treat it with the utmost respect. Women do not let grains of maize fall on the ground or into an open fire. If it happens accidentally, as I saw once, the woman picks it up gently and apologizes to it. The Maya love to talk and laugh, but are generally silent during meals. Most don't know why; it's just the way things have always been done. I once asked an elder about it and he said, 'for us, tortillas are like the Catholic sacramental bread: it is the flesh of god. You don't laugh or speak when taking the flesh of god into your body. The young people are beginning to forget this. They will someday regret it.'

MAYA KINGSHIP

But the creation wasn't a one-time event. The Maya constantly repeated these primordial events in their ceremonies, timed to the sacred calendar. They saw the universe as a living thing. And just like any living thing, it grows old, weakens and ultimately passes away. Everything, including the gods, needed to be periodically recharged with life-bearing power or the world would slip back into the darkness and chaos that existed before the world began. Maya kings were seen as mediators. In countless wall carvings and paintings, monumental stone stelae and altars, painted pottery and other sacred objects, the Maya depicted their kings dressed as gods, repeating the actions of deities at the time of creation.

A common theme was the king dressed as the Maize God himself, bearing a huge pack on his back containing the sacred bits and pieces that make up the world, while dancing them into existence. A beautiful example of this may be seen on the painted *Buena Vista Vase,* one of the true masterpieces of Maya art. Discovered at Buenavista el Cayo, a small

For a lively discussion of Maya religion and the creation, pick up a copy of *Maya Cosmos* by David Freidel, Linda Schele and Joy Parker.

For an incredibly beautiful and searchable collection of photographs of painted vases, monuments and other works of ancient Maya art, visit the Kerr Archives at www.famsi.org/research /kerr/index.html.

The Maya hieroglyphic writing system is one of only five major phonetic scripts ever invented – the others being cuneiform (used in ancient Mesopotamia), Egyptian, Harappan and Chinese.

site in the Cayo District of Belize, right on the river (north side) close to the border with Guatemala, it is now one of the gems of the Maya collection housed in the Department of Archaeology, Belize City. These rituals were done at very specific times of the year, timed to match calendric dates when the gods first performed them. For the Maya, these ceremonies were not merely symbolic of the rebirth of the cosmos, but a genuine creative act in which time folded in on itself to reveal the actions of the divine creators in the primordial world.

In Maya theology, the Maize God is the most sacred of the creator deities because he gives his very flesh in order for human beings to live. But this sacrifice must be repaid. The Maya, as 'true people', felt an obligation to the cosmos to compensate for the loss of divine life, not because the gods were cruel, but because gods cannot rebirth themselves and need the intercession of human beings. Maya kings stood as the sacred link between their subjects and the gods. The king was thus required to periodically give that which was most precious – his own blood, which was believed to contain

If you are curious about how scholars unlocked the secrets of Maya hieroglyphics, read Michael Coe's Breaking the Maya Code. It reads like a detective novel.

HOLLYWOOD VS HISTORY *Mara Vorhees*

The Maya is not one of the world's better-known ancient civilizations. We learn about the Egyptians and the Romans at school, but when it comes to indigenous American history, common knowledge is pretty much nil.

That's why historians, archaeologists and anthropologists were outraged by *Apocalypto*, Mel Gibson's 2006 film about the ancient Maya civilization – not only due to its historical inaccuracy but also its cultural insensitivity.

To his credit, Gibson did employ Amerindian actors who actually spoke the Yucatec Mayan language. And the film did capture many elements of the Maya culture, from the elaborate tattoos on their bodies to the jungle setting of their cities. But, according to most scholars, these small details pale in comparison to the vast misrepresentation of the civilization and the inherently colonialist message of the film.

Nobody denies that violence was an integral part of the ancient Maya culture. Yes, they were known to kill off a few people here and there to keep Chaac happy (see p50). But human sacrifice did not take place in the mass quantities depicted in the movie, and there is no evidence of mass graves at Maya sites. Rather, this is an aspect of the Aztec culture that was co-opted for the film. Most victims of Maya sacrifice were rulers of rival kingdoms who were killed after their capture, or individuals that had been groomed for the honor. (According to one critic, when it came to human sacrifice, the Maya placed their emphasis on quality, not quantity.)

Also absent from Maya society: slavery. *Apocalypto* depicts crowds of slaves toiling under harsh conditions. But when you go to Tikal and Caracol, you learn that these cities were likely built by ordinary citizens, who may have been conscripted or may have volunteered for the job.

So Gibson added a few of his own elements to spice up his story, but he left out some others: art, architecture, astrology, spirituality, hieroglyphics, calendar and more. The Maya civilization endured for thousands of years and its accomplishments were many; *Apocalypto* ignores that.

Apocalypto ends with the arrival of the Spanish, who offer the first and only moment of peace in the entire film. Indeed, the Spanish rescue our hero Jaguar Paw from his bloody fate. The implication is that the Spanish save the Maya from the violence they are perpetrating upon themselves.

Never mind the jumbled timeline: in reality, the Maya cities (with the exception of Lamanai) had long since been abandoned by the time the Spanish arrived. What's worse is that the film completely overlooks the horrific violence the Spanish would inflict on the Maya in the coming years. Some experts estimate that the Maya population declined by as much as 90% within 100 years of the arrival of the Spanish, yet here they are perceived as saviors.

So, viewer, beware: *Apocalypto* is a heart-racing, gut-wrenching, action-adventure film; a history lesson, it is not.

THE HERO TWINS *Mara Vorhees*

According to the *Popol Vuh*, the Lords of Xibalbá (the Underworld) invited Hun Hunahpu and his brother to a game in the ball court. Upon losing the game, the brothers were sacrificed and their skulls were suspended from a calabash tree as a show of triumph.

Along came an unsuspecting daughter of Xibalbá. As she reached out to take fruit from the tree, the skull of Hun Hunahpu spat in her hand, thus impregnating her. From this strange conception would be born the Hero Twins, Hunahpu and Ixbalanque.

The Hero Twins would go on to have many adventures, including vanquishing their evil half-brothers. Their final triumph was overcoming Xibalbá and avenging the death of their father – first by defeating the Lords in a ball game, and then by sacrificing them. After this, the twins ascended into the sky, being transformed into the sun and moon. They were considered the original ancestors of the ruling dynasties of the ancient Maya.

---

the essence of godhood itself. Generally, this meant that members of the royal family bled themselves with stingray spines or stone lancets. Males did their bloodletting from the genital area, literally birthing gods from the penis. Women most often drew blood from their tongues. This royal blood was collected on sheets of bark paper and then burned to release its divine essence, opening a portal to the other world and allowing the gods to emerge to a new life. At times of crisis, such as the end of a calendar cycle, or upon the death of a king and the succession of another, the sacrifice had to be greater to compensate for the loss of divine life. This generally involved obtaining noble or royal captives through warfare against a neighboring Maya state in order to sacrifice them.

Altar 23 from Caracol shows two captive lords from the Maya cities of B'ital and Ucanal, on the Guatemala-Belize border, with their arms bound behind their backs in preparation for sacrifice, perhaps on that very altar. If this were not done, they believed that life itself would cease to exist.

The beauty of Maya religion is that these great visions of creation mirror everyday events in the lives of the people. When a Maya woman rises early in the morning, before dawn, to grind maize for the family meal, she replicates the actions of the creators at the beginning of time. The darkness that surrounds her is reminiscent of the gloom of the primordial world. When she lights the three-stone hearth on the floor of her home, she is once again striking the new fire that generates life. The grains of maize that she cooks and then forms into tortillas are literally the flesh of the Maize God, who nourishes and rebuilds the bodies of her family members. This divine symmetry is comforting in a world that often proves intolerant and cruel.

Like ancient Greece, there was no unified Maya empire. Each city had its own royal family and its own patron gods. Warfare was often conducted not for conquest, but to obtain captives who bore within their veins royal blood to be sacrificed.

MAYA HIEROGLYPHIC WRITING

More than 1500 years prior to the Spanish Conquest, the Maya developed a sophisticated hieroglyphic script capable of recording complex literary compositions, both on folded screen codices made of bark paper or deer skin, as well as texts incised on more durable stone or wood. The importance of preserving written records was a hallmark of Maya culture, as witnessed by the thousands of known hieroglyphic inscriptions, many more of which are still being discovered in the jungles of Belize and other Maya regions. The sophisticated Maya hieroglyphic script is partly phonetic (glyphs representing sounds tied to the spoken language) and partly logographic (glyphs representing entire words), making it capable of recording any idea that could be thought or spoken.

Ancient Maya scribes were among the most honored members of their society. They were often important representatives of the royal family and, as

HOW THE MAYA CALENDAR WORKED

The ancient Maya used three calendars. The first was a period of 260 days, known as the Tzolkin, likely based on the nine months it takes for a human fetus to develop prior to birth. Traditionalist Maya priests still undergo a 260-day period of training before they are 'reborn' as priests worthy to interpret the ancient calendar on behalf of petitioners. The second Maya calendar system was a solar year of 365 days, called the Haab. Both the Tzolkin and Haab were measured in endlessly repeating cycles. When meshed together, a total of 18,980 day-name permutations are possible (a period of 52 solar years) called the Calendar Round.

Though fascinating in its complexity, the Calendar Round has its limitations, the greatest being that it only goes for 52 years. After that, it starts again and so provides no way for Maya ceremony planners to distinguish a day in this 52-year Calendar Round cycle from the identically named day in the next cycle, or in the cycle after that. Thus the Maya developed a third calendar system that we call the Long Count, which pinpoints a date based on the number of days it takes place after the day of creation on August 13, 3114 BC.

Let's use the example of the day on which I am writing this chapter. The Maya Long Count date corresponding to today, Monday, March 31, 2008, is 12.19.15.3.14, 2 Uayeb 7 Ix.

The first number, '12,' of this Long Count date represents how many *baktuns* (400 x 360 days or 144,000 days) that have passed since the day of creation (thus 12 x 144,000 = 1,728,000 days). The second number, '19,' represents the number of *katuns* (20 x 360 or 7200 days) that have passed, thus adding another 19 x 7200 = 136,800 days. The third number, '15,' is the number of *tuns* (360 days), or 5400 days. The fourth number, '3,' is the number of *uinals* (20 days), or 60 days. Finally the fifth number, '14,' is the number of whole days. Adding each of these numbers gives us the sum of 1,728,000 + 136,800 + 5400 + 60 + 14 = 1,870,274 days since the day of creation.

The Maya then added the Calendar Round date: the Haab date (2 Uayeb) and the Tzolkin date (7 Ix). If that weren't precise enough, the Maya would also often mention the dates from various planetary cycles (which lord of the night was in place etc).

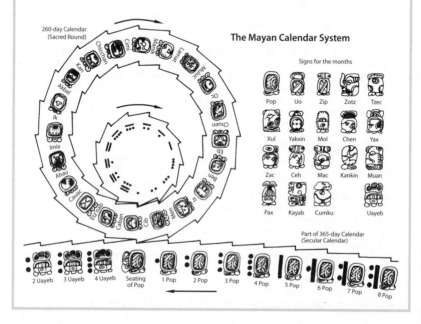

260-day Calendar (Sacred Round)

The Mayan Calendar System

Signs for the months

Pop Uo Zip Zotz Tzec
Xul Yaxkin Mol Chen Yax
Zac Ceh Mac Kankin Muan
Pax Kayab Cumku Uayeb

Part of 365-day Calendar (Secular Calendar)

2 Uayeb 3 Uayeb 4 Uayeb Seating of Pop 1 Pop 2 Pop 3 Pop 4 Pop 5 Pop 6 Pop 7 Pop 8 Pop

such, were believed to carry the seeds of divinity within their blood. Among the titles given to artists and scribes in Maya inscriptions of the Classic Period were *itz'aat* (sage) and *miyaatz* (wise one).

COUNTING SYSTEM

Maya arithmetic was elegantly simple: dots were used to count from one to four, a horizontal bar signified five, a bar with one dot above it was six, a bar with two dots was seven etc. Two bars signified 10, three bars 15. Nineteen, the highest common number, was three bars stacked up and topped by four dots.

The Maya didn't use a decimal system (which is based on the number 10), but rather a vigesimal system (that is, a system that has a base of 20). The late Mayanist Linda Schele used to suggest that this was because they wore sandals and thus counted not only their fingers but their toes as well. This is a likely explanation, since the number 20 in nearly all Mayan languages means 'person.'

To signify larger sums the Maya used positional numbers – a fairly sophisticated system similar to the one we use today and much more advanced than the crude additive numbers used in the Roman Empire. In positional numbers, the position of a sign and the sign's value determine the number. For example, in our decimal system the number 23 is made up of two signs: a 2 in the 'tens' position and a 3 in the 'ones' position; two tens plus three ones equals 23.

In the Maya system, positions of increasing value went not right to left (as ours do) but from bottom to top. So the bottom position showed values from one to 19 (remember that this is a base-20 system so three bars and four dots in this lowest position would equal 19); the next position up showed multiples of 20 (for example four dots at this position would equal 80); the next position represents multiples of 400; the next, multiples of 8000 etc. By adding more positions one could count as high as needed.

Such positional numbers depend upon the use of zero, a concept that the Romans never developed but the Maya did. The zero in Maya numbering was represented by a stylized picture of a shell or some other object – but never a bar or a dot.

When the Spaniards arrived, Christian missionaries zealously burned all the Maya hieroglyphic books they could find. Only four are known to have survived and are held in Dresden, Madrid, Paris and Mexico City.

CALENDAR SYSTEM

The Maya counting system was used by merchants and others who had to add up many things, but its most important use – and the one you will most often encounter during your travels – was in writing calendar dates. The ancient Maya calendar was a way of interpreting the order of the universe itself. The sun, moon and stars were not simply handy ways of measuring the passage of time, but living beings that influenced the world in fundamentally important ways. Even today, the Maya refer to days as 'he.' The days and years were conceived as being carried by gods, each with definite personalities and spheres of influence that colored the experience of those who lived them. Priests carefully watched the sky to look for the appearance of celestial bodies that would determine the time to plant and harvest crops, celebrate certain ceremonies, or go to war. The regular rotation of the heavens served as a comforting contrast to the chaos that characterizes our imperfect human world.

In some ways, the ancient Maya calendar – still used in parts of the region – is more accurate than the Gregorian calendar we use today. Without sophisticated technology, Maya astronomers were able to ascertain the length of the solar year as 365.2420 days (a discrepancy of 17.28 seconds per year from the true average length of 365.2422 days). The Gregorian

The Maya likely used their counting system from day to day by writing on the ground, the tip of the finger creating a dot. By using the edge of the hand they could make a bar, representing the entire hand of five fingers.

calendar year works out to be 365.2425 days. Thus the Maya year count is 1/10,000 closer to the truth than our own modern calendar.

Maya astronomers were able to pinpoint eclipses with uncanny accuracy, a skill that was unknown among the brightest scholars in contemporary medieval Europe. The Maya lunar cycle was a mere seven minutes off today's sophisticated technological calculations. They calculated the Venus cycle at 583.92 days. By dropping four days each 61 Venus years and eight days at the end of 300 Venus years, the Maya lost less than a day in accuracy in 1000 years!

If you would like to convert a modern Gregorian date, such as your birthday or anniversary, to the Maya Long Count and Calendar Round calendars, you could use the Maya Date Calculator found at www.halfmoon.org.

The ancient Maya believed that the Great Cycle of the present age would last for 13 *baktun* cycles in all (each *baktun* lasting 144,000 days), which according to our calendar will end on December 23, AD 2012. By my count we have 1728 days left. By the time you read this, it will be less. The Maya saw the end of large cycles of time as a kind of death, and they were thus fraught with peril. But both death and life must dance together on the cosmic stage for the succession of days to come. Thus the Maya conducted ceremonies to periodically 'rebirth' the world and keep the endless march of time going. These ceremonies continue today among traditionalist Maya, so likely we have nothing to fear.

The Maya never expected the end of this Great Cycle to be the last word for the cosmos, since the world regularly undergoes death and rebirth. Koba Stela 1 (the first stela from the site of Koba) records a period of time equivalent to approximately 41,341,050,000,000,000,000,000,000,000 of our years! (In comparison, the Big Bang that is said to have formed our universe is estimated to have occurred a mere 15,000,000,000 years ago.)

Environment

With Belize's sparse human population and history of relatively low-key human impact, more than 70% of the country still has natural vegetation cover, a much higher proportion than in most other Central American countries. The hot, moist climate and varied topsoil have yielded a vast diversity of animal and plant species, many of which are able to live undisturbed in their natural habitats. Thanks to an admirable conservation agenda pursued by governments and nongovernmental organizations (NGOs) since Belizean independence in 1981, more than 40% of the national territory is under environmental protection. All of this makes Belize a particularly fascinating destination for anyone interested in nature, be it the marine life of the coral reefs, the vegetation and animal life of the forests or the hundreds of bird species that soar, flutter and swoop through the skies.

THE LAND

At 8866 sq miles, Belize is certainly a small country – only slightly bigger than Massachusetts or Wales – but it harbors great geological variety. If you were a magnificent frigate bird flying in westward over the Caribbean toward Belize, the first breaks you'd notice in the surface of the waters would be the three offshore atolls of Lighthouse Reef (p157), Glover's Reef (p227) and Turneffe Atoll (p156). These broken rings of coral reef, dotted with low islands, surround shallow inner lagoons. They're the tips of tall, steep, underwater mountains pushed up by the action of the Caribbean tectonic plate (to their south) sliding past the North American plate on which Belize sits. The sea floor drops away rapidly to great depths around the atolls – to 6000ft within 5 miles east of Lighthouse Reef, for instance.

West of the atolls you'll see Belize's barrier reef breaking the water surface for 160 miles parallel to nearly the entire coastline of the country, ranging between 10 and 25 miles off the mainland. Like the atolls, the reef sits atop geological fault blocks, with steep drop-offs on its eastern side but shallow waters inshore, where the sea floor is a continuation of the continental shelf and rarely more than 15ft deep. The reef itself, and the area between it and the mainland, are dotted with hundreds of islands known as cayes (pronounced 'keys'). The inshore cayes – mainly the northern cayes – tend to be mangrove-lined, while the islands on and beyond the reef are generally sandy with palm trees.

On the mainland, low-lying plains spread across the northern half of the country and the coastal areas of the south. Belize's uplands, stretching southwest from the center of the country to just across the Guatemalan border, are the Maya Mountains. Their highest peak is Doyle's Delight (3687ft) in the southwest. Another well-known landmark is Victoria Peak (3675ft), on the fringe of the Cockscomb Basin (p235) on the northeast side of the mountains.

Numerous rivers drop down off the mountains to snake their way south, east or north across the plains to the Caribbean. None of them is of huge magnitude, but all the country's bigger towns lie on the rivers, which have always been key trade and transportation routes. The biggest is the Belize River, running west to east across the middle of the country, from its source in San Ignacio (see Branch Mouth, p198) to Belize City.

The central core of the Maya Mountains is hard granite, laid down 125 million or more years ago, but the northern, western and southern fringes of the range – such as Belize's northern plains – are limestone, evidence that

Doyle's Delight is named after Arthur Conan Doyle, author of *The Lost World*, who wrote 'there must be something wild and wonderful in a country such as this, and we're the men to find it out!.'

Belize switched to driving on the right in the 1960s, partly because Hurricane Hattie had wiped out most of the lefty cars.

these areas were once under warm, shallow seas. The erosive action of water on the relatively soft limestone has produced numerous underground rivers and caves. Many of the caves were ritual sites for the ancient Maya and they can be visited today (see Cave-Tubing, p186; Actun Tunichil Muknal, p191; Barton Creek Cave, p193; and Che Chem Ha, p210).

The interior of the country, including most of the Maya Mountains, is still mostly covered in moist, tropical broadleaf forests, which are highly diverse and shelter a great range of wildlife. Pines and savannah break out west of Belize City and on Mountain Pine Ridge (p211), a northwestern spur of the Maya Mountains. Nearer the coast you'll find littoral forests with tougher-leaved, salt-tolerant trees.

WILDLIFE

Belize's animal and plant life are the stars of the country, thanks to the conservation of its forests and reefs. Getting to see the animals and to identify and understand the plant life is in large measure a matter of having a knowledgeable guide. Resorts, lodges, hotels and tour agencies throughout

HURRICANE WATCH

Hurricanes have long bedeviled the Belizean coast, leaving their marks in very visible ways. For example, the Split on Caye Caulker (p141) was created when Hurricane Hattie whipped through here and split the island in two. This is the same storm that motivated the Belizean government to build a new inland capital (see Belmopan, p188).

The effects of these tropical storms are not only physical: hurricane season is engrained in the brains of the residents, who long remember the last evacuation and always anticipate the next one. The most treacherous events are even recorded in Belizean literature, providing the setting for crucial scenes in *Beka Lamb* by Zee Edgell and *Belize* by Carlos Ledson Miller.

Any visitor to Belize is likely to engage in at least one conversation about the most recent tempest (more, if it was a bad one). Here are a few of the lowlights from Belizean hurricane history:

- **Hurricane Dean (2007)** Residents feared the worst, and thousands of people were evacuated from Belize City, Caye Caulker and Ambergris Caye in anticipation of this Category-5 hurricane. Thankfully, Hurricane Dean was a near miss, as it made landfall about 40 miles north of the Belizean–Mexican border. Nonetheless, there was millions of dollars worth of damage done in Corozal and Orange Walk, as well as severe repercussions for the sugar and papaya industries.

- **Hurricane Iris (2001)** This devastating Category-4 storm made landfall in southern Belize, destroying many rural Maya villages and leaving upward of 10,000 people homeless. Off the coast south of Belize City, a live-aboard dive ship capsized, killing 20 people. Joe Burnworth recounts the tragic tale in his book *No Safe Harbor*.

- **Hurricane Hattie (1961)** This history-making hurricane killed 275 people and destroyed much of Belize City. Afterward, survivors apparently roamed the rubble-strewn streets in search of food and shelter. Many moved to refugee camps, which later morphed into permanent settlements (the origins of Hattieville; see Belize Central Prison, p113). Hurricane Hattie provides the backdrop for Carlos Ledson Miller's novel *Belize*.

- **Hurricane Five (1931)** One of the deadliest seasons in Atlantic-coast hurricane history, 1931 also saw the highest death toll in Belize. Hurricane Five hit the coast of Belize on September 10, a national holiday, meaning that emergency services were slow to respond. The entire northern coast of the country was devastated, and around 2500 people were killed.

Recent scientific evidence suggests that the strength of hurricanes increases with the rise of ocean temperatures. So as our climate continues to change, countries such as Belize are likely to experience more frequent and more intense hurricane hits.

the country offer a range of tours, nature walks, birding trips, botanical trails and other activities for nature lovers.

Good guides will show you a surprising variety of creatures and plants, many of which you would never spot otherwise. Night forest walks can be especially (and literally) illuminating, as you use flashlights to check out kinkajous, crocodiles and other nocturnal creatures. Birds, of course, are everywhere, but again guides will spot and identify far more than you likely would alone.

Animals
MAMMALS
Felines

Everyone dreams of seeing a jaguar in the wild. Even though Belize has healthy numbers of the biggest feline in the Western hemisphere (up to 6ft long and 250lb in weight), your best chance of seeing one, as with many other species, is still at the Belize Zoo (p113). They're widely distributed, living almost anywhere that has large expanses of thick forest. The biggest populations and most frequent reported sightings are in the Chan Chich area (p171) and Rio Bravo Conservation & Management Area (p169). You stand a good chance of seeing their tracks and maybe the remains of their meals in Cockscomb Basin Wildlife Sanctuary (p235), which was established as a jaguar reserve in the 1980s, when the then highly endangered jaguar became protected in Belize.

Belize has four smaller wildcats, all elusive like the jaguar: the puma (aka mountain lion or cougar), almost as big as the jaguar but a uniform gray or brown color (occasionally black); the ocelot, spotted similarly to the jaguar but a lot smaller; the margay, smaller again and also spotted; and the small, brown or gray jaguarundi.

Most jaguars have yellow-brown fur, with black spots known as rosettes; jaguars with black fur (known as black panthers) also have rosettes, though they are less visible.

Monkeys

The endangered black howler monkey exists only in Belize, northern Guatemala and southern Mexico. Its population has made a comeback in several areas, especially in the Community Baboon Sanctuary (p108), set up in the 1980s specifically to protect this noisy animal. The sanctuary is now home to some 3000 individual monkeys. Other places where you stand a good chance of seeing and hearing howlers include: the Lamanai ruins (p167); Cockscomb Basin Wildlife Sanctuary (p235); Chan Chich Lodge (p171); and the Rio Bravo area (p169). There is also a healthy population in Tikal National Park (p263) in Guatemala. The howler's eerie dawn and evening cries – more roars than howls – can carry two miles across the treetops.

Less common, though you may still spot some in similar areas, are the smaller, long-tailed spider monkeys.

Other Land Mammals

Related to the horse but with shorter legs and tail, a stouter build and small eyes, ears and intellect, the Baird's tapir (or mountain cow) eats plants, bathes daily and runs like mad when approached. It's shy and seldom seen in the forest.

You may well see a peccary, a sort of wild pig that weighs 50lb or more; it is active by day and tends to travel in groups. There are two types, whose names – white-lipped peccary and collared peccary – define their differences.

Resembling a large spotted guinea pig, up to 2ft long and weighing up to 22lb, the nocturnal gibnut (or paca) is a rodent that often lives in pairs. The agouti is similar but diurnal and more closely resembles a rabbit, with strong back legs.

SPOTTING WILDLIFE

Nature viewing with a guide can be thrilling, but it's even more exciting when you start to develop the skills to spot animals on your own.

Birds and other animals will ignore you if you stay fairly still and don't make too much noise: move slowly, avoid sudden movements and keep your voice low. Most animals are well camouflaged, so they're not going to stand out against their natural background. Look for unusual movement in trees, on the ground or on the surface of water. Keep your binoculars around your neck – they're useful only if you can get to them quickly and with little movement. With or without binoculars, a good trick is to scan the horizon rather than peer at one spot.

Listen carefully, because noises in the forest can be very telling. Your best chance of spotting most birds and animals is early in the morning when they're having their early meal. Don't overlook the little things such as bugs, ants, small reptiles or small birds and crabs – they can be some of the most interesting and accessible wildlife on any excursion.

The tayra (or tree otter) is a member of the weasel family and has a dark-brown body, yellowish neck and 1ft-long tail. The coatimundi (or quash) is a rather cute-looking, rusty brown, raccoon-like creature with a long nose and striped tail that it often holds upright when walking. You stand a chance of seeing a coatimundi in daylight on the sides of roads or trails. Also in the raccoon family is the nocturnal kinkajou (or nightwalker), mainly a tree-dweller.

Aquatic Mammals

West Indian manatees can be seen at river mouths, in coastal lagoons and around the cayes. The sure-fire places to spot these gentle, slow-moving creatures are Southern Lagoon, near Gales Point Manatee village (p115), and Swallow Caye (p144), off Belize City. Manatees are the only vegetarian sea mammals in existence. Just a few hundred survive in Belizean waters. They are threatened by increased boat traffic (you'll see some with scars from propellers) and erosion that threatens their feeding areas. Typically 10ft long and weighing 1000lb, adults eat 100lb to 150lb of vegetation, especially sea grass, daily. For more on manatees, see the boxed text on p145.

The best all-in-one wildlife guide is Belize & Northern Guatemala: The Ecotravellers' Wildlife Guide *by Les Beletsky, offering helpful descriptions along with full-color drawings and photographs.*

REPTILES

The protected green iguana is a dragon-like vegetarian lizard that can grow to 6ft in length and is often spotted in trees along riverbanks. You can also see it in iguana houses at Monkey Bay Wildlife Sanctuary (p114) and the San Ignacio Resort Hotel (p198).

Of Belize's two crocodile species, the American crocodile can live in both saltwater and freshwater, while the smaller Morelet's crocodile lives only in freshwater. Both are on the endangered species list. The American usually grows to 13ft, the Morelet's to 8ft. Belizean crocs tend to stick to prey that's smaller than the average adult human. Still, it's best to keep your distance.

Hawksbill, loggerhead, leatherback and green sea turtles can be seen in the waters of Belize. They live at sea and the females come ashore only to lay their eggs. Sea turtles are victims of poaching and egg hunting, as their eggs are believed by the uninformed to be an aphrodisiac. However, while all sea turtles are endangered, the hawksbill, which was hunted for its shell, is the only one currently protected in Belize. Turtle-viewing trips are organized in the May to October laying season from Gales Point Manatee village (p115).

Up to 60 species of snake inhabit the forests and waters of Belize and, of these, only a handful are dangerous (see p304). The nasties include the (sometimes fatally) poisonous fer-de-lance (commonly known as the yellow-jaw tommygoff), which is earth toned and a particular threat to farmers when they're clearing areas of vegetation; the coral snake, banded with bright red, yellow and black stripes; the tropical rattlesnake; and the boa constrictor, which kills by constriction but can also give you a mean (but venomless) bite.

OTHER MARINE LIFE

Belizean waters are home to whale sharks – notably Gladden Spit (p228), near Placencia. Between March and June, most commonly during the 10 days after the full moon, these filter-feeding behemoths come in close to the reef to dine on spawn. These are the world's largest fish (yes, they're sharks not whales), growing up to a whopping 60ft (although the average length is 25ft) and weighing up to 15 tons. Whale sharks can live up to 150 years. They're gray with random light-yellow spots and stripes, and are quite harmless to humans.

Other sharks – nurse, reef, lemontip and hammerhead – and a variety of rays often make appearances around the reefs and islands. They tend to leave divers and snorkelers alone.

Sharing the coral with the larger animals is a kaleidoscope of reef fish, ranging from larger barracuda and groupers to parrotfish, angelfish, butterfly fish and clown fish (they're the ones who like to nestle into the anemones). Belizean waters host nearly every species of fish and coral found in the Caribbean, plus an amazing variety of sponges. The total number of fish and invertebrate species is around 600, and there are over 40 species of coral, from hard elkhorn and staghorn coral (named because they branch like antlers) to gorgonian fans and other soft formations that sway with the current.

Just in case you're wondering what you've just seen, most dive and snorkel boats have laminated fish-identifier cards on board.

BIRDS

Almost 600 bird species have been identified in Belize, 20% of them winter migrants from North America. Even if you are not a 'bird nerd,' you'll be amazed by the unusual and colorful species that guides will show you on any nature trip.

You're likely to see interesting birds almost anywhere at any time, although February to May are particularly good months in many places. Wetlands, lagoons, forested riverbanks and forest areas with clearings (the setting of

> Belize finally got its own birding guide with the publication in 2004 of the comprehensive *Birds of Belize* by H Lee Jones, which is well illustrated by Dana Gardner.

TOP PICKS – BIRDING DESTINATIONS

- Caracol (p213)
- Caye Caulker (p147)
- Chan Chich Lodge (p171)
- Cockscomb Basin Wildlife Sanctuary (p235)
- Crooked Tree Wildlife Sanctuary (p110)
- El Pilar (p204)
- La Milpa Field Station (p171)
- Lamanai and New River (p167)
- Aguacaliente Wildlife Sanctuary (p252)
- Poustinia Land Art Park (p209)
- Sittee River (p234)

many jungle lodges and Maya ruins) are propitious for observing a variety of birds. Some lodges proudly announce how many hundreds of species have been spotted in their areas: these are likely to be places with a focus on birding, providing reference materials and good guides.

Sea Birds

Magnificent frigate birds are constantly soaring over the coastline on pointed, prehistoric-looking wings with a span of up to 6ft. They have difficulty taking off from the ground, so their method of hunting is to plummet down and catch fish as they jump from the sea. They often hang out around fisherfolk and other birds so that they can swoop in on discarded or dropped catches. Males have red throats that are displayed during courtship.

Sharing a habitat with the frigate birds is a colony of red-footed boobies living out at Half Moon Caye (p158). They dive from great heights deep into the sea to catch fish. The frigate birds often try to snatch their catch away as they resurface.

Raptors & Vultures

Raptors usually hunt rodents and small birds. The most common species in Belize include the osprey (look for their huge nests atop houses and telephone posts), peregrine falcon, roadside hawk and American kestrel. Most of these birds of prey are territorial and solitary. The majestic harpy eagle is rarely seen in the wild, but is a resident at the Belize Zoo (p113), as is the ornate hawk eagle, a beautiful large raptor with a black crest, striped tail and mottled breast.

Inland along the sides of the road and flying overhead you'll see large turkey, black and king vultures. Their job is to feast on dead animals. The turkey vulture has a red head, the king has a black-and-white color scheme with a red beak, and the black vulture appears in black and shades of gray.

Other Well-Known Birds

The beautiful scarlet macaw, a member of the parrot family, is highly endangered. Belize's small population – possibly under 200 – lives most of the year in remote jungles near the Guatemalan border, but from January to March scarlet macaws can be seen at the southern village of Red Bank (p239), where they come to eat fruit.

Biodiversity in Belize (www.biological-diversity.info) has a wealth of information about Belizean fauna, flora, ecosystems and more, including plenty of species lists.

The jabiru stork is the largest flying bird in the Americas, standing up to 5ft tall and with wingspans of up to 12ft. Many of the 100 or so remaining Belizean jabirus gather in Crooked Tree Wildlife Sanctuary (p110) in April and May. They feed by wading in shallows, enjoying fish, frogs, snails and the occasional snake.

Belize's national bird, the keel-billed toucan, is black with a yellow face and neck and is widely distributed around the country. Its huge multicolored bill is very light and almost hollow, enabling it to fly with surprising agility and to reach berries at the end of branches. Toucans like to stay at treetop level and nest in holes in trees.

You'll also have the chance to see (among others) many colorful hummingbirds, kingfishers, motmots, parrots, woodpeckers, tinamous, tanagers and trogons.

Plants

Belize is home to over 4000 species of flowering plant, including some 700 trees (similar to the total of the USA and Canada combined) and 250 orchids. Nonspecialists can usefully distinguish three chief varieties of forest in the country: coastal forests (19%), moist, tropical broadleaf forests (68%) and pine and savannah (13%).

COASTAL FORESTS

Coastal forests comprise both the mangrove stands that grow along much of the shoreline and the littoral forests slightly further inland. Mangroves serve many useful purposes as fish nurseries, hurricane barriers and shoreline stabilizers, and they are credited with creating the cayes: when coral grows close enough to the water surface, mangrove spores carried by the wind take root on it. Mangrove debris eventually creates solid ground cover, inviting other plants to take root and eventually attracting animal life. There are four common species of mangrove: red, buttonwood, white and black.

Trees of the littoral forests typically have tough, moisture-retaining leaves. They include the coconut palm, the Norfolk Island pine, the sea grape and the poisonwood, whose sap causes blistering, swelling and itching of the skin, as well as (happily) the gumbo-limbo, with its flaky, shredding bark that acts as an antidote to poisonwood rashes! These forests often provide a key refuge for migrating birds. The sandy bays off the coast are covered in sea grass, including turtle grass, manatee sea grass and duckweed sea grass.

> The tropical broadleaf is often called rainforest, although technically only far southwestern Belize receives enough rain to officially support rainforest.

TROPICAL BROADLEAF FOREST

Tropical broadleaf grows on thin clay soils where the principal nutrients come not from the soil but from the biomass of the forest – that is, debris from plants and animals. Buttressed trunks are a common phenomenon here. These forests support a huge diversity not only of plants but also of animal life.

One of the fascinating elements of these forests is their natural layering. Most have at least three layers: ground cover (a ground or herb layer); a

---

MAYA MEDICINE

The Maya have not only long depended on the forest for food and shelter, but also for hygiene and healing. These days in Belize, tour guides are quick to recommend an herbal remedy for everything from stomach ills to sexual failures. But there are only a few remaining healers who are skilled and knowledgeable in the science of Maya medicine. If you are curious about this holistic and natural approach to medicine, consult a professional (eg at the Chaa Creek Rainforest Medicine Trail, p207, or the Masewal Forest Garden in Bullet Tree Falls, p202). Here is a sampler of what might be prescribed:

- **Bay cedar** (*Guazuma ulmifolia*) The bark is boiled and used to calm the stomach and to treat dysentery.
- **Cockspur** (*Acacia cornigera*) The tea from cockspur thorns is used to treat acne, while the bark can be used to treat some snake bites.
- **Cohune palm** (*Orbignya cohune*) The oil is used for cooking and as a skin moisturizer. The shell was used for fuel, as charcoal.
- **Guava** (*Psidium guajava*) Boil the bark of a guava and drink the tea as an antidote for dysentery or diarrhea.
- **Gumbo-limbo tree** (*Bursera simaruba*) The gumbo-limbo tree always grows near poisonwood, which causes an itchy rash similar to poison ivy. The sticky inner bark of the gumbo-limbo is effective treatment for the poisonwood rash.
- **Skunk root** (*Petiveria alliacea*) The skunk root – boiled into a tea – is an effective way to treat stomach ulcers.

Source: Rainforest Remedies: One Hundred Healing Herbs of Belize, by Rosita Arvigo & Michael Balick

---

BELIZE'S WORLD HERITAGE SITE

In 1996 Unesco designated the **Belize Barrier Reef Reserve System** as a World Heritage site. The World Heritage listing covers seven separate reef, island and atoll areas, not all of which include bits of the barrier reef. The seven sites (in the following list) were recognized for demonstrating a unique array of reef types (fringing, barrier and atoll) and a classic example of reef evolution; for their exceptional natural beauty and pristine nature; and for being an important habitat for internationally threatened species, including marine turtles, the West Indian manatee and the American crocodile.

- Bacalar Chico National Park & Marine Reserve (p126)
- Blue Hole Natural Monument (p157)
- Half Moon Caye Natural Monument (p158)
- Glover's Reef Marine Reserve (p227)
- South Water Caye Marine Reserve (p226)
- Laughing Bird Caye National Park (p228)
- Sapodilla Cayes Marine Reserve (p247)

---

canopy layer formed from the crowns of the forest's tallest trees; and, in between, shorter subcanopy or understory trees. Throughout the layers grow hanging vines and epiphytes, or 'air plants,' which are moss and ferns that live on other trees but aren't parasites. This is also the habitat for over 300 species of orchids, including the national flower, the black orchid.

The national tree in Belize is the majestic mahogany, known for its handsome hardwood. Also important is the ceiba (the sacred tree of the Maya), with its tall gray trunk and fluffy kapok down around its seeds. The broad-canopied guanacaste (or tubroos) is another tree that can grow over 100ft high, with a wide, straight trunk and light wood used for dugout canoes (its broad seed pods coil up into what look like giant, shriveled ears). The strangler fig has tendrils and branches that surround a host tree until the unfortunate host dies. The flowering calophyllum, sometimes called the Santa Maria tree, is used for shipbuilding, while its resin has medicinal uses.

PINE & SAVANNAH

The drier lowland areas inland of Belize City and the sandy areas of the north are designated as lowland savannah and pine forest. Growth here is mostly savannah grasses and Honduran and Caribbean pine, as well as Paurotis palm, giant stands of bamboo and some oak and calabash.

The Mountain Pine Ridge (p211) is a fascinating phenomenon. As you ascend these uplands, the forest changes abruptly from tropical broadleaf to submontane pine, due to a transition to drier, sandier soils. Predominant species include Mexican white pine, Pino amarillo (or Mexican yellow pine) and Hartweg's pine.

NATIONAL PARKS & PROTECTED AREAS

Just over 40% of Belizean territory, a little over 3600 sq miles, is under official protection of one kind or another. Belize's protected areas fall into six main categories:

Forest reserve Protects forests, controls timber extraction and conserves soil, water and wildlife resources.

Marine reserve Protects and controls extraction of marine and freshwater species; also focuses on research, recreation and education.

National park Preserves nationally significant nature and scenery for the benefit of the public.

Natural monument Protects special natural features for education, research and public appreciation.

Nature reserve Maintains natural environments and processes in an undisturbed state for scientific study, monitoring, education and maintenance of genetic resources; not usually open to the general public.

Wildlife sanctuary Protects nationally significant species, groups of species, biotic communities or physical features.

ENVIRONMENTAL ISSUES

The Belize government and the populace recognize that their forests and reefs are natural treasures that need to be preserved – not only for their intrinsic ecological value, but also for attracting tourism. Early on, the government developed a large network of national park and reserve areas, but these are only as inviolable as the degree to which the community is able to protect them. Belizean natural heritage is threatened by lack of management, lack of money and the ever-present temptation to sell out to developers, prospectors and other investors.

Ecotourism

A simple definition of ecotourism is tourism that benefits – or at least minimizes its impact on – the environment. This means small-scale and slow-moving, usually with a focus on investigating the natural environment without disturbing it. Belize practically invented the concept. Its ecolodges allow guests to live in luxury but also in harmony with the creatures and plants in their midst. Its educational tours and activities allow travelers to learn about the forest and the reef without harming these fragile ecosystems. Conscientious enterprises minimize their environmental impact by employing alternative and renewable energy sources; avoiding destruction of surrounding habitats; effectively managing waste and employing recycling programs; and using locally grown produce whenever possible. Dedicated entrepreneurs also give back to the community by employing local people and investing in local causes, thus sharing the wealth.

Ecotourism depends on a precarious balance: welcoming tourists, but not too many of them; allowing access to natural sights, but not too much access; maintaining an infrastructure to support the visitors, but not having too much infrastructure. Belize is constantly struggling to maintain this balance, with varying degrees of success.

The recent increase in cruise-ship traffic in Belizean waters has shocked and outraged many conservationists and concerned citizens, who see the huge numbers of tourists disturbing wildlife, overwhelming the infrastructure and even threatening the tourism industry (see p22 for more).

Development along the coast – catering to the growing demands of tourists – continues unchecked. A 2007 study suggests that as much as 80% of coastal property is foreign-owned, with construction planned or underway. Construction of buildings and pavement of the roads on Ambergris Caye has dramatically changed the aesthetics and the atmosphere of that island, once a sleepy outpost and now a destination for package-tourists and partiers. In a recent struggle, San Pedro developers petitioned to eliminate the protected status of the southern portion of Bacalar Chico National Park & Marine Reserve (p126). The petition, thankfully, was rejected.

Even on Caye Caulker – which somehow seems immune to the changes sweeping the nation – snorkel guides have noticed that the increased tourism can lead to overfishing, which depletes the reef (see boxed text, p146).

Of course, there is no hard and fast rule about how many tourists are too many or how much development is too much. Many Belizeans compare their

Jaguar: One Man's Struggle to Establish the World's First Jaguar Preserve is the story of American zoologist Alan Rabinowitz' efforts to set up what has become the Cockscomb Basin Wildlife Sanctuary (p235).

The Belize Audubon Society's website (www.belizeaudubon .org) is a fine resource for information on protected areas and other environmental topics.

BELIZE'S PROTECTED AREAS AT A GLANCE

Protected Area	Features	Activities	Best Time to Visit
Actun Tunichil Muknal (p191)	spectacular cave with ancient Maya sacrificial remains	caving	year-round
Bacalar Chico National Park & Marine Reserve (p126)	northern Ambergris Caye barrier reef & surrounding waters	diving, snorkeling, birding & wildlife watching	year-round
Blue Hole Natural Monument (p157)	400ft-deep ocean-filled sinkhole, home to sharks	diving, snorkeling	Dec-Aug
Caracol Archaeological Reserve (p213)	Belize's biggest & greatest ancient Maya city	exploring ruins, birding	year-round
Caye Caulker Marine Reserve (p144)	barrier reef reserve with plentiful marine life	diving, snorkeling	year-round
Cockscomb Basin Wildlife Sanctuary (p235)	large rainforest reserve established for jaguars, with huge range of wildlife	hiking, wildlife & plant observation, river-tubing	Dec-May
Community Baboon Sanctuary (p108)	forest sanctuary for black howler monkeys	wildlife watching, birding, horseback riding	year-round
Crooked Tree Wildlife Sanctuary (p110)	wetland area with huge bird population	birding, walking, canoeing, horseback riding	Feb-May
Gales Point Wildlife Sanctuary (p115)	inland lagoons with Belize's colony of manatees	manatee & turtle observation, birding, fishing, sailing	year-round
Gladden Spit & Silk Cayes Marine Reserve (p228)	barrier reef & island reserve visited by whale sharks	diving, snorkeling, kayaking	Mar-Jun
Glover's Reef Marine Reserve (p227)	beautiful atoll with coral-filled lagoon & seas swarming with marine life	diving, snorkeling, swimming, fishing, sailing, kayaking	Dec-Aug
Guanacaste National Park (p187)	small forest park centered on huge guanacaste tree	birding, swimming, plant identification	year-round
Half Moon Caye Natural Monument (p158)	lush bird-sanctuary atoll island with spectacular underwater walls offshore	diving, snorkeling, birding, kayaking	Dec-Aug
Hol Chan Marine Reserve (p126)	waters off Ambergris Caye with the famous Shark Ray Alley	diving, snorkeling	year-round

country to Cozumel or Cancun and they are proud of the way that ecotourism is preserving their paradise. On Ambergris, few locals would stop the construction of condos and resorts that is taking place up and down the coast. Only the expats – who came to Belize to 'escape civilization' – complain about the rampant development. Locals, by contrast, appreciate the influx of cash into the economy – the jobs, the roads, the restaurants – not to mention the constant flow of tourists who keep bringing money to spend.

Deforestation

Despite the impressive numbers about the area of protected territories, deforestation in Belize is occurring at an alarming rate. Agriculture and aquaculture, development and illegal harvesting all contribute to the felling of the forests, which is taking place at a rate of 2.3% per year (twice the rate of Central America overall).

This contradiction is a result of poor management and monitoring. Protection requires money and even at the best of times Belizean governments are short of cash. Underfunding means understaffing, which doesn't help the fight against poaching and illegal extraction. Many protected areas are dependent on funding and management from local and international NGOs; others go unchecked.

Protected Area	Features	Activities	Best Time to Visit
Laughing Bird Caye National Park (p228)	island on unusual faro reef in waters full of marine life	diving, snorkeling	Dec-Aug
Mayflower Bocawina National Park (p229)	rainforest park with hills, waterfalls, howler monkeys & hundreds of bird species	hiking, birding, swimming	year-round
Monkey Bay Wildlife Sanctuary (p114)	small private sanctuary on savannah & tropical forest	birding, wildlife watching, canoeing, caving	year-round
Mountain Pine Ridge Forest Reserve (p211)	upland area with rare pine forests & many waterfalls	walking, swimming, birding, horseback riding	year-round
Nohoch Che'en Caves Branch Archaeological Reserve (p186)	stretch of Caves Branch River running through caverns	river-tubing	year-round
Port Honduras Marine Reserve (p247)	inshore islands & coastal waters important for marine life	diving, snorkeling	Dec-May
Rio Bravo Conservation & Management Area (p169)	large rainforest reserve with great wildlife diversity	birding, wildlife watching, trail hikes, canoeing	year-round
St Herman's Blue Hole National Park (p218)	small rainforest park with cave & swimming hole	swimming, caving, hiking, birding	year-round
Sapodilla Cayes Marine Reserve (p247)	beautiful barrier reef islets with healthy coral & abundant marine life	diving, fishing, kayaking snorkeling, swimming	Dec-May
Shipstern Nature Reserve (p180)	wetlands & rare semideciduous hardwood forests with diverse wildlife, including wood-stork colony	wildlife observation	year-round
South Water Caye Marine Reserve (p226 & p226)	large reserve encompassing parts of barrier reef & inshore islands	diving, snorkeling, fishing, swimming, birding, kayaking	Dec-May
Swallow Caye Wildlife Sanctuary (p144)	small island with permanent manatee population in surrounding waters	manatee observation	year-round
Temash-Sarstoon National Park (p255)	rainforests, wetlands & rivers with huge variety of wildlife	wildlife observation, walks, boat trips	Dec-May

There is a perception in Belize that illegal Guatemalan immigrants are responsible for many of these incursions into protected areas. The ongoing territorial dispute between Guatemala and Belize exacerbates the situation, as many Guatemalan peasants believe they have a right to hunt and harvest there.

Oil

The discovery of sweet crude oil in Belize in 2002 caused dollar signs to start flashing inside the minds of Belizean officials and international prospectors. At least 17 oil companies obtained licenses for exploration all around the country, sometimes without conducting any sort of environmental impact survey or community involvement campaign. Sadly, there is significant overlap between the petroleum map and the protected areas map, so the prospects for striking it rich are threatening the sanctity of those spots.

In 2006 explorers in Spanish Lookout (p192) found what they were looking for: the first oil field with commercially viable quantities. Under pressure from local communities and conservationists, the government of Belize responded by instituting a 40% tax on oil production profits, declaring that the 'petroleum fund' would be used to improve education, fight poverty and strengthen the Belizean dollar. Oil companies balked at this, of course, and it still remains to be seen exactly how much will be paid and to whom.

TOP PICKS – ECOLODGES

- Capricorn Resort (p136), Ambergris Caye
- Driftwood Lodge (p152) Caye Caulker
- Calypso Beach Retreat (p159), Long Caye
- Chan Chich Lodge (p171), Orange Walk District
- Cerros Beach Inn (p179), Copper Bank
- Pook's Hill Lodge (p191), Cayo District
- Lodge at Chaa Creek (p208), Cayo District
- Thatch Caye Resort (p228), Central Cayes
- Hickatee Cottages (p248), Punta Gorda
- Cotton Tree Lodge (p257), the Deep South

Conservationists fear the environmental degradation that is sure to result from further oil exploration and extraction. At the very least, they argue, the government of Belize should utilize a percentage of oil income to establish a fund for environmental protection.

Environmental NGOs

Many environmental organizations are active in Belize, providing funding, monitoring protected areas and conducting research related to biodiversity and sustainability. Environmental organizations of interest to travelers include the following:

Belize Audubon Society (Map pp96-7; ☎ 223-5004; www.belizeaudubon.org; 12 Fort St, Belize City) Prominent NGO involved in the management of eight protected areas and campaigning on environmental issues.

Friends of Nature (☎ 523-3377) Placencia-based NGO co-managing Laughing Bird Caye National Park (p228) and Gladden Spit & Silk Cayes Marine Reserve (p228).

Oceanic Society (☎ 220-4256; www.oceanic-society.org; Blackbird Caye) Paying volunteers can assist with natural history research, collecting data and documenting the incredibly diverse wildlife (manatees, crocodiles, bottle-nosed dolphins and hawksbill sea turtles among others) that lives in the Turneffe Islands (p156).

Programme for Belize (Map pp96-7; ☎ 227-5616; www.pfbelize.org; 1 Eyre St, Belize City) Owns and manages Rio Bravo Conservation & Management Area (p169).

Toledo Institute for Development & Environment (TIDE; ☎ 722-2274; www.tidebelize .org; Mile 1 San Antonio Rd, Punta Gorda) Punta Gorda–based organization involved in managing the Port Honduras Marine Reserve (p247) and other projects.

Wildlife Conservation Society (in USA ☎ 718-220 5100; www.wcs.org) US-based international conservation body involved in research and conservation at Glover's Reef (p227).

Belize Outdoors

If you want it, Belize has got it. The extraordinary array of national parks and wildlife and marine reserves provides an incredible stage for the adventure traveler.

Ever since the days of Jacques Cousteau, Belize has been famous for the spectacular diving and snorkeling along its 160-mile barrier reef and around its coral atolls. More recently, Belize has blossomed as a perfect place to pursue other saltwater activities, too: kayakers, sailors and windsurfers whiz across the surface of those crystal-clear Caribbean waters, and anglers from around the world are starting to discover that there are other fish in the sea (not to mention the rivers, estuaries and lagoons).

Inland, the cool waters of Belize's network of rivers provide plenty of refreshing swimming holes, as well as jungle-clad routes for canoeing and river-tubing. Some of these waterways wind their way through caves, adding a little extra adventure to your canoeing or tubing trip.

Out of the water, the Maya Mountains and the dense forests provide an incredible, exotic setting for jungle treks and mountain bike excursions. Bird and wildlife enthusiasts will be wowed by the amazing array of life that inhabits this tiny country. And, of course, if your idea of 'outdoor activities' is sunbathing on a sandy beach, you can do that, too.

Most of the outdoor activities in Belize are available year-round, although some seasons are better than others. In general it's preferable to avoid the wettest months (June to November in most parts of the country). There is no shortage of activity-oriented lodges and resorts, as well as capable, knowledgeable guides who are eager to facilitate your Belizean adventure.

DIVING & SNORKELING

For divers and snorkelers Belize is a world-class destination. The world's second-longest barrier reef parallels the country's entire coastline from north to south.

Although tourism is big business in Belize, the development of the diving industry has been slower than in other Caribbean destinations. This is good news for divers, as it means fewer people and more pristine reefs. Scattered among more than 450 cayes and small islands, the sites provide an amazing variety of diving. Here you will find dazzling coral reefs, some of the most spectacular walls in the Caribbean region and the sensational Blue Hole (p157), first made famous on TV by Jacques Cousteau and the *Calypso*.

PUTTING DOWN THE GUIDE

No, we're not talking about insulting the local guy who is leading you through the rainforest. We're talking about closing this book that you have in your hands and leaving it behind. We're talking about following your own path, discovering your own dive site and paddling up your own stream. It is bound to be an adventure more memorable than the one you'll find along the tourist trail.

We at Lonely Planet are dedicated to providing comprehensive coverage of every country and region that we research, but we recognize the sometimes detrimental effect of places being 'discovered.' Even more than that, we are dedicated to creating a sustainable global traveler culture, and we recognize the universal benefit of 'discovery.'

So put your guidebook down for a day or – even better – a week. Explore the places that are not covered in the pages of this guidebook. And discover your own lonely planet.

The diving and snorkeling in Belize can be divided into four main areas – the Northern Cayes, Central Cayes, Southern Cayes and offshore atolls – each of which offers a variation. Some sites are particularly suited to snorkeling and free diving, but whatever your level of experience or taste, you can find a location that will allow you to do both.

The majority of dive sites are accessible only by boat. A few dives can be reached from the shore on Tobacco Caye, South Water Caye and the atolls. Most operators offer two-tank dive trips in the morning and afternoon, plus a night dive, which means it is usually possible to do four or five dives a day from your island base. Choosing a live-aboard boat gives you the opportunity for up to five dives a day if you have the energy.

Northern Cayes

The two main centers in this northern sector of the barrier reef are Ambergris Caye (p126) and Caye Caulker (p145), both of which are a short flight or boat ride from Belize City. Ambergris Caye is the largest offshore island and the most developed, so it attracts most of the visiting divers. Many choose Ambergris for its variety and quality of accommodations and nightlife, though it is pretty laid-back compared with other Caribbean destinations. The hub of diving activity is the town of San Pedro, at the southern end of the island. Many of the accommodations that are strung along the shoreline have their own dive shops on site.

Caye Caulker, a few miles to the south of Ambergris Caye, is smaller and less developed. It is a popular choice for travelers on a budget and there are a few dive shops. It is also possible to dive these reefs and the atolls on a daily basis from a base in Belize City (p95), where there are currently two major dive operators.

The barrier reef is only a few minutes by boat from either island. Diving here is quick and easy, though visibility is not always prime and the water can be somewhat surging. Some divers will put up with a longer boat ride to get better visibility and drop-off clarity. Most of the dive shops offer similar deals in terms of the sites they visit and the prices of their packages. All of the dive shops take boats out to the offshore atolls.

At the southern end of Ambergris Caye is Hol Chan Marine Reserve (p126), which was established more than two decades ago. The profusion of marine life is a testament to the reserve's success. A lot of Hol Chan Marine Reserve is shallow and in many cases the sites are better for snorkeling, but divers have the opportunity to explore a sunken ship at Amigos Wreck (p131). While the reef is fishier in the south of this section, the north holds more formations, with deep spur-and-groove cuts and interesting terrain. See p130 for more information on the best dive and snorkel sites in the Northern Cayes.

Undertaking a search for the illusive jaguar shark, Bill Murray stars in The Life Aquatic with Steve Zissou, *a hilarious parody of Jacques Cousteau.*

LIVE-ABOARD BOATS

If you are a truly dedicated diver wanting to maximize the number of dives during your trip, then choosing a live-aboard boat is the only way to go. Your 'hotel' moves with you to the dive site, which gives you the opportunity to dive four or five times a day, including night dives. The boats that operate in Belizean waters are comfortable and well equipped and will even pamper you with hot showers on the dive deck and warm towels to wrap up in. If you do not need dry land and nightlife, then this is definitely the way to see the best that the barrier reef has to offer. All boats depart from Belize City and operators organize all ground transfers for you. Live-aboard boats in Belize include the *Belize Aggressor II* (www.aggressor.com), *Sun Dancer II* (www .peterhughes.com) and *Nekton Pilot* (www.nektoncruises.com).

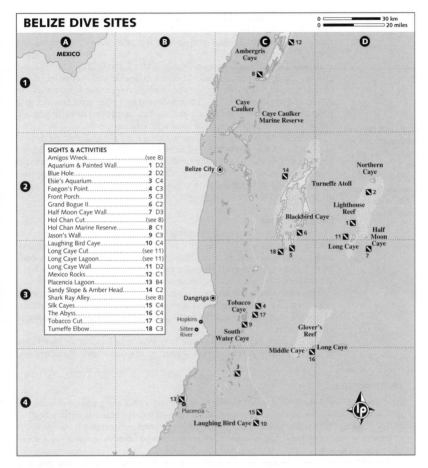

BELIZE DIVE SITES

0 — 30 km
0 — 20 miles

SIGHTS & ACTIVITIES
Amigos Wreck.......................................(see 8)
Aquarium & Painted Wall.............**1** D2
Blue Hole.......................................**2** D2
Elsie's Aquarium..........................**3** C4
Faegon's Point..............................**4** C3
Front Porch...................................**5** C3
Grand Bogue II.............................**6** C2
Half Moon Caye Wall..................**7** D3
Hol Chan Cut...............................(see 8)
Hol Chan Marine Reserve..........**8** C1
Jason's Wall..................................**9** C3
Laughing Bird Caye.....................**10** C4
Long Caye Cut.............................(see 11)
Long Caye Lagoon.......................(see 11)
Long Caye Wall............................**11** D2
Mexico Rocks...............................**12** C1
Placencia Lagoon.........................**13** B4
Sandy Slope & Amber Head........**14** C2
Shark Ray Alley............................(see 8)
Silk Cayes.....................................**15** C4
The Abyss......................................**16** C4
Tobacco Cut.................................**17** C3
Turneffe Elbow............................**18** C3

Central Cayes

Close to the big city but far enough away to be another world apart, the small isles and resorts on the Central Cayes are idyllic and convenient for barrier reef divers. They're normally not as busy as the reefs further north; it is quite possible to go the whole day and not see another dive boat.

Dangriga (p220), Hopkins (p229) and Sittee River (p234) provide fine shore bases for exploring a range of dive sites on a daily basis. A boat ride to the dive sites from the mainland is about 30 minutes on good days. Beautiful on sunny, calm days with sandy flats, reefs and old staghorns peeking above the surface, the dives are done in the deep passes in the middle of the reef. Near here there are nine passes or cuts; the dive involves a descent to between 35ft and 55ft and then a swim along the deep drop-off looking for denizens.

If your primary interest is diving, depart from Dangriga for the offshore resorts on the Central Cayes, including Tobacco Caye and South Water Caye. Tobacco Caye (p226) is a tiny 5-acre island only 10 miles from Dangriga. Dotted with rustic hotels and guesthouses, it offers a low-key atmosphere. This caye sits right on the edge of the barrier reef, provides

There is only one decompression chamber in Belize, on Ambergris Caye. You will be asked to support it by donating BZ$2 for every tank used. Be sure to use a decompression computer and dive well within safe limits.

excellent snorkeling and is one of the few beach-diving locations in Belize. There is a variety of reef topographies to be explored, ranging from shallow-water coral gardens to spur-and-groove formations, and, of course, the drop-offs from the reef edge.

A little further south, toward South Water Caye (p226), the spur and grooves change to what is locally known as a double-wall reef system. Here there are two separate systems, the first of which slopes sharply seaward from depths of 40ft down to 120ft. This is followed by a wide sand channel with isolated coral outcrops and pillars, and then a second coral reef rising to 60ft before it plunges over the wall beyond scuba diving depths.

Part of a set of three, *Reef Creature Identification and Reef Fish: Florida, Caribbean, Bahamas* by Paul Humann and Ned Deloach is invaluable to snorkelers or divers wishing to identify marine life.

The reef systems in this area are considered unique, and Tobacco Caye has been the base for an **Earthwatch** (www.earthwatch.org) reef-study project for several years; in fact, both Tobacco Caye and South Water Caye are designated as marine reserves. South Water Caye is a little larger and offers more expensive accommodations, but also sits on the crest of the barrier reef, offering beach diving and spectacular snorkeling.

Southern Cayes

The Southern Cayes are developing into a diving hot spot. The sandy Placencia peninsula (p237) has some of the best beaches in Belize, while laid-back restaurants, colorful beach huts and even some five-star Hollywood-name hideaways have been erected among the tiny Garifuna villages. Most of the swanky spots are being developed north of town, while budget hotels and guesthouses are still on the beachfront. Dive shops are scattered around town, as well as being connected with specific resorts. Divers will find the waters full of marine life and the reefs slightly less crowded than the popular northern sites.

The big draw here is the 13-mile-long Placencia Lagoon, an incubation area for virtually every creature found on the outer reef. Manatees and

---

LEARNING TO DIVE

Have you ever wondered what it would be like to swim along a spur-and-groove reef system, to tunnel through underwater caves or to peer over a drop-off into the blue and watch schools of fish cruise by? Your trip to Belize is a great opportunity to find out. Learning to dive is not as difficult as you might think, and most of the larger dive centers offer 'try dives' to see if the sport appeals to you.

The PADI system is now the most popular certification program worldwide. The first step is the basic Open Water qualification, which usually requires three days of instruction. It is possible to complete the full three-day program while you are in Belize, or you might undertake your basic theory training close to home and complete your open-water dives in Belize under the PADI referral system. You can hire everything from fins and mask to a full scuba kit, which saves on baggage weight and provides the opportunity to test different equipment before investing in your own.

Belize's best spots for novice divers include the following:

- **Mexico Rocks** off Ambergris Caye (p130)
- **Hol Chan Cut** south of Ambergris Caye (p131)
- **Half Moon Caye Wall** in Lighthouse Reef (p157)
- **Faegon's Point** and **Tobacco Cut** near Tobacco Caye (p226)
- **Jason's Wall** or **Elsie's Aquarium** near South Water Caye (p226)
- **Long Caye Lagoon** and **Long Caye Cut** at Glover's Reef (p227)
- Any site near **Laughing Bird Caye** (p228)

RESPONSIBLE DIVING

Please consider the following tips when diving and help preserve the ecology and beauty of reefs:

- Never use anchors on the reef, and take care not to ground boats on coral.

- Avoid touching or standing on living marine organisms or dragging equipment across the reef. Polyps can be damaged by even the gentlest contact. If you must hold on to the reef, only touch exposed rock or dead coral.

- Be conscious of your fins. Even without contact, the surge from fin strokes near the reef can damage delicate organisms. Take care not to kick up clouds of sand, which can smother organisms.

- Practice and maintain proper buoyancy control. Major damage can be done by divers descending too fast and colliding with the reef.

- Take great care in underwater caves. Spend as little time within them as possible as your air bubbles may be caught within the roof and thereby leave organisms high and dry. Take turns to inspect the interior of a small cave.

- Resist the temptation to collect or buy corals or shells or to loot marine archaeological sites (mainly shipwrecks).

- Ensure that you take home all your rubbish and any litter you may find as well. Plastics in particular are a serious threat to marine life.

- Do not feed fish.

- Minimize your disturbance of marine animals. *Never* ride on the backs of turtles.

bottlenosed dolphins come to mate, feed and raise their young in these protected waters. Myriad fish do the same, and juveniles can be seen in profusion. Located between the mainland and the Placencia peninsula, it is not yet designated as a protected area and there is some development taking place along the inner banks.

The northernmost point of this reef area is Gladden Spit (p228). Blue-water action takes the form of whale sharks, bull sharks, hammerheads, dolphins and shoaling fish, all due to the seasonal spawning of cubera snapper. Looking for whale sharks in blue water is hard work, however, and not always fruitful. The April through June spawning season (about 12 miles off the barrier reef) is always exciting, with plenty of fish aggregations, along with their predators. Nurse sharks stack one atop another in sandy channels and big groups rise up from the depths.

All year round, dives can produce sightings of spotted eagle rays, turtles, moray eels, southern stingrays, large grouper, barracuda, king mackerel, dolphins and several shark species, as well as many smaller tropical reef fish and invertebrates. Manta rays appear with more frequency during winter months when the water temperatures drop, starting in December and January.

The reef table here is much wider and so it takes a little longer to reach the barrier reef by boat; however, the numerous islands with large expanses of coral reef and connecting channels between them are a bonus, providing a host of alternative dive and snorkeling sites on the way to/from the reef.

Dedicated to diving in Belize, www.scubadiving belize.com is very useful for detailed information about specific areas and dive sites.

LAUGHING BIRD CAYE FARO REEF SYSTEM

Laughing Bird Caye appears to be all that is left of another submerged atoll, its approximately 2.5 acres of land seemingly diminishing with passing storms and wave action. The caye got its name from the many laughing gulls that once nested here, but most of their nesting areas have since been swallowed by the rising sea. Pelicans and osprey still use the island as nesting grounds, as do sea turtles. Laughing Bird Caye (p228) is one of Belize's national parks and a part of the Belize Barrier Reef Reserve System World Heritage site (see p64), which includes the island and surrounding reefs.

Within the faro is a system of patch reefs and coral ridges boasting luxuriant hard-coral growth and a variety of sponges and soft corals. The tremendous diversity of fish and invertebrate life in the inshore waters around the island make them ideal for both snorkeling and diving. There are several dive sites at the north and south of the island, all with basically the same marine life and terrain, although in the north it is possible to go a bit deeper.

Offshore Atolls

Diving & Snorkeling Belize by Mark Webster (Lonely Planet) describes 66 of the best dive and snorkeling sites in the Northern Cayes, Central Cayes, Southern Cayes and offshore atolls.

There are only four atolls in the Caribbean and three of them are right here in Belize. All three – Turneffe Atoll, Lighthouse Reef and Glover's Reef – lie offshore from the barrier reef, rising from great depths to just a few feet above sea level. You can dive them on day trips from the main islands, choose one of the atoll-based resorts or take a live-aboard boat, which concentrates on diving the atolls.

TURNEFFE ATOLL

Turneffe Atoll (p156) is the largest of the offshore trio and comprises a series of islands that runs north–south. Here you will find an area dominated by purely mangrove islands, where juveniles of every marine species are protected until they make their way into the wider waters. Sand flats, shallow gardens and life-filled walls are all highlights of Turneffe dives.

The Elbow is the most beloved Turneffe dive site, with its enormous schools of pelagic fish and pods of dolphins. Visibility varies widely depending mostly on the wind direction. A lot of wave action can stir things up in the mangroves, carrying nutrients into the water and reducing visibility. But more often, the deep water around the atolls guarantees excellent visibility and some of the most thrilling wall-diving you'll find anywhere.

SURF SAFARI BIG FIVE

While African adventurers have long had their famed 'Big 5' list of must-see big game animals, the Caribbean now boasts its own version for those who prefer a surf safari. For the wet set, the Big 5 includes a selection of the coral reef's most notorious predators. With a couple of trips out to the reef and a little luck, you should be able to complete this checklist. In fact, one visit to Shark Ray Alley (p131) will get you nearly halfway home.

- **Shark** – even the nurse shark that you are most likely to encounter will on first sight cause a Spielbergian shiver, but that should soon pass after you watch your guide tickle its belly.

- **Stingray** – these demons of the deep come armed with venomous spike-tipped tails. The spotted eagle ray is the bigger and badder ray; it cruises the coral in Belize and is more rare to see.

- **Barracuda** – reaching 6ft in length and possessing powerful jaws with multiple rows of razor-sharp teeth, meet the pit bull of the reef, capable of a thrusting propulsion when it makes a deadly strike.

- **Moray eel** – easily concealing their 5ft-long bodies in a dark pocket of the reef or a crevice in the sea floor, these elongated serpents lie in wait for a quick-strike ambush on passing prey.

- **Octopus** – with eight arms to hold you, the most cunning of the reef's predators is armed with a sharp beak for biting into fish and suction cups to pry open shellfish. It is also prey for barracudas, sharks and eels, which it eludes in a cloud of ink.

SAFETY GUIDELINES FOR DIVING

Before embarking on a scuba diving, skin diving or snorkeling trip, carefully consider the following points to ensure a safe and enjoyable experience:

- Possess a current diving certification card from a recognized scuba diving instructional agency (if scuba diving).

- Be sure you are healthy and feel comfortable diving.

- Obtain reliable information about physical and environmental conditions at the dive site (eg from a reputable local dive operation).

- Be aware of local laws, regulations and etiquette about marine life and the environment.

- Dive only at sites within your realm of experience; if available, engage the services of a competent, professionally trained dive instructor or dive master.

- Be aware that underwater conditions vary significantly from one region, or even site, to another. Seasonal changes can significantly alter any site and dive conditions. These differences influence the way divers dress for a dive and what diving techniques they use.

- Ask about the environmental characteristics that can affect your diving and how local trained divers deal with these considerations.

The northwest site moorings such as Sandy Slope and Amber Head normally sit in 35ft to 40ft of water and the reef becomes a spur-and-groove system that leads to a vertical wall. This drops to a sandy shelf around 100ft to 120ft at most sites, then falls off again past sport-diving limits. The northwest side is protected from the occasional strong eastern and southeastern winds that sometimes blow in.

When the wind shifts to the north-northwest, blowing down from the US Gulf, conditions are better to dive on the east side, at sites such as Grand Bogue II and Front Porch. This reeftop and wall starts a bit deeper, in the 40ft to 60ft range, and is known for being less of a slope and quite sheer in some spots. The reeftop also has interesting swim-throughs and some tight spurs and grooves.

Being the closest atoll to the coast, Turneffe is a quick trip from Ambergris Caye and Caye Caulker, although there are also resorts on Blackbird Caye (part of Turneffe Atoll; see p156).

LIGHTHOUSE REEF

At 50 miles offshore, Lighthouse Reef (p157) is the atoll that lies furthest to the east. Lighthouse Reef is probably the best-known atoll in Belize and it is certainly the most popular, due to the Blue Hole Natural Monument (p157). While this icon of Belize diving makes the atoll a major attraction, it is really the stunning walls, many swim-throughs and superb blue water that make it a favorite with both longtime, experienced Belize divers and complete novices.

Lighthouse Reef is home to Half Moon Caye Natural Monument (p158), a national park managed by the Belize Audubon Society, where a colony of rare red-booted boobies can be observed up close. There are a few fantastic dive sites nearby, such as Aquarium and Painted Wall. Other sites in the vicinity include the coral-covered Long Caye Wall.

The easiest way to see the sites and sights of Lighthouse Reef is via a live-aboard boat. The commute from site to site is minimal, and divers can take advantage of early morning dives and fascinating night dives. There are a few small lodges on Long Caye (p158), while camping is allowed on Half Moon Caye.

Three Adventures: Galapagos, Titicaca, the Blue Holes is a classic book about Jacques Cousteau's underwater explorations.

GLOVER'S REEF

In southern Belize, divers will find the third of the Belizean atolls. Of the three, Glover's Reef (p227) sees the least amount of human contact and remains largely unexplored. Glover's Reef Atoll was named after the 17th-century pirate John Glover, who used the remote islands as a base for raids against treasure-laden Spanish galleons heading to and from the Bay Islands of Honduras.

First recognized as a bird sanctuary in 1954, it has long been atop the conservation list, getting various conservation designations in 1978 before finally being declared a complete marine reserve in 1993, then a Unesco World Heritage site in 1996. There is a marine research station on Middle Caye and the remains of an ancient Maya settlement are being studied on Long Caye.

Located about an hour's boat ride from Hopkins or Placencia, Glover's Reef rises from abyssal depths of well over 2000ft; indeed, a dive site located midway between Long Caye and Middle Caye is known as The Abyss. Oval in shape, it is comprised of more than 700 patch reefs within a 100-sq-mile lagoon. Just to the south is one of the Caribbean's deepest valleys, where depths reach 10,000ft.

There are several rustic outpost resorts here for divers and fishers, each occupying its own island and offering an eco-friendly existence. Otherwise, there is day-boat diving from Dangriga, Hopkins, Sittee River, Tobacco Caye and South Water Caye, and live-aboard boats occasionally cruise this far south.

The chance of seeing dolphins, mantas and whale sharks keep adventurous divers coming back for more. The spectacular walls and hard-coral formations are just a few minutes from the islands that fringe the eastern side of the atoll. If you get the chance, dive the west side of the atoll as well to explore some wonderful swim-throughs and caves.

Destinations Belize (www.destinationsbelize.com) is full of useful information on fishing in Belize, including fish guides, tide charts and fishing location descriptions.

FISHING

This angler's paradise is home to 160 miles of barrier reef, hundreds of square miles of flats and dozens of jungle-lined rivers and lagoons – all of which are teeming with a great variety of fish. The best months are May through July, with their hot sunny weather, though every species has its ideal time and place. Spin fishing, fly-fishing and trolling can all be enjoyed year-round.

Tarpon, snook and jacks inhabit the estuaries, inlets and river mouths, while bonefish, permit and barracuda are found out in the lagoons and flats. The coral reefs support grouper, snapper and jacks, and the deeper waters beyond are home to sailfish, marlin, pompano, tuna and bonito. The flats off the cayes and mainland raise realistic hopes of the angler's 'Grand Slam' of permit, tarpon and bonefish all in one day. Catch-and-release is the norm for these fish and for most snook. Check with your guide or hotel about the regulations for your area and season.

The most popular fishing bases are in the Northern Cayes, especially San Pedro (p128) and Caye Caulker (p147), but there are also fishing outfits in Sarteneja (p179) and Belize City (p95).

For tarpon and bonefish, Belize's southern waters, from Placencia to Punta Gorda, are gaining popularity. It's easy to charter a boat in places such as Glover's Reef (p227), Hopkins (p230), Placencia (p238) and Punta Gorda (p247).

River fishing for big tarpon, snook, cubera snapper and 35lb to 100lb jewfish is also practicable year-round. The Sibun and Belize Rivers and Black Creek are the most frequently fished rivers, but the Deep, Monkey, Temash and Sarstoon Rivers in the south are good, too.

TOP PICKS – SNORKEL SITES

Northern Cayes

- Hol Chan Cut (p131)
- Shark Ray Alley (p131)
- Mexico Rocks (p130)

Southern Cayes

- Laughing Bird Caye (p228)
- Silk Cayes (p228)

Central Cayes

- South Water Caye (p226)
- Tobacco Caye (p226)

Offshore Atolls

- Half Moon Caye (p158)
- Glover's Reef (p227)

Expect to pay about BZ$500 to charter a boat (for up to four people) with an experienced guide for a day's fishing. Lodges and guides may have equipment to rent but it's best to bring your own tackle.

KAYAKING & CANOEING

The translucent waters of the Caribbean are as inviting for kayakers as they are for divers and snorkelers. It's amazing how much underwater life is visible from above the surface! And you can enjoy snorkeling and bird-watching as you go.

If you fancy some kayaking, consider staying at one of the resorts or hotels on the Placencia peninsula or Ambergris Caye, many of which provide free kayaks for guests. At San Pedro, Caye Caulker, Hopkins, Placencia village and Punta Gorda, you can rent a kayak for anywhere between BZ$30 and BZ$60 per day. Glover's Atoll Resort (p227) rents out single/double touring kayaks by the week for BZ$272/382.

If you would like to see Belize from the seat of a kayak – guided or not – check out the kayaking organizations listed in the boxed text, p78.

Canoes are more common than kayaks on inland rivers, especially the Mopan and Macal Rivers near San Ignacio. Both have some rapids, so be sure to choose a stretch of river that's right for your level. Many lodge accommodations in the area rent out canoes (around BZ$50 per half day), and tour outfits in San Ignacio (p198) will also take you out on guided trips.

One of the most unusual canoe trips is the underground river through Barton Creek Cave (p193). Another nice place to use a canoe is the bird paradise of Crooked Tree Lagoon (p110). For information on La Ruta Maya Belize River Challenge, an annual 170-mile canoe race, see p195.

SAILING

A day's sailing on crystal-clear Caribbean waters, with a spot of snorkeling or wildlife watching topped with an island beach barbecue, is a near-perfect way to spend a day. These tours depart from San Pedro (p129), Caye Caulker (p146) or Placencia (p238). The going rate is around BZ$150 per person.

Some of these companies offer multiday sailing and camping trips, as well as popular boozy sunset and moonlight cruises. Raggamuffin Tours and Seahawk Sailing (p147) both do relatively economical island-hopping sails to Turneffe Atoll, Lighthouse Reef and Placencia. At San Pedro (p129) you can rent small craft by the hour or longer for light sailing on your own.

On longer sailing trips you can reach not only Belize's hundreds of islands but also the attractive Guatemalan ports of Lívingston and Río Dulce, Honduras' Bay Islands and much of the rest of the eastern Caribbean.

BELIZE FROM THE SEAT OF A KAYAK

If you want to see Belize with a paddle in your hands, a number of Belize- and North America–based firms offer recommended kayaking holidays:

- **Belize Kayak Rentals** (☎ in USA 800-667-1630; www.belizekayaking.com; s/d per day BZ$66/110, per week BZ$420/700) If you prefer to go it alone on your kayaking expedition, this branch of Island Expeditions (following) rents out kayaks from its base camp in Dangriga. Also offers weekly packages, which include a boat charter out to the cayes.

- **GAP Adventures** (☎ in USA 800-465-5600; www.gapadventures.com; 8-day trip BZ$2450) Using Placencia as a base, GAP's trip gives you four nights of island-hopping on the cayes.

- **Island Expeditions** (☎ in USA 800-667-1630; www.islandexpeditions.com; 5-/10-day package BZ$3060/4180) This ecologically minded company takes tours departing from Dangriga and spending the night at rustic lodges on Tobacco Caye, Southwater Caye and Coco Plum Caye. Island also does a tasty 10-day Coral Jaguar Expedition, which includes four days of hiking in the Cockscomb Basin and then six days of paddling around the islands.

- **Slickrock Adventures** (☎ in USA 800-390-5715; www.slickrock.com; 5-/9-night package BZ$2590/3950) These top-class water sports holidays are based on Long Caye, Glover's Reef, combining sea kayaking, surf kayaking, windsurfing, snorkeling and diving. Accommodations are in stilt cabanas, and the meals are notably good.

- **Toadal Adventure** (☎ 523-3207; www.toadaladventure.com; 4-/6-day package BZ$1890/2760) Take your pick between sea kayaking and snorkeling and sleeping on an island, or paddling through the rainforest rivers and watching for wildlife. Based in Placencia.

Belize Sailing Charters (☎ 523-3138; www.belize-sailing-charters.com; Placencia) and **Sailing Belize** (www.sailingbelize.com) offer a variety of crewed and bareboat charters on catamarans and monohulls. A crewed yacht for up to six people will cost BZ$1200 to BZ$1500 (plus a per-person charge) per night; seven nights bareboat for four to eight people can run anywhere from BZ$4000 to BZ$12,000.

The Lodge Hopper's Special of **Under the Sun** (☎ 523-7127, in USA 800-285-6967; www.underthesunbelize.com; Hopkins; 8-day trip BZ$4400) is an outstanding eight days of Caribbean cruising on an 18ft Hobie Cat, with plenty of stops for snorkeling, fishing, kayaking and hammocking, and instruction provided for novice sailors. Accommodations in lodges on the cayes, food, a guide and support boat are all included in the price.

The recommended Caribbean charter specialist **TMM Yacht Charters** (☎ 226-3026, in USA 800-633-0155; http://sailtmm.com; San Pedro; per week BZ$7800-18,000) has bases in San Pedro and Placencia for its fleet of catamarans and monohulls. Placencia is also the Belizean base for the luxury catamaran charters of **Moorings** (www.moorings.com).

Freya Rauscher's *Cruising Guide to Belize and Mexico's Caribbean Coast* provides comprehensive information for anyone navigating these complicated waters as well as Guatemala's Río Dulce.

RIVER-TUBING

River-tubing is the latest rage in Belize, blessed as the country is with many fairly gentle and temperate watercourses working their way through gorgeous scenery. You may wonder what exactly is involved, but it's not too complicated: it requires sitting in an inflated inner-tube and floating or paddling along a river. You go downstream most of the time and the only technique that needs to be learnt is how to avoid getting beached, eddied or snagged on rocks while continuing to face the right direction.

The Mopan River near San Ignacio is a popular spot for river-tubing, and you can leave from Bullet Tree Falls (p202) or San José Succotz (p205). Most lodges offer tubes and transportation for their guests, or you can rent tubes at the river's edge and go it alone.

The best of all Belizean tubing adventures is the float in and out of a sequence of caves on the Caves Branch River inside the Nohoch Che'en Archaeological Reserve (p186). People come on day trips from all over Belize for this (it costs around BZ$130 from San Ignacio). If you can get here on your own, you can do it for BZ$70 with the guides that hang around the park entrance.

WINDSURFING & KITESURFING

With a light-to-medium warm easterly breeze blowing much of the time and the barrier reef offshore to calm the waters, conditions on Caye Caulker (p147) and Ambergris Caye (p129) are ideal for windsurfing. Regulars here boast occasional runs of 10 miles. You do have to take care with the boat traffic though, especially at San Pedro. More mellow windsurfing beaches can be found in Hopkins (p230), home to a small but dedicated group of windsurfers.

Sailboard rentals run at about BZ$40 per hour or BZ$130 per day, with classes around BZ$100 per hour. Winds are biggest (typically 10 to 17 knots) from February through April.

Kitesurfers also use sailboards but they catch the wind with a kitelike sail high in the air, to which they're attached by a harness and long cords. You can do introductory courses on Ambergris Caye or Caye Caulker from around BZ$300.

> The remote Chiquibul cave system, south of Caracol, is possibly the biggest cave system in the Western Hemisphere. Because of difficult access, it remains largely unexplored.

CAVING

The karstic geology of parts of western Belize has produced many extensive and intricate cave systems, which are fascinating, challenging and awesome to investigate. To the ancient Maya, caves were entrances to Xibalbá, the underworld and residence of important gods. Many Belizean caves today still contain relics of Maya ceremonies, offerings or sacrifices. This archaeological element makes cave exploration doubly exciting. One of the few caves in the country that you can enter without a guide is St Herman's Cave (p218), but even there you are required to take a guide if you want to go more than 300yd into the cave.

The most exciting caves in the west of the country include Actun Tunichil Muknal (p191), with its evidence of human sacrifice; Barton Creek Cave (p193), which you explore by canoe; Che Chem Ha (p210), with its vast array of ancient pottery; and the caves in the Nohoch Che'en Archaeological Reserve (p186). All of these can be visited with guides, and tours to most of them run from San Ignacio (p198).

Remember that caves and their contents are extremely fragile. Don't disturb artifacts or cave formations, and try to avoid tours with large groups of people. For your own well-being, check the physical demands of a cave

---

TOP PICKS FOR KIDS

- Cave-tubing at Nohoch Che'en Caves Branch (p186)
- Canoeing into Barton Creek Cave (p193)
- Snorkeling at the southern dock on Caye Caulker (p147); Long Caye, Lighthouse Reef (p158); Laughing Bird Caye (p228); or Glover's Reef (p227)
- Horseback riding at Banana Bank (p187) or Crystal Paradise (p194)
- Sailing at Caye Caulker (p146)
- Going on a night safari at Belize Zoo (p113)

MORE THAN JUST A WALK IN THE PARK: MARCOS CUCUL

Mr Marcos Cucul is a well-known figure in Belize's travel scene. Over the past several years, he's expanded his work to include not just cave-tubing and day trips, but also multiday jungle survival expeditions into the deepest jungles that Belize offers. We spoke to Marcus about the intensity of his tours: 'My tours come in different levels. The most hard-core of these entail basically going into the jungle with nothing, just a machete, a first aid kit and a two-way radio for emergency communications. Everything that we use for the duration of this tour is gotten from the jungle itself. On our tours we make hammocks by weaving together vines and barks, and we string them between the trees. We learn what kind of leaves to use for blankets to keep us warm. It's really something.

'Some of the people I've taken into the jungle have been military people, police and firefighters. But I've also led courses with many middle-aged people, couples and families. Not long ago I went out with a family, a mother, father and daughter. The daughter was 21. They wanted to experience the jungle at the most primitive level. For this one we brought in some food, some rice and other easily carried food to cook. But most of their diet consisted of what we were able to catch ourselves in the streams: fish, snails, even freshwater lobster!

'Another component of my tours is learning about medicinal plants and herbs, about what things are good to eat and what to leave alone. People come away realizing that the jungle can be safe, and on the other hand it can be dangerous.

'On one of these tours we see every kind of wildlife that Belize has, from snakes to howler monkeys, spider monkeys, owls, coatimundis and many, many birds. A big percentage of the animals in Belize's jungles is nocturnal, so spending several days and nights in the jungle is a unique way to get to experience all that Belize has to offer. Some people come on tours just to experience the wildlife. It is quite different from a trip to the zoo!

'By the end of a four- or six-day course like this, participants are very comfortable with making their own shelter and foraging for their own food, making do with what the jungle has to offer. An experience like this really opens people's minds. When they come out of it, they do so with a new respect for both the jungle and for themselves. This is the essence of the course.

'Our ancestors thought highly of their surroundings. Their religion was based on nature, and on contact with the natural world. A lot of what I have learned was passed on to me from elders in the community, from conversations around the fire with parents and grandparents.

'My son is also a guide. I didn't push him into the life; it was his choice. He likes the job and at the same time he understands the importance of both protecting the ecosystem and preserving our Maya culture. I'm very proud of him.'

Marcos Cucul is a native of Belize from the Kekchi Maya tribe; he runs his jungle treks through Maya Guide (p219).

trip beforehand, and remember that some caves are subject to flash floods during rainy periods. An extra flashlight and a spare set of batteries is never a bad idea. And finally, if you have claustrophobic tendencies or are terrified of the dark (or bats), it's no shame to admit that caves are not for everyone!

CYCLING

Belize is in the tropics, and mostly at low altitude, so temperatures are high and not terribly conducive to strenuous cycling. But the generally flat terrain of most of the country is good for leisurely touring of local areas and short excursions.

Some coastal accommodations provide free bikes for their guests. Otherwise you can rent bikes, usually for around BZ$20 a day, in places such as San Pedro (p129), Caye Caulker (p155), Corozal (p172), Sarteneja (p182), Copper Bank (p179), Hopkins (p233), Sittee River (p234), Placencia (p244) and Punta Gorda (p250).

In Cayo, Pacz Tours (p198) offers a day-long mountain-biking tour to the Mennonite village of Spanish Lookout, while Belize Explorer (p198) provides bikes and support vehicles for multiday biking adventures. Casa Maya Jungle Resort (p205) also rents out mountain bikes to its guests.

There are many different long-distance bike races in Belize, some of which have only been instituted in recent years, including the following:

Krem New Year's Day Bicycle Classic Three different races commence at different places in northern Belize (the elite racers in Corozal, juniors in Orange Walk and women in Crooked Tree) and converge in Belize City.

Temple to Temple (www.templetotemple.com) A one-week race from Lubaantun to Caracol in late January.

Tour of Belize (www.tourofbelize.com) A five-day, six-stage road race that traverses 500 miles in mid-February.

HIKING, BIRDING & WILDLIFE WATCHING

In Belize, hiking usually means guided walks in search of birdlife, as well as other flora and fauna. Many lodges have access to trails on their own or nearby properties that you can walk on your own. Among these are Chan Chich Lodge (p171), Macaw Bank (p194), Black Rock River Lodge (p208) and Blancaneaux Lodge (p215). Hidden Valley Inn (p215) is especially well placed and well designed for hikers, who can take advantage of 90 miles of signposted trails. But more often lodge walks are with a guide who'll show you the animals and plants along the way. Several places offer night walks, which can be real eye-openers!

Two areas with well-developed and well-maintained jungle trail networks that you can walk with or without guides are Cockscomb Basin Wildlife Sanctuary (p235), with a 12-mile network, and Mayflower Bocawina National Park (p229).

It gets hot and bug-infested out in the bush, so carry enough water, a hat and sunscreen, and protect yourself from mosquitoes (with long pants and sleeves as well as bug spray). Compact binoculars are always a plus, as is swimming gear when you reach those welcome swimming holes!

HORSEBACK RIDING

Belize has an active equestrian community. A growing number of lodges offers rides to their guests and – in some cases – nonguests. Often you'll be riding jungle trails. Preeminent is Banana Bank Lodge (p187) near Belmopan,

---

TOP PICKS – WILDLIFE WATCHING

Go where the wild things are:

- **Crooked Tree Wildlife Sanctuary** (p110) The best birding in the country. Giant jabiru storks congregate here in April and May.

- **Community Baboon Sanctuary** (p108) Surefire encounters with black howler monkeys.

- **Chan Chich Lodge** (p171) or the **Rio Bravo Conservation & Management Area** (p169) Excellent chance of seeing coatimundis, peccaries, kinkajous and spider or howler monkeys. Even jaguars are regularly sighted around Chan Chich.

- **Gales Point Manatee** (p115) or **Swallow Caye** (p144), home to small communities of West Indian manatees, which are often sighted from boats cruising in these areas.

- **Cockscomb Basin Wildlife Sanctuary** (p235) The world's first jaguar reserve is home to 40 or 50 jaguars, but you'll probably just see their footprints.

- **Belize Zoo** (p113) Get up close and personal with many of Belize's indigenous species. Great for photos!

with a well-tended stable of 150 horses, where you can enjoy anything from a two-hour ride to a multiday riding package. Windy Hill Resort (p205) near San Ignacio has another large stable.

Also near San Ignacio is Mountain Equestrian Trails (p193), offering rides and riding-based holidays that combine lowland jungles and Mountain Pine Ridge. Other good riding spots include Crystal Paradise Resort (p194), duPlooys' Jungle Lodge (p208) and Black Rock River Lodge (p208), all located around San Ignacio; Crooked Tree Wildlife Sanctuary (p110) is also good. A two- to three-hour ride can cost anywhere from BZ$50 to BZ$130, while full-day outings start at around BZ$150.

Food & Drink

Rare is the tourist who raves about Belizean food. On the other hand, rare is the tourist who complains about it. Belize has never developed an elaborate cuisine of its own, but rather borrows from its Caribbean neighbors, as well as from Mexico, England and the United States. But Belizean food puts these adopted flavors and recipes to good use, incorporating plenty of tropical fruits, fresh seafood and other local delights. It's available at every kind of establishment, from the stand-up snack bar to the classy café and the occasional ritzy restaurant.

Mexican, Chinese and Indian restaurants exist throughout the country. Nowadays, the high level of immigration from Europe and the US ensures an ample array of international cuisine, from straightforward travelers' favorites to gourmet *haute cuisine*.

Mmm… A Taste of Belizean Cooking brings together about 100 recipes from chefs around the country, some of whose food you'll probably eat while you're in Belize.

STAPLES & SPECIALTIES

Belizeans love it and most of them would happily eat it every day. Most non-Belizeans think it's filling and inexpensive but not very exciting. What is it? It's rice and beans. It comes in two varieties: 'rice and beans,' where the two are cooked together; and 'beans and rice,' or more politely 'stewed beans with rice,' where beans in a soupy stew are served separately in a bowl (the idea is to spoon them over the rice). Both variations are prepared with red beans, which distinguishes them from other countries' rice and beans. Rice and beans is usually accompanied by a serving of chicken or seafood, plus coleslaw, potato or fried plantain as a garnish. Both kinds of rice and beans are flavored with coconut milk.

Just like their Caribbean and Central American neighbors, Belizeans like to cook with habaneros, jalapeños and other peppers. Most restaurants have a bottle of hot chili sauce on the table next to the salt and pepper so guests can make their meals as spicy as they like.

Not surprisingly, most restaurant menus feature a variety of creatures from the sea, with lobster playing the starring role. Distinguished from the American and European lobster by their lack of claws, the Caribbean crustaceans are no less divine, especially when grilled. Lobster is widely available in coastal towns, except from mid-February to mid-June, when the lobster season is closed.

Conch (pronounced 'konk') is the large snail-like sea creature that inhabits conch shells. Much like calamari, it has a chewy consistency that is not universally appreciated. From October to June, it is often prepared as *ceviche* or conch fritters (and it's considerably cheaper than lobster).

Cow-foot soup is supposed to be 'good for the back,' in other words, an aphrodisiac.

Belizeans really know how to prepare their seafood, be it barbecued, grilled, marinated, steamed or stewed. A common preparation is 'Creole-style,' where seafood, peppers, onions and tomatoes are stewed together. Snapper and other fillets are good, reasonably priced fish choices.

Belizeans do not eat a lot of beef, but they do love cow-foot soup. This is a glutinous concoction of pasta, vegetables, spices – and an actual cow's foot. It's particularly popular as a way to refuel in the small hours after a night out.

Belizean breakfast is usually simple and hearty, often featuring eggs, fried jacks (deep-fried dough) slathered with beans or fresh-baked johnnycakes (biscuits) smothered in butter. In small towns, the best breakfast is usually found at the local taco vendor's cart, where tortillas stuffed with meat and lettuce are sold.

SHARP ON THE TONGUE

Belizean meals are not usually very spicy, but your table and your meal are always enlivened by the inimitable presence of Marie Sharp's fiery sauces, accurately labeled 'Proud Products of Belize.'

Marie Sharp got into the hot-sauce business in 1981. One season she and her husband found themselves with a surplus of habanero chili peppers at their family farm near Dangriga. Hating to see them wasted, Marie experimented with sauce recipes in her own kitchen. She felt that other bottled hot sauces were often watery and sometimes too hot to be flavorful. She wanted one that would complement Belizean cuisine and would not have artificial ingredients. She tried out some of her blends on her friends and family, and by far the favorite was one that used carrots as a thickener and blended the peppers with onions and garlic.

Once she had her formula, Sharp embarked on a guerrilla marketing campaign, carrying samples of the sauce, along with corn chips and refried beans, door-to-door to shopkeepers all over Belize. When proprietors liked what they tasted, Marie asked them to put the sauce on their shelves and agreed to take back the bottles that didn't sell. The sauce, initially bottled under the name Melinda, caught on and was soon not only in stores but also on restaurant tables all over the country.

Marie bottled the sauces from her kitchen for three years, finally bringing in a couple of workers to help her mix the zealously guarded formula. She eventually hybridized her own red habanero pepper – a mix of Scotch bonnet and Jamaican varieties – which contributes to the distinctive color of her sauces. She opened her own factory in 1986 with two three-burner stoves and six women to look after her pots, and moved to her current factory outside Dangriga (see p222) in 1998.

Today, Sharp's hot red-habanero sauces come in six heat levels ('Mild', 'Hot', 'Fiery Hot', 'No-Wimps-Allowed', 'Belizean Heat' and 'Comatose'), and Sharp also produces a range of mixed sauces (habaneros with prickly pears or citrus fruit), pepper jellies and tropical fruit jams. Peruse the selection at www.mariesharps.us.

Other Mexican snacks, such as *salbutes, garnaches, enchalades* and *panades* – all variations on the tortilla, beans and cheese theme (*salbutes* usually add chicken, *panades* generally have fish) – are available in eateries around the country and as snacks from food carts. You'll also come across burritos and tamales (wads of corn dough with a filling of meat, beans or chilies).

Maya Specialties

Foods of the Maya by Nancy & Jeffrey Gerlach focuses on the Yucatán, but it provides an excellent guide to the food, flavors and recipes of the Maya culture.

Maya meals are sometimes on offer in the villages of southern Belize and in Petén, Guatemala. *Caldo* is a spicy stew, usually made with chicken (or sometimes beef or pork), corn and root vegetables. Served with tortillas, it is hearty and delicious. Ixpa'cha is steamed fish or shrimp, cooked inside a big leaf. The Maya also make Mexican soups-cum-stews such as *chirmole* (chicken with a chili-chocolate sauce) and *escabeche* (chicken with lime and onions), though these are not specific to the Maya.

Garifuna Specialties

Garifuna dishes may appear on numerous restaurant menus, but there are few actual Garifuna restaurants (although see the boxed text, opposite). If you have a chance to try a Garifuna meal, you shouldn't pass it up. The most common dish on menus is 'boil-up,' a stew of root vegetables and beef or chicken. Less common is *alabundiga*, a dish of grated green bananas, coconut cream, spices, boiled potato and peppers served with fried fish fillet (often snapper) and rice. *Sere* is fish cooked with coconut milk, spices and maybe some root vegetables. *Hudut* is a stew with similar ingredients including mashed plantain.

DRINKS
Nonalcoholic Drinks

Delicious and refreshing fruit juices – lime, orange, watermelon, grapefruit, papaya and mango – are available throughout Belize.

'Seaweed shakes' sold by street vendors – a blend of condensed milk, a few spices and extract of *Eucheuma isoforme,* which grows underwater as a tangle of yellow branches – are claimed to have aphrodisiac and many other restorative properties.

In recent years, Belize has started catering to coffee drinkers with its own homegrown beans. Although Belize lacks the high altitudes that benefit other Central American coffee-growing countries, some lodges in Mountain Pine Ridge (p211) have begun experimenting with growing their own beans to serve fresh coffee to their guests. On a *finca* (farm) in Orange Walk, a local company called Gallon Jug is producing shade-grown beans for commercial distribution. Caye Coffee in San Pedro gets its beans from Guatemala, but roasts them in its facility right in San Pedro, producing such popular blends as Belizean Roast and Maya Blend.

'Belikin' is Mayan for 'road to the east' and the main temple of Altun Ha is pictured on the label.

Alcoholic Drinks

Belikin is the native beer of Belize. You'll be hard-pressed to find any other beer available, as there are severe import duties levied on foreign brews. Fear not, however, as Belikin is always cold and refreshing. Most commonly served is Belikin Regular, a lager, but Belikin also brews a lower-calorie, lower-alcohol beer, called Lighthouse Lager. There is also a stronger Belikin Stout and Belikin Premium, in a bigger bottle but the same strength as Belikin Regular. Beer usually costs around BZ$3 to BZ$5 a bottle, although this can vary from place to place.

THE ROOTS OF GARIFUNA COOKING: MRS DELONE JONES-LINO *Joshua Samuel Brown*

When people talk about Belizean food, they think of rice, beans and stewed chicken. But to get the real flavor of Belize, you have to go to a genuine Garifuna restaurant. In Dangriga, I spoke with local chef Mrs Delone Jones-Lino about what makes Garifuna food so good.

'Garifuna people are very indigenous people. We have our own food, our own dances, our own beliefs and our own music. And we definitely have our own food! Our culinary traditions come from St Vincent. When the Garifuna people came here, we brought our traditions, our recipes, and even our crops with us.

'Cassava is a Garifuna staple. Cassava is a starch, like a sweet potato. Here we make cassava bread from it. Then we have something called *varasa*; it's like a tamale, but it's made from a kind of cross between a banana and a plantain, picked while it's still hard and cooked until it's soft.

'*Hudut* is the one food that everyone loves. We serve it here on Wednesday and Friday, and people come from miles around for it. *Hudut* is made from plantain, cooked until tender and mashed with a big mortar and pestle. Then we cook it up with local fish like snapper and co-conut milk.

'The best day to come and try Garifuna food is definitely on Garifuna Settlement Day (p222). That's when we have something called a "boil-up." We have all the traditional foods of our people, and a variety of beverages, sometimes rum or other alcoholic beverages.

'People come to Roots Kitchen from all over the world. When they find us, and see what a small restaurant we are, they're sometimes surprised. A lot of Belizeans go overseas to work, you know. But when they come home, the first thing they want is to eat some traditional Belizean food. Because it doesn't matter how rich you are, outside of Belize you can't get food like this anywhere!'

An expert in Garifuna cuisine, Mrs Delone Jones-Lino is the head chef at Roots Kitchen (p223) in Dangriga.

TOP PICKS FOR FOODIES

- **Hanna's** (p200), San Ignacio – Belizean and Indian fare that also caters for vegetarians
- **Wild Mango's** (p137), San Pedro – fresh seafood and Cajun spices on the island beachfront
- **Capricorn** (p139), San Pedro – high-end nouvelle cuisine in an open-air setting
- **Agave** (p154), Caye Caulker – a delightful blend of Caribbean and Mediterranean flavors
- **Roots Kitchen** (p223), Dangriga – *the* place to experience a traditional Garifuna feast
- **Earth Runnins'** (p249), Punta Gorda – where food presentation becomes an art form
- **Cerros Beach Inn** (p179), Cerros – eco-friendly enterprise *and* the best chocolate cake in Belize

---

In a Caribbean country that produces so much sugarcane, it's not surprising that rum is Belize's number one liquor. The country has four distilleries; the Travellers distillery in Belize City has won several international awards with its thick, spicy One Barrel rum.

Cuba libre (rum-and-coke) and piña colada are the most popular ways of diluting your fermented sugarcane juice. But according to Belize bartenders, the national drink is in fact the 'panty-ripper' or 'brief-ripper,' depending on your gender. This concoction is a straightforward mix of coconut rum and pineapple juice, served on the rocks.

CELEBRATIONS

Belizeans are mad for rice and beans at any time, but on Sunday it is a compulsory ritual. Before Christmas most folks get baking: rum-flavored, dark fruit cakes are popular. On Christmas Day, many Belizeans consume a more elaborate version of rice and beans – perhaps with turkey or ham instead of chicken. The Maya love their tamales and prepare these at Christmas, while Mestizos might tuck into roast pork and gravy with their corn tortillas.

Several festivals around the country focus chiefly on food. Beach communities celebrate the opening of the lobster season with Lobster Festivals: the last weekend of June in Placencia (p240), the first weekend of July on Caulker (p149), and the second weekend of July in Ambergris (p132). Punta Gorda has a weekend Fish Fest in November (p247), and Crooked Tree celebrates the cashew harvest at its Cashew Festival in May (p111).

For thousands of classic and creative cocktails made with rum, visit www.rumcocktail recipes.com.

WHERE TO EAT & DRINK

Belizean eateries are a wide-ranging lot but you can distinguish between two main types. At the lower end (pricewise) of the scale are the straightforward places aimed at a local clientele, offering mainly Belizean favorites – rice and beans, fried chicken, fried or grilled fish, burgers, Mexican soups and snacks and the occasional Garifuna dish. In such down-to-earth diners you can usually eat for BZ$10 to BZ$20 per person.

At the upper end are the fancier places geared to tourists and middle-class customers, where you can dine on steaks, lobster and shrimp; Italian, Thai, Arabic, Tex-Mex and Indian cuisines; gourmet salads; and whole foods and vegetarian preparations. The classier places are mostly at the upscale jungle lodges in Cayo District, on the cayes, and around Belize City and Placencia. These places are catering to foreigners, so you can expect to pay international prices. Ambergris is particularly expensive, and it is easy to spend upwards of BZ$40 per person.

Of course plenty of eateries bridge the gap, serving a selection of Belizean and international fare. In a class of their own are the many

Chinese restaurants, some of which are dingy, flyblown dives while others are sparkling places serving tasty food.

On the whole, service in Belizean restaurants is friendly and fairly prompt and efficient. A tip of around 10% is normal in the fancier places, unless the service charge is already included. In humbler establishments tips are not necessarily expected but are still appreciated.

Typical restaurant mealtimes are 7am to 9:30am for breakfast, 11:30am to 2pm for lunch and 6pm to 8pm for dinner. Belizeans themselves tend to eat at the early ends of those ranges. In Belize City and tourist haunts, many places don't close between meals and may stay open late at night. Opening hours of bars are very diverse. Some open from about noon to midnight, others just for a few evening hours, and yet others from early morning to early evening.

Quick Eats

All around the country you'll encounter street vendors selling a variety of light eats – tacos, tamales, conch fritters, johnnycakes, meat pies – and even fuller fare such as rice and beans or barbecued chicken. Some of this food can be very tasty, and it's always cheap (usually BZ$2 to BZ$5 per item). Pick stands that look clean and are patronized by others – they're likely to provide the tastiest and most hygienic fare.

Get the scoop on the San Pedro Lobster Festival at www.sanpedrolobster fest.com.

VEGETARIANS & VEGANS

Vegetarians will rejoice at the wide variety of tropical fruits and fresh fruit juices. Also delicious and filling are the Belizean baked goods: banana bread, coconut bread, pumpkin bread etc.

In short, non-meat-eaters will have no problem feeding themselves. But if you're on an organized tour or participating in a beach barbeque you should make your requirements known beforehand. Be prepared for rice, beans, tortillas and plantains. Potato salad and coleslaw crop up regularly, but fresh greens (read: iceberg lettuce) can be elusive. Stewed beans are often prepared with ham or bacon, so double-check. Maya and Mestizo foods generally

JOHNNYCAKES

There is no more satisfying Belizean breakfast than a fresh-baked johnnycake with a pat of butter and a slice of cheese. These savory biscuits – straight from the oven – steal the show when served with eggs or beans.

Ingredients
2lb flour
6 teaspoons baking powder
½ cup shortening
½ cup margarine
1 teaspoon salt
2 cups coconut milk or evaporated milk

Method
Sift dry ingredients. Heat oven to 400°F. Use fingertips or knife to cut margarine and shortening into flour. Gradually stir in milk with a wooden spoon. Mix well to form a manageable ball of dough. Roll out dough into a long strip and cut into 1½in to 2in pieces. Shape into round balls and place on greased baking sheets. Flatten lightly and prick with a fork. Bake in hot oven for 10 minutes or until golden brown.

contain meat but tamales *de chaya* (spinach and cheese tamales) and *garnaches* (tortillas with beans, cabbage and cheese) are vegetarian fare.

In tourist areas you'll often find entire menu sections devoted to vegetarian dishes, with an awareness of whole-food cooking in places like Ambergris Caye and at some of the Cayo jungle lodges. Be on the lookout for Thai and Italian restaurants, which usually have good vegetarian selections. Lots of vegetarian dishes will use dairy products so vegans will need to check this.

EATING WITH KIDS

Rice and Beans (www
.riceandbeansindc
.blogspot.com) is a blog
about mindful eating,
written by a Belizean
('I love me some spicy
food') with organic roots
('I want my food straight
from the dirt').

You won't have to work hard to feed your children, who will probably be happy to eat most everyday Belizean foods such as sandwiches, rice and beans, fried chicken, hamburgers and fruits. Bakery goods, pasta and pizzas are additional favorites with kids. Most children will happily quaff a *licuado* (blended fruit juice). If you want to prepare soft foods for infants, you can mash bananas and avocados and other tropical fruits.

HABITS & CUSTOMS

Belizeans love their food (anxiety about weight is rare here). They view the act of sitting down to eat with family and friends as a deserved pleasure.

Belizeans usually eat their main meal at noon, and many offices, shops and even schools close from noon to 1pm so that people can go home and eat lunch with their families. Rice and beans is almost always the staple of this meal, earning the lunch hour the nickname 'rice hour.' Dinner for Belizeans is usually a lighter meal, taken early (around sundown, at 6pm to 6:30pm).

It is not uncommon for Belizeans to eat and drink at restaurants and at street vendors, although most meals are taken at home with family. Community and church events often center around barbecues, where people cook and eat together.

Belize District

What contrast offers the district that shares its country's name! On one hand, you've got Belize City, a seaside urban jungle replete with neighborhoods so gritty that any inner-city denizen would feel right at home. On the other, you've got the area that surrounds the city on three sides and stretches for long and largely unpopulated miles, comprising majestic savannah, wildlife-filled jungles and lagoons, and some of the hemisphere's most breathtaking natural beauty.

Separating the city from the district is mere semantics; Belizeans themselves, referring to a given location, use the term 'Belize' interchangeably, as in 'Altun Ha is up in Belize (District)' or 'I got carjacked in Belize (City).' For the purpose of this book, we've put both Belize (the city) and Belize (the district) as a chapter called simply 'Belize District.'

Just a few miles out of the city center, Belize City's gritty Caribbean urbanism crumbles and evaporates in a great puff of savannah country to the north, jungle to the west, and a verdant gumbo of mangrove lagoon and jungle to the south. This is where, to most travelers and Belizeans alike, the real Belize can be said to begin. There is plenty to see and do in Belize District, so much in fact that a visitor with only a week could spend it all here, gleaning samples of Belize's Maya heritage, Creole culture and ecotourism, all within an hour's drive of Belize City.

HIGHLIGHTS

- Visiting **Belize Zoo** (p113) during the day then coming back for a night tour to check out nocturnal wildlife
- Spending a night surrounded by the roar of howler monkeys at the **Community Baboon Sanctuary** (p108) or **Spanish Creek Wildlife Sanctuary** (p109)
- Bird-watching at **Crooked Tree Wildlife Sanctuary** (p110)
- Soaking up Belize's fascinating history at the **Museum of Belize** (p94) in Belize City
- Learning about the area's fascinating bio-diversity through an internship at **Monkey Bay Wildlife Sanctuary** (p115) or **Spanish Creek Rainforest Reserve** (p110)

■ POPULATION:	■ MONTHLY RAINFALL:	■ HIGHEST ELEVATION:
93,215	Jan 5.5in, Jun 10.2in	300ft

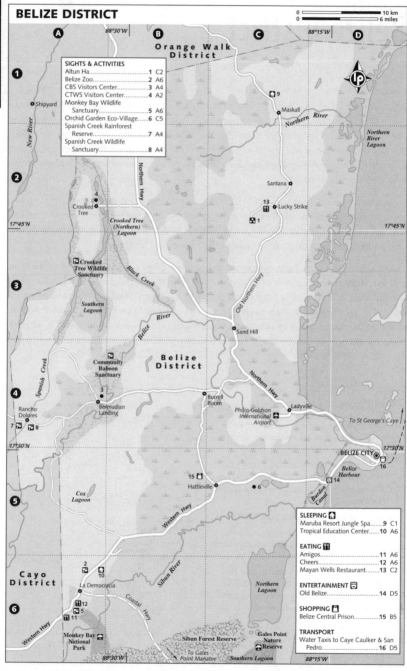

BELIZE DISTRICT

0   10 km
0   6 miles

SIGHTS & ACTIVITIES
Altun Ha.....................................1 C2
Belize Zoo................................2 A6
CBS Visitors Center..............3 A4
CTWS Visitors Center..........4 A2
Monkey Bay Wildlife
  Sanctuary.............................5 A6
Orchid Garden Eco-Village......6 C5
Spanish Creek Rainforest
  Reserve..................................7 A4
Spanish Creek Wildlife
  Sanctuary.............................8 A4

SLEEPING 🏠
Maruba Resort Jungle Spa.......9 C1
Tropical Education Center......10 A6

EATING 🍴
Amigos...................................11 A6
Cheers....................................12 A6
Mayan Wells Restaurant.......13 C2

ENTERTAINMENT 🎭
Old Belize...............................14 D5

SHOPPING 🛍
Belize Central Prison..............15 B5

TRANSPORT
Water Taxis to Caye Caulker & San
  Pedro..................................16 D5

Orange Walk
District

Shipyard

New River

Maskall

Northern River

Northern River Lagoon

Santana

Lucky Strike

Crooked Tree

Crooked Tree (Northern) Lagoon

Northern Hwy

Crooked Tree Wildlife Sanctuary

Southern Lagoon

Black Creek

Belize River

Sand Hill

Old Northern Hwy

Spanish Creek

Community Baboon Sanctuary

Belize District

Rancho Dolores

Bermudian Landing

Burrell Boom

Ladyville

Philip Goldson International Airport

Northern Hwy

To St George's Caye

BELIZE CITY

Belize Harbour

Burdon Canal

Cox Lagoon

Hattieville

Western Hwy

Cayo District

La Democracia

Coastal Hwy

Sibun River

Northern Lagoon

Monkey Bay National Park

Western Hwy

To Gales Point Manatee

Sibun Forest Reserve

Gales Point Nature Reserve

Southern Lagoon

BELIZE CITY

pop 63,670

A fair percentage of tourists in Belize choose to spend as little time as possible in Belize City, the country's only major urban area. This may be explained by the fact that, on the whole, the country's main attractions are natural and nautical, making any kind of prolonged visit to its only metropolis superfluous. But another (and equally likely) explanation is this: outside of certain spots, the city itself just isn't a very safe place for anyone, let alone cash-and-camera toting tourist types. 'Dodgy' is the word many travelers use to describe Belize City, and even those who admire its raffish charms and cultural vibrancy (and, to be fair, there's plenty of this) admit that the city – unlike the rest of the country – is anything but relaxed.

That being said, Belize City is still the historical (if no longer the actual) capital of the nation, making it an interesting place to spend a day or two for those interested in the nation's history and culture. Its ramshackle streets are alive with colorful characters who represent every facet of Belize's ethnic variety, especially the Creoles. The urban scenery encompasses not just malodorous canals and grungy slums, but also handsome colonial houses, seaside parks, bustling shopping areas and sailboats bobbing at the mouth of Haulover Creek. You might find Belize City menacing, but you won't find it dull.

HISTORY

Belize City owes its existence to the harbor at the mouth of Haulover Creek, a branch of the Belize River, down which the Baymen (early British woodcutters) floated lumber from their inland camps. It had little significance until the Spanish briefly captured St George's Caye, the Baymen's first main settlement, in 1779. 'Belize Town' then became and remained the British headquarters in Belize. Popular lore has it that the settlement, at first just a few huts surrounded by mosquito-ridden swamps, grew on a landfill of mahogany chips and rum bottles deposited by the Baymen, who would come to the coast after the rainy season to dispatch their lumber overseas and spend most of the proceeds on rum.

During the 19th century the town grew on both sides of Haulover Creek, with the British merchants' homes and buildings of the ruling elite clustered along and near the southern seafront. African slaves and their descendants lived in cabins inland of here. By the 1880s the town had a population of around 5000; the great majority being Creoles descended from the British and their slaves – though whites still held all the power and wealth. Belize City witnessed most of the significant events on the long road to Belizean independence, including riots in 1894, 1919 and 1950.

The city was devastated by hurricanes in 1931 and 1961. It was 1961's Hurricane Hattie that spurred the government to build a new capital at Belmopan, 52 miles inland. This left Belize City, and the Creole population in general, feeling rather neglected; it was then that people started to emigrate to the USA to seek an escape from overcrowding, unemployment and poor sanitation in Belize City.

Drug-related gangsterism kicked in during the 1980s and 1990s, which helped keep conditions pretty tough for the city's underemployed working class. Middle-class residential areas have developed on the northern and northwestern fringes of the city, while the central areas either side of Haulover Creek remain the country's cultural and commercial hub.

The biggest change to the city's face in the 21st century has been the invasion of cruise-ship tourists: cruise liners anchoring off Belize City brought 850,000 passengers in 2004, up from almost zero five years previously. Most cruise-ship tourists come ashore at the city's new Tourism Village, located at the mouth of Haulover Creek. Generally, the passengers wander around the downtown area for a few hours or head off on excursions to inland attractions.

ORIENTATION

Haulover Creek, running across the middle of the city, separates the downtown commercial area (focused on Albert St) from the slightly more genteel Fort George district to the northeast. Hotels, guesthouses and places to eat are found on both sides of the creek, with the majority of the city's high-end hotels being in Fort George.

The Swing Bridge (the hub of the city, and – some reckon – the heart of Belize itself) crosses Haulover Creek to link Albert St with Queen St. The Caye Caulker Water Taxi Terminal stands by the north side of the bridge.

West of Albert St is Southside, the poorest part of the city. The main bus station and other bus stops are found here, right next to the Collet Canal. It's safest to take taxis to and from these bus points, even during the day. East of Albert St is Regent St and the Southern Foreshore; you'll be able to see cruise ships on the horizon from this coastal avenue on most days. This area is generally OK during the day, but be wary at night.

North, up the coast from the Fort George district, are the Newtown Barracks and Kings Park neighborhoods, home to some of the city's best restaurants and entertainment venues.

The Philip Goldson International Airport is some 11 miles northwest of the city center, off the Northern Hwy; the Municipal Airstrip is 2 miles north of the center. Take a taxi to or from either.

INFORMATION
Bookstores

You'll be able to find some Belize-related books at the National Handicraft Center (p103), Brodie's department store (p103) and at the up-market gift shops; however, the following places have the more comprehensive selections.

Angelus Press (Map pp96-7; ☎ 223-5777; 10 Queen St; ⏱ 7:30am-5:30pm Mon-Fri, 8am-noon Sat) Office-supply store and internet café with a reasonable supply of books with Belizean themes.

Book Center (Map pp96-7; ☎ 227-7457; 4 Church St; ⏱ 8am-noon & 1-5:30pm Mon-Thu, till 9pm Fri, till 6pm Sat) New and secondhand English literature, maps, guidebooks and books on Belizean history, society and natural history.

Image Factory (Map pp96-7; ☎ 203-4151; 91 N Front St; ⏱ 9am-5pm Mon-Fri) This art gallery has the country's best range of books, including international literature and titles on Belizean and Caribbean society and history.

Cultural Centers

Institute of Mexico (Map p93; ☎ 223-0193/4; http ://portal.sre.gob.mx/belice_eng; cnr Newtown Barracks Rd & Wilson St) This is the consular, cultural and educational section of the embassy of Mexico in Belize (the actual embassy itself is in Belmopan). Come here to check out a variety of programs, exhibitions, concerts and films.

Emergency

Ambulance (☎ 90, private ambulance 223-3292)
Crime Stoppers (☎ 922, 224-4646) To report crimes.
Fire Service (☎ 90, 227-2579)
Police (☎ 90, 911, tourist police 227-6082) Tourist police wear a special badge on the left shoulder and patrol central areas of the city. There are police stations located on Queen St (Map pp96-7) and Racoon St (Map pp96-7).

Internet Access

Angelus Press (Map pp96-7; ☎ 223-5777; 10 Queen St; per hr BZ$7; ⏱ 7:30am-5:30pm Mon-Fri, 8am-noon Sat)
KGS Internet (Map pp96-7; ☎ 207-7130; 60 King St; per hr BZ$5; ⏱ 8am-7pm Mon-Fri, 8am-6pm Sat, 9:30am-2:30pm Sun) Will also burn CDs for BZ$3.50.
M Business Solutions (Map pp96-7; ☎ 223-6766; 13 Cork St; per hr BZ$10; ⏱ 8am-5pm Mon-Fri) High-speed internet access, in the Great House hotel building.
Maya Coffee (Map pp96-7; ☎ 223-4788; 158 N Front St; per hr BZ$7; ⏱ 8am-5pm Mon-Fri) Kevin Chen's coffeeshop, just across from S&L Travel, sells souvenirs and books, as well as peddling internet access.

Laundry

G's Laundromat (Map pp96-7; ☎ 207-4461; 22 Dean St; wash per load BZ$10; ⏱ 7:30am-5:30pm) Wash and dry in about 1½ hours. Most hotels can arrange laundry service at similar prices.

Medical Services

Belize Medical Associates (Map p93; ☎ 223-0302/3/4; 5791 St Thomas St; ⏱ 24hr emergency services) Private hospital in Kings Park district with a good reputation among expats.
Brodie's (Map pp96-7; ☎ 227-7070; 2 Albert St; ⏱ 8:30am-7pm Mon-Thu, 8:30am-8pm Fri, 8:30am-5pm Sat, 8:30am-1pm Sun) This department store has a very well-stocked pharmacy.
Karl Heusner Memorial Hospital (Map p93; ☎ 223-1548/64; Princess Margaret Dr; ⏱ 24hr emergency services) A public hospital in the north of town that enjoys a less-than-stellar reputation.

Money

The following banks exchange US or Canadian dollars, British pounds and, usually, euros. The ATMs at Belize Bank downtown and First Caribbean International Bank will accept foreign Visa cards and, in Belize Bank's case, MasterCard, Cirrus and Plus cards. Most ATMs are 24-hour, though it's highly recommended that you visit them during daylight hours.

Belize Bank Downtown (Map pp96-7; ☎ 227-7132; 60 Market Sq; ⏱ 8am-3pm Mon-Thu, 8am-4:30pm Fri); Philip Goldson International Airport (⏱ 8:30am-1pm & 2-4pm Mon-Fri) The downtown branch's ATM is on the east side of the building.
First Caribbean International Bank Downtown (Map pp96-7; ☎ 227-7211; 21 Albert St; ⏱ 8am-2:30pm Mon-Thu, 8am-4:30pm Fri)
Scotiabank Downtown (Map pp96-7; ☎ 227-7027; cnr Albert & Bishop Sts; ⏱ 8am-2:30pm Mon-Thu, 8:30am-4pm Fri, 9am-noon Sat)

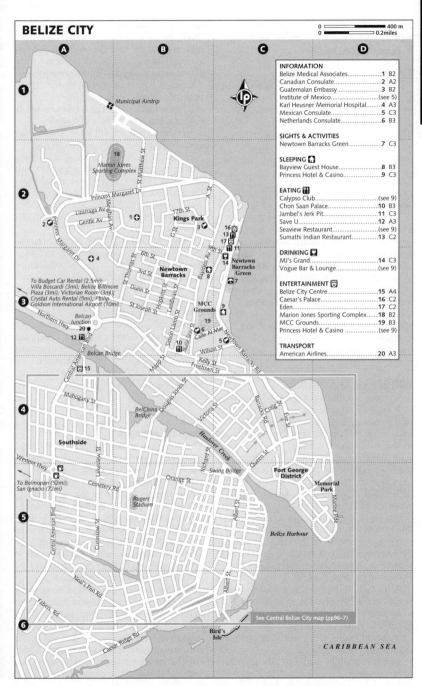

BELIZE CITY

0 — 400 m
0 — 0.2 miles

INFORMATION
Belize Medical Associates...................**1** B2
Canadian Consulate.........................**2** A2
Guatemalan Embassy........................**3** B2
Institute of Mexico.........................(see 5)
Karl Heusner Memorial Hospital...........**4** A3
Mexican Consulate...........................**5** C3
Netherlands Consulate.....................**6** B3

SIGHTS & ACTIVITIES
Newtown Barracks Green.................**7** C3

SLEEPING 🏠
Bayview Guest House.......................**8** B3
Princess Hotel & Casino...................**9** C3

EATING 🍴
Calypso Club.................................(see 9)
Chon Saan Palace..........................**10** B3
Jambel's Jerk Pit...........................**11** C3
Save U......................................**12** A3
Seaview Restaurant.......................(see 9)
Sumathi Indian Restaurant..............**13** C2

DRINKING 🍷
MJ's Grand.................................**14** C3
Vogue Bar & Lounge......................(see 9)

ENTERTAINMENT 🎭
Belize City Centre.........................**15** A4
Caesar's Palace............................**16** C2
Eden..**17** C2
Marion Jones Sporting Complex.........**18** B2
MCC Grounds..............................**19** B3
Princess Hotel & Casino ....(see 9)

TRANSPORT
American Airlines...........................**20** A3

Post

Main post office (Map pp96-7; ☎ 227-2201; N Front St; ⏱ 8am-5pm Mon-Thu, 8am-4:30pm Fri)

Telephone

Public card-operated phones can be found around the city. You can also rent a cell phone from the Radisson Hotel (p100) for BZ$22 per day plus usage charge.

BTL (Map pp96-7; ☎ 227-7085; 1 Church St; ⏱ 8am-6pm Mon-Fri) Has indoor booths for phone-card calls, country-direct calls to Canada and the UK, and collect calls.

Tourist Information

Belize Tourism Board (Map pp96-7; ☎ 227-2420/17; www.travelbelize.org; 64 Regent St; ⏱ 8am-5pm Mon-Fri) This is the brand-spanking-new (as of January, 2008) head office of the BTB, where you can pick up maps, magazines, and all sorts of information relating to travel around Belize.

Belize Tourism Industry Association (BTIA; Map pp96-7; ☎ 227-5717/1144; www.btia.org; 10 N Park St; ⏱ 8am-noon & 1-5pm Mon-Fri) The BTIA is an independent association of tourism businesses, actively defending 'sustainable ecocultural tourism'. The office provides leaflets about the country's regions, copies of its *Destination Belize* annual magazine (free), and information on its members, which include many of Belize's best hotels, restaurants and other tourism businesses. The website is a plethora of information.

DANGERS & ANNOYANCES

Not to put too fine a point on it, but Belize City isn't exactly the relaxed place the rest of the country is. Hotel windows are barred and, in many hotels, front doors are kept locked even during the day. Street crime is fairly common, and if you look like a tourist the chances of being harassed are fairly high. On the other hand, the city is fairly safe in comparison to other urban areas in Central America. Most violent crime occurs in the Southside district, south of Haulover Creek and west of Southside Canal. Take a taxi when you're going to or from the main bus station or other bus stops in this area. Even in the middle of the day these streets can have a threatening atmosphere.

After dark, it's best to take a taxi anywhere you go in the city. If you must walk, even just a couple of blocks, get advice from your hotel about safety in specific neighborhoods. Stay on better-lit major streets and don't go alone if you can help it.

East of Southside Canal you're in the downtown commercial area – Albert St, Regent St and their cross-streets. Though tourists are sometimes the victims of robberies around here, statistically speaking you're more likely to simply be harassed for a dollar or two (usually in rapid succession by the same person). After dark, your odds of being separated from your valuables increase markedly.

The Fort George district is generally safe in daylight, but you should still stay alert.

In contrast to the rest of Belize, any stranger who attempts to engage you in conversation – even just by shaking your hand or claiming they have seen you before – is almost certainly after your money. Don't be afraid to shake these people off rapidly. Tricksters may just try to pressure you for a 'gift' or 'tip,' but they may also be aiming to pick your pockets or worse.

Police maintain a fairly visible presence in the main areas frequented by tourists in Belize City, and will intervene to deter hustlers and other shady characters, but you can't rely on them to always be where you need them. Take the commonsense precautions that you would in any major city. Don't flash wads of cash, cameras, jewelry or other signs of wealth. Don't leave valuables lying around your hotel room. Don't use illicit drugs and avoid deserted streets, even in daylight.

See p282 and p290 for more tips on avoiding trouble in Belize.

SIGHTS
Museum of Belize

This excellent modern **museum** (Map pp96-7; ☎ 223-4524; Gabourel Lane; admission BZ$10; ⏱ 9am-5pm Mon-Fri) in the Fort George district is a must-see for anyone interested in the story of Belize. Housed in the country's former main jail (built of brick in 1857), the museum preserves one cell in its original state, complete with inmates' graffiti; if you thought your hotel room was cramped, think again! Fascinating historical photos and documents bear testimony to the colonial and independence eras and the destruction wrought by hurricanes.

The Maya Treasures section, upstairs, is rather light on artifacts (most of Belize's finest Maya finds were spirited away to other countries) but makes up for that with informative models and explanations. Other sections of the museum are devoted to Belize's highly colorful postage stamps, and its insect life, with full detail on the disgusting manner in which the human botfly uses living human flesh to nourish its larvae! The museum also has a good little gift shop.

Government House

Fronting the sea down at the end of Regent St, this handsome two-story wooden **colonial mansion** (House of Culture; Map pp96-7; ☎ 227-3050; Regent St; admission BZ$10; ☽ 9am-4pm Mon-Fri) served as the residence of Britain's superintendents and governors of Belize from its construction in 1814 until 1996. The house, one of the oldest in Belize, is now a cultural center and museum – well worth a visit for its historical exhibits, colorful displays of modern Belizean art, spacious colonial ambience and grassy gardens. It was here at midnight on September 21, 1981 that the Union Jack was ceremonially replaced with the Belizean flag to mark the birth of independent Belize. Displayed in the gardens is the tender from Baron Bliss' yacht.

St John's Cathedral

Immediately inland of Government House stands **St John's Cathedral** (Map pp96-7; ☎ 227-2137; Albert St; ☽ 6am-6pm), the oldest Anglican church in Central America. It was built by slave labor between 1812 and 1820 using bricks brought from Britain as ballast. Notable things to see inside are the ancient pipe organ and the Baymen-era tombstones that tell their own history of Belize's early days and the toll taken on the city's early settlers.

A block southwest lies **Yarborough Cemetery**, where you'll see the graves of less prominent early citizens – an even more turbulent narrative of Belize, which dates back to 1787.

Swing Bridge

This heart and soul of Belize City life, crossed by just about everyone here just about every day, is the only remaining working **bridge** (Map pp96–7) of its type in the world. Its operators manually rotate the bridge open, usually at about 6am and 5:30pm, Monday to Saturday, just long enough to let tall boats pass, bringing vehicles and pedestrians in the city center to a halt. It's quite a procedure, and if you're in the right place at the right time, you might even get to help out. The bridge, a product of Liverpool's ironworks, was installed in 1923, replacing an earlier bridge that had opened in 1897.

Downstream from the bridge, Haulover Creek is usually a pretty sight, with numerous small yachts and fishing boats riding at anchor.

The Swing Bridge is ground zero for hustlers looking to part tourists from their valuables. You will very likely be approached by seemingly friendly sorts with outstretched hands asking, 'Where you from?' Be advised that the chances of said encounter resulting in a mutually beneficial cultural exchange are slim to none.

Image Factory

The country's most innovative and exciting **art gallery** (Map pp96-7; www.imagefactory.bz; ☎ 203-4151; 91 N Front St; admission free; ☽ 9am-5pm Mon-Fri), near the Caye Caulker Water Taxi Terminal, stages new exhibitions most months, usually of work by Belizean artists. Opening receptions are usually held early in the month; cocktails are served on the Image Factory's deck, which looks out on Haulover Creek. The adjoining shop sells art, gifts and the country's best range of books.

Baron Bliss Tomb

At the tip of the Fort George peninsula lies the granite **Baron Bliss Tomb** (Map pp96–7), the final resting place of Belize's most famous benefactor (see the boxed text, p98), who never set foot on Belizean soil while alive. Next to the tomb stands the **Fort George Lighthouse**, one of the many benefits the baron's munificence has yielded the country.

Coastal Zone Museum

Next door to, and entered from, the Caye Caulker Water Taxi Terminal, this small **museum** (Map pp96-7; N Front St; admission adult/student/child BZ$4/2/2; ☽ 8:30am-4:30pm) has a limited number of pictures, models and carapaces of Belizean aquatic life, plus summary information on the Belize Barrier Reef World Heritage sites and a few dioramas of marine ecosystems. The museum merits a peek if you're in the area.

ACTIVITIES

Although most divers and snorkelers base themselves out on the cayes, it is actually quicker to access some of the best sites direct from Belize City. Some hotels in the city offer their guests diving and snorkeling outings. Other reputable operators include Sea Sports Belize (p98) and Hugh Parkey's Belize Dive Connection (p98).

BELIZE DISTRICT

CENTRAL BELIZE CITY

Ⓐ **Ⓑ** **Ⓒ** **Ⓓ**

INFORMATION
Angelus Press.............................1 F3
Belize Bank................................2 E3
Belize Global Travel Services......3 E4
Belize International Travel Services.4 E4
Belize Tourism Board..................5 F5
Belize Tourism Industry
　Association..............................6 G3
Book Center................................7 E4
BTL..8 E3
Discovery Expeditions.............(see 39)
First Caribbean International Bank.9 E3
French Consulate......................10 E1
German Consulate.....................11 F5
G's Laundromat.........................12 E4
KGS Internet..............................13 E4
M Business Solutions..............(see 39)
Main Post Office........................14 F3
Mexican Embassy.......................15 H3
Police Station.............................16 F3
Police Station.............................17 B4
Programme for Belize................18 G3
S&L Travel.................................19 F3
Scotiabank................................20 E4

SIGHTS & ACTIVITIES
Baron Bliss Tomb.......................21 H5
Belize Audubon Society.............22 G4
City Hall....................................23 F3
Coastal Zone Museum................24 F3
Fort George Lighthouse.............25 H5
Government House.....................26 F6
Hugh Parkey's Belize Dive
　Connection.............................27 H4
Image Factory...........................28 F3
Museum of Belize......................29 G2
St John's Cathedral....................30 E6
Sea Sports Belize......................31 F3
Swing Bridge.............................32 F3

SLEEPING
Bakadeer Inn.............................33 E1
Belcove Hotel............................34 E3
Bellevue Hotel...........................35 F4
Caribbean Palms Inn..................36 F4
Chateau Caribbean Hotel...........37 H3
Coningsby Inn...........................38 E5
Great House..............................39 H4
Hotel Mopan.............................40 E5
Ma Ma Chen Guesthouse...........41 G2
Radisson Fort George Hotel........42 H4
Seaside Guest House..................43 F4
Three Sisters Guesthouse...........44 F1

EATING
Big Daddy's...............................45 F3
Bird's Isle Restaurant ....(see 51)
Brodie's ....(see 58)
Dit's Restaurant........................46 E4
Le Petite Café...........................47 H4
Ma Ma Chen Restaurant.........(see 41)
Macy's.......................................48 E4
Nerie's II Restaurant..................49 F2
St George's Dining Room........(see 42)
Smoky Mermaid.....................(see 39)
Stonegrill Restaurant.............(see 42)
Wet Lizard................................50 G4

DRINKING
Baymen's Tavern....................(see 42)
Bird's Isle Restaurant................51 E6
Maya Coffee..............................52 F3
Radisson Poolside Bar............(see 42)

ENTERTAINMENT
Bliss Centre for the Performing
　Arts.......................................53 F4
Rogers Stadium.........................54 C4

SHOPPING
Augusto Quan............................55 E3
Belize Photo Lab........................56 E4
Belize Tourist Village.................57 G4
Brodie's.....................................58 E4
National Handicraft Center........59 G3

TRANSPORT
Caye Caulker Water Taxi............60 F3
Continental Airlines...................61 E5
Euphrates Auto Rental...............62 D6
Grupo TACA..........................(see 3)
Hertz..63 G4
Jex & Sons Bus Stop..................64 E3
Main Bus Station.......................65 C3
Pound Yard Bus Stop.................66 C3
R-Line Bus Stop.........................67 D3
Sarteneja Bus Line....................68 F3
Tikal Jets..................................69 E4
Triple J Express.........................70 F4
US Airways...........................(see 3)

Douglas Jones St
BelChina Bridge
Unidos Al
Vernon St
Logwood St
Magazine Rd
Johnson St
Bagdad St
Banak St
Fuel Station
Pound Yard Bridge
Mosul St
Orange St
Constitution Park
Cemetery Rd
Cemetery Rd
Pound Yard Bus Stop
Collet Canal
Cairo St
Rogers Stadium
King St
Gibnut St
Hiccatee St
West St
George St
Iguana St
Dolphin St
Bocotora St
Dean St
Racoon St
W Chcl Canal St
E Collet Canal St
Allenby St
Basra St
Armadillo St
Amara Ave
Euphrates Ave
Tigris St
Rocky La
Southside
Kut Ave
Kut Ave
Mex Ave
Southside Canal
Racecourse St
Yarborough Cemetery
Queen Charlotte St

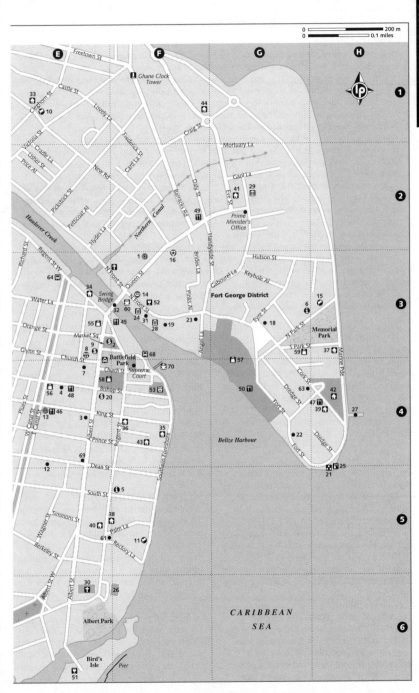

BLISS OF BELIZE

Only Belize could have an annual holiday in honor of a national benefactor with a name like Baron Bliss. Born Henry Edward Ernest Victor Bliss in Buckinghamshire, England, in 1869 (the title 'Baron' was hereditary), Bliss was a man with a powerful love of the sea, and of sailing. So much so, in fact, that he left his wife and his native land for the Caribbean in 1920, spending the next six years living aboard his yacht *Sea King II* off the Bahamas and Trinidad. After a bad bout of food poisoning in Trinidad, the baron took up an invitation from Belize's Attorney General, Willoughby Bullock, and dropped anchor off Belize on January 14, 1926.

Sadly, Baron Bliss' health took a decisive turn for the worse before he could leave his yacht; his doctors pronounced that the end was nigh. On February 17, 1926, the baron signed a will aboard the *Sea King II*, leaving most of his one-million-pound fortune to Belize. On March 9 he died. He had, apparently, fallen in love with Belize without ever setting foot on its soil.

The testament decreed that a Baron Bliss Trust be set up to invest his bequest, and that all income from it be used for the permanent benefit of Belize and its citizens, while the capital sum was to remain intact. No churches, dance halls or schools (except agricultural or vocational schools) were to be built with Bliss Trust moneys, nor was the money to be used for any repairs or maintenance to the Trust's own projects!

Over the decades the Baron Bliss Trust has spent more than US$1 million on projects such as the Bliss Centre for the Performing Arts (p103), the Fort George Lighthouse (beside which lies the baron's tomb; see p95) and the Bliss School of Nursing, which are all in Belize City; and several health centers and libraries around the country. An annual national holiday, Baron Bliss Day, is celebrated on or close to March 9, the anniversary of the good man's death.

The usual destinations are the barrier reef (p64), Turneffe Atoll (p74) and Lighthouse Reef (p75). Prices (including equipment) range from around BZ$240 for a two-tank dive at the barrier reef to BZ$400 or so for a three-tank dive at Lighthouse Reef (usually including the Blue Hole). A day's snorkeling runs from around BZ$150 to BZ$300. Sea Sports Belize can also take you sea or river fishing.

TOURS

Popular day-trip activities and destinations from Belize City include cave-tubing at Jaguar Paw (p188); visits to the Maya ruins at Lamanai (p167), Altun Ha (p167), Xunantunich (p205) and even Tikal (p205) in Guatemala; Crooked Tree Wildlife Sanctuary (p110); the Community Baboon Sanctuary (p108) and Belize Zoo (p113). Trips such as these vary in cost; expect to pay between BZ$120 and BZ$200 per person. Several hotels offer tours to their guests. Tour companies include the following:

Belize Global Travel Services (Map pp96-7; ☎ 227-7185/7364; www.belizeglobal.com; 41 Albert St; ☒ 8am-noon & 1-5pm Mon-Fri, 8am-noon Sat) Amex representative and full-service travel agency.

Belize International Travel Services (Map pp96-7; ☎ 227-1701; 18 Bishop St; ☒ 8am-noon & 1-5pm Mon-Fri, 8:30am-noon Sat) Agent for American Airlines, Continental, Maya Island Air and Tropic Air.

Discovery Expeditions (Map pp96-7; ☎ 223-0748; www.discoverybelize.com; 13 Cork St) Has offices at the Great House hotel and Philip Goldson International Airport.

Hugh Parkey's Belize Dive Connection (Map pp96-7; ☎ 223-4226; www.belizediving.com; inside of Radisson hotel) Offers diving and snorkeling tours to most nearby cayes and reefs, as well as kayaking and wildlife tours.

S&L Travel (Map pp96-7; ☎ 227-7593/5145; www .sltravelbelize.com; 91 N Front St) A very reputable agency run by the Tillett family, who also run a lovely guesthouse in Crooked Tree (p111). The shop also has internet access at BZ$0.10 per minute.

Sea Sports Belize (Map pp96-7; ☎ 223-5505; www .seasportsbelize.com; N Front St) A dive shop that also specializes in wildlife-encounter tours, river cruises, barrier-reef snorkeling and manatee- and dolphin-spotting.

Many taxi drivers in town are part-time tour guides; they may give you a sales pitch as they drive you around the city. These cabbies/guides can be quite knowledgeable and personable and may suit you if you want a customized tour; in general, you can negotiate such tours for around BZ$200 per day. Hotel staff can often make personal recommendations of cabbies known to them. Make sure your guide has a Belize Tourism Board (BTB) license.

FESTIVALS & EVENTS

Belize International Film Festival (www.belize filmfestival.com; takes place annually, check website for details) At the Bliss Centre for the Performing Arts.

Baron Bliss Day (March 9) Festivities include a regatta in front of Fort George Lighthouse.

September Celebrations (September 10 to 21) Celebrations all over the city lasting from National Day (September 10) to Independence Day (September 21), including a huge carnival parade, bands, parties, music and dancing, with many of the country's top bands playing on Newtown Barracks Green on September 21.

SLEEPING

Accommodations are found both north and south of Haulover Creek. The top-end places are to the north, and most of the midrange and budget places are to the south.

Budget

ourpick Seaside Guest House (Map pp96-7; ☎ 227-8339; 3 Prince St; dm/s/d BZ$30/40/50, VIP room BZ$90; ▯) Under new management since the last update, this long-time budget-traveler favorite has a mellow vibe befitting its classic two-story wooden Caribbean exterior (painted in a very groovy lilac and white). Dorms are more than adequate, if a tad on the small side, and the VIP room (with its own bathroom) is quite nice. There's a breezy verandah facing the sea and cool game- and book-filled chill-out spots on the 1st and 2nd floors. Great meals are available for a nominal charge.

Caribbean Palms Inn (Map pp96-7; ☎ 227-0472; www .thecaribbean-palmsinn.com; 26 Regent St; r BZ$36-140; ✕ ✖) This friendly, homy hotel occupies a rambling two-story house a few minutes' walk south of the Swing Bridge. Furnished with attractive wrought iron and wood, the rooms vary in size and light: those upstairs at the front are among the biggest and brightest, but being on the street side, they're also the noisiest. Most rooms have a private bathroom, but the cheapest ones have bathrooms out in the hall. There's also a nice rear terrace where you can hang out (though the bar that once was there has closed), and a comfy indoor sitting area providing plenty of chill-out and social space.

Ma Ma Chen Guesthouse (Map pp96-7; ☎ 223-4568; 7 Eve St; r BZ$60) Rooms are small and cell-like at this Taiwanese-owned budget guesthouse north of the Swing Bridge but, on the bright side, they've all got cable TV and are cheap and close enough to the center of town to be convenient. Best of all, the Chen family run a great vegetarian café in the same building (p101).

Three Sisters Guesthouse (Map pp96-7; ☎ 203-5729; 55 Eve St; s/d BZ$55/63) This is a friendly place with large rooms. It's on a quiet residential street, a short distance north of the center of town, and is a solid budget choice for those who want to be a bit further from the rougher edges of the Haulover Creek/Regent St areas.

Bayview Guest House (Map p93; ☎ 223-4179; www .belize-guesthouse-hotel.com; 58 Baymen Ave; s with fan BZ$40, d with air-con BZ$80; ✕ ✖) Located in the quiet northern end of town in Newtown Barracks, this guesthouse is part of a family home run by the Huang family from Taiwan. Its eight rooms are very clean and simply furnished; all have their own small bathrooms. The large, gated yard, filled with fruit trees, is a great place to decompress after a day hanging out in the city. Apartments can be rented by the month for BZ$375.

Belcove Hotel (Map pp96-7; ☎ 227-3054; www .belcove.com; 9 Regent St W; s/d with shared bathroom BZ$55/70, r with private bathroom BZ$104, r with air-con & private bathroom BZ$109; ✕ ✖) A comfortable – if somewhat ramshackle – hotel near the south end of the Swing Bridge, the Belcove offers cheaper rooms with mosquito-netted windows and fans, and five higher priced rooms with air-con and TV. Overlooking the river, the upstairs terrace is a good place to chill. Management offers free luggage storage and transportation to the airport for BZ$40 (book ahead). They can also help with diving, snorkeling and tour bookings. While the hotel itself has decent security, the surrounding area is fairly dodgy; keep alert.

Midrange

Hotel Mopan (Map pp96-7; ☎ 227-7351; www.hotelmopan .com; 55 Regent St; s/d BZ$78/98, s/d with air-con BZ$98/118; ✕ ✖ ▯) Recently refurbished, this big, old, Caribbean-style hotel provides spacious, clean rooms (all nonsmoking) with good bathrooms, comfortable beds and cable TV. Broad verandahs provide sitting space and there's a large dining room with breakfast available. The best rooms are on the top floor, where you can get a rooftop view of the city. A range of day and half-day trips can be booked at reception.

ourpick Coningsby Inn (Map pp96-7; ☎ 227-1566; www.coningsby-inn.com; 76 Regent St; d/tr BZ$119/131; ✖ ▯) A friendly and comfortable small hotel in an attractive colonial-style house, the Coningsby is unbeatable for midrange value. Rooms are sparkling clean and decent-sized, all with bathtub, phone, cable TV and air-con, and breakfasts (BZ$10) are served in a lovely dining room upstairs. Like the Bakadeer, the Coningsby has wireless internet and 24-hour security.

Bellevue Hotel (Map pp96-7; ☎ 227-7051/2; belle vue@btl.net; 5 Southern Foreshore; r BZ$120; ✵ ☎) The rambling seafront Bellevue has all the hallmarks of a place that's seen better decades, but it's still good value for money. Clean, though threadbare, rooms come with air-con, private bathrooms and cable TV. The nicest is room 127, which has bay windows and an ocean view. There's an airy verandah up front, which droops at an odd angle off the building itself. The pool and pool bar at the back are perhaps this hotel's biggest plus, though that area seems to need maintenance as well.

Bakadeer Inn (Map pp96-7; ☎ 223-0659; www.baka deerinn.com; 74 Cleghorn Street; s/d BZ$120/131; ✵ ▫) Located on a quiet side street north just north of the Haulover Creek, the Bakadeer's rooms are comfortable and basic, though the ones on the 1st floor are a bit on the dark side. The hotel has wireless internet and tight security, making it a good base for those traveling with laptops.

Villa Boscardi (off Map p93; ☎ /fax 223-1691; www .villaboscardi.com; 6043 Manatee Dr, Buttonwood Bay; s/d with breakfast BZ$130/150; ✖ ✵ ▫) Set in a secure middle-class suburb, this guesthouse and its charming hosts will smooth away any stresses that Belize City's rougher edges might induce. The six rooms are large and elegant, built with Belizean materials with plenty of comfortable touches, including big beds, cable TV and hair dryers. Two of the rooms have bathtubs. Children under eight stay free. About 4 miles west of the city center and 7 miles from the international airport; airport pickup is available for BZ$40.

Chateau Caribbean Hotel (Map pp96-7; ☎ 223-0800; www.chateaucaribbean.com; 6 Marine Pde; s/d/tr/ste BZ$158/178/198/218; ℙ ✵) This converted colonial mansion in the Fort George district offers a spacious lobby, bar and dining room overlooking the Caribbean. Rooms are breezy and gracefully appointed with big beds, large windows with white curtains, and wicker furniture from which to sit with a suitably colonial beverage (gin and tonic, anyone?) and enjoy the view. The 2nd-floor bar is equally

lovely, though the food at the restaurant isn't anything to write home about.

Top End

Princess Hotel & Casino (Map p93; ☎ 223-0638; www .princessbelize.com; Newtown Barracks Rd; s/d BZ$262/284, ste from BZ$327; ℙ ✖ ▫ ☎) This six-story, seafront hotel in the north of the city is also an entertainment and social center, with plenty of bustle in its lively lobby and public areas – in fact more of a place to visit for a bit of diversion than a place to base yourself. Clocks at reception show the time in Las Vegas, Miami and Cancún. The rooms are ample, pretty much what you'd expect for the price at a seaside casino. Prices for all rooms include breakfast.

The hotel boasts two restaurants, the Seaview and the Calypso Club (p102), as well as an Olympic-size pool, marina, casino, cinema (Belize's only movie theatre!), bowling alley and a lively lounge bar (p102).

Radisson Fort George Hotel (Map pp96-7; ☎ 223-3333; www.radisson.com/belizecitybz; 2 Marine Pde; s BZ$260-300, d BZ$280-340; ℙ ✖ ▫ ☎) The city's top hotel has 102 conservatively decorated rooms with all the comforts. While offering top international-class service, the Radisson avoids the cultural detachment that often comes with such a package. Local woods, furnishings and decorations confer genuine Belizean character.

There are three classes of room here (all with high-speed internet connection): Club Tower (the fanciest option, in a glass tower where the marble-floored rooms all enjoy a full sea view); Colonial (in the original hotel structure, with fine wooden furnishings and partial sea views); and Villa (the least expensive, across the street from the main hotel). Besides two swimming pools, two restaurants (the Stonegrill, p102, and St George's Dining Room, p102) and bars (p102), the hotel has its own dock, home to Hugh Parkey's Belize Dive Connection (see p98).

Great House (Map pp96-7; ☎ 223-3400; www.great housebelize.com; 13 Cork St; s/d BZ$250/300; ℙ ▫ ✖) A gorgeous, four-story, colonial-style mansion built in 1927 on a piece of prime Fort George real estate, the Great House features individually decorated, hardwood-floored rooms, all fully equipped with air-con, phone, safe, big-screen cable TV and refrigerators. A full range of land and offshore day trips are available to guests. The hotel usually reduces room rates from May to October, and in November and December if business is a bit slow. The Great House is also where you'll find Habanos Cigars, a great place to stock up on Cuba…er, Honduran cigars to bring back home.

EATING

Belize City's restaurants are a good sampler of Belizean eating options, from plain but satisfying rice-and-beans-based local meals to plenty of good seafood and meat and a few more exotic possibilities from the Caribbean, Asia or Europe. Most of the fancier and more upmarket restaurants are in the Fort George and Newtown Barracks districts, north of the Swing Bridge, while you'll find some reliable local restaurants in the commercial area south of the Swing Bridge.

Budget

Dit's Restaurant (Map pp96-7; ☎ 227-3330; 50 King St; snacks BZ$3, mains BZ$6-12; ☼ breakfast, lunch & dinner Mon-Sat, lunch & dinner Sun & public holidays) Dit's is a local favorite, a fine place to get rice-and-bean Belizean standards, sandwiches and Mexican dishes such as *panades* and *salbutes* (variations on the tortilla). Especially good are the desserts, coconut and lemon pies, milk shakes and juices. The surrounding neighborhood is a bit dicey.

Big Daddy's (Map pp96-7; ☎ 227-0932; 2nd fl, Commercial Center, Regent St; lunch BZ$7-10; ☼ breakfast & lunch) You'll get hearty, low-priced meals and friendly service here. At breakfast, fry-jacks (lightly fried pancake slices), eggs, bacon, sausage and a fresh juice are under BZ$8. Lunch is served cafeteria-style from 11am until the food is gone. Rice-and-beans and vegetable-and-rice dishes are the stock in trade, and the view over Haulover Creek from the upper deck is free.

Ma Ma Chen Restaurant (Map pp96-7; ☎ 223-4568; 7 Eve St; Meals from BZ$5 ☼ breakfast, lunch & dinner) Looking for an antidote for meat-heavy Belizean cuisine? Look no further: Ma Ma Chen's is a genuine Taiwan-style vegetarian restaurant, serving tofu, brown rice and vegetable dishes. The Chen's also run a guesthouse of the same name (p99).

Macy's (Map pp96-7; ☎ 207-3419; 18 Bishop St; mains BZ$8-14; ☼ breakfast, lunch & dinner Mon-Sat) Macy's provides consistently good Creole cooking, with friendly service and good prices. The menu changes daily, but you're always likely to find chicken, fish fillets and stewed beef or meatballs. Game, such as boar, gibnut and deer, often makes an appearance.

Nerie's II Restaurant (Map pp96-7; ☎ 223-4028; cnr Queen & Daly Sts; mains BZ$8-15; ☼ 7:30am-10pm) Nerie's offers most imaginable accompaniments to rice and beans, including curried lamb, stewed cow foot, lobster, gibnut and deer. You can start things off with a choice of soups, including chicken, *escabeche* (with chicken, lime and onions), *chirmole* (with chicken and a chili-chocolate sauce) or (again!) cow foot, and round it off with cassava pudding.

Midrange

Le Petite Café (Map pp96-7; Cork St; pastries BZ$1-5, sandwiches BZ$11-14; ☼ breakfast, lunch & dinner) For muffins, croissants, cookies and a wide variety of coffee drinks, stop in at this excellent little café and bakery run by the Radisson.

Wet Lizard (Map pp96-7; ☎ 223-5973; Fort St; dishes BZ$12-18; ☼ breakfast & lunch cruise-ship days only) Inside the Belize Tourist Village (p104) but also accessible directly from the street, the Wet Lizard provides solid serves of mainly Belizean and Tex-Mex food amid bright tropical colors, '70s rock and plenty of cruise-ship passengers. Its upper-deck setting is breezy.

Jambel's Jerk Pit (Map pp96-7; ☎ 223-1966; 164 Newtown Barracks Rd; mains BZ$12-30; ☼ lunch & dinner) Jambel's recent move from the city center to the northern outskirts is a good example of why Belize City deserves its reputation for danger: despite his restaurant having long been a neighborhood fixture, the owner decided to pack it in after a robbery at the former location on King St ended with him being shot in the stomach. Jambel's new location on the coast is far more pleasant, and his food, blending the best of Jamaican and Belizean culinary traditions, is still tops. Try the jerk fish, jerk chicken, or jerk family platter. Vegetarians won't want to miss Jambel's jerk tomato pasta. Is there anything this man can't jerk?

Chon Saan Palace (Map p93; ☎ 223-3008; cnr Kelly & Nurse Seay Sts; dishes BZ$12-30; ☼ 11:30am-2pm & 5-11:30pm Sat-Thu, till 1am Fri) Considered the best Chinese restaurant in Belize City, Chon Saan would probably be considered mediocre in most US cities. Though portions are ample, meals are uninspired, and tacking BZ$5 per person on the bill for Chinese tea bumps the restaurant into a price bracket disproportionate to its culinary quality.

Sumathi Indian Restaurant (Map p93; ☎ 223-1172; 190 Newtown Barracks Rd; dishes BZ$18-38; ☻ 11am-11pm Tue-Sun) Belize City's best Indian restaurant provides a huge range of flavorsome curries, tandooris and *biryanis* (spicy rice and meat-or-vegetable dishes), with plenty of vegetarian options, all in generous quantities. Bollywood films on the TV intensify the mood. It does meals to go if you prefer.

Stonegrill Restaurant (Map pp96-7; ☎ 223-3333; www.radisson.com/belizecitybz; Radisson Fort George Hotel, 2 Marine Pde; mains BZ$20-35; ☻ 11am-10pm; P) At this thatched poolside restaurant at the Radisson hotel you get to grill your own meal – steak, fajitas, shrimp, chicken satay and the like – on super-hot volcanic stones. It's fun, tasty and free of added fat.

Smoky Mermaid (Map pp96-7; ☎ 223-4759; 13 Cork St; mains from BZ$20; ☻ 6:30am-10pm; P ✿) Attached to the Great House hotel, the Smoky Mermaid serves tasty Caribbean and international food on a lovely patio with tinkling fountains and towering tropical trees. The meals are dependably good and the servings satisfying.

St George's Dining Room (Map pp96-7; ☎ 223-3333; www.radisson.com/belizecitybz; Radisson Fort George Hotel, 2 Marine Pde; lunch buffet BZ$26, mains BZ$26-38; ☻ breakfast, lunch & dinner; P) The main restaurant at the Radisson serves hearty buffet lunches with a different theme daily (Mexican, Caribbean, Asian etc) and a mainly Mediterranean dinner menu, with plenty of seafood and some vegetarian options. There are also buffets on Friday, Saturday and Sunday nights, and a big Sunday brunch. Dishes are reliably good.

Calypso Club (Map p93; ☎ 223-2670/2663; www.princessbelize.com; Princess Hotel & Casino, Newtown Barracks Rd; mains BZ$25-50; ☻ 11am-10pm; P) A waterfront restaurant at the Princess Hotel & Casino (p100), Calypso serves ample portions of Belizean- and Caribbean-style seafood. Burgers, pasta and salads provide lighter and more economical options – but a regular Belikin is BZ$6.

Self-catering

Brodie's (Map pp96-7; ☎ 227-7070; 2 Albert St; ☻ 8:30am-7pm Mon-Thu, 8:30am-8pm Fri, 8:30am-5pm Sat, 8:30am-1pm Sun) This department store has the best downtown grocery.

Save U (Map p93; ☎ 223-1291; Sancas Plaza, Belcan Junction; ☻ 8am-9pm Mon-Sat, 8am-2pm Sun & public holidays; P) This modern supermarket is convenient for loading up on supplies before heading out into the wilds of Belize.

DRINKING

Top-end hotel bars, especially on Friday evening, are a focus of Belize City social life, and more fun than they might sound, pulling in a range of locals, expats and tourists. Outside the hotels there are only a few dependably respectable places to drink, but plenty of others you might stick your head into.

Vogue Bar & Lounge (Map p93; ☎ 223-2670/2663; www.princessbelize.com; Princess Hotel & Casino, Newtown Barracks Rd; ☻ noon-midnight Sun-Wed, noon-2am Thu-Sat) This 40-seat lounge at the Princess gets lively later in the week, especially on Friday night when a mixed young crowd launches a new weekend. A DJ helps things get moving from 9pm Thursday to Saturday.

Radisson Poolside Bar (Map pp96-7; ☎ 223-3333; www.radisson.com/belizecitybz; Radisson Fort George Hotel, 2 Marine Pde; ☻ 11am-10pm) The Friday happy hour (5pm to 9pm) is very popular; often there is live music and sometimes there's a DJ.

Belize Biltmore Plaza (off Map p93; ☎ 223-2302; www.belizebiltmore.com; Mile 3½ Northern Hwy; ☻ 11am-10pm) The Friday happy hour (5pm to 8pm) at the Biltmore's poolside bar is a fun session, with a great steel band. There's often live music or cabaret other nights too.

Baymen's Tavern (Map pp96-7; ☎ 223-3333; www.radisson.com/belizecitybz; Radisson Fort George Hotel, 2 Marine Pde; ☻ 10am-10pm) The main bar at the Radisson is friendly and sociable, with a pleasant outdoor deck.

Bird's Isle Restaurant (Map pp96-7; ☎ 207-2179; Bird's Isle; ☻ 10am-midnight Mon-Sat) Located at the end of Bird's Isle, a park-like oasis on the southern coast of town, this open-air restaurant is one of the prettiest settings for an outdoor bar you're likely to find in Belize City. In addition to beer, wine and cocktails, the restaurant serves well-prepared burgers, snacks and Belizean fare. Thursdays from 8:30pm to 1am is karaoke night; the bar also has live music occasionally.

MJ's Grand (Map p93; 170 Newtown Barracks Rd; ☻ 4pm-1am Mon-Fri, 4pm-3am Sat & Sun) You may get to enjoy some funky Belizean rhythms here, but karaoke starts up at 10pm most nights. MJ's is popular with locals both for its indoor pool tables and outdoor terrace tables overlooking Newtown Barracks Green; the atmosphere is relaxed.

ENTERTAINMENT

The hub of Belize City nightlife is, fortuitously enough, located in the relatively safe

Newtown Barracks area in the north of town. It's here where you'll find the Princess Hotel & Casino entertainment complex and the best nightclubs, as well as some of the city's best restaurants. The local press publicizes upcoming events.

Nightclubs

Caesar's Palace (Map p93; ☎ 223-7624; 190 Newtown Barracks Rd; ⏲ 10pm-late Thu-Sat) The music and crowd here have a strong Latino element. People start turning up at about 10:30pm, and the action on and around the small dance floor can get pretty lively on Friday and Saturday.

Bellevue Hotel (Map pp96-7; ☎ 227-7051/2; bellevue@ btl.net; 5 Southern Foreshore) The karaoke at the pool bar here on Wednesday, Friday and Saturday nights can be fun for participants (including some tourists), but may be less so for the occupants of neighboring rooms!

Casino, Bowling & Cinema

Princess Hotel & Casino (Map p93; ☎ 223-0638; Newtown Barracks; ⏲ noon-4am; Ⓟ) The casino at the Princess Hotel is an informal and fun place to try to boost your budget (set yourself a limit on what you're prepared to lose), with roulette, poker and blackjack tables, plus hundreds of slot machines and a floor show with dancing girls kicking up their heels at 10pm. You need to show ID such as your passport or driver's license to enter (minimum age is 18).

The complex is also where you will find Belize's only eight-lane (or any-lane, for that matter) **bowling alley** (per person for 2 games BZ$14; ⏲ 11am-11pm; ✕).

The two-screen **movie theater** (☎ 223-7162; admission BZ$10; screenings usually at 6pm or 7pm & 8pm or 9pm, plus 3pm Sat & Sun) shows first-run Hollywood films, though usually a bit later than their US release dates.

Music & Theater

To find out what's on, watch for posters, read the local press or drop by the following venues.

Bliss Centre for the Performing Arts (Map pp96-7; ☎ 227-2458/2110; Southern Foreshore) The revamped Bliss Centre has a fine 600-seat theater that stages a variety of events, including concerts of traditional Belizean music and other shows that celebrate Belize and its culture. The annual Belizean Film Festival is held here, and the Children's Art Festival in May. The Bliss Centre is also a likely spot in the

city for any major cultural happenings (such as this year's memorial concert for Belizean musician Andy Palacio, which brought the city to a standstill for hours). As they don't yet have a website to promote upcoming events, your best bet is to call or drop by during business hours to learn what's going on during your visit.

Belize City Centre (Map p93; ☎ 227-2051/2092; Central American Blvd; Ⓟ) This is the main venue for tours too large for the Bliss Centre.

Government House (House of Culture; Map pp96-7; ☎ 227-3050; Regent St) Some cultural events, including classical concerts, are held here.

Sports

The main venues are the **MCC Grounds** (Map p93; cnr Newtown Barracks Rd & Calle al Mar), for football and cricket; **Rogers Stadium** (Map pp96-7; Dolphin St) for softball; and the **Marion Jones Sporting Complex** (Map p93; Princess Margaret Dr), which is used for various events.

SHOPPING

Albert St and its side streets are the main shopping streets, with stores dealing in everything from clothes and domestic appliances to spices and music.

Augusto Quan Ltd (Map pp96-7; ☎ 227-8000; quan belize@earthlink.net; 13 Market Sq) An excellent hardware store stocking tools, camping gear, sports gear and even the kitchen sink (really…they sell plumbing supplies). A good place to hit before heading into the bush.

National Handicraft Center (Map pp96-7; ☎ 223-3636; 2 S Park St; ⏲ 8am-5pm Mon-Fri, 8am-4pm Sat) This store carries the best stock of Belizean crafts, at fair prices. Attractive buys include carvings in the strikingly streaked hardwood zericote, slate relief carvings of wildlife and Maya deities, and CDs of Belizean music.

Brodie's (Map pp96-7; ☎ 227-7070; 2 Albert St; ⏲ 8:30am-7pm Mon-Thu, 8:30am-8pm Fri, 8:30am-5pm Sat, 8:30am-1pm Sun) Brodie's is the biggest department store in the country. Some of the 'departments' are pretty small, but it's still a good place to look for many things.

Image Factory (Map pp96-7; ☎ 203-4151; www.image factory.bz; 91 N Front St; ⏲ 9am-5pm Mon-Fri) Some original Belizean art lurks among the handicrafts and books here.

Belize Photo Lab (Map pp96-7; ☎ 227-4428; photo lab@btl.net; cnr Bishop & E Canal Sts) The best place in town for photographic supplies.

Belize Tourist Village (Map pp96-7; ☎ 223-7789; 8 Fort St; ♡ 8am-4pm, cruise-ship days only) This waterfront complex exists for the convenience of cruise-ship passengers, who disembark here on their land trips. Non-cruise tourists may enter from the street with a temporary pass, obtainable on presentation of an identity document such as a passport. Most of the stores are gift shops, liquor stores, jewelers or pharmacies offering Viagra without prescription. Some items are cheaper than elsewhere in the city; others are more expensive. You'll know when it's open from the crowds of hawkers, hustlers and tour agents thronging the street outside.

You'll find similar gift shops at the Museum of Belize (see p94), the Radisson (p100), Princess (p100) and Belize Biltmore Plaza (p102) hotels, and Old Belize (p112). For a most unique handicraft shopping experience, check out Belize Central Prison (p113).

GETTING THERE & AWAY
Air

Belize City has two airports: Philip Goldson International Airport (BZE), which is 11 miles northwest of the city center off the Northern Hwy; and the Municipal Airstrip (TZA), around 2 miles north of the center. All international flights use the international airport. Domestic flights are divided between the two airports, but those using the Municipal Airstrip are cheaper (often significantly). See p291 and p294 for further information on flights to, from and around Belize. The following airlines fly from Belize City:

American Airlines (Map p93; ☎ 223-2522; www .aa.com; Sancas Plaza, Belcan Junction) Direct flights to/from Miami and Dallas/Fort Worth.

Continental Airlines (www.continental.com) Downtown (Map pp96-7; ☎ 227-8309; 80 Regent St); Philip Goldson International Airport (☎ 225-2263) Direct flights to/from Houston.

Delta Air Lines Philip Goldson International Airport (☎ 225-3429; www.delta.com) Direct flights to/from Atlanta.

Grupo TACA (www.taca.com); Downtown (Map pp96-7; ☎ 227-7363/4; Belize Global Travel Services, 41 Albert St); Philip Goldson International Airport (☎ 225-2163) Direct flights to/from Houston and San Salvador (El Salvador).

Maya Island Air (www.mayaairways.com); Municipal Airstrip (Map p93; ☎ 223-1140); Philip Goldson International Airport (☎ 225-2219) Direct flights to Caye Caulker, Dangriga, Placencia, Punta Gorda and San Pedro (Ambergris Caye).

Tropic Air (www.tropicair.com); Philip Goldson International Airport (☎ 225-2302); Municipal Airstrip (Map p93;

☎ 223-5671) Direct flights to Caye Caulker, Dangriga, Placencia, Punta Gorda, San Pedro and Flores.

US Airways (Map pp96-7; ☎ 225-3589; www.usairways .com; Belize Global Travel Services, 41 Albert St) Direct flights to Charlotte, North Carolina.

Boat

Caye Caulker Water Taxi (Map pp96-7; ☎ 203-1969, 226-0992; www.cayecaulkerwatertaxi.com; Caye Caulker Water Taxi Terminal, 10 N Front St) provides the main service that connects Belize City with Caye Caulker and San Pedro (Ambergris Caye). Departures to Caye Caulker (one-way/return BZ$15/30, 50 minutes) and San Pedro (one-way/return BZ$20/40, 1½ hours) are at 8am, 9am, 10:30am, noon, 1:30pm, 3pm and 4:30pm.

If there are more than enough passengers for one boat, one will go direct to San Pedro. An extra boat, to Caye Caulker only, goes at 5:30pm. On request from passengers the boats will stop at Long Caye or Caye Chapel (both one-way BZ$15).

Triple J Express (Map pp96-7; ☎ 207-7777, 223-3464; Court House Warf) has a similar service from Belize City to Caye Caulker and San Pedro leaving at 8am, 10:30am, 1:30pm and 4:30pm; their terminal is across the creek in front of the court house. Though their prices are exactly the same, Triple J occasionally offers discounts (of around BZ$5) to compete with the more well-known Caye Caulker Water Taxi.

You can actually get all the way to Corozal, Sarteneja and Cerros by transferring at San Pedro and continuing north on a Thunderbolt boat (p177).

Bus

The story of Belize's bus system is either a good example of the effectiveness of what acolytes of unfettered capitalism call 'the invisible hand of the free market' – or a bad one. Since the bankruptcy of Belize's main long-distance bus service, Novelo's (the story of which might make a good argument *against* an unrestrained free-market), a dozen or so smaller companies have stepped in to fill the gaps. The southern Belize City–Punta Gorda route is pretty straightforward, as only three companies (James, National and Usher) really service the south, with James being the most reliable (see p105 for a bus schedule).

North to Corozal and west to San Ignacio is where the majority of the little fish have stepped in to meet the needs of the market. While there are plenty of buses servicing both

BUS TIMETABLE: BELIZE CITY TO PUNTA GORDA

Belize City	Belmopan	Dangriga	Independence	Punta Gorda	Service
5:30am	6:30am	8am	9:30am	10:30am	Express
6am	7:30am	9am	10:30am	12:30pm	Regular
8am	9:30am	11am	12:30pm	2:30pm	Regular
9am	10:30am	noon	1:45pm	3:30pm	Regular
10am	11:30am	1pm	2:45pm	4:30pm	Regular
11am	12:30pm	2pm	4pm	5:30pm	Regular
noon	1:30pm	3pm	5pm	7pm	Regular
3pm	4:30pm	5:30pm	7pm	8:30pm	Regular
3:30pm	4:30pm	5:30pm	7pm	8:30pm	Express

routes from morning to night, trying to decipher the schedules (a series of yellowing handwritten charts glued to the wall, with endless barely legible additions and deletions) can be difficult. As it's fairly doubtful whether today's schedule will even be relevant when this book comes out, we'll instead opt for giving generalized information along with a hearty Belizean reassurance: 'Relax, you'll get there.' Prices listed are approximate for regular and express services, and are subject to change.

Belmopan (BZ$4 to BZ$7, 1¼ hours, 52 miles) Lots of buses daily; nearly all buses heading south, and all heading west, pass through Belmopan. Any bus heading to Belmopan can drop you anywhere along Western Hwy.

Benque Viejo del Carmen (BZ$8 to BZ$12, 2½ to three hours, 80 miles) Plenty of buses.

Chetumal (BZ$10 to BZ$14, 3½ hours to 4½ hours, 102 miles) Several each day; Buses pass through Belize City en-route from Flores, Guatemala. Tickets are sold by the same outlets as for Flores buses (see right).

Corozal (BZ$9 to BZ$12, 2½ to 3¼ hours, 86 miles) Plenty of buses daily; all buses to Chetumal stop in Corozal.

Crooked Tree (BZ$3.50, one hour, 36 miles) From the Pound Yard bus stop at 4:30pm and 5pm, Monday to Saturday, and from the corner of Regent St W and W Canal St (Map pp96–7) at 10:45am from Monday to Saturday; can also take any northern bus and hitch from turnoff.

Dangriga (BZ$10 to BZ$14, 2½ to three hours, 107 miles) Many daily buses; all southern buses stop in Dangriga. See (see p250 for a schedule).

Gales Point Manatee (BZ$5 to BZ$7, two to 2½ hours, 65 miles) Gales Point has lost a significant amount of its bus service since Novelo's bankruptcy; currently, two buses per week pass through each way; see p118 for schedule.

Orange Walk (BZ$5 to BZ$7, 1½ to two hours, 57 miles) Many daily buses; all buses to Corozal, Chetumal and Sarteneja stop in OW.

Punta Gorda (BZ$20 to BZ$22, six to seven hours, 212 miles) The terminus for James Bus' southern line; see p250 for a schedule. A few other services also go to Punta Gorda.

San Ignacio (BZ$14 to BZ$22, two to 2½ hours, 72 miles) Many daily buses.

Belize City's **main bus station** (Map pp96-7) is the old Novelo's terminal next to the canal, now painted Rastafarian red, gold and green, and still bearing the Novelo's name. Most buses leave from here or from the next-door **Pound Yard bus stop** (Map pp96-7; Cemetery Rd). **James bus line** (☎ 702-2049, 722-2625) has the most reliable schedule:

Other bus lines leaving from Belize City:

Jex & Sons (Map pp96-7; ☎ 225-7017) Runs buses to Crooked Tree (BZ$3.50, one hour, 36 miles).

R-Line buses (Map pp96-7; cnr of Euphrates Ave & Cairo St) Buses to Bermudian Landing (BZ$3, one hour, 27 miles) go at 12:15pm, 4pm and 9pm, Monday to Friday, and noon and 5pm Saturday.

Sarteneja bus line (Map pp96–7; off Regent St) departs for Sarteneja (BZ$9, 3½ hours, 96 miles) At noon and 4pm, Monday to Saturday from the north side of Supreme Court building; you can also catch this bus in Orange Walk (p163).

TO FLORES, GUATEMALA

Buses to Flores (five hours, 145 miles) leave from the Caye Caulker Water Taxi terminal. The Línea Dorada/Mundo Maya company has the most reliable reputation: you can get tickets for a bus to Tikal leaving at 9:30am (BZ$30, daily) or one to Flores (BZ$40) at **Mundo Maya Deli** (☎ 223-0457) or **Khan Store** (☎ 223-7611), both inside the water-taxi terminal.

Car & Motorcycle

The main roads in and out of town are the Northern Hwy (to the international airport, Orange Walk and Corozal), which heads northwest from the Belcan Junction, and the Western Hwy (to Belmopan and San Ignacio), which is the westward continuation of Cemetery Rd. Cemetery Rd gets its name from the ramshackle Lord's Ridge Cemetery, which it bisects west of Central American Blvd.

Auto rental firms in Belize City include the following:

Avis (☎ 225-2385; www.avis.com) Offices at Philip Goldson International Airport and in Ladyville.

Budget (off Map p93; ☎ 223-2435/3986; www .budget-belize.com; Mile 2½ Northern Hwy) There is also an office at Philip Goldson International Airport.

Crystal Auto Rental (off Map p93; ☎ 223-1600; www .crystal-belize.com; Mile 5 Northern Hwy) One of the best local firms; allows vehicles to be taken into Guatemala. There's another branch at Philip Goldson International Airport.

Euphrates Auto Rental (Map pp96-7; ☎ 227-5752, 614-6967; www.ears.bz; 143 Euphrates Ave, Southside) Local firm that offers some of the best deals in town.

Hertz (Map pp96-7; ☎ 223-0886/5395; www.hertz.com; 11A Cork St, Fort George District) Hertz also has a branch at Philip Goldson International Airport.

GETTING AROUND

Though many of the spots where travelers go are within walking distance of each other, it's always safest to take a taxi after dark.

To/From the Airports

There is no public transportation to or from either airport. The taxi fare to or from the international airport is BZ$40. An alternative is to walk the 1.6 miles from the airport to the Northern Hwy, where fairly frequent buses pass heading to Belize City. Taxis from the Municipal Airstrip to the center of town cost around BZ$10.

Car & Motorcycle

Belize City has the heaviest traffic in the country, as intense as that of a medium-sized country town in North America or Europe. There's a limited one-way system, which is easy to work with. If you need to park on the street, try to do so right outside the place you're staying. Never leave anything valuable on view inside a parked car.

Taxi

Cabs cost around BZ$7 for rides within the city, give or take; if it's a long trip from one side of town to the other, expect to be charged a bit more. Confirm the price in advance with your driver. Most restaurants and hotels will call a cab for you.

NORTHERN BELIZE DISTRICT

The Northern Hwy stretches from Belize City and into Orange Walk District, passing through the communities of Ladyville and Burrell Boom (west of which you'll find the Community Baboon Sanctuary and Spanish Creek Wildlife Sanctuary). At Sand Hill the road forks. To the west, the Northern Hwy continues to Orange Walk, passing the turnoff for the Crooked Tree Wildlife Sanctuary. To the east, the Old Northern Hwy leads to the Maya ruins of Altun Ha.

ALTUN HA

The ruins that have inspired Belikin beer labels and Belizean banknotes, **Altun Ha** (admission BZ$10; ☺ 8am-5pm) stands 34 miles north of central Belize City, off the Old Northern Hwy.

Altun Ha was a rich and important Maya trading and agricultural town with a population of 8000 to 10,000 at its peak in the Classic Period (AD 300–1000). The entire site covered some 1500 acres, but what visitors today see is the central ceremonial precinct of two plazas surrounded by temples, excavated in the 1960s and now looking squeaky clean following a stabilization and conservation program from 2000 to 2004.

Altun Ha existed by at least 200 BC, perhaps even several centuries earlier, and flourished until the mysterious collapse of Classic Maya civilization around AD 900. Most of the temples date from around AD 550 to 650, though, like many Maya temples, most of them are composed of several layers, having been built over periodically in a series of renewals.

In Plaza A, structure A-1 is sometimes called the **Temple of the Green Tomb**. Deep within it was discovered the tomb of a priest-king dating from around AD 600. Tropical humidity had destroyed the garments of the king and the paper of the Maya 'painted book' buried with him, but many riches were intact: shell necklaces, pottery, pearls, stingray spines used in bloodletting rites, ceremonial flints and the nearly 300 jade objects (mostly small beads and pendants) that gave rise to the name Green Tomb.

The largest and most important temple is the **Temple of the Masonry Altars** (B-4). The restored structure you see dates from the first half of the 7th century AD and takes its name

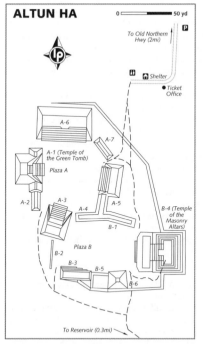

ALTUN HA

0 ——— 50 yd

To Old Northern
Hwy (2mi)

Shelter

Ticket
Office

A-6

A-7

A-1 (Temple of
the Green Tomb)

Plaza A

A-2

A-3

A-4   A-5

B-4 (Temple
of the
Masonry
Altars)

B-1

Plaza B

B-2

B-3   B-5

B-6

To Reservoir (0.3mi)

from altars on which copal was burned and beautifully carved jade pieces were smashed in sacrifice. This is the Maya temple that's likely to become most familiar during your Belizean travels, since it's the one depicted (in somewhat stylized form) on Belikin beer labels.

Excavation of the structure in 1968 revealed several priestly tombs. Most had been destroyed or desecrated, but one, tomb B-4/7 (inside the stone structure protruding from the upper steps of the broad central staircase), contained the remains of an elderly personage accompanied by numerous jade objects, including a unique 6in-tall carved head of Kinich Ahau, the Maya sun god – the largest well-carved jade object ever recovered from a Maya archaeological site. (Look for the jade head illustration in the top left corner of Belizean banknotes.)

A path heading south from structure B-6 leads 600yd through the jungle to a broad pond that was the main **reservoir** of the ancient town.

Modern toilets, and drinks and souvenir stands are near the ticket office, and the site has good wheelchair access.

Sleeping & Eating

Mayan Wells Restaurant (Map p90; ☎ 220-6039; www
.mayanwells.com; Altun Ha Rd; camping per person BZ$10,
r BZ$60, lunch BZ$12; ☑ breakfast & lunch Mon-Fri; ℗ 💻)
Mayan Wells is 1.4 miles from the ruins, on the road in from the Old Northern Hwy, and makes a fine stop for lunch or refreshments. Traditional Belizean lunches of rice, beans, stewed chicken and a drink are served under a *palapa* (thatched-roof shelter) beside a cenote amid lovely tropical gardens. If you fancy staying there, there's a cozy mosquito-netted cabana with private bathroom and hammock-slung verandah, accommodating up to four adults – or you can camp. Free internet is available to people staying here. Birders and other nature lovers will particularly enjoy this hospitable place.

Maruba Resort Jungle Spa (Map p90; ☎ 322-2199,
in USA ☎ 713-799-2031, 800-627-8227; www.maruba-spa
.com; Mile 40½ Old Northern Hwy; s/d from BZ$400/440, ste
BZ$540-1400; ℗ 🎾 🏊) Maruba, 2 miles north of Maskall village (13 miles from Altun Ha), takes the jungle-lodge-and-spa concept to extremes of expensive pampering. There are luxurious amenities and a slew of health and rejuvenation treatments. Lush tropical grounds harbor individually designed rooms in a variety of African, Creole, Maya and even Gaudíesque styles – including honeymoon and 'fertility' suites and a jungle tree house. There are two pools and a tree-house restaurant that serves good seafood, game and salads to nonguests as well as guests. For the active, there are a range of adventures and tours on offer.

Getting There & Away

Many tours run to Altun Ha from Belize City, Caye Caulker, or from San Pedro on Ambergris Caye.

To get here in your own vehicle, turn off the Northern Hwy 20 miles from Belize City at a junction signed 'Altun Ha,' then drive 11.5 miles along the paved but narrow and often potholed Old Northern Hwy to Lucky Strike village, where a better paved road heads off west to Altun Ha (2.4 miles).

Buses to Maskall, four times daily from the main bus station in Belize City (see p104), will drop you at Lucky Strike. Heading back to the city, buses leave Maskall at 5:30am, 6am, 6:30am and 7am, passing through Lucky Strike 20 to 30 minutes later. Traffic along the jungle-lined Old Northern Hwy tends to be light, so if you're hitchhiking prepare to wait.

NIGHT OF THE LIVING HOWLER MONKEYS *Joshua Samuel Brown*

They roared periodically through the night; at times the sound seemed far away, and at other times it was as if the howlers were right on the grounds of the lodge in which we were staying. Although I knew the howling wasn't directed at me – my being a different order of primate entirely – it still sent chills down my spine. Something about the growling roar of the black howlers was not merely eerie, but eerily familiar. I couldn't figure out what it was.

The next day I ran into a sound engineer who was vacationing a few miles away at the Spanish Creek Rainforest Sanctuary. He'd set up a high-quality digital audio recording device out in the jungle specifically to capture the monkeys' howling, and let me listen to some excerpts through his headphones. Then and there I realized exactly why the howls sounded so familiar to me: in every one of George Romero's *Living Dead* films (I'm a big fan, and have seen them all many times) there's always at least one scene – usually mid-way or towards the end – in which Romero tries to get the audience to feel the survivors' terror; they are, after all, hopelessly outnumbered by walking corpses. The camera pans out to show the endless horde, and the audio…it's the same in every movie, an echoing cacophony of growls, bone-chilling and inhuman.

This is exactly the sound of the howler monkeys. Have filmmakers been coming to Belize to sample their growls for the benefit of horror-film geeks such as myself? Quite possibly – art does imitate life.

(For readers who might be dissuaded from visiting, don't be. The howler monkeys are not undead. Also, they're vegetarians.)

COMMUNITY BABOON SANCTUARY

No real baboons inhabit Belize, but Belizeans use that name for black howler monkeys. Though howler monkeys live throughout Central and South America, the endangered black howler exists only in Belize, northern Guatemala and southern Mexico. The **Community Baboon Sanctuary** (CBS; Map p90; www .howlermonkeys.org) is spread over several long-established Creole villages in the Belize River valley. The sanctuary has engineered a big increase in this primate's population and is doubly interesting because it's a completely community-run, grassroots conservation operation. In addition to the near-certainty of seeing some of these fascinating primates, the sanctuary offers river trips (day and night) and horseback riding. There are also nearly 200 bird species here to keep wildlife watchers busy.

The sanctuary takes up approximately 20 sq miles; however, the black howlers have made an amazing comeback in the area, and the monkeys now roam freely all around the surrounding area. While you're most likely to see the monkeys in the sanctuary (the ones who live here are the most socialized, and least prone to shun humans,) you'll probably hear their distinctive howls at dusk and dawn in places such as Spanish Creek Wildlife Sanctuary (several miles to the west; opposite) or in other areas of Belize District that offer the monkeys the broadleaf-forest habitat in which they thrive.

The **CBS visitors center** (☎ 220-2181; admission BZ$10; ◷ 8am-5pm), in Bermudian Landing, has a number of good exhibits and displays on the black howler, the history of the sanctuary, and other Belizean wildlife. Included with the admission fee is a one-hour guided nature walk on which you're likely to encounter a resident troop of black howlers. Along the way the trained local guides also impart their knowledge of the many medicinal plants. Lodge staff can connect you with a wide variety of touring options, as can Edward and Melissa Turton at the nearby Howler Monkey Lodge (opposite).

Sleeping & Eating

With the closing of the CBS restaurant, the only choices for eating while in the Community Baboon Sanctuary are to bring in your own food, get snacks at the local grocery store on the main road, or to have your hotel/resort arrange meals for you. Luckily, they all do this – some exceedingly well. **Bed & Breakfast** (d incl 2 meals BZ$49) is available in local homes or specially built visitor cabanas in several Community Baboon Sanctuary villages. Conditions are rustic (not all places have showers or flush toilets), but there's no better way to experience Creole village life. Book at the visitors center.

Howler Monkey Lodge (☎ 220-2158; www.howler monkeylodge.com; s/d/tr cabanas BZ$50/90/120; P 🐾) Owned and operated by Edward and Melissa Turton, the lodge consists of seven cabins set on 20 acres on a jungle-filled patch of land above a bend in the Belize River. Like the nearby CBS visitors center (just 400yd away), the lodge has regular visits from local howler monkeys. Cabins are BZ$120, 'jungle cabins' are BZ$90 and what they call their 'purple berry cabins' (covered by blackberries), which are three rooms with a shared bath, rent out for BZ$50. There's a lodge serving three meals a day, but only if requested beforehand (the Turtons are excellent cooks).

Nature Resort (☎ 223-3668; naturer@btl.net; cabanas BZ$60-130; P 🐾) Right next to the visitors center, this is the most comfortable place to stay, with friendly management and clean, well-maintained cabanas holding up to four people, spread around an attractive lawn area with some trees. Most have private bathrooms (with unheated water); one is air-conditioned.

Getting There & Away

Bermudian Landing is 28 miles west of Belize City. Leave the Northern Hwy at the turnoff for Burrell Boom. Turn right after 3 miles, into Burrell Boom village, then carry straight on to Bermudian Landing, 9 miles beyond. If you're heading to western Belize after you visit the sanctuary, save time by taking the direct road 8 miles south from Burrell Boom to Hattieville on the Western Hwy.

R-Line buses run between Belize City and Bermudian Landing (BZ$4, one hour). See p105 for details of departures from Belize City. Departures from Bermudian Landing to Belize City are at 6:20am, 6:30am and 4pm Monday to Friday, and 6:30am and 6:45am Saturday.

SPANISH CREEK WILDLIFE SANCTUARY

Several miles past the Community Baboon Sanctuary sits this amazingly pristine 5900-acre sanctuary managed by the **Rancho Dolores Environmental and Development Group** (RDEDG; ☎ 220-2191). Another of Belize's protected areas, Spanish Creek Wildlife Sanctuary is part of the biological corridor that runs through much of the nation, allowing once-highly endangered animals such as howler monkeys and pumas to roam and breed. The sanctuary runs 5 miles along the length of the

Spanish Creek beginning by the small Creole/Maya community of **Rancho Dolores** (population 200). Though the village is traditionally agricultural, many families also work locally in the tourism sector.

Activities

Visitors to SCWS will find a number of excellent opportunities to mix recreation with tropical education. Canoes are available for rent (half-/full day BZ$10/$20), and trips up-river by motorboat go for about BZ$50 for up to six people. There are lovely riverside paths for **hiking**, and locals will be glad to 'hook you up' with a hand line to fish the creek. Another Belizean activity you can try in the area is **dory poling**; similar to a canoe, the Belizean dory is hand-carved from a single log. Though the dory can be paddled with a hand-carved cedar paddle, the more traditional method of movement is pushing it with a bamboo pole. The catch, you ask? Whoever's poling the dory has to remain standing. Horses can also be rented for trail rides for around BZ$15 per hour.

Sports fans take note: Rancho Dolores is a hotbed of cricket and softball, with the former being played in town every other Saturday from January through June and the latter every other Sunday. Food and drinks are usually available at the games.

Sleeping & Eating

Though there are no hotels in Rancho Dolores, RDEDG offers a homestay program with families throughout the village. In addition to providing room and meals, host families will often act as guides and liaisons between guests and the general community. Contact RDEDG for details of price and availability. RDEDG also arranges internships for volunteers (p110) to help with both conservation work inside the Spanish Creek Wildlife Sanctuary and education through the local primary school.

Getting There & Away

Rancho Dolores is located 17 miles from the junction at Burrell Boom. You will pass through several villages along the way and Rancho Dolores is at the end of the road. **Russell's Bus** (☎ 610-5164, BZ$4) leaves Belize City at 5pm Monday to Friday and 1pm Saturday from the R-Line bus stop, corner of Euphrates Ave and Cairo St, and gets to Rancho Dolores

---

INTERNSHIP OPPORTUNITY: SPANISH CREEK RAINFOREST RESERVE

An excellent place where those looking for a deeper understanding of the area can be found at the **Spanish Creek Rainforest Reserve** (☎ 670-0620, 668-3290 www.belizebamboo.com). Begun in 2004 by Sol Tucker and Marc Ellenby, the 2000-acre solar-powered farm cultivates the largest collection of noninvasive clumping bamboo in Central America, using no pesticides, herbicides or energy-intensive irrigation. The farm also has hundreds of tropical fruit trees including avocados, mangoes, and jackfruit. Interns on the farm can learn farming techniques and study medicinal rainforest plants while living in one of the most undisturbed corners of Belize. There's plenty of time left over for reading and relaxation, observation of wildlife, canoeing, meditation and exploration. The cost of the program is BZ$50 per day, which includes comfortable accommodations and gourmet organic meals. Casual travelers are also welcome with advanced notice.

---

about an hour later. The same bus departs Rancho Dolores at 5am Monday to Saturday. You can also call **Cyril Smith** (☎ 606-4627), proprietor of the one licensed taxi service of Rancho Dolores, to arrange pick up from just about anywhere.

CROOKED TREE WILDLIFE SANCTUARY

Thirty-two miles up the Northern Hwy from Belize City lies the turnoff to the **Crooked Tree Wildlife Sanctuary** (CTWS; Map p90; admission BZ$8). Quite possibly one of the best birding areas in Belize (perhaps even all of Central America), the sanctuary isn't merely a park for nature enthusiasts, but a living community of about 900 folks, mostly of Creole descent, who were farming and fishing the area long before the word 'ecotourism' was ever coined. It is well worth a visit for anyone who loves nature or fancies experiencing a peaceful rural community with an interesting history and a beautiful setting. It's best to stay the night so you can be here at dawn, when the birds are most active. The village has several midrange and budget accommodations. Don't forget your binoculars – though if you do local guides should be able to lend you a pair.

The story goes that **Crooked Tree village** got its name from early logwood cutters who boated up Belize River and Black Creek to a giant lagoon marked by a tree that seemingly grew in every direction. These 'crooked trees' (cashew trees, in fact) still grow in abundance around the lagoon. Founded in the early 18th century, Crooked Tree may be the oldest village in Belize. Until the 3½-mile causeway from the Northern Hwy was built in 1984, the only way to get here was by boat, so it's no wonder life still maintains the slow rhythm of bygone centuries.

Migrating birds flock to the lagoons, rivers and swamps each year between December and May. The best **bird-watching** months are usually February to May, when many migrants stop over on their way north, and the low level of the lagoon draws thousands of birds into the open to seek food in the shallows.

Bird-watchers are in for hours of ornithological bliss. Boat-billed, chestnut-bellied and bare-throated tiger herons, Muscovy and black-bellied whistling ducks, snail kites, ospreys, black-collared hawks and all of Belize's five species of kingfisher are among the 286 species recorded here (see a near-complete list at www.belizeaudubon.org/parks/ctws .htm). Jabiru storks, the largest flying bird in the Americas, with wingspans of up to 12ft, congregate here in April and May and a few pairs nest in the sanctuary in the preceding months.

The **CTWS visitors center** (⏰ 8am-4:30pm), with good displays and a range of books and information materials for sale, stands at the entrance to the village, just off the causeway. It's here that you'll be asked to pay your admission fee. The helpful, knowledgeable staff will give you a village and trail map and answer questions on anything to do with visiting the sanctuary, including information on expert local bird guides.

The obvious reference point in the village is the 'Welcome to Crooked Tree' sign, at a junction 300yd past the visitors center as you enter the village from the causeway.

A series of reasonably well-signposted **walking trails** weave along the lakeshores and through and beyond the village. About 3 miles north of the village center are an excellent 700yd boardwalk and an observation tower, allowing access to swampy areas of thick, low vegetation around the lagoon's edge. From

December or January to May you can reach the boardwalk by driving and walking; the rest of the year you'll need a boat to reach it.

If you can afford it, take a **boat tour** as well as walking. A two- to three-hour boat tour, costing around BZ$150 for up to four people, can be arranged at the main accommodations (see below). A boat trip gets you out onto the lagoon and into the surrounding swamps.

You can also explore Spanish Creek and Black Creek, leading south out of the main lagoon, which, with their thick tree cover, harbor plenty of birds all year. Black Creek is also home to black howler monkeys, Morelet's crocodiles, coatimundi and several species of turtle and iguana; Spanish Creek gives access to **Chau Hix**, an ancient Maya site with a pyramid 80ft high.

Festivals & Events

Crooked Tree is home to a great number of cashew trees and the village's annual **Cashew Festival**. Happening the first weekend in May, the festival celebrates the cashew harvest in a big way, with music, dancing and lots of cracking, shelling, roasting and stewing of cashews, not to mention the making of cashew cake, cashew jelly, cashew ice cream, cashew wine (not unlike sweet sherry) and cashew you-name-it. The harvest season continues into July.

Sleeping & Eating

Rhaburn's Rooms (☎ 225-7035; s/d BZ$20/35; P)
The four wooden rooms here are on the small and rustic side, but clean and neat nonetheless. All have fans and a shared hot-water bathroom and verandah. Owners Owen and Maggie Rhaburn are friendly and welcoming, which is a good thing, as the rooms are above their own home. Go south of the 'Welcome to Crooked Tree' sign and after 300yd cross the cricket field on the right immediately past the Church of the Nazarene. Follow the track through the trees from the far left corner of the cricket field and you'll see the Rhaburn's sign on the first bend. The house is the cream-colored one on the left side of the broad lawn area.

Sam Tillett's Hotel & Tours (☎ 220-7026; samhotel@ btl.net; s/d/f BZ$60/80/150, d with air-con BZ$110, breakfast/ lunch/dinner BZ$8/12/16; P 🛇) The Tilletts are a local Crooked Creek clan; Patriarch Sam Tillet (who passed away last year) was one of the most celebrated bird guides in the country.

The 10 thatched rooms and cabanas here are clean and well furnished with private bathrooms. All of the rooms and cabanas have beautiful murals depicting local avian life (the place is, after all, for the birds), painted by local Belizean artists. Sam's is beside the main street, 500yd north of the 'Welcome to Crooked Tree' sign.

Bird's Eye View Lodge (☎ 205-72027, 203-2040, in USA 570-588-0844; www.birdseyeviewlodge.com; camping per person BZ$12, s/tw/d/tr/q downstairs BZ$120/140/160/180/200, s/d/tr upstairs BZ$160/200/220, meals BZ$20-30; P 🛇 🛇)
Aptly named, this lodge has the best spot in the village for viewing birds, especially the waterfowl that inhabit the sanctuary's main lagoon on whose banks the lodge is set. The furthest from the entrance of the park's lodgings, Bird's Eye View is at the south end of the village, 1 mile from the 'Welcome to Crooked Tree' sign. Comfortable and clean without being impersonal, the lodge is especially popular with birdwatchers and nature lovers. Rooms are of ample size, with good beds, bathrooms, fans and reading lights; upstairs rooms have patios that look out on the lagoon. Good meals are served in a bright dining room. Room rates are reduced by up to one-third from May 15 to October 30. The lodge offers lagoon boat tours, nature walks with experienced bird guides (per person per hour BZ$10), horseback riding (per hour BZ$20) and canoe rental (per person per hour BZ$10).

Cearrie's Kitchen (☎ 205-7076; meals from BZ$5; 🕙 10am-9pm Mon-Thu, 10am-11pm Fri & Sat) Serves Creole and Belizean specialties such as rice and beans, stewed chicken and jerked pork, cooked just the way locals like.

There are two other eateries inside the village as well.

Getting There & Away

Driving to Crooked Tree is the easiest way to get here, though nearly all listed accommodations will arrange transfers to and from Belize City or the international airport for between BZ$90 to BZ$160, depending on group size. Jex & Sons runs buses from Belize City (BZ$3.50, one hour); see p105 for details of departures from Belize City. Departures to Belize City from Crooked Tree are at 5am, 6:30am and 7am Monday to Saturday. Alternatively, you can get a bus on the Northern Hwy to the Crooked Tree turnoff, then thumb it the 3.5 miles to the village.

SOUTHERN BELIZE DISTRICT

Most of the southern Belize District's attractions are along the Western Hwy, which stretches from Belize City through Belmopan and out to Guatemala. It's in this area where you'll find the Belize Zoo, Monkey Bay and perhaps Central America's strangest gift shop. This is also where you'll find more kitsch than you can shake a stick at in 'Old Belize'.

OLD BELIZE

You know that one really famous American roadside attraction that straddles the North Carolina–South Carolina border, the one you always wanted to stop at when you were a kid because highway signs hype it for about a thousand miles in either direction, but your parents said no because they knew it was just a tourist trap, causing you and your siblings to whine for, like, 50 miles until dad just gave in and said, 'Fine, stop whining, we'll stop at South of the Border...I need some coffee anyway.'

If you liked it, despite the overwhelming kitsch, you'll love **Old Belize** (Map p90; ☎ 222-4129/4286; www.oldbelize.com; Mile 5 Western Hwy; adult/child BZ$15/7.50, children under 6 free; ⏰ 8am-4pm Tue-Sat, 10am-4pm Sun & Mon). Initially designed to provide hurried cruise-ship tourists with a neatly encapsulated version of Belizean history and culture, this place is so tourist-trap plastic that in a weird sort of way it's actually fun.

After paying your (rather hefty) ticket price, you'll be allowed to enter the Old Belize museum, where plastic models of trees (representations of the same trees you'll find in the rainforest just a few miles south) sit beneath speakers through which the songs of (presumably) Belizean birds are piped. You'll then walk through a series of other plastic exhibits depicting genuine scenes of old Belize – plastic Maya people frozen in amber, plastic Garifuna people settling on plastic shores, and plastic workers working in plastic recreations of the sugarcane, chicle and logging industries of an early 20th-century Plastic Belize (or 'Plastic British Honduras,' as it would have been known back then). Lest visitors get the idea that plastic was actually in use in actual old

Belize, the exhibit also includes a number of genuine artifacts, including a sugarcane press and a steam tractor used for dragging logs. Your trip through the plastic bowels of Old Belize ends at the gift shop, which is actually pretty well stocked with interesting knick knacks, including T-shirts, rum, gum made of chicle, and Cuban cigars.

Old Belize's partly open-air restaurant, **Sibun Bite Bar & Grill** (mains BZ$12-25; ⏰ 9am-9pm), serves up good burgers and grilled shrimp and chicken dishes. It overlooks the beach, which has a good swimming area and plans to boast three more attractions: a 750,000-gallon salt-water pool filled with a faux-reef (and presumably real fish) for snorkelers who can't make it to an actual reef; a 50ft-high water slide; and a zip-line from which adventurous types will be able to descend at high speeds over the water from a 50ft platform. Yowza!

Any Belmopan-bound bus will drop you at the Old Belize entrance (BZ$1, 10 minutes from Belize City).

ORCHID GARDEN ECO-VILLAGE

This **eco-village** (OGEV; Mile 14.5 Western Hwy; ☎ 225-6991; www.trybelize.com; 1st-night package s/d/tr/q BZ$200/280/360/440; ✖ P) is in many ways the exact opposite of Old Belize; whereas the latter attempts to encapsulate the essence of Belize as an easily grasped, photo-friendly model, the Taiwan-born proprietors have done so by creating a natural microcosm of the nation. On the grounds of their village, visitors can walk around in beautifully cultivated gardens, visit geological exhibits, and learn about the complicated web of flora and fauna that makes up Belize's ecosystem.

Built in a natural setting encompassing 43 acres of jungle savannah (half of which is designated as a protected sanctuary), OGEV offers not just a place to stop by for a quick overview of Belize, but also a convenient place from which to be based in Belize District. The eco-village's onsite hotel is lovely and understated; the rooms are large and subtly decorated, with double beds, wardrobes, and bathrooms (but no TV), giving the place a 'meditation center' feel. This fits well with the ethos of OGEV's owners, whose stated aim is to 'promote a way of life for people of different cultures to live in harmony with nature on both a physical and spiritual level.'

The village's location – 15 miles outside of Belize City – makes it an excellent choice for those looking to avoid staying in Belize City itself. The proprietors offer a wide variety of nature- and culture-oriented day trips all over central Belize, including meals and transportation. The eco-village's Orchid Garden Restaurant is also excellent, serving dishes prepared using vegetables and herbs from the family's own organic garden. Vegetarian dishes are especially excellent (in fact, the website offers a seven-day 'vegetarian tour' of Belize).

The main focus of Orchid Garden seems to be on multiday packages that include meals and tours; check their website for full rates and details.

BELIZE CENTRAL PRISON

Only in a country as laid-back as Belize could a fully functioning **prison** (Mile 2 Burrell Boom Rd, Hattieville) also be considered a tourist attraction. It's the only prison in Belize (the name 'Hattieville' is to Belizeans what 'San Quentin' is to Americans) and, as such, houses criminals of all stripes, from pickpockets to murderers. But don't come looking for some sort of American-style corporate-owned Supermax with imposing concrete walls topped with electrified razor ribbon and manned guard towers every 20 yards. The 'Hattieville Ramada' (as it's called on the streets) looks more like a summer camp, its main prison buildings set back from the road and surrounded by farmland (where the prisoners work). This is surrounded by a fence about as daunting as what you'd find surrounding a suburban junkyard. According to a few Belizeans we've spoken to, Hattieville residents have been known to break out at night to go drinking with nearby friends only to return in the morning before head-count. So what makes the prison worth a visit?

Two words: gift shop.

Belize Central Prison has an amazing **gift shop** (☎ 225-6991; ☒ 9am-3pm), filled with items from the reformatory's renowned woodshop. Inside the small shop (located on the road and outside of the actual prison itself) you'll find hand-carved walking sticks, traditional masks, religious icons such as crucifixes, statues depicting saints and a host of carved Jesus figures, and even beautifully crafted wooden doors. All items in the shop are meticulously crafted by the prisoners themselves from locally grown woods including mahogany, teak and sandalwood. There's also a fine variety of

smaller items, including jewelry, cards, calendars, hammocks, clothing and other assorted knick knacks, all of which have been made by the prisoners themselves.

This most unusual penal facility is part of the larger vision of an organization called the **Kolbe Foundation** (☎ 225-6190, www.kolbe.bz), which took over the management of the once-notorious government prison and restructured it in a way that would be more in line with the foundation's Christian philosophy. Rather than merely punishing criminals by sequestering them from society, the Kolbe approach focuses more on rehabilitation through education and development of skills. In addition to the various craft-making shops inside the prison, there are also a number of small-scale animal farms and gardening operations, from which the prison gets some of its food. One of the long-term goals of the foundation is for the prison to be self-sustainable; as such, all funds earned by gift-shop sales go back to the maintenance of the prison, meaning that your purchases directly assist in the rehabilitation of Belize's criminal element (who might otherwise wind up robbing you on your next visit to Belize).

While the gift shop is open to the public, the prison itself isn't. Plans are in the works to expand operations to include a snack stand.

BELIZE ZOO

Anyone with an interest in wildlife, and Belize's wildlife in particular, should place a visit to this amazingly well-cared-for **zoo** (Map p90; ☎ 220-8004; www.belizezoo.org; Mile 29 Western Hwy; adult/child BZ$15/7; ☒ 8:30am-5pm, closed major public holidays) high on their Belize 'to do' list. Set in natural forest, 31 miles from Belize City along the Western Hwy, the Belize Zoo is a must-visit even for people who don't like zoos.

The origin of Belize Zoo begins with filmmaker Richard Foster, who shot a wildlife documentary entitled *Path of the Raingods* in Belize in the early 1980s. Sharon Matola – a Baltimore-born biologist, former circus performer and former US Air Force survival instructor – was hired to take care of the animals. By the time filming was over, the animals had become partly tame and Matola was left wondering what to do with her 17 charges. So she founded the Belize Zoo, which displays native Belizean wildlife in natural surroundings on 29-acre grounds. From these beginnings, the zoo has grown to provide homes for animals endemic to the region that have been injured, orphaned at a young age or bred in captivity and donated from other zoos.

Many of the animals in Belize Zoo are rescue cases, that is, wild animals that were kept as pets by individual collectors. The zoo makes every attempt to recondition such animals for a return to the wild, but only when such a return is feasible. In cases where return is impossible (as is the case with most of the zoo's jungle cats, who've long since forgotten how to hunt, or never learned in the first place), they remain in the zoo: perhaps not the best life for a wildcat, but better than winding up in Zsa Zsa Gabor's closet.

The zoo has many animals you're unlikely to see elsewhere – there are two fat tapirs (a Belizean relative of the rhino), gibnuts, a number of coatimundi (they look like a cross between raccoons and monkeys), scarlet macaws, white-lipped peccaries, pumas, and many others. But what really sets Belize Zoo apart is that the zoo itself – and in some cases, even the enclosures of individual animals – are relatively porous. This means that the wildlife you'll see inside enclosures are outnumbered by creatures who've come in from the surrounding jungle to hang out, eat, or – just maybe – swap tales with incarcerated brethren. Among the animals you'll see wandering the grounds are Central American agouti (also called bush rabbits), huge iguanas, snakes, raccoons, squirrels, and jungle birds of all sorts.

Take a night tour (one of the best ways to experience Belize Zoo, as many of the animals are nocturnal) and you'll be just as likely to see a gibnut outside enclosures as in. You'll also be able to hear ongoing long-distance conversations between the zoo's resident black howler monkeys and their wild brethren just a few miles away.

If most zoos are maximum security wildlife prisons, than the Belize Zoo is more like a 'country-club jail'. Some would even call it a halfway house for wild animals that can't make it on the outside. We call it a must-visit.

Sleeping & Eating

The **Tropical Education Center** (TEC; ☎ 220-8003; tec@belizezoo.org; Mile 29 Western Hwy; camping per person BZ$15, dm/cabana/guesthouse BZ$32/70/75, meals BZ$10-12; **P**) is the zoo's environmental education center. It's situated just over a mile away and is an excellent accommodation option for travelers, set on 84 acres of tropical savannah with lush gardens and good birding (with a treetop viewing platform), especially for those who want to do night tours at the zoo.

Sleeping options run from electricity-free dorms to neat, modern 'tent cabanas' (made of wood, on stilts, with electricity and fan), and two 'VIP guesthouses' with private bathrooms and kitchens overlooking the center's own small lake (home to Morelet's crocodiles). All options have good mosquito screens. If you want meals here, you need to request them in advance.

The TEC also offers nocturnal zoo visits (adult/child US$10/6, with a minimum of five people), and canoe trips on the nearby Sibun River (half-/full day per two-person canoe US$30/40). The TEC is 0.9 miles off the Western Hwy, from a signposted turning 50yd east of the zoo. If you're staying, staff can pick you up from the zoo.

Juice, snacks, and other assorted items (including Red Bull) are available in the zoo's **gift shop** (8:30am-5pm, closed major public holidays). It's an easy drive a couple of miles along the highway to one of the good restaurants near Monkey Bay Wildlife Sanctuary (see opposite).

Getting There & Away

Any nonexpress bus from Belize City heading along the Western Hwy will drop you at the zoo entrance (BZ$3, 45 minutes).

MONKEY BAY WILDLIFE SANCTUARY

Monkey Bay Wildlife Sanctuary (Map p90; ☎ 820-3032; www.monkeybaybelize.org; Mile 31½ Western Hwy; camping per person BZ$15, tent rental BZ$6, bunkhouses per person BZ$25, cabanas per person BZ$35; **P** **X** **□**) is a wildlife sanctuary and environmental education center offering lodging and activities for casual travelers, as well as internship activities for those with a more long-term interest in Belize (see opposite). Established in the 1980s by Matthew and Marga Miller, the 1.7-sq-mile sanctuary stretches from the Western Hwy to the Sibun River, encompassing areas of tropical forest and savannah and providing an important link in the biological corridor between coastal and inland Belize.

Across the river is the remote **Monkey Bay National Park**, which together with the sanctuary creates a sizable forest corridor in the Sibun River Valley. The park gets its name from a bend in the river – in Belize called a 'bay' – once noted for its resident black howler monkeys. Though the species had all but disappeared in the area, they have returned in

---

INTERNSHIP OPPORTUNITY: MONKEY BAY WILDLIFE SANCTUARY

Those with more long-term interest in the area may be interested to learn about **Monkey Bay's internship program** (☎ 820-3032; www.monkeybaybelize.org/intern.html). Generally speaking, the program is geared towards university students (though not exclusively). Internships can be of varying lengths, but should be no shorter than a month. ('It takes about that long for a new intern to get into the swing of things,' says staff member Anna Zabrowski.)

Interns can study a variety of disciplines, working alongside staff members and getting exposed to all the various tours offered to guests; interns are also encouraged to explore the country on their own. Interning at Monkey Bay is an excellent way to experience in depth what Belize has to offer, while having both a support network and base of operations; the general price for internship is BZ$50 per day. Internship applications are available on the website.

---

sizable numbers, thanks in no small part to the work done at the sanctuary.

Accommodations at the sanctuary range from camping out on offground decks to mosquito-screened bunkhouses or cabanas for three with fans. The amenities demonstrate ecological principles in action, with biogas latrines producing methane for cooking, rainwater catchment and partial solar energy. Independent visitors can partake of group meals if a group is present: otherwise you can make your own meals.

Around 230 bird species have been identified at the sanctuary. Larger wildlife such as pumas and coatimundi have been spotted on the 2-mile track running down beside the sanctuary to the river. A well-stocked library provides plenty of reference and reading matter on natural history and Belize. Also at the site is a splendid green iguana enclosure – these monarchs of the lizard world can grow to 6ft long.

Casual visitors should contact the sanctuary in advance to find out what activities will be available at the time of their visit. Possibilities include canoe and caving trips and dry-season trips to Cox Lagoon, about 12 miles north, which is home to jabiru storks, deer, tapir, black howlers and lots of crocodiles.

Eating & Drinking

Meals are available within the sanctuary but should be arranged at least a day in advance. Within a few hundred yards along the Western Hwy on either side of Monkey Bay Wildlife Sanctuary are two fun eateries that are often filled with just-off-the-plane travelers happily adjusting to the fact that they're on holiday. They're also worth noting if you're spending the afternoon at the Belize Zoo (just a few miles north; p113).

Amigos (Map p90; ☎ 822-3031; Mile 31¾ Western Hwy, 200yd west of sanctuary turnoff; mains BZ$12-22; ☯ 8am-10pm) Amigos serves both American and Belizean cuisine in a distinctly Belizean setting (a mosquito-screened *palapa* house) drenched in pure American whimsy (walls covered in kitschy signs and bumper stickers). Carnivores should order the BBQ pork ribs (BZ$22); those with a serious sweet tooth won't want to miss Amigo's desserts.

Cheers (Map p90; ☎ 614-9311; Mile 31¼ Western Hwy; mains BZ$10-20; ☯ breakfast, lunch & dinner) This large, airy and friendly place serves hearty meals, from all-day breakfasts to French-dip roast beef sandwiches to excellent Cuban tilapia. Naturally, rice, beans and stew chicken are served as well. It's about 500 yards east of the Monkey Bay turnoff.

Getting There & Away

Any nonexpress bus doing the Belize City–Belmopan run will drop you at the sanctuary turnoff (around 220 yards from the main entrance) or at Cheers or Amigos (BZ$3, 50 minutes from Belize City).

GALES POINT MANATEE

pop 450

The Creole village of Gales Point Manatee sits on a narrow peninsula that juts out about 2 miles into the **Southern Lagoon**, one of a series of interconnected lakes and waterways between Belize City and Dangriga. The village was initially founded by runaway slaves from Belize City escaping south into jungle and lagoon country around 1800. A more beautiful spot you'd be hard pressed to find; to the west, jungle-clad limestone hills rise above the plains that end on the shores of the Southern Lagoon; to the east, also across the lagoon, sits the narrow stretch of forest and mangrove swamp

DRUM MASTER SPEAKS WITH HIS HANDS: MR EMMETH YOUNG *Joshua Samuel Brown*

I'd come to Gales Point Manatee to interview Emmeth Young, one of Belize's most respected Creole drummers. Finding his school wasn't hard; it's a house on stilts behind his wife's restaurant, a wooden shack dreamily painted in sky-and-ocean blue hues with a sign on the door reading 'Open: Honk o' Halla.' The interview itself was also easy; relaxed and effusive, Young is as friendly an interview subject as a reporter could hope for. It was only later, when I went home to type up the recordered session, that I realized that putting our conversation on paper might present a special challenge.

For while Young, oral historian of his village, is a master of the spoken word, drums are a different beast entirely. And when it comes to talking drums, Emmeth Young speaks with his hands.

Tell me a little about what kind of drumming you do.

I play traditional Creole drums; there are many of these. The Sanbai, the Goomba, the Sabaia…

(I point to a the largest drum in the school; as wide as a mature tree-trunk, the drum reaches up to Young's waist.) What's this drum called?

Ah, this one here is the Sanbai.

It looks like it's made of a single piece of wood.

Yes, it's made of a coconut trunk, and the head is made of deer skin, caught by hunters not far from here.

(Young places the drum between his legs, and I begin to suspect that our interview will not be carried by words alone. I ask him if he can give me an example of a traditional Creole rhythm, and within seconds the sounds of drumming flood the room, a rhythm deep and steady. As he drums, Master Young begins to speak.)

This is the main rhythm. It is very significant, you see. This rhythm is part of the fertility dance that takes place in the days surrounding the full moon. It begins two days before the full moon, and everyone in the village will join, some dancing, some drumming. The rhythm will continue through the full moon, and until two days after. First the men will play, dance and sing. Then the women will play, dance and sing. If the energy is right, the rhythm can go on for five days straight.

(Young continues drumming, singing in Creole as he plays. I can't understand the words, and can only imagine the thunderous rythm that would be produced by an entire village during a session running around the clock for five days.)

that separates the lagoon from the Caribbean Sea. Gales Point Manatee has some superlative wildlife attractions. Chief among them is the highest concentration of West Indian manatees in the Caribbean (an estimated 70 of these gentle aquatic giants are present in the lagoon). The 14-sq-mile **Gales Point Wildlife Sanctuary** covers the Southern and adjoining lagoons. The nearby beaches are the primary breeding ground for hawksbill turtles in Belize, and there's excellent bird-watching too.

Orientation & Information

Getting lost in Gales Point Manatee would be difficult – the town's only street runs about 2.5 miles north from the Coastal Hwy to the tip of the peninsula, and if you walk too far either east or west you'll be wading in the lagoon. Once you hit town from the south (the only way you can hit town barring an amphibious landing), you'll pass by the police

station, Ionie's Bed & Breakfast, Gentle's Cool Spot and the Sugar Shack (behind which you'll find the Maroon Creole Drum School) before winding up at Manatee Lodge at the end of the peninsula.

Activities

Nature tours bring most visitors to Gales Point Manatee, and for the majority of these you'll need to hire a guide with a boat; all accommodations can set you up with one (your hosts will certainly be able to connect you with a guide, if they aren't guides themselves). In addition to fishing, the lagoons surrounding Gales Point Manatee are specifically noted for birding, turtling, and of course, manatee-ing. (Are those last two even words? They should be!)

MANATEE-WATCHING

Manatees graze on sea grass in the shallow, brackish Southern Lagoon, hanging out around

Do you also have some Garifuna drums? (Young picks up a smaller drum.)

Actually, in the house here I don't really have any that are skinned up like Garifuna drums. But this one is similar, though if this were a true Garifuna drum it would have a snare going across the top.

So a Garifuna rhythm would be very different...

Yes yes, and the technique itself is actually different. They play with a lot of drumrolls. This is the Punta rhythm of the Garifuna people. (Picking up a new drum, Young Plays for me a typical Garifuna rhythm, something slightly more complex than the previous Creole sounds, a rhythm punctuated by quick fingertip rolls along the edge of the drum head.)

Definitely a different sound. What sort of person comes to your school?

Well, I get a wide variety of people. I get people from the United States, from Canada and from Europe. Some of them come for drum class and some take a workshop so they can make their own drum.

How long would it take – I mean, if I were coming to make my own drum, how long would I stay? And how much would it cost?

A medium-sized drum takes three to four days, and maybe it would cost about two-fifty, or maybe three hundred Belize dollars. It depends on the size.

How long have you been making drums?

I've been making drums since I was 13, and now I'm 40. And I've been playing the drums since I was eight years old.

Belize has got these three strong cultures; the Maya, Garifuna and Creole. Are there any bands in Belize that mix together these styles?

Sometimes the Creole and Garifuna mix their styles together, but I don't know about the Maya. Once I had an intern down here and he did something with all three.

Do you feel that young people in Belize are interested in drumming?

Yes, that is what I do. There are young people in Belize who want to learn about drumming and other cultural things and that is why I am here. I am here sharing the drums and sharing the culture so they can carry on when I'm not here. So the drumming can live on through them.

Joshua's interview with Emmeth Young can be read online at lonelyplanet.com,
with audio samples of Mr Young's drumming.

the **Manatee Hole**, a depression in the lagoon floor near its east side that is fed by a warm freshwater spring. They rise about every 20 minutes for air, giving views of their heads and sometimes their backs and tails. A 1½-hour manatee-watching boat trip costs BZ$100 for up to four people. Manatee-watching can also be combined with other activities.

TURTLE-WATCHING

Around 100 hawksbill turtles, which are protected in Belize, as well as loggerheads, which aren't, lay their eggs on the 21-mile beach straddling the mouth of the Bar River, which connects the Southern Lagoon to the sea. For both species, this is the main nesting site in the country. Turtle-watch outings from Manatee Lodge (p118) during the nesting season (May to October) involve a boat trip down the river, then a 4-mile nocturnal beach walk looking for nesting turtles (BZ$350 for up to four people).

BIRD-WATCHING

In the **Northern Lagoon**, about 45 minutes from Gales Point Manatee by boat, is **Bird Caye**, a small island that is home to many waterfowl, including frigate birds, great egrets, and toucans. Gentle's Cool Spot (p118) combines trips here with a stop at the Manatee Hole for BZ$190.

FISHING

Large tarpon quite often break the surface of the Southern Lagoon. You can also fish for snook, snapper, jack and barracuda in the lagoon and rivers. A half-/full-day trip for up to three people costs around BZ$350 from Manatee Lodge (p118).

CREOLE DRUMMING

Lest culture be given short shrift over nature, Gales Point Manatee is also home to one of Belize's pre-eminent Creole drummers and

IBO ECHOES

Gales Point Manatee is believed to have been founded over 200 years ago by runaway slaves from Belize City, of Nigerian Ibo (or Ebo) origin, and is probably the only place in Belize where the Ibo *sambai* dance rhythm – traditionally beaten out with drums under the full moon – survives. Creole rhythms such as the *sambai* are quite distinct from the Garifuna rhythms you hear in Dangriga or Hopkins.

drum-makers, Emmeth Young. Young runs the **Maroon Creole Drum School** (☎ 603-6051, www.maroondrumschool.com; lessons BZ$20), teaching traditional percussion when he isn't touring with his band, Fore Afrique (Black Africa). His very cool studio-on-stilts is a renowned center of learning, both cultural and musical. It's here where Young – the village *griot* (a Creole word meaning 'oral historian') – teaches visitors from around Belize and abroad about Creole culture and history using music and words (see the boxed text, pp116). Young is also known as a master craftsman who both builds custom drums and teaches students the art of drum-making. Typically a student can build their own drum from scratch in about three days. Traditional Creole drums include the Sambai, Sabaya, Djembe, Kenkeni, Sangban and Dunumba, and materials range from Mahogany to cashew wood and coconut wood. Rates vary depending on the type of drum and material used.

Tours

Manatee Lodge (right) offers a wide range of trips at fixed prices; rates elsewhere can be lower. One licensed guide who comes recommended is **John Moore** (☎ 608 3373 johnsmoorebz@yahoo.com). A native of Gales Point, John has a Mexican Pelican boat, and does both birding and fishing tours. Prices for the former are BZ$250 per couple, and the latter BZ$300. Both tours take a half day, and extra people (up to six, total) can be added for an additional BZ$50 per person. Another guide with a good reputation in town is Raymond Gentle of Gentle's Cool Spot (below).

Sleeping & Eating

Gentle's Cool Spot (☎ 609-4991; d/tr BZ$30/50, mains BZ$6; P) Three kinds of dingy rooms with cold-water showers, double bed, a tiny window and little else go for BZ$30. A somewhat nicer room with three double beds in a higher house on stilts goes for BZ$50. Ms Gentle also does hair braiding for BZ$40. Anyone with hair long enough to braid and an hour and a half to kill is welcome.

Sugar Shack (☎ 603-6051, camping per person BZ$10, cabana BZ$30, meals BZ$5-8; ☺ breakfast, lunch & dinner) Jill, the wife of Creole drummer Emmeth Young, operates this establishment, cooking up excellent vegetarian cuisine from a small and colorful shack that doubles as a gift shop. The couple also have a couple of cool stilt cabanas for rent out back, as well as space for camping. Look for the wooden shack with the sign reading 'Open: Honk o' Halla' on the door. Many of Emmeth's drum students wind up staying here while studying or making drums.

Ionie's B&B (☎ 220-8066; s/d BZ$33/38) This B&B is run by friendly Ionie Samuels (also a justice of the peace, if you've matrimony in mind). Rooms are in a house on stilts, and have fans and shared bathrooms with cold showers. Good-sized Belizean meals (BZ$5 to BZ$9) include a drink.

Manatee Lodge (☎ 220-8040, from USA 877-462-6283; www.manateelodge.com; r BZ$180; P ☺ 🖵) The only mid-priced lodge in the area, Manatee Lodge takes up the tip of the Gales Point peninsula and is situated in a beautiful garden surrounded on three sides by the Southern Lagoon. The eight rooms, spread over two floors, are spacious and comfortable, with bathtubs and lots of varnished wood. There is a large sitting/reading room with a lovely, breezy verandah that overlooks the lagoon. There is also a dining room for guests of the lodge (breakfast/lunch/dinner BZ$22/18/32). A wide range of activities is on offer, and canoes and a sailboat are provided free for guests.

Getting There & Away

Gales Point Manatee is located about 1 mile off the Coastal (Manatee) Hwy; the turnoff is 22 miles off the Western Hwy and 14 miles from the Hummingbird Hwy. The Coastal Hwy and the road into the village are mostly unpaved, but quite drivable in a normal car during the dry season. In the rainy season, those without a 4WD risk getting stuck in the mud.

Bussing it requires a bit of scheduling flexibility, as the once-daily bus from Dangriga now only passes through twice a week. You can catch a bus leaving Dangriga at 5am on Monday and Friday, arriving at Gales Point Manatee around 6am before heading out to Belize City. Coming the other way, you can catch a bus from Belize City at 5pm on Monday and Friday, which should reach Gales Point Manatee around 7pm before heading south to Dangriga. The whole trip is around BZ$5.

The best way to travel to or from Gales Point Manatee for those who can afford it is by boat via a network of rivers, canals and lagoons stretching from Belize City. The trip takes about two hours, and costs around BZ$350 for up to four people. John Moore makes the trip with advanced notice, and arrangements can also be made through Manatee Lodge, Gentle's Cool Spot and some agencies in Belize City.

Northern Cayes

Daydream a little. Conjure up an image of your ultimate tropical island fantasy – the postcard 'paradise' that you always dreamed about. With over a hundred enticing isles and two amazing atolls, chances are that one of the northern cayes can bring your fantasy to life. If you imagined stringing up a hammock on an otherwise deserted beach, there is an outer atoll with your name on it. Pining to be pampered? You have your choice of an ever-growing glut of ritzy resorts on Ambergris Caye. San Pedro is prime for sipping cocktails and dancing the night away to a reggae beat; Caye Caulker moves at a slower pace, exuding a friendly village vibe.

But this is only the beginning. The richest resource of the northern cayes lies below the surface of the sea. Only a few miles offshore, the barrier reef runs for 80 miles, nearly uninterrupted. For snorkelers and divers, Belize offers unparalleled opportunities to explore caves, canyons and coral gardens, to come face to face with nurse sharks and stingrays in their natural habitat, and to swim with schools of fish, painted every color of the palette. Much of the reef is protected by various marine sanctuaries, ensuring the continued vibrancy of this underwater world.

You might be shocked by prices in the northern cayes (especially Ambergris), which are noticeably higher than the rest of Belize. But it's not outrageously expensive compared with other destinations in the Caribbean. Anyway, that's the price you pay for paradise.

HIGHLIGHTS

- Cycling up the sandy coast of the **North Island** (p129) on Ambergris Caye and stopping for a refreshing smoothie at **Beach n' Kitchen** (p138)

- Being surrounded by nurse sharks and stingrays at **Shark Ray Alley** (p131)

- Watching the sun set while relaxing on the upper deck of the **Driftwood Lodge** (p152) on Caye Caulker

- Catching sight of a West Indian manatee frolicking in the shallow waters off **Swallow Caye** (p144)

- Cruising out to Lighthouse Reef to descend into the darkness of the **Blue Hole Natural Monument** (p157) and spying on the rare red-footed booby at **Half Moon Caye** (p158)

★ North Island
★ Beach n' Kitchen
★ Shark Ray Alley
★ Driftwood Lodge
★ Swallow Caye
Blue Hole Natural Monument ★
★ Half Moon Caye

| POPULATION: 12,000 | MONTHLY RAINFALL: Jan 4in, Jun 8in (San Pedro) | HIGHEST ELEVATION: 50ft |

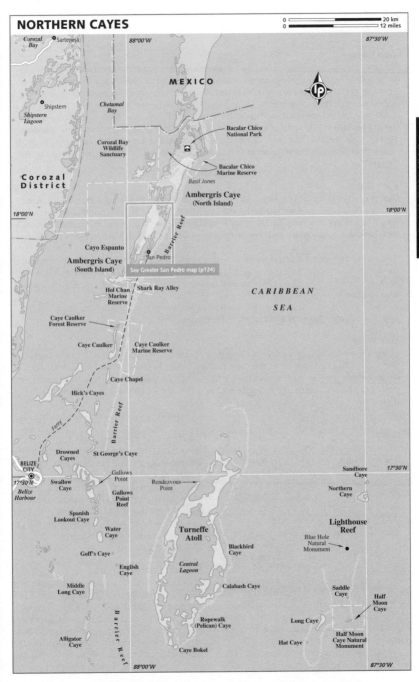

NORTHERN CAYES

| 0 | 20 km |
| 0 | 12 miles |

Corozal Bay
Sarteneja
Shipstern
Shipstern Lagoon

M E X I C O

Chetumal Bay

Bacalar Chico National Park

Corozal Bay Wildlife Sanctuary

Bacalar Chico Marine Reserve

Basil Jones

C o r o z a l D i s t r i c t

Ambergris Caye (North Island)

18°00'N
88°00'W
87°30'W
18°00'N

Cayo Espanto

Ambergris Caye (South Island)

San Pedro

See Greater San Pedro map (p124)

C A R I B B E A N

S E A

Hol Chan Marine Reserve
Shark Ray Alley

Caye Caulker Forest Reserve

Caye Caulker

Caye Caulker Marine Reserve

Caye Chapel

Hick's Cayes

Barrier Reef

Ferry

Drowned Cayes
St George's Caye

BELIZE CITY

17°30'N
Sandbore Caye
17°30'N

Gallows Point

Belize Harbour

Swallow Caye

Rendezvous Point

Gallows Point Reef

Northern Caye

Spanish Lookout Caye

Water Caye

Turneffe Atoll

Lighthouse Reef

Goff's Caye

Blackbird Caye

Blue Hole Natural Monument

English Caye

Central Lagoon

Middle Long Caye

Calabash Caye

Saddle Caye

Half Moon Caye

Alligator Caye

Ropewalk (Pelican) Caye

Long Caye

Half Moon Caye Natural Monument

Caye Bokel

Hat Caye

88°00'W
87°30'W

NORTHERN CAYES IN...

Two Days

With only two days, spend them on Caye Caulker, where you can get the most tranquil experience for your time. Start day one with breakfast at **Amor Y Café** (p153), then spend the day snorkeling or diving at **Hol Chan Marine Reserve** (p126). In the evening, catch the shuttle boat up to the restaurant at **Driftwood Lodge** (p152) for sunset drinks and a seafood dinner.

On your second day you can settle in for some serious relaxation. Rent a bike and pedal to the **public dock** (p147) south of town to soak up some sun and sea. Have lunch at the **Bamboo Grill** (p153) and retreat to a hammock for the afternoon. As the sun sets, ride around the airstrip in search of birds. Dine at **Habaneros** (p154), then wind down with reggae and rum at the **I&I Reggae Bar** (p154).

Four Days

With four days to spare, you may want to start in San Pedro, beginning with a big breakfast at **Celi's Deli** (p137) or **Estel's Dine by the Sea** (p137). Snorkel at **Hol Chan Marine Reserve** (p126) and **Shark Ray Alley** (p131). Enjoy a leisurely lunch at any one of the beachfront bars, then hang out on the beach and stroll back to town with the sunset. Head to **Fido's** (p139) bar for the rest of the evening.

Start day two with a take-out breakfast from **Ruby's Café** (p137) then cycle north, stopping for a drink and a swim wherever you fancy. Lunch at **Capricorn Restaurant** (p139). Cycle on as far as you wish then dine at **Mambo Restaurant** (p139). Finally, put your bicycle on a boat back to town.

Spend days three and four on Caye Caulker, with a snorkeling or diving trip to one of the outer atolls, either **Turneffe Atoll** (p156) or **Lighthouse Reef** (p157).

One Week

Spend a few extra days on each island, engaging in your favorite water sports. On Caye Caulker, you'll have time to kayak up to the **Caye Caulker Forest Reserve** (p144) and look for birds. On Ambergris, you can learn to **windsurf** (p129) or enjoy a **sunset sail** (p129). Don't miss the chance to take a manatee tour to **Swallow Caye** (p144) and watch these gentle giants feasting on sea grass.

History

The history of the northern cayes is essentially that of Ambergris Caye (p123), the main population center since Maya times. The northern part of the island, with its position at the mouth of Chetumal Bay, was a hub in the Maya trade network, and a port of call for traders coming down from the Yucatán Peninsula.

The Maya evaporated during the era of the whalers and the British buccaneers. Small treasure troves have been discovered on the island, and gold coins and old bottles have been washed ashore, evidence of pirates using the island for its fresh water, abundant resources and hidden coves. These swashbucklers turned into mainland loggers who partly depended on manatees and turtles from the northern cayes for their survival.

Following on from the buccaneers came the ancestors of today's residents, who were fisherfolk and worked on the coconut plantations. The 20th century was dominated by the lobster industry and the arrival of tourism. Today the northern cayes are fast catching up on technology. Tourism, high-speed internet and satellite telephones have increased contact with the outside world. While life goes slow on the cayes, the population is acquiring the accoutrements of the Western world in the 21st century.

Getting There & Around

Scheduled flights and regular passenger boats go from Belize City to San Pedro (on Ambergris Caye) and Caye Caulker, and from Corozal to San Pedro. Caye Chapel and Northern Caye (Lighthouse Reef) also have airstrips. No scheduled boats run to/from the outer islands, but most of the lodges located there provide transportation for their guests.

AMBERGRIS CAYE

pop 11,308

When Madonna sang about dreaming of San Pedro, she was referring to the captivating capital of Ambergris Caye, which has since adopted the inevitable nickname La Isla Bonita. Of course, it was more than 20 years ago when Madonna crooned about all the nature being wild and free. She might not recognize the place today, with condos being constructed on every corner and golf carts whizzing through the streets.

Nonetheless, Ambergris (am-*ber*-griss) Caye exudes the atmosphere of a tropical island paradise, where sun-drenched days are filled with fruity drinks and water sports. The island is long and thin, measuring 25 miles long and five miles across at its widest point, though much of it is less than half a mile across. Although resorts are being erected up and down the coast, its outer reaches are still uninhabited. The remote northern extremity abuts Mexican territory, and the Hispanic influence is evident in language, customs, food and fiestas.

Though the entire island is often called **San Pedro**, technically that is the name of the town at the southern tip. Once a laid-back little village dotted with colorful Caribbean houses, San Pedro is starting to resemble a typical tourist town, lined with souvenir shops and beach bars. The sandy streets were recently replaced with concrete, rapidly increasing the number of cars and golf carts on the roads (not to mention the speeds at which they drive). The beach is built up, though thankfully no buildings are higher than three stories.

Despite the over-development complaints, San Pedro has protected its most valuable asset, the barrier reef, which is only a half-mile offshore. If you are passionate about water sports, San Pedro will seduce you: dive operators lead tours to more than 35 sites, both local and beyond. And if you don't want to look at the fish, surely you'll want to eat them, as San Pedro is home to the country's most imaginative and appetizing dining scene.

History

Once the southern tip of the Yucatán Peninsula, Ambergris Caye was an important Maya trading post. Around 1500 years ago, in order to open up a better trade route between the Yucatán coast and mainland Belize, the Maya dug the narrow channel at Bacalar Chico that now separates Ambergris from Mexico.

As with the Maya on the mainland, the inhabitants gradually retreated to the bush as contact with the Europeans became more frequent. Whalers in the 17th century probably gave the island its current name, which derives from the waxy gray substance used in perfume production that comes from the intestines of sperm whales. According to folklore, British, French and Dutch pirates used the island's many coves as hideouts when ambushing Spanish ships, so they may also be responsible for the title.

Ambergris Caye was not significantly populated until the War of the Castes (see In Living Color: British Honduras, p34), when the war in the Yucatán first forced Mestizos, and then Maya, across Bacalar Chico and onto the island. The town of San Pedro (named for Peter, the patron saint of fishermen) was founded in 1848.

Ownership of the island was bandied about between a group of wealthy British mainlanders. Finally, in 1869, James Hume Blake purchased the land for US$625 with the gold of his wife, Antonia Andrade, a rich Spanish refugee widow from the Yucatán. The Blake family converted much of the island to a coconut plantation, conscripting many of the islanders to work the land.

The coconut business thrived for less than a century. By the 1950s it had been all but destroyed by a series of hurricanes. In the 1960s, the Belize government forced a purchase of Ambergris Caye and redistributed the land to the islanders.

While the coconut industry declined, the island's lobster industry began to develop. The market for these crustaceans skyrocketed once refrigerated ships came to the island. San Pedro lobster catchers formed cooperatives and built a freezer plant on their island.

Inevitably, the waters close to Ambergris Caye were over-fished. Fisherfolk looked to supplement their income by acting as tour, fishing and dive guides for the smattering of travelers who visited the island. Today lobster stocks have partly recovered with the aid of size limits and an annual closed season, but tourism and real estate are the booming businesses on Ambergris.

GREATER SAN PEDRO

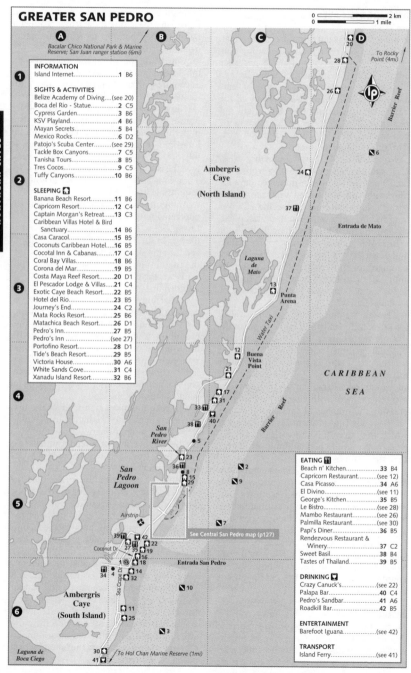

0 ——— 2 km
0 ——— 1 mile

Ⓐ   **Ⓑ**   **Ⓒ**   **Ⓓ**

Bacalar Chico National Park & Marine
Reserve; San Juan ranger station (6mi)

To Rocky
Point (4mi)

Barrier Reef

INFORMATION
Island Internet......................**1** B6

SIGHTS & ACTIVITIES
Belize Academy of Diving....(see 20)
Boca del Rio - Statue..........**2** C5
Cypress Garden...................**3** B6
KSV Playland......................**4** B6
Mayan Secrets.....................**5** B4
Mexico Rocks.......................**6** D2
Patojo's Scuba Center.........(see 29)
Tackle Box Canyons............**7** C5
Tanisha Tours.....................**8** B5
Tres Cocos..........................**9** C5
Tuffy Canyons....................**10** B6

SLEEPING
Banana Beach Resort............**11** B6
Capricorn Resort..................**12** C4
Captain Morgan's Retreat....**13** C3
Caribbean Villas Hotel & Bird
  Sanctuary......................**14** B6
Casa Caracol.......................**15** B5
Coconuts Caribbean Hotel....**16** B5
Cocotal Inn & Cabanas.........**17** C4
Coral Bay Villas...................**18** B6
Corona del Mar....................**19** B5
Costa Maya Reef Resort.......**20** D1
El Pescador Lodge & Villas....**21** C4
Exotic Caye Beach Resort.....**22** B5
Hotel del Rio.......................**23** B5
Journey's End.....................**24** C2
Mata Rocks Resort...............**25** B6
Matachica Beach Resort.......**26** D1
Pedro's Inn.........................**27** B5
Pedro's Inn ....(see 27)
Portofino Resort..................**28** D1
Tide's Beach Resort..............**29** B5
Victoria House.....................**30** A6
White Sands Cove................**31** C4
Xanadu Island Resort..........**32** B6

**Ambergris
Caye**

(North Island)

*Laguna
de
Mato*

Entrada de Mato

Water Taxi

*San
Pedro
River*

*San
Pedro
Lagoon*

Airstrip

Coconut Dr

Seagrape Dr

Buena
Vista
Point

Punta
Arena

CARIBBEAN

SEA

Barrier Reef

Entrada San Pedro

See Central San Pedro map (p127)

**Ambergris
Caye**

(South Island)

*Laguna de
Boca Ciego*

To Hol Chan Marine Reserve (1mi)

EATING
Beach n' Kitchen.................**33** B4
Capricorn Restaurant...........(see 12)
Casa Picasso.......................**34** A6
El Divino.............................(see 11)
George's Kitchen.................**35** B5
Le Bistro............................(see 28)
Mambo Restaurant..............(see 26)
Palmilla Restaurant.............(see 30)
Papi's Diner........................**36** B5
Rendezvous Restaurant &
  Winery...........................**37** C2
Sweet Basil........................**38** B4
Tastes of Thailand...............**39** B5

DRINKING
Crazy Canuck's...................(see 22)
Palapa Bar..........................**40** C4
Pedro's Sandbar..................**41** A6
Roadkill Bar........................**42** B5

ENTERTAINMENT
Barefoot Iguana..................(see 42)

TRANSPORT
Island Ferry........................(see 41)

Orientation

A narrow channel splits Ambergris Caye in two segments, known as South Island and North Island. The northernmost section of the North Island constitutes Bacalar Chico National Park, and the surrounding waters form Bacalar Chico Marine Reserve (see p126). The western shore has mangroves and wildlife along much of its length.

Most services and many hotels, as well as the airstrip, are within walking distance of each other in San Pedro's town center, on the South Island. Water taxis from Belize City and Caye Caulker dock on the reef side of the island right in San Pedro's center. The Thunderbolt boat service from Corozal and Belize City docks on the lagoon side.

San Pedro has three main north–south streets: Barrier Reef Dr (formerly Front St, to the east); Pescador Dr (formerly Middle St); and Angel Coral Dr (formerly Back St, to the west). South of the airstrip, Coconut Dr goes to Victoria House and beyond (with Sea Grape Dr running parallel for a short distance).

North of town at Pescador Dr, the hand-crank ferry across the channel has been replaced by a toll bridge (BZ$2). From here, a dirt road, suitable for 4WDs, golf carts and bicycles, runs north for at least 8.5 miles. Rumor has it that it won't be long before this road is paved and runs all the way to the southern edge of Bacalar Chico National Park (13 miles).

Many hotels and resorts are strung out along the coast both north and south of town. Cycling is a very convenient way to get around. Otherwise, a water shuttle runs between Fido's Dock and the North Island resorts.

Information

EMERGENCY
Medical, fire & police (☎ 911)
Police (Map p127; ☎ 226-2022; Barrier Reef Dr)

INTERNET ACCESS
Caribbean Connection (Map p127; ☎ 226-4664; cnr Barrier Reef Dr & Black Coral St; per hr BZ$20; ☼ 7am-10pm; 🖳) High-speed connections, CD burning, international phone calls, excellent coffee, unique jewelry.
Island Internet (Map p124; ☎ 226-3777; Coconut Dr; per hr BZ$20; ☼ 7:30am-10pm) Convenient for the southern end of town.
Mousepad (Map p127; ☎ 226-3690; 29 Barrier Reef Dr; per hr BZ$10; ☼ 10am-7pm) Cheap internet access, as well as printing and burning CDs.

INTERNET RESOURCES
Ambergris Caye (www.ambergriscaye.com) Excellent island information and a lively message board.
GoAmbergriscaye.com (www.goambergriscaye.com) Detailed information including comprehensive accommodations listings.

LAUNDRY
Candace's Laundromat (Map p127; ☎ 226-2052; Barrier Reef Dr; DIY wash & dry per load BZ$15; ☼ 8am-9pm Mon-Fri, 10am-6pm Sun) Also offers a full service wash and dry, per load BZ$20.
Nellie's Laundromat (Map p127; ☎ 226-2454; Pescador Dr; full service per lb BZ$2; ☼ 7am-9pm Mon-Sat)

MEDIA
Two rival weekly newspapers keep readers informed about news and events. Both are printed on Thursday.
Ambergris Today (www.ambergristoday.com)
San Pedro Sun (www.sanpedrosun.net) Includes a weekly column on the birds of Ambergris Caye.

MEDICAL SERVICES
Hyperbaric Chamber (Map p127; ☎ 226-2851, 684-8111; Lion St; ☼ 24hr) Center for diving accidents, next door to the Lion's Club.
Lion's Club Medical Clinic (Map p127; ☎ 226-4052, 600-9071; Lion St) Across the street from the Maya Island Air terminal at the airport.
San Carlos Medical Clinic, Pharmacy & Pathology Lab (Map p127; ☎ 226-2918, emergencies 614-9251; Pescador Dr) Treats ailments and does blood tests.

MONEY
You can exchange money easily in San Pedro, and US dollars cash and traveler's checks are widely accepted.
Atlantic Bank (Map p127; ☎ 226-2195; Barrier Reef Dr; ☼ 8am-2pm Mon-Fri, 8:30am-noon Sat) Near Buccaneer St; cash advances cost BZ$10 per transaction.
Belize Bank (Map p127; ☎ 226-2450; Barrier Reef Dr; ☼ 8am-3pm Mon-Thu, to 4:30pm Fri) At the north end of San Pedro; one of two ATMs that are plugged into international networks.

POST
Post office (Map p127; ☎ 226-2250; Alijua Bldg, Barrier Reef Dr; ☼ 8am-noon & 1-4pm Mon-Fri)

TOURIST INFORMATION
San Pedro Tourist Information Center (Map p127; ☎ 226-2198; Barrier Reef Dr; ☼ 10am-1pm Mon-Sat) Next to the town hall, this tourist information center has plentiful giveaway information.

Sights

HOL CHAN MARINE RESERVE

At the southern tip of Ambergris, the 6.5-sq-mile **Hol Chan Marine Reserve** (off Map p124; park admission BZ$20) is probably Belize's most oft-visited site. Its spectacular coral formations and abundance and diversity of marine life, not to mention its proximity to the cayes, make it the country's number one spot for diving and snorkeling.

Hol Chan is Mayan for 'Little Channel,' which refers to a natural break in the reef, also known as **Hol Chan Cut**. The channel walls are covered with colorful corals, which in turn harbor an amazing variety of fish life including moray eels and black groupers.

Although the reef is the primary attraction of Hol Chan, the marine reserve also includes sea-grass beds and mangroves. The sea grass provides a habitat for nurse sharks and southern stingrays, which lend their name to **Shark Ray Alley** (see p131). Snorkelers are guaranteed the chance to get up close and personal with both species, due mainly to the fact that the animals are used to getting fed by tour boats.

All dive operators and nautical tours offer trips to Hol Chan; see right and p129. For information and displays on marine life, visit the **Hol Chan Visitor Center** (Map p127; ☎ 226-2247; Caribeña St).

BACALAR CHICO NATIONAL PARK & MARINE RESERVE

At the northern tip of Ambergris Caye, **Bacalar Chico** (☎ 226-2247; tours BZ$180, park admission BZ$10) is part of the Belize Barrier Reef Reserve System World Heritage site, declared in 1996. At the time of research, the park was only accessible by a 90-minute boat ride from San Pedro.

On the way up north, boats might stop at **Cayo Iguanu**, better known as 'bird island,' as it is the nesting ground for the roseate spoonbill and the reddish-brown egret. The next stop is the **San Juan ranger station**, at the northern tip of the island, where there is a nature trail and some small Maya ruins to explore. From here, the boat motors through the **ancient channel** that was dug by sea-faring Maya about 1500 years ago. Now the narrow channel separates Ambergris Caye from the Mexican mainland.

Boat trips to Bacalar Chico usually make several snorkel stops along the way. The coral is extra colorful around here, as there is sig-nificantly less damage from boats and tourists. Besides the bountiful fish and bird life, you have the chance of seeing crocodiles and man-atees, as well as green and loggerhead turtles.

If the waters are calm, boats go to **Rocky Point**, notable as one of the only places in the world where land meets reef.

In theory, the return trip is on the east side of the island, but this requires a quick detour outside the reef, so in rough seas the boats travel up and down the western side of the island.

Not all tour operators run trips to Bacalar Chico, due to the long travel distance, so plan ahead and inquire in advance about trips. Companies that are likely to run this tour include the following:

Searious Adventures (Map p127; ☎ 226-4202, 662-8818; www.ambergriscaye.com/searious)

Tanisha Tours (Map p124; ☎ 226-2314; www.tanishatours.com)

Activities

If you're into water sports, you'll be in ec-stasy on Ambergris. The town is awash with tour companies and individuals organizing scuba diving, snorkeling, windsurfing, sailing, swimming and fishing trips.

DIVING

Many hotels have their own dive shops that rent equipment, provide instruction and organize diving excursions. Numerous dive sites are within a 10- to 15-minute boat trip from town. Most popular (and affordable) is undoubtedly Hol Chan Marine Reserve (see opposite), south of the island.

Following is a list of some reputable inde-pendent dive operators; a few also run a full range of nondiving tours.

Ambergris Divers (Map p127; ☎ 226-2634; www.ambergrisdivers.com) Offers half-day trips including one tank at Hol Chan and a snorkeling stop at Shark Ray Alley (BZ$130). Also offers night dives (BZ$110) and full-day trips to north Ambergris (BZ$200 to BZ$260) and the offshore atolls (from BZ$370).

Amigos del Mar Dive Shop (Map p127; ☎ 226-2706; www.amigosdive.com) Runs two local trips each day, one departing at 9am and another at 2pm. Also specializes in day trips to Turneffe and Blue Hole.

Belize Academy of Diving (Map p124; ☎ 226-2873; www.belize-academy-of-diving.com) Specializing in lesser-visited dive sites; 7 miles north of San Pedro.

Belize Diving Adventures (Map p127; ☎ 226-3082; www.belizedivingadventures.net) Highlights include the

NORTHERN CAYES

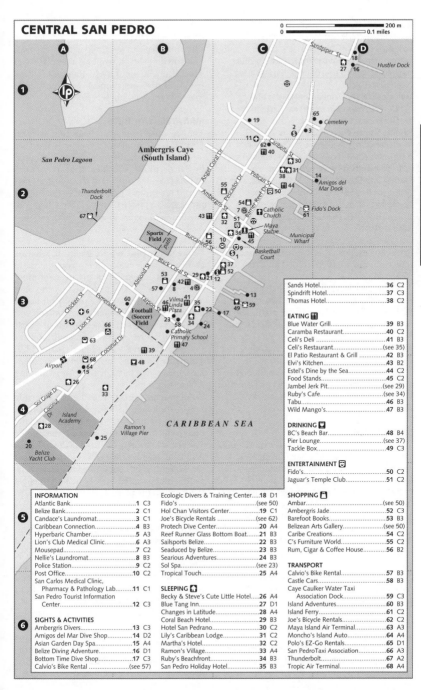

CENTRAL SAN PEDRO

San Pedro Lagoon

Ambergris Caye
(South Island)

Thunderbolt
Dock

Sports
Field

CARIBBEAN SEA

Ramon's
Village Pier

Island
Academy

Belize
Yacht Club

Airport

Football (Soccer)
Field

Catholic
Church

Maya
Statue

Municipal
Wharf

Basketball
Court

Catholic
Primary School

Cemetery

Amigos del
Mar Dock

Fido's Dock

Hustler Dock

Sandpiper St

Blue Hole (BZ$500) and the Turneffe Elbow (BZ$270). Single-/double-/triple-tank dives run BZ$80/130/180, while a night dive is BZ$90.

Bottom Time Dive Shop (Map p127; ☎ 226-2014; www.sanpedroholiday.com) On the dock in front of San Pedro Holiday Hotel.

Ecologic Divers & Training Center (Map p127; ☎ 226-4118; www.ecologicdivers.com) Divers receive a free CD with photos from their dive.

Patojo's Scuba Center (Map p124; ☎ 226-2283; www.ambergriscaye.com/tides) Connected with Tide's Beach Resort; a small, family-run operation offering knowledgeable and personal service. Dive packages available.

Protech Dive Center (Map p127; ☎ 226-3008; www .protechdive.com; Belize Yacht Club) With three boats ranging from 28ft to 38ft, this is the only technical dive outfit in Belize. Offers courses in recreational and technical diving at all levels.

Prices do not include admission to the marine reserves, which is BZ$20 for Hol Chan and BZ$80 for Blue Hole.

A one-tank local dive, without equipment, costs BZ$80 to BZ$100; with two tanks it's BZ$130 to BZ$150. Night dives are BZ$90 to BZ$110, including a headlamp. Four-day full-certification courses cost about BZ$700, including equipment. A one-day Discover Scuba Diving course costs BZ$300 to BZ$320.

Day trips further afield to the Blue Hole and Lighthouse Reef (three dives) or Turneffe Elbow (three dives) cost from BZ$370 to BZ$400.

SNORKELING

The most popular destinations for snorkeling excursions include Hol Chan Marine Reserve and Shark Ray Alley (BZ$90 including park fee) or Mexico Rocks and Tres Cocos (BZ$50 to BZ$80). Snorkeling operators usually offer two daily half-day trips (three hours, two snorkel stops), departing at 9am and 2pm.

Full-day trips go to the northern tip of Ambergris (six hours, three stops) for BZ$150 to BZ$170. Trips to Bacalar Chico (p126) also make several snorkel stops. Most of the dive operators (p126) and all of the tour companies (opposite) offer various versions of these snorkeling trips.

Most dive boats take snorkelers along if they have room on their boats, but snorkelers sometimes get lost in the shuffle on dive boats, so you are better off joining a dedicated snorkel tour whenever possible. Unfortunately, snorkel tours do not often run to Blue Hole (p157), so if you have your heart set on snorkeling around the edge of this World Heritage site, you'll have to tag along with the divers.

If you don't want to opt for a tour, you can snorkel under the dock at Ramon's Village (p134). It does not support the extensive life that the reef does, but it is free.

MANATEE-WATCHING

The best offshore manatee-watching (day trip US$90) is off Swallow Caye near Belize City (see p144). Tanisha Tours (p126) and Seaduced by Belize (p130) offer these trips for BZ$105 to BZ$115, including park fees and a snorkel stop. This trip is slightly cheaper (and travel times are less) from Caye Caulker, where folk are also working on manatee conservation.

SWIMMING

While sandy beaches are plentiful, seagrass at the water line makes entry from the shore unpleasant, so you'll mostly be swimming from piers in waters protected by the reef. When you do this, watch carefully for boats: while there's plenty to see down under if you snorkel, you often can't see or hear if a boat is coming your way. Have someone look out for you. Ramon's Village Pier (Map p127), distinguished by its four *palapas* (thatched-roof open-sided huts), is good for swimming and snorkeling.

All beaches are public and most waterside hotels are generous with their deck chairs, but a proprietorial air is developing about the piers, which are also supposed to be public. The beach in front of the Banana Beach Resort is clear of seagrass and the nearby pier is good for swimming. Of course, the further north or south you go on the island, the fewer people there are on the piers.

FISHING

San Pedro draws fishing enthusiasts who are anxious to take a crack at Belize's classic tarpon flats, which cover over 200 sq miles. The ultimate angling accomplishment is the Grand Slam: catching bonefish, permit (best from March to May) and tarpon (best from May to September) all in one day. In the reef, fishers get bites from barracuda, snapper, jacks and grouper.

Deep-sea fishing is less of a drawcard; most people are here for the reef. There are, however, stories of giant marlin caught out in the deep beyond. In December there is a deep-sea fishing tournament hosted by the Belikin beer company.

Fishing is mostly on a catch-and-release basis, but your fishing guide might clean and cut your catch if you intend to eat it. Companies offering fishing outings include the following:

Ambergris Divers (Map p127; ☎ 226-2634; www .ambergrisdivers.com) Charter a boat for up to four people for a half-/full day of reef fishing for BZ$420/620, or a half-/full day of deep-sea fishing for BZ$850/1320.

Amigos del Mar Dive Shop (Map p127; ☎ 226-2706; www.amigosdive.com) A half-/full day of fishing on the reef or flats for BZ$410/600.

The Rock Fishing Team (☎ 601-3865; www.belize fishfinder.com) Specializing in deep-sea fishing. Half-/full-day outings start at BZ$900/1800, while an all-day fishing excursion in Turneffe Atoll is BZ$2400.

SAILING, WINDSURFING & KITESURFING

Ambergris is ideal for wind-powered sports: the offshore reef means the waters are always flat, but there is no shortage of breeze to power your craft. The windiest time of year is between January and June, when the wind speed is usually between 12 and 20 knots.

Right in front of San Pedro Holiday Hotel, you'll find the seaside 'office' of **Sailsports Belize** (Map p127; ☎ 226-4488; www.sailsportsbelize.com). This is the place that will put the breeze in your sail. You can sign up for sailing lessons for BZ$122 per hour, or if you're already your own captain, rent a Laser Pico (BZ$44 per hour) or a Hobie (BZ$76 to BZ$98 per hour) and set sail. Windsurfers cost BZ$44 per hour, or you can get a lesson for BZ$98 per hour. More comprehensive instruction packages are also available.

Kitesurfing is the new craze, where the sail floats high up in the sky and pulls the surfer across the waves at alarming speeds. Two instructional courses are required before you can do it on your own: kite control skills (BZ$330, 2½ hours) and board control skills (BZ$330, 2½ hours). After that you can rent equipment (BZ$30 per half day) and fly with the wind.

If you want somebody else to man the rig, see Tours, right.

PARASAILING

This is the sign that San Pedro is going the way of Daytona Beach. Feel the wind in your face as you soar high above the island, powered by a motor boat below. Look for the parachutes or stop by **Fido's** (Map p127; ☎ 226-3513; www.para sailingbelize.com; s/d/tr BZ$140/240/330). The flight lasts for about 10 or 15 minutes.

BIKING

The North Island is a wonderful place for a cycle. With the breeze off the ocean and the palms shading your path, you can ride all the way up to Matachica Beach Resort and beyond. Just follow the sandy path that runs along the beach from Reef Village. You have a few places to stop for a fruit smoothie or an ice-cold Belikin beer along the way. Rent bikes at the following places:

Calvio's Bike Rental (Map p127; ☎ 661-7143; www .belizeextremeadventure.com; Pescador Dr)

Joe's Bicycle Rentals (Map p127; ☎ 226-5371; cnr Pescador Dr & Caribeña St; 3hr/24hr/week US$6/9/40; ⏰ 8am-6pm)

SPAS

If you have come to Ambergris Caye for a bit of rest and relaxation, you may want to schedule a day at the spa.

Asian Garden Day Spa (Map p127; ☎ 226-4072; www.asiangardendayspa.com; Coconut Dr) Specializing in Thai Massage (per hour BZ$160), this lovely garden spot also offers reflexology, facials and body wraps. Evenings are reserved for couples' massage (per hour BZ$340) at 5pm with a view of the setting sun or at 6:30pm under a starlit sky.

Mayan Secrets (Map p124; ☎ 226-3584; www.mayan secrets.com; Casa Tropicana, North Island; treatments BZ$90-220) All treatments include a tropical drink and a soak in the garden mineral bath.

Sol Spa (Map p127; ☎ 226-2410; www.solspa.com; Vilma Linda Plaza, Tarpon St; ⏰ 9am-6pm Mon-Sat) Sol Spa offers the whole range of body work and facial treatments, but the specialty is the Maya abdominal massage (BZ$190), a noninvasive technique inspired by Ix Chel, the goddess of medicine and fertility.

Tropical Touch (Map p127; ☎ 226-4666, 600-1031; www.tropicaltouchspaworks.com) With a prime waterfront location, this thatched-roof cabana is the perfect place to indulge in a Bomba mud massage or a seaweed sugar scrub. Therapists are also trained to give Maya abdominal massage treatments.

Tours

NAUTICAL TOURS

Most nautical tours include snorkeling, swimming and sunning at various destinations; full-day trips also include lunch, and often a beach barbecue.

El Gato (☎ 226-2264, 602-8552; www.ambergriscaye .com/elgato; half-/full-day cruise BZ$60/100) Sail to Caye

---

AROUND AMBERGRIS: WHERE TO DIVE & SNORKEL

You may not have too much choice about where to drop anchor, as dive masters usually choose the best sites based on weather conditions. Depending where you end up, here is what you'll find.

Mexico Rocks

This site (Map p124) 4.5 miles north of San Pedro is a unique patch reef at the northern end of the island. Snorkelers will find an incredible array of corals, including the *Montastrea annularis* corals, which are unique to the Northern Shelf Lagoon. Many small creatures inhabit the turtle grass and coral heads, including flounders, walking hermit crabs, conch, stingrays and hogfish. Schooling fish take refuge in the larger corals, while banded shrimp and Pederson shrimp have cleaning stations.

Boca del Rio (Statue)

The underwater terrain at Boca del Rio (Map p124), 2 miles northeast of San Pedro, is a spur-and-groove system, featuring rolling coral hills and sandy channels. This is one of the few sites with healthy staghorn coral, as well as plate corals. Around 90ft, there are big coral heads, barrels and tubes, and turtles are often spotted here. Near the mooring (in the shallows at 60ft) is a statue of Christ, which gives this site its alternative name of 'Statue.'

Tres Cocos

Tres Cocos (Map p124) is a bit deeper than most, with coral heads rising up to 50ft and a wall with spurs that spill out from 90ft to 120ft. The marine life here is wonderful, with thick growths of star corals, big plating corals, red rope sponges and soft sea whips, and gorgonians on the upper reaches of the spurs. The place is renowned for shoals of schooling fish, including snapper, horse-eye jack and spotted eagle rays.

Tackle Box Canyons

One mile offshore from the Tackle Box pier is this great site (Map p124) with big, steep coral grooves. There are swim-throughs in many places along the drop-off on the way to the outer reef. Gray angels, redband and stoplight parrotfish, and blue chromis hang out along the outer wall.

Caulker aboard the *El Gato*, stopping to snorkel if you like. Also offers sunset cruises (BZ$90).

Reef Runner Glass Bottom Boat (Map p127; ☎ 226-2172; www.ambergriscaye.com/reefrunner; Barrier Reef Dr) Here's a way to get a look at the reef without getting wet (if you don't want to). Visit Hol Chan and Shark Ray Alley (adult/child BZ$80/35) or Tuffy and San Pedro Cut (BZ$50/30). Snorkeling is optional.

Seaduced by Belize (Map p127; ☎ 226-2254; www.seaducedbybelize.com; Vilma Linda Plaza, Tarpon St) Offers family discounts, a range of sailing trips, including a sunset and full-moon cruise, and manatee tours; child-friendly. Don't miss the full-day trip to Mexico Rocks and Robles Beach, complete with snorkel stops and beach barbecue (BZ$140).

Searious Adventures (Map p127; ☎ 226-4202; www.ambergriscaye.com/searious) On the beach in front of Ruby's Beachfront hotel.

Tanisha Tours(Map p124; ☎ 226-2314; www.tanisha tours.com) On the beach, near the cut. Offers a wide range of tours, including snorkeling, watching the manatees and inland trips.

MAINLAND TOURS

Many visitors to Belize use San Pedro as their base and make excursions by plane or boat to other parts of the country. Mainland trips are operated by many of the dive and boat-tour firms.

Altun Ha (p106), the closest Maya ruin to the cayes, is one of the most popular day trips. If you have just one day and wish to see a sample of mainland attractions, you can pair Altun Ha with one or two other stops (BZ$150 to BZ$225). Trips go by boat across the San Pedro Lagoon, up the Northern River to Bomba village and then by bus to Altun Ha. One trip pairs Altun Ha with a stop at the exotic Maruba Resort Jungle Spa (p107). The pause at Maruba can be filled with lunch

Tuffy Canyons

Tuffy Canyons (Map p124), about 1.6 miles south of San Pedro, is marked by deep grooves and a long narrow tunnel. This high-walled passage leads to an opening at 80ft to 90ft onto the reef drop-off. Look for some attractive sponges in the deeper reaches, and the occasional eagle ray passing by. Marauding nurse sharks hang around the entire dive. *Tuffy* was the name of a shrimp boat that met its demise here, and you may see some pieces at around 20ft.

Cypress Garden

Within the Hol Chan Marine Reserve, Cypress Garden (Map p121) is home to resting nurse sharks, turtles, black grouper and tiger grouper. The pronounced undercuts provide habitat for arrow crabs and various shrimps, as well as drums of all sizes. The coral growth here includes flower corals, thin leaf lettuce corals and some nice stands of the rare pillar corals.

Hol Chan Cut

Four miles south of San Pedro, this site (Map p121) is famous for its ample sea life, including eagle rays, stingrays and shoaling schools of fish. The channel is lined with large corals, which hide black snapper, chubs, schoolmasters and mutton snappers, as well as moray eels and channel crabs. At the channel mouth, groupers, rays and sapper ride the current. Yellowtails are ubiquitous, but you might also spot tarpon.

Shark Ray Alley

Only snorkeling is allowed at this perennially popular spot, which is part of the Hol Chan Marine Reserve. Shark Ray Alley (Map p121) was a place for local fishers to clean fish and the creatures attracted to the fish guts soon became a tourist attraction. As the name implies, the area is known for the big southern stingrays and mooching nurse sharks, which come right up to the boat when it first arrives. See the boxed text, p132 for more information.

Amigos Wreck

The one and only wreck on the reef is in Hol Chan Marine Reserve. Amigos Wreck (Map p121) is a 60ft barge, intentionally sunk to provide a marine habitat, now home to nurse sharks and large, green moray eels.

(BZ$30), then swimming, horseback riding or a spa (at extra cost).

If you're interested in seeing more wildlife, you might combine Altun Ha with a trip to the Community Baboon Sanctuary (p108), Crooked Tree Wildlife Sanctuary (p110) or Belize Zoo (p113).

Altun Ha is lovely, but it doesn't have the importance or architectural variety of Lamanai (p167). If you want a closer look at Maya history and ruins, consider the Lamanai River Trip (BZ$310), which takes you up the Lamanai River (lots of bird and croc spotting) to the spectacular ruins. This is a great tour, but it makes for a long day trip in a variety of vehicles – ocean boat, van, river boat and then back again.

Another option is a cave-tubing adventure (BZ$350 to BZ$460) at Nohoch Che'en Caves Branch Archaeological Reserve (p186). Tours combine a river-tube float and a tour of a cave, where you'll see stalagmites and stalactites and possibly pottery shards and other evidence of the ancient Maya. At some point during the tour, the group spends a few spooky moments in total darkness. This tour is often packaged with a trip to the Belize Zoo or the Zip-line Canopy Tour (p187).

Tours going all the way west to San Ignacio, Xunantunich and Mountain Pine Ridge are available from San Pedro, but you'll spend most of the day getting to/from these sites. It's better to spend a few days in the west instead of trying to visit from the cayes.

Festivals & Events

Costa Maya Festival (☎ 226-3462; www.ambergris caye/festival) Formerly known as the Sea & Air Festival, this celebration is a highlight of Ambergris festivities. During the first weekend in August, participants from El

FEEDING THE FISH

To feed or not to feed? That seems like it is always the question.

Feeding is common at Shark Ray Alley (p131) and other sites, as guides want to be able to guarantee a good time for their guests. Fish feeds usually mean close-up views, more interaction and – sometimes – incredible photographs.

Purists argue that feeding changes a fish's natural behavior; it may be harmful to their natural abilities to forage for food if they become dependent on humans. It certainly makes them more vulnerable to the hand that feeds them. For example, the wrong kind of food can be harmful.

For some people, fish feeds have a tinge of falseness, lessening the thrill of interacting with the creatures in their natural habitat.

This is one controversy that will undoubtedly continue as long as there are snorkel guides and dive masters who want to entertain their clients. One thing that is certain is that feeding should be left to the professionals: lurking barracuda can shred a hand in seconds; poor-sighted moray eels can leave an awful tear to the skin; aggressive stingrays can give you a mean hickey. And we all remember what happened to that Crocodile Hunter.

These (and other) fish are inherently dangerous and frequently present at fish-feeding sites. Professional guides know how to look out for fish that could pose a threat – and they know how to respond when somebody scary shows up. If there is going to be fish feeding on your snorkel or dive outing, leave it to the guide so you can come home with all of your digits working!

Salvador, Guatemala, Honduras, Mexico, Costa Rica and Nicaragua join Belize in celebrating their shared heritage. The streets are filled with music, parades, dancing and drinking, culminating in a bodybuilding contest and the crowning of a festival queen.

San Pedro Lobster Festival (☎ 226-3115; www .sanpedrolobsterfest.com) As of 2007, the third week in June is dedicated to the spiny tail. San Pedro re-opens lobster season with a block party, featuring live music, delicious seafood and the crowning of the Lobsterfest king and queen.

San Pedro for Kids

Whether swimming, snorkeling or building sand castles, there's no end to the fun in the sun for your kids in San Pedro. On cloudy days, take them to **KSV Playland** (Map p124; ☎ 206-2061; Blake St), a kids' fantasyland. From kiddie rides and minitrains all the way up to trampolines and ATVs, there is an adventure for every age. Pool, foosball, air hockey and other table games cater for competitive spirits.

Sleeping

Reservations are recommended for the winter season, between December and May. Almost all hotels accept major credit cards, though you may pay a steep surcharge. For more apartments, suites and condominiums, check www.ambergr iscaye.com.

SAN PEDRO

While it's fun to be in the middle of the action, some of the places right in the center can be noisy. If you are on a tight budget you may have no other choice.

Budget

Ruby's Beachfront (Map p127; ☎ 226-2063; www.amber griscaye.com/rubys; Barrier Reef Dr; s BZ$36-50, d without/with air-con BZ$80/100; ✹) This white-with-red-trim hotel near the water taxi dock is a local landmark. The most attractive feature of the long-standing backpacker fave is the large terraces, giving guests plenty of opportunity to enjoy the beachfront location. Unfortunately the rooms themselves are pretty tired, with shabby decor and shoddy mattresses. Thin walls do little to block out the revelries of your neighbors, so you might as well join the party.

Martha's Hotel (Map p127; ☎ 206-2053; www.amber griscaye.com/marthas; Pescador Dr; s/d/tr/q BZ$47/70/94/114) Apart from needing a lick of paint, this ramshackle wooden house has a great vibe. All rooms have private bathrooms and there's hot water most of the time – a budget hotel rarity, as is the daily cleaner service that keeps the place spotless. Tempting as the sea-view rooms are, you might want to reconsider – the hotel backs onto one of the hotter discos in town, and these rooms can get noisy.

If these budget options are booked, there are a couple more affordable choices right next door to each other on Barrier Reef Dr: **Thomas Hotel** (Map p127; ☎ 226-2061; Barrier Reef Dr; s/d with fan BZ$35/70, d with air-con BZ$93; ✹) Rooms are equipped with TV and minifridge. The comfy little balcony out back sports a wonderful view of the building next door.

Hotel San Pedrano (Map p127; ☎ 226-2054; san pedrano@btl.net; Barrier Reef Dr; s/d/tr BZ$76/87/87, with air-con BZ$96/107/107; 🕸) There are no views from this 2nd-story, streetside hostelry, but you might catch the breeze from the balcony. Relatively spacious rooms have two or three beds.

Midrange

Sands Hotel (Map p127; ☎ 226-2510; www.ambergriscaye .com/sands; Barrier Reef Dr; d from BZ$100; 🕸) Set on a busy stretch of Barrier Reef Dr, Sands Hotel is set back from the road, protected by lush gardens. Friendly and functional, the family-run place offers six affordable rooms with mismatched furniture and tile floors, a wide shady porch and panoramic views from the rooftop. Note the location next door to an all-night party spot.

ourpick Hotel del Rio (Map p124; ☎ 226-2286; www.ambergriscaye.com/hoteldelrio; d without/with air-con BZ$90/130, cabana BZ$140-180; 🕸) Just south of the cut, this little lodge has a perfect spot on a quiet stretch of beach, which still provides easy access into town. Three categories of rooms vary in size and layout. Most enticing, the thatched-roof cabanas (sleeping two to four people) are clustered around the sandy grounds, with a central *palapa* that's ideal for socializing or swinging in a hammock. In the background, the two-storey Casa Azul houses the cheapest rooms, but even these have access to a shared balcony with cooling sea breezes and captivating sea views.

Coral Beach Hotel (Map p127; ☎ 226-2013; www .coralbeachhotel.com; cnr Barrier Reef Dr & Black Coral St; s/d with fan BZ$96/114, with air-con BZ$114/138; 🕸) If you want to be in the middle of the action, consider the Coral Beach Hotel. It doesn't get more central than this location, upstairs from the popular Jambel Jerk Pit (p137) and one block from the water taxi dock. A communal balcony provides an excellent vantage point to watch the goings-on. Stylish, spacious rooms are trimmed in dark polished wood and equipped with flat-screen TVs.

Spindrift Hotel (Map p127; ☎ 226-2018, 601-8977; www.ambergriscaye.com/spindrift; cnr Barrier Reef Dr & Buccaneer St; d BZ$107, d with patio/sea view BZ$170/220, beachfront apt BZ$350; 🕸) This is a big concrete block in the middle of town – not the most attractive place, but the service is efficient and staff are warm and welcoming. Rooms are clustered around a central patio, decked

with potted plants; pay more for the ones with sea views. On the ground floor, the Mexican restaurant Caliente is a popular spot.

Lily's Caribbean Lodge (Map p127; ☎ 226-2059; www.ambergriscaye.com/lilys; cnr Barrier Reef Dr & Caribeña St; s BZ$110-130, d BZ$130-150; 🕸) A long-standing favorite, Lily's has a prime beach location and a long wooden balcony offering views of it all. Rooms are spacious and simple, with a modicum of style; if you get one facing the sea, the big, breeze-inducing windows are all you need. Downstairs, guests tend to congregate in the highly recommended beachfront restaurant. The slow-moving, sweet-talking Felipe Paz is your knowledgeable friendly host.

Changes in Latitude (Map p127; ☎ 226-2986; www .ambergriscaye.com/latitudes; Coconut Dr; d BZ$250; 🕸) Unique in San Pedro for its intimate atmosphere, this B&B is a short block from the beach. The six rooms are small but stylish, with wood and bamboo adding Belizean flair. All rooms overlook a well-tended garden with an exotic flower-covered pagoda – a perfect place for guests to sip fruity cocktails and swap snorkeling tales. Other perks include a common kitchen and use of the pool and dock at the Belize Yacht Club next door.

Tide's Beach Resort (Map p124; ☎ 226-2283; www .ambergriscaye.com/tides; s/d incl breakfast BZ$234/272, r with kitchenette BZ$314-370; 🕸 🕸 🕸) Set in a classic, colonial-style wooden building, Tides is an ultrafriendly place that caters to divers, due to its affiliation with Patojo's Scuba Center (p128). But everyone will appreciate the classy rooms with high ceilings, polished wood floors and king-sized beds with funky, hand-painted headboards. A wooden balcony runs the width of the building, giving everyone access to ocean views. Out front, a palm-shaded deck surrounds the swimming pool and the bartender serves up drinks to guests and locals alike.

San Pedro Holiday Hotel (Map p127; ☎ 226-2014; www.sanpedroholiday.com; Barrier Reef Dr; r BZ$252-288, apt BZ$400; 🕸) The central location is both a bonus and a shortcoming. Sure, there's great people-watching and easy access to everything, but this is a busy stretch of beachfront. So even though a painted picket fence surrounds a patch of sand that's only for guests, they still don't get much privacy. Nonetheless, it's a pretty little place, with intricate wooden trim adorning the porches and decks. Light-filled rooms are simple but spacious, and there is an excellent restaurant on site.

Top End

our pick **Blue Tang Inn** (Map p127; ☎ 226-2326, in USA 866-337-8203; www.bluetanginn.com; Sandpiper St; ste with garden/ocean view BZ$327/392, deluxe ste BZ$458; 🕸 🖳) Named for one of the brightest and most beautiful fish on the reef, the Blue Tang lives up to this enticing image. Each of the suites at this beachside retreat includes kitchen facilities, dining furniture and living space. Big windows and vaulted ceilings make the rooms seem even bigger than they are. Many rooms have good sea views, but for the best of all, make your way upstairs to the rooftop – one of the highest vantage points on the island – for the true 360-degree panorama.

Becky & Steve's Cute Little Hotel (Map p127; ☎ 226-2071; www.ramons.com/stevebecky.html; Coconut Dr; d BZ$338; 🕸 🖳) However unfortunate the name, it does indeed describe this hidden gem. Tucked into a tiny, tree-filled courtyard, the resort has quaint, colorful colonial-style cabins. It's away from the beach, which means less foot traffic and more peace and quiet. This place is owned and operated by Ramon's Village, so guests have access to all of the facilities of its big brother across the street.

Ramon's Village (Map p127; ☎ 226-2071; www.ramons .com; Coconut Dr; cabanas garden-view/seaside/beachfront BZ$392/425/490, ste from BZ$556; 🕸 🖳) Guests love the exotic, faux-jungle setting at this luxurious beach resort, with a giant Maya mask known as 'Rey Ramon' overlooking the grounds. Thatched-roof cabanas are surrounded by lush greenery and flowering hibiscus and bougainvillea, allowing for plenty of privacy. Beachfront cabanas are front and center, on the beach, with uninhibited Caribbean vistas; seaside cabanas are set back a bit, with a partially blocked view of the water. Ramon's also boasts one of the best beachfronts on the island, with a dock for swimming and lounge chairs for sunning.

Casa Caracol (Map p124; ☎ 602-6370, 226-2370; www.casacaracol.com; d/q BZ$407/470; 🕸 🖳) Ideal for families and groups, this beachfront house has two apartments, each with two or three bedrooms and bathrooms, a fully equipped kitchen, a private verandah and a comfy living area. Everything is clean and contemporary, with a tropical vista of a quiet stretch of beach on the north side of town. The place offers all the services of a regular hotel, including laundry, housekeeping and local information.

SOUTH OF TOWN

If you need a vacation from your vacation, get out of San Pedro. South of town, you can enjoy more peace and privacy, although you still have easy access to the restaurants and facilities in town. If you don't feel like making the trek (more than a mile in some cases), a few restaurants and bars cater to the southerners.

Pedro's Inn (Map p124; ☎ 226-3825, 206-2198; www .backpackersbelize.com; Sea Grape Dr; s/d with shared bathroom BZ$20/40, r with private bathroom & air-con BZ$70; 🕸 🖳) Pedro is a saint for opening the cheapest and friendliest budget option on the island. Sleep in clean, plain rooms with fresh paint jobs, take cold showers, play poker and eat pizza at the sports bar on site, use the internet for free and save your money for drinking and diving (and other important things).

our pick **Caribbean Villas Hotel & Bird Sanctuary** (Map p124; ☎ 226-2715; www.caribbeanvillashotel.com; Sea Grape Dr; r BZ$170-214, ste from BZ$376; 🕸) These simple, sophisticated studios and suites are the best bargains on the island. Brightly painted walls, tile floors and wood trims adorn the oceanfront accommodations, all of which are equipped with kitchenettes. The suites range in size, so this is an ideal spot for families or groups. The jungly grounds of the Caribbean Villas are home to a bevy of birds, which you can observe from the 'people perch' (also ideal for sunrises). Best of all, the pier protects some algae-covered equipment and local sedimentary rock, forming a sort of artificial reef that attracts a flurry of fish – a great snorkel spot just off your doorstep!

Corona del Mar (Map p124; ☎ 226-2055; www.amber griscaye.com/coronadelmar; Coconut Dr; s/d from BZ$214/284, ste BZ$358, additional person BZ$46; 🕸 🖳 ♿) Friendly and efficient, this 12-room hotel is removed from San Pedro's hustle and bustle. Tile floors, wicker furniture and cool white hues give the rooms an appealing tropical atmosphere (also aided – in some cases – by beautiful ocean views). Woody's Wharf stretches out from the white sandy beach into the sea, offering a perfect place to swim, sunbathe or swing in a hammock.

Coconuts Caribbean Hotel (Map p124; ☎ 226-3500; www.coconutshotel.com; Coconut Dr; s/d/tr/q incl breakfast BZ$231/283/304/325, ste BZ$347-546; 🕸 🖳 🖳) Coconuts scores low on the subtlety scale (as you might expect, with a name like Coconuts), but it's not a bad place for a beach holiday. The true-blue concrete building forms a horseshoe around a central patio, giving all 30 rooms easy access to the pool (with swim-up bar) and the sea beyond. Rooms are rather nondescript, but are equipped with TVs, telephones, fridges and coffee makers.

Mata Rocks Resort (Map p124; ☎ 226-2336; www.mata rocks.com; Sea Grape Dr; s/d/tr/q from BZ$261/282/303/324, ste from BZ$355/366/387/408; 🔀 🖳 🛎) Modern and minimalist, this intimate 17-room hotel is a little oasis on a pretty stretch of beach. The contemporary design gives every room a bit of an ocean view, plus hardwood or tile floors, stucco walls and high ceilings.

Banana Beach Resort (Map p124; ☎ 226-3890; www.bananabeach.com; Sea Grape Dr; r BZ$284, ste poolside/oceanfront BZ$313/460, oceanfront apt from BZ$730; 🔀 🖳 🛎) This place may be too Daytona Beach for some tastes, but nobody can deny the excellent value it offers. It's a big, three-story concrete building with rooms set around two swimming pools or facing a clean stretch of beach. Attractive rooms have rattan furniture, ceramic artwork and woven tapestries; suites have fully-equipped kitchens that are ideal for long-term stays. Indeed, the place offers excellent week-long package deals.

Coral Bay Villas (Map p124; ☎ 226-3003; www.coral baybelize.com; Coconut Dr; r BZ$314; 🔀 🖳) This attractive colonial-style hotel is set back from the ocean, which means that a wide, sandy swathe is free for sunbathing, sandcastle building and hammock swinging. What's better, the beach gets very little foot traffic this far south, so it feels like you have the whole place to yourself. Six deluxe condos are equipped with full kitchens, wireless internet access, cable TV and – lest you forget where you are – private verandahs with sea views. Bikes and kayaks are available for guest use.

Exotic Caye Beach Resort (Map p124; ☎ 226-2870; www.belizeisfun.com; Coconut Dr; 1-bedroom condos BZ$344-450, 2-bedroom condos BZ$490-720; 🔀 🖳 🛎) By 'exotic,' the owners mean beachfront thatched-roof cabanas, freshwater swimming pool and friendly beach bar. The condos are nothing fancy (certainly not exotic), but the guaranteed views of the Caribbean's sparkling waters more than make up for this. Divers, note the resort's on-site dive shop offers both technical and recreational diving.

Victoria House (Map p124; ☎ 226-2067, in USA 800-247-5159; www.victoria-house.com; Sea Grape Dr; state r BZ$372, casitas BZ$616, plantation r/ste BZ$638/773; 🔀 🖳 🛎) Two miles south of the airport, this elegant beach resort is one of the oldest on the island. A beautiful beach and grassy grounds are shaded by a healthy stand of palm trees. Rooms are in thatched-roof casitas, with colorful Caribbean themes, or colonial-style 'plantation' houses, with a sophisticated white-on-white scheme that oozes luxury.

Xanadu Island Resort (Map p124; ☎ 226-2814; www.xanaduresort-belize.com; Sea Grape Dr; ste BZ$408-452, loft BZ$538-580, 2-bedroom apt BZ$580-860; 🔀 🖳 🛎) When the Travel Channel's Samantha Brown came to San Pedro, she stayed at Xanadu, so you know this place has something going for it. Ms Brown stayed in the oceanfront deluxe apartment, but you might opt for a slightly simpler studio or loft apartment. It doesn't really matter, as they are all fitted with every amenity and an atmosphere of rustic luxury. The thatched-roof cabanas are clustered around an enticing freshwater swimming pool, shaded by palm trees. Bicycles, kayaks and snorkel gear are complimentary.

NORTH ISLAND
The North Island is where you want to go if you really want to get away from it all. These resorts are all top end and mainly accessible by boat; you can travel in and out by golf cart to at least as far north as the Portofino Resort, but the island ferry is probably a more pleasant way to go (see p125).

Cocotal Inn & Cabanas (Map p124; ☎ 226-3077; www.cocotalbelize.com; d BZ$262-314, ste BZ$523; 🔀 🛎) A wonderful new addition to the North Island, the Cocotal has four rental units, each with a kitchenette. Look for a cool colonial atmosphere, with fans hanging from high mahogany ceilings, potted plants, tile floors and wicker furniture. The most charming unit is the cupola-topped casita, with sunlight pouring through the skylights. It's all very secluded and sophisticated and good value to boot.

Costa Maya Reef Resort (Map p124; ☎ in USA 877-451-1240; www.costamayareef.com; 1-/2-bedroom condos BZ$390/540; 🔀 🖳 🛎) Big rotunda-style buildings house 30 contemporary condos (which sleep four to six people). The place is pretty innocuous, but all of the activities and amenities are here, including snorkeling and scuba, beachfront bar, free bikes and kayaks, and loads of activities for kids. Costa Maya is 6.5 miles north of San Pedro, accessible only by the island ferry (see p141).

Captain Morgan's Retreat (Map p124; ☎ 226-2567; captmorgan@btl.net; casitas/villas BZ$435/545; 🔀 🖳 🛎) All you need to know is that Captain Morgan's

Retreat was the filming location for the first season of the reality TV show *Temptation Island* (if you're not familiar with this show, be grateful). Enjoy thatch cabins with private porches, two swimming pools and lots of reggae music. Beware the timeshare sales pitch!

Journey's End (Map p124; ☎ in USA 800-460-5665; www.journeysendresort.com; lagoon-view/garden-view/beachfront r BZ$440/528/583, meal plan per person BZ$132; ❄ 🖳 🌊) Whether you want a view of the crystal-blue Caribbean or the emerald-green garden, your lodging at Journey's End is spacious and sophisticated, with big windows, high ceilings and romantic four-poster mahogany beds. A dive shop, spa, restaurant and bar are at your doorstep. Add on BZ$270 per person for a private transfer from Belize City. Besides pampering its guests, Journey's End makes a point of caring for its environs. Guests appreciate the biodegradable shampoos and soaps in the bathroom, and the homegrown, organic ingredients in the kitchen. Other efforts go unseen, such as the water conservation policy that includes collecting rainwater and reusing graywater.

White Sands Cove (Map p124; ☎ 226-3528; www.whitesandscove.com; 1-bedroom condos BZ$470-512, 2-bedroom condos BZ$637-721; ❄ 🖳 🌊) If you want to get away from it all without giving up any of the comforts of home, White Sands Cove – about 2.5 miles north of San Pedro – is for you. Condos are furnished with fully equipped kitchens, gas grills, spacious living areas (where you can watch one of 60 channels on your big TV) and high-speed internet. The beach bar, freshwater pool and tropical spa ensure optimal relaxation, while active types can take advantage of the on-site dive shop or the complimentary bikes and kayaks. Receives rave reviews for above-and-beyond service.

El Pescador Lodge & Villas (Map p124; ☎ 226-2398; www.elpescador.com; standard r BZ$492, 1-/2-/3-bedroom villas BZ$784/1150/1515; ❄ 🖳 🌊) With the atmosphere of a charming old-time fishing lodge and the amenities of a luxury hotel, this 21-acre property is a sweet retreat for anglers and adventurers. Set in an intimate, colonial-style building, the sea-facing standard rooms have polished hardwood floors and colorful handwoven tapestries. The villas are nothing short of vast – perfect if you have family or friends in tow. Located 2.6 miles north of the cut.

our pick Capricorn Resort (Map p124; ☎ 226-2809; www.capricornresort.net; d BZ$537; ☽ closed mid-Sep–mid-Oct; ❄) Unexpectedly luxurious, Capricorn has three sweet but sumptuous cabanas. Decorated in rich jewel tones and handmade artisan crafts, they feature romantic details such as private porches and showers built for two. Capricorn heats up for a few hours each evening, when people from town boat up to dine at the outstanding restaurant. The grounds are a botanical wonderland, bursting with blooms of Belize's native plant species. The small size means that the local habitat was barely disturbed by the construction of the cabanas, which are made from hardwoods and thatch.

Matachica Beach Resort (Map p124; ☎ 220-5010; www.matachica.com; sea-breeze bungalows BZ$580, sea-view ste BZ$710, beachfront casitas $865, luxury villas for 4 BZ$1515, all incl breakfast; ❄ 🖳 🌊) Vying for the title of 'swankiest resort,' Matachica is extravagant, exotic and eclectic. This place is serious about the idea of tropical luxury, so down duvets and Frette linens cover the mosquito-netted beds, and each thatched-roof cottage has a private patio, hung with hammocks, of course. Other highlights include the award-winning Mambo Restaurant and the indulgent Jade Spa. It's 5 miles north of San Pedro.

Portofino Resort (Map p124; ☎ 220-5096; www.portofinobelize.com; beachfront cabanas BZ$635, treetop ste from BZ$735, meal plan per person BZ$132; ❄ 🖳) Who knew a thatched-roof cabin could be so chic? With high ceilings, huge picture windows, Mexican tiles and Guatemalan rugs, these lodgings are at once primitive and plush. The resort's total capacity is 32, making it wonderfully intimate. Gourmands come up from San Pedro by the boatload to dine at the world-class restaurant Le Bistro (p138).

Eating

Although there are plenty of options for cheap street food, pizza and sandwiches, it's hard to sit down at a San Pedro restaurant without paying as much as BZ$50 per person. Dining on Ambergris is startlingly expensive, especially in comparison with the rest of Belize. That said, diners usually get their money's worth, as Ambergris is home to the country's freshest seafood and most innovative chefs.

SAN PEDRO

For the budget conscious traveler, several small cafés in the town center serve cheap, simple meals. Try the food stands in front of the park, where a plate of chicken with rice and beans, barbecue meat or fish and other delicacies is under BZ$10.

Budget

Papi's Diner (Map p124; ☎ 226-2047; Pescador Dr; breakfast & lunch BZ$2-10, mains BZ$20-40; ☺ breakfast, lunch & dinner) At the far north end of town, this small, friendly place is an excellent budget option. For breakfast, choose from burritos, *huevos rancheros*, omelettes or bacon with hash browns. For lunch and dinner, it offers elaborate main courses but the bargains are in the burgers, chicken, pork chops and fish fillets.

our pick Ruby's Café (Map p127; ☎ 226-2063; Barrier Reef Dr; pastries BZ$3-5; ☺ 6am-6pm) This tiny place is packed with locals during the morning hours. Nobody can resist the sweet and sticky cinnamon rolls, chicken-filled Johnny cakes, homemade banana cake, hot tortillas filled with ham, cheese and beans, and more. There is no place to sit so grab your breakfast to go and find a shady spot on the beach.

Celi's Deli (Map p127; ☎ 226-2014; Barrier Reef Dr; deli items BZ$3-10, restaurant mains BZ$16-30; ☺ deli 6am-6pm, restaurant lunch & dinner) A fantastic find for breakfast or lunch, Celi's Deli serves food to go – sandwiches, meat pies, tacos, tamales and homemade cakes. You can take your snack across the street and eat on the deck in front of the San Pedro Holiday Hotel. This is where you will find Celi's Restaurant, which is also recommended (especially for the Wednesday night beach barbecue).

Tabu (Map p127; ☎ 226-2254; Vilma Linda Plaza, Tarpon St; meals BZ$10-20; ☺ 7am-5pm; ☷) When you can't take the heat, retreat to this friendly café and sandwich shop. At breakfast, you can indulge in pancakes, waffles or French toast, topped with fresh fruit and doused in syrup. For lunch, choose from the selection of interesting sandwiches and burgers, as well as fresh salads and other vegetarian options. There is also a good menu of espresso drinks, making this an inviting place to relax and do the coffee shop thing, tropical style.

Estel's Dine by the Sea (Map p127; ☎ 226-2019; Pelican St; meals BZ$10-30; ☺ 6am-5pm) This long-standing breakfast favorite is basically an extension of the beach – complete with sandy floors and ocean breezes. Stop by for a breakfast burrito, fruit-filled jacks or an eye-opening coffee.

Midrange & Top End

Caramba Restaurant (Map p127; ☎ 226-4321; www .ambergriscaye.com/caramba; Pescador Dr; burgers BZ$9-12,

mains BZ$20-40; ☺ lunch & dinner Thu-Tue) Caramba is the busiest place in town due to its excellent food, fun atmosphere and attentive service. Mexican and Creole dishes focus on fresh fish and seafood cooked in at least 10 tasty ways. There are a few tables on the street, but the tropical decor inside only enhances your seafood feast.

El Patio Restaurant & Grill (Map p127; ☎ 226-3898; Black Coral St; lunch mains BZ$10-20, dinner mains BZ$30-50; ☺ lunch & dinner Wed-Mon) Potted plants, flowing fountain and a candlelit interior make this sand-floored *palapa* an inviting setting for a romantic dinner. Grilled meats and seafood are the specialty, accompanied by fresh-squeezed, thirst-quenching fruit juices or ice cold Belikin beers.

Blue Water Grill (Map p127; ☎ 226-3347; www .bluewatergrillbelize.com; Sun Breeze Beach Hotel, Coconut Dr; starters & salads BZ$10-30, mains BZ$20-50; ☺ 7am-9:30pm) It's hard to resist the huge open-air restaurant on this beachfront property, and almost everybody who comes to San Pedro ends up eating here at some point. Few are disappointed. The menu is wide-ranging, including some safe options such as pizza and pasta, as well as more adventurous Asian-influenced seafood dishes. The place is always busy, but it's big so you probably won't have to wait for a table, however, service can be slow once you are seated.

Jambel Jerk Pit (Map p127; ☎ 226-3515; Coral Beach Hotel, Barrier Reef Dr; mains BZ$16-30; ☺ 10am-10pm) Spice it up at the Jambel Jerk Pit, specializing in Jamaican jerk with Belizean flare. Whether you want fish, chicken or pork – or the famous Jamaica Mi Crazy Shrimp – your order will be as spicy as you like it. Wednesday nights feature an all-you-can-eat buffet that will sate the hungriest Rasta Mon.

Elvi's Kitchen (Map p127; ☎ 226-2176; Pescador Dr; mains BZ$20-50; ☺ lunch & dinner) This San Pedro institution has been around since the early days, serving up local specialties such as shrimp creole, fried chicken and conch ceviche. The funky tropical decor, loud marimba music and expensive T-shirts for sale (not to mention the overpriced entrées) give it a Disney-like atmosphere. But it's a good place to sample some authentic and filling local cuisine.

our pick Wild Mango's (Map p127; ☎ 226-2859; Barrier Reef Dr; mains BZ$30-50; ☺ lunch & dinner) Exuding a carefree, casual ambience (as a beachfront restaurant should), this open-air restaurant manages to serve up some of the island's most consistent and creative cuisine. With a hint of the Caribbean and a hint of Mexico, the dishes showcase fresh seafood, Cajun spices and local fruits and vegetables. The place is always packed – come early or make a reservation.

SOUTH OF TOWN

George's Kitchen (Map p124; ☎ 226-2974; Coconut Dr; meals BZ$6-12; ☽ breakfast, lunch & dinner Wed-Mon) Opposite the entrance to Corona del Mar, this little seafood and sandwich shack is one of San Pedro's hidden food gems. An excellent option for breakfast, with big omelettes and other hearty egg dishes.

El Divino (Map p124; ☎ 226-2444; www.bananabeach .com; Banana Beach Resort, Coconut Dr; breakfast BZ$10-16, mains BZ$20-40; ☽ breakfast, lunch & dinner) This street-side eatery gets heaps of praise, especially for its filling breakfasts, steaks and wood-fired pizzas. The beach-themed decor is not exactly subtle, as you will notice as soon as you catch a glimpse of the reef mural on the wall (or, even better, the sunset vista in the martini lounge). Staff members dressed in brightly colored tropical uniforms ensure a fun and friendly ambience.

Casa Picasso (Map p124; ☎ 226-4507; tapas BZ$10-30; ☽ dinner Mon-Sat) Combining the flavors of the Caribbean and the Mediterranean, Casa Picasso is a semi-swanky place for tapas and pasta (taking full advantage of local seafood, of course). If that's not hip enough for you, add some jazzy music or a fruit-flavored martini. This place is slightly off the beaten track – head south on Coconut Dr and turn right at the intersection near Island Internet – but it's worth the extra effort. Reservations recommended.

Tastes of Thailand (Map p124; ☎ 226-2601; Sea Grape Dr; mains BZ$20-50; ☽ dinner Mon-Sat) In an appealing, traditional house, this is a tiny place with only six tables and arguably tacky decor. But vegetarians and meat-eaters alike will rejoice at the menu of authentic Thai favorites, including tofu or cashew dishes, satays and *tom yum* (spicy soup with lemongrass, prawns etc).

Palmilla Restaurant (Map p124; ☎ 226-2067; www.victoria-house.com; Sea Grape Dr; mains BZ$30-60; ☽ breakfast, lunch & dinner) The classy, candlelit restaurant at Victoria House is overseen by New York–trained chef José Luis Ortega, who ensures high-quality cuisine for his discriminating guests. At lunchtime, you might prefer Admiral Nelson's Beach Bar, the hotel's casual, open-air café on the beachfront.

NORTH ISLAND

Some visitors take the dirt road only as far as the Sweet Basil restaurant for lunch or the Palapa Bar for drinks, before heading back to San Pedro. Others travel up the coast by launch for an exotic starlit evening at one of the North Island's excellent restaurants. You can expect unusual menus featuring excellent seafood dishes. See p141 for the schedule and prices for the island ferry.

ourpick Beach n' Kitchen (Map p124; ☎ 226-4456; fruit smoothies BZ$4, mains BZ$10-20; ☽ breakfast & lunch) If you are cycling up the coast, this sweet spot is a perfect pit stop; place your order and take a seat on the breezy deck. Look for fresh squeezed fruit juices, homemade cookies, cold soups and hearty sandwiches. On Saturday and Sunday, an all-day brunch menu includes eggs Benedict, cinnamon bread, French toast with fruit topping and – of course – a Bloody Mary or mimosa to start the day right.

Sweet Basil (Map p124; ☎ 326-2113; mains BZ$15-30; ☽ 11am-9pm) A quarter of a mile north of the cut, this high-end gourmet deli has an attractive but unlikely location overlooking the lagoon. The open-air restaurant is set in a wooden, Victorian-style home amid a flower-filled tropical garden. It prepares light meals of sandwiches made with home-baked bread, pâtés, platters of imported cheeses and meats, and pasta dishes. International wines are available.

Le Bistro (Map p124; ☎ 220-5096; Portofino Resort; mains BZ$20-40; ☽ breakfast, lunch & dinner) With a chef trained in French and Italian cuisine and a brilliant Belizean setting, the European-Caribbean fusion cuisine at Le Bistro makes perfect sense. The all-sauté menu features freshly caught snapper, lobster and other seafood prepared with diverse (and divine) sauces. A new vegetarian menu caters for animal-free eaters. If you're feeling really romantic, inquire about private dining on the pier. A complimentary shuttle boat leaves Fido's Dock at 6:30pm; reservations recommended.

Rendezvous Restaurant & Winery (Map p124; ☎ 226-3426; www.ambergriscaye.com/rendezvous; mains BZ$40-60; ☽ lunch & dinner) Four miles north of town, Rendezvous is unique in San Pedro – if not Belize. Set in a ramshackle house on the beach, this colonial-style place artfully blends the flavors of French and Thai cuisine, with exquisite results. Try Thai pepper pork with roasted garlic chips or fresh fish with coconut cream sauce with saffron and cilantro. House wines are made at the winery on the grounds.

Mambo Restaurant (Map p124; ☎ 220-5011; Matachica Beach Resort; mains BZ$40-80; ☒ breakfast, lunch & dinner) The Matachica Beach Resort's award-winning restaurant is as eclectic and exotic as the resort itself. Specializing in Mediterranean fare such as pasta and paella, the menu does not skimp on fresh seafood and local seasonal produce. While you are here, be sure to stroll around the grounds to thoroughly appreciate this tropical fantasy. Reservations required.

our pick Capricorn Restaurant (Map p124; ☎ 226-2809; Capricorn Resort; mains BZ$50-70; ☒ Thu-Tue) This restaurant's nouvelle cuisine has long been considered among the best in Belize. By day you can chill out under the *palapa* at the beach bar; at night the open-air restaurant is lit by festive twinkling lights. Dinner specials change daily, but they might include stone-crab claws with a garlic and herb dip, filet mignon with portobello mushroom sauce or grilled lobster tail painted with garlic butter. The most requested item is a sensational appetizer: sun-dried tomato pesto drizzled over cream cheese and basil leaves, served with homemade bread. Reservations are essential; book a table and it's yours for the night.

Drinking

Most hotels have comfortable bars, often with sand floors, thatched roofs and reggae music. The following bars open from late morning till late at night (unless otherwise noted).

BC's Beach Bar (Map p127; ☎ 226-3289; ☒ 9am-midnight) This little shack on the beach is one of the hottest spots on the island for cool breezes and cold drinks. There's not much of a menu, but Sunday afternoon sees a hoppin' beach barbecue and jam session. Local bands also play on Thursday nights.

Tackle Box (Map p127; ☎ 226-3235; Water Taxi Pier) Right next to the water taxi dock, the Tackle Box extends a warm welcome (usually with a reggae beat) to everyone arriving in San Pedro. It is a popular first stop, allowing patrons to have a drink, unwind and get into the island frame of mind.

Palapa Bar (Map p124; ☎ 226-3111; North Island) This over-the-water *palapa* is about a half-mile north of the San Pedro River. If you're hungry you can nosh on pulled-pork sandwiches and fresh fish tacos. Otherwise, it's a fantastic place for tropical drinks and cold beers any time of day. Happy hour is from 4pm to 6pm daily.

Pier Lounge (Map p127; ☎ 226-2002; Spindrift Hotel, cnr Barrier Reef Dr & Buccaneer St; ☒ 10am-midnight Mon-Sat, 11am-11pm Sun) This otherwise innocuous sports bar has made a name for itself by hosting the weekly World Famous Chicken Drop (6pm Wednesday), giving new insight to the origin of the term 'chicken shit.' (Sort of like bingo with chickens, the floor is divided into numbered squares and a chicken is put in the middle of it; participants place bets on where it will drop a turd.) Give people enough alcohol and they are amused by anything. This place also has a giant plasma TV, bingo and karaoke.

Other recommended drinking spots south of town include the following:

Crazy Canuck's (Map p124) Open to cooling sea breezes. Staff are friendly and regular patrons welcoming.

Pedro's Inn (Map p124; ☎ 206-2198; Sea Grape Dr) Come to eat pizza, play pool and watch sports on the big screen.

Roadkill Bar (Map p124) Live music at 7pm Monday; Roadkill BBQ Monday eve and Saturday morning.

Entertainment

Fido's (Map p127; ☎ 226-2056; www.fidosbelize.com; 18 Barrier Reef Dr; ☒ 11am-midnight) This enormous *palapa* – decorated with seafaring memorabilia – attracts crowds for drinking, dancing and hooking up. There's plenty of seating, an extensive food menu and an ample-sized dance floor. Live music is on every night at 8pm – classic and acoustic rock, reggae and the occasional record spin. For those staying at the southern end of the island, **Fido's Sandbar** (☎ 226-4220; 1 Seagrape St) is on the grounds of the Royal Caribbean Resort. The *palapa* bar offers good vibes, cold beers and beach bowling!

Jaguar's Temple Club (Map p127; ☎ 226-4077; Barrier Reef Dr; ☒ 9:30pm-3am Thu-Sat) You can't miss this surreal Maya temple, complete with jaguar face, across from the central beachside park. The place does its very best to create a 'wild' atmosphere, with jungle dioramas setting the stage and lighting effects keeping it spooky. Hip-hop and breakbeat music keeps dancers on their feet. When you need to take a break, check out the streetside Rehab Lounge (open 3pm to midnight Tuesday to Sunday).

Barefoot Iguana (Map p124; ☎ 226 2927; Coconut Dr; ☒ from 10pm Wed & Sat) This high-energy club evokes the more whimsical side of the rainforest, with an indoor waterfall and plenty of faux greenery. Loud music with heavy bass, dark dance floors with funky lighting effects and an endless flow of alcohol guarantee a good time for those with fancy feet.

Shopping

Plenty of gift shops in the hotels and on and around Barrier Reef Dr sell T-shirts, beachwear, hammocks, jewelry and ceramics. But there are also interesting boutiques, fancy gift stores, art galleries and woodwork shops. Prices are high but you might find unique and artistic souvenirs. Sometimes artisans sell their woodwork and handicrafts from stalls on the street near the central park or on the beach.

Ambar (Map p127; ☎ 226-3101; Fido's, 18 Barrier Reef Dr; ☺ 9am-9pm Mon-Sat) Beautiful handmade jewelry in interesting and diverse styles, including plenty of options out of the namesake stone.

Ambergris Jade (Map p127; ☎ 226-3311; 45 Barrier Reef Dr) The Maya valued jadeite for its iridescent beauty and perceived powers. Different varieties were believed to enhance creativity, stimulate positive energy and offer protection from evil spirits. This so-called 'Jade & Maya History Museum' carries a wide variety of beautiful Guatemalan jade in the form of jewelry and other carved objects. Also offers appraisal services.

Barefoot Books (Map p127; ☎ 226-3563; www .barefootbooks-belize.com; Pescador Dr; ☺ 9am-9pm) The biggest and best bookstore in Belize, with an excellent selection of travel books and reference books about Belize history and culture. This is also the place to trade in your used paperbacks and pick up a new novel to peruse on the beach.

Belizean Arts Gallery (Map p127; ☎ 226-3019; www .belizeanarts.com; Fido's, 18 Barrier Reef Dr; ☺ 9am-10pm Mon-Sat) This is one of the country's best shops for local art and handicrafts, selling ceramics, woodcarvings, Garifuna drums and antiques alongside affordable and tasteful knick knacks. You'll also find a decent selection of paintings by local and national artists. Rainforest-flora beauty products, including soaps, are on sale.

Caribe Creations (Map p127; ☎ 226-2803; Barrier Reef Dr) Take a bit of Belizean style home with you; here you'll find custom-made clothes with Caribbean flare, ranging from beach coverups and do-rags to silky sarongs and wedding gowns, all in free-flowing fabrics with a distinctive 'island' design.

C's Furniture World (Map p127; ☎ 226-4037; Pescador Dr; ☺ 10am-6pm Mon-Sat) If you are heading further into Belize, you are better off buying your wood products and furniture in Cayo, where prices are lower and the selection is more diverse. But otherwise, stop by C's to see the handiwork with mahogany, rosewood and teak.

Rum, Cigar & Coffee House (Map p127; ☎ 226-2020; Pescador Dr; ☺ 9am-9pm) Catering to all of your vices, with a good selection of fresh roasted coffee beans, local rums and cigars from all over the Caribbean. Stop by for a taste test, which will give you the chance to sample several coffee and fruit-flavored liqueurs.

Getting There & Away

Tropic Air (☎ 226-2338; www.tropicair.com) offers hourly flights to/from the Belize International Airport (BZ$126, 20 minutes) and the Belize City municipal airstrip, 12 miles closer to town (BZ$70, 20 minutes). About half the flights stop at Caye Caulker (BZ$70, five minutes, six daily). Additional flights depart for Corozal (BZ$95, 20 minutes, five daily). All flights depart between 7am and 5pm daily.

Maya Island Air (☎ 226-2435; www.mayaairways .com) has a similar schedule, with hourly flights to Belize International Airport (BZ$126, 15 minutes) and the Belize City municipal airstrip (adult/child BZ$70/52, 25 minutes). Six flights a day stop at Caye Caulker (adult/child BZ$70/52, 10 minutes), while four go to Corozal (adult/child BZ$95/69, 25 minutes).

Caye Caulker Water Taxi Association (☎ 226-0992; www.cayecaulkerwatertaxi.com; Shark's Dock) runs boats between San Pedro, Caye Caulker and Belize City, with stops at Caye Chapel (BZ$20) upon request. Boats to Belize City (adult/child BZ$20/10, 1½ hours) via Caye Caulker (BZ$15/10, 45 minutes) leave San Pedro at 8am, 9:30am, 11:30am, 1pm, 2:30pm and 3:30pm (also 4:30pm Friday through Sunday and holidays). An express boat goes direct to Belize City at 7am.

The **Thunderbolt** (☎ 422-0026; www.ambergris caye.com/thunderbolt; Thunderbolt Dock) departs San Pedro's lagoon-side dock at 7am and 3pm for Corozal (one-way/round-trip BZ$45/85, two hours), stopping at Sarteneja upon request.

Getting Around

You can walk into town from the airport in 10 minutes or less, and the walk from the boat docks is even shorter. **San Pedro Taxi Association** (☎ 206-2076) drives minivans. From the airport one or two people pay BZ$6 to any place in town, or BZ$8 to BZ$10 to the hotels south of town. Taxis are prohibited from crossing the toll bridge (BZ$2) to the North Island, but bicycles and golf carts are allowed.

BICYCLE

Many hotels and resorts provide bikes for their guests for a small fee or for free. Otherwise, you can rent a bike at **Joe's Bicycle Rentals** (Map p127; ☎ 226-5371; cnr Pescador Dr & Caribeña St; 3hr/24hr/week US$6/9/40; ☷ 8am-6pm) or **Calvio's Bike Rental** (Map p127; ☎ 661-7143; www.belizeextremeadventure.com; Pescador Dr).

BOAT

The **Island Ferry** (☎ 226-3231) operates an Ambergris-only water-taxi service north and south from Fido's Dock. In the high season, boats depart every two hours from 7am to 5pm and hourly from 6pm to 10pm, stopping at the north-end resorts. There are midnight and 2am runs on Wednesday, Friday and Saturday nights. The return trip is 45 minutes later (7:45am, 9:45am etc). The ferry also runs south to Fido's Sandbar (just south of Victoria House) four times a day.

The cost is BZ$15/10 per adult/child one way to Journey's End, BZ$25/15 to resorts north of Journey's End. Southbound, passengers pay BZ$7 each way to/from Fido's Sandbar. Special runs out of hours cost BZ$40 from Fido's Dock to Journey's End for one to three people and BZ$60 to resorts beyond Journey's End. North Island resorts also frequently run their own shuttle services for guests to/from San Pedro.

GOLF CART

These days, traffic jams are not unusual in San Pedro due to the glut of golf carts cruising the streets. Note that some golf carts are battery-powered and others run on gas; the former being more ecologically sound and the latter having greater endurance. If you are addicted to motorized transport, you can get yours at any of the following rental agencies:

Castle Cars (Map p127; ☎ 226-2421; www.castlecars belize.com; 1 Barrier Reef Dr) Gas-powered carts are BZ$115 for a half-day (eight hours), BZ$131 for a full day (24 hours) or BZ$540 for one week (seven days). One tank of gas is included, plus a free refill on long-term rentals.

Island Adventures (Map p127; ☎ 226-4343; www .islandgolfcarts.com; Coconut Dr) Rent a four-seater for BZ$132/550 per day/week or a six-seater for BZ$192/696.

Moncho's Island Auto (Map p127; ☎ 226-3262; www .monchosrentals.com; Coconut Dr) Rents out battery-powered carts for a half-/full day for BZ$88/129 or gas-powered carts for BZ$108/143 (including gas). Moncho's will deliver your vehicle to your hotel for your convenience.

Polo's EZ-Go Rentals (Map p127; ☎ 226-5542; Barrier Reef Dr) Rents out four-seaters for one/eight/24 hours for BZ$50/90/120.

CAYE CAULKER
pop 1300

'No Shirt, No Shoes…No Problem.' You'll see this sign everywhere in Belize, but no place is it more apt than Caye Caulker. Indeed nothing seems to be a problem on this tiny island, where mangy dogs nap in the middle of the dirt road and suntanned cyclists pedal around them. The only traffic sign on the island instructs golf carts and bicycles to 'go slow,' a directive that is taken seriously.

The one thousand or so residents have traditionally made their living from the sea, specifically from the spiny lobsters and red snapper that inhabit its warm waters. It has also long been a budget travelers' mecca, part of a classic backpacker route from Tulum, Mexico to Tikal and Antigua, Guatemala. In recent years, the economy has been shifting, as tourists of all ages and incomes are beginning to appreciate the island's unique atmosphere. On Caye Caulker, there are no cars, no fumes and no hassles, just white sandy beaches, balmy breezes, fresh seafood, azure waters and a fantastic barrier reef at its doorstep.

Caye Caulker offers fewer amenities than Ambergris, but that is part of the charm of this place. All the residents know each other and it won't take long before they know you, too.

The easygoing attitude is due in part to the thriving Rastafarian culture on the Caye, which pulses to a reggae beat. If it's not Bob Marley blaring from a boom box on the beach, it's the latest in punta rock. Drumming groups gather on the beach and at local bars to get their Afro-Caribbean groove on. They play for themselves, but anybody is welcome to gather around and soak up the good vibes.

The island is an ideal base for snorkeling and diving adventures at the nearby reef. The northern part of the island – a tempting destination for kayakers – is mostly mangroves, which are home to an amazing variety of birdlife. Other than that, all visitors should be sure to schedule in plenty of time for swinging on a hammock and enjoying the breeze (which is indeed a legitimate activity on Caye Caulker).

NORTHERN CAYES

History

Caye Caulker was originally a fishing settlement. It became popular with 17th-century British buccaneers as a place to stop for water and to work on their boats. Like Ambergris Caye, it grew in population with the War of the Castes (see In Living Color: British Honduras, p34), and is known mainly as a Mestizo island. It was purchased in 1870 by Luciano Reyes, whose descendants still live on the island. Reyes parceled the land out to a handful of families, and to this day descendants of those first landowners still live in the general vicinities of those original parcels. These islanders were self sufficient and exported turtle meat until the turtle population was decimated.

During much of the 20th century, coconut processing, fishing, lobster trapping and boat building formed the backbone of the island's economy. Caulker was one of the first islands to establish a fisherfolk cooperative in the 1960s, allowing members to receive fair prices for the lobster and other sea life pulled from their waters.

Caye Caulker remains a fishing village, and boat design and construction continue, but tourism is taking over the economy. Tourism began in the late 1960s and 1970s when small numbers of hippies found their way to the island. Today, international visitors come in steady numbers, however, although many islanders operate tourism-related businesses, there are no plans for large-scale development. Caulker residents enjoy the slow rhythm of life as much as visitors do.

Orientation

Caulker village has three main north–south streets: from east to west these are the Front, Middle and Back Sts. The streets are now officially called Avenidas Hicaco, Langosta and Mangle, though you're unlikely to hear the new names used. The main dock street runs east–west through the center of the village. There are another 15 or so east–west streets; some of them might have names but they are not used.

In 1961 Hurricane Hattie carved 'the Split' through the island just north of the village. (Some locals contend that this waterway is actually man-made; indeed, some villagers maintain that they were involved in the dredging!) North of the Split is mostly undeveloped (although not for much longer, as the land has been subdivided for housing and a path cuts through here). A few folk live on the North Island just over the Split. The most northerly part of Caulker is the Caye Caulker Forest Reserve (p144).

From the dock street north to the Split is around half a mile. The village stretches another half-mile or so south from the dock street to the airstrip and there are a few houses south of the airstrip. Though most of the tourist facilities are on the east side of the village, there are a couple of places to stay and a restaurant or two 'to the back.' Here you get lovely sunsets and seclusion, but you pay with a longer walk into civilization and extra bugs.

Information

EMERGENCY
Police (☎ 911, 226-0179; Front St)

INTERNET ACCESS
Caye Caulker Cyber Café (Front St; per hr BZ$14; ⏱ 7am-10pm) Air-conditioned; has a bar with happy hour from 3pm to 6pm.
Cayeboard Connection (Front St; per hr BZ$15; ⏱ 8am-9pm) In an air-conditioned prefab building; also has a book exchange.
Taj Internet (☎ 226-0034; Front St; per hr BZ$10) The computers are not equipped with timers, so you are better off keeping track of your own usage. This place also acts as an agent for Linea Dorada and San Juan Express bus services to Guatemala and Mexico.

INTERNET RESOURCES
www.cayecaulker.org Includes links to an active message board, travel hints and loads of info.
www.cayecaulkerbelize.net The village council's site, which has news of upcoming events.
www.cybercayecaulker.com Besides the typical information about tours and accommodations, also hosts links to local artists, galleries and other souvenir specialists.
www.gocayecaulker.com The official site of the Caye Caulker branch of the Belize Tourism Industry Association (BTIA).

LAUNDRY
Caye Caulker Coin Laundromat (the dock st; wash, dry & soap per load BZ$20; ⏱ 7am-9pm)
Marie's Laundry (Middle St; per 8lb BZ$10)

MEDICAL SERVICES
Caye Caulker Health Center (☎ 226-0166) Just off Front St, two blocks south of the dock street. Operates on a donation basis.

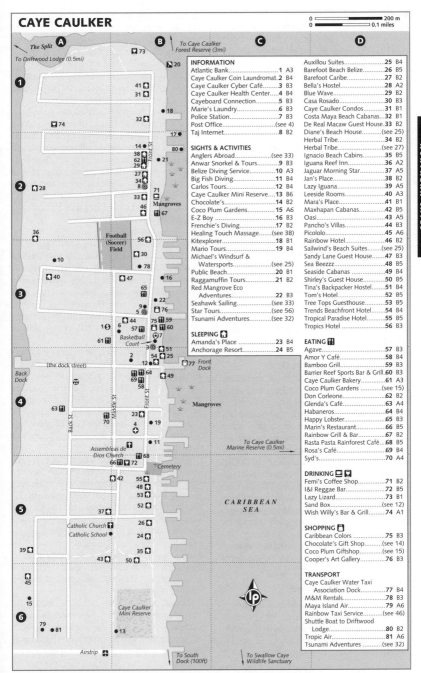

CAYE CAULKER

The Split
To Driftwood Lodge (0.5mi)
To Caye Caulker Forest Reserve (3mi)
To Caye Caulker Marine Reserve (0.5mi)
To Swallow Caye Wildlife Sanctuary
To South Dock (100ft)
Airstrip
Back Dock

INFORMATION
Atlantic Bank..........................1 A3
Caye Caulker Coin Laundromat.2 B4
Caye Caulker Cyber Café........3 B3
Caye Caulker Health Center....4 B4
Cayeboard Connection...........5 B3
Marie's Laundry....................6 B3
Police Station.......................7 B3
Post Office.....................(see 4)
Taj Internet.........................8 B2

SIGHTS & ACTIVITIES
Anglers Abroad..................(see 33)
Anwar Snorkel & Tours..........9 B3
Belize Diving Service............10 A3
Big Fish Diving....................11 B4
Carlos Tours.......................12 B4
Caye Caulker Mini Reserve....13 B6
Chocolate's........................14 B2
Coco Plum Gardens.............15 A6
E-Z Boy............................16 B3
Frenchie's Diving.................17 B2
Healing Touch Massage....(see 38)
Kitexplorer........................18 B1
Mario Tours........................19 B4
Michael's Windsurf &
  Watersports.................(see 25)
Public Beach......................20 B1
Raggamuffin Tours...............21 B2
Red Mangrove Eco
  Adventures.....................22 B3
Seahawk Sailing..............(see 33)
Star Tours......................(see 56)
Tsunami Adventures.........(see 32)

SLEEPING
Amanda's Place 23 B4
Anchorage Resort.................24 B5

Auxillou Suites.....................25 B4
Barefoot Beach Belize...........26 B5
Barefoot Caribe....................27 B2
Bella's Hostel......................28 A2
Blue Wave..........................29 B2
Casa Rosado........................30 B3
Caye Caulker Condos...........31 B1
Costa Maya Beach Cabanas...32 B1
De Real Macaw Guest House.33 B2
Diane's Beach House........(see 25)
Herbal Tribe........................34 B2
Herbal Tribe....................(see 27)
Ignacio Beach Cabins...........35 B5
Iguana Reef Inn....................36 A2
Jaguar Morning Star.............37 A5
Jan's Place..........................38 B2
Lazy Iguana.........................39 A5
Leeside Rooms....................40 A3
Mara's Place........................41 B1
Maxhapan Cabanas..............42 B5
Oasi..................................43 A5
Pancho's Villas....................44 B3
Picololo.............................45 B4
Rainbow Hotel.....................46 B2
Sailwind's Beach Suites....(see 25)
Sandy Lane Guest House.......47 B3
Sea Beezzz.........................48 B5
Seaside Cabanas..................49 B4
Shirley's Guest House...........50 B5
Tina's Backpacker Hostel......51 B4
Tom's Hotel........................52 B4
Tree Tops Guesthouse...........53 B5
Trends Beachfront Hotel........54 B4
Tropical Paradise Hotel.........55 B5
Tropics Hotel 56 B3

EATING
Agave................................57 B3
Amor Y Café........................58 B4
Bamboo Grill.......................59 B3
Barrier Reef Sports Bar & Grill.60 B3
Caye Caulker Bakery.............61 A3
Coco Plum Gardens ....(see 15)
Don Corleone......................62 B2
Glenda's Café......................63 A4
Habaneros..........................64 B3
Happy Lobster.....................65 B3
Marin's Restaurant...............66 B5
Rainbow Grill & Bar..............67 B2
Rasta Pasta Rainforest Café..68 B5
Rosa's Café.........................69 B4
Syd's.................................70 A4

DRINKING
Femi's Coffee Shop...............71 B2
I&I Reggae Bar.....................72 B5
Lazy Lizard.........................73 B1
Sand Box.......................(see 12)
Wish Willy's Bar & Grill.........74 A1

SHOPPING
Caribbean Colors 75 B3
Chocolate's Gift Shop.......(see 14)
Coco Plum Giftshop.........(see 15)
Cooper's Art Gallery.............76 B3

TRANSPORT
Caye Caulker Water Taxi
  Association Dock...............77 B4
M&M Rentals.......................78 B3
Maya Island Air...................79 A6
Rainbow Taxi Service........(see 46)
Shuttle Boat to Driftwood
  Lodge.............................80 B2
Tropic Air...........................81 A6
Tsunami Adventures ....(see 32)

NORTHERN CAYES

MONEY
Atlantic Bank (☎ 226-0207; Middle St; ☼ 8am-2pm Mon-Fri, 8:30am-noon Sat) Offer cash advances, as well as an ATM that functions on Cirrus and other international networks.

POST
Post office (Caye Caulker Health Center Bldg; ☼ 8:30am-4:30pm Mon-Fri)

Sights

CAYE CAULKER MARINE RESERVE
Declared a marine reserve in 1998, the 61-sq-mile Caye Caulker Marine Reserve includes the portion of the barrier reef that runs parallel to the island, as well as the turtle grass lagoon adjacent to the Caye Caulker Forest Reserve. Although the reef is regenerating after patchy hurricane damage, it is rich with sea life, including colorful sponges, blue-and-yellow queen angel fish, Christmas tree worms, star coral, redband parrotfish, yellow gorgonians and more. Between April and September, snorkelers and divers might even spot a turtle or a manatee.

All local snorkel and dive operators lead tours to the Caye Caulker Marine Reserve; see opposite.

CAYE CAULKER FOREST RESERVE
The northernmost 100 acres of the island constitute the Caye Caulker Forest Reserve, also declared in 1998. The littoral forest on Caye Caulker is mostly red, white and black mangrove, which grows in the shallow water. The mangroves' root systems support an intricate ecosystem, including sponges, gorgonians, anemones and a wide variety of fish. Besides the mangroves, the forest contains buttonwood, gumbo-limbo (the 'tourist tree'), poisonwood, madre de cacao, ficus and ziracote. Coconut palms and Australian pines are not native to this region, but there is no shortage of them.

Birdlife is prolific in the mangrove swamp, especially wading birds such as the tricolored heron and songbirds including the mangrove warbler. Somewhat rare species that can be spotted include the white-crowned pigeon, rufus-necked rail and black catbird. Inland lagoons provide habitat for crocodiles and turtles, all five species of crabs, boa constrictors, scaly tailed iguanas (locally called 'wish willies'), geckos and lizards.

The forest reserve is only accessible by boat, but it's an excellent (if ambitious) destination for a kayaker. Many places to stay have kayaks available for their guests; otherwise, you can rent one from Chocolate's (p146). You may prefer to paddle up the calmer, west side of the island to avoid strong winds and rough seas. There is a visitors/research center and picnic area, and a platform trail through the mangrove forest.

SWALLOW CAYE WILDLIFE SANCTUARY
Southwest of Caye Caulker, the vast **Swallow Caye Wildlife Sanctuary** (☎ 226-0151; www.swallowcayemanatees.org; adult/child BZ$10/5) spans nearly 9000 acres, including Swallow Caye and some parts of nearby Drowned Caye. Here, the ocean floor is covered with turtle grass beds, which support a small population of **West Indian manatees**.

For years, guides have been bringing tourists to this spot, in the hope of catching a glimpse of these gentle creatures as they chow down on the turtle grass. But the constant traffic put stress on the habitat, having the unintended effect of harming the manatees. After tireless efforts on the part of conservationists and guides, a wildlife sanctuary was finally established in 2002.

Now, strict guidelines are in place to protect the manatee and to encourage them to stay in the area. Swimming with manatees is now forbidden by the Belizean authorities and signs have been posted to dissuade boat operators from using their motors near the manatees and from speeding through the area. (Propeller injuries are one of the chief causes of manatee deaths.) There is a permanent caretaker in these waters, although some complain that this is not enough to adequately enforce regulations.

Nonetheless, those who monitor the manatees are encouraged by the increase in numbers at Swallow Caye. Patient visitors are usually rewarded with several sightings of breeching and feeding manatees, often including a mother and calf swimming together.

THE CAYE TO THE STINK

An acrid smell may arise from your bathroom or your freshly laundered clothes. This is from desalinated seawater or ground water, which is used for everything other than bathing, drinking and cooking.

SEA ELEPHANTS

Belonging to a unique group of sea mammals comprising only four species worldwide, manatees are thought to be distantly related to elephants. However, with at least 55 million years separating the two, their kinship is only apparent in a few fairly obscure anatomical similarities and a broadly similar diet. Like elephants, manatees are herbivores and require huge amounts of vegetation each day. Grazing on a wide variety of aquatic plants, a large adult can process as much as 50kg every 24 hours, producing a prodigious amount of waste in the process – fresh floating droppings (similar to a horse's) and almost continuous, bubbling streams of flatulence are useful ways to find them. (Not too appetizing, but it does make them easier to spot.) The best places for a chance to observe manatees are around 'blowing holes' or *sopladeros* (deep hollows where manatees congregate to wait for the high tide).

Manatees are reputed to have excellent hearing, but they're most sensitive to fairly high frequency sounds, such as their squeaking vocalizations. Apparently, the engine of a motorboat is not a high-frequency sound, which means that quiet approaches are often rewarded with good viewing, although sadly it also makes them vulnerable to collisions with motorboats.

Chocolate Heredia was one of the first Caulker fishermen who began ferrying backpackers out to Swallow Caye on his fishing boat. He has also played a crucial role in the establishment of the wildlife sanctuary and continued protection of the sea mammals. **Chocolate's** (☎ 226-0151; chocolate@btl.net; Front St) still leads excellent and informative tours, however sporadically. Other tour operators that take groups to Swallow Caye include **Red Mangrove Eco Adventures** (☎ 226-0069; www.mangrovebelize.com; Front St) and **E-Z Boy** (☎ 226-0349; e-zboytours@yahoo.ca).

Activities

Activity on the island focuses on water sports and sea life.

DIVING

Common dives made from Caye Caulker include two-tank dives to the local reef (BZ$120); two-tank dives in the Hol Chan Marine Reserve area (BZ$160, plus a BZ$20 marine park fee); three dives off Turneffe Atoll (BZ$230 to BZ$300); and three-dive trips to the Blue Hole Natural Monument and Half Moon Caye (BZ$250, plus BZ$80 for park fees). For more information about Turneffe Atoll, Blue Hole and Half Moon Caye, see p156, p157 and p158 respectively.

Recommended dive companies include the following:

Belize Diving Service (☎ 226-0143; www.belize divingservice.com) Professional and highly recommended dive shop that runs PADI certification courses and Advanced Open Water courses. It specializes in excellent trips to Turneffe Elbow, but doesn't go to the Blue Hole.

Big Fish Diving (☎ 226-0450; www.bigfishdivebelize .com; Front St) Caulker's largest dive outfit, offering daily trips to the Blue Hole, as well as outings to Turneffe and other local dives.

Frenchie's Diving (☎ 226-0234; www.frenchiesdiving belize.com) Offers full-day trips (three dives) to Blue Hole and Turneffe and half-day trips (two dives) to Hol Chan, Caye Chapel or Spanish Bay. Night dives at Caye Caulker Marine Reserve cost BZ$100. Promises groups of 10 divers or fewer.

SNORKELING

It is possible to snorkel around the Split and off the pier near the airstrip (see Swimming, p147), but to really experience life under the sea it's necessary to sign up with a tour operator and go out to the reef. Even though it is only a short boat ride offshore, only licensed guides are permitted to take snorkelers out to the reef, which aids in protecting this fragile ecosystem. Most guides are knowledgeable about the reef and adept at spotting and identifying many hidden creatures.

The most popular destination for snorkeling trips is Hol Chan Marine Reserve and Shark Ray Alley (see p126). Half-day trips (BZ$60) leave at 9:30am or 10:30am and 2pm. Full-day tours (BZ$90) include a stop in San Pedro for lunch (not included in the price).

Other half-day snorkeling trips visit the Caye Caulker Marine Reserve (opposite; BZ$50), leaving at 10:30am and 2pm. Destinations include Coral Gardens, the Swoosh (a stand of coral near an opening in the reef where the current and swells attract a good variety of marine life) and **Shark Ray Village**, Caulker's own shark and ray habitat.

FISHING WITH YOUR EYES: CARLOS AYALA   *Mara Vorhees*

Carlos Ayala knows that people come to Caye Caulker to see the reef, and he is more than willing to show them – and teach them. Once a fisherman, he is now a snorkel guide, underwater photographer and jewelry designer. His favorite fish are the nurse shark, queen triggerfish, scrawled filefish and queen parrotfish. And the octopus (but that's a mollusk).

'Even though I am a city boy, I have always loved the sea. I am an earth sign – Taurus – so my opposite is a water sign (Scorpio). Opposites attract. So, I used to be a fisherman, but now I only fish with my eyes.

'Caye Caulker is a small village, but it's growing. An influx of tourism can change the whole island. More hotels mean more people, more restaurants and more fishing, which depletes the reef. Most tourists come to see the reef, but if they eat all the fish, we won't have anything to show them!

'Without proper management, it could be a disaster. Now there is little or no management of the marine reserves. Over-fishing is a real problem due to lack of oversight. For example, there is a new regulation that has increased the minimum size of a lobster tail caught in these waters. But it is the co-op that enforces the rule; the co-op will not accept any lobster tail smaller than 4oz. So what do you think fishers do if they cannot sell their lobster to the co-op? They turn around and sell it directly to a restaurant! There is nothing to stop them doing this, no patrol boats, no other enforcement.

'Many people ask me if my job is dangerous, especially after the Crocodile Hunter, Steve Irwin, was killed by a stingray. I have been bitten by a moray eel. A couple of times I have been nipped by a shark in the midst of a feeding frenzy. But I am not afraid of the animals in the water. I always approach the animals with respect, but I am not afraid.'

Carlos is the owner of Carlos Tours (below), which gives him ample opportunity to photograph the fish.

Some tour operators also take snorkel groups to Turneffe Atoll (p156), a longer trip that promises a more pristine reef and an even greater variety of fish. Dedicated snorkel tours to Blue Hole (p157) and Lighthouse Reef (p157) are rare, although snorkelers are usually welcome to tag along with dive boats (see p145).

All of the tour operators (see p148) take groups snorkeling, as do the sailing companies (right). Specialized snorkel tour operators include the following:

Anwar Snorkel & Tours (☎ 226-0327; liznovelo@ hotmail.com; Front St) Well recommended.
Carlos Tours (☎ 226-0458; carlosayala10@hotmail .com; Front St) Carlos is an accomplished underwater photographer and he offers all of his guests a CD featuring photographs from their snorkel outing. See also the boxed text, above.
Mario's Tours (☎ 226-0056, 602-1773; mariostours@ yahoo.com; Front St)

MANATEE-WATCHING

Tours to monitor the manatees journey to Swallow Caye Wildlife Sanctuary (p144), followed by one or two snorkeling stops and a lunch break at Sergeant's Caye or Goff's Caye. If you didn't have luck spotting manatees in the morning, the boat might return to Swallow Caye in the afternoon to give it another go. Most of Caulker's tour operators can organize this trip for BZ$120 to BZ$130, although the specialist is Lionel 'Chocolate' Heredia, of **Chocolate's** (☎ 226-0151; chocolate@ btl.net; Front St), pioneer of manatee tours and champion of this creature's cause.

SAILING

Several companies organize sailing trips, most of which are organized in a similar fashion to the snorkel tours, visiting two or three different sites – usually Caye Caulker Marine Reserve and Hol Chan Marine Reserve – and stopping somewhere for lunch. The difference is that your journey will be wind powered. In general, the sailboats are large, meaning they can take larger groups than the little motorboats other tour operators might use.

In addition to the snorkeling trips, these companies might offer sunset cruises (BZ$40) and moonlight sailing trips (BZ$60). Island-hopping trips include overnight excursions to Lighthouse Reef or Turneffe Atoll (BZ$556), as well as multiday trips to the southern cayes and Placencia. These tours usually involve one or two nights camping on the beach, as well as plenty of snorkel stops.

Recommended companies:

Raggamuffin Tours (☎ 226-0348; www.raggamuffin
tours.com; Front St) Three-day sailing trips to Placencia
depart every Tuesday and Friday. Raggamuffin has a
reputation as a party boat!

Seahawk Sailing (☎ 607-0323; www.seahawksailing
belize.com; Front St)

SWIMMING

Hurricanes Mitch and Keith in 1998 and 2000
left strips of sand on Caye Caulker where there
once were sea shrubs, and local authorities
have also built up sandy beaches. However,
seagrass is under the water along much of
the shore, which doesn't make for pleasant
wading or swimming. The best swimming
is off the end of the docks that line the east
side of the island. The docks are supposed
to be public, but hotel owners have become
proprietorial, putting up gates to give privacy
to their guests who use the sun lounges and
deck chairs provided.

Caye Caulker's **public beach** is at the northern
end of the village at the Split. It's a popular spot
for both tourists and locals, who drink at the
Lazy Lizard and do cannonballs from the new
diving board. The beach is small and scattered
with debris; sunbathers lounge on a broken
seawall that is crumbling into the ocean. But
the water is cool and clean, thanks to the currents passing through the Split. You can snorkel around here, but beware of boats cruising
through deeper water on the north shore.

If you prefer to catch your rays without
the clamor of crowds, there is a lesser-known
public dock south of town, near the airstrip. The
end of the dock looks like it was wiped out by
one of the hurricanes that passed through, but
there is still plenty of space for sunbathing and
swimming. The water is clear of seagrass, but
fish hover in the shade underneath the dock,
making for decent snorkeling. That said, getting out of the water is a bit precarious. There
is no ladder, so you must wade in through the
foliage or try to climb out onto the dock.

The surf breaks off the shore on the barrier
reef and is easily visible from the eastern shore
of Caye Caulker. Don't attempt to swim out
to it as powerful boats speed through these
waters. Crocodiles live in the waters on the
west side of the island.

WINDSURFING & KITESURFING

With an easterly wind blowing much of the
time, and shallow waters protected by the

barrier reef, Caulker has superb conditions
for these sports, especially between November
and July. To rent equipment or sign up for
lessons, try the following:

Kitexplorer (☎ 623-8403; www.kitexplorer.com; Front
St) Offers a three-hour introductory course or a nine-hour
basic course, as well as equipment rental. Located at the
northern end of the island near the Split.

Michael's Windsurf & Watersports (☎ 226-0452;
www.staycayecaulker.com/wind.html) Rents out long
boards for windsurfing for BZ$40/130/420 per hour/day/
week, while lessons are BZ$80 to BZ$90 per hour. Kitesurfing equipment is BZ$30/90/250 per hour/day/week, or
take a five-hour introductory lesson for BZ$300.

FISHING

Just about any skipper will take you fishing,
and it's cheaper than from Ambergris Caye.
Grand Slams are not unusual (catching permit,
tarpon and bonefish all in one day); other fish
often caught include snook, barracuda, snapper and shark, usually on a catch-and-release
basis. If you venture out for deep-sea fishing,
look for wahoo, sailfish, kingfish, snapper,
grouper, jacks, shark and barracuda.

Half-/full-day fly-fishing or deep-sea
fishing trips for two to three people run at
BZ$400/600. The following operators will take
anglers out for fishing in the deep water, flats
or reef:

Anglers Abroad (☎ 226-0303; www.anglersabroad
.com; Front St)

Big Fish Diving (☎ 226-0450; www.bigfishdivebelize
.com; Front St)

Raggamuffin Tours (☎ 226-0348; www.raggamuffin
tours.com; Front St)

Tsunami Adventures (☎ 226-0462; www.tsunami
adventures.com; Front St)

HIKING, BIKING & BIRDING

The Caye Caulker Forest Reserve (p144) at the
northern end of the island has a short trail that
leads through the mangrove forest. It is an
excellent place to spot water birds, including
rails, stilts and herons, as well as ospreys and
mangrove warblers.

Houses are being built along the coastline
south of the airstrip, but this southern part
of the island is relatively undeveloped, especially in the interior. A rough trail suitable
for hiking or biking follows the perimeter
of the **southern tip**, beginning and ending at
the airstrip. The airstrip itself is flanked on
both sides by swampy marshland, making
it a fantastic place to spot birds, including

GULLS, GULLS, GULLS

While the fish are the main attraction, the northern cayes are also prime real estate for birds. But unless you are a certifiable birder, it can be tricky to know what you are looking at. Here is a primer for the ornithologically challenged.

Level One: stationary, Belikin in hand, chair facing water

Don't get up – there are plenty of opportunities to observe nature from your seat. Check out the aerial acrobatics and fishy give-and-take of the pelicans, frigates, terns and gulls, gulls, gulls. The medium-sized one with the black head and black-tipped wings who won't shut up is the laughing gull.

Everyone knows the pelican (his beak can hold more than his belly can). What you see here are brown pelicans, the smallest and most abundant of the species. They can spot a small fish from 50ft up and their beaks have an elastic sac holding the 3 gallons of water that are gulped in a dive.

Higher up, cruising on the thermals are the magnificent frigate birds. They are more likely to steal a fish from a pelican than catch one themselves. The males are all dark colored, and you might see a red balloon-like growth on their necks – this means they're thinking about something other than fish.

Is that a white heron standing knee-deep in the shallows looking for lunch? If it is tall with a yellow beak and black legs, it's the great egret; if it's smaller with a black beak and black legs with yellow feet, then you're looking at the snowy egret.

Level Two: sea kayak rented, exploratory mission to mangroves

Just north of the Split, on the leeward side, lives a couple of osprey, big birds of prey with white heads and black bodies. They like to hang out on dead tree branches near the water's edge – very photogenic.

---

the killdeer, the black-neck stilt, the common black hawk and herons of all kinds. Be on the lookout for airplanes that fly in and out of here without paying much heed to who or what might be on the airstrip.

Just north of the airstrip, the **Caye Caulker Mini Reserve** is run by the Caye Caulker branch of the BTIA. The small **visitors center** (☎ 226-2251; ⏱ 9am-noon) has information on the island's flora and fauna, while a short interpretative trail (always open) runs through the littoral forest.

SPAS

After swimming, snorkeling and sunning, you may be in need of a little hands-on healing.

Coco Plum Gardens (☎ 226-0226; www.cocoplum .typepad.com; ⏱ 8am-5pm) From chakra balancing and tarot readings to tropical fruit facials and body massages. The octagon-shaped day spa was built from indigenous hardwoods and is set amidst the lush garden of the Coco Plum.

Healing Touch Massage (☎ 206-0080; Front St; ⏱ 9am-5pm) Ms Eva McFarlane can take care of all your beauty and body needs, including manicures and pedicures, Reiki, reflexology and aromatherapy.

Tours

Although most tour operators have their own specialties (see Diving, p145, Snorkeling, p145, and Sailing, p146), many offer similar versions of the same trips. Prices are also similar. Most tour operators work closely together, consolidating tours on slow days and juggling overflow at busier times. Snorkel gear, water and fruit are included in the price of most boat trips.

Aside from the boat tours, some companies also organize trips to the Belizean mainland, including zip-lining, cave-tubing and visiting Maya sites at Lamanai and Altun Ha. For more information on trips to the mainland, see p130.

The following recommended companies are generalists, offering a wide variety of tours by land and sea:

E-Z Boy (☎ 226-0349; e-zboytours@yahoo.ca; Front St)

Red Mangrove Eco Adventures (☎ 226-0069; www .mangrovebelize.com; Front St)

Star Tours (☎ 226-0374; www.startours.bz; Tropics Hotel, Front St)

Tsunami Adventures (☎ 226-0462; www.tsunami adventures.com; Costa Maya Beach Cabanas, Front St)

Now quietly slip into one of the small creeks and study the mangrove edge for shy waders:

- Green heron – seems short for a heron; brown-and-green body with yellow legs. Won't wait for you to focus.
- Tricolored heron – lanky slate-bluish body with white belly, honks as it flies away from your lens.
- Boatbill heron – stouter than the others, with a broad boat-like bill, quietly chilling in the back shade of the undergrowth. You can get its photo but it won't come out very well.
- Yellow-crowned night heron – medium height; cool black-and-white striped head with lilty fringe on top. Not as shy as its feathered friends – you might just get its picture.
- Kingfisher – small bluish-green and white bird, dive-bombing into creeks. A cousin of the woodpecker. Don't even think about shooting.
- White ibis – find an opening in the mangroves that reveals a muddy flat and you might catch a glimpse of these guys hanging out in groups and honking. You might also get a photo of them flying overhead, but you will have to tell your friends what it is.
- Roseate spoonbill – like an ibis, except…it's self-explanatory. They are in there somewhere; good luck finding one.

That was a pretty good bird outing to the mangroves. God knows what those lovely little yellow warbling birds were. Don't you wish you remembered your insect repellant?

Level Three: binoculars around neck, 445-page *Birds of Belize* **book in hand**
Why are you wasting your time reading this box? Book a trip to Half Moon Caye to get up close to the fabulous red-footed, blue-beaked boobies in all their guano-splattered glory.

Festivals & Events

Caulker hosts the original northern cayes' **Lobsterfest**, which kicks off lobster fishing season in the first weekend in July. The streets are filled with punta drumming, Belikin beer and grilled lobster. Other activities include a fishing tournament, canoe races, dance performances and – of course – the Lobster Festival Pageant.

Sleeping

Golf-cart taxis meet boats and flights upon arrival; they will take you around to look at a few places to stay. It's best to book in advance if you're coming at Christmas and Easter.

IN TOWN

As you wander up Front St, you will see that there is an endless array of accommodation options (mostly budget), as local business owners rent out one or two rooms above or behind their shops.

Budget

Bella's Hostel (☎ 226-0360; monkeybite38@yahoo.com; dm/d BZ$20/45; 🖳) On the back side of the island,

Bella's is a hideaway for the backpacker set, who can camp on the shady grounds or snag a bunk bed in the basement dorm. You are likely to see travelers sharing a meal in the kitchen or playing cards on the balcony.

Tina's Backpacker Hostel (☎ 226-0351, 206-0019; www.auxilloubeachsuites.com/tinashome.html; Front St; dm/d BZ$22/45) This fun and funky hostel is just a few steps from the water taxi dock, giving it a prime location in the center of town and at the water's edge. Tina's takes full advantage of its beachfront property, reserving a dock for guests and stringing up hammocks in the leafy garden nearby. Rooms are clean and crowded; the vibe is low-key and laid-back. Shared facilities include a fully equipped kitchen and outdoor showers.

Sandy Lane Guest House (☎ 226-0117; www.toucan trail.com/sandy-lane-guest-house.html; r BZ$40) It doesn't get more basic than this, but the concrete cottages are clean and comfortable, with fans and private bathrooms. The grill-covered windows don't do much for the atmosphere, but at least the place is safe. The rooms are pretty small, so you'll want to take advantage of the pleasant porches, complete with Adirondack chairs, where you can sit back and admire the view of the sandy lane.

Tropics Hotel (☎ 226-0374; www.thetropicshotel.com; Front St; r BZ$40-60, with air-con BZ$100-110; 🌀) You can't miss this citrus-colored concrete block that occupies a prime location between the dock street and the Split. With a shady porch running the length of the building and a big sandy front yard, it's an unbeatable spot to watch the Caye Caulker commotion (or lack thereof). Unfortunately, the sand-colored rooms are bland by comparison, as is the lukewarm reception at the front desk.

Trends Beachfront Hotel (☎ 226-0094; www.trends bze.com; cnr 'dock' & Front Sts; BZ$76-87) Trimmed in pink and blue, Trends is the first place you'll see when you step off the water taxi. With wide porches and vast, shady grounds, it is a fantastic spot for watching the comings and goings on the island (and to the island, and from the island…). Rooms are simple and fresh. They are equipped with two double beds, ceiling fan and minifridge, but not much in the way of decoration. The idea – undoubtedly – is to get outside and enjoy the view!

Mara's Place (☎ 206-0056; www.toucantrail .com/maras-place.html; 27 Front St; d BZ$85; 🌀) The eight guest rooms in this two-story wooden structure are simple but spotless, cramped but comfortable. Not exactly luxurious, they nonetheless include a few perks you would not expect, such as a private veranda, complete with hammock and reading material. The sandy beach is right across the street, where Mara's also has a private dock with lounge chairs and hammocks.

Midrange

Blue Wave (☎ 206-0114; www.toucantrail.com/blue-wave -guest-house.html; Front St; d with shared/private bathroom BZ$40/150; 🌀 ♿) Look for the attractive log cabin–style house overlooking Front St, and you'll know you've arrived at the Blue Wave, an inviting guesthouse with several different accommodation options. 'Deluxe' rooms are spacious and stylish, with air-con, televisions, private bathrooms and breezy balconies overlooking Front St. Beneath the owners' clapboard house, there are three cheaper rooms with shared facilities.

our pick Leeside Rooms (☎ 226-0020; www.caye caulkerrentals.com; r BZ$77-88; 🌀 🖥) Boasting the island's most beautiful sunset view, these simple rooms have small verandas overlooking a private beach and dock. Located on the

back side of the island, there is less noise and less light than on Front St. The stylish interior design features high beds, tile floors and walls hung with old maps. Your welcoming committee includes the very talkative resident parrot, Polly-O.

De Real Macaw Guest House (☎ 226-0459; www.de realmacaw.com; Front St; r BZ$100-140, apt BZ$260; 🌀 🖥) Whether the cabanas built from primenta sticks or the beachfront rooms with thatched-roof verandas, all of the rustic lodgings dotting the leafy grounds here are inspired by the jungle. The decor continues with swinging hammocks and woven tapestries, but these rooms are also equipped with modern conveniences such as TVs, fridges and coffee makers. The main property is in a great central spot opposite the beach; additional apartments are in a less appealing location on Back St.

Costa Maya Beach Cabanas (☎ 226-0432; www.tsu namiadventures.com; Front St; d BZ$110, q with kitchenette BZ$143-154; 🌀 🖥) Eight two-story hexagon-shaped cabanas are clustered around a sandy courtyard here. The wood-paneled interiors of the cheaper units are gloomy but each unit has a porch, perfect for catching sea breezes. The pricier beachfront units are kitted out with kitchenettes, cable TV and air-con. Guests enjoy complimentary bicycles, beach chairs and kayaks, as well as discounts on tours at Tsunami Adventures.

Casa Rosado (☎ 226-0029; www.cayecaulkerrentals .com; cabanas BZ$142-164, cabanas with kitchenette BZ$207; 🌀) Painted in pastels and trimmed with a seashell theme, these sweet cabins occupy a (usually) quiet spot overlooking the soccer field. Each is equipped with a shady porch and a comfy hammock, though they lack the ocean breezes.

Rainbow Hotel (☎ 226-0123; www.rainbowhotel -cayecaulker.com; Front St; d without/with air-con BZ$142/208; 🌀) Bright blue paint, a couple of rainbows for decoration and upgraded rooms make this bunker-like concrete building relatively appealing, but the rooms are cell-sized. Bottom-floor rooms open right onto the street; some folks sit on a chair out front and enjoy the street life. For privacy, choose a room on the top floor or rent one of the cottages (BZ$460 to BZ$550 for up to four people) at the back.

Barefoot Caribe (☎ 226-0161; www.barefootcaribe resort.com; Front St; r/ste BZ$145/186; 🌀) A big blue building trimmed in white, Barefoot Caribe is an attractive and affordable place to crash. Rooms are sparse but spotless, with white-washed walls and cool tile floors. Handy features such as fridge and fan are appreciated, as is the open-air deck upstairs. Note that the 'sea view' rooms have their view partially blocked by buildings across the street.

Pancho's Villas (☎ 226-0304; www.panchosvillasbelize .com; Pasero St; d BZ$186; ✖ 💻) Resembling a big square wedding cake with lemon-yellow frosting, Pancho's Villas is a little out of place on this quiet side street. The brand new building is decked out with all the modern amenities such as kitchenettes, cable TV and the rest. Big on comfort and convenience, but small on style and sophistication.

Amanda's Place (☎ 226-0029; www.cayecaulker rentals.com; Front St; r from BZ$198; ✖ 💻 💱) The owner is the energy behind Caye Caulker Rentals. Besides renting out other people's houses, Amanda offers two art-filled apartments with kitchenettes and a cozy casita of her own. Only a block back from the beach, the grounds are leafy and the attractive apartments each have a little porch from where you can watch street life and see the ocean.

Top End

Caye Caulker Condos (☎ 226-0072; www.cayecaulker condos.com; Front St; ste BZ$230-272; ✖ 💻) While the concrete block is not the most attractive building on Front St, the eight swanky suites inside are sweet retreats. Each is equipped with a full kitchen, satellite TV, and fancy bathrooms with romantic, stone, two-person showers. Suites each have a private balcony, but the rooftop terrace trumps them all with its 360-degree views, taking in part of the North Island.

Seaside Cabanas (☎ 226-0498; www.seasidecabanas .com; r BZ$230, cabanas BZ$262; ✖ 💻 💱) Sun-yellow stucco buildings shaded by thatched-palm roofs exude a tropical atmosphere at this beachfront beauty. The interior decor features desert colors, rich fabrics and plenty of pillows. Most of the rooms occupy the main building facing the ocean; closer to the sea, concrete cabanas hold further high-quality lodgings with big comfy beds and cable TV.

Jan's Place (☎ 226-0273; www.jansplace.net; Front St; ste BZ$250; ✖ 💻) This charming yellow clapboard house has two self-contained apartments facing the sea (private porches with hammocks ensure maximum appreciation of this gorgeous view). They contain kitchenettes, dining area, two full-sized beds and wood furniture – not fancy but very functional.

our pick **Iguana Reef Inn** (☎ 226-0213; www.iguana reefinn.com; standard r BZ$260-270, deluxe r BZ$300-320, all incl breakfast; ✖ 💻 💱) Set on sandy grounds fringed with palms, the Iguana Reef is both upscale and informal. It's the kind of place you can roam around barefoot by day, but you might dress up for dinner. Bamboo furniture, Mexican tapestries and local artwork adorn the jewel-toned rooms. Outside, you can lounge poolside or swing in a hammock; at the end of the day, take your pick from the extensive menu of tropical cocktails in the *palapa* bar and watch the sunset.

Auxillou Suites (☎ 226-0370; www.auxilloubeach suites.com; ste BZ$270; ✖ 💻) Steps from the sea, Auxillou is one in a string of florescent-colored houses just north of the water taxi dock. These modern suites offer excellent value, with king-size beds, cable TV, kitchenettes and spacious decks.

You'll get a similar deal next door at **Diane's Beach House** or **Sailwind's Beach Suites** (☎ 226-0826; www.staycayecaulker.com), which are also owned by the Auxillou family.

SOUTH OF TOWN

South of the cemetery, Caye Caulker is noticeably quieter and the beach sees much less foot traffic. Almost all of the accommodations south of town are in the midrange price bracket.

our pick **Ignacio Beach Cabins** (☎ 226-0175; reyes reubbenreyes@yahoo.com; d BZ$27-45, ste BZ$110) In the far south of town, Ignacio offers simple waterfront lodging in weathered cabins on stilts. There is little foot traffic this far south, so it feels private and pristine. The cabins all have easy access to the beach, but the pricier ones are at the water's edge, catching cool breezes and salty scents. If you like the location but not the rusticity, spring for the spacious suite, with stylish furnishings and a breezy balcony.

Tom's Hotel (☎ 226-0102; www.toucantrail.com /toms-hotel.html; d with shared bathroom BZ$30, cabanas BZ$60; ✖) Owned by a local fisher family, this trim hotel south of the cemetery has long been a budget favorite, thanks to the private pier, rooftop deck and always affable management. The cheapest rooms are in the concrete building, with a wide shady verandah to meet your fellow travelers and enjoy the sea breeze. Otherwise, upgrade to the cozy cabanas with private facilities.

Tropical Paradise Hotel (☎ 226-0124; www.tropical paradisehotel.com; Front St; r BZ$90-113, cabins BZ$130-155,

---

NORTH OF THE SPLIT

On Punta Arena Beach, surrounded by mangrove forests and a large lagoon, the **ourpick** **Driftwood Lodge** (Map p121; ☎ 626-2925; www.driftwood.bz; d incl breakfast BZ$250-355, mains BZ$40, cocktails BZ$15; ☺ restaurant 11am-10pm Tue-Sun) is the only place to stay or eat north of the Split. There are three exquisite cabins, each named for the local hardwood used to construct it (machiche, bullet tree and chechem). Nature is highlighted throughout, with slate countertops, polished wood floors, plenty of sunlight and sea breezes. Cathedral ceilings and private porches facing the sea ensure a constant flow of cool air into the space. The best part is that the place is solar powered, while rainwater supplies the bathrooms and showers.

Even if you're not staying here, it's worth catching the boat shuttle (BZ$10; departs from the pier opposite Chocolate's) or kayaking up for lunch or dinner. The gorgeous two-story restaurant has beautiful views of the ocean and lagoon, not to mention a constantly changing menu of seafood and other delicacies. Once a month, this lodge hosts a full-moon party, with Garifuna drummers and bonfires on its little beach.

---

ste BZ$202-238; ⊠) With an ideal location just south of the cemetery, Tropical Paradise Hotel is Caulker's 'original beach resort.' It was one of the first places to clean out a stretch of sand, furnish it with painted lounge chairs and entice guests with fruity cocktails. These days there are plenty of more stylish places to stay, but these colorful clapboard cottages still offer decent value. The restaurant is a perennially popular place for guests to meet.

Jaguar Morning Star (☎ 226-0347; www.jaguar morningstar.com; r BZ$98-115; ⊠) From his perch inside the mural on the side of the building, a friendly jaguar overlooks the quiet garden and the schoolyard next door. Run by a gracious Belizean-Canadian couple, this little guesthouse has only three rooms in total, two on the top floor of the three-story house, and one cabana in the garden. Amenities are comfortable, and the position, a few blocks back from the beach and a few blocks south of the dock street, is improved by renting a bicycle.

Maxhapan Cabanas (☎ 226-0118; maxhapan04@ hotmail.com; s/d incl breakfast BZ$100/120; ⊠) In an unexpected location south of town, Maxhapan has sweet yellow cabanas clustered around a shady courtyard. At its center, a big *palapa* has hammocks and a bring-your-own bar, where guests can gather. Natural light floods the comfortable cabins, which are equipped with fridges, fans and televisions. The only drawback is that it's not on the water, which explains why it's such a bargain.

Tree Tops Guesthouse (☎ 226-0240; www.tree topsbelize.com; r with shared/private bathroom from BZ$102/131, ste BZ$200; ⊠ ▦) Doris and Terry are hospitable and helpful, but they sure run a tight ship. Once you have the rules down,

you will enjoy cool, clean rooms decorated with international themes and original artistic touches. Set back from the beach, the three-story building is fronted by a pleasant palm-shaded garden. A roof terrace with panoramic vistas towers over the treetops, which gives the place its name.

Sea Beezzz (☎ 226-0176; www.seabeezzz.com; d BZ$109; ☺ Nov-Apr) Chuck and Bonnie Balfour are a fun-loving couple that rents out quaint clapboard cabins on stilts. Small and very simply furnished, the cabins are clustered around a sandy yard, the centerpiece of which is a flourishing orchid tree (come in December to see it in full bloom). Bonnie is your chef, Chuck is your bartender, and your job is to sit back and enjoy.

Shirley's Guest House (☎ 226-0145; www.shirleys guesthouse.com; r with shared/private bathroom BZ$109/142, cabins with private bathroom BZ$188) At the far end of the island, just north of the airstrip, is this sweet and secluded spot for adults only. Five rooms are housed in the cottages that dot the sandy grounds, each with a sensational sunrise view. The dock out front would be ideal for swimming, but it was falling into the sea at the time of research. Otherwise, the grounds are lush and lovingly maintained. Be sure to make advance arrangements as the proprietor is not always on hand.

ourpick **Barefoot Beach Belize** (☎ 226-0205; www .barefootbeachbelize.com; r BZ$144-165, ste BZ$270, cottages BZ$303; ⊠ ▦) Painted in candy colors, this perky place is on a quiet stretch of beach at the southern end of the village. Suites and cottages have kitchens and living space, with direct access to beach breezes; rooms are smaller but still spacious, with fridges, fans and coffee makers. The whole place has a tropical theme, with plenty of floral prints and sea-themed artwork. Hammocks hang under a thatched-roof *palapa* at the end of a long deck, offering a perfect place to while away an afternoon.

Anchorage Resort (☎ 206-0304; www.anchorage resort.com; d BZ$164; ✂) This is not the place to come for style or swank, but if you're in search of a hammock strung from a coconut palm or a wooden pier stretching out to the sea for swimming, snorkeling or fishing, look no further. With floral bedspreads and dormitory furniture, the rooms are not going to win any design awards, but they are equipped with plenty of perks, such as king-size beds, cable TV and private balconies with glorious sea views. The resort boasts one of the most beautiful stretches of beach on the island (nonguests can rent a lounge chair for BZ$10 per day).

Lazy Iguana (☎ 226-0350; www.lazyiguana.net; d BZ$230; ✂ 💻) On the island's southwest side, this place is off the beaten track and away from the beach. But you won't miss out on sea views: just head up to the rooftop patio for 360-degree panoramas. The four guest rooms – fitted with dark wood furniture and tile floors – are prettily decorated in tones of gold, sage and cream. Common space includes two cool and comfy lounges, as well as a leafy garden overflowing with orchids.

The back streets at the south end of town are known as 'Gringo Heights,' for this is where many expats have bought property and built houses. With names such as 'Hummingbird Hideaway' and 'Canuck Cottage,' many of them are available for longer-term rentals (three days or more) via **Caye Caulker Rentals** (www.cayecaulkerrentals.com).

The following properties offer apartments (bedroom, living space, kitchen) that are modern, clean and comfortable:

Oasi (☎ 623-9401; www.holidaybelize.com; Ave Mangle; apt BZ$160; ✂ 💻) Set around a tropical garden.

Picololo (☎ 226-0371, 662-5337; http://picololo .googlepages.com; apt BZ$150; ✂) Includes complimentary use of bike.

Eating

Indulge in the creatures of the sea, including spiny tail lobsters, shrimp, conch and all the fish of the reef. Seafood lovers take note: lobster season is closed from mid-February to mid-June, and conch season is closed from July to September.

BUDGET

Glenda's Café (☎ 226-0148; Back St; mains BZ$4-8; ✂ breakfast & lunch Mon-Fri) Glenda's serves traditional Belizean food in a clapboard house on the island's west side. It has the best cheap breakfasts in town, from cinnamon rolls and orange juice to full breakfasts of eggs, bacon or ham, bread and coffee. Burritos, tacos, sandwiches and chicken with rice and beans are offered for lunch. Get there early for breakfast.

our pick Amor Y Café (☎ 601-1458; Front St; mains BZ$8-12; ✂ breakfast Tue-Sun) There's no contest about the most popular breakfast spot on the island. It's always busy, but you won't have to wait long for a table on the shaded porch overlooking Front St. Take your pick from fresh-squeezed juices, scrambled eggs or homemade yogurt topped with fruit, but don't miss out on the fresh-brewed coffee. If you have to pack a lunch, sandwiches are available to go.

Rosa's Café (☎ 226-0407; dock st; mains BZ$8-16; ✂ breakfast, lunch & dinner) This friendly streetside café has an inviting *palapa* out the back, where you can feast on grilled lobster and other fruits of the sea.

Marin's Restaurant (☎ 226-0104; Middle St; mains BZ$10-20; ✂ breakfast & dinner, bar open all day) Dine in the open air at treetop level on hearty Belizean fare, seafood dishes and more at Marin's, one of the oldest restaurants on the island. There is nothing too creative about this cooking, but it is filling and cheap.

If you want a quick breakfast to go, stop by the **Caye Caulker Bakery** (Middle St; ✂ 7:30am-noon & 2-7pm Mon-Sat) to pick up fresh bread, rolls and buns (baked goods cost under BZ$2).

MIDRANGE

Rainbow Grill & Bar (☎ 226-0281; mains BZ$8-30; ✂ lunch & dinner Tue-Sun) Perched on a deck over the turquoise waters, this local favorite is evidence of Caulker's agreeable temperatures. By day, nibble on vegetarian plates, burgers, quesadillas, burritos and sandwiches. At night fancier fare includes fish, shrimp, conch and lobster cooked how you like it, from simple lemon with butter to Jamaican jerk or oriental style.

our pick Bamboo Grill (☎ 607-1514; mains BZ$15-25; ✂ lunch & dinner) Arguably the best location on the island, this casually cool bar and grill sits right on the beach, with swings hanging from the rafters and tables set up in the sand. Besides the Cajun specialties, you can feast on a huge seafood burrito or a delectable grilled fish sandwich, washed down with a fruit smoothie.

Syd's (☎ 206-0294; Middle St; mains BZ$15-30; ☺ lunch & dinner Mon-Sat) Syd's is a longstanding favorite for its good-value meals and convivial atmosphere. Out back, there is a flower-filled patio, where you can dine to the soothing sounds of a gurgling fountain. Otherwise, the dining room is rather nondescript. No matter where you sit, you will be sated by the big plates of Belizean and Mexican food.

Happy Lobster (☎ 226-0064; Front St; mains BZ$18-30; ☺ breakfast, lunch & dinner Fri-Wed) The lobster at this Caulker institution is actually not that happy. But you will be after eating big plates of fresh fish, spiced up with Creole flavoring or sweetened with coconut. The place has plenty of vegetarian options, as well as a popular breakfast menu. The front porch is a pleasant place to catch the breeze off the ocean and watch the activity on Front St.

Barrier Reef Sports Bar & Grill (☎ 226-0077; www .belizesportsbar.com; Front St; mains BZ$18-30; ☺ 9am-midnight; ☐) This unlikely spot – Canadian run – has surprisingly delicious food and good prices. And not just pub grub (although that's good, too); you won't be disappointed by lasagna, burritos, seafood specials and salads. Service is nonchalant, at best. If you don't like the multiple TVs blaring sports interviews into the atmosphere, take a seat out front and enjoy the breeze off the ocean.

Rasta Pasta Rainforest Café (☎ 206-0356; Front St; mains BZ$20-30; ☺ breakfast, lunch & dinner Thu-Tue) No longer located on the beach, Rasta Pasta is still serving up its extensive menu of seafood, veggie dishes, desserts and fruity cocktails. The always affable service is a highlight, as is the home-brewed ginger beer, a delectable concoction that cures all stomach woes. Note that – despite the name – there are not many pasta dishes on the menu.

Coco Plum Gardens (☎ 226-0226; mains BZ$20-30; ☺ breakfast Mon-Sat) The highlight of the Coco Plum is the beautiful garden setting, overgrown with hibiscus, sea grape and coco plum (spot the ceiba tree at the entrance). Off Back St near the airstrip, Coco Plum is off the beaten track but worth the walk for home-baked breads and wholesome breakfasts. From 6pm to 9pm on Friday or Saturday nights, it sometimes hosts a tropical garden party (mains BZ$25 to BZ$40), with live acoustic music or drumming.

TOP END

Don Corleone (☎ 226-0025; Front St; breakfast dishes US$7, mains BZ$30-50; ☺ lunch & dinner) One of Caulker's unexpected gems, Don Corleone is Dutch owned and Italian flavored. Decor is sophisticated and the service impeccable. Whatever you order lives up to management's promise to make you a meal you can't refuse, be it one of the gorgeous salads, a pasta with an aromatic sauce or a more substantial fish or meat main. Finish off with an excellent strong espresso.

our pick **Agave** (☎ 226-0403; Front St; mains BZ$25-40; ☺ lunch & dinner) This new super-suave place has a prime location on Front St, with a wide porch overlooking the traffic. The sophisticated menu has a selection of seafood dishes that blends Caribbean and Mediterranean influences, utilizing fresh fruits and local spices. Service can be a bit slow – all the more time to savor the flavors and enjoy the view.

Habaneros (☎ 226-0487; cnr Front St & dock st; mains BZ$25-50; ☺ dinner Fri-Wed) Caulker's 'hottest' restaurant, named for the *habanero* chili, is located in a brightly painted clapboard house in the center of town. Here chefs prepare gourmet international food, combining fresh seafood, meat and vegetables with insanely delicious sauces and flavors. Wash it down with a fine wine or a jug of sangria. Sit in the funky bar and sip a fruity cocktail or enjoy the buzz and eat by candlelight at the tables on the verandah. Reservations are recommended.

Drinking & Entertainment

Femi's Coffee Shop (Luciano Reyes St; ☺ 7am-late) Femi's is a coffee shop and so much more. By all means, come here for your morning dose of caffeine – perhaps in the form of fresh-brewed Belizean coffee or a frozen coffee mocha. Come in the afternoon for a fruit smoothie or an energy shake. And if you need a shot of something extra, take your pick from the vast menu of frozen fruity cocktails. Prime waterfront spot!

I&I Reggae Bar (☎ 625-0344; ☺ 6pm-midnight) I&I is the island's most hip-hop happening spot after dark, when its healthy sound system belts out a reggae beat. Its three levels each offer a different scene, with a dance floor on one and swings hanging from the rafters on another. The top floor is the 'chill-out zone,' complete with hammocks and panoramic views. Great place for a sunset drink.

Lazy Lizard (☎ 226-0280; the Split; ☽ 11am-11pm)
The Lazy Lizard is described as a 'sunny place
for shady people' – and there is no shortage
of the latter hanging about. It mainly serves
beer to swimmers and sunbathers, but has
some food items as well.

Sand Box (☎ 226-0200; Front St; ☽ 8am-late) With
outdoor seating facing the dock, and a happy
hour from 3pm to 6pm, the Sand Box is an
island institution. Locals and expats gather to
socialize and catch up on gossip. If you can't
check into your hotel straight away, make this
your first stop coming off the water taxi.

Wish Willy's Bar & Grill (☽ 5pm-late) This funky
place is named for a scaly tailed iguana. On
the back side of the island, it's a great place
to watch the sunset, whether you're sipping a Belikin beer or feasting on the day's
BBQ special.

Herbal Tribe (Front St; ☽ 11am-late) A large
open-air restaurant and hip reggae joint
with great pizzas. Happy hour (6pm to 8pm)
fills the place with merry folks drinking
and chatting.

Shopping

Caulker has a few shops selling T-shirts, beach
gear and souvenirs, but this is not the best
place for shopping. Keep your eye out for
colorful paintings and handmade jewelry by
local artists.

Caribbean Colors (☎ 206-0208; www.caribbean-colors
.com; Front St) This shop stocks a collection of
silk-screened fabrics, jewelry and paintings
by the owner Lee Vanderwalker and the artist
Nelson Young. You'll also find a small selection of homemade soaps and body oils made
from natural products, as well as a friendly
coffee counter.

Chocolate's Gift Shop (☎ 226-0151; Front St)
Chocolate's wife Annie has souvenirs with
international flare: gorgeous hand-woven
textiles from Mexico and Guatemala; sarongs and clothing from Indonesia and
Malaysia; and jewelry made from precious
and semiprecious stones.

Coco Plum Giftshop (☎ 226-0226; www.cocoplum
.typepad.com) Sometimes a spa and sometimes a
restaurant, the Coco Plum is also – sometimes –
a gift shop. There is an eclectic assortment of
tropical-themed paintings, unique jewelry,
carved wood pieces and reference books on
natural healing.

Cooper's Art Gallery (☎ 226-0330; Front St; ☽ noon-
8pm Wed-Sun) Debbie Cooper's primitive paint-

ing style is a huge hit with tourists, who
appreciate her colorful depictions of island
life. The whimsical frames are designed and
painted by her husband.

Getting There & Away

AIR

Both **Maya Island Air** (☎ 226-0012; www.maya
airways.com) and **Tropic Air** (☎ 226-0040; www.tropicair
.com) stop at Caye Caulker en route from San
Pedro (adult/child BZ$61/46) to Belize City
International Airport (one-way BZ$109).
Each company has flights four or five times a
day. The airline offices are at Caye Caulker's
newly renovated airstrip. **Tsunami Adventures**
(☎ 226-0462; www.tsunamiadventures.com; Front St) can
also book tickets.

BOAT

Caye Caulker Water Taxi Association (☎ 226-0992;
www.cayecaulkerwatertaxi.com) runs boats from
the main dock on Caulker to Belize City
(one-way/round-trip BZ$15/30, one hour)
at 6:30am, 7:30am, 8:30am, 10am, noon,
1:30pm, 3pm and 4pm (and 5pm Saturday,
Sunday and holidays). Boats to San Pedro
(one-way/round-trip BZ$15/30, 20 to 30 min-
utes) go at 7am, 8:45am, 9:50am, 11:20am,
12:50pm, 2:20pm and 3:50pm.

Water taxis also run to St George's Caye
and Caye Chapel, but you must request these
stops and arrange pick-up in advance.

Getting Around

Caulker is so small that most people walk
everywhere. If need be, you can rent a bicycle
or golf cart at **M&M Rentals** (☎ 226-0229; bicycles per
hr/day/week BZ$4/15/60, golf carts per hr/day BZ$30/100).
The golf-cart **Rainbow Taxi Service** (☎ 226-0123;
Front St) costs BZ$10 for a one-way trip any-
where on the island.

OTHER NORTHERN CAYES

Most visits to the other northern cayes are
made by day trip from Caye Caulker or San
Pedro, usually as part of a trip to snorkel or
dive the Turneffe Elbow or the world-famous
Blue Hole. But you can stay on a number of
the smaller and outlying islands if you don't
mind being stranded on an otherwise deserted
island. Serious divers and fishers, nature lovers and honeymooners are the most common
customers at the camps and resorts on these
cayes, which are generally available as weekly
(or partial-week) all-inclusive packages.

Transportation by charter boat or flight is usually provided by the lodge; inquire about transportation when you book.

Cayo Espanto

Billed as 'A Private Island,' the ultra sumptuous **Cayo Espanto** (☎ in USA 888-666-4282, 910-323-8355; www.aprivateisland.com; villas incl all meals from BZ$2688; ⚇ 💻 🏊) resort has six delightful villas (total capacity 16), each designed for maximum privacy and panoramic views. Each casa is ridiculously decked out, with king-size beds dressed in high-thread-count designer sheets and draped in mosquito netting. Each one also has a private dock *and* a private plunge pool, and – in some cases – an alfresco shower. The most unusual option is Casa Ventanas, which is perched out at the end of a long dock, surrounded by 360 degrees of crystal blue loveliness.

One of the highlights of staying at Cayo Espanto is the exceedingly attentive service (all packages include the services of a personal house attendant). Prior to arrival, guests are invited to fill out a preferences survey, which is used to prepare for all aspects of the visit, including the menu. Chefs create artistic dishes according to your personal tastes and serve them in the privacy of your villa.

Cayo Espanto is three miles west of Ambergris Caye. It's not uncommon for celebrities to frequent this 'Private Island,' which has hosted the likes of Robert De Niro, Harrison Ford and Tiger Woods. Leonardo DiCaprio loved it so much that he bought neighboring **Blackadore Caye** to build his own environmentally friendly island resort. Stay tuned.

Caye Chapel

Just south of Caye Caulker, **Caye Chapel Island Resort** (☎ 226-8250, in USA 800-901-8938; www.cayechapel.com; casitas from BZ$750, villas from BZ$2500; ⚇ 💻 🏊) is a private 265-acre island with an 18-hole golf course and a super-deluxe corporate retreat center. Room rates include all meals and unlimited golfing. The golf course (☎ 226-8250) is open to the public by reservation. The cost is BZ$300 for the day, which includes unlimited golf, golf carts, clubs, poolside Caribbean lunch and use of the resort's swimming pool complex, hot tub and private beach. Arrange boat transportation in advance with boats going to/from San Pedro or Caye Caulker with the Caye Caulker Water Taxi Association (p155).

Turneffe Atoll

Belize is home to three of the four coral atolls in the Western Hemisphere: Lighthouse Reef (opposite); Glover's Reef (p76); and Turneffe Atoll, the largest of the offshore trio and the closest to the Belize coastline. The Turneffe Islands Atoll is the largest of the offshore trio and the closest to the Belize coastline. At 30 miles long and 10 miles wide, Turneffe Atoll is alive with coral, fish and large rays, making it a prime destination for **diving**, **snorkeling** and **fishing**.

This area is dominated by mangrove islands. Mangroves are what make Belize diving special, as they are the nurseries on which almost all marine life depends to ensure juvenile protection and biological productivity.

Although the atoll is best known for its walls, there are also many shallow sea gardens and bright sand flats inside the reef that are excellent sites for novice divers and snorkelers.

Undoubtedly, the highlight of Turneffe Islands diving is a spot called the **Turneffe Elbow**, where the current attracts big hungry fish in large numbers and affords one of the only drift dives in Belize. Other sites include **Front Porch**, in front of the Turneffe Island Lodge; **Myrtle's Turtle**, named for the resident green turtle that appears annually; and **Triple Anchor**, marked by three anchors remaining from a wreck. See p74 for more on diving in this region. Fishing enthusiasts are attracted by the flats, which are ideal for saltwater fly-fishing.

Turneffe Atoll is usually visited by day trip, as it's within easy reach of Caulker, Ambergris and Belize City to the north, and Glover's Reef and Hopkins village to the south. Even Placencia dive boats occasionally make the trip to Turneffe Elbow, at the southern tip of the islands. On rough days it's favored by San Pedro dive operators (p126), because much of the trip can be made behind the barrier reef, protecting passengers from choppy open seas.

Incredibly, the Turneffe Islands have as yet no environmental protection. However, Belize University's Institute of Marine Studies monitors environmental impacts from a field station on Calabash Caye.

SLEEPING & EATING

The lodging available on the Turneffe Islands is at all-inclusive resorts, which usually include diving, snorkeling and/or fishing tours for a minimum of one week.

Turneffe Flats Lodge (☎ 220-2046; www.tflats.com; Blackbird Caye; weekly diving/fishing packages BZ$2696/7986; 🕸) Although its principal fame is as a fishing retreat with expert guides, this lodge also offers dive trips that are often far less crowded than those from other resorts (because most of the other guests are out fishing). Accommodations are in spacious, terracotta-tiled duplex apartments, each with balcony and dramatic views of the waves crashing on the nearby reef. As a bonus, guests can feel assured that at least some of their money is going to a good cause, as Turneffe Flats Lodge donates 1% of its revenues to organizations that are working to promote conservation.

Oceanic Society (☎ 220-4256; www.oceanic-society .org; Blackbird Caye; weekly research programs from BZ$3780) The society has a field station about five minutes' walk from Blackbird Caye Resort. Accommodations here are in basic but comfortable white, wooden beachfront cabanas with private porches. Participants spend eight days helping with natural history research, collecting data and documenting the incredibly diverse wildlife (manatees, crocodiles, bottle-nosed dolphins and hawksbill sea turtles among others) that lives in the Turneffe Islands. Special family-education programs are worthwhile.

Blackbird Caye Resort (☎ 223-2772; www.blackbird resort.com; Blackbird Caye; weekly diving/fishing/snorkeling packages BZ$4230/5630/3830; 🕸) Blackbird offers fishing and diving as well, but is popular with snorkelers as it has two dedicated snorkeling boat trips per day. Enthusiasts can kayak out to the reef for even more snorkeling. Accommodations are in separate roomy cabanas with stereo systems, and meals are eaten in a huge *palapa* restaurant near the main dock.

Turneffe Island Lodge (☎ 220-4142, in USA 800-874-0118; www.turneffelodge.com; Caye Bokel; weekly fishing/diving/beachcomber packages BZ$10,340/5940/5060; 🕸 🕸) At the southern tip of the atoll, the fanciest of the Turneffe resorts offers gorgeous cabanas with screened porches (where your morning coffee will be delivered), wooden floorboards, and indoor and outdoor showers, all set amid coconut palms just yards from the beach. Proximity to the famous Elbow dive site means trips go there frequently; some of the best tarpon fishing is a three-minute

boat ride away. What's more, you can fish at the Turneffe Island Lodge with a clear conscience, as the fishing schedule operates according to a rigorous flats conservation and management program.

Lighthouse Reef

At 50 miles out, Lighthouse Reef is the furthest of the three atolls from the coastline. But it is probably the most visited, thanks to the allure of the mysterious Blue Hole Natural Monument (below). While this icon of Belize diving makes the atoll a major attraction, it is the stunning walls, heavily adorned with swim-throughs and clear blue water that make it a favorite of both longtime divers and complete novices.

Besides the Blue Hole, there is no shortage of fantastic dive sites, as well as a spectacular stop for bird enthusiasts. In addition to what follows, other sites in Lighthouse Reef include **Painted Wall**, named for the plethora of painted tunicates found here; the **Aquarium**, often visited as a second stop after Blue Hole; and the **Cathedral**, known for its amazing variety of sponges. **Half Moon Caye Wall** is probably the best of the lot for its variety of coral formations along the wall, and within canyons and swim-throughs. Of particular interest is a field of garden eels found on the sand flats near the wall. Snorkelers don't despair: the shallows around these sites are interesting as well. For more on diving and snorkeling at Lighthouse Reef, see p75.

In addition to Half Moon Caye (p158) and Long Caye (p158), other islands in the atoll include Northern Caye, Sandbore Caye, Saddle Caye and Hat Caye. Northern Caye is a small but lovely island, home to **Lighthouse Reef Resort** (www.scubabelize.com), which was closed at the time of research, while the others are popular with mosquitoes and crocodiles.

BLUE HOLE

At the center of Lighthouse Reef is the world-famous **Blue Hole Natural Monument** (marine fee BZ$80). The Blue Hole is an incomparable natural wonder and an unparalleled diving experience. It may not be the best dive in Belize, but it certainly ranks among the most popular. The image of the Blue Hole – a deep blue pupil with an aquamarine border surrounded by the lighter shades of the reef – has become a logo for tourist publicity and a symbol of Belize.

NORTHERN CAYES

MAKING OF A BLUE HOLE

A Unesco World Heritage site and a Belizean Natural Monument, the celebrated sinkhole is around 400ft deep and 1000ft across. To dive it is to take a journey back into geological history. For millions of years the Blue Hole was a dry cave where huge stalactites and stalagmites slowly formed. When the last ice age ended, sea levels rose 350ft, flooding the cave. At the same time, its ceiling collapsed, leaving the hole you see today.

Inside a sheer-sided wall drops about 100ft to an undercut filled with stalactites. Deep blue in the center the hole forms a perfect 1000ft-diameter circle on the surface. Inside, it is said to be 430ft deep, but as much as 200ft of this may now be filled with silt and other natural debris.

You drop quickly to 130ft where you swim beneath an overhang, observing stalactites above you and, usually, a school of reef sharks below you. You might see four or five varieties of shark. Although the water is clear, light levels are low as you wend your way through the formations. A good dive light will enable you to appreciate the sponge and invertebrate life. Because of the depth, ascent begins after eight minutes; the brevity of the dive does disappoint some divers.

This trip is usually combined with other dives at Lighthouse Reef. Experienced divers will tell you that those other dives are the real highlight of the trip. But judging from its popularity – most dive shops make twice-weekly runs to the Blue Hole – plenty want to make the deep descent.

On day trips the Blue Hole will be your first dive, which can be nerve-racking if you're unfamiliar with the dive master and the other divers, or if you haven't been underwater lately. It may be worth doing some local dives with your dive masters before setting out cold on a Blue Hole trip. An alternative is to take an overnight trip to Lighthouse Reef. For dive outfits and tour details see p126 and p145.

Snorkelers can enjoy a trip to the Blue Hole, too, as there's plenty to see around the shallow inner perimeter of the circular reef. But it's an expensive trip and you'll probably have to tag along on a dive boat.

Note: this trip involves two hours each way by boat in possibly rough, open waters. Also, there's a BZ$80 marine-park fee for diving or snorkeling at the Blue Hole, usually separate from the dive fees.

HALF MOON CAYE
Nesting ground of the rare red-footed booby, this island is the **Half Moon Caye Bird Sanctuary** (park fee BZ$20). It is the most oft-visited of the Lighthouse Reef's cayes.

The caye has a **lighthouse**, excellent **beaches** and spectacular submerged walls teeming with marine flora and fauna. Underwater visibility can extend more than 200ft here.

Rising less than 10ft above sea level, the caye's 45 acres hold two distinct ecosystems. To the west is lush vegetation fertilized by the droppings of thousands of sea birds, including some 4000 red-footed boobies, the magnificent frigate bird and 98 other bird species. The east side has less vegetation but more palms. Loggerhead and hawksbill sea turtles, both endangered, lay their eggs on the southern beaches.

A **nature trail** weaves through the southern part of the island to an observation platform that brings viewers to eye level with nesting boobies and frigate birds. Along the path you'll see thousands of seashells, many inhabited by hermit crabs.

Organized boat trips, mainly from San Pedro and Caye Caulker, stop at Half Moon Caye on their way to/from the nearby Blue Hole. Camping is sometimes permitted and there is a picnic area and toilets, but you need to bring all your water. The Belize Audubon Society has a visitors center where you must register and pay a BZ$20 park fee on arrival. This part of the island is also used as a base camp for kayaking, snorkeling and diving holidays by adventure-tour company Island Expeditions (see p78).

LONG CAYE
The contemporary version of a hippy commune, **Long Beach at Lighthouse Reef** (☎ 223-2077; www.belizeisland.com) is an idyllic private island, 2.5 miles long and 3.25 miles wide, with white sandy beaches and plentiful coconut palms. It has been earmarked as an ecovillage, with strict eco-guidelines for anyone who wants to purchase property. The idea is to build using materials that are collected on site; to utilize alternative sources of energy, such as solar

and hydro; to minimize waste by recycling and composting; to minimize the impact of human presence on the local ecosystem; and to demonstrate that development can be managed in a sustainable way.

This is a project in progress, but there are already a couple of places to stay, a medical center with a decompression chamber, some houses and a couple of docks. Boardwalks, many already built, are to be used around the island to protect the wildlife underneath. Package prices include transfer from Belize City; otherwise, make arrangements for boat transport with your lodge (BZ$360).

The **Lighthouse Reef Cabins** (☎ in USA 703-297-1571; www.lighthousereef.net; 3-day diver/non-diver packages BZ$2090/1100 Lucky Dog Cabin per week BZ$4900, all incl meals; ☐) are simple beachfront cabins furnished with queen-size beds, as well as single bunks if you want to bring the family. The kitchen is fully equipped, and a boat (and captain) is at your disposal. The latter includes a 26ft console boat and captain who acts as your guide. For groups (up to six), the Lucky Dog Cabin is an excellent affordable alternative that utilizes wind-powered electricity.

Calypso Beach Retreat (☎ in USA 303-523-8165; www .calypsobeachretreat.com; Long Caye; r incl breakfast BZ$272, beachcomber/snorkel packages per week BZ$1733/2823; ☐) is on the northeast corner of the island. This B&B is built from tropical hardwoods, housing four charming guest rooms with priceless Caribbean sea views. Sleep in four-poster beds and feel the breeze off the ocean. The packages include all meals, or you can pay by the night and utilize the shared kitchen facilities. Diving and fishing packages are also available (weekly diving/fishing package BZ$3920/4350), as are other combinations.

Northern Belize

Northern Belize is probably the most passed-through region in the country. Many travelers save themselves a small chunk of change by flying into Chetumal or Cancun in Mexico and bussing straight down into Belize City and out to the cayes. Their general take on the transitory sojourn is less than complimentary. 'Flat terrain, farmland and uninspiring towns,' some have said. To these travelers, we say, 'Have fun in San Pedro!'

Are they gone yet? Excellent!

Now we can talk about the beautiful, chilled-out stretch of Belize that the masses miss entirely, keeping paths un-beaten, and hotel and food prices close to half that of the rest of Belize.

Northern Belize comprises two districts: Corozal and Orange Walk. From the road down from Mexico, the terrain of both appears to be mostly farmland and sparse jungle, with attractions for tourists thin on the ground. While the Northern Hwy lacks the gorgeous curves and panoramic vistas of the Hummingbird or Southern Highways, off this main road lie a plethora of places to explore, including pretty fishing villages, pristine jungles and ancient Maya cities.

Then there's the food! With its close proximity to Mexico, cuisine in Belize's north is far more colorful and diverse than it is down south; if you're ready to trade stew beans, rice and rum for ceviche, empanadas and tequila, you'll definitely want to head north.

Beautiful, inexpensive, untouristy and tasty: in a nutshell, that's northern Belize!

HIGHLIGHTS

- Taking a riverboat tour through the jungles and winding up at the magnificent Maya ruins of **Lamanai** (p167)

- Hanging out in the saltwater breezes and Spanish colonial charm of **Corozal Town** (p172)

- Enjoying the panoramic ocean views from atop the pyramid at the beachfront Maya ruins of **Cerros** (p178)

- Enjoying exceptional birding and wildlife watching at the **Rio Bravo Conservation & Management Area** (p169)

- Chilling in the laid-back fishing town of **Sarteneja** (p179)

| ■ POPULATION: 84,500 | ■ MONTHLY RAINFALL: Jan 4in, Jun 5in (Corozal) | ■ HIGHEST ELEVATION: 777ft |

History

On the eastern fringe of the ancient Maya heartland, northern Belize supported many settlements through history without producing any cities of the size or grandeur of Caracol, further south in Belize, or Tikal in Guatemala. It was home to important river trade routes linking the interior with the coast: the north's major Maya site, Lamanai, commanded one of these routes and grew to a city of up to 35,000 people.

A Spanish expedition into northern Belize from the Yucatán in 1544 led to the conquering of many of the region's Maya settlements and, later, the creation of a series of Spanish missions distantly controlled by a priest at Bacalar in the southeastern Yucatán. Maya rebellion was fierce, and after a series of battles the Spanish were driven out of the area for good in 1640.

British loggers began moving into the region in search of mahogany in the 18th century. They encountered sporadic resistance from the now weakened and depleted Maya population, who had been ravaged by European-introduced diseases.

In 1847 the Maya in the Yucatán rose up against their Spanish-descended overlords in the War of the Castes ('Guerra de Castas' in Spanish), a vicious conflict that continued in diminishing form into the 20th century. Refugees from both sides of the conflict took shelter in northern British Honduras (as Belize was then called), with people of Spanish descent founding the towns of Orange Walk and Corozal, and the Maya moving into the forests and countryside. It wasn't surprising that intermittent hostilities took place in British Honduras. One group of Maya, the Icaiché, were repulsed from Orange Walk after fierce fighting in 1872. The border between Mexico and British Honduras was not agreed between the two states until 1893.

Caste War migrants from the Yucatán laid the foundations of modern northern Belize by starting the area's first sugarcane plantations. Despite the sugar industry's many vicissitudes, it is now the backbone of the northern Belize economy, with some 900 cane farms in the region.

Language

Because of northern Belize's proximity to Mexico and Guatemala's Petén, and the

---

NORTHERN BELIZE IN...

One Day
Take a trip up the bird-rich New River to the jungle-clad Maya ruins at **Lamanai** (p167).

Three Days
Spend a day chilling out on the cheap in **Corozal Town** (p172) before heading out by **solar-powered boat** (p177) for a day of Maya exploration at **Cerros** (p178) and another day of carbon-neutral decadence at **Cerros Beach Inn** (p178).

Five or Six Days
Follow the three-day agenda with an additional two days of horseback riding and jungle exploration at **Backpacker's Paradise** (p180) in Sarteneja. Spend the last day traveling slowly overland to **Orange Walk Town** (p163) and indulge in some street food followed by pastries at **Panificadora La Popular** (p166).

Mexican or Guatemalan origins of many of the people living here, Spanish is the first language of many northerners, be they Maya, Mestizo of Mexican origin or more-recent immigrant workers from El Salvador and Guatemala. See the boxed text, p262, for a quick Spanish lesson. However, nearly everybody speaks English as well.

Getting There & Around

The Northern Hwy links Belize City with the Mexican border via the region's two main towns, Orange Walk and Corozal. Several bus companies service the route, with some going as far as Chetumal, 7 miles into Mexico. Since the bankruptcy of Novelo's (once the flagship bus company of Belize), half a dozen companies have stepped in to service the region, and approximately 30 daily buses run each way from Belize City to Corozal Town. There are also daily buses connecting Orange Walk Town with Sarteneja (though the nicest way to get to Sarteneja is by boat from Corozal Town). Daily flights connect Corozal Town with Sarteneja and San Pedro (Ambergris Caye). At San Pedro you can connect with flights to and from Belize City. Presently, there are no regular flights servicing Orange Walk Town.

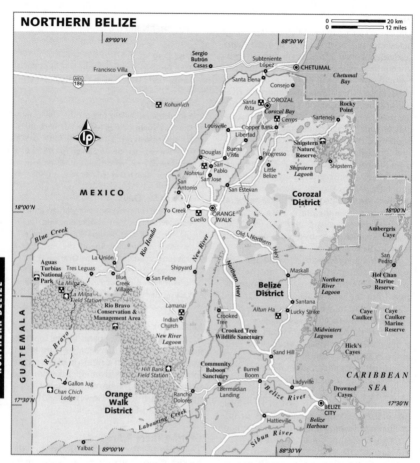

NORTHERN BELIZE

ORANGE WALK DISTRICT

Orange Walk is one of the more spread out and thinly populated districts in Belize. The Northern Hwy cuts through the panhandle that is the district's population center in its far northeast, and most of the communities and attractions scattered west of this are connected by a network of (mostly) unpaved roads. A casual glance at the government-produced Belize Travel Map shows a fairly extensive series of grid-roads west of the Northern Hwy that stretches out into towns with names like Shipstern and August Pine Ridge. Though this gives the impression of larger communities in rural Orange

Walk, these are actually Mennonite farming communities; the neatly drawn lines represent farming roads and boundaries created by the farmers themselves, and not major towns bustling with activity.

Further west and to the south, these grid roads disappear entirely, and you're in what Belizeans refer to as 'deep bush,' the backwoods jungle country that makes up most of Orange Walk District. It's here you'll find the vast Rio Bravo Conservation and Management Area (p169) and, further out still, the village of Gallon Jug and the ultra exclusive Chan Chich Lodge (p171). Most casual visitors – those without a good 4WD or the hefty funds needed to visit the lodge – restrict their exploration of the district to places within reasonable striking distance of Orange Walk Town.

ORANGE WALK TOWN
pop 15,990

Orange Walk Town is many things to many people: agricultural town, economic hub of northern Belize, meeting place of Mennonites, good place for street eats…but it generally isn't thought of as a tourist town. And chances are pretty good that this won't change any time soon. No, this town of 16,000 souls – just 57 miles from Belize City – doesn't have much to keep travelers around for more than a day or two, but what it does have makes it an excellent base from which to make the superlative trip to the ruins of Lamanai (p167) and longer

excursions into the wilds of northern Belize. Orange Walk has a fine location beside the New River, which meanders lazily along the east side of town, and there are a few very nice (and reasonably priced) hotels and restaurants for visitors who choose to hang around for a bit before leaving for other parts of Belize.

Orientation & Information

It's easy to find your way around Orange Walk Town. The Northern Hwy (known as Queen Victoria Ave while it passes through town) is the main thoroughfare. A recently built bypass now keeps the lumbering sugarcane trucks out of the town center, making the town considerably more peaceful than in years past. Central Park is in the center of town, on the

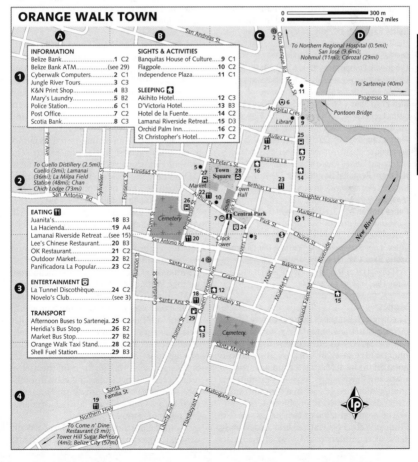

ORANGE WALK TOWN

0 ——————— 300 m
0 ——————— 0.2 miles

INFORMATION
Belize Bank....................................1 C2
Belize Bank ATM..................(see 29)
Cyberwalk Computers...................2 C1
Jungle River Tours........................3 C3
K&N Print Shop.............................4 B3
Mary's Laundry.............................5 B2
Police Station................................6 C1
Post Office.....................................7 C2
Scotia Bank...................................8 C3

SIGHTS & ACTIVITIES
Banquitas House of Culture.........9 C1
Flagpole.......................................10 C2
Independence Plaza....................11 C1

SLEEPING
Akihito Hotel................................12 C3
D'Victoria Hotel...........................13 B3
Hotel de la Fuente......................14 C2
Lamanai Riverside Retreat..........15 D3
Orchid Palm Inn..........................16 C2
St Christopher's Hotel.................17 C2

EATING
Juanita's.......................................18 B3
La Hacienda.................................19 A4
Lamanai Riverside Retreat....(see 15)
Lee's Chinese Restaurant...........20 B3
OK Restaurant.............................21 C2
Outdoor Market..........................22 B2
Panificadora La Popular..............23 C2

ENTERTAINMENT
La Tunnel Discothèque................24 C2
Novelo's Club........................(see 3)

TRANSPORT
Afternoon Buses to Sarteneja....25 C2
Heridia's Bus Stop.......................26 B2
Market Bus Stop..........................27 B2
Orange Walk Taxi Stand.............28 C2
Shell Fuel Station.........................29 B3

NORTHERN BELIZE

THE WAR OF THE CASTES COMES TO ORANGE WALK

Orange Walk Town was born as a logging camp in the 18th century, from where mahogany was floated down the New River to Corozal Bay. It began to develop as a town around 1850, when Mexican refugees from the War of the Castes arrived. These migrants, whose agricultural experience was welcomed by the British colonial authorities, started northern Belize's first sugar boom (which lasted from the 1850s to the 1870s).

The complex War of the Castes itself reached Orange Walk in 1872, when a force of some 150 Icaiché Maya attacked the town's British garrison. After several hours of fierce fighting the Icaiché were repelled, and their leader Marcos Canul was fatally wounded in the attack, which has gone down in history as the last significant armed Maya resistance in Belize. The Icaiché had been at odds with the British for several reasons, including encroachments by British loggers into lands that the Icaiché considered their own around the Rio Hondo (which today forms Belize's border with Mexico), and arms supplies from British Honduras to the Cruzob Maya (bitter enemies of the Icaiché).

---

east side of Queen Victoria Ave. Orange Walk lacks an official tourism information center, though hotels can provide local information.

Belize Bank (☎ 322-2019; 34 Main St; ⌚ 8am-3pm Mon-Thu, 8am-4:30pm Fri) Accepts all major credit cards with BZ$2 fee and BZ$500 per day limit.

Cyberwalk Computers (☎ 322-3024; 115 Otro Benque; internet per hr BZ$4; ⌚ 8am-9pm Mon-Sat, 8am-5pm Sun) On the northern edge of town.

K&N Print Shop (☎ 322-0294; Queen Victoria Ave; internet per hr BZ$4; ⌚ 8am-noon, 2-5pm & 7-9pm Mon-Sat, 8am-5pm Sun) Downtown internet access.

Mary's Laundry (☎ 322-3454; Progresso St; washing per pound BZ$1; ⌚ 7am-5pm) Washes, dries and folds laundry, just like you wished mom would.

Northern Regional Hospital (☎ 322-2072; Northern Hwy; ⌚ 24hr emergency services) At the north end of town, beside the Northern Hwy.

Police station (☎ 322-2022; Hospital Cres) Across from the library.

Post office (☎ 322-2345; cnr Queen Victoria Ave & Arthur St; ⌚ 8am-noon & 1-4:30pm Mon-Thu, till 4pm Fri)

Scotia Bank (☎ 322-2194; cnr Park & Main Sts; ⌚ 8am-3pm Mon-Thu, till 4:30pm Fri) Accepts all cards without fee; limit per day BZ$800.

Sights

The modern **Banquitas House of Culture** (☎ 322-0517; Banquitas Plaza; admission free; ⌚ 10am-6pm Tue-Fri, 8am-noon Sat) has an attractively displayed exhibit on Orange Walk's history. It's especially good on the local Maya sites and has artifacts, maps and illustrations, as well as exhibits that change monthly. It's set in a pleasant, small, riverside park with an amphitheater.

The scant remains of two British forts in Orange Walk, Fort Cairnes and Fort Mundy, serve as reminders of the War of the Castes

conflict. A **flagpole** behind Orange Walk's town hall is the only remnant of Fort Cairnes, while **Independence Plaza** marks the site of Fort Mundy.

Close to Orange Walk Town, **Cuello** (*kway-yo*) is one of the earliest-known settled communities in the Maya world, probably dating back to around 2400 BC, although there's not very much left to show for it. The Maya of Cuello, a small farming community, were excellent potters and prolific farmers, and though archaeologists have found plenty here, only Structure 350, a nine-tiered pyramid, is of much interest to the non-expert. The pyramid was constructed around AD 200 to AD 300 but its lower levels date from before 2000 BC. The site is on private property owned by **Cuello Distillery** (☎ 320-9085; Yo Creek Rd), 2.5 miles west of Orange Walk (take San Antonio Rd out of town). The rum distillery, on the south side of the road, is unmarked except for a gate; the site is through and beyond it. The distillery is free to explore, but ask permission at the gate. A taxi to Cuello from Orange Walk costs about BZ$25, roundtrip.

Meaning 'Great Mound' in Mayan, **Nohmul** (noh-*mool*) was, in its day, a much more important site than Cuello. In the late Classic Period this was a town of some 3000 people. The vast site covers more than 7 sq miles, though most of it is overgrown with grass and sugarcane. Although the ruins themselves aren't exactly spectacular, the view from the lofty acropolis of Structure 2 is; you can see clear across Orange Walk District, over endless fields of cane.

From the northern edge of Orange Walk, drive 9.6 miles north on the Northern Hwy to the village of San Jose. At the north end of the village look for the sign directing you 1.3 miles west to Nohmul. The dirt road slightly forks twice – keep your eyes on the odometer and stay right; the actual site is not well marked. If you don't have a car, you can take a bus to San Jose, and walk the dirt road. A taxi from Orange Walk is about BZ$30, roundtrip.

Tours

Sugarcane and street-tacos aside, the main reason travelers come to Orange Walk is to head out to the Maya ruins at Lamanai. We know of two reputable companies that do full day trips by riverboat there and back; both have guides who know their birds as well as their archaeology. They usually require a minimum of four people to make the trip, and you should reserve your place the day before, although you may be lucky on the morning you want to go. It's also feasible to take this tour on a long day trip from as far away as Belize City or Corozal.

One of the oldest ecotourism specialists is **Jungle River Tours** (☎ 302-2293; lamanai mayatour@btl. net; 20 Lovers' Lane). Its Lamanai tour, which costs BZ$90 per person, includes a buffet lunch and site admission. The Novelo brothers (of the same clan as the owners of the financially troubled Novelo's bus company) also do a variety of other tours from Orange Walk, including cave-tubing.

Offering similarly priced tours, **Reyes & Sons** (☎ 322-3327, 610-1548) also does river tours to Lamanai; Mr Reyes will also do a guided tour sans refreshments for BZ$55. Reyes & Sons are not based right in Orange Walk Town (they keep their boat docked by the Northern Hwy bridge over the New River, 5 miles south of town), but they'll pick you up at your hotel with advanced notice.

Sleeping

Akihito Hotel (☎ 302-0185; 22 Queen Victoria Ave; d/tr with private bathroom BZ$45/55; ✹ 🖳) If you've never experienced the no-star ambiance of a low-budget hotel in China, comrades, here's your chance. This Chinese-owned (perhaps formerly Japanese-owned, judging by the name?) guesthouse has a similar feel to the thousands of hundred-yuan hotels from Guangzhuo to Urumuqi. There's cheap Chinese food downstairs, too.

D'Victoria Hotel (☎ 322-2518; 40 Queen Victoria Ave; s/d/tr with fan BZ$50/65/90, with air-con BZ$80/92/115;

(🅿 ✹ 🖳) The overall vibe of this medium-sized hotel is a bit drab, like a rust-belt Motel 6 that's seen better days. Rooms are clean, boxy and basic. There's cable TV, tiled private bathrooms with hot showers, and a backyard pool (empty on our last visit).

Lamanai Riverside Retreat (☎ 302-3955; Lamanai Alley; r BZ$80; 🅿 ✹ 🖳) Located right on the river, the Lamanai has three wooden rooms, each with two beds, private bathroom and cable TV. Adjoining the retreat is one of Orange Walk's more picturesque eating and drinking spots (see p166), so the place can get a bit noisy in the evenings. The owner is involved in the cataloging and protection of the area's crocodile population, and will be glad to tell you all about the crocs and other animals that call the river home. Being right on the river, boats to Lamanai will pick you up here.

St Christopher's Hotel (☎ 322-2420; rowbze@btl.net; 10 Main St; r with fan/air-con BZ$60/90, garden- or river-view with fan/air-con BZ$70/100; 🅿 🖳 ✹) This yellow-painted, well-run hotel offers large and clean rooms with private bathroom, tiled floors and cable TV. The newer, off-street, garden rooms are the nicest and quietest. You can embark right here for the boat trip to Lamanai.

Hotel de la Fuente (☎ 322-2290; www.hoteldela fuente.com; 14 Main St; s/d BZ$55/120; 🅿 ✹ 🖳) Readers speak highly of this newly opened hotel in the heart of Orange Walk, and with good reason. The staff are friendly and helpful, and the rooms clean and cozy with comfy foam mattresses. All rooms come with air-con, free wireless, fridge and coffee maker. The cheapest room is a good deal, no less comfortable but fan-cooled only, and the most expensive one – the 'junior suite' – has a separate living room, full kitchenette with all utensils, and two beds. The latter is also rented monthly. Owners can arrange tours and point visitors in the right direction during their stay in Orange Walk.

Orchid Palm Inn (☎ 322-3947; www.orchidpalminn com; 22 Queen Victoria Ave; s/d BZ$60/130; 🅿 ✹ 🖳 ♿) Another new and clean little hotel in Orange Walk, it has the quaint feel of a small-town family-owned hotel (which it is). The Inn (winner of the coveted Belize Tourism Board's 2007 Small Hotel of the Year Award) has eight well-furnished and nicely decorated rooms that come in a variety of configurations, from one-bed singles to two-bed doubles with kitchenettes. The management provides free wireless internet, fruit and coffee in the morning, and offers discounts for guests opting out of air-con.

Eating

Though a quick drive through town may not reveal it, Orange Walk is actually pretty good for eats. While there aren't many of what you'd call 'five-star eateries' in this working-class town, the place is known for its street food. Surrounding the town square are tiny cafés, snack stalls, fruit stands and pushcarts offering a veritable smorgasbord of northern Belizean and Mexican foods, including rice and beans, tacos, enchiladas, stewed chicken, ice cream and more. Everything is super cheap, between BZ$1 and BZ$5, and hygiene standards are generally pretty good. As for the food, put it this way: we have friends in Corozal who come to Orange Walk on Saturdays 'just to hang out and eat.'

ourpick **Panificadora La Popular** (☎ 322-3229, Belize Rd; ⏰ 6:30am-8pm Mon-Sat, 7:30am-noon & 3-6pm Sun) Should you find yourself in Orange Walk during daylight hours, *do not pass go, do not collect 200 dollars*; stop in at this amazing family-run bakery and get anything (and perhaps everything) chocolate on the shelves – the more gooey the better. Trust us on this one.

Juanita's (☎ 322-2677; 8 Santa Ana St; dishes BZ$5-8; ⏰ 6am-2pm & 6-9pm) You can tell by the dedicated locals who flock here that the food is satisfying. A simple, clean and very well-priced place, Juanita's serves eggs and bacon for breakfast, and rice and beans and other local favorites, such as cow-foot soup, during the rest of the day.

La Hacienda (☎ 302-3955, 322-0740; Northern Hwy; dishes BZ$7-10; ⏰ 11am-10pm Sun-Thu, 11am-midnight Fri & Sat) Travelers speak highly of this steak restaurant on the south end of town.

Come n' Dine Restaurant (☎ 302-3420; Belize Rd; BZ$7-12; ⏰ breakfast, lunch & dinner, closes at 10pm Fri & Sat) Located right next to the gas station on a crook on the Northern Hwy just a couple of miles south of town, this friendly restaurant serves up excellent stews, steaks & stir-fries. Stephanie Perry is one of the chefs at this fine place, and she's been cooking for missionaries around Belize for years. It serves some of the best Belizean food you'll find around.

OK Restaurant (☎ 322-1489; Queen Victoria Rd; mains BZ$8-12; ⏰ 10am-10pm, closes 3pm Tue) A place with a name that sets the bar at mediocre deserves kudos for well exceeding expectations; this Chinese restaurant north of the park isn't merely 'OK', it's actually pretty darned good, serving up fine American-style Chinese dishes. There isn't much on the menu for vegetarians, but they'll happily make meat-free dishes on request.

Lee's Chinese Restaurant (☎ 322-2174; 11 San Antonio Rd; dishes BZ$10-40; ⏰ 11am-midnight) Another of Orange Walk's Chinese eateries, Lee's serves up a slightly superior range of Hong Kong–style dishes. The black bean crab is a good and spicy choice, as is anything with conch or lobster. Ambiance is somewhat more upscale, with a stylish dragon-theme decor kept cool by whirring ceiling fans. There's a bar with slot machines next door, owned by the same family, if you feel the need for some post-meal gambling.

Lamanai Riverside Retreat (☎ 302-3955; Lamanai Alley; mains BZ$12-25; ⏰ 8am-10pm) With its breezy deck and tables right by the river, you might expect more from this place. Though the menu is large and varied, meals are uninspired and overpriced. A nice place to hang out for the riverside view alone, but best to stick to drinks and appetizers.

Entertainment

Orange Walk is a town where farmers from all over northern Belize (including the area's sizable Mennonite population) come to swap tales, sell produce and eat Chinese food. If watching men in straw hats with Abe Lincoln beards lounging on the sidewalks isn't your idea of entertainment, there are a few other options. **La Tunnel Discothèque** (South Park St) is located just up from the office of Jungle Tours. The place is lively at night but dead in the day. And the Novelo brothers have a **club** right next to their Jungle Tours office where live music often plays (especially during political rallies). The bar at Lamanai Riverside Retreat is popular and usually fairly crowded on the weekends.

Getting There & Away

Orange Walk is the major northern Belize bus hub for buses plying the Corozal–Belize City route. At last count there were six companies servicing this route and between 25 and 30 buses a day going in each direction. All buses pass through the center of town before stopping on the west side of Central Park or around the market to pick up and drop off customers. Buses heading north from Orange Walk begin at 7am and run until 9pm. Heading south to Belize City, buses begin at 5am and run until 8:45pm. The trip to Belize City takes between 1½ and two hours, and costs between BZ$5 and BZ$7; the trip to Corozal is slightly quicker and cheaper.

Buses to outlying regions depart from various points around the market (generally behind it), and schedules are subject to change. Your best bet for finding one of these buses is to go behind the market and look for a school bus bearing either the company name, destination name, or both. Heridia's buses depart for Copper Bank (BZ$4, one hour, 11:30am and 5pm Monday to Saturday) from their **bus stop** half a block south of the market. Tillett's buses run out to Indian Church, less than a mile from Lamanai (BZ$5, 1½ hours, 3:30pm Monday, Wednesday and Friday) from the **market bus stop**. Also from the market, Sarteneja buses go to Sarteneja (BZ$5, 1½ hours, hourly from noon to 5pm Monday to Saturday). On Sunday, there's only one bus to Sarteneja (3pm).

LAMANAI

Perhaps the most fascinating Maya site in northern Belize, **Lamanai** (admission BZ$10; ⏰ 8am-5pm) lies 24 miles south of Orange Walk Town up the New River (or 36 miles by unpaved road). The ruins are known both for their impressive architecture and marvelous setting, surrounded by dense jungle overlooking the New River Lagoon. Most visitors approach Lamanai by guided river trip from Orange Walk not just to avoid the long and bumpy road, but to take advantage of the **river trip** itself, which goes deep into the home of the countless colorful and unusual birds that live in the area. Most guides who do the 1½-hour river trip are experts in both archaeology and the area's wildlife, making it an especially worthwhile experience. The river voyage passes through some of the most beautiful jungle and lagoon country in northern Belize, and the Mennonite community of **Shipyard**, before reaching Lamanai itself. There are a number of excellent tour guides in Orange Walk who specialize in the journey (see p165).

History

Lamanai not only spans all phases of ancient Maya civilization but also tells a tale of ongoing Maya occupation and resistance for centuries after the Europeans arrived. This adds up to the longest known unbroken occupation in the Maya world. Lamanai was inhabited at least as early as 1500 BC, and was already a major ceremonial center, with large temples, in late Preclassic times.

It seems to have surged in importance (perhaps thanks to its location on trade routes between the Caribbean and the interior) around 200 or 100 BC, and its major buildings were mostly constructed between then and AD 700, although additions and changes went on up until at least the 15th century. At its peak it is estimated to have had a population of around 35,000.

When the Spanish invaded northern Belize from the Yucatán in 1544, one of the most important of the missions they set up was Lamanai, where they had found a thriving Maya community. But the Maya never readily accepted Spanish overlordship, and a rebellion in 1640 left the Lamanai mission burned and deserted. Maya continued to live here until the late 17th or 18th century when they were decimated by an epidemic, probably smallpox.

Archaeological excavations commenced as early as 1917, but large-scale digging, by David Pendergast of Canada's Royal Ontario Museum, only began in 1974. The painstaking work of uncovering more than 700 structures found here will take several lifetimes, not to mention huge amounts of funding.

Sights

Arriving at Lamanai by boat, you'll probably first be brought to the small **museum**, which exhibits some beautiful examples of pottery and obsidian and jade jewelry. Then you'll head into the jungle, passing gigantic guanacaste (tubroos), ceiba and ramón (breadnut) trees, strangler figs, allspice, epiphytes and examples of Belize's national flower, the black orchid. In the canopy overhead you might see (or hear) some of the resident howler monkeys. A tour of the **ruins** takes a minimum of 90 minutes, but can be done more comfortably in two or three hours, and encompasses a number of fascinating structures.

JAGUAR TEMPLE

This temple (Structure N10-9), fronting a 100yd-wide plaza, was built in the 6th century AD and modified several times up to at least the 15th century – a fine example of

NORTHERN BELIZE

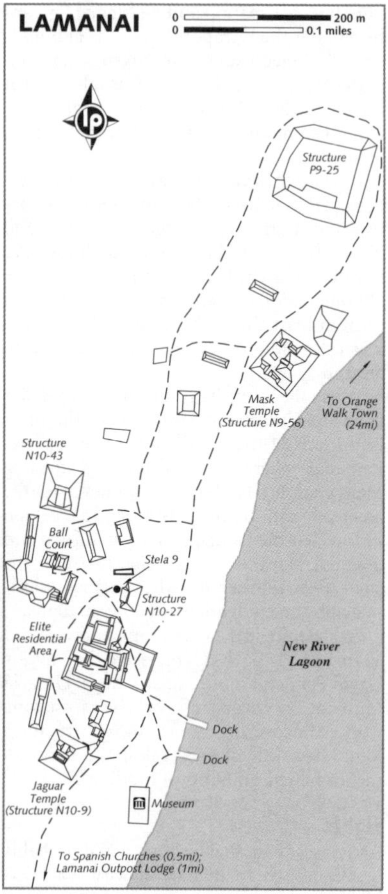
LAMANAI
0
200 m
0
0.1 miles
Structure P9-25
Mask Temple (Structure N9-56)
To Orange Walk Town (24mi)
Structure N10-43
Ball Court
Stela 9
Structure N10-27
Elite Residential Area
New River Lagoon
Dock
Dock
Jaguar Temple (Structure N10-9)
Museum
To Spanish Churches (0.5mi); Lamanai Outpost Lodge (1mi)

the longevity of the Lamanai settlement. The stone patterning on the lowest-level turns depict two cleverly designed jaguar faces, dating from the initial 6th-century construction. On the opposite (north) side of the plaza is a set of buildings that were used as residences for Lamanai's royal elite.

STELA 9

North of the elite residential complex, this intricately carved standing stone in front of Structure N10-27 was erected in AD 625 to commemorate the accession of Lord Smoking Shell in AD 608. He is shown in ceremonial regalia, wearing a rattlesnake headdress with quetzal feathers at the back, and holding a double-headed serpent bar diagonally across his body, with a deity emerging from the serpent's jaw at the top. The remains of five children – ranging in age from newborn to eight – were buried beneath the stela. Archaeologists believe the burial must have been highly significant, since offerings are not usually associated with the dedication of monuments.

BALL COURT

Not far west of Stela 9 is Lamanai's ball court, one of the smallest in the Maya world – but with the largest ball-court marker found yet! A ceremonial vessel containing liquid mercury, probably from Guatemala, was found beneath the marker.

STRUCTURE N10-43

North of the ball court, across a plaza shaded by trees, is Structure N10-43, the highest at Lamanai, which rises 125ft above the jungle canopy. Few large buildings in the Maya world were built as early as this one, which was initially constructed around 100 BC. This grand ceremonial temple was built from nothing on a site that had previously been residential, which indicated a dramatic surge in Lamanai's importance at the time. You can climb to its summit for fabulous panoramas over the rest of Lamanai, the New River Lagoon and plains and forests stretching out on all sides.

MASK TEMPLE

To the northeast along a jungle path, the Mask Temple (Structure N9-56) was begun around 200 BC and was modified several times up to AD 1300. It has a 13ft stylized mask of a man in a crocodile headdress emblazoned on the southern part of its west face. The name Lamanai meant Submerged Crocodile in the language of its ancient inhabitants, and this animal clearly had great significance for them.

Dating from about AD 400, this is one of the finest big masks in the Maya world and unusual in that it is made of limestone blocks rather than plaster. A similar mask is hidden beneath the façade on the northern side. Deep within this building archaeologists found the tombs of a man adorned with shell and jade jewelry, and a woman from almost the same date. The pair are thought to be a succession of leaders – perhaps a husband and wife, or brother and sister.

STRUCTURE P9-25

At the far north end of the Lamanai site, and often missed by tour groups, this large platform, 120yd by 100yd in area, supports several large buildings up to 92ft high. Next to it is a river inlet that once formed an ancient harbor.

COLONIAL STRUCTURES

Some 400yd south of Jaguar Temple are the remains of the thick stone walls of two Spanish churches, which were built from the remains of a temple by Maya forced labor. The southern church was built in 1544, and the northern one in the 1560s. Both were destroyed by the Maya, the second one in the 1640 rebellion. Unknown to the Spanish, the Maya placed sacred objects such as crocodile figurines inside the churches while building them.

A 300yd path opposite the churches leads to the partly overgrown remains of a 19th-century sugar mill.

Sleeping & Eating

Lamanai Outpost Lodge (☎ 223-3578, in US ☎ 888-733-7864; www.lamanai.com; 2-/3-/4-night package for 2 from BZ$3000/4000/5000; P 🖳) For those who can afford it, the best option for fully exploring Lamanai is one of the package tours offered by this place. About 1 mile south of the ruins, this classy lodge is perched on a hillside just above the lagoon, and boasts panoramic views from its bar and gorgeous open-air dining room. The 20 thatched-roof bungalows, each with fan, private bathroom and verandah, are cozy and perfectly suited to the casual jungle atmosphere. Packages include meals, most drinks, transfers to/from Belize City and three guided, small-group activities per day. The list

of activities ranges from visiting the ruins to observing howler monkeys to starlight canoeing to nocturnal crocodile encounters. Birding is big here: almost 400 species have been documented within 3 miles of the lodge. Discounts are sometimes available online.

Getting There & Away

If you decide to go without a guide, you can get to Indian Church (next to Lamanai) from Orange Walk via Yo Creek and San Felipe via Tillett's Bus (p167). Returning to Orange Walk, you'll need to leave Indian Church at 4am.

RIO BRAVO CONSERVATION & MANAGEMENT AREA

If you're looking for true, wild tropical rainforest, this is it. Encompassing 406 sq miles in northwest Belize, the Rio Bravo Conservation & Management Area (RBCMA) takes up 4% of Belize's total land area. The area is managed by the Belizean nonprofit organization Programme for Belize (PFB; see below), and while independent trips are possible, PFB prefers travelers coordinate any visits to the area through them. The RBCMA harbors astonishing biological diversity – 392 bird species (more than two-thirds of Belize's total), 200 tree species, 70 mammal species, including all five of Belize's cats (jaguar, puma, ocelot, jaguarundi and margay). Rio Bravo is said to have the largest concentration of jaguars in Central America.

Parts of the territory of the RBCMA were logged for mahogany and other woods from the 18th century until the 1980s, but distance and inaccessibility helped to ensure the survival of the forest as a whole. The area also contains at least 60 Maya sites, including **La Milpa**. In the northwestern corner of the area

---

THE 4-1-1 ON THE PFB

The creed of ecotourism has always been to leave nothing but footprints (and light ones at that) and take away nothing but photos and memories. Established in 1988, **Programme for Belize** (PFB; Map pp96-7; ☎ 227-5616/1020; www.pfbelize.org; 1 Eyre St, Belize City; ☉ 8am-5pm Mon-Fri) is a Belizean nonprofit organization that works with individual conservationists, private landowners and the Belizean government to demonstrate that the long-term benefits of land preservation outweigh the short-term profits of resource exploitation.

To this end, PFB has helped in the establishment of the Rio Bravo Conservation and Management Area. By planning your visit to Rio Bravo through PFB, you'll not only be assuring that your tourist dollars are redirected into conservation of the land; you'll be demonstrating the power that tourism has for promoting the change from resource exploitation to sustainable land use. PFB also offers a number of other programs, both for individual travelers and student groups. Contact the Belize City office for more information.

itself, La Milpa is the third-largest Maya site in Belize, believed to have had a population of 50,000 at its peak between AD 750 and AD 850. Its 5-acre Great Plaza, one of the biggest of all Maya plazas, is surrounded by four pyramids up to 80ft high.

At the RBCMA the PFB seeks to link conservation with the development of sustainable land uses. Programs include tree nurseries, extraction of nontimber products such as chicle, thatch and palm, experimental operations in sustainable timber extraction, and ecotourism. The thousands of visitors annually include many Belizean and international students.

History

Maya lived in this area as early as 800 BC. When Spanish expeditions first journeyed here the Maya were still using the same river trade routes, though by then their population was seriously depleted. Mahogany loggers moved into the area by the mid-18th century but were subject to intermittent attacks by the Maya for at least a century. By the late 19th century the Belize Estate and Produce Company (BEC) owned almost all of the land in northwestern Belize. The company carried out major timber extractions, floating mahogany and Mexican cedar out through the river system to the coast.

With the advent of rail systems and logging trucks, operations flourished until overcutting and a moody market finally prompted the BEC to stop cutting trees in the early 1980s.

Intensive chicle tapping also took place throughout the 20th century, and you can still see slash scars on sapodilla trees throughout the RBCMA.

Belizean businessman Barry Bowen, owner of the Belikin brewery and the country's Coca-Cola distribution rights, bought the BEC and its nearly 1100 sq miles of land in 1982. He quickly sold off massive chunks to Yalbac Ranch (owned by a Texan cattle farmer) and Coca-Cola Foods. Meanwhile the Massachusetts Audubon Society was looking for a reserve for migrating birds. Coca-Cola donated 66 sq miles to support the initiative (a further 86 sq miles followed in 1992), and Programme for Belize was created to manage the land. Bowen also donated some land, and PFB, helped by more than US$2 million raised by the UK-based World Land Trust, bought the rest, bringing its total up to today's 406 sq miles.

Sleeping & Eating

It's a long trek out here, so most visitors stay overnight at one of the two field stations. **Hill Bank Field Station** (dm/cabana per person

---

KNOW THY MENNONITES *Christopher Nesbitt*

Visitors to Belize rarely fail to notice the abundance of one particularly interesting group of people. You'll see them all over, groups of Caucasians in this primarily non-Caucasian nation. Some will be dressed in quaint mid-19th century outfits, the women wearing head coverings and the men driving horses and buggies. Others may look more like extras in a country and western video. Sometimes entire families seem to be wearing clothes made from the same roll of cloth.

These are the Mennonites, an Anabaptist group with similar religious leanings to the Amish. Arriving in Belize in the 1950s, after fleeing persecution in Paraguay and Mexico, the Mennonites found in Belize a nation more than willing to give them refuge. Since then, these Mennonites have become a central part of the economy, producing much of the food eaten in Belize.

Belize is home to about 4000 Mennonites, with Mennonite communities spread throughout the nation. The largest of these are in Orange Walk and Cayo Districts, but there are also smaller communities at Springfield near Belmopan and at Pinehill in Toledo District.

Though to the outsider they may seem to be cut of the same cloth, there are in fact a number of different schools of thought among Belize's Mennonite communities. The main dividing line in the Mennonite community is between the Old Order Mennonites and the Progressive Mennonites. Old Order Mennonites drive horses and buggies. The men wear broad-brimmed hats, suspenders, long sleeved shirts and beards; and the women wear very dour clothes, completely covering the body except for the face and hands. They are isolationist communities, engaged in agriculture using horses and buggies, and coming out to engage in business with the rest of Belize. They live lives that seem timeless. With their quaint manner of dressing, and their rejection of modern conveniences, including electricity and internal combustion engines, their communities resemble the set of *Little House on the Prairie*, only with palm trees. In general, they are respected and

incl meals BZ$200/230; ⓟ) is in the southeastern part of the RBCMA beside the New River Lagoon (upstream from Lamanai), on the site of an abandoned logging station where old wooden buildings and antique steam engines remain. **La Milpa Field Station** (dm/cabana per person incl meals BZ$200/230; ⓟ) is in the northwest of the RBCMA, 3 miles from La Milpa Maya site. The birding at La Milpa is exceptional, and spider and howler monkeys, coatimundi, peccaries and agoutis (as well as jaguar and ocelot tracks) are all commonly seen in the area.

Visiting arrangements for either place must be made in advance through the PFB. The stations' lovely thatched cabanas come complete with private bathroom, hot water, fresh linens, verandah and mosquito nets. The four-person dorm rooms incorporate eco-technology such as solar power and graywater recycling. There are plenty of hammocks in which to lie back and listen to birdsong.

The prices include all meals and two guided tours of your choice from the selection on offer: trail hikes, early morning bird walks, a visit to La Milpa archaeological site (from La Milpa Field Station), canoeing or nighttime crocodile-spotlighting at Hill Bank. At an extra cost you can visit nearby communities or Lamanai from La Milpa Field Station, or take a lagoon boat tour from Hill Bank Field Station. There are also opportunities to meet visiting researchers and archaeologists.

Getting There & Away

Most visitors rent a vehicle to get to either field station: it's about a three-hour drive from Belize City to La Milpa (via Orange Walk, Yo Creek, San Felipe, Blue Creek and Tres Leguas), or two hours to Hill Bank (via Burrell Boom, Bermudian Landing and Rancho Dolores). Call Programme For Belize for detailed directions and advice on road conditions (the later stages of both trips involve sections on unpaved roads, which can be impassable after heavy rains). PFB can also help arrange transit for you from Belize City to La Milpa or Hill Bank.

CHAN CHICH LODGE

One of Belize's original ecolodges, **Chan Chich Lodge** (☎ /fax 223-4419, in US ☎ 800-343-8009; www .chanchich.com; cabanas from BZ$470, package deals available; ⓟ 🖥 🌐) is located in the remote far west of Orange Walk District. Distance makes Chan Chich something of a destination in and of itself; many Chan Chich visitors come here via charter flight from Belize City and spend the whole of their Belize visit right here. The

admired as very hard workers by most Belizeans, despite the fact (or perhaps because of it) that they religiously refuse to take part in Belizean politics.

Progressive Mennonites tend to wear overalls and plastic cowboy hats. The women still dress modestly, but not as severely as the Old Order Mennonites. They are involved in broad-acres agriculture, growing soybean and corn, working in construction and business, and are more fully integrated into the rest of Belize (though they still shun politics). Because these progressive Mennonites use modern farm equipment, drive, and don't share their more conservative brethren's aversion to mechanization, they're sometimes known locally as 'Mecha-nites.' Their communities, with their large, spread-out farms, auto parts and farm equipment dealerships, closely resemble parts of Iowa, only with palm trees.

Another group of Belizean Mennonites are those who immigrated more recently from the USA and Canada. Less conservative, but more scripturaly observant than the Progressive Mennonites, this is the only group who engage actively in both proselytizing and the affairs of the non-Mennonite community. These more modern Mennonites live in communities that are not primarily Mennonite, and engage in mechanical work and agrochemical sales. Most Mennonites of this sect are based in Toledo District. One member of this community, Mr Laban Kroppf, runs a great bakery in St Margaret's village on the Hummingbird Hwy that ships cookies and pastries throughout the country.

Certain beliefs are central to all Mennonites, most notably simplicity in dress, modesty in behavior, and pacifism. Despite their small numbers, the Mennonites are a large part of the Belizean economy, providing foods, goods and services, helping to make Belize the country it is.

Christopher Nesbitt is an organic farmer who operates the Maya Mountain Research Farm in Toledo District (p253).

setting is picture perfect for a jungle lodge. Thatched cabanas – each with bathroom, fan, two queen-size beds and a wraparound verandah – share space with partly excavated ruins of an ancient Maya plaza. Its distance from anywhere deters drop-ins, and the limited number of cabanas (not to mention the price) keeps it uncrowded and helps maintain the feeling that you're really in the middle of nowhere.

Chan Chich lies within a private reserve of over 200 sq miles known as the Gallon Jug Parcel, maintained by Belizean businessman Barry Bowen after his purchase of the BEC's lands in the 1980s (see p170). Intensive agriculture is practiced in a small part of the reserve, but the rest is subject to strict conservation. The lodge offers guided walks, vehicle tours and other activities throughout the day (and some at night), and 9 miles of trails invite independent exploration. One tour goes to Gallon Jug, the center of the reserve's very orderly agricultural operations. Crops grown here include corn, soybean, cacao and organic coffee bean, and another program aims to raise the quality of local beef using embryo transfer technology from English Herefords.

The lodge is about 25 miles south of La Milpa Field Station (see p171) and 4 miles from the Guatemalan border. It's most easily reached by chartered plane from Belize City (about BZ$500 per person roundtrip). Some make the drive from Belize City via Orange Walk Town (four hours, 130 miles), though the 73 miles from Orange Walk to the lodge are mostly unpaved. Reliable sources tell of a much shorter – and reasonably smooth – road reaching from Yalbac (10 miles north of the Western Hwy) to Gallon Jug, but said road has yet to appear on any map. If this road exists, it would cut travel time considerably. In any event, Chan Chich management will be glad to help arrange details of your voyage from start to finish.

COROZAL DISTRICT

Peaceful and secluded, Corozal is Belize's northernmost district. Its proximity to Mexico gives it a certain Spanish charm, while its distance from the rest of the country keeps it well off the beaten tourist track. More compact (by far) than Orange Walk District, most of the sights of Corozal District are well within striking distance – by boat or road – of Corozal Town itself.

The chunk of land that spreads south and eastward across the bay from Corozal Town is at once one of the least-visited and most visit-worthy spots in Belize. Though topographically not as dramatic as the west or the south (most of northern Belize is fairly flat), this part of the country is sparsely populated and filled with lovely jungle, not to mention the cool seaside town of Sarteneja and the amazing coastal Maya ruins at Cerros.

COROZAL TOWN
pop 9100

South of Mexico by 9 miles and 29 miles north of Orange Walk Town, Corozal Town has a vibe different from any other town in Belize. For one thing, though it feels prosperous (especially by Belizean standards), most of the town's wealth comes from its position as a commercial and farming center, not tourism. So while Corozal is a fine place to be a tourist, it escapes that 'tourist plantation' vibe that haunts so many other places in Belize.

With ocean breezes, a selection of budget and midrange hotels, good food and easy access to all of northern Belize, Corozal is a good place to spend a few days either on the way to or from Mexico. The whole town is situated on Corozal Bay, and the waterfront is filled with parks, picnic tables, and beachside *palapas* (thatched-roof, open-air huts). Though the water is clearer on the other side of the bay (thanks to prevailing tides and a river bringing silt from western farmland), this side of the bay is fine for swimming as well.

History

The ruins of the Postclassic Maya trading center, now called Santa Rita (probably the original Chetumal), lie beneath parts of modern Corozal. Across the bay, Cerros was a substantial coastal trade center in the Preclassic Period.

Modern Corozal dates from 1849, when it was founded by Mexicans fleeing the War of the Castes. The refugees named their town Corozal after the Spanish word for cohune palm, a strong symbol of fertility.

For years Corozal had the look of a typical Mexican town, with thatched-roof homes. Then Hurricane Janet roared through in 1955 and blew away many of the buildings. Much

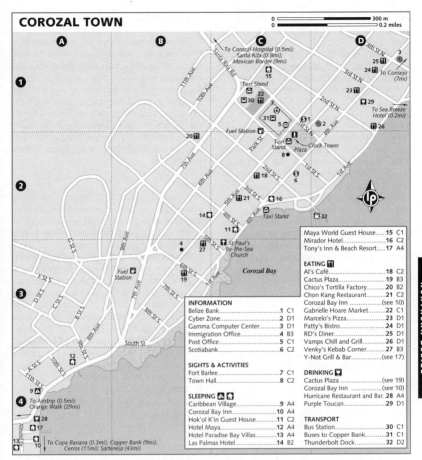

COROZAL TOWN

Maya World Guest House.....**15** C1	
Mirador Hotel............................**16** C2	
Tony's Inn & Beach Resort.....**17** A4	

EATING 🍴
Al's Café.................................**18** C2	
Cactus Plaza.........................**19** B3	
Chico's Tortilla Factory........**20** B2	
Chon Kang Restaurant..........**21** C2	
Corozal Bay Inn ....(see 10)	
Gabrielle Hoare Market........**22** C1	
Marcelo's Pizza......................**23** D1	
Patty's Bistro.........................**24** D1	
RD's Diner..............................**25** D1	
Vamps Chill and Grill.............**26** D1	
Venky's Kebab Corner............**27** B3	
Y-Not Grill & Bar...................(see 17)	

INFORMATION
Belize Bank..............................**1** C1	
Cyber Zone...............................**2** D1	
Gamma Computer Center........**3** D1	
Immigration Office..................**4** B3	
Post Office................................**5** C1	
Scotiabank................................**6** C2	

SIGHTS & ACTIVITIES
Fort Barlee...............................**7** C1	
Town Hall.................................**8** C2	

SLEEPING 🛏
Caribbean Village.....................**9** A4	
Corozal Bay Inn.....................**10** A4	
Hok'ol K'in Guest House..........**11** C2	
Hotel Maya.............................**12** A4	
Hotel Paradise Bay Villas.......**13** A4	
Las Palmas Hotel...................**14** B2	

DRINKING 🍸
Cactus Plaza ....(see 19)	
Corozal Bay Inn ....(see 10)	
Hurricane Restaurant and Bar.**28** A4	
Purple Toucan.......................**29** D1	

TRANSPORT
Bus Station.............................**30** C1	
Buses to Copper Bank............**31** C1	
Thunderbolt Dock..................**32** D2	

NORTHERN BELIZE

of Corozal's wood-and-concrete architecture dates from the late 1950s.

Like Orange Walk, the Corozal economy is based on sugarcane farming (though there's also quite a bit of trade with nearby Chetumal in Mexico as well). A large sugar refinery operated at Libertad, a few miles south of Corozal, from 1935 to 1985, but today all of Belize's cane is processed at Tower Hill near Orange Walk.

Orientation & Information

Corozal is arranged around a town square (encompassing the plaza, post office and bus station). The main highway passes through town as Santa Rita Rd and 7th Ave, briefly skirting the sea at the south end of town.

Belize Bank (☎ 422-2087; cnr 5th Ave & 1st St N; ☼ 8am-1pm Mon-Thu, 8am-4:30pm Fri) Situated on the plaza; ATM accepts all international credit cards, with BZ$500 limit and BZ$2 fee.

Corozal.com (www.corozal.com) Lots of links to local businesses.

Corozal Hospital (☎ 422-2076) This hospital is located northwest of the center of town on the way to Chetumal (Mexico).

Cyber Zone (☎ 602-6255; N Park St; internet per hr BZ$4; ☼ 9am-9pm) Good internet service.

Gamma Computer Center (☎ 442-0225; 22 4th Ave; internet per hr BZ$4; ☼ 8am-8pm Mon-Sat, 9:30am-1:00pm Sun) Internet & computer supplies.

Immigration Office (5th Ave, ☼ 8:30am-noon & 1-4pm Mon-Fri) Provides 30-day visa extensions for most nationalities.

lonelyplanet.com

Post office (☎ 422-2462; 5th Ave; ⏱ 8:30am-noon & 1-4:30pm Mon-Thu, till 4pm Fri) On the site of Fort Barlee, facing the plaza.

Scotiabank (☎ 422-2046; 4th Ave; ⏱ 8:30am-2:30pm Mon-Thu, 8:30am-4pm Fri, 9am-noon Sat) Currency exchange and cash advances; ATM accepts all international cards with BZ$800 daily limit and no fee.

Sights

ARCHITECTURE

If you enjoy looking at interesting architecture, then you'll want to spend a few hours walking around Corozal, as the town has a number of beautiful homes (in various states, from crumbling to fully restored) with a lovely Spanish Colonial feel. The coastal walk itself offers several fine examples of old Belize (not to be confused with Old Belize, p112), such as Corozal's old **market and customs house**, built in 1886 and one of only 11 buildings spared by Hurricane Janet. This building was once the town's museum but, alas, is currently vacant. There are a few dozen other lovely homes along the waterfront, and many more scattered throughout town.

Predating the customs house is (what's left of) **Fort Barlee**, built by Caste War refugees in 1849, for protection from attacks by hostile Maya. Remains of the brick corner turrets are still visible on the fort site.

TOWN HALL

A colorful and graphic mural depicting Corozal's history by Belizean-Mexican artist Manual Villamor Reyes enlivens the lobby of the **town hall** (☎ 422-2072; 1st St S; admission free; ⏱ 9am-noon & 1-5pm Mon-Sat), which faces the plaza. Episodes depicted in the mural include the War of the Castes, with the talking cross and the fall of Bacalar; the flight of refugees into British Honduras; the founding of Corozal; and Hurricane Janet.

SANTA RITA

These are the remains of an ancient coastal town that once occupied (give or take) the same strategic trading position as present-day Corozal Town, namely the spot between two rivers – the Rio Hondo (which now forms the Belize–Mexico border) and the New River (which enters Corozal Bay south of town, bringing with it much silt). Though at present much of Santa Rita remains unexcavated, the part that is restored is well worth the time you'll spend finding it.

To get to the restored **Maya temple** (admission free) of Santa Rita, head north on the main highway, about 1200yd from the bus station, then turn left at the Super Santa Rita store. Some 350yd past the store you'll find a wooded area on the right, and in the middle of this is the medium-sized and partially restored pyramid offering an amazing view of the surrounding town and bay. There's no visitors center, and you can pretty much visit whenever you want. If you can't find it, just ask a local where the ruins are; someone will tell you.

Tours

A popular destination for fishing enthusiasts and jungle explorers, Corozal is the base of operations to a number of good guides. If you're looking for plane tickets, contact Rosita at the Hotel Maya (see opposite).

Vitalino Reyes (☎ 602-8975; www.cavetubing.bz) is the man to meet if you're looking for a deeper understanding of the nature and culture of Belize. In addition to being a pioneer of cave-tubing (p219), Vitalino also leads tours to various Maya ruins including Cerros, Lamanai and Altun Ha, as well as taking visitors on jungle tours around Sarteneja. What makes Vitalino so unique is that he's constantly mingling the practical and historical aspects of local lore: one minute he'll be telling you about foraging techniques of the Ancient Maya, and the next he'll have you tasting jungle grasses, tree bark, and even termites (surprisingly refreshing, they taste like after-dinner mints). For a real treat, ask Vitalino to teach you about proper tarantula-handling techniques. Vitalino specializes in one- and two-day package tours combining popular Belize District destinations such as Tikal, Altun Ha and the Belize Zoo with cave-tubing expeditions. This is a great way to arrange group transit from Corozal to the Belize District, as Vitalino drives a large van.

The **Saldivar Brothers** (☎ 623-3920), Robert and Richard, specialize in nautical outings around Corozal. With their 40hp outboard motor, mahogany-outfitted skiff, they're well equipped to bring visitors around the coastal villages from Cerros to Sarteneja. The brothers are also expert fly fishermen, and lead fishing expeditions from Corozal Bay to the northern cayes and reefs. Rates vary depending on time and distance, with the ballpark figure for a full day going for BZ$200 for a group of two or three.

Sleeping
CAMPING

Caribbean Village (☎ 422-2725; www.belizetransfers .com; 7th Ave, South End; camping per person BZ$10, RVs BZ$40) You can't miss this place; it's the plot of land right off the main road on the south end of town with all the RVs parked on it. Lot spaces include all connections (water, electricity, sewage); there's an additional charge of BZ$10 for each person over two per rig. There's also a campground with toilets and cold showers. Internet is BZ$5 per hour, and owners Henry and Joan Menzies are licensed travel agents who can help you book tickets throughout Central America.

BUDGET

ourpick Sea Breeze Hotel (☎ 422-3051; 605-9341; www .theseabreezehotel.com; 23 1st Ave; r BZ$35-55; P ☒ ☐) Definitely our favorite budget hotel in all of Belize, the Sea Breeze is reminiscent of the kind of cheap and pleasant Key West hotel where Ernest Hemingway might have spent his last years. The hotel has 11 rooms, each with a queen-sized bed, desk and chair, and en suite with hot shower. The more expensive rooms have air-con, and all have cable TV and wireless internet. The feature that would have appealed most to Papa Hemingway might well have been the fully stocked bar on the second floor, complete with indoor and outdoor seating and a stunning view of Corozal Bay. Good food and strong coffee available on request.

Maya World Guest House (☎ 422-0191, 626-0131; byronchuster@gmail.com; 16 2nd St North; s/d BZ$45/53) An offbeat and artistically done guesthouse, Maya World consists of two houses and an enclosed courtyard. The front house is a restored two-story colonial home with a wraparound verandah complete with hammock; the one out back is a one-story building with four simple but functional rooms. The rooms in front are a bit brighter, but the ones in back have all been painted with scenes of splendor representing different places in Taiwan, the ancestral home of owner Chu Baoshan ('Byron'). All rooms have shared bathrooms with solar-heated showers. The garden in the center is at once fragrant and functional, containing herbs, vegetable plants, and a tall Neem tree, reputed to have many healing qualities. Guests have full run of the kitchen, and Byron will

cook you up some Taiwanese dishes if he has the time. Byron is also the proud owner of *The Loon*, Belize's only solar-powered speedboat. Ask him to take you on an eco-friendly tour of Corozal Bay!

Hotel Maya (☎ 422-2082; www.hotelmaya.net; 7th Ave, South End; s/d/tr/q BZ$68/75/89/89, s/d/tr/q with air-con BZ$89/100/100/126; ☒ ☒) Run by the very friendly Rosita May, the Hotel Maya is a long-time budget favorite. Rooms are clean and enlivened by colorful bedspreads and paintings done by local artists. The attached restaurant serves a great breakfast, and lunch and dinner are available on request for groups. In addition to being a licensed travel agent, Rosita is also a great source of local information.

Hotel Paradise Bay Villas (☎ 422-0209; shanny belize@hotmail.com; 7 Almond Dr; villas BZ$80; ☐) Run by a German named Hermann, this place offers fully furnished European-style apartments with two bedrooms, bathroom, living room, broadband internet and full kitchens. Honeymooners take note: master bedrooms have king-sized beds and mirrored ceilings.

MIDRANGE

Mirador Hotel (☎ 422-0189; www.mirador.bz; 4th Ave & 3rd St S; s/d/tr BZ$70/90/110, s/d/tr with air-con BZ$100/120/150; ☒ ☐) A stately hotel resembling a miniature Belizean version of New York City's famed Flatiron Building, the 20 rooms of the four-story Mirador are all clean and nicely arranged, with hot shower and cable TV, and most with lovely ocean views. The rooftop patio is a sight to behold, offering hammocks, lounge chairs, and views clear out to Mexico.

Hok'ol K'in Guest House (☎ 422-3329; www.corozal .net; 89 4th Ave; r with fan BZ$76-114, with air-con BZ$92-135; ☒ ☐) With a Maya name meaning 'rising sun,' this modern, well-run, small hotel overlooking the bay may well be the best value in town. The large, impeccably clean rooms are designed to catch sea breezes. Each has two double beds, a bathroom and a balcony with hammock. There's also a family suite available (BZ$190) and a rather small economy room (BZ$42). Hok'ol K'in also serves meals at reasonable prices (breakfasts are particularly good).

Las Palmas Hotel (☎ 422-0196, 602-5186; www .nestorshotel.com; 123 5th Ave S; s/d/q BZ$90/100/150; P ☒ ☐) Formerly known as Nestor's, this newly renovated hotel has rooms with a crisp, minimalist feel, with white stucco walls, wooden furniture and a southwestern motif. The hotel has good security, though this does give it a bit of a gated community feel.

our pick Corozal Bay Inn (☎ 422-2691; www.corozal bayinn.com; Almond Dr; cabanas BZ$120; P ⊠ ☐ ☒) Fronting the sea at the far south end of town, this relaxed, family-run place has cozy, tiled, mosquito-netted, air-con cabanas set around a broad sandy area. Each has a fridge, coffee maker, cable TV and hot shower. Hospitable staff, a good restaurant (see right), a sociable outdoor bar, good pool and informal atmosphere make this a hugely enjoyable place to stay.

Copa Banana (☎ 422-0284; www.copabanana.bz; 409 Bayshore Dr; r BZ$120; P ⊠ ☒) The Copa Banana has five suites, which are more like full-service apartments, set in off the beach on the far southern end of Corozal. Each has clean and comfortable themed rooms (palms, beach, nautical etc), shared kitchen, washing machine, and dining and sitting areas. All are cable-TV and internet equipped. The owners offer weekly rates, free bicycles and free pickup from the bus station or the airstrip.

Tony's Inn & Beach Resort (☎ 422-2055; www .tonysinn.com; Almond Dr; r BZ$164; P ⊠ ☐) Another of the southside Corozal resorts, Tony's has similar standards to the Corozal Bay Inn with a slightly more formal atmosphere. Uniform rooms are on two floors of a building surrounding a small garden, and have all the amenities you'd expect at this price range.

Eating

Travelers who are using Corozal as a way station before heading into Southern Belize may want to spend an extra day in Corozal just to eat some great food before heading out into the land of stew chicken and rice and beans. Check out the second floor of the **Gabrielle Hoare Market** (6th Ave; ⏰ 6:30am-5:30pm Mon-Sat, till 3pm Sun) for cheap eats in a lovely setting.

BUDGET
Chico's Tortilla Factory (25 7th Ave; tortillas per dozen BZ$1.25; ⏰ 6am-5pm) Not a sit-down restaurant, but a fun place to go to watch flour tortillas being made; there's a small vegetable market outside where you can buy stuff to put in 'em for a meal on the cheap.

Vamps Chill & Grill (☎ 402-2141; ice cream BZ$2-5; ⏰ 10am-9pm Tue-Sun) This cute waterfront ice creamery has cones, banana splits, and other sundae-type stuff. A good place to bring the

kiddies to cool off and watch movies on the overhead TV.

Al's Café (☎ 422-3654; 5th Ave; snacks BZ$1-2, mains BZ$5-8; ⏰ 8am-2pm Mon-Sat & 6-10pm Mon, Wed, Fri & Sat) A popular small sidewalk café, Al's does tasty Mexican snacks. Try the burritos with beans, chicken, cheese and very hot green sauce! No alcohol is served.

Romantic Restaurant (☎ 422 0013; cnr 4th Ave & 2nd St S; meals BZ$6-10; ⏰ 8am-midnight) Downstairs from the Mirador Hotel (p175), this big Chinese restaurant on the first floor is worth a visit should you get hungry for egg rolls or conch chowmein.

Marcelo's Pizza (☎ 422-3275; 25 4th Ave; pizzas BZ$7-16; ⏰ 8am-midnight; ☒) This pizzeria serves decent pizza, hamburgers, fried chicken and fish in small-town, fast-food joint ambiance.

Venky's Kabab Corner (☎ 402-0546; 5th St S; dishes BZ$8-15; ⏰ 10:30am-9:30pm) Chef Venky is the premier – and, as far as we know, the only – Hindu chef in Corozal, cooking excellent Indian meals, both meat and vegetarian. The place is not much to look at on the inside, but the food is excellent and filling. Two main dishes and a few sides easily serve three people.

MIDRANGE
Corozal Bay Inn (☎ 422-2691; Almond Dr; dishes BZ$6-25; ⏰ 7am-11:30pm) There's a wide variety of food on the menu here at the Inn's outdoor restaurant. Particularly good are the ceviche, garlic butter shrimp, and grilled steaks. Cheapest dishes tend to be Belizean standards such as stew chicken and rice and beans.

Cactus Plaza (☎ 422-0394; 6 6th St S; snacks BZ$3-5, mains BZ$8-20; ⏰ 6pm-1am Wed-Sun) Cactus Plaza serves light Mexican meals from a building that looks like a cross between a Christmas tree and a Mexican fruitcake. There are tacos, *salbutes* and *panuchos* (fried corn tortillas with fillings), *caldos* (broths), as well as shrimp, sea-snail or mixed-seafood ceviches. There are also plenty of good drinks including *licuados con leche* (milkshakes) and fresh fruit juices. This place also has a disco from Friday to Sunday (see opposite).

Y-Not Grill & Bar (☎ 422-2055; Almond Dr; dishes BZ$8-32; ⏰ 11am-11pm or midnight) Well-prepared meat and seafood dishes served under a breezy thatch-roofed *palapa* right on the waterfront, with dockside seating stretching out into the bay. The bar offers a fine selection of not just booze-boat drinks, but virgin ones as well.

RD's Diner (☎ 422-3796; 25 4th Ave; meals from BZ$10; 7:30am-9:30pm) Earth tones and high ceilings complement a menu offering a mix of Belizean, Mexican and straight-up continental fare such as burgers, salads and fried seafood. Service is a bit slow, and the coffee weak. The pastries are good, however.

Patty's Bistro (☎ 402-0174; 13 4th Ave; meals from BZ$10; 7:30am-9:30pm) Another Corozal favorite, Patty's is best known for its conch soup (BZ$12), a thick potato-based chowder with vegetables and chunks of conch meat that's a meal in itself. Patty's also has good Belizean and Mexican dishes.

Chon Kang Restaurant (☎ 422-0169; 32 5th Ave; dishes BZ$10-30; 10:30am-11:30pm;) Formerly known as Chon Saan Palace, this is considered one of the better Chinese eateries in town. Look for the Laughing Buddha statue at the door. There are also several other Chinese restaurants (Both Taiwanese and Cantonese run) scattered around town. Corozal's 'Chinatown' district is centered around Park St, one block north of 5th Ave and south of the central market (Gabrielle Hoare Market).

Drinking & Entertainment

Cactus Plaza (☎ 422-0394; 6 6th St S; 9pm-3am or 4am Fri-Sun) The disco at this unique-looking restaurant features a DJ on Saturday and karaoke on Friday and Sunday. Colorful low-relief murals demonstrate the same amusing taste as the building itself.

Corozal Bay Inn (☎ 422-2691; Almond Dr; 7am-late) With a fully stocked bar beneath a lovely enclosed and air-conditioned *palapa* offering outdoor ocean-front seating as well, the Corozal Bay Inn's bar is a very chilled spot in which to drink. An overhead disco ball and a full stage give rise to the notion that dancing and/or live entertainment may at times erupt. Food is also served well into the wee hours.

Hurricane Restaurant and Bar (South End; 4-11pm) A green beachside hut with outdoor seating, this newly opened place on the south end of town serves beer, booze and good bar grub.

Purple Toucan (☎ 422-2727; 52 4th Ave; 6pm-midnight) One of the more respectable bars in town, the Toucan has a pool table, dartboard and small backyard beer garden. Some food items are also available. Smaller items are good, but stay away from the steaks.

Shopping

Corozal isn't as flush with handicraft shops as most of the Garifuna-dominated southern Belizean towns. A cultural thing? Perhaps. Nonetheless, you won't want to leave without checking out the **Gabrielle Hoare Market** (6th Ave; 6:30am-5:30pm Mon-Sat, till 3pm Sun) where you'll find craftspeople selling handicrafts among stalls selling fruits, vegetables and fish. The 2nd floor has stores selling food and locally made clothing. In addition, many of Corozal's hotels have shops selling handicrafts. If you're really desperate for retail therapy, your best bet might well be a quick trip up to the 'Free Trade Zone' (see p178) on the Belize–Mexico border.

Getting There & Around

AIR

Tropic Air (☎ 422-0356; www.tropicair.com) and **Maya Island Air** (☎ 422-2333; www.mayaairways.com) both fly from Corozal to San Pedro (one-way/return BZ$90/$180, 25 minutes) and Belize City (via San Pedro; one-way/return BZ$200/$390, one hour) four or five times daily. Some flights stop at Sarteneja (BZ$70, 10 minutes) en route. Corozal's airstrip (CZH) is about 1 mile south of the town center. Taxis (BZ$10) meet incoming flights. Rosita at the Hotel Maya (p175) sells tickets for both airlines.

BOAT

Corozal is the natural jumping off point for trips to Cerros, Sarteneja and San Pedro. The largest water taxi service is **Thunderbolt** (☎ 422-0026, 226-2904), which runs regular skiffs with triple 250hp outboard motors and interior seating to Sarteneja (one-way/return BZ$25/50, 30 minutes) and San Pedro (one-way/return BZ$45/85, two hours) from its dock on 1st Ave. Call or stop by the dock for schedules. Boats leave from both sides (Corozal and San Pedro) at 7am and 3pm, and stop by Sarteneja from either direction. They'll also stop in Cerros if asked in advance. Your guesthouse should also be able to connect you with a guide and boat for group trips to either Cerros or Sarteneja.

One of the coolest – and definitely most environmentally friendly – ways you can get across the bay is by calling **Byron Chu** (☎ 422-0191, 626-0131; byronchuster@gmail.com), owner of both the Maya World Guest House (p175) and *The Loon*, Belize's only (to our knowledge) solar-powered boat. *The Loon* seats eight, runs silently, and gets across the bay in about twice

---

THE FREE TRADE ZONE?

Straddling the Belize–Mexico border at Santa Elena–Subteniente López, 9 miles north of Corozal Town, is a curious experiment in global capitalism going by the moniker 'The Free Trade Zone.' Though the name implies a kind of free-market free-for-all, with shops and stalls selling goods from both sides of the border at discounted rates to consumers from both sides of the border, the reality is, well…different. In practice, the Free Trade Zone resembles a shopping mall comprised of uninspired Wal-Mart clones and second-world duty-free shops, selling second-rate consumer goods from China, India and other export nations, and staffed partially by a combination of Belizean and Mexican workers. The last part, apparently, is where the notion of 'free trade' comes in (ie both Belizeans and Mexicans are free to work there). But not to shop, as Belizeans can't just drive in, shop and go home (as can their Mexican counterparts) due to restrictive import regulations and duties on the Belizean side of the border. In essence, the Free Trade Zone is pretty much a bargain-basement shopping mall for consumers on the Mexican side of the border – one that Belizean customers can only utilize with some degree of bureaucratic wrangling.

Surely though, there must be something there for intrepid non-Belizean travelers heading into Belize? Perhaps hefty discounts on consumer goods that can be gifted to Belizean friends down the road, or at least the promise of a few cheap cases of Guinness to be stowed in the trunk of the rental car for later beachside consumption? Think again. The Free Trade Zone is not the Duty Free Zone, at least not as far as the Belizean side is concerned. All items bought within are subject to duty and tax, and any purchase of liquor or tobacco above the allowable limit will be confiscated.

About the only thing the Free Trade Zone is good for, at least from the traveler's point of view, is this: according to one border guard on the Belizean side, leaving and returning via this crossing is a good way to renew your visa for 30 days for only BZ$37.50 (the normal fee for exiting Belize by land) as opposed to the BZ$50 it would cost you at the Immigration Office in Corozal.

---

the time (and at a fraction of the cost) of a gas-powered boat.

BUS

Corozal is a main stop for nearly all of the myriad bus lines that ply the Northern Hwy down to Belize City, all of which stop at the town's main bus station. At last count, 30 buses daily were doing the 2½-hour run from Corozal Town to Belize City, from 3:45am until 7:30pm; in the other direction, a similar number do the 15-minute run to the Mexican border.

In Chetumal, Mexico, buses from Corozal stop at the Nuevo Mercado (New Market), about 0.75 miles north of the town center. A few continue to Chetumal's inter-city bus station, a further 0.6 miles north, where buses leave for other destinations in Mexico. A taxi from the Nuevo Mercado to the bus station or town center is US$1. From Chetumal to Corozal, buses leave from the north side of the Nuevo Mercado from about 4:30am to 6pm.

If you're shooting straight through to Flores in Guatemala (eight to nine hours), the Línea Dorada (BZ$40) and San Juan Travel

(BZ$50) buses from Chetumal both stop at Corozal's Hotel Maya (p175) at 7am – the hotel sells tickets.

Buses to Copper Bank (BZ$2, 30 minutes) depart from behind the post office at 11am and 4pm Monday to Friday and 10:30am Saturday.

CERROS

This **Maya site** (Cerro Maya; admission BZ$10; ☺ 8am-5pm) is the only major ruin in Belize that also sits on beachfront property. In late Preclassic times, Cerros' proximity to the mouth of the New River gave it a key position on the trade route between the Yucatán coast and the Petén region.

The ruin is comprised of a series of temples built from about 50 BC. The temples are larger and more ornate than any others found in the area, and archaeologists believe Cerros may have been taken over by an outside power at this time, quite possibly Lamanai. Cerros flourished until about AD 150, after which it reverted rapidly to small, unimportant village status.

While the site is mostly a mass of grass-covered mounds, the center has been cleared and consolidated. Climbing Structure 4 (a funerary temple more than 65ft high) offers stunning panoramic views of the ocean and Corozal Town just across the bay. Northwest of this, Structure 5 stands with its back to the sea. This was the first temple to be built and may have been the most important. Large stucco masks flanking its central staircase have been covered over by stone walls for their protection. Southwest of Structure 5, Structure 6 exhibits a 'triadic' arrangement (one main temple flanked by two lesser ones, all atop the same mound) that is also found in Preclassic buildings at Lamanai and El Mirador in the Petén.

Cerros is about 2.5 miles north of the village of Copper Bank, which is 8.5 miles from Corozal. All-weather roads run from Corozal to Copper Bank, punctuated by two rivers forded by hand-cranked cable ferry (see p180) and on to Cerros. Bus schedules to Copper Bank don't permit day trips to Cerros, so most people visit on a guided tour from Corozal (typically costing BZ$80 per person) or trek here from the Cerros Beach Inn (see below), just a couple of miles down the road.

Cerros can get buggy, especially during the rainy season; cover up and don't skimp on the bug spray!

COPPER BANK

On the coast, a mile or so north of Copper Bank (and within striking distance of Cerros) sits our new favorite spot in northern Belize, **Cerros Beach Inn** (☎ 623-9530, 623-9763; cabanas d/q BZ$80/120; P 💻). What makes us love this place isn't just its location, set as it is on the white-sand shore of the crystal blue side of Corozal Bay. Neither is it just the amenities: four beautiful, well-decorated thatched-roof cabanas

with fans, lovely beds, hot shower and sea-facing porch, on-site kayaks and fully wireless internet 24/7. Nor is it just the food (restaurant mains BZ$8 to BZ$20), prepared by the owner, a former pastry chef from Miami who makes not only the best ceviche we've ever had but also the most decadent chocolate cake. What makes us wish we could spend months here is a combination of all these things, plus one other factor: Cerros Beach Inn is (almost) totally ecologically sustainable (see the boxed text, p181). Come for the kayaking, cake and ceviche; stay for the low-carbon footprint.

For those without wheels of their own, getting to Copper Bank and Cerros is best done by boat. See opposite for information on buses from Corozal to Copper Bank, and p166 for buses from Orange Walk. Buses to both places leave from Copper Bank at 6:30am (Monday to Saturday) and 1:30pm (Monday to Friday).

SARTENEJA & AROUND

Sarteneja (sar-ten-*eh*-ha) is a fishing village near the northeast tip of the Belizean mainland, and a hidden gem for those looking for a beautiful and inexpensive place from which to explore both the nautical and jungle treasures of the region. The village spreads just a few blocks back from its long, grassy seafront, and it's from this lovely seaside setting that visitors can head out to the Shipstern Nature Reserve and take birding, snorkeling, fishing and manatee-watching trips all along the fabulous coast of northern Belize. Of course, just chilling out in town is a good option. Sarteneja is also where you'll find Backpacker's Paradise (p180), a newly opened 27-acre jungle reserve that's quickly becoming a destination for the young (and young at heart) looking for vacations off the beaten path.

NORTHERN BELIZE

GETTING TO MEXICO

The border crossing at Santa Elena (Belize) and Subteniente López (Mexico) is 9 miles north of Corozal and 7 miles west of Chetumal. If you are crossing from Mexico to Belize you will normally have to hand in your Mexican tourist card to Mexican immigration as you leave. If you plan to return to Mexico within the card's period of validity you are entitled to keep it and reuse it for your return visit. Officials at this border may charge US$10 to allow you to keep the card; this is still cheaper than the US$20 you would have to pay for a new card on your return.

Travelers departing from Belize by land have to pay BZ$37.50; this includes both the exit fee and a government-imposed conservation fee.

Bus travelers, heading in either direction, have to get off the bus and carry their luggage through customs.

Information

Tiny's Internet Cafe (☎ 660-2977; tino_bz@yahoo.com; internet per hour BZ$8; ⏰ 6am-8pm Mon-Fri, 6am-5pm Sat & Sun) With four computers, a printer/scanner combo, sandwiches, coffee and fresh pastry.

Sights

SHIPSTERN NATURE RESERVE

This large **nature reserve** (admission BZ$10; ⏰ 8am-5pm) has its headquarters 3.5 miles southwest of Sarteneja on the road to Orange Walk. The reserve protects 43 sq miles of semideciduous hardwood forests, wetlands and lagoons and coastal mangrove forests. Lying in a transition zone between Central America's tropical forests and a drier Yucatán-type ecosystem, its mosaic of habitats is rare in Belize.

All five of Belize's wild cats and a score of other mammals can be found here, and its 250 bird species include ospreys, roseate spoonbills, white ibis and a colony of 300 pairs of American woodstorks, one of this bird's few breeding colonies in Belize. The reserve is owned by a Belizean nonprofit organization, Shipstern Nature Reserve Belize, funded by the Swiss- and Dutch-based **International Tropical Conservation Foundation** (www.papiliorama.ch).

Admission allows access to both a small **museum** and **butterfly house** at the headquarters and a botanical trail. More exciting are tours using the reserve's safari-type vehicles. Charges for these are reasonable compared with many other 'ecotourism' operations in Belize, and can be split between up to eight people. The **Xo-Pol** area, 40 minutes from the headquarters, has a treetop hide overlooking a large forest-surrounded pond where you can hope to see crocodiles, waterfowl, peccaries, deer and, if you're lucky, a tapir. As always, you'll see most in the early morning. Any guesthouse in Sarteneja can help you arrange these longer tours, and the reserve staff will

transport up to eight people from Sarteneja for BZ$10 roundtrip. Don't forget your long sleeves, pants and bug spray!

Sleeping & Eating

Sarteneja Village has a handful of small hotels, most of which also double as restaurants. There are also a couple of bakeries, grocery stores and bars scattered around the village.

Backpacker's Paradise (☎ 403-2051; www.cabanasbelize.com; Sarteneja; camping BZ$5, cabanas with shared/private bathroom BZ$20/35) Peaceful, beautiful, affordable even by Central American standards, and run by some of the nicest folks you'd ever want to meet. Backpacker's is an idyllic 27-acre patch of unspoiled jungle and tropical farmland with camping, cabins and a great little restaurant. It's no surprise that all sorts of travelers (not just backpackers) are making the trek into northern Belize just to spend a few days here, walking on jungle trails, eating tropical fruit from the trees, swimming in the nearby ocean, or just lounging in hammocks in the screened-in communal spaces. The cabanas are screened-in huts with thatched roofs and king-sized beds. There's a communal kitchen, and owners Christian and Nathalie Genest (both excellent chefs) serve up a number of French and Belizean favorites. Horses and bicycles are available for rent, and there's plenty around Sarteneja to do, which helps make Backpacker's Paradise everything the name suggests and more.

Oasis Guesthouse (☎ 661-8631, 660-9621; Lagunita St; d BZ$60; **P**) This new two-story guesthouse has four clean and comfortable double guestrooms with hot showers and TV. The rooftop patio offers a spectacular view of the bay and surrounding village.

Fernando's Seaside Guesthouse (☎ 423-2085; www.cybercayecaulker.com/sarteneja.html; N Front St; s/d BZ$60/80) This small and colorful hotel has three rooms

---

CRANK YANKING

If you're driving or riding through the back bush of Corozal District from Corozal Town to Sarteneja, you'll wind up fording two rivers in a distinctly Belizean way – via hand-cranked ferries that run along thick cables strung from riverbank to riverbank. This throwback to the early days of industrialization owes its existence to the low traffic density plying the roads. With too few vehicles to make building a bridge feasible, the low-tech (and low impact) human-powered cable ferry was seen as a fine way to ensure that cars, bikes and motorcycles could get where they needed to go (even if only two at a time). The first is between Corozal and the town of Copper Bank, and the second on the way out of Copper Bank towards Sarteneja. They're slow, fun and, according to locals, run 24 hours a day. Best of all, they're free.

SUSTAINABLE FROM SCRATCH: BILL BELLERJEAU *Joshua Samuel Brown*

There's no shortage of resorts in Belize jumping on the ecotourism bandwagon by slapping 'Environmentally Friendly' onto brochures and business cards. In some cases, the heart is in the right place and the company makes (and keeps) promises to move from nonrenewable to sustainable energy practices.

Bill and Jenny Bellerjeau, owners of Cerros Beach Inn (p179), decided to go a different route. Instead of transforming an existing hotel, Bill built theirs from scratch, solar powered and completely off the grid. Lonely Planet spoke with Bill and found out how…and why:

How did you decide on this piece of land?

We started here two years ago, and there was no road, just bush. The first time my wife and I came here, we had to cut our way through the jungle with a machete. When we got to this patch of land by the beach, something told us that this was the place.

So three years ago there was nothing but jungle here, no pre-existing infrastructure to work with?

Just jungle. I stayed here for a year, building first our house and then the restaurant, living in a tent on the beach for the first two months. After that, I built the cabanas.

When it came time to decide on a power source, why did you go with solar?

There aren't any wires out here, so it was either that or burn diesel, and I felt that solar was cleaner, more sustainable. I'm also planning to incorporate wind power into the system in the near future.

What was the initial expense?

For the solar panels and batteries it cost around US$16,000. We figure we'll have made it back after five years, judging by our average energy expenditure. I mean, we built this place to be very comfortable. We have 500 channels of cable TV, wireless internet, and the same conveniences of any other beachside hotel. We're a bit remote, but hardly spartan. To me, solar power is the best way to be both remote, energy independent, and totally comfortable.

Before opening up the Inn, did you consider yourself an environmentalist?

I've always cared about the environment, and I've been interested in solar power since I was a kid. Learning to set up a totally solar-powered system here was a necessity, which really made me jump into it with both feet. Now I'm a total believer. After two years, the solar system meets almost all of the Inn's needs. We're running cabanas, pumps, computers, stereos, a whole kitchen…all from solar power.

What parts of your operation aren't solar?

My showers are still heated by propane; I needed to set something up for hot water quickly, and solar water heaters work differently than photovoltaic (solar electricity) systems. But I'm planning to switch over to pure solar by the end of the year. I'll also be installing a 100% solar-powered Jacuzzi.

…which brings us to the subject of water. Where does yours come from?

We have two different systems: utility water for toilets and showers come from a solar-powered pump, and we also have rainwater stored in a water tank.

With so many places in Belize jumping on the 'eco-friendly' bandwagon, it's nice to see a place like Cerros Inn that's independent of the energy grid.

If I have my way, it always will be.

Innkeepers Bill and Jenny Bellerjeau are former professional chefs from the United States.

NORTHERN BELIZE

with two double beds, private bathrooms with hot showers and ceiling fans. The larger room has a thatched roof and tiled floor. Fernando can also help arrange snorkeling, fishing and other trips around the area, including to the Shipstern Nature Reserve.

Krisami's Bayview Lodge (☎ 423-2283; www.krisamis .com; N Front St; r BZ$80; ⓟ ⌨ 🖳) Next door to Candelie's on the west end of the waterfront street, Krisami's has comfortable, good-sized rooms with big bathrooms, cable TV and large wooden beds. The Verde family that owns both Krisami's and Candelie's are caterers, so home-cooked meals (BZ$10 to BZ$12) are available on request; the family can also arrange tours and transport around the area.

Candelie's Sunset Cabanas (☎ 423-2005; candelies cabanas@yahoo.com; N Front St; cabana with fan/air-con BZ$80/120; **P** 🔀 🖳) At the west end of the waterfront street, Candelie's has two comfortable cabanas, the air-con Wood Stork and fan-cooled Brown Pelican. Both are big and breezy, with two wooden queen-sized beds, huge showers, wireless internet and cable TV. There's also a dining room with an amazing mural depicting Sarteneja's history, and another room big enough to host workshops and meetings. Meals are available on request.

Getting There & Around

Sarteneja is 40 miles northeast of Orange Walk by a mostly unpaved all-weather road passing through the village of San Estevan and the scattered Mennonite community of Little Belize. Several buses per day run from Orange Walk, and at least one per day runs from Belize City. See p166 for information on buses from Orange Walk and p104 for buses from Belize City.

Tropic Air (☎ 422-0356; www.tropicair.com) flies at least twice daily to/from San Pedro (BZ$80,

10 minutes) and Corozal (BZ$70, 10 minutes). Other flights between San Pedro and Corozal may stop here on request.

The **Thunderbolt** (☎ 422-0026, 610-4475) ferry that does the San Pedro–Corozal run twice daily will stop in Sarteneja with advanced notice. The ride to Corozal takes 30 minutes and costs BZ$30; to San Pedro you're looking at an hour and a half at sea and BZ$50. Call for scheduling.

Five daily buses do the Sarteneja–Orange Walk run (BZ$5, 1½ hours, hourly from noon to 5pm Monday to Saturday), returning the same day. On Sunday, there's only one bus from Sarteneja.

Drivers from Corozal Town can reach Sarteneja (43 miles) by taking the road toward Copper Bank but turning right 6 miles from Corozal at a junction signposted to Progresso and Sarteneja. This road meets the road from Orange Walk Town shortly before Little Belize.

You can rent good bicycles at Fernando's Seaside Guesthouse or Backpacker's Paradise for BZ$4 per hour or BZ$20 per day.

Cayo District

Welcome to the Wild West of Belize. Covered with jungle, woven with rivers and dotted with Maya sites, Cayo District is a magnet for hikers, bikers, birders, canoeists, kayakers, cavers and archaeologists. The lush environs of San Ignacio are peppered with Maya ruins, ranging from small, tree-covered hills to massive, magnificent temples. Connoisseurs of the pre-Columbian era will have a field day, roaming around unexcavated mounds, crawling into empty tombs and ascending the heights at Cahal Pech, Xunantunich and El Pilar.

The mother of all Belizean Maya sites is Caracol, the mighty empire that defeated Tikal. Caracol towers atop the Pine Mountain Ridge, a dense forest that blankets the mountains in southern Cayo. Getting to this remote site is an adventure in itself, especially when it entails stopping for a swim in one of the many pools or waterfalls that decorate the countryside. The Maya also left traces of their age-old rituals in caves all around the region. There is no adventure more thrilling than climbing, crawling, canoeing, tubing, swimming or scrambling through a dark cavern, only to come across artifacts and skeletons from rituals over 1000 years old.

Besides its ancient history, Cayo District is teeming with life in the here and now. Wander around the Belize Botanic Gardens or a butterfly house to see it up close and personal, or take your binoculars out into the wild to be amazed by the flora and fauna that flourish there. You can live it up in luxury in an exotic jungle lodge or pick a lower-priced place in San Ignacio, or even pitch your tent alongside the Macal River. No matter where you set up camp, you are sure to sleep well after a day of action and adventure in Cayo.

CAYO DISTRICT

HIGHLIGHTS

- Discovering the artifacts from ancient Maya rituals deep in the darkest depths of **Actun Tunichil Muknal** (p191)
- Spotting a toucan twosome atop the High Temple at the Maya ruins at **Caracol** (p213)
- Floating in a river-tube along the **Mopan River** (p206) or through the caves of the **Nohoch Che'en Caves Branch Archaeological Reserve** (p186)
- Witnessing the intersection of art and nature at **Poustinia Land Art Park** (p209)
- Exploring the jungle on horseback with guides and horses from **Mountain Equestrian Trails** (p193) or **Banana Bank Lodge** (p187)

| POPULATION: 62,000 | MONTHLY RAINFALL: Jan 4.7in, Jun 9.1in | HIGHEST ELEVATION: 3640ft |

History

In ancient Maya times, the Belize River valley was a key trade route between the Caribbean coast and cities such as Tikal and Naranjo. Cahal Pech (p196) on the outskirts of San Ignacio is the oldest site in the valley, settled between 1500 and 1000 BC. Both Cahal Pech and nearby Xunantunich reached their peak in the 7th and 8th centuries AD, in late Classic times. The more splendid Xunantunich (p205) probably controlled the valley during these final centuries of Classic Maya civilization. But the most important ancient city of western Belize – indeed of all Belize – lay 23 miles south of Xunantunich, up on the Vaca Plateau. This was Caracol (p213), which conquered the mighty Tikal in AD 562 and grew to a city of perhaps 150,000 people (far bigger than modern-day Belize City) in the succeeding century.

Classic Maya civilization ended abruptly in western Belize, as elsewhere, around AD 850–900, although Xunantunich remained occupied a little longer. When the Spanish arrived in the 16th century, the town of Tipu, now on the site of Negroman Farm south of San Ignacio (not open to visitors), was capital of the Postclassic Maya province of Dzuluinicob. A Spanish expedition from the Yucatán in 1544 conquered Maya settlements as far inland as Tipu. But the Tipuans never really accepted Spanish political or religious control, rebelling several times and burning down their Catholic church in 1618. Tipu was the epicenter of a major rebellion beginning in 1638 that drove the Spanish out of most of Belize for good. The Spanish had the final victory over Tipu, however, returning to rebaptize more than 600 people in 1680, and eventually resettling the Tipuans on Lago de Petén Itzá, near Flores (p272), Guatemala, in 1707.

Mahogany cutters moved up the Belize River into western Belize in the late 18th century, suffering attacks from Maya who were scattered in the forests. The town of San Ignacio (p195), near the confluence of the Macal and Mopan Rivers, was founded as a collecting point for mahogany and, later, chicle, which were floated downriver to the coast. Work in the mahogany camps was one reason people began to move into the area from Guatemala in the 19th century. River and mule remained Cayo District's only means of contact with the outside world until the Western Hwy was built in the 1930s.

CAYO DISTRICT IN...

Two Days

Stay in the best lodge or hotel you can afford and take your pick from the jungle activities on offer, such as birding, canoeing or horseback riding. Finish off with dinner at **Hannah's** (p200) or **Erva's** (p200). On your second day, visit one of the Maya sites – either **Xunantunich** (p205) or **Caracol** (p213).

Four Days

Follow the two-day itinerary, but spend an extra day engaging in the jungle activities of your choice. On your remaining day, explore the amazing ritual cave of **Actun Tunichil Muknal** (p191)

One Week

If you have a week at your disposal, you can split your time between San Ignacio and a more remote jungle lodge, indulging in the best of the area's attractions. Follow all of the activities outlined in the four-day itinerary. In addition, you can wander around **Poustinia Land Art Park** (p209) and cave-tube at **Nohoch Che'en Caves Branch Archaeological Reserve** (p186).

Ten to 12 Days

Add further activities and attractions to the one-week itinerary, such as horseback riding at **Banana Bank Lodge** (p187) or canoeing through **Barton Creek Cave** (p193). Avid archaeology fans should visit **Cahal Pech** (p196) and **El Pilar** (p204), while nature lovers might prefer **Belize Botanic Gardens** (p207) or the Green Iguana Exhibit & Medicinal Trail (p198).

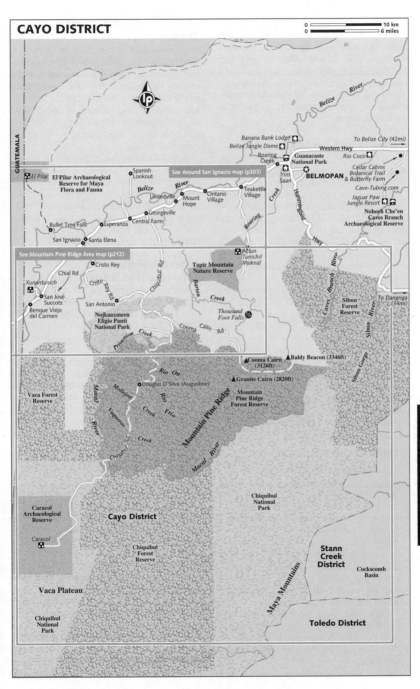

CAYO DISTRICT

0 — 10 km
0 — 6 miles

GUATEMALA

Belize River

To Belize City (42mi)

Banana Bank Lodge
Belize Jungle Dome
Roaring Creek
Western Hwy
Rio Coco
Guanacaste National Park
Yim Saan
BELMOPAN

Cedar Cabins Botanical Trail & Butterfly Farm
Cave-Tubing.com
Jaguar Paw Jungle Resort
Nohoch Che'en Caves Branch Archaeological Reserve

El Pilar
El Pilar Archaeological Reserve for Maya Flora and Fauna
Spanish Lookout
See Around San Ignacio map (p203)
Belize River
Unitedville
Mount Hope
Ontario Village
Teakettle Village
Georgeville
Central Farm
Bullet Tree Falls
Esperanza
San Ignacio
Santa Elena

Hummingbird Hwy

Roaring Creek

Caves Branch River

Sibun Forest Reserve

To Dangriga (34mi)

See Mountain Pine Ridge Area map (p212)
Cristo Rey
Chial Rd
Xunantunich
San José Succotz
Benque Viejo del Carmen
Cristo Rey Rd
San Antonio
Nojkaaxmeen Eligio Panti National Park
Privassion Creek
Chiquibul Rd
Barton Creek
Cooma Cairn Rd
Thousand Foot Falls
Actun Tunichil Muknal
Tapir Mountain Nature Reserve

Sibun Gorge
Sibun River

Cooma Cairn (3126ft)
Baldy Beacon (3346ft)
Granite Cairn (2820ft)

Vaca Forest Reserve

Macal River
Vaqueros Creek
Privassion Creek
Chiquibul Rd
Douglas D'Silva (Augustine)
Rio On
Rio Frito
Mollejon Creek
Mountain Pine Ridge
Mountain Pine Ridge Forest Reserve
Macal River

Caracol Archaeological Reserve
Caracol

Cayo District

Chiquibul Forest Reserve

Chiquibul National Park

Stann Creek District

Cockscomb Basin

Vaca Plateau

Chiquibul National Park

Maya Mountains

Toledo District

CAYO DISTRICT

As the logging and chicle industries declined in the 20th century, Cayo turned to cattle ranching and agriculture, growing sorghum, fruit and vegetables. The selection of Belmopan (p188) as the site of the new national capital in 1971 gave the region a big push forward, and since the 1980s tourism has proved an increasingly important addition to the local economy.

Getting There & Around

The Western Hwy is the region's artery, running across the country from Belize City through San Ignacio and Benque Viejo del Carmen and on to the Guatemalan border. The Hummingbird Hwy diverges southward 2 miles northwest of Belmopan. Buses run along the Western Hwy between Belize City and Benque Viejo del Carmen, stopping in Belmopan and San Ignacio. Bus travelers going between western and southern Belize need to change in Belmopan.

Unpaved or partially paved roads head off the main highway to villages, farms and remote lodges and attractions, the most important of these routes being Chiquibul Rd, which heads up and over the Mountain Pine Ridge, and Cristo Rey Rd, which links Chiquibul Rd directly with San Ignacio.

There are few bus services off the main highway. To access isolated lodges and attractions, if you don't have your own vehicle, you need to take tours from San Ignacio (or from the lodges themselves).

CRUISING FOR A BRUISING

Assuming you are not coming off a cruise yourself, you would be wise to avoid the Caves Branch Reserve and Jaguar Paw resort in the middle of the week. Tuesday, Wednesday and Thursday are the days that cruise ship passengers descend on Belize by the boatload; many of them squeeze into river-tubes and harnesses, in the hope of getting some action. Hundreds of people get herded through the caves and along the zip-line on these days; worse, prices are higher due to the increase in demand.

Remember, these people have been eating at buffets all week long – you don't want to mess with them. Better to do your cave-tubing and zip-lining between Friday and Monday.

BETWEEN BELIZE DISTRICT & BELMOPAN

West of the Belize District, the Western Hwy speeds along for about 50 miles on smooth, unbroken pavement. This is probably the country's most heavily trafficked road. It leads to the capital, of course, but even more significantly, it carries busloads of island-based tourists and cruise ship passengers to inland adventures such as cave-tubing, zip-lining and horseback riding.

About 11 miles east of Belmopan, a turn-off leads south to the Nohoch Che'en Caves Branch Archaeological Reserve and the Jaguar Paw Jungle Resort, two perennially popular attractions. In 2007 this road was paved, making it a quick and easy drive from the coast and exponentially increasing the number of visitors to the region.

Sights & Activities

BOTANICAL TRAIL & BUTTERFLY FARM

Less than a mile from the Western Hwy, an area formerly used for timber extraction is now the **Cedar Cabins Botanical Trail & Butterfly Farm** (☎ 821-5020; www.cedarcabinsbelize.com; Mile 47 Western Hwy). This recreation area – an excellent spot for families – features a 1-mile trail through the mahogany, chicle, yemeri and palm trees; bromeliads, ferns, orchids and other epiphytes are also abundant. The trail is also excellent for birding, with almost 30 different species in residence. Nearby, a 2000-sq-ft butterfly house is home to 25 different species, as well as a caterpillar growing area. Cedar Cabins also has a restaurant, gift shop and campsites on the grounds.

CAVE-TUBING

River-tubing is all the rage in Belize, and why not? What more pleasant way to spend a hot day than sitting inside an inflated river-tube and floating down a cool, calm river? How about floating down a river through a series of dark, mysterious caves?

The country's most popular cave-tubing site is the **Nohoch Che'en Caves Branch Archaeological Reserve** (admission BZ$10), east of Belmopan. Here, the Caves Branch River flows through five caves, taking tubers between the open air and cool caverns, and giving them an up-close view of stalactites, stalagmites, crystalline formations and artifacts from ancient Maya rituals. The extensive network allows for exploration of side passages, which sometimes lead to other caves, such as the spectacular **Crystal Cave**.

Independent cave-tubing guides gather just inside the entrance to Nohoch Che'en Caves Branch Archaeological Reserve. You can choose between the full five-cave float (BZ$70 per person, two hours) or a shorter two- or three-cave venture (BZ$50). Both involve a jungle walk to your starting point. Some guides also offer exhilarating night-tubing trips.

Prices include river-tubes, headlamps and life vests, but admission to the park must be paid separately. Bring your own swimming costume, tennis shoes and sun block, as well as a set of dry clothes to change into afterward. Beware: prices double on cruise-ship days (Tuesday, Wednesday and Thursday)!

More organized outfits that cater to cruise-ship traffic include the Jaguar Paw Jungle Resort (p188) and **Cave-Tubing.com** (☎ 222-5523, 605-1575; www.cave-tubing.com; per person BZ$90). Tour companies in San Ignacio (p198) can also arrange this trip with transfers from San Ignacio for about BZ$130.

To reach Nohoch Che'en Caves Branch Archaeological Reserve, turn south off the Western Hwy, 11 miles east of Guanacaste National Park (look for the signs to Jaguar Paw Jungle Resort). Follow this road south for 6 miles until you come to the reserve's entrance.

ZIP-LINING

On the grounds at Jaguar Paw Jungle Resort (p188) is the **Zip-line Canopy Tour** (BZ$110), where you zoom through the treetops from platform to platform on six linked cable runs up to 200ft long. Trained guides give you a safety briefing and help you into your harness. The tour takes about two hours, but on busy cruise-ship days, you'll be rushed through in less than an hour.

HORSEBACK RIDING

Belize's largest equestrian center is **Banana Bank Lodge** (☎ 820-2020; www.bananabank.com; Mile 47 Western Hwy; 2/4hr jungle tour BZ$120/180), set on a jungle- and pasture-covered property of more than 6 sq miles. Banana Bank has over 100 well-tended horses enjoying an extensive grazing area and state-of-the-art stables. Besides miles of jungle and riverside trails, facilities include a round pen and a large arena for training and exercising the horses. Owner

John Carr has lived and worked with horses all his life, having grown up on a Montana ranch and worked as a rodeo rider and cattleman before coming to Belize in the 1970s. See below for directions to Banana Bank.

GUANACASTE NATIONAL PARK

Belize's smallest national park is **Guanacaste National Park** (Map p185; admission BZ$5; ☼ 8am-4:30pm), named for the giant guanacaste tree on its southwestern edge. Somehow, possibly thanks to the odd shape of its trunk, the tree survived the axes of canoe-makers and still rises majestically in its jungle habitat. Festooned with bromeliads, ferns and dozens of other varieties of plants, the great tree supports a whole ecosystem of its own.

The guanacaste (tubroos) tree is one of Central America's largest trees. Its light wood was used by the Maya to make dug-out canoes. The tree is identifiable by its wide, straight trunk and broad, flat seed pods that coil up into what looks like a giant, shriveled ear (you'll see fallen 'ears' on trails throughout Belize).

Perched at the junction of the Western and Hummingbird Hwys, this 250,000-sq-yd park is an excellent place to break a drive. At the confluence of Roaring Creek and the Belize River, the park contains 2 miles of hiking trails that will introduce you to the abundant local trees and colorful birds. Birding is best here in winter, when migrants arrive from North America. After your hike, you can head down to the river for a dip in the park's good, deep swimming hole.

Sleeping & Eating

Rio Coco (☎ 621-3328; www.rio-coco.com; Mile 45 Western Hwy; d BZ$100; ℗) Although it's billed as a 'private resort,' this place is more like a private house, available for rental by the room or as a whole. La Casa Grande contains four bedrooms, two bathrooms and a big kitchen with comfy living space. A gazebo hung with hammocks is at the doorstep, as is a wooden walkway leading into the overgrown surrounding jungle. Although Rio Coco is right on the Western Hwy, it is in a funny no-man's-land a few miles east of Belmopan.

our pick **Banana Bank Lodge** (☎ 820-2020; www.bananabank.com; Mile 47 Western Hwy; chalet s/d/tr/q BZ$144/168/192/216, standard s/d/tr BZ$240/284/316, cabana s/d/tr/q BZ$250/316/370/425, ste s/d/tr BZ$327/382/436, all incl breakfast; lunch/dinner BZ$22/33; ℗ ✖ 💻 ♨) This wonderful lodge and equestrian center (see p187) sits on the banks of the Belize River, 4 miles from Belmopan. Each of the mahogany-and-thatch cabanas has a unique two-bed-room design, with sitting room, bathtub, mosquito nets, ceiling fans and wrought-iron or carved-mahogany bedsteads. Now Banana Bank also has the budget conscious 'chalet,' with three rooms sleeping five people.

With a fascinating history as an old logging-company headquarters and the scene of colonial-era horse races, Banana Bank is an expression of the personalities and interests of its owners, horseman John Carr and his artist wife Carolyn. For nonequestrians, the lodge has a bird observation tower overlooking a lagoon, an orchadia with over 50 species of orchids and some small unexcavated Maya ruins on site.

The turnoff to Banana Bank is 1 mile east along the Western Hwy from Guanacaste National Park. About 1 mile north of the highway, you reach a metal gong hanging beside a path leading down to the river. Bang the gong and someone will come from the lodge (on the opposite bank) to get you in a hand-operated ferry. It's also possible to drive to the lodge via a vehicle ferry over the Belize River just west of Roaring Creek village.

Belize Jungle Dome (☎ 822-2124; www.belizejungle dome; Mile 47 Western Hwy; standard/junior/ste/upper terrace r BZ$231/297/352/396; breakfast/lunch/dinner BZ$18/22/44; ⓟ ⓧ ⓛ ⓡ) This is, undoubtedly, an architectural oddity, but the signature dome deserves a mention, its skylights allowing sunlight to filter, reflecting off the polished mahogany interior. Standard rooms, suites and terraces are fully equipped with modern conveniences such as air-con, cable TV and internet access, and have easy access to the central swimming pool. There's also an organic fruit orchard, an orchid house and an enticing treetop café from which to survey the domain. Drive to Belize Jungle Dome via the village of Roaring Creek.

Jaguar Paw Jungle Resort (☎ 820-2023, in USA 877-624-3770; www.jaguarpaw.com; s/d BZ$384/440; breakfast BZ$10-16, lunch dishes BZ$16-20, dinner mains BZ$30-50; ⓟ ⓧ ⓛ ⓡ) Set in the midst of the jungle, Jaguar Paw is just 200yd from where the Caves Branch River issues from one of its caves. You're right on the spot for cave-tubing and zip-lining, and 9 miles of trails wind around the property. The resort decor is over-the-top, with each of the 16 rooms following a different theme, ranging from English Country Garden to Wild West. The grounds, lush with vegetation, also contain an aviary, a small butterfly farm and several restaurants. Drive past the entrance to Nohoch Che'en Caves Branch Archaeological Reserve and follow signs on the jungle road up the hill to the resort.

BELMOPAN
pop 17,570

In 1961 Hurricane Hattie all but destroyed Belize City. Certain that a coastal capital would never be secure from further terrible hurricanes, the government decided to move. In 1971 the government declared its intention to build a new capital in the center of the country, which would become Belmopan.

A grand new National Assembly was built to resemble a Maya temple and plaza, with government offices around it. Government needs have since outgrown these core buildings and a variety of less-uniform government offices is spread out around the central green.

The capital was slow to come to life; a lot of people still prefer to commute from Belize City or San Ignacio. But increasing numbers are seeing the plus points of the broad, leafy streets of Belmopan's quiet suburbia, and the population has increased significantly in recent years. Many government ministries and other organizations are based here, as well as a few embassies, giving the place an unexpected international atmosphere.

There has long been talk of opening a branch of the Museum of Belize in the capital, but there has been little movement on that front. In the meantime, this is a common place to change buses, but there is little reason to linger.

Orientation

Belmopan is located 1 mile east of the Hummingbird Hwy, reached by either of two turnoffs, 1 and 2 miles south of the Hummingbird's junction with the Western Hwy, 50 miles from Belize City. Belmopan is a small place that is easily negotiated on foot. A ring road encircles the central area of town. The bus terminal and the main commercial area are within the west side of this ring.

The government buildings at the heart of town are surrounded by grassy lawns and are vehicle-free, but look like a drab college campus of concrete bunkers. The square

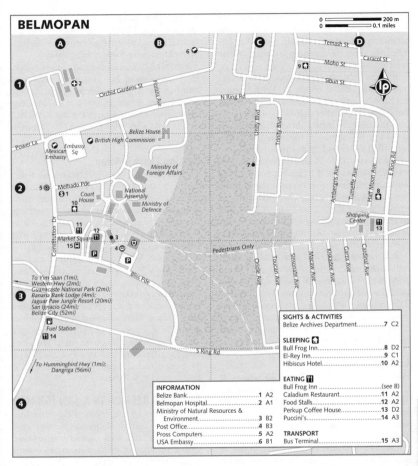

BELMOPAN

SIGHTS & ACTIVITIES
Belize Archives Department.............**7** C2

SLEEPING
Bull Frog Inn..**8** D2
El-Rey Inn...**9** C1
Hibiscus Hotel...................................**10** A2

EATING
Bull Frog Inn.................................(see 8)
Caladium Restaurant......................**11** A2
Food Stalls..**12** A2
Perkup Coffee House......................**13** D2
Puccini's...**14** A3

TRANSPORT
Bus Terminal.....................................**15** A3

INFORMATION
Belize Bank...**1** A2
Belmopan Hospital............................**2** A1
Ministry of Natural Resources &
   Environment....................................**3** B2
Post Office...**4** B3
Pross Computers................................**5** A2
USA Embassy......................................**6** B1

National Assembly building occupies the highest point of the area, surrounded by various ministry buildings.

Information

Belize Bank (☎ 822-2303; Constitution Dr; 8am-3pm Mon-Thu, to 4pm Fri) ATM and currency exchange.

Belmopan Hospital (☎ 822-2264; off N Ring Rd) Just north of the center, this is the only emergency facility between Belize City and San Ignacio.

Ministry of Natural Resources & Environment (☎ 822-2226; www.mnrei.gov.bz; 8am-noon & 1-4:30pm Mon-Fri) The Land Information Center here sells the best topographic maps of Belize available, including 1:50,000 sheets.

Post office (8am-noon & 1-5pm Mon-Thu, to 4:30pm Fri)

Pross Computers (☎ 601-3529; Constitution Dr; per hr BZ$6; 9am-7pm Mon-Fri, to 6pm Sat) Internet access.

Sights
BELIZE ARCHIVES

The **Belize Archives Department** (☎ 822-2247; www.belizearchives.gov.bz; 26-28 Unity Blvd; 8am-4:30pm Mon-Fri) has rotating displays on hurricanes, the Garifuna, Belmopan, Baron Bliss and other subjects. The extensive collections of photographs, newspapers, books, maps, documents and sound and video archives are also open to the public.

Sleeping

El-Rey Inn (☎ 822-3438; www.belmopanhotels.com; 23 Moho St; r BZ$54; P) An affordable option

CAYO DISTRICT

for budget travelers is just outside the ring road, northeast of the green. Named after the affable owner, 'Elroy' Garbutt, the El-Rey has 12 plain, clean rooms equipped with private bathrooms and fans.

Hibiscus Hotel (☎ 822-1418; www.belmopanhotels .com; Market Sq; s/d BZ$85/105; P ✗) With easy access to the bus station and everything that Belmopan has to offer (as limited as that may be), the friendly little Hibiscus Hotel offers good value. Rooms are spacious and clean, with tiled floors and freshly painted walls.

Yim Saan (Map p185; ☎ 822-1356; Hummingbird Hwy; s/d/tr BZ$94/94/120; P ✗) This big hotel on the outskirts of Belmopan represents the Chinese population in the capital. Clean, crisp rooms are sparsely decorated, with breezy balconies overlooking the parking lot. The downstairs restaurant serves a steaming and satisfying *lo mein* (noodles).

Bull Frog Inn (☎ 822-2111; www.bullfroginn.com; 25 Half Moon Ave; s/d BZ$130/160; P ✗ ☐ ☐) On the edge of the village green, just inside the ring road, the Bull Frog is a cheerful, civilized place. The 25 rooms are void of any special atmosphere, but they are spacious and comfortable, complete with telephones and cable TV, while big bathrooms have strong, hot showers.

Eating & Drinking

For a cheap meal, you can't go wrong at the food stalls just east of the bus station. They serve Mexican snacks such as burritos and *salbutes* (mini tortillas, usually stuffed with chicken) amid the sounds of rhythm and blues.

Caladium Restaurant (☎ 822-2754; Market Sq; mains BZ$8-12; ☺ 7:15am-8pm Mon-Fri, 8am-7pm Sat; ✗) Just across the street from the bus station, the Caladium is one of Belmopan's longest-standing family businesses. It offers a dependable menu of Belizean favorites such as fried fish and coconut rice, conch soup and barbeque chicken.

Perkup Coffee House (☎ 822-0001; 4 Shopping Center, E Ring Rd; mains BZ$10-22; ☺ 9am-9pm Wed-Mon; ☐) With excellent food, great coffee and desserts, and free wireless internet, it's no wonder the Perkup seems to be Belmopan's in spot. From breakfast bagels (perhaps the only bagels in Belize?) to steak sandwiches to lasagna, the place has a fairly wide culinary bandwidth. Leave room for cappuccino and cake!

Bull Frog Inn (☎ 822-2111; www.bullfroginn.com; 25 Half Moon Ave; mains BZ$15-20; ☺ breakfast, lunch & din-

ner) This popular and breezy hotel-restaurant serves up good steaks and seafood. The adjoining bar is a popular watering hole, livened up by karaoke and live mariachi music.

Puccini's (☎ 822-1366; Constitution Dr; mains BZ$15-30; ☺ lunch & dinner; ✗) This lively restaurant and bar has a great selection of pasta and other Italian dishes, as well as a few Mexican specialties. Take a seat at the open-air bar, or sit inside and enjoy the air-con. Service is friendly but slow.

Getting There & Away

The **bus terminal** (☎ 802-2799; Market Sq) is a stop for all buses operating along the Western and Hummingbird Hwys, including those operated by James bus line and National Transportation Services, Ltd (NTSL). Along the Western Hwy, buses head east to Belize City (BZ$4, one hour) and west to San Ignacio (BZ$4, one hour) and Benque Viejo del Carmen (BZ$6, 1½ hours) every half-hour from 6am to 7pm. Along the Hummingbird Hwy, buses go south to Dangriga (BZ$6, two hours) once or twice an hour from 6:45am until 7:15pm. Three of these southbound buses continue to Placencia (BZ$18, 8:30am, 2pm and 3pm). Almost all of the other Dangriga buses continue on to Punta Gorda (BZ$18, 5½ hours), including one express bus (BZ$22, four hours) at 4:30pm.

BETWEEN BELMOPAN & SAN IGNACIO

The 22 miles of the Western Hwy between San Ignacio and the Belmopan turnoff wind through verdant, well-shaded countryside, with a number of villages strung along the road. The road to Actun Tunichil Muknal (opposite) heads off south at Teakettle Village, midway between the two larger cities. About 6 miles from San Ignacio, at Georgeville, Chiquibul Rd (p193) turns south off the highway heading to Barton Creek and the Mountain Pine Ridge. It joins with Cristo Rey Rd (p194), which circles back to the Western Hwy in Santa Elena. Almost as soon as you turn off the highway, you enter another ecosystem, as these unpaved roads wind through the broadleaf forest, occasionally intersecting with a village or jungle lodge, but not much else.

Right on the highway, east of Georgeville, **Orange Gifts** (Map p203; ☎ 824-2341; www.orangegifts .com; Mile 60 Western Hwy) is one of the best gift shops in the country. It has a wide selection

CAYO DISTRICT

of Belizean souvenirs and handicrafts, including fine hardwood furniture, kitchen wares and sculptures made right here in the family's own workshop. The owner and founder of this place – Caesar Sherrard – designed the comfortable folding 'clam chair' that now furnishes just about every resort in Belize.

Behind Orange Gifts, **Caesar's Guesthouse** (Map p203; ☎ 824-2341; www.belizegifts.com/guesthouse; Mile 60 Western Hwy; s/d/tr/q BZ$80/100/110/120, with air-con BZ$110/130/140/150; breakfast & lunch BZ$14, dinner BZ$28; **P** ✖ 🖳) is a friendly, family-run inn. The excellent restaurant serves Belizean and international food; much of the produce is grown on site. The rooms are good and clean, if not luxurious, and there's a sweet swimming hole in Barton Creek at the bottom of its grounds. Besides being a master woodworker, Caesar is a jazz musician and his band Mango Jam plays here on the first Saturday of each month.

Garden of Eve Resort (Map p203; ☎ 824-3688; www.gardenofeveresort.com; Mile 62 Western Hwy, Central Farm; ste BZ$174-218; **P** ✖ 🖳 🐾) is a lovely, romantic resort set in the foothills of the Maya mountains. What is its claim to fame? No, it's not irresistible apples or a rascally resident snake… It's the swimming pool, which is apparently the largest in Cayo District. Aside from this swanky place for a swim or a soak, Garden of Eve boasts spacious suites with separate sleeping and living areas, as well as private porches. Also on the grounds are a small fitness center in a *palapa* (thatched-roof shelter), a playground and a campsite.

Actun Tunichil Muknal

One of the most unforgettable and adventurous tours you can make in Belize, the trip into 'ATM' (Map p203) takes you deep into the underworld that the ancient Maya knew as Xibalbá. The entrance to the **3-mile-long cave** lies in the northern foothills of the Maya Mountains, approximately 8 miles south of Teakettle Village on the Western Hwy. The trip is moderately strenuous, starting with an easy 45-minute hike through the lush jungle and across Roaring Creek (your feet will be wet all day). At the wide, hourglass-shaped entrance to the cave, you'll don your helmet, complete with headlamp. To reach the cave entrance, you'll start with a frosty swim across a deep pool (about 15ft across), so you must be a satisfactory swimmer. From here, you will follow your guide, walking, climbing, twisting and turning your

way through the blackness of the cave for about an hour.

Giant shimmering flowstone rock formations compete for your attention with thick calcium-carbonate stalactites dripping from the ceiling. Phallic stalagmites grow up from the cave floor. Eventually you'll follow your guide up into a massive opening, where you'll see hundreds of pottery vessels and shards, along with human remains. One of the most shocking displays is the calcite-encrusted remains of the woman who Actun Tunichil Muknal (Cave of the Stone Sepulcher) is named for.

Although it was discovered earlier, ATM was officially reported in 1989 and investigated in detail in the 1990s by Belizean and North American archaeologists. The researchers found some 200 ceramic vessels and the skeletal remains of 14 humans (seven of them children), all almost certainly sacrificial victims. The people and the pottery are all believed to have been offerings to the rain god Chaac (who dwelt in caves) in supplication for rain at a time of drought in the second half of the 9th century.

In the cave's Main Chamber, you will be required to remove your shoes. Make sure you wear socks – not only to protect your feet from sharp rocks, but also to protect the artifacts from the oils on your skin.

In view of the unique value and the fragility of the cave's contents, visits are strictly controlled. The common belief is that it won't be long before the ATM is closed to the public, so check it out now, while you still can. At the time of writing, only two companies were licensed to take groups of six to eight people: **Pacz Tours** (Map p197; ☎ 824-0536; www.pacztours.net; 30 Burns Ave, San Ignacio), the original ATM company, and **Mayawalk Tours** (Map p197; ☎ 824-3070; www.mayawalk.com; 19 Burns Ave, San Ignacio), also recommended.

The trip takes about 10 hours from San Ignacio, including a one-hour drive each way. Both companies charge BZ$160 per person, including lunch and equipment. Most hotels and lodges can book these trips for you (although they may charge more). Bring closed-toe shoes (not sandals), socks and a change of clothes.

Off the dirt road that leads to ATM, **our pick** **Pook's Hill Lodge** (Map p203; ☎ 820-2017; www.pookshilllodge.com; s/d/tr cabanas BZ$294/404/468; breakfast/lunch/dinner BZ$22/22/44; **P**) is a gorgeous

CAYO DISTRICT

WELCOME TO XIBALBÁ

The limestone outcrops of the northern foothills of the Maya Mountains have been eroded over millennia by the action of water running off the older crystalline rocks of the range's central core. Absorbing carbon dioxide from the atmosphere when it falls as rain, and more carbon dioxide from the decaying plant material on the ground, the water becomes a weak acid that dissolves into limestone, eventually producing what is known as a karst landscape, characterized by caves, sinkholes and underground rivers.

To the ancient – and many modern – Maya, caves were entrances to the underworld, Xibalbá, and the homes of all-important deities such as the agricultural fertility god and Chaac, the rain god. The Maya entered caves to present the ritual offerings considered necessary to keep the gods happy: pottery, tools, pine needles and food such as corn, chili peppers, and cacao seeds. Very few known caves in Belize do not contain some evidence of ancient Maya ritual activity more than a millennium ago. The most important offerings were human blood and human lives. Caves in western Belize such as Barton Creek Cave (opposite) and Actun Tunichil Muknal (p191) contain the remains of many children and adults, the majority almost certainly sacrificial victims, although some may have been interred in a form of ancestor worship.

Ritual activity in caves seems to have increased in the last century of Classic Maya civilization, from about AD 750. This was a time of growing stress and discord in the Maya world, leading to the Classic Maya collapse of 850–900. If, as recent research suggests, it was a series of devastating droughts that destroyed Classic Maya civilization, then it would be no more than logical for the Maya to have been redoubling their efforts to propitiate their rain god at this time.

Visiting caves is a relatively new and extremely exciting tourist activity in Belize. In addition to the fascinating Maya history, you'll be awed by the geomorphological structures where undulating flowstone decorates the walls, stalactites and stalagmites grow like ancient trees, bats flit in and out of ceiling nooks and darkness prevails.

When visiting, do remember that the caves themselves and their contents are very fragile. Take special precautions so as not to disturb the artifacts, which are left in situ. In some cases, you may be requested to remove your shoes and/or wear socks to reduce the inevitable erosion. At all times, stay close to your guide and follow instructions carefully.

---

lodge on the site of a small Classic Period Maya residential complex. Round, thatch-and-stucco cabanas sport wrap-around windows and immaculate natural-stone bathrooms. They are well spaced, allowing plenty of privacy. Set within a 300-acre private reserve, the grounds are lush with life, excellent for swimming, river-tubing and horseback riding. The birding is also superb, from the lodge verandah or along the forest trails or river frontage on Roaring Creek.

Spanish Lookout

A thriving Mennonite community, Spanish Lookout (population 2000) is located about five miles north of the Western Hwy, accessed from a turnoff at Central Farm. A hand-crank ferry transports cars across the Belize River.

Spanish Lookout is an excellent place to see the Mennonites' industriousness in action. Surprisingly, this road is paved; not surprisingly, it was the Mennonites – not the government – who paved it. They are the country's primary producers of dairy, meat, poultry and produce: here in Spanish Lookout you will find Quality Chicken, the biggest poultry producer, as well as Western Dairy, the only commercial dairy.

Since 2006, Spanish Lookout has been in the news related to the discovery of commercial quantities of oil in its environs. Understandably, drilling was highly controversial in this conservative community. A Mennonite spokesperson was quoted in the local press as saying: 'We would prefer not to have any production in our lands rather than money. Our way of life means more than money. Because of the laws of Belize we have to allow oil drilling.' The Mennonites have since come to an agreement to share profits with the landowner and oil companies, but the developments promise to bring big changes to this community.

Several buses a day go to Spanish Lookout (BZ$6, one hour) from San Ignacio, via Bullet Tree Falls.

Chiquibul Road

Chiquibul Rd (sometimes called Pine Ridge Rd) turns south off the Western Hwy at Georgeville, heading for the Mountain Pine Ridge and the Vaca Plateau to the far south. If you are heading to Mountain Pine Ridge from Belize City or Belmopan, this is the route you'll take. After 9 miles, Chiquibul Rd hooks up with Cristo Rey Rd, coming east from San Ignacio and Santa Elena.

SIGHTS & ACTIVITIES
Barton Creek Cave

Barton Creek rises high in the Mountain Pine Ridge and flows north to join the Belize River near Georgeville. Along the way it dips underground for a spell, flowing through the Barton Creek Cave (Map p203). During the Classic Period, the ancient Maya interred at least 28 people and left thousands of pottery jars and fragments and other artifacts on 10 ledges. Today, the cave is only accessible by canoe.

This peaceful trip takes you (in groups of six or fewer) about 750ft into the cave so you can get a look at the crystal cave formations, as well as the spooky skulls, bones and pottery shards that remain from the Maya. You must be accompanied by a guide to enter the cave.

If you have your own vehicle, you can drive yourself to Barton Creek and hook up with a guide at **Mike's Place** (Map p203; ☎ 670-0441; per person BZ$60), the restaurant in front of the cave entrance.

Be aware that this is a precarious drive. The narrow and very rough 4-mile track to Barton Creek Cave heads east off Chiquibul Rd, abut 5 miles south of the Western Hwy. Along the way you pass through the scattered traditional Mennonite farming community of Upper Barton Creek and ford both Barton Creek itself then one of its tributaries. Between the two fords a turning to the right leads to the friendly **Barton Creek Outpost** (Map p203; ☎ 607-1813; dishes BZ$10-16; ☻ 10am-5pm), which has home-prepared food and a few inviting hammocks on a deck by a cool swimming hole.

Coming from the other direction (via El Progresso), take the fork to the left as you exit the village. Heading down to the river, the steep incline and hairpin turns absolutely require 4WD. If you are not up for driving yourself, most of the jungle lodges and San Ignacio tour agencies (p198) can organize this trip. The half-day trip (4½ hours) costs between BZ$80 and BZ$90, including transportation.

Green Hills Butterfly Ranch

If butterflies make your heart flutter, don't miss the chance to see 30-plus exotic and exquisite species at **Green Hills Butterfly Ranch** (Map p203; ☎ 820-4017; http://biological-diversity.info/greenhills.htm; Mile 8 Western Hwy; adult/child BZ$10/5; ☻ 8am-4pm), which is 8 miles off the Western Hwy. Biologists Jan Meerman and Tineke Boomsma breed the butterflies, mostly for export to butterfly houses in the USA. Research activity includes tracking interaction between different species and compiling a field guide, as well as cultivating a botanical garden that supports the butterfly population.

On the guided tours, knowledgeable guides will walk you around the largest live butterfly display in Belize. You will come away with a good understanding of the insects' life cycle from egg to caterpillar to pupa to butterfly. A minimum of two people are required for the tour; the last one leaves at 3:30pm.

Horseback Riding

Explore the jungles and river valleys of Cayo on horseback by joining a tour with **Mountain Equestrian Trails** (Map p203; ☎ 820-4041, in USA 800-838-3918; www.metbelize.com; Mile 8 Chiquibul Rd; half/full day BZ$126/166). On a half-day ride, you might visit the ruins of the ancient city of **Pacbitun** or the secluded Vega river valley (excellent for birding). Full-day rides include Barton Creek Cave (including canoeing into the cave), Big Rock Falls and Mountain Pine Ridge. Horseback riding trips include a picnic lunch and breaks for swimming and exploring, making for a glorious day away from civilization. Wear long pants and closed-toe shoes or boots. You might go riding in the 1500-hectare **Slate Creek Preserve**. This private land in the Upper Barton Creek area is protected by the efforts of a community-based conservation group that MET is an active part of. Slate Creek provides an important buffer zone for Mountain Pine Ridge in the south and Tapir Mountain Nature Reserve in the north.

SLEEPING & EATING

Gumbolimbo Village Resort (Map p203; ☎ 665-3112; www.gumbolimboresort.com; Mile 2 Chiquibul Rd; r BZ$240; breakfast/lunch/dinner BZ$18/14/40; Ⓟ ▢ ⓡ) The namesake gumbo-limbo tree is known locally as the 'tourist tree,' due to its red, peeling bark. The resort is perched high atop a hillside that is covered with such trees. Indeed, visitors to the Gumbolimbo are particularly vulnerable to the trees' fate, because they will be loath to leave the swimming pool and spectacular vista over the valley. Four modern cabins surround the pool, with cool white interiors and large glass doors. Rooms are sparse but spacious, with plenty of room for extra beds (sleeping up to four people). This place is surprisingly green (with the exception of the too-blue swimming pool), running completely on solar power.

Mountain Equestrian Trails (Map p203; ☎ 820-4041, in USA 800-838-3918; www.metbelize.com; Mile 8 Chiquibul Rd; s/d/tr/q BZ$264/316/370/422; breakfast/lunch/dinner BZ$16/22/40; P) After a day of horseback riding, rest your weary body in the spacious thatched-roof cabanas, decorated with beautiful Maya tapestries and boasting lovely forest views. Kerosene lamps light the way (as there is no electricity), making for a particularly romantic atmosphere. Good home-style meals are served in the cantina, while a wide deck offers wonderful views of the valley. Turn off Chiquibul Rd immediately opposite Green Hills Butterfly Ranch and drive about 0.75 miles on the unpaved road. Multiday packages and transfers also available.

Cristo Rey Road

Cristo Rey Rd turns south off the Western Hwy in Santa Elena and winds up through the forests and villages of **Cristo Rey** and **San Antonio** to meet Chiquibul Rd after 12.5 miles. You'll come this way if you're heading to the Mountain Pine Ridge from San Ignacio.

Buses from San Ignacio to San Antonio (see p201) run along the Cristo Rey Rd. Return buses leave San Antonio at 6am, 7am, 1:15pm and 4:15pm.

Half a mile before San Antonio, the colorfully painted facade on the left side is the **García Sisters' Place** (Map p203; ☽ 7am-7pm), which displays and sells a wide assortment of black slate carvings. These five sisters – born and raised right here in San Antonio – invented this craft, which is now widely imitated around Belize. Their carvings, selling for between BZ$10 and BZ$200, depict a variety of subjects including local wildlife and Maya deities. You are likely to meet at least one of the sisters (or their wizened mother) working in the shop, doing their part to keep local traditions alive.

SLEEPING & EATING

Cristo Rey Rd has an excellent choice of lodges, ranging from affordable to opulent.

The location is within striking distance of many of Cayo's best adventures. The relative remoteness also means that there is adventure right at your doorstep, in the forests and rivers in the immediate surrounding area.

Mango Walk Inn (Map p203; ☎ 609-8892; www.mango walkinn.com; Cristo Rey Rd; cabanas per person incl dinner BZ$50; P) Set on 20 acres of rain forest and fruit trees, at the edge of the Macal River, this family-owned lodge is about 2 miles south of Cristo Rey village. The grounds are ideal for horseback riding, canoeing and birding. Rustic thatched-roof cabanas overlook the river. Be sure to contact the family in advance, so somebody is here to greet you upon arrival.

Crystal Paradise Resort (Map p203; ☎ 820-4014; www.crystalparadise.com; Cristo Rey Rd; non-thatched s/d/tr BZ$120/186/250, garden-view BZ$164/230/294, valley-view BZ$208/278/338, all incl breakfast & dinner; P ▣) Spread out over well-tended gardens just above the Macal River, Crystal Paradise is one of the few Cayo lodges owned by a local family. All of the members of the large Tut family get in on the fun, with the various sons acting as nature guides and the daughters cooking up hearty Belizean meals. Son Jeronie is a top-class bird guide who runs Paradise Expeditions (p198). Of the various cabanas and rooms, all are utilitarian but comfortable, the best ones sporting palm-thatched roofs (although the valley views are not worth paying for). Most of the guests come here on packages that incorporate preplanned tours, including horseback riding, canoeing, Maya ruins and other activities.

Maya Mountain Lodge (Map p203; ☎ 824-2164; www.mayamountain.com; 9 Cristo Rey Rd; r small/large BZ$140/236, cottages BZ$142; breakfast & dinner BZ$52; P ⌘ ▤) A long-standing favorite in Cayo, this lovely lodge is set on beautiful grounds less than a mile from Santa Elena. The gardens are lush, with a trail leading to a small, ancient Maya ceremonial site. Eight thatched cottages have tile floors and porches hung with hammocks. The rooms are less attractive but perfectly acceptable, opening up to a shared verandah. Owners Bart and Suzi Mickler pioneered many of the tours that are now widely offered throughout. One way they share their unbridled enthusiasm for the region is by asking their guests to subscribe to a simple ecological 'code of ethics,' which is presented upon arrival.

ourpick Macaw Bank Jungle Lodge (Map p203; ☎ 608-4825; www.macawbankjunglelodge.com; off Cristo

---

CANOE-SERVATION

One morning in March the waters of the Macal River beneath San Ignacio's Hawkesworth Bridge are the gathering place for a colorful flotilla of three-person canoes. They are assembled for the start of **La Ruta Maya Belize River Challenge** (www.larutamayabelize.com; registration fee BZ$250), a grueling four-day race down the Belize River to Belize City, where contestants arrive on Baron Bliss Day, a national holiday in memory of a great Belizean benefactor (see boxed text, p98). From relatively humble beginnings in 1998, the race has grown rapidly into Central America's biggest canoe event, attracting international as well as Belizean canoeists.

Even though it's all downstream, this is no gentle paddle. The fastest teams cover the river's 170 or so winding and beautiful miles from San Ignacio to Belize City in around 19 hours, while the slowest take around 36 hours. The race is divided into four one-day stages: Hawkesworth Bridge to Banana Bank Lodge near Belmopan (around 50 miles); Banana Bank to Bermudian Landing (60 miles including Big Falls Rapids); Bermudian Landing to Burrell Boom (35 miles); and Burrell Boom to Belcan Bridge, Belize City (25 miles).

In addition to being Belize's largest competitive sporting event, La Ruta Maya is an impressive conservation effort, as all proceeds are donated to local environmental efforts to revitalize and sustain Belizean waterways.

Rey Rd; d small/large BZ$140/272; (P)) Getting to these gorgeous grounds – spread out along the Macal River – is an adventure in itself. Turn off Cristo Rey Rd about 3 miles south of the village, then drive another 3 miles on the narrow, overgrown dirt track. Once you're here, you won't want to leave, as this place is a wildlife wonderland, teeming with birds and other animals. Hike the network of trails or float down the river in a tube, then retire to your rustic, kerosene-lit cabin, decorated with hand-hewn furniture and woven tapestries. A restaurant is on site, but meals must be ordered in advance.

Table Rock Camp & Cabanas (Map p203; ☎ 670-4910; www.tablerockbelize.com; Cristo Rey Rd; d BZ$250-294; camping incl tent BZ$60; breakfast/lunch/dinner BZ$18/22/40; (P)) This exquisite little resort has only three classy cabanas, each named for an exotic bird you might see on the grounds. The Kiskadee, Aracari and Motmot rooms are all furnished with custom-made four-poster beds, tile floors and thatched roofs. Or get up close and personal with the sounds and scents of the jungle when you pitch a tent alongside the Macal River. Delicious meals are served in the open-air *palapa*. Your hosts – Alan and Colleen Spring – built this place from scratch and are committed to preserving its pristine environment. They produce their own electricity, grow their own fruits and vegetables and use purified rain water. Athough this used to be farmland, the Springs are actively working to return it to its natural state by planting native mahogany trees.

Mariposa Jungle Lodge (Map p203; ☎ 670-2113; www.mariposajunglelodge.com; Cristo Rey Rd; d BZ$310; (P)) Luxe it up at this new jungle lodge near the turnoff to Mountain Pine Ridge. Each named for a jungle creature, the beautiful bamboo cabins feature handmade thatched roofs and hardwood furniture. Enjoying views of the rain forest or the mountain ridge, the screened porch is a perfect place to hang a hammock. King-size canopy beds are dressed with Egyptian linens and mosquito nets. And if all this is just a little too rustic for your tastes, you can retreat to the main lodge to watch your favorite program on the big-screen TV.

SAN IGNACIO
pop 19,084

Travelers to Cayo spend their time swimming in jungle-clad rivers, canoeing or crawling through mysterious caves, spying on birds, butterflies and other creatures, and learning the secrets of the ancient Maya. And at the end of the day, many of them make their way back to San Ignacio to rest up for the next day's adventure.

Together with neighboring **Santa Elena**, on the east bank of the river, San Ignacio forms the chief population center of Cayo District. Staying here is generally the more economical option for travel in Cayo; furthermore, there is no shortage of tour operators who are willing to show you the attractions and activities in the surrounding area. It is a friendly, functional base for your explorations in the region.

But San Ignacio is not one of those towns that exist only for tourists. It has a very positive local vibe, with a bustling market and a steady influx of immigrants. Residents are Mestizos, Maya and Garifuna, as well as a bunch of free-spirited expatriates from Europe and North America. They are easygoing and outgoing. Sure, they might try to make a buck off you, but there is no hard sell and they are just as likely to engage you in a discussion or invite you for a beer.

San Ignacio is located on the west bank of the Macal River a couple of miles upstream from its confluence with the Mopan River – a meeting of waters that gives birth to the Belize River. This once-remote location between two rivers gives San Ignacio its alternative name of Cayo – a Spanish word meaning 'island.'

Orientation

Two bridges cross the Macal – the Hawkesworth Bridge (a suspension bridge) to the south and the lower, wooden New Bridge to the north. Traffic is normally westbound over the wooden bridge and eastbound over the Hawkesworth. So if you're coming into San Ignacio along the Western Hwy from Belmopan or Belize City, you'll pass through Santa Elena first and then cross the wooden bridge, entering San Ignacio at the north end of its football ground. Sometimes during the rainy season the northern bridge floods and traffic goes both ways across the Hawkesworth Bridge.

Burns Ave, running north–south, is San Ignacio's main street, running past the football field and terminating at the traffic circle in the south, where you'll find the town hall and the police station. There is no bus terminal in San Ignacio, but most buses stop in the market square, just east of Burns Ave.

Information

EMERGENCY
Police station (☎ 824-2022; cnr Missiah & Buena Vista Sts)

INTERNET ACCESS
Café C@yo (☎ 824-2709; Burns Ave; per hr BZ$6; ◷ 10am-10pm)
Cocopelle Bar (8 Hudson St; per hr BZ$6; ◷ 10am-midnight) Free internet access with purchase of a drink.
Tradewinds (☎ 824-2396; cnr Waight's Ave & West St; per hr BZ$5; ◷ 7am-11pm Mon-Sat, 10am-10pm Sun) Reduced rates for students.

MEDICAL SERVICES
La Loma Luz Hospital (☎ 804-2985, 824-2087; Western Hwy; ◷ emergency services 24hr) This Adventist hospital in Santa Elena is one of the best in the country.

MONEY
Belize Bank (☎ 824-2031; 16 Burns Ave; ◷ 8am-1pm Mon-Thu, to 4:30pm Fri, 9am-noon Sat) The ATM here accepts international Visa, MasterCard, Plus and Cirrus cards.
Scotiabank (☎ 824-4190; cnr Burns Ave & King St; ◷ 8am-2:30pm Mon-Thu, to 4pm Fri, 9am-noon Sat)

POST
Post office (☎ 824-2049; Hudson St; ◷ 8am-noon & 1-5pm Mon-Thu, to 4pm Fri)

Dangers & Annoyances

San Ignacio is not a dangerous place, but travelers should always exercise caution, especially after dark. The area north of Market Sq – especially around the football ground – can be pretty dark and desolate after hours. A reader reported an attack and attempted robbery that took place in the evening on Burns Ave, north of Waight's Ave.

Sights & Activities

CAHAL PECH
High atop a hill on the southern outskirts of San Ignacio, **Cahal Pech** (☎ 824-4236; admission BZ$10; ◷ 6am-6pm) is the oldest known Maya site in the Belize River valley, having been first settled between 1500 and 1000 BC. It is, perhaps, less impressive than Xunantunich (p205) or Caracol (p213), but it's still a fascinating example of Preclassic Maya architecture. It was a significant Maya settlement for 2000 years or more.

Cahal Pech (kah-*hahl* pech) is Mopan and Yucatec Mayan for 'Place of Ticks,' a nickname earned in the 1950s when the site was surrounded by pastures grazed by tick-infested cattle. Today it's a pleasantly shady site with plenty of trees and few tourists. Its core area of seven interconnected plazas has been excavated and restored since the late 1980s.

The earliest monumental religious architecture in Belize was built here between 600 and 400 BC, though most of what we see today dates from AD 600–800, when Cahal Pech and its peripheral farming settlements had an estimated population of between 10,000 and 20,000. The place was abandoned around AD 850.

SAN IGNACIO

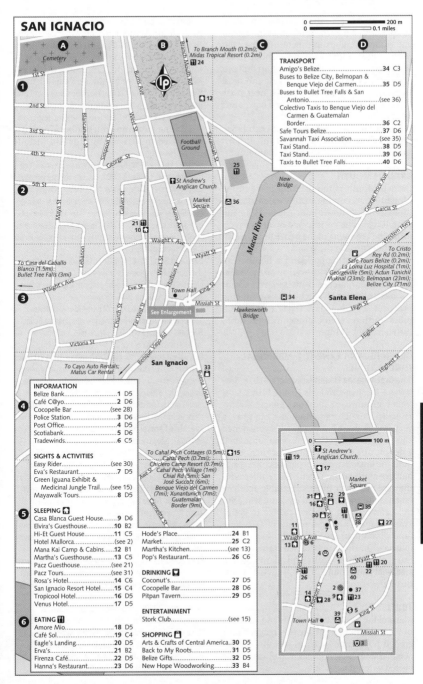

0 — 200 m
0 — 0.1 miles

Cemetery

To Branch Mouth (0.2mi);
Midas Tropical Resort (0.2mi)

To Casa del Caballo
Blanco (1.5mi);
Bullet Tree Falls (3mi)

To Cayo Auto Rentals;
Matus Car Rental

Football
Ground

St Andrew's
Anglican Church

Market
Square

New
Bridge

George Price Ave

García St

Western Hwy

Town Hall

Missiah St

Hawkesworth
Bridge

Santa Elena

High St

Higher St

Highest St

To Cristo
Rey Rd (0.2mi);
Safe Tours Belize (0.2mi);
La Loma Luz Hospital (1mi);
Georgeville (5mi); Actun Tunichil
Muknal (23mi); Belmopan (23mi);
Belize City (71mi)

San Ignacio

To Cahal Pech Cottages (0.5mi);
Cahal Pech (0.7mi);
Chiclero Camp Resort (0.7mi);
Cahal Pech Village (1mi);
Chial Rd (5mi); San
José Succotz (6mi);
Benque Viejo del Carmen
(7mi); Xunantunich (7mi);
Guatemalan
Border (9mi)

TRANSPORT
Amigo's Belize.............................**34** C3
Buses to Belize City, Belmopan &
  Benque Viejo del Carmen.............**35** D5
Buses to Bullet Tree Falls & San
  Antonio..................................(see 36)
Colectivo Taxis to Benque Viejo del
  Carmen & Guatemalan
  Border..................................**36** C2
Safe Tours Belize........................**37** D6
Savannah Taxi Association..........(see 35)
Taxi Stand................................**38** D5
Taxi Stand................................**39** D6
Taxis to Bullet Tree Falls............**40** D6

INFORMATION
Belize Bank...................................**1** D5
Café C@yo....................................**2** D6
Cocopelle Bar ....(see 28)
Police Station.................................**3** D6
Post Office.....................................**4** D5
Scotiabank....................................**5** D6
Tradewinds...................................**6** C5

SIGHTS & ACTIVITIES
Easy Rider.................................(see 30)
Eva's Restaurant.............................**7** D5
Green Iguana Exhibit &
  Medicinal Jungle Trail......(see 15)
Mayawalk Tours..............................**8** D5

SLEEPING
Casa Blanca Guest House................**9** D6
Elvira's Guesthouse.......................**10** B2
Hi-Et Guest House.........................**11** C5
Hotel Mallorca..........................(see 2)
Mana Kai Camp & Cabins...............**12** B1
Martha's Guesthouse.....................**13** C5
Pacz Guesthouse.......................(see 21)
Pacz Tours................................(see 31)
Rosa's Hotel.................................**14** C6
San Ignacio Resort Hotel................**15** C4
Tropicool Hotel............................**16** D5
Venus Hotel.................................**17** D5

EATING
Amore Mio...................................**18** D5
Café Sol......................................**19** C4
Eagle's Landing............................**20** D5
Erva's...**21** B2
Firenza Café................................**22** D5
Hanna's Restaurant.......................**23** D6

Hode's Place................................**24** B1
Market..**25** C2
Martha's Kitchen........................(see 13)
Pop's Restaurant..........................**26** C6

DRINKING
Coconut's....................................**27** D5
Cocopelle Bar...............................**28** D6
Pitpan Tavern...............................**29** D5

ENTERTAINMENT
Stork Club.................................(see 15)

SHOPPING
Arts & Crafts of Central America...**30** D5
Back to My Roots.........................**31** D5
Belize Gifts.................................**32** D5
New Hope Woodworking................**33** B4

0 — 100 m

St Andrew's
Anglican Church

Market
Square

Waight's Ave

West St

Hudson St

Wyatt St

King St

Missiah St

Town Hall

CAYO DISTRICT

A small visitors center explains some of the history of Cahal Pech. Sometimes independent guides hang around here offering **tours** (2hr tours BZ$20). Otherwise, walk about 150yd to the area of excavated and restored plazas and temples. **Plaza B** is the largest and most impressive complex; **Structure A1**, near plaza A, is the site's tallest temple. Two ball courts lie at either end of the restored area.

Cahal Pech is 1 mile south of central San Ignacio. Head up Buena Vista St and turn left immediately before the Texaco station.

BRANCH MOUTH

Branch Mouth is the meeting place of the Mopan River, coming from Guatemala, and the Macal River, flowing down from Mountain Pine Ridge. The confluence of these rivers forms the beginning of the Belize River, which flows northeast to the sea.

The surrounding parkland is home to an abundance of **birdlife** as well as an **iguana reserve**. The confluence of these rivers forms a sweet **swimming hole**, which is an enticing prospect on a hot day. Cycle or walk 1.5 miles north on scenic Branch Mouth Rd to the Hammock Bridge.

GREEN IGUANA EXHIBIT & MEDICINAL JUNGLE TRAIL

The **Green Iguana Exhibit** (admission BZ$11; ⊗ 8am-noon & 1-4pm, tours every hr) is in the lush Macal Valley grounds of the San Ignacio Resort Hotel (p200). The green iguana can grow a very impressive 6ft long, but it's threatened chiefly because the eggs were once considered a delicacy (it's now illegal to eat them or to hunt the iguanas). This program collects and hatches iguana eggs, raising the reptiles until they are past their most vulnerable age. The iguanas are then released into the wild, but not before giving guests a chance to get to know them. You'll get plenty of face time (and photo ops), as well as fun facts about iguanas. On the way back from the exhibit, learn about local herbs and plants on the **medicinal jungle trail** (⊗ 8am-4pm) that winds through the forest.

Tours

Many of the most exciting sights and activities in Cayo District are most easily reached on a guided trip; some (such as Actun Tunichil Muknal and Barton Creek Cave) cannot be visited without a guide.

Typical day-trip prices per person are BZ$160 for Actun Tunichil Muknal, BZ$60 to BZ$90 for a half-day trip to Barton Creek Cave, BZ$140 to BZ$180 to Caracol, BZ$130 for a cave-tubing trip to Nohoch Che'en, BZ$60 to BZ$90 for Mountain Pine Ridge and BZ$200 to BZ$240 (plus border fees) for Tikal in Guatemala. Most agencies can pick you up from hotels and lodges for an extra fee.

Leading tour companies or booking agencies based in or near San Ignacio include the following:

Belize Explorer (☎ 624-8071; www.belizex.com; Central Farm; tours per day BZ$200, support vehicles per day BZ$500) Besides all the regular tours, Belize Explorer also organizes custom-designed mountain- and jungle-biking expeditions, which generally feature three to six hours of riding each day, and warm Maya hospitality in local homes at night. Hard-core adventurers may want to engage in '30 days of nonstop action.'

Belizean Sun (☎ 824-4841, 601-2630; www.belizeansun.com) Offers canoeing or river-tubing, jungle hikes, horseback riding. Also organizes trips to any of the nearby Maya ruins, including Tikal.

Easy Rider (☎ 824-3734; 24 Burns Ave; half-day tour BZ$60) Highly recommended horse-riding trips to Bullet Tree Falls or Cahal Pech. Two person minimum. Inquire inside Arts & Crafts of Central America (p201).

Eva's Restaurant (☎ 804-2267; www.evasonline.com; 22 Burns Ave) Eva's is a San Ignacio institution, now under new ownership. It's better for information than for eating, although it's a fun place to hang out in the late afternoon as groups return from their outings. Offers all of the standard tours, including hiking, biking, birding and trips to Caracol.

Everald's Caracol Shuttle (Map p203; ☎ 804-0090, 604-5097; info@crystalparadise.com; Crystal Paradise Resort, Cristo Rey Rd;) Knowledgeable guide Everald Tut organizes day trips to Caracol (per person BZ$150). Tour groups may be large, as he takes guests from the resort, as well as other organized groups and independent travelers.

Mayawalk Tours (☎ 824-3070; www.mayawalk.com; 19 Burns Ave) Mayawalk is one of the biggest and best established tour companies, offering everything from canoeing, cave-tubing and horseback riding to Maya ruins and ATM trips.

Pacz Tours (☎ 824-2477; www.pacztours.net; 30 Burns Ave) The original tour company for Actun Tunichil Muknal. This company has new ownership, but trips are reliably excellent. Check out the bike trip to Spanish Lookout (p192; per person BZ$120), a local Mennonite community.

Paradise Expeditions (Map p203; ☎ 820-4014, 610-5593; www.birdinginbelize.com; Crystal Paradise Resort, Cristo Rey Rd) Run by the accomplished local bird guide Jeronie Tut, offering trips for both the 'casual and serious birder.' Operates from Crystal Paradise Resort (p194).

River Rat Expeditions (☎ 824-2166, 605-4480; www.riverratbelize.com) Specialist in kayaking, river-tubing and cave trips. Enjoy a relaxing paddle down the Mopan River near Clarissa Falls, or take on some white water near Paslow Falls. Also books multiday kayaking and camping adventures, but arrangements must be made in advance.

Sleeping

San Ignacio accommodations are mostly in the budget bracket but there are also some excellent value establishments here. More luxurious options can be found at lodges out of town.

BUDGET

Pacz Guesthouse (☎ 604-4526; Far West St; dm BZ$15, r with shared bathroom BZ$20, s/d/tr with private bathroom BZ$30/40/45) There is not much to say, except this is the cheapest place in town. It's a tiny 2nd-floor hostelry – stark but spotless – with a few private rooms, plus one three-bed dorm. Owner Ramón Rosado is a friendly face, but this place is bare-bones basic.

Tropicool Hotel (☎ 824-3052; 30 Burns Ave; s/d/tw/tr with shared bathroom BZ$23/28/33/38, cabins with private bathroom s/d/tw/tr BZ$56/56/63/67) The rooms in the main building are stark but clean and equipped with fans and mosquito screens. The cabins in the back are more appealing, with private bathrooms, televisions and breezy verandahs overlooking a shady garden. Check in at the gift shop next door.

Hi-Et Guest House (☎ 824-2828; thehiet@btl.net; 12 West St; s/d from BZ$25/45) The friendly, funky Hi-Et occupies two adjacent and connected houses, each with its own verandah overlooking the busy street below. Some rooms have shared bathrooms, but all are clean and comfy. Bonus: free coffee in the mornings!

Venus Hotel (☎ 824-3203; emorfing@btl.net; 23 Burns Ave; s/d with shared bathroom BZ$28/32, s/d/tr with private bathroom BZ$49/59/75, s/d/tr with private bathroom & air-con BZ$85/85/105; 🖳) The dark hallway and reception area are not overly inviting, but the rooms at the Venus Hotel are well maintained and comfortable (if unspectacular). Tile bathrooms and cable TV are some of the available perks in the pricier rooms.

Elvira's Guesthouse (☎ 804-0243, 620-5940; 6 Far West St; r with shared bathroom BZ$30, r with private bathroom BZ$40-55; 🖳) Simple and spacious rooms all have colorful paint jobs and warm woven blankets. The guesthouse is upstairs from Elvira's cool and cozy café, an excellent place

for coffee, cakes, sandwiches and snacks (whether or not you are staying here).

Mana Kai Camp & Cabins (☎ 824-2317, 624-6538; Branch Mouth Rd; d BZ$45; 🅿) Just north of the football grounds, Mana Kai is a big swath of swampy land with colorfully painted cottages. There is plenty of space to spread out, with hammocks strung up around the grounds and an open-air wood stove for cooking. Inside, the cabins have few perks, but they are basic and clean. It's an excellent, affordable option if you are feeling stifled by the big city of San Ignacio.

Rosa's Hotel (☎ 804-2265; www.toucantrail.com/rosas-hotel.html; Hudson St; s/d incl breakfast BZ$45/50; 🖳) It's not much to look at, but Rosa's has been around for a long time. It attracts long-term residents, who appreciate the friendly management, the free continental breakfast and the view of the rooftops from the shared balcony. The rooms themselves are pretty bare, but they do have the basic necessities.

Hotel Mallorca (☎ 824-2960; mallorcahotel@gmail.com; 12 Burns Ave; s/d BZ$45/55) Aside from the colorful quilts that cover the firm beds, the dark spacious rooms at the Hotel Mallorca are unadorned. Super service is provided by managers Yolanda and Carlos, who live upstairs. All guests have access to the kitchen, a pleasant lounge area and a tiny balcony overlooking Burns Ave.

Casa Blanca Guest House (☎ 824-2080; www.casablancaguesthouse.com; 10 Burns Ave; s/d/tr BZ$50/60/70, s/d with air-con BZ$80/100; 🖳) Intimate and immaculate, the Casa Blanca gets rave reviews for its simplicity and hospitality. Decent sized rooms have clean white walls and crisp fresh linens. Guests have a comfy sitting area, a clean kitchenette and a breezy rooftop terrace, from which to watch the world go by.

MIDRANGE & TOP END

our pick Martha's Guesthouse (☎ 804-3647; www.marthasbelize.com; 10 West St; r BZ$80-90, r with air-con BZ$100-110, all incl breakfast; 🖳 🖳) This family-run guesthouse has bright, sparkling clean rooms, each with a private balcony. Woven Maya tapestries accent the mahogany walls and furniture, while tile floors keep the rooms cool. Hotel amenities include a laundry and an excellent restaurant (p201). Offers a perfect blend of comfort, class and congeniality.

Midas Tropical Resort (☎ 824-3172, 824-3845; www.midasbelize.com; Branch Mouth Rd; s/d with fan BZ$96/107, with air-con BZ$118/129; 🅿 🖳 🖳 🖳) Both exotic and convenient, this affable, affordable option is surrounded by jungly wilderness on the bank of the Macal River, but it is only a five-minute walk from the center of San Ignacio. Bright, breezy cabanas are lined up in a colorful row, each with a porch overlooking the shady grounds. You can cool off in the river, just 100yd away, or stroll into town and take a dip at its sister property, Venus Hotel (p199).

Chiclero Camp Resort (☎ 824-3132; www.chiclerocamp.com; Cahal Pech Hill; d without/with air-con BZ$108/131; P ⊠) Just past Cahal Pech, this little resort is on quiet grounds, shaded by palms. The cheaper rooms are in thatched-roof cabanas with tile floors, ceiling fans and modern bathrooms. They are actually more appealing than the dark, pricier rooms in the cement structure nearby. A pleasant restaurant and bar, as well as a communal kitchen are on site.

Cahal Pech Cottages (☎ 620-4366; www.cahalpechcottages.com; Cahal Pech Rd; r BZ$120; P ⊒) Heading up the hill toward Cahal Pech, you can't miss these concrete cottages, which are built to optimize the panoramic view over the town of San Ignacio. Simple rooms feature plenty of hardwood, and every cottage has a screened-in porch hung with a hammock.

Cahal Pech Village (☎ 824-3740; www.cahalpech.com; Cahal Pech Hill; d/q BZ$182/225; P ⊠ ⊒ ⊠) Atop Cahal Pech hill, 1.25 miles up from the town center, you can enjoy splendid views from this upscale resort. Choose between bright, tile-floored, air-con rooms in the large main building or comfortable cabanas with thatched roofs and varnished wood floors. Wherever you stay, you'll enjoy a view of the Maya Mountains or surrounding villages from your verandah. The on-site restaurant serves good international food (mains BZ$12 to BZ$20), so you don't need to trek into town for dinner. In summer the place is very popular with groups of archaeology students, who spend their days doing fieldwork.

San Ignacio Resort Hotel (☎ 824-2034; www.sanignaciobelize.com; 18 Buena Vista St; s/d balcony r BZ$228/296, regal r BZ$376, ste BZ$684; P ⊠ ⊒ ⊠) About 400yd uphill from the town center, this is as upscale as it goes in San Ignacio. The lobby is graced with a gorgeous mahogany staircase, marble floors and huge bouquets of orchids and bromeliads. Newly renovated, luxurious rooms boast hardwood floors, down comforters and views of the forest covered hillside. The lush grounds on the Macal River are lovely, with

excellent birding from the terrace and an on-site jungle trail, leading to the Green Iguana Exhibit (p198). Also on site: a restaurant, bar and casino.

Eating

Head to the market on Savannah St for San Ignacio's best fruit, vegetables, jams and dairy products. Farmers sell from all over the Cayo District – you can't get fresher than this. There is also a string of stand-up food stalls strung along this road, offering breakfast, burritos and other cheap eats.

Pop's Restaurant (☎ 824-3366; West St; breakfast BZ$8-10; ⏰ 6:30am-2pm & 6:30pm-10pm Thu-Tue, 6:30am-2pm Wed; ⊠) This small, friendly diner is a good choice for a filling, slightly greasy breakfast at a good price, served all day.

our pick Hanna's Restaurant (☎ 824-3014; 5 Burns Ave; breakfast BZ$8-12, Belizean dishes BZ$10-12, Indian dishes BZ$15-20; ⏰ 6am-9pm) Hanna's is the most popular spot in town, any time of day. Go for fresh-squeezed juices, hearty omelettes and homemade yogurt at breakfast; rice and beans or filling sandwiches for lunch; or Hanna's delectable spicy ginger rum shrimp for an unbeatable dinner. Indian dishes and other meatless options cater to vegetarians.

Erva's (☎ 824-2821; 2 Far West St; mains BZ$8-16; ⏰ breakfast, lunch & dinner) Locals recommend Erva's for top-notch Belizean food and super-friendly service. Try the local Cayo specialty known as *chaya*, which is a leafy green, often sautéed with butter and garlic. The interior of this place is pretty nondescript; take a seat on the tiny terrace and enjoy the breeze while you wait for your meal.

our pick Café Sol (☎ 824-2166; West St; mains BZ$12-20; ⏰ 7am-9pm Tue-Sat, to 2:30pm Sun) The menu at Café Sol is eclectic, with Greek salad wraps, pineapple ginger chicken and Thai noodle shrimp salad, making it a delightfully delicious place to eat. But the café also enjoys an easygoing coffee shop atmosphere, with artwork on the walls and plush sofas in the corner, so you might be just as inclined to order coffee and dessert or a fruit smoothie while you read and relax.

Hode's Place (☎ 804-2522; Branch Mouth Rd; mains BZ$12-20; ⏰ 10am-midnight) Locals love this rambling place north of the center. A large terrace restaurant opening onto a citrus orchard and kids' playground, it's a popular spot for families (a jukebox and games room also help). Friendly service and satisfying food – from burritos and fajitas to steaks, seafood and rice and beans – complete the successful recipe.

Firenza Café (☎ 601-6537; Wyatt St; mains BZ$12-20; ☽ dinner) Please your palate with daily changing seafood specials, handmade Italian sausage or fresh pasta. There is an inviting seating area on the back patio, but be warned: you can't avoid the aromas wafting from the pizza oven, so it's virtually impossible not to order one of the specialty pies!

Amore Mio (☎ 602-8365; JNC Mall, Market Sq; mains BZ$15-20; ☽ lunch & dinner Tue-Sun) Who can resist homemade pizza and pasta dishes made by a *real* Italian chef? On an inviting terrace overlooking Market Sq, Amore Mio's husband-wife team – Fabio and Simonetta – serves up crispy-crust pies and pasta al dente. Wash it down with a swig of vino *rosso* and you might forget you are in Central America.

Martha's Kitchen (☎ 804-3647; 10 West St; mains BZ$15-20; ☽ 6:30am-3pm & 4-11pm) Martha's receives all-round rave reviews, not only for its well-appointed rooms, but also for the diverse and delectable menu. Highlights run the gamut, from tasty pizza and delicious fish burritos, to juicy steaks and vegetarian kebabs. Take a seat inside the wood-accented dining room or outside on the foliage-fronted terrace, but don't be surprised if you have to wait.

To eat local food and hang out with local people, stop by **Eagle's Landing** (☎ 824-0378; Wyatt St; ☽ 24hr).

Drinking & Entertainment

Pitpan Tavern (JNC Mall, Market Sq; ☽ 2pm-midnight Tue-Sun) This tiny little bar is a great local hangout, just behind Market Sq. Excellent atmosphere, by day or night. Come for cold drinks, hot music and plenty of local flavor.

Cocopelle Bar (8 Hudson St; ☽ 10am-midnight) A friendly place for drinks, pool, foosball and loud music. The deck out back is a great place for a drink on a warm night.

Stork Club (☎ 824-2034; San Ignacio Resort Hotel, 18 Buena Vista St; ☽ bands & DJs 9:30pm-2am Fri & Sat) This hotel is a bit of a social hub, attracting tourists and expats but not too many locals. There is often live music on Saturday; otherwise, DJs play on Friday and Saturday nights.

Another option is **Coconut's** (10 Savannah St), which was undergoing a name change at the time of research. It attracts a steady stream of regulars.

Shopping

Back to My Roots (☎ 824-2740; 30 Burns Ave) Offers cool handmade jewelry, including silver, amber and other semiprecious stones. The name of the place refers to the drums and other Rasta gear for sale.

Belize Gifts (☎ 824-4159; JNC Mall, 21 Burns Ave) This place has an excellent selection of high quality souvenirs, including beautiful salad bowls, jewelry boxes and other wooden items. There is also a small selection of books and guidebooks about Belize, including the useful *Guide to the Maya Sites of Belize* by Jaime Awe.

New Hope Woodworking (☎ 824-2188; Buena Vista St) South of the center, this carpentry workshop is a worthwhile stop if you are in the market for wooden furniture, cabinetry or smaller items made from mahogany or native woods. Be prepared to check it with your luggage, because it is prohibitively expensive to ship.

Arts & Crafts of Central America (☎ 824-2253; 24 Burns Ave) This little shop sells a wide variety of handmade jewelry, handbags and textiles, mostly from Guatemala. This is also the place to book your tours with Easy Rider (p198).

Getting There & Around
TO/FROM THE AIRPORT

All of the local tour agencies (p198) will provide transfers to/from the Philip Goldson International Airport in Ladyville (near Belize City); Belizean Sun charges BZ$50 per person (minimum three people). For slightly cheaper rates, check out Cocopelle Bar (p196) or Tropicool Hotel (p199).

BUS

For information about bus schedules, stop by the stand for the **Savannah Taxi Association** (☎ 824-2155) in the center of Market Sq. This is where buses stop en route to/from Belize City (BZ$6, two hours), Belmopan (BZ$4, one hour) and Benque Viejo del Carmen (BZ$3, 30 minutes). Buses run in both directions just about every half-hour from 7am to 9pm, with less frequent service on Sunday. One bus a day goes to Dangriga (BZ$12, three hours), Friday to Monday only.

Alternatively, **Amigo's Belize** (☎ 622-0283; www.amigosbelize.com; Missiah St), across the Hawkesworth Bridge, is affiliated with San Juan Travel and Línea Dorada. Twice a day, buses go to Chetumal, Mexico (BZ$40, 8:30am and 10:30am) via Belize City. An additional bus comes from Flores, Guatemala and continues on to Belize City (BZ$20, 11am).

From a vacant lot on Savannah St, buses leave for Bullet Tree Falls (BZ$1, 15 minutes) at 10:30am, 11am, 11:30am, 12:30pm, 3:30pm, 4pm and 5pm, Monday to Saturday. From the same spot, buses go to San Antonio (BZ$3, 45 minutes) at 10:45am, 1:15pm, 3:15pm and 5:15pm, Monday to Saturday.

CAR
Rates include third-party insurance and unlimited mileage at the following agencies:
Cayo Auto Rentals (☎ 824-2222, 610-4779; www .cayoautorentals.com; 81 Benque Viejo Rd) Daily rates start at BZ$164 for a Kia Sportage; rent six days and the seventh day is free.
Matus Car Rental (☎ 824-2005, 663-4702; www .matuscarrental.com; 18 Benque Viejo Rd) Rates start at BZ$115/630 per day/week for a Suzuki Sidekick or Kia Sportage.
Safe Tours Belize (☎ 824-4262, 670-4476; 278 Western Hwy, Santa Elena; ☼ 7am-9pm) Rents vehicles for BZ$164 per day; inquire at the office just north of Hanna's.

TAXI
Several taxi stands are dotted around the town center. Sample fares are BZ$20 to the Guatemalan border (9 miles) or Crystal Paradise Resort (5 miles), BZ$60 round-trip to Xunantunich, and BZ$80 to BZ$100 one-way to the Mountain Pine Ridge lodges.

Colectivo taxis (charging per person and leaving when they have a full car) head from a vacant lot on Savannah St to Benque Viejo del Carmen (BZ$4) and the Guatemalan border (BZ$6). Taxis to Bullet Tree Falls (*colectivo/ private* BZ$4/15) go from Wyatt St, just off Burns Ave.

NORTHWEST OF SAN IGNACIO
A paved road leads northwest out of San Ignacio, through green pastures and farmland to Bullet Tree Falls, a pretty little town straddling the Mopan River. Beyond Bullet Tree Falls, a rough track covers the 8 miles to the remote Maya site of El Pilar on the Guatemalan border.

Bullet Tree Falls
Bullet Tree Falls is a quiet and quaint little village, home to a few laid-back lodges overlooking the Mopan River. Although it's on the edge of the jungle, it offers easy access into San Ignacio, even if you don't have your own

vehicle. There is also a handful of outdoor adventure activities at your doorstep, including hiking in the nearby forests and river-tubing down the Mopan.

As you come into the village you'll see the bus stop at the junction of a road to the right (which leads to Iguana Junction and Cohune Palms). Straight ahead, the main road continues 200yd to the bridge over the Mopan.

Eighty yards past the bus stop, **Be Pukte Cultural Center** has a display on El Pilar, with a model of the site and booklets for sale. It also sells tickets for El Pilar and can arrange a taxi there (BZ$50 round-trip with one hour at the site). Unfortunately, it is open sporadically, so don't come here with high expectations.

Up the road to the left, you'll find the **Masewal Forest Garden** (admission BZ$5), an herbal and botanical garden that is maintained by the local healer Heriberto Cocom. For the price of admission, he will also offer a consultation and remedy for whatever ails you.

A few knowledgeable local guides lead tours in the area, including tours to El Pilar (BZ$40 per person including transportation), as well as river-tubing trips (BZ$25 per person) on the Mopan River and guided hikes along the medicine trail. Contact cousins **Teddy Waight** (☎ 669-2255; vlteddy@yahoo.com) or **Anthony Chuc** (☎ 667-6060; keepitsecret@gmail.com).

SLEEPING & EATING
Casa del Caballo Blanco (☎ in USA 707-97-4942; www .casacaballoblanco.com; Bullet Tree Rd; s/d/tr BZ$266/310/353, breakfast/dinner BZ$21/47; ℗) Midway between San Ignacio and Bullet Tree Falls, the 'House of the White Horse' is a concrete yellow ecolodge set on 23 acres of rolling hills and forest overlooking the Mopan River valley. Guests stay in spacious thatched-roof cabanas that are sparingly decorated with hardwood furniture and Maya fabrics. Homegrown veggies and locally produced baked goods cover the tables at meal time. Aside from the sweeping views, the highlight of the White Horse is the bird sanctuary, an impressive facility that is used for the rehabilitation and release of native species.

The following places are listed in order from west to east along the Mopan River.

Iguana Junction (☎ 824-2249; www.iguanajunction .com; r with shared bathroom BZ$66, cabanas with private bathroom BZ$88) Now under new ownership, the Iguana Junction was recently revamped with a fresh coat of paint, new landscaping

AROUND SAN IGNACIO

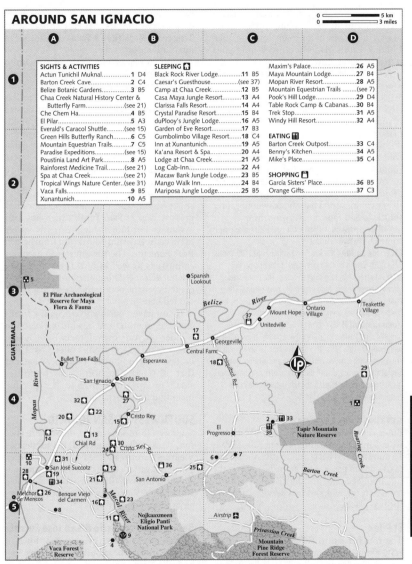

0 — 5 km
0 — 3 miles

A **B** **C** **D**

1
2
3
4
5

GUATEMALA

CAYO DISTRICT

El Pilar Archaeological
Reserve for Maya
Flora & Fauna

Spanish
Lookout

Belize *River*

Mount Hope Ontario
Village

Teakettle
Village

Unitedville

Georgeville

Central Farm

Bullet Tree Falls

Esperanza

San Ignacio Santa Elena

Cristo Rey

Chial Rd

Cristo Rey Rd

San José Succotz

San Antonio

Melchor
de Mencos

Benque Viejo
del Carmen

Mopan *River*

Macal *River*

Chiquibul Rd

El
Progresso

Tapir Mountain
Nature Reserve

Barton *Creek*

Roaring *Creek*

Nojkaaxmeen
Eligio Panti
National Park

Airstrip

Privassion Creek

Mountain
Pine Ridge
Forest Reserve

Vaca Forest
Reserve

and a gorgeous, spacious riverside deck. All accommodations are simple and clean, but the cabanas feature delightful details such as locally made furniture and lamp shades. The central *palapa* is generously draped with hammocks, making it the ultimate hang-out place. The on-site restaurant is now open only for guests.

our pick **Cohune Palms** (☎ 600-7508, 609-3728; www.cohunepalms.com; s/d/tr BZ$128/172/216; breakfast/lunch BZ$16/24; P ⚏) Always laid-back but absolutely lovely, Cohune Palms is set on the riverbank, surrounded by its namesake tree. Four spacious cabanas – all topped with a thatch roof – have high ceilings, wood carvings, tile floors and woven tapestries. They share access to a shady deck, where meals are served. Spend the day swinging in a hammock or sign up for one of the many tours on offer. Cohune Palms also offers week-long yoga retreats several times a year.

Parrot Nest Jungle Lodge (☎ 820-4058, 602-6817; www.parrot-nest.com; d with shared/private bathroom BZ$100/120; breakfast BZ$8-12, dinner BZ$22; **P**) If you ever wanted to live like the monkeys, here is your chance to sleep in the branches of a massive guanacaste tree. Five cabins – some on stilts, some in trees – all have sturdy wood construction, thatch roofs and shared bathroom; one larger cabin has a private bathroom and inviting verandah. The overgrown grounds are a haven for wildlife watching, river swimming and hammock swinging. Free shuttle to San Ignacio every morning.

Other options in Bullet Tree Falls are open somewhat sporadically:

Riverside Lodge (☎ 824-3580; cabanas BZ$100; meals BZ$15-20) Sitting by the north side of the bridge, this place is better for eating than sleeping. The *palapa* restaurant serves decent food in a lovely river setting. Three light-filled cabanas have wood accents and tile floors, but the place does not seem prepared for visitors.

Hummingbird Hills (☎ 614-4699; www.humming birdhills.com; Paslow Falls Rd; cabanas with shared/private bathroom BZ$109/175; **P**) The verdant 12-acre grounds are dotted with a dozen cute cabanas and a funky tree house, all constructed with bamboo, thatch and hardwood. It's 500yd along the road to the left between Be Pukte Cultural Center and the bridge.

GETTING THERE & AWAY
Buses run seven times daily (except Sunday) from San Ignacio to Bullet Tree Falls (BZ$1, 15 minutes) and back. Alternatively, *colectivo* taxis pick up passengers at the bus stop at the junction. See p201 for details on departures from San Ignacio and taxi services between the two places.

El Pilar
The rough road to **El Pilar** (Map p203; admission BZ$10; ☺8am-4pm) heads off to the left 400yd past the bridge in Bullet Tree Falls. Be prepared for a bumpy ride: 4WD is required for the 7-mile jungle trek.

El Pilar was occupied for at least 15 centuries, from the middle Preclassic Period (around 500 BC) to the late Classic Period (about AD 1000). Long before present-day political borders, El Pilar stretched to modern-day Pilar Poniente in Guatemala, and the

two countries are now working as partners to preserve the area. **El Pilar Archaeological Reserve for Maya Flora & Fauna** straddles the international boundary.

With 25 plazas and 70 major structures, El Pilar was more than three times the size of Xunantunich (opposite). Despite excavations since 1993, not much of El Pilar has been cleared; this has been to avoid the decay that often follows clearing of ancient buildings. While appreciating El Pilar's greatness requires some imagination, this may actually help to give you the feeling that you're discovering the place rather than following a well-worn tourist trail.

Six archaeological and nature trails meander among the mounds. The most impressive area is **Plaza Copal**, which has four pyramids 45ft to 60ft high. A partly visible Maya causeway runs 500yd west from here to Pilar Poniente. The site attracts archaeology enthusiasts as well as bird nerds. Toucans, orioles, toucanets, hummingbirds, woodpeckers and even the occasional scarlet macaw are sighted here.

If you have your own vehicle, it's an incredible, remote and rewarding place to wander on your own. Otherwise, you can hire a taxi (BZ$50 from Bullet Tree Falls) or take a tour. Bullet Tree local **Anthony Chuc** (☎ 667-6060; keepitsecret@gmail.com) brings small groups here (BZ$40 per person, including transportation).

SOUTHWEST OF SAN IGNACIO
Southwest from San Ignacio, the Western Hwy runs across rolling countryside toward Benque Viejo del Carmen and the Guatemalan border. There is a variety of places to stay strung out along the highway. Buses between San Ignacio and Benque Viejo del Carmen will drop you anywhere along this stretch.

Between San Ignacio & San José Succotz
As the Western Hwy heads out of town, it passes through the suburbs of San Ignacio – basically a series of resorts scattered around the forested hills. The location is ideal, as the highway provides easy access into town, but the atmosphere feels like it's far from anywhere.

Bamboo Crafts & Furniture (☎ 624-0808; www.bam boobelize.com) is a small family-run business with a showroom in the village of Callow Creek, about 7 miles out of San Ignacio. Stop by to see how the bamboo is cultivated and harvested, then crafted into fine furniture. This sustainable practice results in uniquely rustic pieces that are reasonably priced (if you can figure out how to get them home). Turn north off the Western Hwy and follow the signs.

SLEEPING & EATING

Clarissa Falls Resort (Map p203; ☎ 824-3916; www.clarissa falls.com; Mile 70 Western Hwy; camping per person BZ$15, cottages per person BZ$65, ste BZ$350; meals BZ$10-20; **P**) In an idyllic setting on the banks of the Mopan River, this rustic little ranch welcomes guests and makes them feel like part of the family. The lodging is in cement blocks with thatched roofs and no windows, meaning very little natural light gets in, but it is simple, clean and comfortable. Ample activities are at your doorstep, including horseback riding, river rafting and river-tubing. Located about 1 mile off the Western Hwy.

Log Cab-Inn (Map p203; ☎ 824-3367; www.log cabinns-belize.com; Mile 68 Western Hwy; s/d BZ$142/164, incl meals BZ$233/347; **P** **X** **L** **L**) Despite the unfortunate name, the Log Cab-Inn is a wonderful, welcoming resort on a scenic hillside, almost opposite Windy Hill. The cabins are indeed built from mahogany logs, and much of the furniture is crafted at the carpentry workshop on site. Orange and palm trees dot the grounds, which also feature an open-air restaurant and bar. Kids under 12 stay free with parents.

Casa Maya Jungle Resort (Map p203; ☎ 820-4020; www.casamayaresort.com; Mile 68½ Western Hwy; s/d cabanas BZ$220/240, incl meals BZ$298/318; **P** **X** **L**) Follow the signs about 1.4 miles off the highway to this extensive resort, spread out over the back slope of the Maya Mountains. White stucco cabanas have hardwood frames and bay leaf palm–thatched roofs, all of which is harvested sustainably from the local jungle. On the grounds, you can explore nature and medicinal trails, ride mountain bikes and admire the birds from the beautiful hilltop *palapa*. A full range of tours and activities is offered, including multiday wilderness treks.

Ka'ana Resort & Spa (Map p203; ☎ 824-3350; www .kaanabelize.com; Mile 69 Western Hwy; d/q BZ$600/800, breakfast BZ$16-24, lunch & dinner BZ$40-60; **P** **X** **L** **L**) If you are in the market for some indulgence, this new boutique resort and spa is a good place to start. Luxurious rooms and casitas are fully equipped with high-thread-count sheets, down comforters, LCD televisions and classy,

contemporary decor. Private terraces overlook the lush grounds. The gourmet restaurant offers innovative, organic local cuisine and a well-stocked wine cellar. Most tempting is the full menu of spa treatments at the Caribbean Spa (open 7:30am to 8:30pm), ranging from facials and pedicures to mud wraps and the signature couples' massage. Nonguests also welcome at the spa.

Windy Hill Resort (Map p203; ☎ 824-2017; www .windyhillresort.com; Mile 68 Western Hwy; 3-night/4-day packages s/d/tr/q from BZ$2634/3046/3424/3800; **P** **X** **L**) Windy Hill, set on – yes – a breezy hillside located 1 mile west of the edge of San Ignacio, is a family-run resort for the interested and active. Packages (three to seven days) cover all of the major sights and activities of western Belize combined with lodging, meals and airport transfers. Accommodations are in attractive wooden cottages spread across manicured gardens, all with custom-made furniture, local art and hand-woven rugs. Plentiful meals are served in a large *palapa*; the bar, games room and fitness center will fill any spare moments. Reduced rates for kids.

San José Succotz

There's not much to this little village, located 6.5 miles west of San Ignacio on the Western Hwy. On the way from San Ignacio to the Guatemalan border, Succotz gets plenty of people passing through, many of whom stop to spend a morning at Xunantunich, an impressive and easily accessible Maya site (see below). A handful of restaurants and mini-resorts is strung out along the Western Hwy to cater to archaeology buffs and other adventurers. It's easy to visit Xunantunich on an outing from San Ignacio, or you may prefer to use this slow-paced barrio as your base for exploring Cayo and Guatemala. The bus between San Ignacio and Benque Viejo del Carmen will drop you here.

SIGHTS & ACTIVITIES
Xunantunich

Set on a leveled hilltop, **Xunantunich** (Map p203; admission BZ$10; ☼ 7:30am-4pm), pronounced shoo-nahn-*too*-neech, is one of Belize's most easily accessible and impressive Maya archaeological sites. To reach the ruins, take the free, hand-cranked ferry across the Mopan River. From the ferry, which comes and goes on demand, it's about 1 mile uphill to the parking lot and ticket office. It's a semi-strenuous walk with

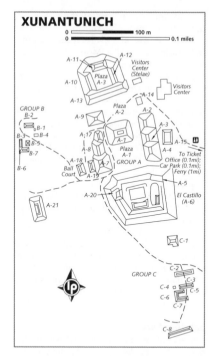

XUNANTUNICH

great opportunities for sighting birds and butterflies. At the end, your reward is a complex of temples and plazas that date back to the 7th century.

Xunantunich may have been occupied as early as 1000 BC but was little more than a village. As mentioned, the large architecture that we see today began to be built in the 7th century AD. From AD 700 to 850, Xunantunich was possibly politically aligned with Naranjo, 9 miles west in Guatemala. Together, they controlled the western part of the Belize River valley, although the population probably never exceeded 10,000. Xunantunich partially survived the initial Classic Maya collapse of about AD 850 (when nearby Cahal Pech was abandoned), but was deserted by about AD 1000. A good visitors center, located between the ticket office and the hilltop ruins, explains this history.

The site centers on **Plazas A-2** and **A-1**, separated by Structure A-1. Just north of Plaza A-2, Structure A-11 and **Plaza A-3** formed a residential 'palace' area for the ruling family. The dominant **El Castillo** (Structure A-6) rises 130ft high at the south end of Plaza A-1. El Castillo may have been the ruling family's ancestral shrine, where they were buried and/or represented in sculpted friezes. Structures A-1 and A-13, at either end of Plaza A-2, were not built until the 9th century and would have had the effect of separating the ruling family from the rest of the population, possibly a response to the pressures that came with the decline of Classic Maya civilization at that time.

You can climb to the top of El Castillo to enjoy a spectacular 360-degree view. Its upper levels were constructed in two distinct phases. The first, built around 800, included an elaborate **plaster frieze** encircling the building; the second, around 900, covered over most of the first and its frieze. The frieze on the east end of the building and part of the western one have been uncovered by archaeologists; these depict a series of Maya deities, with Chac, the rain god, probably being the central figure at the east end. The friezes you see today are actually replicas, with the originals underneath for safe keeping.

South of El Castillo is a partly overgrown area of lesser structures (Group C) that were abandoned as the city shrank after 900, leaving El Castillo (formerly at the center of the ancient city) on the southern edge of the occupied area.

Tropical Wings Nature Center

Perhaps you are looking for something to do on a rainy day or you need a low-key afternoon activity after spending an exhausting morning at Xunantunich? Look no further than the **Tropical Wings Nature Center** (Map p203; ☎ 823-2265; www.thetrekstop.com; Mile 71 Western Hwy; adult/child BZ$6/3; ⏱ 9am-5pm). The interactive ecology exhibits are aimed at kids, but even adults will enjoy the butterfly house and medicinal gardens. If you crave some more active recreation, try your hand at **Frisbee golf** (per person BZ$6), a newfangled sport that requires floating the disk through the trees and into baskets. It's all on the grounds of the Trek Stop (opposite).

River-Tubing

Between San José Succotz and Clarissa Falls, the Mopan River twists and turns through green pastures and lush jungles, teeming with wildlife, birds and butterflies. Women do their washing on the rocks and kids play in the cool rapids. You can see it all from the comfy perch of a **river-tube** (BZ$20) as you float along the 2-

mile route. There is no cooler way to spend a hot afternoon. Look for the 'tubing' sign just northeast of the ferry; price includes pick-up at Clarissa Falls Farm.

SLEEPING & EATING

our pick Trek Stop (Map p203; ☎ 823-2265; www.the trekstop.com; Mile 71 Western Hwy; camping per person BZ$11, s/d/tr/q with shared bathroom BZ$33/52/83/96, d/tr/q with private bathroom BZ$83/109/131; breakfast BZ$5-10, main dishes BZ$10-15; ☒ restaurant 7am-8pm; P ☐) The Trek Stop offers a unique combination of ecolodge and backpackers' outpost, perfectly located to provide a remote jungle setting and easy access to all the local sites. Hand-hewn cabins have simple wood furnishings and private verandahs. Toilets are self-composting. There is plenty of hang-out space, including a shady hammock lounge, a self-catering kitchen and a highly recommended (and affordable) restaurant. The entrance to the Trek Stop is right on the Western Hwy (just before San José Succotz), but its 22 acres extend back into the wilds, where you can enjoy Frisbee golf, nature trails and other jungle activities.

Inn at Xunantunich (Map p203; ☎ 624-5262, 662-2036; info@innatx.com; Mile 72 Western Hwy; r BZ$60-90; meals BZ$10-15; ☒ breakfast, lunch & dinner; P ☒ ☐ ☒) Opposite the ferry to Xunantunich, this hotel provides brightly colored rooms set around a pool. The atmosphere is enhanced by carved wood masks and totems, perched up on the bar and around the patio. The rooms are rather plain, though the pricier options have more space and some Maya masks for decoration. The 2nd-floor dining terrace overlooks the river, making it a lovely place to lunch after exploring the ruins at Xunantunich.

Benny's Kitchen (Map p203; ☎ 823-2541; Mile 72 Western Hwy; meals BZ$10-20; ☒ 7am-10pm Sun-Thu, to midnight Fri & Sat) Sample the local specialties at Benny's, just a few steps from the Xunantunich ferry. Come for tangy *escabèche* (spicy chicken and onion stew), spicy BBQ or – only in Belize – cow foot soup! It's about 50m off the Western Hwy; turn off the road that heads south in Succotz.

Chial Road

Chial Rd, heading southeast off the Western Hwy, 5 miles from San Ignacio, gives access to three exquisite lodges on the west bank of the Macal River. In operation for as long as 30 years, these are some of the region's longest established and best-loved lodges. Aside

from the rather luxurious accommodations, they also offer an extensive range of activities, including some unique nature attractions that are open to nonguests.

Getting here is half the fun: Chial Rd is unpaved and very bumpy, traversing miles of agricultural fields, orange and lemon orchards and untamed wilderness. A 4WD may be required, especially outside the driest months. If you don't have your own vehicle, any of the lodges can provide airport transfers.

SIGHTS & ACTIVITIES
Belize Botanic Gardens

On the grounds at duPlooy's Jungle Lodge (p208), the **Belize Botanic Gardens** (Map p203; ☎ 824-3101; www.belizebotanic.org; per person unguided/ guided tour BZ$10/20, self-guided tour booklet BZ$15, guided tour with transport BZ$30; ☒ 7am-3pm) is one of the region's highlight attractions. The bountiful 45-acre zone boasts 2 miles of trails, many fruit trees and four different Belizean habitats: wetlands, rainforest, Mountain Pine Ridge (with a lookout tower) and plants of the Maya. Two ponds attract a variety of waterfowl; Hamilton Hide allows birders to bring their binoculars and spy on various species. Highlighting native species, Belize Botanic Gardens has a native orchid house and a special exhibit on the products and uses of native palms.

It's easy to while away a day (or a half day) at the botanic gardens. Sign up in advance for the **Early Bird Tour** (per person BZ$45; ☒ 6am), which includes transportation, guided tour and breakfast. Or spend a **Day at the Gardens** (per person BZ$65), which includes transportation, guided tour and your choice of horseback riding or canoeing.

Chaa Creek

North along the Macal River, the Lodge at Chaa Creek (p208) also has extensive grounds and facilities that are open to nonguests.

Running through the jungle just above the river, the **Rainforest Medicine Trail** (guided tours BZ$10; ☒ tours hourly 8am-5pm) was established by Dr Rosita Arvigo (see boxed text, p209). This is just one of a series of projects, which aim to spread knowledge of traditional healing methods and preserve the rainforest habitats, from which many healing plants come. It identifies about 100 medicinal plants used in traditional Maya and/or modern medicine. A gift shop near the start of the trail sells a guide to the trail's plants and some of Dr Arvigo's books.

From here, hike up the tree-covered hillside to the **Chaa Creek Natural History Center & Butterfly Farm** (Map p203; guided tours BZ$10; ☺ tours hourly 8am-4pm), a small nature center with displays on Belize's flora and fauna, as well as the early Maya. The highlight is the butterfly farm, which breeds the dazzlingly iridescent blue morpho *(Morpho peleides)* for export.

On the crest of the hill, the **Spa at Chaa Creek** (Map p203; ☎ 824-2037; www.chaacreek.com; 1-day packages BZ$474) overlooks the 365-acre grounds, offering a spectacular panorama of the Macal River valley. Enjoy the view while indulging in a massage, facial, aromatherapy, body wrap or some other sensual treat.

SLEEPING & EATING

ourpick **Black Rock River Lodge** (Map p203; ☎ 824-2341; www.blackrocklodge.com; d with shared bathroom BZ$152, river view/deluxe d BZ$240/316, extra person BZ$22; breakfast BZ$20, lunch items BZ$8-10, dinner BZ$80; P) High up the Macal in beautiful Black Rock Canyon, this is a stunning setting for a jungle adventure. Comfortable slate-and-wood cabins look down on the river, where there are sandy beaches for swimming. From here you can hike a signed trail up the mountain behind the lodge, ride a horse to Vaca Falls up the Macal, or bike to the little-visited Flour Camp Cave, with its abundant ancient Maya pottery, stalactites and stalagmites. The vast dining area and deck, covered by a *palapa*, is fantastic for birding, but you may also spot howler monkeys, otters and iguanas. The electricity here is solar and hydro. Black Rock River Lodge is at the end of a good, well signposted, 6-mile unpaved road that leaves Chial Rd 0.8 miles off the Western Hwy.

duPlooy's Jungle Lodge (Map p203; ☎ 824-3101; www.duplooys.com; r BZ$431, bungalows BZ$540, ste & casitas BZ$695, all incl breakfast; 3 meals BZ$92; P ✗ 🖳) Relaxed but well-managed, duPlooy's is a family-run lodge that sits in large and lovely grounds above the Macal. Founded in 1989 it's one of the longest-running Cayo lodges. Rooms and bungalows are spacious and comfortable, sleeping up to four people in two queen- or king-size beds. The suites and the casita can comfortably sleep as many as eight people, and they also include a kitchen and living space. All lodging options have private verandahs overlooking the jungle grounds. Guests can enjoy swimming or canoeing in the river, hiking along the jungle trails, and coffee and bird observation from the bar in

the morning, all for free. To reach duPlooy's, turn right off Chial Rd after 2.5 miles and go on for 1.7 miles. Another perk is free access to the Belize Botanic Gardens (p207), on the grounds here.

Lodge at Chaa Creek (Map p203; ☎ 824-2037, 820-4010; www.chaacreek.com; cottages s/d/tr BZ$512/714/820, ste BZ$833, all incl breakfast; lunch/dinner BZ$22/70; P 🖳) Consistently rated among the best lodges in Belize, Chaa Creek's tropical gardens and beautifully kept thatched cottages spread across a gentle slope above the Macal, 3 miles from the highway. Owned and operated by Lucy and Mick Fleming since 1977, Chaa Creek blossomed from an overgrown farm into Belize's original jungle lodge. The cottages, richly decorated with Maya textiles and local crafts, all have good decks, fans and private bathrooms. An array of tours and activities is offered, and Chaa Creek is proud of its state-of-the-art spa on a hilltop overlooking the river. Chaa Creek is one of the original ecolodges, with its rainforest medicinal trail (p207) and organic Maya farm.

The **Camp at Chaa Creek** (Map p203; Macal River Camp; per person incl dinner & breakfast BZ$130) is Chaa Creek's more economical alternative, half a mile away on the banks of the river. Wooden cabins on stilts are screened on all sides, with comfy cots inside and a shady verandah outside. The place is not landscaped, but rather inhabits the jungle without disturbing the environs. They all share clean bathrooms and excellent hot showers. A campfire is lit nightly, creating an atmosphere of camaraderie. To reach the Camp at Chaa Creek, you'll have to park in the designated area and hike in through the jungle for about half a mile. Room rates at both the Lodge and the Camp include canoeing, guided bird walks and visits to the on-site rainforest medicine trail, natural history center and butterfly farm.

Benque Viejo del Carmen

About a mile from the Guatemalan border and 7 miles from San Ignacio, Benque Viejo del Carmen (population 6700) is a small town with a surprisingly sophisticated cultural scene. Aside from the interesting attractions in the vicinity, it is home to the **Benque Viejo House of Culture** (☎ 823-2697; 64 St Joseph St; ☺ 9am-4pm Mon-Fri), which hosts exhibits, and **Stone Tree Records** (www.stonetreerecords .com), which produces some of Belize's best known music.

RAINFOREST REMEDIES: ROSITA ARVIGO

Rosita Arvigo is doing her part to bring the wisdom of the Maya to the whole wide world. She has been studying herbal healing and rainforest remedies for more than a quarter of a century.

She credits much of her knowledge to the wisdom of Don Eligio Panti, one of the last known Maya natural healers, from San Antonio village. In decades of healing, Don Eligio had treated thousands of patients who traveled from all over Belize to seek his help with physical, emotional and spiritual ailments. To Arvigo, it seemed that the illiterate Don Eligio had an almost magical power to heal. But she knew that this healing power didn't come out of thin air; rather, it came from plants, flowers and the Maya spirits that lived high on tree branches, under bushes and in the ground. So she convinced Eligio to pass on his knowledge to her. She studied and worked with Eligio for 14 years, gathering plants from the forests and knowledge from the old man's wisdom, until his death in 1996, at age 103.

In the meantime, Arvigo also began working with Dr Michael Balick, director of the Institute of Economic Botany at the New York Botanical Garden. Together, under the Belize Ethnobotany Project, they identified, cataloged and collected 3560 plants, some of which are being investigated in the US for potential use in the fights against cancer and AIDS. Arvigo is adamant that natural healing should not replace conventional medicine, but rather complement it. They both serve their purposes, she insists.

Arvigo set up the Ix Chel Tropical Research Foundation (named for the Maya goddess of healing and medicine), with a mandate to preserve traditional healing methods and conserve the rainforest through research and education. At her farm she established the Rainforest Medicine Trail (p207), now operated by Chaa Creek, which demonstrates the medicinal values of Belize's plant life. Arvigo was also involved in starting Rainforest Remedies, a San Ignacio enterprise whose herbal remedies are on sale throughout Belize. These remedies, with names such as 'Belly Be Good,' help everything from backaches and colds to traveler's diarrhea and frayed nerves.

More recently Dr Arvigo has focused on abdominal massage, using ancient Maya techniques, which repositions organs that have dropped, seeking to restore the body's balance (see www .arvigomassage.com).

Arvigo tells her fascinating story in her book *Sastun: My Apprenticeship with a Maya Healer*, coauthored by Nadine Epstein. She has also coauthored *Rainforest Remedies: One Hundred Healing Herbs of Belize* and *Rainforest Home Remedies: The Maya Way to Heal Your Body & Replenish Your Soul*. To learn about some of her remedies, see p63.

The centerpiece of the town is **Our Lady of Mount Carmel Church**, visible from all corners. On Good Friday (the Friday before Easter), the church hosts a dramatic procession through town. In mid-July, Benque breaks out of its tropical somnolence, when the **Benque Viejo del Carmen Fiesta** celebrates the town's patron saint with several days of music and fun.

SIGHTS & ACTIVITIES
Poustinia Land Art Park

Drive about 2.5 miles south of Benque Viejo along the unpaved, overgrown Hydro Rd, and you will come to one of the hidden jewels of Western Belize. **Poustinia Land Art Park** (Map p203; ☎ 822-3532; www.poustiniaonline.org; Mile 2½ Hydro Rd; admission by appointment only BZ$20) is a highly unexpected avant-garde sculpture park in 60 acres of rainforest. Created by Benque brothers Luis and David Ruiz, it displays some 30 works by Belizean and international artists. Poustinia was conceived as an environmental art project, where, once in place, the exhibits – including a car, a greenhouse and a strip of parquet flooring – become subject to the action of nature, which may rot, corrode or otherwise transmute them.

One piece, *Stone Labyrinth*, is set on top of an unexcavated Maya mound with views to Xunantunich (p205). Poustinia is best enjoyed if you have time to contemplate the art and the natural environment it's set in. Allow at least two hours, preferably more.

Make arrangements and buy your admission ticket at Benque Viejo House of Culture (opposite), just off Campo Santo Memorial Park. The House of Culture can also arrange for a taxi cab to take you to Poustinia (BZ$20). Otherwise, turn south off George Price Blvd

CAYO DISTRICT

GETTING TO GUATEMALA

The Belize–Guatemala border is 1 mile beyond Benque Viejo del Carmen. If you are crossing the border on foot, it is advisable to do so in the morning, as onward transportation dwindles with the approach of nightfall. If you are traveling on a through bus en route to Flores, you will have to unload your luggage and carry it across the border, stop at passport control desks for both countries, then reboard your bus on the other side.

Travelers leaving Belize must pay a departure tax of BZ$30, plus a conservation fee of BZ$7.50. Pay this fee on the Belizean side of the border, before passing through passport control. You do not have to pay any fees in Guatemala; see p260 for information on Guatemalan visa requirements.

There are no banks on either side of the border (nor in Benque Viejo del Carmen), but money changers on both sides buy and sell Guatemalan, Mexican, Belizean and US currencies at decent rates. See p260 for information about money in Guatemala.

Taxis run to the border from San Ignacio and Benque Viejo. On a *colectivo* basis you pay BZ$4 to/from San Ignacio and BZ$2 to/from Benque. A private taxi costs about BZ$20 to/from San Ignacio and BZ$10 for Benque.

On the Guatemalan side of the border, you can often charter a taxi or minibus to Flores or Tikal (Q300 to Q350, two hours); chances of this are best in the morning. Otherwise, walk about half a mile to the market in Melchor de Mencos, the border town on the Guatemalan side. From the market there are minibuses to Flores (Q20) about every half-hour from around 5am to 6pm. If you're heading for El Remate, these vehicles can drop you at Puente Ixlú (El Cruce).

---

onto Hydro Rd, beside the Long Luck Super Store, and drive 2.5 miles to the park.

Che Chem Ha

William Morales' dog was busy chasing down a gibnut on his lush property one day in 1989, when the dog seemingly disappeared into a rock wall. Morales pressed into the 'wall' and found it was actually a cave mouth; inside he came upon probably the largest collection of Maya pottery ever discovered. The cave is **Che Chem Ha** (Map p203; ☎ 820-4063; Mile 8 Hydro Rd; tour per person BZ$40), or the 'Cave of Poisonwood Water.'

Morales' family has been farming this land since the 1940s, and today they also conduct tours through the cave, offering lunches and simple lodgings to visitors. The cave, about 800ft long, was used by the Maya for many centuries for food storage and rituals.

Narrow passages wind past ceremonial pots, many of them intact, to a stela at the end of the tunnel. Short ladders enable you to climb up rock ledges. Bring strong shoes, water and a flashlight. The tour lasts about 90 minutes, following an uphill jungle walk of about 30 minutes to the cave mouth. After the cave, you can visit a lovely waterfall on the property and/or hike about 30 minutes down to **Vaca Falls** for a swim in the Macal River.

It's a good idea to ring ahead, and, if you like, order a good home-cooked lunch

(BZ$15). You can also make arrangements for transportation from San Ignacio or Benque Viejo del Carmen; continue south on Hydro Rd, about 5.5 miles beyond Poustinia.

SLEEPING

Mopan River Resort (Map p203; ☎ 823-2047; www .mopanriverresort.com; Riverside North; 3-night packages per person cabanas/ste BZ$1314/1446; ✱ Nov-Jun; ✖ ✚) Set in beautifully manicured gardens on the north bank of the Mopan River (you'll be ferried across from Benque on arrival), this resort specializes in worry-free adventure vacations. Guests get to know each other remarkably easily with the assistance of fruity cocktails (included in the package price)! The packages (from three nights upward) also include meals, airport transfers and daily activities. After an outing exploring archaeological sites, river-tubing, bird-watching or kayaking, guests return to lovely accommodations with hardwood floors and furniture, modern bathrooms with tub, and spacious verandahs. The food is first class, with a different international buffet each night.

Maxim's Palace (☎ 823-2360; cayobenque@yahoo .com; 41 Church Hill St; s/d BZ$80/120; ⓟ ✗) If you are passing through en route to/from Guatemala, considering crashing at chez Maxim. Spacious rooms, warm hospitality and affordable rates make it a decent place to use as a base as you explore the sights around the border.

Benque Viejo del Carmen is the end of the line for most Western Hwy buses from Belize City. Buses depart for San Ignacio (BZ$2, 30 minutes), Belmopan (BZ$6, 1½ hours) and Belize City (BZ$10, 2½ hours) about every half-hour from 7am to 5:30pm (and about every hour on Sundays).

MOUNTAIN PINE RIDGE AREA

South of San Ignacio and the Western Hwy, the land begins to climb toward the heights of the Maya Mountains, whose arching ridge forms the border separating Cayo District from Stann Creek District to the east and Toledo District to the south.

In the heart of this highland area, 200 sq miles of submontane (ie on the foothills or lower slopes of mountains) pine forest is protected as the **Mountain Pine Ridge Forest Reserve**. Unlike the tropical broadleaf forests so prevalent in Belize, whose shallow soils sit on limestone, much of the Mountain Pine Ridge's soil sits on a superficial level of red clay, beneath which lies solid granite, making agriculture almost impossible.

The sudden switch from tropical rainforest to pine trees as you ascend to the Mountain Pine Ridge – a broad upland area of multiple ridges and valleys – is a little bizarre and somewhat startling. Also unexpected is the number of dead pines, the result of an infestation by the southern pine beetle in 2000. Fortunately the forest is growing back, thanks in part to a reforestation program; initial fears that the beetle would kill the entire forest have proved groundless. With luck it will be back to something like its former glory in 20 or 30 years.

The reserve is full of **rivers**, **pools**, **waterfalls** and **caves**; the higher elevation means relief from both heat and mosquitoes. Beyond the Pine Ridge, to the southwest, are the ruins of Caracol (p213), Belize's largest and most important Maya site.

The main road into the Mountain Pine Ridge area is the Chiquibul Rd (also called the Pine Ridge Rd), which heads south off the Western Hwy at Georgeville. The Cristo Rey Rd from Santa Elena (near San Ignacio) meets up with the Chiquibul Rd after 9 miles. Both of these roads and all others in the area (except for the final 12 miles to Caracol) are unpaved and very rough. For the most part, they are drivable in an ordinary car with reasonably high clearance, except in some cases

after a lot of rain. Give priority to any large trucks you meet. Without a car, you can take one of the Mountain Pine Ridge or Caracol tours from San Ignacio (see p198).

At the entrance to the protected area, 1.4 miles up the Chiquibul Rd from the Cristo Rey Rd junction, a warden stops all vehicles and registers names and license plates. This is to control illegal activity and to keep track of who is in the area in case of accidents or bad weather. You can inquire here about road conditions further on.

Dangers & Annoyances

Keep in mind that this massive area is largely uninhabited. The exceptions include a small presence of forestry and dam-construction workers in the village of Douglas D'Silva (also called Augustine), staff at the area lodges, a few archaeologists, occasional troops on training exercises and a smattering of illegal squatters from Guatemala. Nonetheless, Mountain Pine Ridge is one of the country's most remote regions.

In recent years, there were several reported incidents of tourist vehicles being stopped by armed robbers, presumed to be Guatemalan bandits. For this reason, the park instituted a convoy system, where rangers accompany all vehicles traveling to Caracol (see p214). It's an extreme measure that does not allow for much flexibility but it seems to be working.

Sights & Activities
WATERFALLS & CAVES

It's a far cry from the rainforest, but the pine forest is also a thriving ecosystem, covered with flora, traversed by river systems and replete with birds and other wildlife. The Macal River, Rio Frio, Barton Creek and Roaring Creek all start up on Mountain Pine Ridge. From here they flow north to the Belize River and out to the sea, cascading across rocky cliffs and verdant hillsides along the way.

Thousand Foot Falls

Ten miles off Chiquibul Rd, the Thousand Foot Falls are reckoned to be the highest falls in Central America. Access them by turning onto Cooma Cairn Rd, then turning left after 7 miles at the '1000 Ft Falls' sign. What you actually reach is a **lookout point** (admission BZ$4; 8am-5pm) with a view of the falls plunging over the edge of the pine-covered plateau into the tropical broadleaf valley far below. The

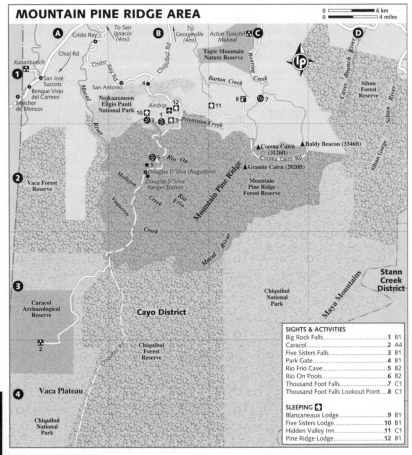

MOUNTAIN PINE RIDGE AREA

falls are in fact around 1600ft high, but the thin long stream of falling water is unlikely to hold your interest for a very long time. Birders should keep their eyes peeled for the rare orange-breasted falcon.

The highest point of the Mountain Pine Ridge is **Baldy Beacon** (3346ft), topped by a cluster of transmitter masts. Follow the signs a further 8 miles from the Thousand Foot Falls turnoff.

Privassion Creek

The shorter (150ft) and wider **Big Rock Falls** on Privassion Creek are more powerful and, for many people, more beautiful and impressive than Thousand Foot Falls. Take the road toward Five Sisters Lodge and, 1.5 miles past

Blancaneaux Lodge, turn along a track to the left where a 'Five Sisters Lodge' sign points straight ahead. The track ends after about 175yd, and a foot trail continues 400yd down to the river. You can swim in the river and the falls are 100yd upstream. There's also a trail to the falls from Blancaneaux Lodge (p215).

Five Sisters Falls, a set of smaller cascades with swimming pools and shelter pavilions at their base, are on the property of Five Sisters Lodge (p215). From the lodge, walk along the trail for about 45 minutes, or take the hydro-powered **mini-tram** (lodge guests/non-guests free/BZ$5; ☼ 8am-5pm). Near the falls, Five Sisters maintains an impressive floral display of hundreds of species of orchids, bromeliads and palmettos.

Rio Frio & Rio On

Just off Chiquibul Rd, 2.5 miles north of Douglas D'Silva, **Rio On Pools** is a series of small waterfalls connecting pools that the river has carved out of granite boulders. It's a beautiful spot: the pools are refreshing for a dip and the smooth slabs of granite are perfect for stretching out on to dry off. A picnic area and outhouse are the only amenities here, but it's a popular spot for tour groups on their way back from Caracol.

In Douglas D'Silva itself, look for the signed turnoff to **Rio Frio Cave**, less than 1 mile away. The river gurgles through the sizeable cave, keeping it cool while you explore.

CARACOL

Once one of the most powerful cities in the entire Maya world, **Caracol** (admission BZ$15; ☺ 8am-4pm) now lies enshrouded by thick jungle near the Guatemalan border, a 52-mile, two-hour drive from San Ignacio.

Sitting high on the Vaca Plateau, 1650ft above sea level, this is the largest Maya site in Belize, having stretched over possibly 70 sq miles at its peak around AD 650. Nearly 40 miles of internal causeways radiate from the center to large outlying plazas and residential areas, and connect parts of the city. At its height, the city's population may have approached 150,000, more than twice as many people as Belize City has today. Though they had no natural water source, the people of Caracol dug artificial reservoirs to catch rainwater and grew food on extensive agricultural terraces. Its central area was a bustling place of temples, palaces, busy thoroughfares, craft workshops and markets. Caracol is not only the preeminent archaeological site in Belize but also exciting for its jungle setting and prolific bird life.

At the ticket office, a small visitors center outlines Caracol's history and has a helpful scale model. A museum under construction will house much of the sculpture found at Caracol. There are toilets, picnic tables and a small gift shop. Be sure to bring food, water and, if you're driving, a spare tire. Overnight stays are not permitted.

Maya History

Caracol was settled by 600 BC but remained a modest place until the Classic Period. What sparked a sudden explosive growth in the 6th century AD was a confrontation with mighty Tikal, some 50 miles northwest. Caracol appears to have been allied with Calakmul (in Campeche state, Mexico), Tikal's major rival in the ancient Maya world. Caracol's Altar 21 (actually a ball court marker) records an 'axe event' in AD 556 that is thought to have been the sacrifice at Tikal of someone from Caracol, triggering hostilities between the two cities.

Altar 21 further records a successful war against Tikal by Caracol's ruler Lord Water in 562. Tikal's ruler Double Bird may have been sacrificed by Caracol at this time. The decades following these events saw a surge of construction and population at Caracol and a halt in the erection of monuments at Tikal. Tikal may have been forced to hand over much of its wealth to Caracol in the form of tribute for a century or more. Caracol's Lord Kan II conquered Naranjo, 25 miles north (in Guatemala), in 631, but Naranjo later turned the tables, defeating Caracol in 680. Thereafter Caracol declined in importance, although a prosperous elite continued to occupy the central area until around 895.

Excavation History

In 1937 a logger named Rosa Mai first stumbled upon the ruins. In 1938 commissioner of archaeology AH Anderson named the site Caracol (Spanish for snail), perhaps because of all the snail shells found in the soil. In 1950 Linton Satterthwaite from the University of Pennsylvania recorded the visible stone monuments, mapped the site core and excavated several tombs, buildings and monuments. Many stelae were removed and sent to Pennsylvania. Since 1985, Drs Diane and Arlen Chase have led the **Caracol Archaeological Project** (www.caracol.org), with annual field seasons conducting surveys and excavations that have revealed Caracol's massive central core and complex urban development. From 2000 to 2004 the Tourism Development Project carried out an excavation and conservation program led by Belizean archaeologist Jaime Awe, and improved the road access to Caracol.

Touring the Site

A system of trails meanders through Caracol, but Plazas A and B are the most excavated. The highlight is **Caana** (Sky-Place), which rises from Plaza B, and at 141ft is still the tallest building in Belize! Caana underwent many

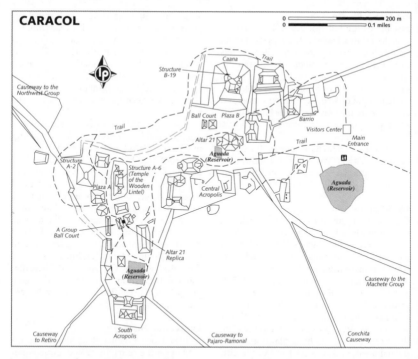

construction phases until its completion in about 800. It supports four palace compounds and three temples. High steps narrowing up to the top probably led to the royal family's compound, where **Structure B-19** housed Caracol's largest and most elaborate tomb, containing the remains of a woman, possibly Lady Batz' Ek from Calakmul, who married into Caracol's ruling dynasty in 584. Climb to the top of Caana to feast upon one of the most magnificent views in all of Belize. On the way down, don't miss the hidden tombs around the back on the left side.

South of Plaza B, the **Central Acropolis** was an elite residential group with palaces and shrines. To its west, Plaza A contained many stelae, some of which are still in place. Atop **Structure A-2** is a replica of a stela found here in 2003 that is engraved with the longest Maya inscription found in Belize. Structure A-6, the **Temple of the Wooden Lintel**, is one of the oldest buildings at Caracol. One of its lintels (the one to the left as you enter the top chamber) is original.

South of the Temple of the Wooden Lintel is the A Group Ball Court where the all-important **Altar 21**, telling us so much about Caracol's history, was found. A replica of the 'altar,' actually a ball court marker, sits in the middle. Further south is one of Caracol's many **reservoirs**, and beyond that the **South Acropolis**, a Classic Period elite residential complex where you can enter two tombs.

Getting There & Away

Most people come on a guided tour but it's possible to drive here on your own, as long as you are prepared for a bumpy ride. All visitors – individuals and groups alike – travel to Caracol in a convoy that departs Douglas D'Silva (Augustine) ranger station at 9:30am every morning. On the return trip, the convoy departs at 2pm. Each car must sign in and out. The convoy is accompanied by two park ranger vehicles to ensure the safety of all passengers.

Most of the vehicles in the convoy are tour buses, driven by experienced drivers and guides. Unless you are used to driving on crazy, bumpy, mind-numbing and muddy roads, you might want to let the more experienced drivers go ahead.

The final 12 miles to the site are paved. Once you cross the bridge over the Macal River you will appreciate the smooth sailing to the parking lot.

Tours

Most tour companies and lodges in and around San Ignacio run tours to the Mountain Pine Ridge and Caracol. On a typical day tour (usually BZ$140 to BZ$180 per person), you'll visit the Rio On Pools, Rio Frio Cave and one of the waterfalls. Caracol trips also stop at Rio On Pools and Rio Frio Cave on the way back, usually for around BZ$150. See p198 for tour operators.

Sleeping & Eating

The Mountain Pine Ridge has a handful of places offering accommodations, meals and tours and activities – including some of the most luxurious lodges in the country. Although you might find a room if you show up unannounced, it's a long way to come for a 'No Vacancy' sign, so it's best to book ahead.

If you don't have your own transportation, you'll need a taxi or lodge transfer to get to/from these places. A taxi from San Ignacio should cost about BZ$100; lodge transfers are BZ$120 to BZ$150 for up to four people.

Pine Ridge Lodge (Map p212; ☎ 606-4557, in USA 800-316-0706; www.pineridgelodge.com; d/tr/q incl breakfast BZ$180/233/286; lunch/dinner BZ$15/43; P) The most rustic of the Pine Ridge lodges has six little cabins decorated with Guatemalan handicrafts and original pieces created by local artists. Screened porches and hammocks are prime spots for relaxation. The Little Vaqueros Creek runs across the bottom of the grassy gardens, which are bursting with orchids. There's no electricity, but you'll come to love your kerosene lantern's soft glow, and the restaurant cooks up delicious meals using butane. The lodge is 4 miles along the Chiquibul Rd from the warden post.

Five Sisters Lodge (Map p212; ☎ 820-4005; www.fivesisterslodge.com; s/d/tr/q BZ$202/250/298/356; breakfast/lunch/dinner BZ$17/19/40; P) This locally owned lodge, 2.5 miles west of Blancaneaux Lodge, is named for five side-by-side cascades on the Privassion Creek at the bottom of its property (see p212). The open-air restaurant has a great view over the falls. Otherwise, a hydro-powered mini-tram and a 45-minute medicinal plant trail will both take you down to the river for swimming and sunbathing. Cozy cabanas were built from pimento sticks and bay leaf thatch roofs, and have beautiful mahogany floors and terraces hung with hammocks. You'll not see a clearer sky, which you can admire from the star-gazing deck.

our pick **Hidden Valley Inn** (Map p212; ☎ 822-3320; www.hiddenvalleyinn.com; s/d/tr BZ$400/462/524; breakfast/lunch/dinner BZ$29/35/72; P 🖳 🖳) Hidden Valley Inn is set on 11 gorgeous sq miles of Mountain Pine Ridge, all for the exclusive use of its guests. The grounds straddle pine and tropical forest ecosystems, and have access to 90 miles of signposted trails, eight sets of waterfalls and some inviting swimming spots and spectacular lookouts. Set out on foot, on a free mountain bike, or get a vehicle drop-off and make your own way back – whichever you choose, you get a map and a two-way radio and, if you like, they'll ensure that no one else is walking your trails at the same time! You can even rent a waterfall for the day, complete with champagne lunch. Birders, look out for the orange-breasted falcon (which nests here), the king vulture and the Stygian owl, as well as heaps of colorful and less rare species. The 12 cottages feature earth-toned tapestries, brick fireplaces and mahogany furniture, creating a warm, intimate atmosphere that extends throughout. The lodge is 4 miles off the Chiquibul Rd, along Cooma Cairn Rd.

Blancaneaux Lodge (Map p212; ☎ 824-3878, 824-4912, in USA 800-746-3743; www.blancaneaux.com; garden-view cabanas s/d BZ$535/619, riverfront cabanas s/d BZ$631/750, honeymoon cabanas BZ$820, 2-bedroom villas from BZ$1190, all incl breakfast; lunch & dinner mains BZ$25-50; P 🖳) This indulgent lodge was formerly a private retreat for its owner, movie director Francis Ford Coppola. Blancaneaux offers 17 thatched cabins and luxury villas, spread around beautifully manicured gardens, with some looking right over the picturesque Privassion Creek. The lodgings feature beautiful tiled bathrooms, with open-air living rooms in the villas, and handicrafts from Belize, Guatemala, Mexico and Thailand. Blancaneaux has its own stables, walking trails and riverside spa with a large hot pool. The restaurant serves Italian cuisine (Coppola's own recipes), gourmet pizzas from the brick oven and wines from the Niebaum-Coppola Estate Winery in California's Napa Valley. Much of the produce comes from the lodge's own organic garden.

Southern Belize

Southern Belize is where open savannah and citrus-filled farmland give way to forested hills dotted with Maya ruins and jungles, with many fine beaches and beautiful tropical islands thrown in for good measure. The area comprises two districts; Stann Creek, ancestral home of the Garifuna people, and Toledo, often referred to lovingly throughout Belize as the country's 'Deep South,' home to an eclectic mix of Maya, Garifuna and Creole people.

Diversity, both cultural and ecological, is the main hallmark of southern Belize, so it's natural that the area appeals to a wide variety of travelers. Adventurers will find no shortage of opportunities to get off the beaten path in the jungles of the Toledo District. Those who like their paths pre-beaten will find Placencia a tourist's paradise. Trekkers who wish to splurge have a number of five-star jungle lodges tucked away in remote corners from which to choose, while those of more modest means will be able to have a great time on the cheap in the small villages and communities of the Deep South.

Lest we forget, the south also has cayes all its own, islands small and large boasting stunning coral reefs, where snorkeling, boating and diving enthusiasts can experience Belize's nautical wonders while avoiding the crowds (and significantly higher price tags) of the northern cayes. Walt Whitman once wrote of himself: 'I am vast; I contain multitudes.' Though not large in size, this region can claim the same: from Dangriga to Baranco and everywhere in between, southern Belize definitely has many sides. Both the land and those who call it home are as diverse as the nation itself.

HIGHLIGHTS

- Camping, chilling and zip-lining into rivers at **Crocodile Isle** (p228)

- Cave-tubing through Belize's dark underbelly at **Cave's Branch** (p219)

- Walking the jungle trails of **Cockscomb Basin Wildlife Sanctuary** (p235) and **Mayflower Bocawina National Park** (p229)

- Learning Garifuna beats and drum making with master drummers in **Hopkins** (p230) and **Dangriga** (p224)

- Exploring the ancient Maya ruins, modern Maya villages and remote rivers, lagoons and forests of the **Deep South** (p250)

■ POPULATION: 57,000	■ MONTHLY RAINFALL: Jan 6.5in, Jun 23.4in	■ HIGHEST ELEVATION: 3687ft

SOUTHERN BELIZE

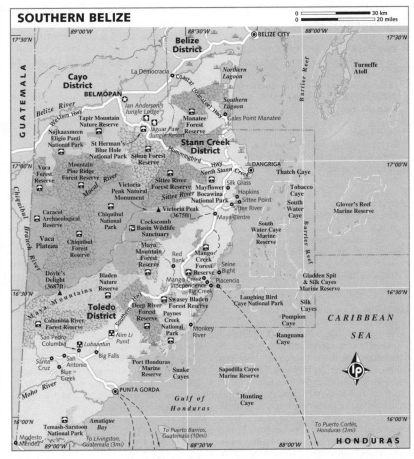

History

Ancient Maya sites in the Deep South such as Lubaantun and Nim Li Punit point to a flourishing Maya society that existed around AD 700–800. Centuries later, it was the Maya of southern Belize who most strongly resisted being conquered by the Spanish, though they eventually succumbed to European germs and diseases rather than bullets. The Maya who survived were driven out by the British to the Alta Verapaz region of Guatemala in the 18th and 19th centuries. In the late 19th century, Maya started moving back to Belize's far south where there are now more than 30 Maya villages.

English buccaneers and North American puritans settled along the Belize coast in the 17th century, and the earliest Creole villages were established near river mouths in the 18th century. Garifuna people started arriving in southern Belize around the same time: the biggest single landing of Garifuna people came on November 19, 1832, when some 200 arrived at Dangriga from Honduras in dugout canoes.

Industries such as small-scale agriculture, fishing and some logging have long been mainstays of the region's economy. Today, the growing and processing of citrus fruit in the Stann Creek Valley, situated west of Dangriga, is a major agro-industry, as is shrimp farming. As in much of Belize, tourism is a major cash generator throughout the southern region.

SOUTHERN BELIZE

SOUTHERN BELIZE IN...

Two Days
Spend a day soaking up Garifuna culture in **Dangriga** (p220) and another listening to the sounds of the jungle in **Cockscomb Basin Wildlife Sanctuary** (p235) or at **Crocodile Isle** (p228).

Four Days
Do the two-day itinerary, spending your extra two days soaking up the sunshine and enjoying ocean breezes at **Thatch Caye** (p228).

One Week
Base yourself in **Punta Gorda** (p245) and explore the jungles, Maya villages and ruins of Belize's **Deep South** (p250). Head to the Garifuna village of **Barranco** (p254) and take a jungle trek through **Temash-Sarstoon National Park** (p255).

Language

Come down south to experience the real linguistic gumbo that is Belize. While English is spoken almost everywhere, at home many Belizeans speak the languages of their own cultures. In Dangriga, Hopkins, Seine Bight and Punta Gorda, expect to hear lots of Garifuna, and, to a lesser extent, Creole. And in villages of the Deep South you're as likely to hear Kekchi or Mopan Mayan as you are English. Spanish is widely spoken as well, both by locals and first- and second-generation immigrants from around Central America. In addition, there's a fair bit of Chinese spoken, mostly Cantonese.

Getting There & Around

Two roads connect southern Belize to the Belize District and Northern Belize: the Hummingbird Hwy (which runs from Belmopan to the start of the Southern Hwy near Dangriga) and the Coastal (Manatee) Hwy, an unpaved road that stretches from the Belize District just south of the zoo to the Hummingbird Hwy west of Dangriga, along the way stretching the very definition of the term 'highway.' Though shorter in terms of miles, unless you're planning to visit Gales Point Manatee (p115) on your way down south, the Manatee isn't worth

the chiropractic trauma. The Southern Hwy meets the Hummingbird west of Dangriga then continues 100 miles south to Punta Gorda. Both the Hummingbird and Southern Hwys are well paved except for a 10-mile stretch of the Southern Hwy around Nim Li Punit.

Buses from Belize City and Belmopan head down the Hummingbird Hwy to Dangriga then on to the Southern Hwy to Independence and Punta Gorda. Other services run from Dangriga to Hopkins and Placencia, and from Punta Gorda to villages around the far south. See p250 and p104 for schedules. Placencia can also be accessed by water-taxi service from Mango Creek, which adjoins Independence.

Daily flights head from Belize City to Dangriga, Placencia and Punta Gorda. Scheduled boat services link Dangriga and Placencia with Puerto Cortés in Honduras, and Punta Gorda with Puerto Barrios and Lívingston in Guatemala. Boats cross to Tobacco Caye from Dangriga daily; boats to the other islands can be organized through tour operators, dive shops, accommodations or boat owners.

Though there isn't officially a land border crossing between southern Belize and Guatemala, unofficial crossings – generally of locals – occur just west of the village of Jalacte. If you cross this way you risk being stuck on the other side without an entry stamp in your visa.

THE HUMMINGBIRD HIGHWAY

Passing through jungle and citrus orchards as it skirts the northern edges of the Maya Mountain range, the Hummingbird offers a near constant procession of postcard-perfect vistas. There are also plenty of reasons to stop and spend a day or two before hitting the Southern Hwy.

Chief among these may well be a visit to some of Belize's most amazing caves, many of which are located in this neck of the jungle. The 575-acre **St Herman's Blue Hole National Park** (admission BZ$10; 8am-4:30pm) contains one of the few caves in Belize that you can visit independently. The visitors center (where flashlights can be rented for BZ$5) is 11 miles along the Hummingbird Hwy from Belmopan. From here a 500yd trail leads to **St Herman's Cave**. A path leads 300yd into the cave alongside an underground river. To explore deeper in the extensive cave system, with its huge caverns and classic Maya ceremonial chambers containing calcified skeletons and artifacts, you must have a guide.

Highly experienced Kekchi Maya guide **Marcos Cucul** (☎ 600-3116; www.mayaguide.bz) can sometimes be found at the visitors center (when he isn't leading jungle survival tours deep in the bush; see the boxed text, p80). With over a decade's experience as an area guide, Cucul enjoys an excellent reputation. A three-hour spelunk costs BZ$100 per person. There's also a 1.5-mile aboveground **jungle loop trail** starting near the cave entrance, with a lookout tower at the area's highest point.

The **Blue Hole** for which the park is named is just off the highway, 1 mile east of the visitors center (an off-road trail connects the two). This is a 25ft-deep sapphire-blue swimming hole inside a 328ft-wide cenote that was formed when the roof caved in on one of the Sibun River's underground tributaries. A popular stop on the Hummingbird Hwy, the Blue Hole always makes for a refreshing dip, except after rain when it's murky and uninviting. An attendant at the Blue Hole parking area will collect your park fee if you don't have a ticket from the visitors center. Buses along the Hummingbird Hwy will drop you at the visitors center or Blue Hole entrance (BZ$2, 20 minutes from Belmopan; BZ$4.50, 1¼ hours from Dangriga).

Perhaps the most iconic of all Belizean caving experiences can be had at **Cave's Branch**, the main staging ground for what is quickly becoming Belize's most popular non-nautical activity, **cave-tubing**. You'll need a guide to go through the area's underground river and cave network. Highly recommended is **Vitalino Reyes** (☎ 602-8975; http://cavetubing.bz), a pioneer of the pursuit who begins his tubing trips with fascinating, information-filled jungle walks. During the walk, Vitalino will show you which plants are good to eat, which ones will hurt you, and which ones will help you if you confuse the first with the second. Vitalino is also an entomologist who delights in introducing his charges to tasty jungle bugs; he also has a penchant for handling tarantulas.

Also licensed for cave-tubing are **Marcos Cucul** (☎ 600-3116; www.mayaguide.bz) and **Ian Anderson's Adventure Company** (☎ 822-2800; www.cavesbranch.com; Mile 41½ Hummingbird Hwy).

Sleeping & Eating

Ian Anderson's Jungle Lodge (Map p217; ☎ 822-2800; www.cavesbranch.com; Mile 41½ Hummingbird Hwy; camping per person BZ$10, dm BZ$30, cabanas/bungalows d BZ$196-390; breakfast/lunch/dinner BZ$24/24/36; **P**) With something for all budget ranges, Ian Anderson's is a 90-sq-mile private jungle estate that acts as both starting point and nerve center for a variety of jungle activities, including horseback riding, mountain biking, nocturnal jungle walks, and day, night (and overnight) cave, jungle and kayak expeditions. Check the website for a full description of what's on offer at the lodge. All employed tour leaders are highly trained, knowledgeable, attentive and enthusiastic. Accommodations are jungle-chic, and the restaurant serves excellent Belizean, Maya & Carribean cuisine.

Jaguar Paw Jungle Resort (Map p217; ☎ 820-2023, in USA 877-624-3770; www.jaguarpaw.com; Hummingbird Hwy; s/d BZ$381/440, breakfast BZ$10-16, lunch BZ$16-20, dinner BZ$30-50; **P** ✕ ☐ ☎) Adventure by day and comfort by night is the motto of Jaguar Paw, and with 16 gorgeous double rooms each done up in its own individual theme (Wild West, English Country Garden, Chinese), the resort certainly follows this motto in style. Jaguar Paw offers a variety of activities,

---

DARK, WET FUN

Picture yourself on a tube on a river, with tamarind trees and Belizean blue skies... Ah, but did we mention that within a few minutes of your trip's launch the sky will be replaced by total darkness as you and your erstwhile comrades are pulled down into the very bowels of the earth? No, this isn't an anti-LSD ad from the sixties. This is **cave-tubing**, possibly the coolest (and most family friendly) thing you can do in the dark. After entering the cave you'll float through bracingly cold water in an underground network and witness – through the light of your headlamp – wonders unseen in the world above, from schools of eyeless cave fish and stalactites to strange Maya paintings high on the cave ceilings. Welcome to the underground, Belizean style!

similar to Ian Anderson's Jungle Lodge, at prices roughly equivalent.

STANN CREEK DISTRICT

Bordering the Belize District to the north, Cayo to the west and Toledo to the south, the Stann Creek District is home to a number of spots popular with visitors, from the coastal villages of Hopkins and Placencia, to amazing inland parks and jungle sanctuaries, to some of Belize's least visited cayes. Dangriga, Belize's second-largest town, is located on the district's northern coastal edge.

DANGRIGA
pop 10,400

Dangriga is the largest town in southern Belize, and the spiritual capital of the country's Garifuna people. Stretching along the coast, Dangriga has a funky vibe about it – tumbledown and mildly untidy – and for this reason it isn't a major stopover point for most tourists. We think this is a shame: despite sharing a similar ramshackle exterior with Belize City, Dangriga exudes little of the larger city's menace. Though a bit rough around the edges (strangers may ask you for money), Dangriga is generally a safe place to explore and has a good deal of cultural cachet with which to entice visitors to stay an extra day. It's a proud, festive town, one that does its best to make the most of its vibrant Garifuna heritage.

The name Dangriga comes from a Garifuna word meaning 'sweet water,' the town's name having been changed from 'Stann Creek Town' in the 1980s. Dangriga is the birthplace of punta rock (a fusion of acoustic Garifuna and electric instruments; see p45), and is home to a number of notable Garifuna artists, artisans and festivals, not to mention Belize's only Garifuna museum. With good access to both the central cayes and the Southern and Hummingbird Hwys, Dangriga is also an excellent place from which to launch nautical or jungle excursions.

Orientation

Dangriga stretches about 2.5 miles along the coast and up to 1000yd inland. North Stann Creek empties into the Caribbean roughly in the middle of town. The main street, stretching most of the length of the town, runs through the names Havana St, St Vincent St and Commerce St. The main bus station is toward its south end (Havana St); most boats to the central cayes and other cayes dock on South Riverside Dr, near the bridge over North Stann Creek. Most accommodations are in the southern half of town, and the airstrip is at the north end.

Information

Belize Bank (☎ 522-2903; 24 St Vincent St; ☷ 8am-3pm Mon-Thu, to 4:30pm Fri) Same as Scotia Bank, but with a BZ$500 daily limit and BZ$2 ATM fee for credit cards..

First Caribbean International Bank (☎ 522-2015; Commerce St; ☷ 8am-2:30pm Mon-Thu, to 4:30pm Fri) ATM accepts international Visa cards.

Immigration Office (☎ 522-3412; St Vincent Street; ☷ 8am-noon & 1-5pm Mon-Thu, 8am-noon & 1-4:30pm Fri) Offers 30-day visa extension stamps for BZ$50.

Police (☎ 90, 911, 522-2022; Commerce St) No longer handles visa extensions; for these, go to the Immigration Office.

Post office (☎ 522-2035; Mahogany Rd; ☷ 8am-noon & 1-5pm Mon-Thu, 8am-noon & 1-4:30pm Fri)

Scotia Bank (☎ 522-2005; St Vincent St; ☷ 8am-3pm Mon-Thu, to 4:30pm Fri) The ATM accepts international Visa, MasterCard, Plus and Cirrus cards with no additional fee; daily limit is BZ$800.

Southern Regional Hospital (☎ 522-2078; Stann Creek Valley Rd) Good-standard public hospital.

Val's Laundry (☎ 502-3324; cnr Mahogany Rd & Sharp St; internet per hr BZ$4, laundry wash & dry per lb BZ$2; ☷ 7:30am-7pm) Get your clothes cleaned, surf the Web (wireless available) and have some of Belize's best homemade ice cream all at the same time. Dana (Val's daughter) also runs the attached Val's Backpacker Hostel (p222).

Sights & Activities
GULISI GARIFUNA MUSEUM

This **museum** (☎ 669-0639; www.ngcbelize.org; Chuluhadiwa Park, Stann Creek Valley Rd; admission BZ$10; ☷ 10am-5pm Mon-Fri, 8am-noon Sat), operated by the National Garifuna Council (NGC), is a must for anyone interested in the vibrant Garifuna people. The museum is 2 miles out of town, but is easily reached by bicycle (stop at Rosalie's, p222, for some tortillas on the way). It brings together artifacts, pictures and documents on Garifuna history and culture, including film of the original punta rockers, Pen Cayetano and the Turtle Shell Band, in Dangriga back in 1983. The museum hosts exhibitions, workshops and Garifuna language courses, schedules for which can be obtained at its musical website.

DANGRIGA

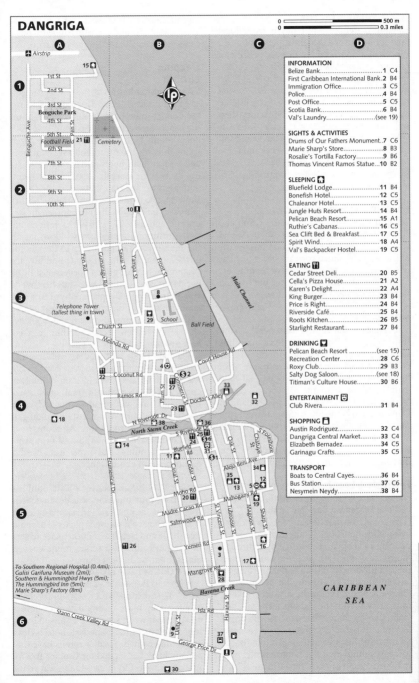

0 _____ 500 m
0 _____ 0.3 miles

INFORMATION
Belize Bank.............................**1** C4
First Caribbean International Bank.**2** B4
Immigration Office...................**3** C5
Police....................................**4** B4
Post Office.............................**5** C5
Scotia Bank...........................**6** B4
Val's Laundry.....................(see 19)

SIGHTS & ACTIVITIES
Drums of Our Fathers Monument..**7** C6
Marie Sharp's Store..................**8** B3
Rosalie's Tortilla Factory............**9** B6
Thomas Vincent Ramos Statue...**10** B2

SLEEPING
Bluefield Lodge.......................**11** B4
Bonefish Hotel........................**12** C5
Chaleanor Hotel......................**13** C5
Jungle Huts Resort..................**14** B4
Pelican Beach Resort................**15** A1
Ruthie's Cabanas....................**16** C5
Sea Clift Bed & Breakfast...........**17** C5
Spirit Wind............................**18** A4
Val's Backpacker Hostel............**19** C5

EATING
Cedar Street Deli.....................**20** B5
Cella's Pizza House..................**21** A2
Karen's Delight........................**22** A4
King Burger............................**23** B4
Price is Right..........................**24** B4
Riverside Café........................**25** B4
Roots Kitchen.........................**26** B5
Starlight Restaurant..................**27** B4

DRINKING
Pelican Beach Resort ....(see 15)
Recreation Center....................**28** C6
Roxy Club..............................**29** B3
Salty Dog Saloon..................(see 18)
Titiman's Culture House............**30** B6

ENTERTAINMENT
Club Rivera............................**31** B4

SHOPPING
Austin Rodriguez.....................**32** C4
Dangriga Central Market............**33** C4
Elizabeth Bernadez...................**34** C5
Garinagu Crafts.......................**35** C5

TRANSPORT
Boats to Central Cayes..............**36** B4
Bus Station............................**37** C6
Nesymein Neydy......................**38** B4

SOUTHERN BELIZE

MARIE SHARP'S FACTORY

Habanero peppers, purchased from local farmers, are turned into the super-hot bottled sauces that adorn tables all over Belize and beyond at **Marie Sharp's Fine Foods** (☎ 520-2087; www.mariesharps-bz.com; ☽ 7am-4pm Mon-Fri), 8 miles northwest of town on Melinda Rd. Casual tours, often led by Marie herself, are offered during business hours, and the factory shop sells hot sauces and jams at outlet prices. If you can't make it to the factory but would still like to peruse the full line of sauces and jams, Marie Sharp's also has a **store** (☎ 522-2370; 3 Pier Rd; ☽ 8am-noon & 1-5pm Mon-Fri) in Dangriga. See also the boxed text, p84.

ROSALIE'S TORTILLA FACTORY

Though there's no indoor seating, you can come to **Rosalie's Tortilla Factory** (☎ 520-2397; 765 Unity St; ☽ 6:30am-5:30pm Mon-Sat), on the outskirts of Dangriga, to watch corn and flour tortillas being made and take a dozen of them to eat on the fly. The best time to get the freshest tortillas is between 9am and noon.

MONUMENTS

The **Drums of Our Fathers Monument**, in the traffic circle south of Dangriga's main bus station, underscores the importance of percussion in Garifuna (and Belizean) life, with its large bronze representations of ritual *dügü* drums and *sisira* (maracas). It was sculpted by Stephen Okeke, a Nigerian resident in Dangriga. Up at the other end of town, at the meeting of Commerce and Front Sts, stands a **statue of Thomas Vincent Ramos** (1887–1955), an early promoter of Garifuna culture who inaugurated Garifuna Settlement Day.

Festivals & Events

Dangriga explodes with celebrations to mark **Garifuna Settlement Day** (November 19), the Garifuna arrival date here in 1832. Dangrigans living elsewhere flock home, and drumming, dancing and drinking continue right through the night of the 18th to 19th, while canoes reenact the beach landing in the morning.

Dangrigans celebrate **Día de los Reyes** (Three Kings' Day; on the nearest weekend to January 6) with the *wanaragua* or *jonkonu* (John Canoe) dance: male dancers with bright feather-and-paper headdresses, painted masks representing European men and rattling bands of shells around their knees move from house to house dancing to Garifuna drums. It's the culmination of two weeks of Christmas-season festivities and may also happen at other times between Christmas and January 6.

Sleeping

BUDGET

Val's Backpacker Hostel (☎ 502-3324; cnr Mahogany Rd & Sharp St; dm/d BZ$19/60; ☐) Quite a find for the budget traveler, Val's is located right on the beach, across from Alejo Beni Park. Val's dorm rooms are fan cooled with a large porch facing the park and ocean, and have bunk beds and separate bathrooms with hot showers. The double room is more like a studio apartment, with its own separate bathroom (with hot shower), two twin beds, comfortable couches and easy chairs, a full dining room set, dresser drawers and color TV with full cable hook-up. Both dorms and studio have windows facing the sea, so you can fall asleep to the sounds of the ocean. Wireless internet and luggage lockers are free for guests (lockers cost BZ$2 per day if you want to leave stuff here while you go traveling). Dangriga native Dana (the eponymous Val's daughter) is a great source of local information. Bicycle rental, book exchange, fresh brewed coffee and more. Your home away from home in 'Griga.

Bluefield Lodge (☎ 522-2742; www.toucantrail .com/bluefield-lodge.html; 6 Bluefield Rd; d with shared/private bathroom BZ$32/44, 2-bed d with shared/private bathroom BZ$42/60) This well-run small guesthouse fills up fast, so book ahead. With good, clean rooms in a pristine colonial-style building, it gets plenty of return visitors. All rooms have fans, some have cable TV. Single occupants may get discounts. The owner has a wealth of information about Dangriga.

Ruthie's Cabanas (☎ 502-3148; 31 Southern Foreshore; cabanas s BZ$54, each additional person BZ$10) Ruthie's comprises four pleasant, seaside, thatched-roof huts on the north side of Havana Creek. It offers hot and cold showers, plenty of coconut tree shade and a chill and cheap place to stay in 'Griga. Ruthie also serves home-cooked meals for an additional charge.

Sea Clift Bed & Breakfast (☎ 502-2350; www .seaclift.com; 15 Mahogany St; s/d incl breakfast BZ$76/100; ☒ ☒ ☐) Looking like a Colorado ski chalet (it's the only place in this nation of homes on stilts that we've seen with a sunken living room), this nice little home-style hotel is clean and family owned. Smaller rooms have mahogany bunk beds, good for two, for BZ$50. All rooms have TV, internet and great views.

There's a shared kitchen, and yes, the sunken living room is also communal.

Chaleanor Hotel (☎ 522-2587; www.toucantrail .com/chaleanor-hotel.html; 35 Magoon St; s/d/tr with shared bathroom BZ$20/30/40, with private bathroom BZ$50/86/108; ✗ ☆) Owned by Chad and Eleanor (hence the name) Usher, Chaleanor is a friendly hotel with a great location on a residential street two blocks from the ocean and Dangriga's main street. Rooms are clean and comfortable, with the ones upstairs having the best views. The owners will also be glad to help you arrange any trips or boat charters. Free coffee and bananas are available all day; ask Chad to see the pair of gibnuts in the backyard.

Jungle Huts Resort (☎ 522-0185; junglehutsresort@ gmail.com; 4 Ecumenical Dr; s/d BZ$58/78, with air-con BZ$78/98; P ✗ ☐ ☆) This riverside resort has 16 rooms and three cabanas. Its secluded feel belies its central location, and its facilities – on-site laundry, restaurant and many hammocks for chilling out – make it a good budget spot.

MIDRANGE

Bonefish Hotel (☎ 522-2243; www.bluemarlinlodge.com; 15 Mahogany Rd; r BZ$107-180; ☆) Located right on the beach, across from Alejo Beni Park. The rooms on the upper floors are clean and not without charm, but the ones on the lower floor are a bit darker. All rooms have two double beds (except for one room that has a king-size bed), fan, air-con and cable TV. Some rooms seem to lack screens in the windows. A decent place, but not the best deal for the money in Dangriga. This place is owned by the same people who run the Blue Marlin Lodge (p226) on South Water Caye, and you can arrange packages and boat trips to that caye from here.

Hummingbird Inn (☎ 522-0512; www.hummingbird innbelize.com; Mile 6 South Stann Creek Valley Road; d standard/deluxe incl breakfast BZ$140/220; P ✗ ☐) Six miles out of Dangriga, this family owned plantation-style house has a charming B&B vibe about it. The doubles are more than comfortable, and the deluxe room (with its soaker tub) is positively decadent. Screened-in verandahs and porches wrapping around both stories of the house make excellent use of the setting, allowing guests to chill out and gaze at some of central Belize's gorgeous scenery. In addition to breakfast, lunch and dinner (prepared by the inn's excellent Maya chef) can also be arranged. David Gobeil, the Hummingbird's manager, is a wealth of local information, offering tours to the many spots within striking distance of the inn.

Spirit Wind (☎ 522-0409; www.spiritwindbelize .com; cabanas incl breakfast BZ$200; ✗) Spirit Wind is hands down the best spot for a romantic weekend getaway in Dangriga, with gorgeous cabanas on the south side of Stann Creek (about half a mile inland; call for directions). All four cabanas have hot and cold water, air-con and big double beds with mosquito nets. Decorations and the design are in a luscious Afro-Caribbean style that is delicately sensual without being over-the-top lewd. Meals are available, and the Spirit Wind is connected to the Salty Dog (p224).

TOP END

Pelican Beach Resort (☎ 522-2044; www.pelicanbeach belize.com; 1st St; s/d BZ$214/278, s/d with air-con BZ$232/297; P ✗ ☐) Set in beachside gardens (with a sandy beach) at the far north end of town, Dangriga's one upmarket hotel has good, spacious rooms and the best restaurant in town. All rooms have phones and many are decorated with colorful art by Dangriga's Pen Cayetano. The owners also run the Pelican's Pouch (p227) on South Water Caye.

Eating

There are several good fast-food shacks and stands along the main street serving beans, rice and chicken, and a number of Chinese restaurants scattered around town run by Cantonese immigrants.

King Burger (☎ 522-2476; 135 Commerce St; dishes BZ$4-15; ⏱ breakfast, lunch & dinner Mon-Sat) No relation to the chain restaurant of the reversed name, King Burger serves reliably fresh though somewhat mediocre breakfasts of eggs, beans and fryjacks for BZ$6.50, as well as hamburgers and plates of fried shrimp. Coffee is instant, but juices are fresh.

our pick **Roots Kitchen** (☎ 601-2519; 2246 Ecumenical Dr; dishes BZ$5-10; ⏱ 6am-10pm) *The* place in Dangriga to eat like the locals do. In addition to the usual Belizean standards, such as beans and rice with stew beef or chicken, Roots is also known for its Wednesday, Friday and Saturday Garifuna feasts, when chef Delone cooks up fish stewed in coconut milk, served with *hudut*, a paste made from plantain. To read what Delone has to say about Garifuna cooking, see p85.

SOUTHERN BELIZE

Karen's Delight (☎ 502-3952; 3 Stanley Dr; dishes BZ$7-10; ⊗ lunch & dinner) Another unassuming, small shack restaurant serving wonderfully prepared local dishes, such as fry fish (caught daily) and stew chicken and beef. Karen makes some of the meanest pickled peppers you'll find in town.

Starlight Restaurant (☎ 522-3398; Commerce St; mains BZ$8-14; ⊗ breakfast, lunch & dinner) The best Chinese restaurant in Dangriga, and probably one of the better ones in Belize. Starlight has been in operation for decades, and serves a good variety of traditional Chinese dishes using local ingredients. For some real Sino-Belizean fusion, try the conch chow mein. Lobster noodles are a surprising bargain.

Cedar Street Deli (☎ 609-5664; Cedar St; mains BZ$8-15; ⊗ lunch) This is a sight for sore eyes in a country where heart-healthy food is hard to come by. Open for lunch only, it serves salads, homemade lasagna and other distinctly non-Belizean dishes. There wasn't a sign on the restaurant the last time we went, so look for the red and green doorway on the lower corner of a yellow house.

Riverside Café (☎ 502-3449; S Riverside Dr; mains BZ$10-25; ⊗ breakfast, lunch & dinner) Just east of the Stann Creek bridge, this café is the place to meet fishers and the folks who do boat tours to the outlying cayes. Food is good and the fish is always fresh. Don't expect a full lobster for BZ$25 (the costliest item on the menu); it's only a Mars Bar–sized tail, tasty but expensive.

Cella's Pizza House (☎ 527-2536; 3 Cemetery Rd; pizzas BZ$24-30; ⊗ lunch & dinner) A cool-looking pizza joint in a private home at the north end of town, Cella's serves good pizza and bottled beer in a fairly untrodden section of Dangriga. A bit pricey, but understandable as all ingredients are imported. (Pizza is definitely not native to Belize!)

The supermarkets on the main street on both sides of North Stann Creek have bread, cheese and lunch-meat, not to mention a wide variety of snacks, both domestic and imported. The largest of these is Price is Right, just south of the bridge.

Drinking & Entertainment

Club Rivera (2 St Vincent St; ⊗ from 9pm Tue-Thu & Sun, from 10pm Fri & Sat) Formerly called Club Griga, Club Rivera usually has live bands on Friday and Saturday night, featuring punta rock and other types of music. It gets a bit of a crowd for midweek karaoke sessions, but things really start jumping at the Friday and Saturday dances.

Roxy Club (Commerce St; ⊗ from 9pm Tue-Thu & Sun, from 10pm Fri & Sat) To quote a pair of Dangriga-based Peace Corps volunteers: 'The Roxy is a good place. Stumpy and Penny are very friendly, and Penny makes great *panatas* (small fish-filled fried tortillas), three for a dollar.' It's at the north end of the city, about three blocks north of the police station in Harlem Sq.

Salty Dog Saloon (☎ 522-0409; www.spiritwind belize.com) This very chilled bar (at Spirit Wind, p223) has the most Jimmy Buffet vibe in Dangriga, though it is a bit out of town. To find it, call or follow the signs for the Salty Dog Saloon beginning on Ecumenical Dr around North Stann Creek.

Titiman's Culture House (☎ 602-2099; sailbelize@ yahoo.com) Poots 'Titiman' Flores is a local Dangriga legend. His laid-back club – located on an unmarked country road two blocks southwest of the Drums of Our Fathers Monument – is a great place to chill out and get down with serious Garifuna culture.

Also recommended are the following:

Pelican Beach Resort (☎ 522-2044; www.pelican beachbelize.com; 1st St) The Friday happy hour from 6pm to 8pm usually pulls in a crowd.

Recreation Center (St Vincent St; ⊗ 4pm-midnight) This piece of earth with a thatched roof, no walls and a mainly local clientele can be a lot of fun.

Shopping

Austin Rodriguez (☎ 502-3752) This master artisan carves Garifuna drums from mahogany, cedar and the mayflower tree in his thatched-roof workshop by the water's edge, southeast of Dangriga Central Market. Though Austin's drums are sold all over Belize, you can cut out the middleman by going straight to the maker himself. Mr Rodriguez will be happy to answer any questions you might have on the drum-making process.

Elizabeth Bernadez (13 Howard St; ⊗ daylight hr) Granddaughter of Austin Rodriguez, Elizabeth sells handmade crafts from her home (next door to the Bonefish Hotel), including beautiful dolls dressed in traditional Garifuna outfits, and acrylic paintings featuring various cultural scenes of traditional Garifuna life. Elizabeth also makes jewelry from jadeite, tiger eye and other local materials. A native of Dangriga ('born here, grown here'), Elizabeth has been doing artwork locally for over 15 years, and is happy to introduce visitors to Garifuna life and culture through the art of its people.

Garinagu Crafts (☎ 522-2596; grigaservices@yahoo .com; 46 Oak St) With the mission statement of 'keeping the black diaspora alive,' Dangriga native Francis M Swaso's shop is part crafts store, part museum. The shop sells a wide range of arts and handicrafts made by Garifuna artists, including drums, maracas, paintings and dolls, and displays a number of historical Garifuna artifacts as well. Garinagu Crafts also carries postcards made from prints by local artist Pen Cayetano.

Dangriga Central Market (Doctor's Alley; ◷ 6am-4pm) An old-school semi-enclosed market. You'll find traders selling shoes, clothing and crockery on the outskirts, while farmers and fishers sell their wares inside and around the main building. Naturally the market is busiest in the morning. You can also get cheap breakfasts here.

Getting There & Away
AIR
From Dangriga airport (DGA), **Maya Island Air** (☎ 522-3475; www.mayaairways.com) and **Tropic Air** (☎ 522-2129; www.tropicair.com) both fly several times daily to Belize City (one-way/return BZ$114/218, 25 minutes) and less often to Punta Gorda via Placencia.

BOAT
Dangriga is the jumping off point for trips to Belize's central cayes, as well as for chartered trips up and down the coast and regularly scheduled trips to Honduras. Boats to the cayes leave from opposite the Riverside Café on South Riverside Dr. Stop by around 9am to 10am, or the afternoon before, to check when boats will be leaving. Some lodges on the islands will organize a boat for you.

The water taxi **Nesymein Neydy** (☎ 522-0062, 522-3227) makes weekly trips from Dangriga to Puerto Cortés, Honduras, departing North Riverside Dr at 9am Saturday. The trip costs BZ$100 and takes from three to four hours. Captain Reyes' boat also stops at Placencia and Big Creek to board passengers, so you can arrange for pick-up from those places as well. Be at the dock around 8am. The return trip from Puerto Cortés is on Tuesday; there are also trips on Saturday, though not every week.

DRUMMED-OUT DANGRIGA?

In bygone days Dangriga was known for spontaneous explosions of Garifuna drumming, not merely around festivals such as Garifuna Settlement Day or Día de los Reyes (p222), but also ad hoc gatherings in parks, on the beach or on the street. This seems to be happening less and less outside of festival times, according to local drum-making legend Austin Rodriguez (opposite). 'Dangriga got kind of drummed out a few years back. Nowadays the kids seem lazier.' This might be the case, or it might be that today's kids are channeling their musical energies into punta rock, which mixes traditional drumming with heavy bass, electric guitar and slamming lyrics.

Topsy's Boat Service (☎ 623-9764, 522-0823) offers trips to all cayes reasonably accessible from Dangriga for decent prices on a sliding scale: the more people you can get for one trip (within reason), the less you can expect to pay per person. Day trips and longer to South Water Caye and Tobacco Caye can be arranged, as can trips to Glover's Reef. Mike, owner of Topsy's, can often be found in front of the Riverside Café when not on his boat.

BUS
A major transit point for all bus companies servicing southern Belize, Dangriga's main bus station is across from the Drums of Our Fathers Monument. See p250 and p104 for schedules.

CENTRAL CAYES
Less crowded (and often less costly) than those in the north, the cayes off Belize's central coast are smack in the middle of some of Belize's most amazing diving, snorkeling and fishing sites. Slackers take note: there's no shortage of tropical breezes and palm-tree-slung hammocks.

Getting There & Away
Dangriga is the natural jumping off point for trips to Tobacco, Thatch and South Water Cayes. Most listed hotels and resorts will arrange your passage; some, such as Thatch Caye Resort, include pick-up from Dangriga airport, van to the dock and boat to the caye in their vacation packages. You can also hire

SOUTHERN BELIZE

a boat yourself in Dangriga at the dock across from the Riverside Café (Map p221); prices vary, so your best bet is to go in a group of four or more. If you're arranging your own trip, make sure to schedule your pick-up, or risk being at the fickle mercies of nautical travel. Glover's Reef can also be reached from Dangriga, though most travelers opt to get there from Glover's Guest House (p235).

Tobacco Caye

Tiny Tobacco Caye, 200yd long, 100yd wide and mainly sandy, sits right on the barrier reef 12 miles off Dangriga. The caye is a great place for **snorkeling**, **diving**, **fishing** or slacking out on a hammock. With half a dozen places to stay, it's popular with travelers on a limited budget looking for the *Gilligan's Island* experience. The atmosphere is sociable and friendly. At most accommodations all guests eat at the same time, and three places have bars open to all. Just west is **Man-O'-War Caye**, an important nesting site for the brown booby and magnificent frigate bird, which you will very likely pass on the way to Tobacco Caye. Both islands are among the dozens within the World Heritage–listed **South Water Caye Marine Reserve**.

Tobacco Caye is close to some of central Belize's premier dive spots. In the vicinity is **Shark Hole** (or Shark Cave), an underwater cave popular with fish, turtles and sharks. The entrance, 42ft down, is about 33ft wide but the cave opens up to about 150ft inside. In its center is a large sandhill around which the sharks circle. Dives can be organized through **Tobacco Caye Diving** (☎ 614-9907; www.tobaccocaye diving.com), which is next to Reef's End Lodge. Local dives cost BZ$60 per day. Various dive packages are available, as are equipment rental and certification. Two-tank outings to Belize's atolls (usually requiring four people) head to other popular spots. Call or check the website for current rates, which are highly sensitive to rising fuel prices.

Of course, if you're more into marine life for its culinary value, there's good fishing for tarpon, bonefish and snook very close to the island. Most accommodations have fishing equipment for rent.

SLEEPING & EATING

Equipment rental and meal packages are available at most lodgings. The only restaurants are at the places to stay.

Tobacco Caye Lodge (☎ 520-5033, in Belize City 227-6247; www.tclodgebelize.com; s/d BZ$90/160) This place on the east side of the island has six simple but clean and fairly spacious rooms with private bathrooms, fans and beautiful verandahs. The dining room serves good food and has a couple of useful marine life identification books. Snorkel gear rental is BZ$20 per day for guests; canoes are free.

Reef's End Lodge (☎ 520-5037, in Dangriga 522-2419; www.reefsendlodge.com; r/cabanas per person BZ$130/150) At the south end of the island, Reef's End has eight sizable rooms plus a couple of lovely cabanas. It also offers a wide variety of diving and snorkeling packages and equipment rental. Inquire about discounts in the off season.

Other recommendations include the following:

Tobacco Caye Paradise (☎ 520-5101; r/cabanas per person incl meals BZ$50/55) At the northern tip, this has the cheapest, most basic rooms and meals, but also two cabanas, with private bathrooms, built over the water (call ahead to secure one of these).

Lana's (☎ 520-5036; s/d BZ$80/120) On the west side of the island with four rather cramped rooms but good meals.

Ocean's Edge Lodge (☎ 601-8537; r per person incl/excl meals BZ$100/50) On the island's southeast edge, the lodge has seven good rooms and a deck over the water. Snorkel gear and boat outings to nearby islands can be arranged through management.

South Water Caye

Five miles south of Tobacco Caye, South Water Caye is three times as big, but home to just three more-expensive resorts. The 15-acre island, often called Water Caye by locals, has excellent **sandy beaches** and an interesting combination of palm and pine trees. Like Tobacco Caye, it is part of the South Water Caye Marine Reserve. A seemingly bottomless 8-mile-long underwater cliff on the ocean side of the reef makes for excellent **wall-diving**, with usually good visibility. Snorkelers will find healthy coral reefs in the lagoon. Trips to Belize's offshore atolls are possible, and there's excellent **fishing** here, too. Passage to South Water Caye is usually arranged through the resorts.

SLEEPING & EATING

Blue Marlin Lodge (☎ 520-5104, in USA 800-798-1558; www.bluemarlinlodge.com) At the northern end of the island, Blue Marlin has its own full-service PADI dive center and a restaurant serving particularly good seafood. The resort has a series of cabanas and rather odd (but cool looking) igloo-shaped 'dome cabanas.' Though the lodge offers single-night rates varying by room and season (from BZ$337), the best deals are the packages including longer stays, meals, transit and diving. Check its website for more details (the rate sheet is rather complicated!), or visit its Dangriga office inside the Bonefish Hotel (p223).

International Zoological Expeditions (IZE; ☎ 520-5030, in USA 800-548-5843; www.ize2belize.com; packages per person per night from BZ$320; ▢) Perhaps the best way to experience the island is through Massachusetts-based IZE, which has a site in the middle of the island with dorms for students and beautiful spacious wooden shoreline cottages for other guests. The main building incorporates a field station (with reference books and videos), an attractive wood-furnished dining room, internet access and a great bar. The basic package (minimum three nights) includes meals, transfers to/from Dangriga, snorkeling and sightseeing boat trips, and use of kayaks and sports equipment. IZE also offers two-site eco-adventure and study packages combining South Water Caye with its Blue Creek Rainforest Lodge in the Toledo District.

Pelican's Pouch (☎ 522-2044; www.southwatercaye .com; s/d BZ$350/520, cottages BZ$440/590, all incl meals) The solar-powered Pelican's eight comfortable wooden cottages at the south of the island are well spaced, giving a feeling of seclusion. Heron's Hideaway is probably the pick of the bunch, with a big porch and two hammocks overlooking the surf crashing onto the reef. The main building (once an island retreat for Belize's Sisters of Mercy) houses the dining room and five guest rooms opening onto long verandahs. If you want to dive from here, book at least a week ahead. Kayaks are available free of charge. Boat transfers to/from Dangriga are BZ$110 per person.

Glover's Reef

Named after 18th-century English pirate John Glover, who attacked Spanish merchant ships from here, Glover's Reef is the southernmost of Belize's three atolls, lying about 27 miles east-southeast of Dangriga and extending 16 miles north–south and up to 7 miles east–west. Half a dozen small cayes of white sand and palm trees are dotted along the atoll's southeastern rim, supporting a handful of low-key resorts and diving and kayaking bases.

The reef's unique position atop a submerged mountain ridge on the edge of the continental shelf makes it home to some of the world's finest **dive sites**. Divers at Glover's regularly see spotted eagle rays, southern stingrays, turtles, moray eels, dolphins, several shark species, large groupers, barracudas and many tropical reef fish. In the shallow central lagoon, 700 coral patches brim with marine life – brilliant for **snorkelers**. Turtles lay eggs on the beaches between June and August. Glover's Reef is included in the Belize Barrier Reef World Heritage listing, and it's also a **marine reserve** with a no-take zone covering most of the southern third of the atoll.

SLEEPING & EATING

Glover's Atoll Resort (☎ 520-5016, 614-8351; www.glovers .com.bz; per person per week camping BZ$198, dm & on-site tents BZ$298, cabins BZ$398-438) This is a ramshackle backpackers' resort on Northeast Caye. If you like getting back to basics, as in no electricity or running water (although there is a well for washing), this could be for you. The weekly prices include cooking facilities and boat transfers on Sundays to/from the owners' mainland Glover's Guest House in the village of Sittee River (see p235), but you also need to think about the cost of water, food, equipment rentals and any excursions. Drinking water costs BZ$2 per gallon on the island (though water from the many coconuts is free).

The open-air thatched restaurant serves breakfast/lunch/dinner for BZ$18/14/24, or you can make your own meals – a few basic groceries plus fish, lobster and conch are available on the island, but the rest (including any alcohol) you must bring yourself. Snorkel gear rents for BZ$60 a week, kayaks from BZ$300 a week, and the resort has a PADI shop offering a range of courses and dives. There's a long list of rules to keep things running smoothly. If a Sunday-to-Sunday stay doesn't suit you, there are nightly accommodation rates but the boat trips there and back will push costs up. A one-way trip on the Sunday boat is BZ$80 per person. The resort may close from September to November.

Isla Marisol Resort (☎ 520-2056, 615-1485; www .islamarisol.com; 1-week diving package per person BZ$4200) The atoll's southernmost caye, Southwest Caye, was split in two by Hurricane Hattie in 1961. On its southern half, this small resort provides sturdy, comfortable cabins with hot showers, a highly recommended PADI dive shop, excellent food and a bar on stilts over the water. During a week's diving you'll probably do around 17 dives, including some at other atolls. Prices include boat transfers to and from Dangriga.

Glover's Reef also houses camps/resorts for the excellent sea-kayak holidays of North American–based **Slickrock Adventures** (☎ in USA 800-390-5715; www.slickrock.com) and **Island Expeditions** (☎ in USA 800-667-1630; www.island expeditions.com), on Long Caye and the northern half of Southwest Caye respectively. See also the boxed text on p78.

Thatch Caye

This privately owned tiny island 8 miles off the coast of Dangriga is home to the newly developed **our pick Thatch Caye Resort** (☎ 603-2414; www .thatchcaye.com; all-inclusive 3-day/4-night packages per person from BZ$1650, camping per person BZ$30). The collective brainchild of Travis Holub, Steven Hewitt and Nancy Engel, Thatch Caye may well be one of the loveliest island resorts in Belize.

What impressed us most about Thatch Caye is the way in which environmental sustainability has been built into every aspect of the resort's design. All structures are built around (in some cases in between) the island's mangroves, giving the place a lovely natural feel. The resort's 11 beautiful thatched-roof cabanas, all built from local hardwoods (hand-carved mahogany doors are a nice touch), are on stilts over the ocean, nicely eliminating the need for air conditioning. Nearly all power used on the island is generated from either solar or wind (a diesel generator is kept at one end for rare periods of neither sunshine nor wind), giving Thatch Caye a further thumbs-up from the very ecoconscious writers of this guide.

Activities range from swimming, snorkeling, fishing, fly-fishing and kayaking in the azure waters surrounding the island, or just hanging out on the island's white sands. Thatch Caye is a great base for nautical excursions to popular (and lesser-known spots) including **Gladden Spit**, Lighthouse Reef (including the Blue Hole) and Glover's Reef. Travis offers rates that are competitive with the resorts in Placencia. Snorkelling trips to Glover's Reef, **Silk Cayes**, **Pompion Caye**, and **Laughing Bird Caye** can be arranged for BZ$170 per person, and two-tank diving trips to the same cayes will cost BZ$300. Both include picnic lunch, and both require a minimum of four people. Travis also leads midnight diving trips to swim with whale sharks on full-moon nights in March, April, and May for BZ$500 per person, four person minimum.

Because of Thatch Caye's close proximity to Tobacco Caye and South Water Caye, snorkelling trips to these places can be done cheaper than out of Placencia. Snorkeling trips in either Tobacco Caye channel or South Water Caye channel go for BZ$60 per person, and diving trips are twice that. A four-person minimum applies for all trips. Full day fly-fishing with guide, boat, and picnic lunch goes for BZ$700 per person.

Visitors with children and animal lovers will especially enjoy interacting with Thatch Caye's resident animals: several families of tame long-nosed coatimundi, rabbits, gibnuts, exotic birds, sea iguanas and two very friendly raccoons (usually found outside the resort's fantastic dining room).

SILK GRASS
pop 550

In days of old, pirates and British sailors would stop and fill their casks with water from Fresh Water Creek in Silk Grass; nowadays, the community has another attraction for travelers.

our pick Crocodile Isle (☎ 661-1559, 614-3328; www .belizecrox.com; admission BZ$10, tents per person BZ$10; ⏰ 8am-dusk) is a 100-acre solar-powered bird and crocodile sanctuary that also happens to be a backpacker's paradise, with one of the best little restaurant-bars in all of Belize.

The brainchild of an Australian adventurer and naturalist (who goes by the moniker Croc), Crocodile Isle was designed from the ground up with sustainability in mind. Everything on the grounds, from the restaurant to the zip-line, is built around the existing contours and conditions of the land. 'We built everything around the trees,' says Croc. 'Even the restaurant is made of locally grown wood, with a tied-on thatch roof made of thousands of palm leaves.'

Difficult to categorize, Crocodile Isle might best be described as an eco-adventure chill-out spot. On the grounds of the park, visitors will find some of southern Belize's best **bird-watching**, **fishing** and **jungle trails**, a fenced-in **crocodile sanctuary** and a lovely restaurant (surrounded by a croc-filled moat, naturally). Management offers various tours of the area, including all-day reef fishing and **snorkeling**, night-time jungle walks, crocodile spotting and **canoeing**.

The park also has a one-of-a-kind 'zip 'n splash' line, a cable stretched across **Fresh Water Creek** on which visitors can zip from a 10m-high platform into the deepest part of the river (don't worry, it's free of crocs). No lifeguard is on duty; however, post-jump swimmers will be guided back to shore gently but firmly by Croc's very cool dog, Daisy May.

Though there are no cabanas yet, large tents – each stocked with a queen-size air mattress, sheets and pillows – are available. When the daytime visitors have left, the whole place sounds like an extended Brian Eno ambient track, as the still air fills with birdsong, the cries of nocturnal animals and the occasional sound of a crocodile, lizard or turtle splashing into a nearby pond.

Croc offers various packages ranging from drop-in **day trips** (incl unlimited zip-lining BZ$10) and **canoe rentals** (per hr BZ$10) to a tour he refers to as **The Five Bs** (Bus, Breakfast, Birding & Back by Boat; per person BZ$80). The latter trip begins and ends in the town of Hopkins, just a few miles down the road.

Crocodile Isle's bar and restaurant is **Snap Jaws Restaurant Bar & Thrill** (☎ 614-3328; meals BZ$6-10; ☯ 11am-7pm Tue-Sun). Snap Jaws is worth the trip for its excellent burritos and hamburgers, which many in the know call 'the best in Belize.' It also serves typical Belizean cuisine such as beans and coleslaw, and spicy wings, along with a few dishes from Australia, including Mr Croc's 'Mighty Meaty Matey Beef Stew.' Snap Jaws is as environmentally friendly as you'd expect from a restaurant on the grounds of an ecopark, with much of its produce grown on site, fertilizer and chemical free. While traveling friends of Bill W sometimes gather here, drinkers will be happy to know that there's also a fully stocked bar.

Silk Grass is about 2 miles off the Southern Hwy and 5 miles north of Hopkins. Get off any highway bus at the Silk Grass turnoff and walk in, or call Croc to arrange transport.

MAYFLOWER BOCAWINA NATIONAL PARK

This beautiful 11-sq-mile park of jungle, mountains, waterfalls, walking trails, swimming holes and small Maya sites lies about 16 miles southwest of Dangriga and 12 miles northwest of Hopkins. The walks are at least as good as the trails most people do at

Cockscomb Basin (p235), and you'll encounter far fewer tourists. You'll see lots of birds, and the park is home to two troops of black howler monkeys.

A 4-mile unpaved access road, leaving the Southern Hwy 2 miles north of Silk Grass village, brings you to a small **visitors center** (☯ 8am-4pm) where you pay a BZ$10 park fee, and the partly excavated **Mayflower Maya site**, with two pyramids and nine other structures, occupied in the late 9th and early 10th centuries. **Antelope Trail** leads down over Silk Grass Creek to the larger, unexcavated, partly tree-covered **Maintzunun temple mound**, 250yd away (built around 800). Continue on a further 1.7 miles – steep and strenuous in places – up to the beautiful 100ft-high **Antelope Falls**, with great panoramas. The less demanding **Bocawina Hill Trail** (1.4 miles) leads to the lower and upper **Bocawina Falls**: there's a cool swimming pool at the foot of the 50ft upper falls. Branch trails, for which a guide is recommended, lead to **Peck Falls** and **Big Drop Falls**.

On a beautiful spacious plot 500yd past the visitors center along the Bocawina Hill Trail (drivable this far) is **Mama Noots Jungle Resort** (☎ 606-4353; www.mamanoots.com; cabins from BZ$300; breakfast/lunch/dinner BZ$15/20/30; P X &.). Some 238 bird species have been identified on this property, which is run entirely on renewable energy (24-hour power). Mama Noots offers some adventurous guided hikes in the national park, and excellent discounts for extended stays. Good Belizean and international food is served in the spacious, thatched-roof restaurant, which welcomes drop-in customers. The colorfully decorated rooms sport artful paintings and ceramics, are wheelchair accessible and have good bathrooms.

Day tours to the park from Hopkins or Maya Centre (p235) cost around BZ$90 per person. A taxi from Dangriga is about BZ$60. If you're staying at Mama Noots, staff there can often pick you up at the highway junction if you call ahead.

HOPKINS
pop 1100

Located off the main southern highway (which can be irksome if you're traveling by bus), the coastal Garifuna village of Hopkins is a fairly popular spot for travelers looking to soak up some sun and culture. Smaller than Dangriga, Hopkins is a good place to meet other travelers and to base yourself for explorations of the surrounding areas. The beaches in Hopkins are decent, though, outside the ones kept clean by the owners of the properties behind them, they aren't always free of trash. Dolphins and manatees are spotted regularly from the beach.

Founded in 1942 by people from Newtown, a nearby Garifuna settlement that was destroyed by a hurricane, the village is named for Frederick Charles Hopkins, a Catholic priest who drowned in the waters here in 1923. Hopkins is a friendly enough place, though some travelers may sense a bit of a hustle vibe from some of the locals (mostly young men engaged in the ganja trade).

Hopkins' emerging place on the tourism map is a mixed bag; an increasing trickle of North Americans have bought homes and plots in the area, and there is an increasing number of high-end resorts springing up to the north and south of town. Some of these have a distinctly gated-community, *Stepford Wives* vibe. The construction – bringing scores of big trucks laden with material and heavy machinery through the town on its one unpaved road – definitely detracts from the serenity. Whether Hopkins can avoid becoming Placencia North is anybody's guess.

Orientation & Information

Hopkins stretches about 1.5 miles along the coast. The road in from the Southern Hwy reaches the village at King Cassava bar, roughly the village's mid-point. There are plenty of guesthouses south of this intersection, either on the beach or the town's single street (hence the lack of street addresses in our listings). The northern end of town is more densely populated, though there are fewer guesthouses and restaurants.

Hopkins Internet (☎ 523-7249; per hr BZ$8; ◷ 1-9pm Fri-Wed) is on the beach 650yd south of King Cassava; internet service is a bit slow, but outside of the expensive resorts down in Sittee Point, this is the only place in Hopkins to check email.

Activities

WATER SPORTS

Like Dangriga and Placencia, Hopkins is a fine place from which to access some of Belize's best **dive sites**. The barrier reef is less than a 40-minute boat ride away, and Glover's Reef is about 1½ hours away. Diving can be arranged at Hamanasi Dive & Adventure Resort

(p234). Hamanasi and Hopkins Inn (p232) offer reef snorkeling trips, as does **Noel's Fishing & Snorkeling** (☎ 523-7219, 609-1991), outside the Watering Hole Restaurant. Noel charges two people BZ$250 for a day's outing. He also rents snorkel sets for BZ$10 a day.

Hopkins also has some good spots for **windsurfing**; two places, Windschief (p232) and Jungle by the Sea (opposite), offer lessons and gear rental.

Several accommodations have **kayaks** available for their guests.

DRUMMING

Lebeha (☎ 608-3143) is an excellent Garifuna drumming school on the north side of town set up by local drummer Jabbar Lambey. Lebeha functions both as an education and cultural center for local kids and as a general happening spot for travelers interested in Garifuna drumming. Drumming lessons for individuals and groups are available for reasonable prices, and there's drumming almost every night beginning at around 7pm. Most definitely Hopkins' 'in' spot, Lebeha is a place that nobody with an interest in Garifuna music and culture will want to miss (see also p233).

Tours

Hopkins is handily placed for day trips to some of southern Belize's top natural attractions. Cockscomb Basin (p235) is the most popular inland trip: tours usually include early morning walks to see birds and nature, followed by a waterfall hike and a river-tube float. Other good trips are to Mayflower Bocawina National Park (p229) and Gales Point Manatee (p115). All these cost around BZ$80 to BZ$120 per person, usually with a three- or four-person minimum.

Two excellent local guides for boating trips are **Noel Nunez** (☎ 523-7219, 609-1991), who offers fishing and snorkeling tours at reasonable prices, and his cousin **Lloyd Nunez** (☎ 662-0873, 603-2970), a professional fly-fisherman who leads expeditions into both the inner and outer cayes (BZ$500 to BZ$600 for two people, depending on the tour). Lloyd also operates a homestay on the south side of town (p232).

Horace Andrews runs a service out of nearby Sittee River called **Belize by Horace** (☎ 603-8358; www.belizebyhorace.com). He has a 26ft skiff and does tours both out to the cayes and through the lagoons and rivers around

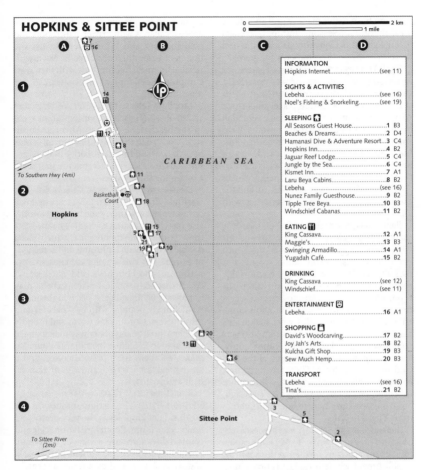

HOPKINS & SITTEE POINT

CARIBBEAN SEA

To Southern Hwy (4mi)

Hopkins

Basketball Court

To Sittee River (2mi)

Sittee Point

INFORMATION
Hopkins Internet..........................(see 11)

SIGHTS & ACTIVITIES
Lebeha ....(see 16)
Noel's Fishing & Snorkeling............(see 19)

SLEEPING
All Seasons Guest House..................**1** B3
Beaches & Dreams............................**2** D4
Hamanasi Dive & Adventure Resort...**3** C4
Hopkins Inn....................................**4** C4
Jaguar Reef Lodge...........................**5** C4
Jungle by the Sea............................**6** C4
Kismet Inn.....................................**7** A1
Laru Beya Cabins............................**8** B2
Lebeha ....(see 16)
Nunez Family Guesthouse................**9** B2
Tipple Tree Beya.............................**10** B3
Windschief Cabanas.........................**11** B2

EATING
King Cassava...................................**12** A1
Maggie's..**13** B3
Swinging Armadillo..........................**14** A1
Yugadah Café..................................**15** B2

DRINKING
King Cassava ....(see 12)
Windschief...................................(see 11)

ENTERTAINMENT
Lebeha...**16** A1

SHOPPING
David's Woodcarving........................**17** B2
Joy Jah's Arts.................................**18** B2
Kulcha Gift Shop.............................**19** B3
Sew Much Hemp..............................**20** B3

TRANSPORT
Lebeha ....(see 16)
Tina's...**21** B2

Sittee River. He also offers trips to Mayflower, Cockscomb and Red Bank. Also offering trips to Cockscomb Basin are the experienced guides from Maya Centre (see Tours, p236), who will be glad to pick you up in Hopkins.

Sleeping

The following accommodations are listed from south to north.

Jungle by the Sea (☎ 523-7047; http://junglebythe sea.com; cabanas BZ$100, cabins BZ$180) A 10-minute walk south of Hopkins takes you to Jungle by the Sea, also known as Jungle Jeanie's. Combining the best of both worlds, Jungle J's offers beautiful hardwood cabins nestled in the trees with lovely sea views. Each has a double bed, futon, bathroom, mosquito

screens and verandah. One has a loft with a second double bed. At the north end of the property are a few older, more basic wooden cabanas with similar amenities. Windsurfing equipment and kayaks are available for guests for a small charge.

All Seasons Guest House (☎ 523-7209; www.all seasonsbelize.com; s/d BZ$86/150; P X X) All Seasons may be the prettiest guesthouse in town, with its octagonal, thatch-covered upstairs porch and its four uniquely decorated rooms with big private bathrooms and usually superfluous mosquito nets (the rooms are spotless and the windows screened). Our favorite is the zebra-striped room, which is great for a couple (and also the cheapest). All rooms have air-con and hot showers. There's a great patio out front with a massive grill and picnic area. Ingrid (All Seasons' European owner) is a delightful person who also has the best bicycles in town – free, but only for guests.

Tipple Tree Beya (☎ 520-7006; www.tippletree.com; camping per person BZ$10, r with cold-water shower BZ$50, s/d/tr BZ$86/100/120, d/q cabanas BZ$108/140; **P**) This sturdy wooden beachside place rents three cozy, clean rooms sharing a sociable verandah beneath the owner's quarters upstairs. Two rooms have private hot-water bathrooms; the third (cheaper at BZ$50 for two) has an unheated shower. The cabana, set a little further back, has a small kitchen. There are bikes (BZ$15 per day) and kayaks (BZ$40), and the owner can set up tours and activities with local guides.

Nunez Family Guesthouse (☎ 662-0873, 603-2970; r BZ$100; **P** 🖳) Lloyd Nunez (p230) and his wife Clarice run a homestay at the south end of town that's really one of a kind. For BZ$100 per day, you get a big, comfortable room with a queen-size bed, private bathroom and huge hot-water shower, and access to an upstairs living room with a full home entertainment system. But what makes this place truly unique is that your rent also gets you three meals a day with the Nunez family, and Clarice is rumored to be one of the best Garifuna chefs in town. There are three guest rooms; double occupancy costs a little more (to cover the cost of meals). There's no sign, but it's a two-story mauve house just across from Yugadah Café.

Hopkins Inn (☎ 523-7013; www.hopkinsinn.com; cabanas incl breakfast BZ$99-199; **P** 🗙) Four cabins right by the beach are on offer at this well-run establishment where breakfast is brought to you. Each cabin has a coffee maker, verandah, mosquito screens and a nice, clean, white-tiled bathroom. A catamaran, bicycles (for BZ$40 and BZ$15 per day, respectively) and free snorkeling gear are available, and owner Greg, a registered tour guide, takes snorkelers out in his boat. The town's only Indian restaurant (excellent, so we've heard, though it keeps irregular hours) is right next door.

Windschief Cabanas (☎ 523-7249; www.windschief .com; small/large r BZ$50/80; **P** 🖳) Run by Oliver and Pamela Guthoff, the Windschief is Hopkins' primary hangout for windsurfers. In addition to renting out windsurfing gear (BZ$20 for the first hour, BZ$10 each hour thereafter), Oliver also offers private wind-surfing lessons for BZ$60 an hour, or BZ$40

per person for groups of two to four. There are two cabanas with private bathrooms and cold showers, and Windschief also has the honor of being the only place in town with reliable internet (free for those with their own computer; see Hopkins Internet, p230, for more details).

Laru Beya Cabins (☎ 523-7229, 666-1973; cabins BZ$109; **P** 🐾) These are four log cabins right by the beach done up in an Afro-Caribbean style. Located in the center of town, all cabins have dark-wood furniture, coffee makers and soft beds. It's a lovely place, but the staff seem a bit on the snarky side.

Lebeha (☎ 608-3143; cabins s/d BZ$30/50) The Garifuna drumming school set up by local drummer Jabbar Lambey and his wife Dorothy also has three cabanas for rent. The nicest of these is the honeymoon suite, which has a double bed, private bathroom and screened-in porch. The two smaller cabanas share a bathroom, and both have cold-water show-ers. A distinctly musical place, Lebeha may not always be the quietest place in town, but it's definitely popular with backpackers and music lovers. Dorothy is a warm and friendly woman who'll go out of her way to help make your stay in Hopkins memorable. She also makes excellent fresh-brewed coffee, and a mean breakfast of fryjack and eggs or granola, fruit and yogurt.

Kismet Inn (☎ 523-7280; www.kismetinn.com; s/d BZ$25/50, f BZ$125) The last guesthouse on the north side of Hopkins is the very pretty and funky Kismet Inn. Rooms are ramshackle and comfortable, and have a view of the ocean. There's a small organic garden in the back, and water is provided by a rainwater catch-ment system. Owner Tricia works hard to ensure all her guests have a genuine cultural experience, while her partner Elvis, a tall Rastafarian fisherman, fishes for the com-munal supper table. The rainbow-gathering, Grateful Dead–tour vibe will no doubt appeal to some travelers while deterring others, but as Tricia herself says, 'if it's kismet, it's meant to be.'

Eating

The village has a number of straightforward, locally run eateries, several of them serving up a good variety of fare, but if you want anything fancy you need to head down to the hotels south of the village. Some families will prepare special Garifuna meals in their homes: inquire at your lodging or at Tipple Tree Beya (opposite).

Maggie's (☎ 669-4463; mains BZ$6-8; ☽ breakfast, lunch & dinner) Maggie's is a funky old shack on the side of the road south of town, but a shack serving the best burritos (chicken, beef and fish) and chocolate coconut pie around. It's open in the morning for pastries as well.

King Cassava (☎ 502-2277; mains BZ$8-20; ☽ 11am-midnight) This great restaurant in the middle of Hopkins serves excellent meat and seafood dishes, from steaks to conch and lobster (in season); naturally, there's no shortage of Belizean standards such as stew chicken, fry fish, and rice and beans. King Cassava is also Hopkins' leading cool spot at night.

Yugadah Café (☎ 503-7255; mains BZ$10-20; ☽ breakfast, lunch & dinner Thu-Tue) With a menu serving Belizean fare, burgers and burritos and a variety of world-class homemade sauces, this place is pretty packed most nights.

Swinging Armadillo (☎ 609-7434; meals from BZ$12; ☽ lunch & dinner) This beachfront yellow shack two blocks south of Lebeha serves up impressively good Garifuna cuisine. Chef Digna Martinez has a small kitchen, so she generally only has a few specials going at any given time. Her fried snapper, rice and plantains is especially good, and folks are known to come from as far away as Dangriga for a bowl of her conch soup.

Drinking & Entertainment

The more expensive resorts at Sittee Point have on-site bars and generally make their own evening fun. In humble Hopkins, people make due with a few local bars. Three of the most happening spots in town:

Windschief (☎ 523-7249) This local watering hole offers all kinds of cocktails, beer and stout. It's owned and operated by the same couple that runs Hopkins Internet, so why not have a drink or six then email your family to tell them how much fun you're having?

King Cassava (☎ 502-2277; ☽ 11am-midnight) In the middle of town, this is a beer, pool and reggae hub for both locals and travelers.

Lebeha (☎ 608-3143) The drumming center is one of the coolest spots in Hopkins to be on any given evening from about 7pm, when local Garifuna drummer Jabbar Lambey hosts drum-ins for friends, students and travelers alike. Lambey also teaches drumming in the day (see p230) and his wife Dorothy runs the attached guesthouse (opposite).

Shopping

Hopkins is an especially good place to buy local crafts. Some restaurants and hotels carry items made by local craftspeople, but to get the real flavor, you'll want to go to the source. With the exception of Sew Much Hemp, all shops listed following are on Hopkins' main street, south of King Cassava.

Joy Jah's Arts (☎ 669-1744) This place is run by George Estrada and his wife Andrea, the artists who painted the huge mural that greets visitors as they arrive into town. It sells lovely paintings, hand-carved wooden statues and other Belizean-flavored curios. You can't miss this shop: it's fluorescent green and has a plaster dolphin and turtle.

David's Woodcarving (South of Joy Jah's) David makes exquisitely carved staffs, masks, canes, mortar-and-pestle sets and wooden jewelry in a workshop behind his shop by night, selling his creations at very reasonable prices during the day. Where he gets the time to sleep is anybody's guess. The shop is inside a little green building with a thatched roof just south of Joy Jah's.

Kulcha Gift Shop (☎ 523-7075) Creole for 'culture,' Kulcha sells drums made by Belizean artists, as well as other arts and crafts. Kulcha is also the place to go for Cuban cigars (BZ$25).

Sew Much Hemp (sewmuchhemp@hotmail.com) This little shop about half a mile south of town (on a dirt road just across from Maggie's) sells all kinds of hemp products, from all-natural bug repellants to skin creams and lotions. Barbara, Sew Much's owner, is a true acolyte of hemp's qualities and is always happy to share her knowledge (and no, this isn't a double entendre; we mean *hemp*, not ganja).

Getting There & Around

If there's no bus passing through Hopkins at a convenient time, it's quite common to hitch to the Southern Hwy junction and pick up a bus there. A taxi to Hopkins from Dangriga costs about BZ$80.

You can rent bicycles at **Lebeha** (☎ 608-3143) for BZ$15 a day, or at Tina's for BZ$10/20 per half/full day. All Seasons Guest House (p231) has some of the nicest bikes in town, but they're only for guests.

SITTEE POINT

About 1.5 miles south of Hopkins village sits Sittee Point. Where Hopkins ends and Sittee

Point begins is subject of mild debate, so we'll leave it to you to decide. The area itself (closer to Hopkins than to Sittee River, with which it should not be confused) has mostly high-end resorts and a few exceptionally pleasant midrange surprises. Too far to walk (for most), Sittee Point is about 20 minutes from Hopkins by bicycle.

Sleeping & Eating

The following reviews are arranged geographically, from north to south.

Hamanasi Dive & Adventure Resort (Map p231; ☎ 520-7073, in USA 877-552-3483; www.hamanasi.com; r BZ$644-878; P ✖ ☐ ⚛) Easily the premier resort of the area, Hamanasi (Garifuna for 'almond tree') combines the amenities of a top-class dive resort with an array of inland tours and activities and a gorgeous 400ft beachfront. All of Hamanasi's 18 large, very comfortable rooms and suites face the sea, except the popular wood-floored tree houses, secluded among the foliage behind the beach. The best deals at this exclusively priced resort are available through packages including room, meals and tours. Hamanasi's professional PADI dive operation can carry divers out to all three of Belize's atolls (Lighthouse, Turneffe and Glover's), as well as the barrier reef's best dive spots, and is equipped with the latest in Nitrox dive technology. Kayaks and bikes are available free for guests, and the on-site bar and restaurant are excellent.

Jaguar Reef Lodge (Map p231; ☎ 520-7040, in USA 800-289-5756; www.jaguarreef.com; cabanas BZ$460, beachfront s/d BZ$632/761; P ✖ ☐ ⚛) A little further down the coast, Jaguar Reef is another luxury resort with a long, sandy beachfront and ample amenities and activities on land and water. It's good for families or wary adventurers with deep pockets. The cabanas are solidly built, with a conservative, familiar design that you would find in Hawaiian or Mexican resorts. As well as snorkeling, birding, diving, jungle hiking, fishing and river kayaking, guests can hang out at Jaguar Reef's day lodge on the nearby Sittee River or take a four-hour outing to its island lodge on Coco Plum Caye, 10 miles offshore. A wide variety of packages are available through the resort's website.

Beaches & Dreams (Map p231; ☎ 523-7259; www.beachesanddreams.com; r incl continental breakfast BZ$262; P ☐) If it's a more personalized family atmosphere you're after, look no further. The family-owned Beaches & Dreams is run by Tony and Angela Marsico, two professional chefs who traded catering in Alaska for running a high-quality inn on the Belizean shore. There are just four rooms in two solid, octagonal wooden cabanas, with king-size beds, tiled bathrooms and futons for lounging. Tony and Angela are renowned for their culinary skills, so even if you're not spending the night, stop in for a delicious Italian or Mediterranean meal (BZ$15 to BZ$40). Bikes and kayaks are available for guests, and discounts are available during the low season. Rum-flavored impromptu jam sessions featuring local musicians often happen on weekend evenings.

SITTEE RIVER

The tranquil Creole village of Sittee River, with an increasing population of North American expats, straggles along the beautiful jungle-lined river of the same name about 3 miles by unpaved road southwest of Hopkins. It's a great bird-watching area, and a couple of good accommodations make excellent stress-free bases for a stay. Sittee River can be buggy, so make sure your accommodations are adequately screened or netted!

Sights & Activities

Nearby **Boom Creek** (inhabited by otters, a few crocodiles and plenty of birds) and **Anderson's Lagoon** make for good canoeing. One good birding spot is the ruined (but under restoration) 19th-century **Serpon Sugar Mill**, 3 miles from the village toward the Southern Hwy.

Sleeping

The following reviews are arranged geographically, from north to south.

Toucan Sittee (☎ 523-7039; www.toucansittee.info; dm BZ$25, d with shared bathroom per person BZ$39, apt with private bathroom per person BZ$50; breakfast/dinner BZ$12/18; P) Popular with backpackers and families on a budget, Toucan Sittee sits in beautiful, tropical riverside gardens surrounded by tropical birds of all sorts. The family running Toucan Sittee is friendly and always eager to help vacationers plan trips around the area. Accommodations are cozy and traditionally built (most of the houses are on stilts) and meals are a good bargain as well, with vegetarian dishes available on request. Night trips up Boom Creek and to Cockscomb Basin Wildlife Sanctuary (opposite) are also offered.

SOUTHERN BELIZE

River House Lodge (☎ 603-0298; www.river houselodge.net; r incl continental breakfast BZ$118-178; P ⊠ ⬛ ⬛) With another lovely riverside setting about 1400yd nearer Hopkins than Toucan Sittee, River House Lodge provides very comfortable air-con rooms with screened verandahs in two-story wooden houses, plus a restaurant, bar and inviting indoor pool. Bikes and kayaks are available free of charge to guests, and the owners also offer daily sailing tours on their 38ft catamaran for BZ$172 per person (20% discounts available for groups of four or more).

Glover's Guest House (☎ 509-7099; www.glovers .com.bz; camping per person BZ$6, dm BZ$16, r with shared/private bathroom BZ$40/56; P) The boat to Glover's Atoll Resort (p227) leaves from this guesthouse in Sittee River. The accommodations are cramped and basic, but at these prices, who's complaining?

Getting There & Away

Buses that serve Hopkins also go through Sittee River at about 1pm and 6pm heading out to the Southern Hwy and on to Placencia, and at around 6:30am (7:45am Sunday) heading to Hopkins and Dangriga.

COCKSCOMB BASIN WILDLIFE SANCTUARY

The **Cockscomb Basin Wildlife Sanctuary** (admission BZ$10) is Belize's most famous sanctuary; at 200 sq miles, it's also one of its biggest protected areas. On some maps the place appears simply as 'jaguar reserve,' though despite the moniker your chances of seeing a jaguar here are slight at best. This great swath of tropical forest became the world's first **jaguar sanctuary** in 1984, thanks to the efforts of American zoologist Alan Rabinowitz. Today, this critical biological corridor is home to an estimated 40 to 50 jaguars and a vast array of other animal, bird and botanical life.

The sanctuary is part of the eastern Maya Mountain range. Most visits are restricted to a small eastern pocket of the sanctuary, which contains a visitors center, the sanctuary's accommodations and a network of excellent walking trails (old timber roads from the time when the region was still being logged). The visitor sighting book does record instances of people spotting jaguars, so it is possible (but it's unlikely). What you can hope to spot are plenty of birds – egrets, toucans and hummingbirds are just a few that live in or pass through the park. You can also expect to see iguanas, local rodents such as gibnuts, and maybe, with a little luck, some jaguar paw prints.

Mornings are the best time for wildlife watching, as most animals seek shelter in the heat of the day. Though many visitors come as part of large (and inevitably noisy) tours arranged through nearby lodges or travel agencies, your best bet for viewing more elusive wildlife is to come alone or in as small and quiet a group as possible. Regardless, the trails are still magnificent.

Despite its size, the sanctuary itself isn't big enough to support a healthy breeding population of jaguars; however, its position adjacent to other reserves and swaths of jungle make it part of a biological corridor that, many believe, offers promise for the jaguar's future in Central America. Belize's four other wild cats, the puma, ocelot, margay and jaguarundi, also reside in and pass through the sanctuary, as do tapirs, anteaters, armadillos (the jaguar's favorite prey – crunchy on the outside but soft and chewy on the inside), brocket deer, coatimundis, kinkajous, otters, peccaries, tayras and other animals native to the area.

The sanctuary is also home to countless birds: over 290 feathered species have been spotted, including the keel-billed toucan, king vulture, great curassow and scarlet macaw. There's also a thriving community of black howler monkeys living close to the visitors center (these were reintroduced here from the Community Baboon Sanctuary, p108, in 1992). If you don't see them near the center, you'll definitely hear their eerie, cacophonous howling should you choose to spend the night. And herpetologists take note: large boa constrictors, small (and deadly poisonous) fer-de-lances and the tiny coffee snake are just some of the snakes that call the sanctuary home.

Cockscomb became a forest reserve and no-hunting area in 1984. A small part of it was given sanctuary status in 1986, and the rest followed in 1990. The people of the small Maya village of Quan Bank were compulsorily relocated as part of the creation of the sanctuary. Many of them now live in **Maya Centre village**, a few miles east, and make a living from the sanctuary, running tourist accommodations or tours, or working as park staff.

Orientation & Information

The unpaved, 6-mile road to the sanctuary starts at the village of Maya Centre, on the

Southern Hwy 5 miles south of the Hopkins turnoff. The **sanctuary office** (☯ 7:30am-4:30pm), where you pay admission, is at the end of the road that begins at Maya Centre. The office has trail maps (BZ$5) plus a few gifts, soft drinks and chocolate bars for sale. You can also rent binoculars (BZ$5 per day).

Activities

A well-maintained 12-mile network of trails fans out from the park office. Most of the walks are flat along the bottom of the basin, but the moderately strenuous **Ben's Bluff Trail** (1.25 miles and steep in parts) takes you up to a lookout point with fantastic views over the whole Cockscomb Basin and the Cockscomb Mountains. It's named for one of the original members of the Cockscomb Jaguar Sanctuary Project, who would make this climb daily to listen for signals from the radio transmitters attached to the jaguars.

An easy 1.4-mile **self-guided nature walk**, looping together the Curassow Trail, Rubber Tree Tail and River Path, can be followed with the trail map from the park office. The **River Path** (0.4 miles) and the **Wari Loop** (a 2.3-mile loop from the office) are good early morning bets for seeing a variety of birds. Jaguar tracks are often spotted on the Wari Loop and the **Victoria Peak Path**. The **Antelope Loop** (a 3.4-mile loop from the office) rises and falls through a variety of terrain and vegetation, and offers a good sample of the basin's geological features.

The office rents tubes (BZ$5) for half-hour **river-tube floats** down South Stann Creek from the River Overlook on Wari Loop.

Tours

Tours can be arranged in Maya Centre, and are usually conducted by Maya who were relocated there when the jaguar reserve was created. This is an interesting situation: not only do the guides show you the animals and the history of the park, they'll also show you where they lived just 20 years ago. Of course, they know the area pretty well and in general they're experienced and professional.

A typical day tour to the sanctuary from Maya Centre costs around BZ$90 per person and includes transportation, a couple of guided walks (usually including a waterfall), lunch and maybe river-tubing. An exciting option is a night tour (BZ$50 per person), which offers increased chances of seeing nocturnal animals such as kinkajous, anteaters, peccaries and possibly even a feline. Guides can also lead tours for people who are staying in the sanctuary. Check whether your fee includes the sanctuary admission cost and, at night, whether flashlights are provided.

Sleeping & Eating

IN THE SANCTUARY

Staying in the sanctuary gives you easy access to the trails, and enables you to experience the sounds of the jungle at night and be up at dawn when wildlife is most active. You'll have to bring all your food and drinks with you. Maya Centre has a couple of grocery stores selling basic supplies, so stock up before you come to the sanctuary (unless you want to live on chocolate bars and Pringles from the visitors center). The accommodation options, most close to the sanctuary office, range from camping under *palapas* (thatched-roof shelters; BZ$10 per person, bring your own tent) through to a 'rustic cabin' with bunks and kerosene lamps (BZ$16 per person). There's also a lovely (and solar powered) dorm with bunks and a compost toilet (BZ$36 per person), and four cabins that sleep up to eight people that go for BZ$96 to BZ$108 each. Use of a communal kitchen is included with all options except camping, where grill pits are available. You can rent kitchen utensils for up to five people for BZ$10 per day.

IN MAYA CENTRE

Nu'uk Che'il Cottages (☎ 615-2091, 520-3033; www .mayacottages.com; camping per person BZ$7, dm BZ$20, d & tr with shared/private bathroom BZ$46/50; dishes BZ$8-16; ☯ restaurant 7am-8pm; P) These accommodations, spread around a verdant garden about 500yd along the sanctuary road, are owned by Aurora Saqui (a niece and apprentice of the legendary Maya healer Eligio Panti) and her husband Ernesto, a former Quan Bank villager who was director of the Cockscomb sanctuary from 1988 to 2004. The rooms are simple but clean, with hot-water bathrooms. Also here are a medicinal plant trail (BZ$5 per person with a self-guiding leaflet, BZ$20 per group for 30-minute guided tours), a craft shop, and a large fan-cooled *palapa* restaurant with Maya dishes available (if ordered ahead), as well as more standard Belizean fare and lovely fresh fruit juices.

Tutzil Nah Cottages (☎ 520-3044; www.maya center.com; s/d BZ$34/45; meals BZ$12-24; P) On the

Southern Hwy 100yd north of the Maya Centre junction, the three Chun brothers, also originally from Quan Bank, provide four neat, clean rooms with shared bathrooms; those in the wooden-stilt building at the rear are airier.

Cockscomb Diner (☎ 520-3042; mains BZ$8-12; ⏰ 6:30am-9pm) Well-prepared Belizean and Maya dishes and good fresh juices are served here, plus lighter eats such as burgers and sandwiches. It adjoins a craft shop and the Maya Centre Women's Group.

Getting There & Away

Any bus along the Southern Hwy will drop you at Maya Centre, but there is no public transportation into the sanctuary. A taxi from Hopkins to Maya Centre or the sanctuary costs around BZ$80. Most of the Maya Centre tour guides offer taxi services to the sanctuary for around BZ$36/60 one-way/return. To walk in takes about two hours (the terrain is relatively flat).

PLACENCIA

pop 600

How you feel about Placencia depends on why you've come to Belize: if it's seaside pleasures and tourists you're after, you've come to the right place. But if you were hoping to get off the beaten path, forget it: the path to Placencia is not merely beaten, it is professionally flogged.

Placencia is where tourists – mostly North Americans – come to swim, snorkel, scuba dive, hang out on the beach and drive around in golf carts holding bottles of Belikin stout at 10 in the morning. There is little of the Garifuna/hippie vibe you'll find in communities such as Hopkins, nor any of the urban hustle of Dangriga. Instead, the village of Placencia feels like an upper crust New England village transported to the Caribbean coast.

The drive to Placencia village down the narrow 4-mile-long peninsula is quite pretty. There are some lovely resorts of varied price ranges on the east-facing beach, and mangrove swamp on the western side. But open land on either side is disappearing at a fast clip as lots are bought up for development, both for upper-end resorts, and for private homes being sold to Americans and Canadians looking for their own slices of heaven in tropical climes.

Like most tropical places existing primarily for tourists, Placencia has a different feel from season to season. In the dog days of summer, the town is quieter, hotels are cheaper (some even close) and the overall tourist vibe much mellower. Peak times for tourists are May, June and July.

Orientation

Placencia village occupies the southernmost mile of the peninsula, with a sandy beach all along its eastern side. The road from the north runs down the western side of the village, ending at the Shell fuel station and the main boat dock (a handful of short piers). Parallel to the road and about 100yd east of it is the Sidewalk, a narrow pedestrian-only footway, with the beach about 100yd further east.

Placencia's airport is about 1 mile north of the village; 6 miles beyond that is the North American expat settlement of Maya Beach. Between the two lie an increasing number of accommodations, including some of the swankest in Belize, not to mention a growing number of luxury housing units.

In between mainland Belize and the village of Placencia is the Garifuna village of Seine Bight. With its shacks, shanties, vegetable stands and cheap restaurants, Seine Bight sticks out on the resort peninsula like a Rastafarian at a GOP fundraiser.

Information

There's no shortage of info on Placencia, both on the Web and around Belize. Check out a copy of the monthly *Placencia Breeze* (also on-line at www.placenciabreeze.com) or **Placencia Online** (www.placencia.com) before you get here.

Belize Bank (Map p241; ⏰ 8:30am-2:30pm Mon-Thu, to 4pm Fri) All cards accepted.

Book Shak (Map p241; ☎ 606-8457; ⏰ 10am-5pm) New and used books at reasonable prices.

Bosun's Chair (Map p241; laundry BZ$8; internet per hr BZ$8; ⏰ 7am-7pm) A beachfront café across from the post office where you can do your laundry, have a beer and check your email. What could be finer?

De-Tatch Café (Map p241; ☎ 503-3385; internet per hr BZ$10; ⏰ 7am-9:30pm) Internet access, coffee and more.

Julia's Laundry (Map p241; ☎ 503-3478; laundry by weight, internet per hr BZ$10; ⏰ 7am-7pm) Located at the Julia & Lawrence Guesthouse in the heart of the popular beachfront, so you can head straight out for a swim when the laundry is done.

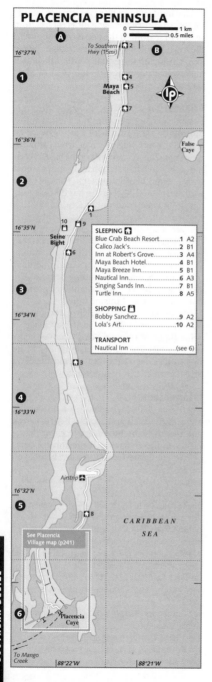

PLACENCIA PENINSULA

0 ——————— 1 km
0 ——————— 0.5 miles

To Southern
Hwy (15mi)

16°37'N

16°36'N

False
Caye

Maya
Beach

16°35'N

Seine
Bight

SLEEPING		
Blue Crab Beach Resort	1	A2
Calico Jack's	2	B1
Inn at Robert's Grove	3	A4
Maya Beach Hotel	4	B1
Maya Breeze Inn	5	B1
Nautical Inn	6	A3
Singing Sands Inn	7	B1
Turtle Inn	8	A5

SHOPPING		
Bobby Sanchez	9	A2
Lola's Art	10	A2

TRANSPORT		
Nautical Inn	(see 6)	

16°34'N

16°33'N

Airstrip

16°32'N

CARIBBEAN
SEA

See Placencia
Village map (p241)

Placencia
Caye

To Mango
Creek

88°22'W   88°21'W

Placencia Office Supply (Map p241; ☎ 523-3205; internet per hr BZ$10; ⏰ 8:30am-7pm) High-speed internet, CD burning, digital card readers.

Placencia Tourism Center (Map p241; ☎ 523-4045; ⏰ 9-11:30am & 1-5pm Mon-Fri) Right by the bus stop and dock, friendly staff are ready to set travelers off on the right foot. Pick up a copy of *Placencia Breeze* to catch up on what's happening.

Purple Space Monkey (Map p241; ☎ 523-4094; internet per hr BZ$10; ⏰ 7am-2pm & 5-9:30pm) Wireless internet and computers for hire; 15 minutes free with meal purchase.

Scotiabank (Map p241; ⏰ 8:30am-2:30pm Mon-Thu, to 4pm Fri) All cards accepted.

Activities

Placencia is close enough to a plethora of cayes, reefs and dive sites to make it a good base for **diving** and **snorkeling**. As fuel prices rise, however, so too do the prices of diving trips, especially to more distant areas. Most operators will charge around BZ$200 per person for a two-tank dive trip to a nearby dive spot. Longer outings to Shark Hole (p226), Glover's Reef (p227) or the Sapodilla Cayes (p247) should be between BZ$250 and BZ$300. For some sites you may need to add admission fees of between BZ$8 and BZ$30. Advanced divers take note: March through June are especially good months to see whale sharks in the area. One of these trips should cost between BZ$300 and BZ$340.

There's no shortage of dive operators in town, and many of these also dabble in fishing, sailing or land tours (for a listing of tour operators, see opposite). Most dive operators also run snorkeling trips. A snorkeling day trip, often with a beach barbecue included, costs around BZ$60 to BZ$90 per person for nearby cayes, increasing in price the further out you go.

Opportunities for **fishing** are equally amazing, and in the waters off Placencia you can troll for barracuda, kingfish or tuna, spincast or fly-fish for tarpon, bonefish or snook, and bottom-fish for snapper or jack. **Sailing** is also popular in the waters around Placencia. As well as Belize's cayes and other ports, Río Dulce in Guatemala and Honduras' Bay Islands are close enough to sail to.

As the whole town is geared toward tourism and aquatic fun, any hotel in Placencia can arrange your tour for you. Most beachside accommodations, particularly the mid-priced ones north of the village, have free **kayaks** or

SOUTHERN BELIZE

canoes for guests' use, and some will even provide fishing poles and bait to use on their private docks.

Tours

Considering its peninsular nature, Placencia isn't too bad a spot to begin land journeys. Some of the more popular expeditions launched regularly from Placencia (in order of their proximity to the area itself) are listed following.

Tours of the **Placencia lagoon** can be arranged through any of the tour companies (right), and shouldn't set you back more than BZ$70 per person. The half-day tours are good for exploring the mangrove ecosystems. Expect to see plenty of birds and, if you're lucky, manatees or dolphins.

A **Monkey River** trip is generally around BZ$80 per person, and includes a short sea cruise to Monkey River Town (actually a village), 14 miles southwest of Placencia. From here, a short trip upriver takes visitors into howler monkey territory. We've heard that sometimes guides smack on the sides of trees to entice the monkeys to howl, which does strike us as a bit intrusive. Crocodile viewing and bird-watching are also on the agenda, as may be a couple of jungle walks and a swim or river-tube float, followed by a Creole lunch in the village. The forests here are still recovering from hurricane damage.

The forest fruits of **Red Bank** village, 14 miles west of Placencia as the crow flies, attract rare and beautiful scarlet macaws from January to March. On a good day you might see 30 of these spectacularly plumaged birds, plus plenty of other species. The trip costs around BZ$130 per person, and takes the whole day.

Day trips to Cockscomb Basin Wildlife Sanctuary (p235) cost approximately BZ$120, and also take the whole day. However, the sanctuary is vast (not to mention interesting) enough to warrant its own separate trip, if you have the time.

TOUR COMPANIES

Author and noted curmudgeon Robert Heinlein coined the phrase 'specialization is for insects.' He might have appreciated the generalist nature of Placencia's guide services, most of which do a little of everything.

Some reputable operators include the following:

Advanced Diving (Map p241; ☎ 523-4037, 615-1233) Does diving, snorkeling and fishing trips.

Joy Tours (Map p241; ☎ 523-3325, in USA 917-446-6610; www.belizewithjoy.com) Offers a variety of fishing, snorkeling and diving activities. Staff will also be glad to arrange hiking tours to Maya ruins around southern Belize.

Next Wave Sailing (Map p241; ☎ 523-3391, 610-5592; www.nextwavesailing.com) Does day sails on a 50ft catamaran out to sandy islands where you can snorkel, swim and lunch (adult/under 12s BZ$176/88); also offers popular sunset cruises (BZ$99/50). Kids under four are free of charge. Departures are from Placencia docks; you can book at the Purple Space Monkey (p243).

Nite Wind Guide Service (Map p241; ☎ 523-3487, 609-6845) Offers a variety of land and nautical tours.

Ocean Motion Guide Service (Map p241; ☎ 523-3162, 512-3363) Does fishing and snorkeling trips.

Sailing Belize (Map p241; ☎ 523-3138; http://sailing belize.com) Day sails on a 50ft monohull (BZ$240 per person).

Sambur Jaguar Adventure Tours (Map p241; ☎ 523-3040, 600-2481; Sidewalk) Friendly little operation with colorful blackboard listing trips.

South Belize Reef & Jungle (Map p241; ☎ 523-3330; southbelize@yahoo.com) A well-known dive operator that also dabbles in jungle tours.

Toadal Adventure (Map p241; ☎ 523-3207; www .toadaladventure.com; Deb & Dave's Last Resort) Led by

---

SEINE BIGHT ART STOP

Most visitors to Placencia just breeze through Seine Bight, the Garifuna village in the center of the tourist peninsula where many who work in the surrounding resorts reside. But if you can, take the time to stop for a while at the shops of two of Seine Bight's resident artists. Painter and sculptor Lola Delgado is the mistress of **Lola's Art** (Map p238; ☎ 523-3342, 601-1913; lolasart@ btl.net), where you'll find paintings, handcrafted jewelry, sculpture and assorted crafts. Many of Lola's pieces adorn the walls and grounds of Placencia's higher end hotels and resorts. Another local craftsman is **Bobby Sanchez** (Map p238; ☎ 601-5096), who builds beautiful Garifuna drums from locally harvested hardwoods and Belizean antelope skins. Lola's shop is in the center of Seine Bight; just follow the signs from the main road. Bobby's place is just north of Seine Bight, down the road from the Blue Crab (p242).

SOUTHERN BELIZE

highly experienced local guide Dave Vernon, who does popular multiday sea-kayaking trips. Call or check the website for packages and pricing. It also rents kayaks for BZ$70 per day.

Festivals & Events

The **Sidewalk Art Festival** (mid-February, nearest weekend to Valentine's Day) features art, crafts and music, with scores of participants from all over Belize.

Lobsterfest (last weekend of June) celebrates the opening of the lobster-fishing season with music, boat races, a fishing contest, a huge variety of lobster dishes to eat and a lot of fun.

Sleeping

Inside the village, lodgings range from budget to midrange; most of these are small and family-run, and there are plenty of beachside cabanas (though your neighbor may be just a few feet away). Out on the peninsula things range from mid-priced cabanas to some of the plushest, most top-end luxury resorts you're likely to see anywhere in Belize. Most places on the peninsula offer free airport pick-ups and a full range of tours and activities, usually at slightly higher prices than the agencies in town.

During the low season, almost all places offer discounts of 10% to 25%.

PLACENCIA VILLAGE
Budget

On Da Beach Camping (Map p241; ☎ 503-3068; camping per person BZ$10) Camping on the beach. Look for a yellow house (but not *the* Yellow House, right) at the northern end of the Sidewalk.

Omar's Guesthouse (Map p241; ☎ 600-8421; dm/s/d BZ$25/30/40) Small and unpretentious, Omar's is a perennial favorite with backpackers and others doing Belize on the cheap. Rooms are fan-cooled, bathrooms are shared and showers are cold. The downstairs café serves good cheap grub.

Charro Hotel (Map p241; ☎ 523-4078, 623-4779; s/d BZ$40/60; P 🖳) No sign marks this square, two-story, gray-stone hacienda with wooden railings and cement columns. It's set on the west side of Placencia's main street, north of Tommy's Restaurant and south of the gas station. Half of the top floor is a private residence; the other half houses four fully furnished long-term apartments. The bottom floor contains six small rooms with private

bathrooms, hot showers and cable TV. Not the most luxurious place, but clean, serviceable and way affordable.

Deb & Dave's Last Resort (Map p241; ☎ 523-3207; debanddave@btl.net; r with shared bathroom BZ$50) One of the cheaper options in town, D&D offers comfortable, compact rooms with fans, surrounded by a leafy garden. Rooms have their own coffee makers and share a screened porch.

Yellow House (Map p241; ☎ 523-3481; ctbze@btl .net; r BZ$50-70; P) Located in a – you guessed it – yellow house, this budget hotel in the center of Placencia has clean and basic rooms with double beds, kitchenettes, bathrooms and ceiling fans.

Seaspray Hotel (Map p241; ☎ 523-3148; www.sea sprayhotel.com; r BZ$50-130; 🖳) Owned and operated by the Leslies (one of Placencia's most established families), this lovely hotel has seven grades of room (all with private hot-water bathroom) of varying degrees of luxury and proximity to the ocean. The best of these are the 'Seaside Cabanas,' which have a porch (with sea view), deck, kitchenette and coffee maker. Even the least expensive ones are quite nice (though without the sea view). Seaspray's website lays out all options nicely.

Julia & Lawrence Guesthouse (Map p241; ☎ 503-3478; r BZ$75-140) A beachfront place on the tightest packed part of the shore, J&L's has a series of clean rooms with private bathrooms. The cheaper rooms, with shared facilities, are in a darker, older building toward the back (but closer to the beach).

Manatee Inn (Map p241; ☎ 523-4083; www.mana teeinn.com; s/d/tr BZ$88/99/110) Hardwood floors and furniture set this lovely budget guesthouse apart from others in its price category. All rooms have ceiling and standing fans, refrigerators and private bathrooms with hot-water showers.

Midrange

Dianni's Guest House (Map p241; ☎ 523-3159; www .diannisplacencia.com; s/d/tr/cabanas BZ$85/118/130/190; ✂ 🈺 🖳) Rooms in this lovely house, a stone's throw from Placencia's southern shore, are good value. Clean – if not a bit on the ascetic side – all have coffee makers, microwaves and refrigerators, and there's a wide, wood-floored verandah with chairs and hammocks for long-term lounging. Cabanas offer more space and full kitchenettes. An on-site gift shop, internet access, bicycle rentals and

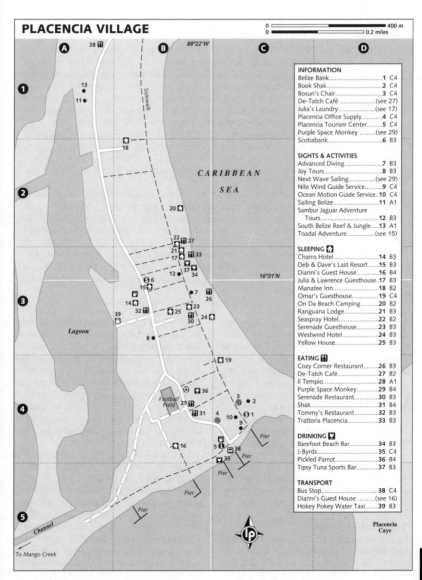

PLACENCIA VILLAGE

0 — 400 m
0 — 0.2 miles

88°22'W

CARIBBEAN
SEA

16°31'N

Lagoon

Football
Field

Channel

To Mango Creek

Pier

Pier

Pier

Pier

Placencia
Caye

INFORMATION
Belize Bank...........................**1** C4
Book Shak...........................**2** C4
Bosun's Chair......................**3** C4
De-Tatch Café....................(see **27**)
Julia's Laundry..................(see **17**)
Placencia Office Supply.........**4** C4
Placencia Tourism Center......**5** C4
Purple Space Monkey........(see **29**)
Scotiabank..........................**6** B3

SIGHTS & ACTIVITIES
Advanced Diving....................**7** B3
Joy Tours..............................**8** B3
Next Wave Sailing.............(see **29**)
Nite Wind Guide Service........**9** C4
Ocean Motion Guide Service..**10** C4
Sailing Belize........................**11** A1
Sambur Jaguar Adventure
    Tours..............................**12** B3
South Belize Reef & Jungle....**13** A1
Toadal Adventure..............(see **15**)

SLEEPING
Charro Hotel.........................**14** B3
Deb & Dave's Last Resort......**15** B3
Dianni's Guest House............**16** B4
Julia & Lawrence Guesthouse...**17** B3
Manatee Inn.........................**18** B2
Omar's Guesthouse..............**19** C4
On Da Beach Camping...........**20** B2
Ranguana Lodge....................**21** B3
Seaspray Hotel.....................**22** B2
Serenade Guesthouse...........**23** B3
Westwind Hotel....................**24** B3
Yellow House........................**25** B3

EATING
Cozy Corner Restaurant.........**26** B3
De-Tatch Café......................**27** B2
Il Tempio.............................**28** A1
Purple Space Monkey............**29** B4
Serenade Restaurant............**30** B3
Shak...................................**31** B4
Tommy's Restaurant.............**32** B3
Trattoria Placencia................**33** B3

DRINKING
Barefoot Beach Bar...............**34** B3
J-Byrds................................**35** C4
Pickled Parrot......................**36** B4
Tipsy Tuna Sports Bar............**37** B3

TRANSPORT
Bus Stop..............................**38** C4
Dianni's Guest House.........(see **16**)
Hokey Pokey Water Taxi........**39** B3

tour and flight bookings make Dianni's a safe choice. Long-term rentals are available.

Serenade Guesthouse (Map p241; ☎ 523-3380; www.belizecayes.com; Sidewalk; r BZ$100-120; ✄ ▯) Wind chimes serenade visitors and passersby alike from the verandah of this big white wooden house just a block off the beach. Wood-floored rooms are cozy, and all have

air-con, private bathroom and cable TV. More expensive rooms have sea views and their own coffee makers. The friendly local owners also run the next-door Serenade Restaurant, which serves some of the finest gibnut stew you're likely to find in Belize.

Westwind Hotel (Map p241; ☎ 523-3255; www .westwindhotel.com; s/d/f ste BZ$131/164/327) Travelers

---

AN OFFER YOU CAN'T REFUSE

Turtle Inn (Map p238; ☎ 523-3244, 824-4912, in USA 800-746-3743; www.turtleinn.com; s/d/tr cottages from BZ$630-850, villas from BZ$1300; P 🖳 🕹 🕭) This is it. The ultra-chic lodge owned by Mr Francis Ford Coppola, where the director himself maintains his own Belizean villa. It's the beachside complement to Coppola's hill-country Blancaneaux Lodge (p215). There is, of course, little need for a lengthy review of this Balinese themed, opulent-in-every-way resort; it is everything you'd expect from a place of both its price-tag range and Hollywood pedigree. (Its cinematic website – perhaps created with input from Coppola himself – paints an accurate picture.)

Yes, it is wonderful, combining luxury with a hint of the rustic, equipped with two beachfront pools, a fully equipped PADI dive shop, and spa complete with Thai masseurs. Would you expect anything less from the man who brought the world *Apocalypse Now*? Of course not. Instead, let's skip to the question you really want to ask, namely: 'How much to live in Mr Coppola's personal villa…the actual one he lives in when he's in town?'

To rent the fabulous Pavilion House, a two-bedroom, two-bathroom villa with private entrance, pool, dining pavilion and personal attendant, costs a mere $2100 per night in the high season (that's in US currency, exclusive of tax or service charges). So, on to your second question: 'At that price, do I get full access to Mr Coppola's private DVD stash, including the *real* director's cut of the *Godfather* trilogy?'

No. While all accommodations at the Turtle come equipped with iHome units where you can plug in your iPod and enjoy your own music to your heart's content, neither the Pavilion House nor any of the villas have TV sets. This is, after all, where the director comes to get away from the movies. And at these prices, shouldn't you, too?

---

speak highly of George and Lisa Westby's Westwind Hotel, a funky two-story wooden place with large, clean rooms and a definite family-run feel. Most rooms face the sea and all have a balcony, terrace or patio and hot-water bathroom. The six-hammock *palapa* out front on the sand is a great place to eat, play board games and chill out in general.

Ranguana Lodge (Map p241; ☎ 523-3112, 610-2287; www.ranguanabelize.com; r with/without sea view BZ$168/160; 🕭) Five good-sized mahogany cabins on a small stretch of lovely beach. Two have kitchens; the others (smaller) have sea views and air-con. All have two double beds, hot-water bathroom, cable TV and microwaves, not to mention lovely verandahs.

PLACENCIA PENINSULA

Accommodations on the peninsula range from mid-priced places such as Singing Sands to ultra-chic resorts such as the Turtle Inn (see boxed text, above). The following are arranged geographically along the peninsula, from south to north.

Inn at Robert's Grove (Map p238; ☎ 523-3565, in USA 800-565-9757; www.robertsgrove.com; r BZ$430-1490, check website for full rates listing; P 🕭 🖳 🕹) From the Grecian fountain in the front driveway to the beautiful beachfront patio bar and restaurant, Robert's Grove is classy all the way. The 51 air-con rooms and suites, set in blocks around the ample grounds, are all spacious, comfortable, terracotta-floored and brightly decorated with colorful art and fabrics. They're complemented by a vast array of amenities, including three pools, a PADI dive center employing three full-time instructors (this is the only place in Placencia offering Nitrox technology, allowing for longer dives), rooftop Jacuzzis, tennis, windsurfers, kayaks, Hobie Cats and a spa full of exotic body treatments.

Nautical Inn (Map p238; ☎ 523-3595; www.nauticalinnbelize.com; Seine Bight; s BZ$232, d BZ$292; P 🕭 🖳 🕹) A pretty little blue-and-white, chalet-type hotel, the Nautical Inn does a good job of capturing the Margaritaville vibe with its maritime theme, laid-back staff and oceanfront pool and bar. Rooms are clean and breezy (air-con is available, but not usually necessary), come with their own coffee makers, and have views and verandahs galore. Wednesday night is beach BBQ night, with Garifuna drumming, all-you-can-eat grill food and everyone's favorite, coconut bowling. The Nautical Inn is a quick hop from the village of Seine Bight.

Blue Crab Beach Resort (Map p238; ☎ 523-3544; www.bluecrabbeach.com; Seine Bight; cabanas BZ$180, r with air-con BZ$200; P 🕭) Offering quaint and quiet cabanas and rooms away from the main house and just a few feet from the sea, the Blue Crab is a great mid-priced place to relax on the peninsula. But what will make your stay at the Blue Crab unforgettable is the gentle fragrance of chocolate wafting in from the small factory across the street; in addition to running this excellent and tranquil family-style resort, Kerry Goss and Linn Wilson are proud proprietors of Goss Chocolate, which produces Belize's finest organic chocolate. The family also owns the patch of mangrove across the road, an excellent place to spot coatimundis, endangered hawksbill turtles and other local wildlife.

our pick **Singing Sands Inn** (Map p238; ☎ 520-8022, 523-8017; www.singingsands.com; Maya Beach; cabanas incl continental breakfast BZ$150-250; P ☐ ☎) Another wonderfully quirky mid-priced choice a bit further north on the peninsula, rooms at the Singing Sands are eclectically decorated with antique furniture and beautiful Maya carvings. The resort's exterior is even more beautiful, with vine-covered trestles connecting the front office to the central restaurant, and surrounded by superbly landscaped gardens, palm trees and driftwood sculptures. Inn proprietors Marti and Eldon have done an amazing job creating a magical space that's at once astonishing and comfortable: with its swimming pool, restaurant, library, beach and dock (fishing gear and kayaks available on request), Singing Sands may be one of the most family-friendly mid-priced resorts in Belize. Climb the exterior spiral staircase to the crow's nest atop the main building to get one of the best views in Placencia!

Maya Beach Hotel (Map p238; ☎ 520-8040, in USA 800-503-5124; www.mayabeachhotel.com; Maya Beach; r BZ$196-218; ☺ restaurant 7am-noon & 5:30-9pm Wed-Mon; P ☒ ☐) It offers good, fresh, clean air-con rooms with custom-made wooden furniture. The major selling point of this hotel is its highly popular bistro, offering excellent (and creative) international dishes using top local ingredients. Try the spicy 'sassy shrimp pot,' with tequila-flambé–caramelized pineapple tossed in coconut curry! Snacks and meals are also available all day at the bar. Kayaks and bikes are free for guests.

Maya Breeze Inn (Map p238; ☎ 523-8012, in USA 888-458-8581; www.mayabreezeinn.com; Maya Beach; s/d/tr incl continental breakfast BZ$198/242/268; P ☒ ☐) This is a great place for the adventurous, as owners Buddy and Tressa Olson offer a full range of land and sea tours as far afield as Actun

Tunichil Muknal (p191) in western Belize and Tikal (p263) in Guatemala. Activities with specially selected guides are also on offer. Beachside cabins come in a variety of sizes, and most have either full kitchens or kitchenettes. Kayaks and bikes are free for guests.

Calico Jack's (Map p238; ☎ 520-8103; www.calicojacksvillage.com; cabanas BZ$210-260, villas BZ$320; P ☒ ☐ ☎) Opened in 2003, Calico Jack's is right by the point where the peninsula meets the mainland. Thatched-roof cabanas are built using an environmentally friendly 'Euroblock' design that reduces the need for air-con, and are beautifully decorated inside. Jack's lovely outdoor bar, with its thatched roof and carved totem-pole-like beams, is a great place to sit and watch the sun go down while smelling the bougainvillea.

Eating

Restaurants are easy to come by in Placencia village, both cheap and expensive. All lodgings on the peninsula have on-site restaurants with prices commensurate to the resort's caliber. There are also some cheap Chinese restaurants and fry-shacks in Seine Bight.

De-Tatch Café (Map p241; ☎ 503-3385; Seaspray Hotel; breakfast & lunch dishes BZ$5-12, dinner mains BZ$12-26; ☺ 7am-9:30pm Thu-Tue) Head to this popular, thatched-roof, open-air beachside place for satisfying Caribbean, Belizean and North American dishes. Favorites include the coconut shrimp curry, charbroiled steaks and chicken in mango-rum sauce.

The Shak (Map p241; ☎ 622-1686; dishes BZ$6-10; ☺ breakfast, lunch & dinner) Indian curries, healthy Mexican dishes and excellent smoothies all served with pride by the lovely Magda. With the exception of the occasional fish dish, all dishes are 100% meat free. For vegetarians, this must be the place.

Purple Space Monkey (Map p241; ☎ 523-4094; breakfast BZ$9-12, dinner mains BZ$10-18; ☺ breakfast, lunch & dinner; ☐) Under new management since our last write-up, this place is garish, done up in wild shades of hot pink, lemony yellows and key lime greens. But what do you expect from a place called Purple Space Monkey? Free internet, good cuisine (Belizean and Western) and a decent book-swap library. Portions aren't huge, but they'll refill your coffee mug (if you ask nicely). Be warned: Wednesday night is karaoke night.

Tommy's Restaurant (Map p241; ☎ 523-3662; dishes BZ$10-20; ☺ lunch & dinner; ☒) A decent Chinese

SOUTHERN BELIZE

restaurant, Tommy's serves up localized Chinese dishes such as conch fried rice and lobster chow mein. Try the fried stuffed crab claw (BZ$30), expensive but tasty.

Serenade Restaurant (Map p241; ☎ 523-3380; lunch & dinner mains BZ$12-26; ⌚ lunch & dinner) Even if you aren't staying at the hotel next door, you'll still be serenaded by its wind chimes at this patio restaurant serving Belizean seafood, chicken and meat dishes. Feeling adventurous? Try the gibnut stew, a specialty of the house.

Cozy Corner Restaurant (Map p241; ☎ 523-3540; mains BZ$18-30; ⌚ 11am-11pm) A popular open-air beachside *palapa*, Cozy Corner scores with generous portions of seafood, steaks, chicken and burgers – and several types of enormous burritos for BZ$10 or less.

Trattoria Placencia (Map p241; ☎ 609-3143; mains BZ$20-28; ⌚ from 5pm Mon-Sat) The trattoria serves great handmade pasta, seafood and salads in a cozy wooden cabin with a terrace opening onto the beach. The fettuccine with smoked chicken and broccoli is hard to beat. Located next to Julia & Lawrence Guesthouse, it is in the busy part of town. Get there by 6pm to 6:30pm to avoid a wait.

Il Tempio (Map p241; ☎ 600-3504; meals BZ$35-40; ⌚ dinner) Multicultural is the first word that comes to mind with this place, built to resemble a cross between a Mexican hacienda and a Maya pyramid, with a set of antique redwood Chinese doors thrown in for good measure. Inside, however, the food is strictly Italian, served by the Roman owner Stefano Parisse. Prices are steep for the area, but meals are expertly prepared. It doesn't get more eclectic than this.

Drinking & Entertainment

Tipsy Tuna Sports Bar (Map p241; ⌚ 7pm-midnight Sun-Wed, to 2am Thu-Sat) Occasional live bands spice up the program at Placencia's shiniest bar, with pool tables, big-screen TV and a concrete apron spreading onto the sands. A fun-loving crowd gathers most nights. Happy hour is 7pm to 8pm.

Barefoot Beach Bar (Map p241; ☎ 523-3515; ⌚ 10am-8pm Thu-Tue) Stroll in for a cooler or light eats. Happy hour is 5pm to 6pm.

J-Byrds (Map p241; ☎ 523-3412; ⌚ 10am-midnight or later; ⛶) This dockside bar can get pretty lively with locals and visitors, especially at the Friday dance party (9pm to 2am).

Pickled Parrot (Map p241; ☎ 604-0278; www.pickledparrotbelize.com; ⌚ noon-midnight or later) This thatched-roof Caribbean-style bar and restaurant a block from the ocean has been a popular spot for locals and tourists alike for 15 years. Happy hour – with half-priced rum drinks – runs from 5pm to 6pm, and Tuesday night is darts night, with bar-tab credit being awarded to high scorers.

Getting There & Away

AIR

From Placencia airport (PLJ), between them, **Maya Island Air** (☎ 523-3475; www.mayaairways.com) and **Tropic Air** (☎ 523-3410; www.tropicair.com) fly around 16 times daily to Belize City (one-way/return BZ$190/328, 35 minutes), 12 times to Dangriga (BZ$90/180, 15 minutes) and eight times to Punta Gorda (BZ$90/180, 15 to 20 minutes), offering big time savings over the much-longer bus rides. The airstrip is just north of town.

BOAT

The **Hokey Pokey Water Taxi** (Map p241; ☎ 601-0271, 523-2376) runs skiffs between the southern tip of Placencia and the town of Independence (also called Mango Creek; one-way BZ$10, 12 minutes, every half-hour from 6:30am to 6pm); from Independence you can connect with any of the buses that traverse the Southern Hwy.

The 45-passenger **Gulf Cruza** (☎ 202-4506, 523-4045, 601-4453) sails from Placencia dock to Puerto Cortés, Honduras (BZ$100, 4½ hours) at 9:30am on Friday. Tickets are sold at the Placencia Tourism Center (p238). The return trip leaves Puerto Cortés at 11am on Monday.

BUS

James bus line runs two daily buses to Belize City (see opposite), passing through Dangriga and Belmopan. Check at the tourist office for transfers to Sittee River and Hopkins. If you're heading south, your best bet is to take the boat to Independence (see above) and catch a south-going James bus from there.

CAR & MOTORCYCLE

The 24-mile road into Placencia from the Southern Hwy is smooth but mostly unpaved. Auto rentals are available at the **Nautical Inn** (Map p238; ☎ 523-3595; Seine Bight; per day BZ$150-180).

Getting Around

Many accommodations north of the village offer free airport transfers and free use of bicycles for guests.

BUS TIMETABLE: PLACENCIA TO/FROM BELIZE CITY				
Placencia	**Dangriga**	**Belmopan**	**Belize City**	**Service**
6am	7:30am	9:30am	10:30am	Regular
2pm	3:30pm	5pm	6:30pm	Regular
Belize City	**Belmopan**	**Dangriga**	**Placencia**	**Service**
8am	9:30am	11am	1:30pm	Regular
2pm	3:30pm	5pm	6:30pm	Regular

Taxis meet many flights. The ride to or from the village costs BZ$5 per person (minimum BZ$10). A taxi from the village costs around BZ$7 per person to Seine Bight (minimum BZ$20) or BZ$10 per person to Maya Beach (minimum BZ$30).

Dianni's Guest House (Map p241; ☎ 523-3159) rents good bicycles for BZ$5/16/26 per hour/half day/day.

TOLEDO DISTRICT

Bordering Guatemala to the south and west and the Stann Creek and Cayo Districts to the north, the 1669-sq-mile Toledo District encompasses an area most Belizeans refer to lovingly as 'The Deep South.' A bucolic place, until recently not even connected by paved road (it still isn't, at least not fully), only 27,000 people live in this huge area. About half the district is under protection as national parks, wildlife sanctuaries, forest reserves or nature reserves.

Toledo's attractions – jungle trails, lagoons, wetlands, rivers, caves, waterfalls, countless birds – and its archaeological heritage are much less trumpeted than those of Belize's other districts, which makes them all the more magnetic to those looking to get off the beaten path. Visitor facilities are increasing, and rural accommodations now range from a smattering of midrange and top-end lodges to an excellent guesthouse program. The people of the district, two-thirds of them Maya, are dedicated primarily to agriculture, and their traditional lifestyles provide a fascinating complement to the natural attractions. Toledo's capital, and only major town, is Punta Gorda.

PUNTA GORDA
pop 5100

Most casual travelers in years past didn't make it as far as Punta Gorda (or PG as it's

called throughout Belize); if they did, they only used this low-key seaside town as a jumping-off point into Guatemala. Recently though, the worm seems to be turning (at a typically slow Belizean pace, naturally), with the number of visitors coming to chill out in this unpretentious southern town increasing. Some base themselves here for longer term trips out to the southern cayes or for lengthy explorations of Belize's deep Maya south.

Though it lacks the beaches of Placencia, there are plenty of docks from which to take a long swim out in the Gulf of Honduras' blue waters. A pretty town, a good part of PG's charm lies in its unassuming character. Though hardly a hub of tourism (a plus to many travelers), PG boasts a good variety of mid-priced guesthouses, hotels and B&Bs, as well as a number of backpacker-budget accommodations. Rainfall and humidity are at their highest down here in the south. From June through February, be ready for at least a short downpour almost daily and some sultry weather in between.

History
PG was founded by Garifuna settlers from Honduras in 1832 and nearly half its population is still Garifuna today. The town once served as an R&R center for the British Army (always a mixed blessing, as anyone who's ever lived in a town favored by the military will attest). After this phase ended (for better or worse) in 1992, tourism in PG went into somewhat of a lull, though in recent years things have picked up significantly, thanks both to increasing interest in the region by casual travelers and a significant number of NGOs basing themselves in and around the town.

Orientation & Information
PG spreads along the Gulf of Honduras, its downtown area stretching lazily for several blocks just in from the coast. The airport is on

PUNTA GORDA

0 — 300 m
0 — 0.2 miles

To Sea Front Inn (0.1mi); Wild Encounters (0.1mi);
Beya Suites (0.3mi); Waluco's (0.8mi);
Nim Li Punit (26mi); Independence (63mi);
Dangriga (105mi)

Airstrip

To Hickatee
Cottages (1mi)

School
School

Gulf of Honduras

INFORMATION
Belize Bank.................................1 C2
Belize Tourism Board....................2 C2
Customs & Immigration................3 D2
Post Office..................................4 C2
Punta Gorda Hospital...................5 A4
Punta Gorda Laundry Service........6 C2
Scotia Bank................................7 C2
Toledo Ecotourism Association...(see 2)
V-Comp Technologies....................8 C2

SIGHTS & ACTIVITIES
Clock Tower.................................9 C2
Galvez's Tours..........................(see 28)
Tide Tours.................................10 C2

SLEEPING
Blue Belize Guest House.............11 B4
Charlton's Inn.............................12 D1
Coral House Inn..........................13 A4
Lux Drive In Guesthouse..............14 D2
Nature's Way Guest House...........15 B3
St Charles Inn............................16 C1
Tate's Guest House......................17 C1

EATING
Earth Runnins'............................18 C1
Emery Restaurant........................19 D1
Gomier's.....................................20 D1
Grace's.......................................21 C1
Hang Cheong Restaurant..............22 B2
Marencos....................................23 C2
Marian's Bayview Restaurant........24 B3
Snack Shack................................25 C2

DRINKING
Bukut Bar.................................(see 18)
PG Sports Bar..............................26 C2

TRANSPORT
Customs Dock.............................27 D2
Galvez's Auto Rental...................28 B2
Galvez's Taxi............................(see 28)
James Bus Line...........................29 D2
Maya Island Air...........................30 B1
Requena's Charter Service............31 D2
Tide Tours.................................(see 10)
Tropic Air...................................32 B1

the inland edge of town, and the town center is a triangular park with a distinctive blue-and-white clock tower. Wednesday, Saturday and, to a lesser extent, Monday and Friday are market mornings, when villagers from the mostly Maya settlements of southern Toledo come to town to buy, sell and barbecue around the central park and Front St. Two informative websites for the area are www.southernbelize .com and www.howlermonkey.com.

Belize Bank (☎ 722-2324; 30 Main St; ☒ 8am-3pm Mon-Thu, to 4:30pm Fri) Exchanges cash and traveler's checks; ATM accepts most international cards, and is accessible after hours.

Belize Tourism Board (BTB; ☎ 722-2531; Front St; ☒ 8am-noon & 1-5pm Tue-Fri, 8am-noon Sat) Staff are knowledgeable and keen to enthuse visitors. The Toledo

Ecotourism Association (TEA; see boxed text, p255) shares the premises.

Emergency (☎ 911, 922)

Post office (Front St; ☒ 8am-noon & 1-5pm Mon-Thu, 8am-noon & 1-4:30pm Fri)

Punta Gorda Hospital (☎ 722-2026; Main St)

Punta Gorda Laundry Service (☎ 702-2273; Main St; wash & dry per lb BZ$1.75; ☒ 8:30am-12:30pm & 1:30-5pm Mon-Sat)

Scotia Bank (☎ 722-0098; 1 Main St; ☒ 8am-2pm Mon-Thu, to 3:30pm Fri, 9am-11:30am Sat) PG's newest bank is a branch of this Canadian financial giant. Exchanges cash and traveler's checks; ATM accepts most international (Visa, MasterCard, Plus and Cirrus) cards, but is located inside the bank itself.

V-Comp Technologies (☎ 722-0093; 29 Main St; internet per hr BZ$8; ☒ 8am-8pm Mon-Sat) Internet access.

SOUTHERN BELIZE

Customs & Immigration (☎ 722-2022; Front St, next to dock; ☯ 9am-5pm Mon-Fri) This is where you'll arrive if you're coming to Punta Gorda by boat from Guatemala or Honduras, or where you'll leave from if you're going to either place. There is a departure tax of BZ$7.50 for leaving via ocean. This is also where you go to get your visa extension.

Activities

Punta Gorda is a cool place to chill out for a few days, but outside of eating, lounging around the park and swimming off various docks, it isn't exactly activity central.

In the town's immediate environs, however, it's a different story: you can kayak on **Joe Taylor Creek**, which enters the sea at the eastern end of town, **hike** in the jungle around Hickatee Cottages (p248) or take **kayak trips** on other rivers, where you may see monkeys, crocodiles and even manatees or dolphins off the river mouths (a typical trip like this costs around BZ$350 for up to four people).

Offshore, some of the islands of the **Port Honduras Marine Reserve**, northeast of Punta Gorda, present good snorkeling and diving, especially the **Snake Cayes** (named for their resident boa constrictors!), 16 miles out, with white-sand beaches. The beautiful **Sapodilla Cayes** on the barrier reef, some 38 miles east of Punta Gorda, are even better, with healthy coral reefs, abundant marine life and sandy beaches. A day trip for four costs around BZ$500 to the Port Honduras Marine Reserve or BZ$650 to Sapodilla Cayes.

Fishing for bonefish, tarpon, permit, snook, barracuda, kingfish, jacks and snapper is superb in the offshore waters and some coastal lagoons and inland rivers: fly- and spin-fishing and trolling can be practiced year-round. Any of the tour operators listed (below) can help you arrange fishing and sailing trips, as well as other activities.

Tours

Ideally located for exploring Belize's Deep South, Punta Gorda has a number of certified tour guides who can arrange day trips to places such as Blue Creek (p254), Lubaantun (p252) and Nim Li Punit (p253), as well as rent out canoes and kayaks. The best of these are **Wild Encounters** (☎ 722-2300; www.seafrontinn .com; 14 Front St), **Tide Tours** (☎ 722-2129; www.tidetours .org; Front St) and **Galvez's Tours** (☎ 722-2402; 61 Jose Maria Nunez St). The BTB office can also direct you to recommended guides.

Festivals & Events

Two days of fishing, beer drinking, punta dancing, kayaking and volleyball contests, plus music, drumming and plenty to eat and drink add up to a big weekend at the **Toledo Fish Fest**, held close to Garifuna Settlement Day (November 19). The **Toledo Cacao Festival**, organized by local organic Cacao businesses, happens at the end of May and beginning of June.

Sleeping

Whether you're traveling on a tight budget or living off a trust fund, you'll have little problem finding suitable accommodations in Punta Gorda.

BUDGET

Nature's Way Guest House (☎ 702-2119; natures wayguesthouse@hotmail.com; 82 Front St; s/d/tr/q BZ$23/33/45/50; 🖳) Clean, safe and affordable, with a terrific breakfast and ocean breezes to die for, Chet Schmidt's guesthouse has been a long-standing favorite of backpackers and students for years. Simple, screened-in, ocean-breeze-cooled wooden rooms are upstairs, and a large airy communal area with TV, music and internet is below. There's also one big communal sleeping area where a bunk with mosquito netting goes for BZ$16. Chet also offers bicycle rental for BZ$10 per day.

Lux Drive In Guesthouse (☎ 722-2080; rosewood studio@hotmail.com; 47 Front St; r BZ$30) They say in business it's all about location; if that's the case, this small seaside guesthouse has a definite advantage, located as it is practically on top of the pier where boats to Guatemala dock. Rooms are a bit on the grotty side, but the ocean views are stellar and the place isn't without its Bukowski-esque charm. Owner Oscar Burke is himself a local character, and runs the attached El Che café, serving breakfast in the morning, and beer, strong stout and music at night.

Tate's Guest House (☎ 722-0147; tatesguesthouse@ yahoo.com; 34 Jose Maria Nunez St; s/d BZ$38/76, extra person BZ$11; 🖾 🖳) Mr Tate is Punta Gorda's postmaster and a man known to run a tight ship. The rooms in his quiet guesthouse are clean and safe, and all come with cable TV and hot showers. The costlier rooms have air-con and kitchenettes, the cheaper ones are fan-cooled. Long-term rental discounts are available.

St Charles Inn (☎ 722-2149; 23 King St; s/d/tr BZ$40/50/65; 🖾) Lilac colored walls, verandahs with hammocks, and budget rooms are the main appeal at this aging guesthouse in the center of Punta Gorda (just down from Grace's Restaurant). The only complaint we've heard concerns noise: the inn's central location might not be overly conducive to a good night's rest. All rooms come with private bathrooms, coffee makers and cable TV.

Charlton's Inn (☎ 722-2197; wagnerdm@btl.net; 9 Main St; s/d/tr BZ$66/77/98; 🕸 🖵) With 25 clean rooms with air-con and cable TV, not to mention a good location at the north end of town, Charlton's is a good choice for those looking for a place in the upper level of the budget category. Triples are more like suites, with two stand-alone bedrooms. Some rooms have their own bathtubs, a rarity in this area.

MIDRANGE

ourpick Hickatee Cottages (☎ 662-4475; www.hickatee .com; duplex cottages s/d BZ$100/140, detached cottages s/d/tr BZ$130/170/170; 🖵) In a world where an increasing number of businesses are flying a green flag to appeal to the ecoconscious crowd, Ian and Kate's Hickatee Cottages are a breath of fresh air. The British couple hasn't printed brochures with the words 'environmentally friendly' emblazoned across the top (they haven't printed brochures, period). Rather, they've gone out of their way to create a beautiful and unique space that leaves as light an ecological footprint as possible. Their three cottages are furnished with beautifully crafted items made of locally harvested wood, and designed for maximum air flow, making air-con superfluous. It's a good thing, too, as Hickatee is totally off the local electrical grid and powered primarily by the sun. The property itself, a mixture of intentional garden and wild jungle space, has a 1.5-mile trail network, home to a wide variety of bird and butterfly species. Ian and Kate encourage visitors to explore Toledo on their well-maintained bicycles, free for guests to use.

Blue Belize Guest House (☎ 722-2678; www .bluebelize.com; 139 Front St; ste BZ$110; 🖵) Taking up the 2nd story of the home of marine biologist Rachel Graham and her husband Dan Castellanos, Blue Belize leaves a light environmental footprint with its high ceilings (which, combined with the ocean-front location, nicely eliminate the need for air-con) and rainwater-fed plumbing system. Plans for switching to solar power are under way. BB's two breezy and beautifully decorated suites

are more like serviced apartments than hotel rooms, offering well-furnished living rooms and kitchenettes, in addition to a comfortable master bedroom. Dan and Rachel have a well-stocked book and DVD library for guests who'd rather lounge than explore. If you're looking for a home away from home in PG, then BB is the place.

Sea Front Inn (☎ 722-2300; www.seafrontinn.com; 4 Front St; s/d BZ$120/150; 🅿 🕸 🖵) A strong contender for the quirkiest-looking hotel in Belize, this four-story gabled construction in stone, wood and concrete was partly inspired by owner Larry Smith's travels in Europe. It's a comfortable and hospitable place, where each of the good-sized, air-con rooms (some boasting their own balconies) has a different theme (jaguar, blue morpho, manatee) – try for the emperor angelfish with its exotic sculptures! The top-floor restaurant serves excellent breakfasts of locally grown tropical fruits. The rear building – no less unusual looking – houses three apartments for medium and long-term visitors.

Beya Suites (☎ 722-2188; www.beyasuites.com; 6 Hopeville; s/d/tr BZ$120/150/180; 🕸) Awarded 'Best Small Hotel of the Year' in 2007 by the Belize Tourism Board, this hotel on the north side of PG is a good find for those looking to balance comfort and economy. The rooms are well appointed and comfortable, with wireless internet, air-con, hot-water bathrooms and private verandahs. It also has a restaurant, and is across the street from the beach.

Coral House Inn (☎ 722-2878; www.coralhouseinn .net; 151 Main St; d incl continental breakfast BZ$165-200; 🕸 🏊) This excellent seaside inn at the southern end of town boasts a lovely garden and an oddly narrow, in-ground swimming pool (perfect for laps or one-on-one water volleyball matches). All rooms in this renovated house are clearly decorated by someone with an eye for style, giving the place a classic (but not at all pretentious) colonial feel. A spacious verandah overlooks the sea on one side and a quaintly picturesque old cemetery on the other. A full range of tours, quiet poolside bar and free bicycles are just some of the options available to guests.

Eating

Grace's Restaurant (☎ 702-2414; 16 Main St; breakfast BZ$5-10, mains BZ$7-12; 🕙 6am-10pm; 🕸) A longtime favorite of locals and travelers alike, Grace's offers a wide range of dishes, from Belizean favorites such as stew chicken, fried fish, and rice and beans to more exotic fare, including Chinese food and even grilled lobster for those with deeper pockets. Breakfasts are especially good value.

Marencos (☎ 702-2572; 57 Main St; mains BZ$7-13; 🕙 9:30am-2pm & 5-10pm Mon-Sat, 5-10pm Sun) For a place in southern Belize, Marencos serves up some suspiciously good American-style food, including fine double cheeseburgers, french fries and Coke floats with vanilla ice cream. If it weren't for the presence of some Belizean dishes on the menu, you might think you'd stepped into a scene from *American Graffiti*.

Marian's Bayview Restaurant (☎ 722-0129; 76 Front St; mains BZ$8-14; 🕙 lunch & dinner) A 3rd-floor outdoor eatery with an amazing view over the Gulf of Honduras, this place is worth visiting for the ambience alone. But add to the mix excellent East Indian cuisine dished up by Marian and her husband Hubert, and some of the wickedest homemade hot sauce south of the Rio Grande (you can bring a bottle home for BZ$5; watch out, it's a slow burn!), and you've got one of the best little restaurants in Punta Gorda. Very popular with locals, visitors and Peace Corps recruits alike.

our pick **Earth Runnins'** (13 Main Middle St; dishes BZ$9-20; 🕙 7am-2pm & 5-11pm Wed-Mon) Every now and then, you come across a restaurant run by someone for whom food preparation is a matter of 'artistry' first and 'business' second. Earth Runnins' is such a place. At this restaurant, a party of four can order four separate dishes, which, though nutritionally similar in composition (meat or fish, starch, vegetable), are completely different in presentation, texture and flavor; each one offers something worth raving about. The decor is also fabulous, with mahogany furniture and walls painted in rich earth tones, and there's a fine bar where you can have a few ice-cold Belikins while waiting for your meal.

Other recommendations:

Gomier's (☎ 722-2572; Main St; ice cream BZ$2-6, meals BZ$6-16; 🕙 11am-2pm & 5:30-10pm) Serves excellent vegetarian cuisine; the tofu-based ice cream is absolutely to die for.

Hang Cheong Restaurant (Main St; dishes BZ$6-18; 🕙 10:30am-2:30pm & 5pm-midnight; 🍴) One of the few Chinese restaurants in town, Hang Cheong seems to enjoy the best reputation (if lunchtime crowd sizes are anything to go by).

The Snack Shack (Main St; mains BZ$10-20; 🕙 11:30am-2pm & 6-10pm Mon-Fri, 6-10pm Sat) A popular outdoor venue serving burgers, burritos, sandwiches and pastries.

Drinking & Entertainment

PG has a fair number of bars, from small waterfront pubs located on Front St to larger places over on Main. The town is also home to some top performers, such as *paranda* (serenading music) maestro Paul Nabor, *brukdown* (19th-century Creole music) queen Leela Vernon, and local punta rock favorites, the Coolie Rebels. Don't miss a chance to hear any of these on their home turf at one of the following bars in town.

Bukut Bar (13 Main Middle St; 🕙 5-11pm Wed-Mon) It's hard to say exactly when the transformation takes place – certainly well after sundown – but when PG is dark, its hippest new eatery Earth Runnins' becomes its coolest new bar, where homemade cocktails are served and local music (sometimes live) heard.

PG Sports Bar (☎ 722-2329; cnr Main & Prince Sts; 🕙 8pm-midnight Tue-Thu, to 2am Fri & Sat) A good-sized, fairly standard bar, incongruously enhanced by a staggering collection of US sports photos and posters. There's usually a DJ or live music on Friday and Saturday.

Waluco's (☎ 702-0073; Front St) If you're wondering where everybody is on Saturday or Sunday afternoon, they're probably out at this big breezy *palapa* a mile northeast of town, swimming off the pier, eating barbecue and knocking back a few Belikins. It's normally open Tuesday to Saturday evenings, too, and Garifuna drummers often play here.

Getting There & Away

AIR

Tropic Air (☎ 722-2008; www.tropicair.com) has flights five times daily to Placencia (one-way/return BZ$90/180, 20 minutes), Dangriga (BZ$120/240, 40 minutes) and Belize City (BZ$218/427, one hour). **Maya Island Air** (☎ 722-2856; www.mayaairways.com) does the same trips three times daily. Ticket offices are at the airstrip (airport code PND).

BOAT

Requena's Charter Service (☎ 722-2070; 12 Front St) operates the *Mariestela*, departing Punta Gorda at 9am daily for Puerto Barrios, Guatemala (BZ$30, one hour), returning at 2pm. Tickets are sold at the office and the

BUS TIMETABLE: PUNTA GORDA TO BELIZE CITY

Punta Gorda	Independence	Dangriga	Belmopan	Belize City	Service
-	-	5am	6:30am	8am	Regular
-	-	6am	7:30am	9am	Regular
-	-	7am	8:30am	10am	Regular
-	6am (Placencia)	7:30am	9am	10:30am	Regular
4am	6am	7:30am	9:30am	10am	Regular
5am	7am	8:30am	10:30am	11:30am	Regular
6am	7:30am	8:30am	10am	11am	Express
6am	8am	9:30am	11:30am	12:30pm	Regular
8am	10am	11:30am	1:30pm	2:30pm	Regular
10am	noon	1:30pm	3:30pm	4:30pm	Regular
noon	2pm	3:30pm	5:30pm	6:30pm	Regular
2pm	3:45pm	5pm	6:30pm	7:30pm	Regular
3pm	4pm	6pm	7:30pm	8:30pm	Regular

customs dock down the street. The Guatemalan **Pichilingo** (☎ 722-2870; one-way BZ$36) sails from Puerto Barrios to Punta Gorda at 10am and returns from Punta Gorda at 2pm. From Puerto Barrios boats leave for Lívingston (BZ$3 to BZ$7, 30 to 90 minutes) until about 5pm. A Guatemalan-operated direct boat to Lívingston (BZ$30, one hour) leaves the customs dock at about 10am Tuesday and Friday. The local Belize Tourism Board can help you buy tickets.

BUS

As with elsewhere in Belize, the slack left by the bankruptcy of Novelo's bus company has been taken up by a number of smaller companies (many of which have bought up old Novelo's buses). The largest of these servicing the south is **James Bus Line** (☎ 722-2625, 702-2049; King St), which runs nine times a day (see table, above) from Punta Gorda to Belize City (BZ$22, seven hours), pulling into Independence (BZ$9, two hours), Dangriga (BZ$14, 3½ hours) and Belmopan (BZ$20, 5½ hours) along the way. The only official express service leaves at 6am daily, and costs BZ$2 more. While the express still stops at all three terminals prior to getting to Belize City, it tends not to pick up passengers at random spots along the road (except when it does), hence the 'express' status. All buses leave from the main bus station on King St and cruise around PG a bit before heading north. A few other companies also do the PG–BC run.

For bus services to the villages of Toledo, see p257.

CAR & MOTORCYCLE

Galvez's Auto Rental (☎ 722-2402; 61 Jose Maria Nunez St) rents Chevy Geo Trackers for around BZ$160 a day.

Getting Around

Tide Tours (☎ 722-2129; Prince St; 🕑 9am-noon & 2-6pm Mon-Wed & Fri, 9am-noon Thu & Sat) rents bikes for BZ$3/12/20 per hour/half day/day. **Galvez's Taxi** (☎ 722-2402; 61 Jose Maria Nunez St) is dependable.

THE DEEP SOUTH

Beautiful, remote and largely untrodden by travelers, Belize's Deep South is a hotbed of culture and history, nature and environmentalism. The region is also home to some of the countries swankest ecolodges.

Visitors to Belize's Deep South have a unique opportunity to simultaneously experience both ancient and contemporary Maya culture. Over 60% of the population of Toledo District is Maya and these people, with more than 30 villages, have done a great deal to keep their culture alive and intact. Those Maya of southern Belize who survived European diseases were mostly driven into Guatemala by the British in the 18th and 19th centuries. But two groups crossed back from Guatemala to southern Belize in the late 19th and early 20th centuries, fleeing taxes, forced labor and land grabs by German coffee growers. The Mopan Maya settled in the uplands of southern Belize, while the Kekchi Maya, from the Alta Verapaz area of Guatemala, settled in the lowlands. The Mopan and Kekchi speak distinct Mayan languages, as well as English and sometimes Spanish.

While Maya men generally adopt Western styles of dress, most women still wear plain, full-length dresses with bright trimmings, or calf-length skirts and embroidered blouses. Rituals and folklore continue to play an important role in Maya life, with masked dances such as the Cortés Dance and Deer Dance performed in some villages at festivals, including All Saints' and All Souls' Days (November 1 and 2) and Easter week. If your village visit coincides with one of these, it will be all the more memorable.

Villages & Ruins
SAN PEDRO COLUMBIA
Around 20 miles northwest of Punta Gorda is the village of San Pedro Columbia, the largest Kekchi Maya community outside of Guatemala. Columbia (as locals call it) was established by Kekchi families who left Pueblo Viejo to look for new farmland around 1905. The village has seen boom and bust cycles with mahogany and cedar felling, chicle collection and, in the 1970s and 1980s, marijuana cultivation. There are currently around 1500 people in Columbia. The village has one restaurant, Maggie's, by the crossroads, which serves uninspired fare and cold beer, and there are several shops where handicrafts and food can be bought.

Two miles up the river is the source of the Columbia branch of the Rio Grande, where water bubbles out from beneath the rocks. Local guides can take you to see the source; it's

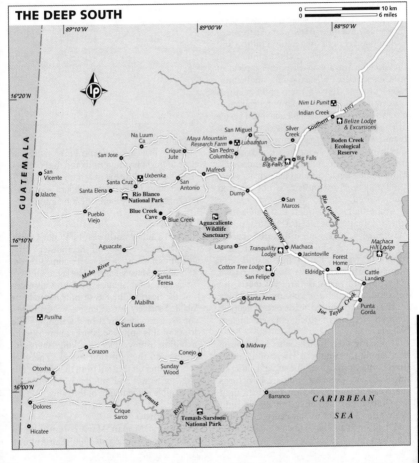

THE DEEP SOUTH

SOUTHERN BELIZE

a 45-minute walk from the center of town (try floating down on a river-tube!). Behind the village, up into the hills, is the **Columbia Forest Reserve**, which has thousands of acres of forest, sinkholes, caves and ruins hidden in the valleys. There are also local guides who can take you there. One of the best is Alphonso Chee, who can be contacted either through Maggie's or the Toledo Ecotourism Association (see boxed text, p255).

Maya Mountain Research Farm (opposite) is just a few miles upriver from the village. Columbia is also close to Lubaantun (below) and 20 minutes by bus from Nim Li Punit (opposite), making the village an ideal place from which to explore two of the area's most complex and amazing ruins.

LUBAANTUN

The Maya ruins at **Lubaantun** (admission BZ$10; 8am-5pm), 1.3 miles northwest of San Pedro Columbia, are built on a natural hilltop and display a construction method unusual in the ancient Maya world (though typical of southern Belize) of neatly cut small limestone blocks. Belize's then–chief medical officer, Thomas Gann, an amateur archaeologist, bestowed the name Lubaantun (Place of Fallen Stones) in 1924. History does not record whether Gann's naming of the site was inspired by his own practice of dynamiting temple tops to remove earth and rocks. More-professional work has taken place since 1970 and much of the site is now cleared and restored.

Archaeologists postulate that Lubaantun, which flourished between AD 730 and 860, may have been an administrative center regulating trade, while nearby Nim Li Punit (opposite) was the local religious and ceremonial center. The Maya site comprises a collection of five **plazas**, three **ball courts** and surrounding structures. Lubaantun is known for the numerous mold-made **ceramic figurines** found here, many of which represent ancient ball players.

If making your own way to Lubaantun, head along the Southern Hwy for 15 miles from Punta Gorda. Continue straight along an unpaved road where the Southern Hwy turns sharp east at Dump junction, then turn right at a 'Lubaantun' sign after 2 miles. Go right again after 2.5 miles in San Pedro Columbia and then left at another 'Lubaantun' sign after 0.6 miles.

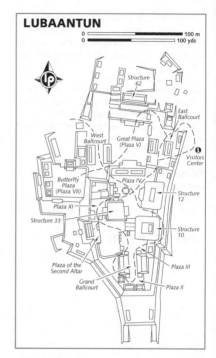

SAN MIGUEL

This Kekchi village of 400 people is on the road close to the Lubaantun ruins and the Southern Hwy. You can walk to Lubaantun or make a little expedition to **Tiger Cave**, 1½ hours' walk away, returning by canoe along the Rio Grande.

LAGUNA

About 13 miles northwest of Punta Gorda, Laguna is just 2 miles off the Southern Hwy and quick and easy to get to. It's home to about 300 Kekchi Maya villagers. The lagoon the village is named for, about a two-hour walk away, is at the heart of the 8.6-sq-mile **Aguacaliente Wildlife Sanctuary**, an extensive wetland area. The area provides great bird-watching, with flocks of ibis and woodstork, many raptors including ospreys, plenty of kingfishers and herons and the odd jabiru stork. There's a visitor center on the trail from the village. The hike can be wet and muddy, and sometimes impassable at the height of the rains.

SAN ANTONIO

The largest Mopan Maya community in Belize (population about 2500), San Antonio was founded in the mid-19th century by farmers from San Luis Rey, in the Petén, Guatemala. A wooden idol (of San Luis) was taken from the church in San Luis Rey by settlers who returned to Guatemala to retrieve their saint. The idol remains in the beautiful **stone church** in San Antonio, which has wonderful stained-glass windows with Italian and Irish names on it belonging to the parishioners of the church in St Louis, (the glass was donated to the church in Belize by parishioners in Missouri, where the glass originated). The **Feast of San Luis**, a harvest festival where the famous Deer Dance is performed, is celebrated in town from about August 15 to 25. There is a TEA (see boxed text, p255) guesthouse in the village, and **Bol's Hilltop Hotel** (r with shared bathroom BZ$15) has very basic rooms. (Meals can be obtained next door at Clara Bol's house.) San Antonio has a large concentration of cacao farmers, growing cacao for export and use in Belizean-made chocolate products.

UXBENKA

Smaller in size and far less developed than Lubaantun and Nim Li Punit, the Maya ruins of Uxbenka are located close to Santa Cruz village on the road from San Antonio. The site is mostly undeveloped and the visible part is merely the center of a larger, yet-to-be excavated city. Archeologists believe

Uxbenka dates back to the Classic Period, with stelae erected in the 4th century. There is evidence that it had a close relationship with Tikal (p263) to the north. The open site has a large plaza with some excavated tombs and sweeping views to the sea. On a clear day it is possible to see the mountains of Honduras and Guatemala. At the time of writing, there were no entry fees for Uxbenka; a local guide can take you, or you can make your own way there.

NIM LI PUNIT

The Maya ruins of **Nim Li Punit** (admission BZ$10; 9am-5pm) stand atop a natural hill 0.5 miles north of the Southern Hwy, 26 miles from Punta Gorda. Buses along the highway will drop you off or pick you up at the turnoff. Only discovered in 1976 by oil prospectors, Nim Li Punit was inhabited from some time in the middle Classic Period (AD 400–700) until some time between AD 800 and 1000. It was probably a town of 5000 to 7000 people at its peak, a political and religious community of some importance in the region.

The site is notable for the 26 stelae found in its southern **Plaza of the Stelae**. Four of the finest are housed in the stela house beside the visitors center. **Stela 14**, at 33ft, is the second-longest stela found anywhere in the Maya world (after Stela E from Quirigua, Guatemala). It shows the ruler of Nim Li Punit

---

INTERNSHIP OPPORTUNITY: MAYA MOUNTAIN RESEARCH FARM

Those interested in learning about permaculture, Maya farming techniques and sustainable living should consider an internship at **Maya Mountain Research Farm** (MMRF; Map p251; www.mmrfbz.org). Located in a beautiful jungle valley 2 miles upriver from San Pedro Columbia, the 70-acre organic farm and registered NGO is run by Christopher Nesbitt and his wife Dawn. With the philosophy of promoting fully sustainable food production, the farm offers internships for those interested in learning about organic farming, biodiversity and alternative energy. Accommodations are simple and beautiful: students can choose from a series of rustic cabanas and thatched-roof *palapas*, all of which come equipped with beds, blankets and mosquito netting. Interns pay BZ$300 for the week, or BZ$1100 for the month, which includes everything.

All aspects of life at MMRF are geared toward environmental sustainability. Interns take part in every stage of meal preparation, from harvesting fruits, vegetables, nuts and herbs to cooking over a wood-burning stove inside the farm's outdoor kitchen (hand-built with stones from the river that marks the border between MMRF and the surrounding farms). Even the toilet – an outhouse with fantastic views of the valley – is set up to recycle nutrients back into the soil.

Rustic, beautiful in the extreme and completely off the grid (phone service, no; satellite internet, yes!), the farm is located in one of the least touristy sections of Belize. Applicants note: this is a tobacco- and drug-free space (with the exception of coffee, brewed in copious quantities). MMRF also offers short-term courses lasting between one and three weeks in both permaculture design and solar electricity management.

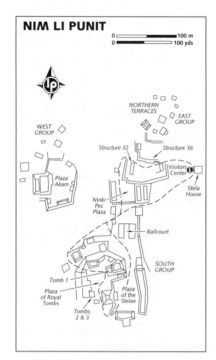

NIM LI PUNIT

in an offering or incense-scattering ritual, wearing an enormous headdress, which is responsible for the name Nim Li Punit ('Big Hat' in Kekchi Maya).

The most interesting part of the Nim Li Punit site is the south end, comprising the Plaza of the Stelae and the **Plaza of Royal Tombs**. The Plaza of the Stelae is thought to have acted as a calendrical observatory: seen from its western mound, three of the small stones in front of the long eastern mound align with sunrise on the equinoxes and solstices. The Plaza of Royal Tombs, with three open, excavated tombs, was a residential area for the ruling family. Archaeologists uncovered four members of this family in Tomb 1, along with several jadeite items and 37 ceramic vessels.

SANTA ELENA
Santa Elena is another Mopan village, 6 miles west of San Antonio, with about 300 people. Just east is the little **Rio Blanco National Park**, containing the spectacular **Rio Blanco Falls** and one of the best swimming holes in the country.

PUEBLO VIEJO
Three miles beyond Santa Elena, the name Pueblo Viejo is Spanish for 'Old Town,' which is appropriate as this was the first settled Mopan village in Belize. Today it is home to about 550 people. It's still an isolated place, without electricity. There are beautiful **waterfalls** close by and you can take **jungle hikes** or go **horseback riding**.

SAN JOSE
Also known as Hawaii (a Mopan word, pronounced ha-wee-ah), this Mopan village of 700, known for practicing organic farming, is located in the foothills of the Maya Mountains. The rainforest surrounding it is among the most pristine in Toledo. You can make jungle hikes to **Gibnut Cave** and a 200ft **sinkhole**. The village honors its patron saint with three days of eating and dancing to marimba and harp music around March 19.

BLUE CREEK
This village of some 250 people, part Kekchi and part Mopan, does indeed have a pretty, blue-tinted river running through the middle. Howler monkeys inhabit the surrounding hilly jungles, otters live along the creek and green iguanas are plentiful. Blue Creek is a tourist stop for the **Blue Creek Cave** (Hokeb Ha Cave; admission BZ$2), a walk of about 0.75 miles along a marked jungle path from the bridge in the middle of the village. The cave has a 'wet side,' where you swim and wade up to an underground **waterfall** (about one hour in the cave), and a 'dry side' where you can try a more difficult venture involving some climbing and emerge at a different entrance. Guides are obligatory inside the cave. Another good hike here is the hill known as **Jungle Height** (about 1½ hours to the top), which affords great views.

Near Blue Creek is the **Tumul'kin School of Learning**, a Maya boarding school that hosts students from throughout Toledo and other parts of Belize, providing a learning venue that inculcates pride in being Maya and gives students an education that values traditional knowledge.

BARRANCO
Barranco is an anomaly indeed, a Garifuna community surrounded by Maya villages. It is both the oldest settlement in Toledo and, despite its distance from major Garifuna

population centers such as Dangriga and Hopkins, a major spiritual homeland of the Garifuna. Though the area was once heavily farmed, nowadays the village supports itself primarily through fishing, as its population has dwindled to about 150 (men of working age head for the cities and better economic opportunities). Still, many are working to revitalize Barranco, both because of its spiritual importance to the Garifuna and its proximity to **Temash-Sarstoon National Park**, an amazing and remote 64-sq-mile protected reserve of rainforest, wetlands, estuaries and rivers lined by towering mangroves and stretching all the way to Guatemala.

The park harbors a huge variety of wildlife, from jaguars, tapirs and ocelots on land to ospreys in the air, large snook and tarpon in the rivers and manatees in the estuaries. Walking trails, developed by the locally run **Sarstoon Temash Institute for Indigenous Management** (SATIIM; www.satiim.org.bz), extend through parts of the park. Two Barranco natives deeply involved in both local tourism and park conservation are **Egbert Valencio** (egbert valencio@yahoo.com) and **Alvin Loredo** (alvinloredo@ yahoo.com); both lead land and river tours into the nearby park, and will be glad to help arrange tours for groups and individuals with a few days' notice.

Other activities available at Barranco include **drumming** and **dory building** (a dory is a traditional Belizean canoe).

Like the surrounding Maya communities, Barranco is connected with the TEA program (see boxed text, below); the Barranco guesthouse has a thatched roof (made from locally harvested comfra palm), electricity and outdoor toilets for BZ$25 per person.

Sleeping & Eating

Tourism is still in its infancy in the area, and outside of the TEA program (see boxed text, below) and the fancy ecolodges, there aren't many hotels in the Deep South. This doesn't mean you'll wind up sleeping in the jungle (although that can be arranged), it just means that you'll have to look a bit harder to find a bed. Some of the larger villages – San Antonio and Columbia, for example – have small hotels not affiliated with the TEA program. In general, if you ask around at the village candy store they'll either find a place for you or direct you to the TEA guesthouse. Nearly every village has at least one small restaurant.

TRAVEL WITH TEA

A unique opportunity to be welcomed into local villages and experience village life firsthand is provided by the **Toledo Ecotourism Association** (TEA; Map p246; ☎ 722-2531, 722-2096; teabelize@ yahoo.com; PO Box 157, Punta Gorda, Toledo District, Belize). TEA is a community organization that manages guesthouse programs in several picturesque Maya villages, offering travelers the chance to really get to know the families and faces that make up the area. Through TEA, travelers can arrange to stay in the homes of Maya families, taking meals with them and participating in a variety of local activities. The villages are gorgeous – simple, neat, clean, surrounded by lovely scenery and usually with a river or stream at their heart – and the villagers friendly without being overly so. Around the villages are waterfalls, caves and ancient Maya ruins that can be best experienced with a local guide. All of the villages listed in this section are affiliated with the TEA program.

Rates vary by village, but are generally around BZ$25 per person per day, well within the budget/backpacker range. In addition to housing, meals prepared in local families' homes are available for around BZ$8 each. Main meals usually consist of tortillas and *caldo* – a stew made from root vegetables and meat, usually chicken – although in Barranco (opposite) you might luck onto some traditional Garifuna food. If you're vegetarian, be sure to specify this clearly and in advance.

Most of the funds collected through the programs go directly to the villages themselves. Activity options range from guided hikes, caving, canoeing and bird-watching to classes in textiles, basket weaving or cooking, or village tours and after-dinner storytelling. Most of these cost around BZ$8 per person per hour. Performances of traditional dance and music (using the harp in Kekchi villages, marimba among the Mopan) can also be arranged. TEA is the brainchild of Chet Schmidt, who runs Nature's Way Guest House in Punta Gorda (p247).

SOUTHERN BELIZE

LIFE ON A PERMACULTURE FARM: CHRISTOPHER NESBITT

In 1985, New York City bicycle messenger Christopher Nesbitt swapped the urban jungle for the real thing, relocating to a mountainous patch of land in southern Belize's Toledo District. Since then, Christopher has spent two decades perfecting organic agricultural techniques and practicing sustainable living. In recent years, the farm (Maya Mountain Research Farm, or MMRF; see p253) has hosted scores of interns from North America, Central America and Europe, as well as local Belizean farmers who've come to Christopher to learn about biodiversity, organic farming, renewable energy and environmental sustainability.

Your website describes MMRF as a farm using 'permaculture principles' – could you define the term? Permaculture is an agricultural and social philosophy that values observation of natural processes, and uses biotic and community-based symbiotic relationships to create sustainable and productive farms and communities.

Farming mountainous terrain seems challenging. What made you choose to start your farm in the mountains of Toledo as opposed to more level ground? This was a working citrus and cattle farm in 1988, and since we had to rehabilitate it for permaculture I was able to get it very cheap. But I found the varied topography very appealing. I especially like the high hill behind most of the cultivated areas, from which you can see both Honduras and Guatemala on a clear day.

What kind of crops grow at MMRF? We have at least 600 types of plants we cultivate, eat, use, foster, encourage or monitor. We have gardens, and we have terraces where we grow vegetables such as corn, beans and squash. Most of what we do is agri-forestry, growing trees that produce food such as avocadoes, mangos, breadnut, breadfruit and bananas, as well as valuable timber, including cedar, mahogany and teak. We also grow coffee and cacao, pineapple and cassava, and

---

There is also a number of small, cheap hotels and bar-restaurants (often called 'cool spots') along the Southern Hwy. On the unpaved roads between villages you may find a few cool spots and/or small grocery stores (usually the same place).

Belize's southern lodges are the epitome of jungle swank; while most are cost-prohibitive to your average backpacker, some offer more reasonable multiday package tours, especially in the low season. Be sure to check the websites before booking.

Tranquility Lodge (www.tranquility-lodge.com; d/tr incl breakfast BZ$100/140; P ⚡) Just north of Jacintoville, 8 miles from PG, this little mid-priced lodge lives up to its name as a tranquil retreat, perfect for relaxing for a couple of days or more. Set amid pretty gardens, the clean, tidy air-conditioned rooms are equipped with hot water and colorful fabrics, and there's a spacious upstairs dining-hangout area where you can enjoy good three-course dinners for BZ$30. Birds abound on the 20-acre grounds and there's a lovely swimming hole on the Jacinto River. Free rides are available to and from PG most days.

Lodge at Big Falls (☎ 614-2888; www.thelodgeatbig falls.com; s/d/tr BZ$250/310/360; breakfast/packed lunch/dinner BZ$10/20/30; P 🖳 🐾) At the village of Big Falls on a loop of the jungle-clad Rio Grande, 18 miles from Punta Gorda (and out of telephone range), sits the eponymous Big Falls lodge, where tiled-floor, palm-thatched cabins are spread about beautifully tended gardens. Popular with birdwatchers (and rightly so, as over 200 species have been spotted here) and butterfly enthusiasts, the lodge is also a fine place from which to enjoy a host of activities, from snorkeling in the southern cayes to caving, fly-fishing and kayaking. It's a good base for excursions into the wilds of southern Belize, too. Meticulously maintained by owners Rob and Marta Hirons (who have recently added an in-ground swimming pool), the Lodge at Big Falls is an island of Anglo-American aristocracy in the jungles of southern Belize. Transfers to or from PG are BZ$100 for up to four people.

Machaca Hill Lodge (☎ 722-0050; www.machacahill .com s/d BZ$381/500) Formerly called 'El Pescador,' Machaca Hill Lodge is a marvelous rainforest and fishing lodge with a superb hilltop setting overlooking miles of protected jungle stretching down to the Gulf of Honduras. Surrounded by the Laughing Falcon Reserve, an 11,000-acre privately owned protected area, the lodge offers comfortable accommodations and access to unparalleled fishing. Experienced fishing guides take anglers out on eight-hour fishing trips and the lodge has

medicinal crops, with an ethnobotanical collection of plants used by our Kekchi Maya neighbors. In the last few years we have established hundreds of vines of vanilla as well.

At any given time you've got a few interns living and working at the farm. What sort of person is a good candidate for internship at MMRF? We like people who are easygoing, hard working and not afraid to get dirty. We like interns who use MMRF to augment their college education, or people taking a gap year before, in the middle of, or after their university studies. We've had interns as young as 16 and as old as 61.

Could you describe a typical day for an MMRF intern? We plant trees and other plants from July through November, our rainy season. During pineapple season we harvest and process pineapple. When we are conducting workshops or training, interns help in facilitating the training. Regardless of the season, much of the day is centered around the kitchen, where the food is processed, prepared or cooked, and eaten. What we do – and what our interns do – pretty much depends on what needs doing at the time.

MMRF runs entirely off solar- and wind-generated electricity, and you've been active in helping others in Belize make the leap from fossil fuels to renewable resources. How would you rate Belize's tourism sector as a whole, as far as its commitment to switching to more sustainable practices goes? Having helped install solar systems for five protected areas in Belize, I can definitely chart the growing interest in renewable energy, especially in the more remote parts of the country. I'm seeing more interest in renewable energy. More green tourism destinations are working to make their practices greener. Some of the hotels now use photovoltaics, wind or microhydro, compost their vegetable wastes and practice energy conservation. That is something I like to see.

a well-stocked fly shop, and fly-fishing gear for rent. On land, there's excellent birding, trails to walk and trips to southern Belize attractions. The 12 beautiful rooms boast solid wood furniture, ceramic-lined bathrooms, two queen-size beds and verandahs overlooking the jungle and sea. Packages include transfers to and from Belize City International Airport. The lodge is 2.4 miles off the Southern Hwy, from a turnoff 3 miles out of PG.

Cotton Tree Lodge (☎ 670-0557, in USA 866-489-4534; www.cottontreelodge.com; luxury cabins incl meals from BZ$400; P ⊠ ⊡) Luxury, environmentalism and intense beauty meet a few miles north of the village of San Felipe and 10 miles from PG. It's here you'll find Cotton Tree Lodge, 100 acres of the swankest jungle savannah you're likely to find anywhere. The property is outstandingly beautiful, with amazing views of the nearby Maya mountain range on the western horizon. All of Cotton Tree's thatched-roof cabins are luxuriously furnished in a superb jungle/hardwood motif, and all (including the remote 'jungle cabin,' nearly 0.25 miles away) are connected to the main restaurant-bar area via a network of elevated wooden boardwalks that spans the entire property. The resort's power (including heating for the Jacuzzi) is partially provided by 15 solar panels, and plans are in the works to commit even further

to alternative energy. Most of the food served in the lodge's excellent restaurant is bought locally, with some of the vegetables coming from the on-site organic garden. Activities include hiking, horseback riding, kayaking, canoeing and bird-watching.

Belize Lodge & Excursions (☎ 223-6324, in USA 888-292-2462; www.belizelodge.com; packages from BZ$570; P ⊡) This fantastically expensive lodge is part of a chain of luxury vacation spots in Belize operated by Belize Lodge & Excursions. All of the beautiful and meticulously designed cabanas on the property (part of the privately owned, 51-sq-mile Boden Creek Ecological Reserve) have airy verandahs overlooking a pair of lakes, and there's a restaurant and beautiful rosewood bar on site. Packages (various ones are available) combine stays in the main lodge and Jungle Camp, tours and all meals, including five-course dinners.

Getting Around

Chun's Bus Service (☎ 016-4257; Punta Gorda airstrip) is the main transport provider connecting Punta Gorda to the surrounding villages. Its current route goes from Punta Gorda to the Guatemalan border at Jalacte, stopping in the villages of Eldridge, Dump, Mafredi, San Antonio, Santa Cruz, Santa Elena and

HITCHHIKING IN BELIZE

Guidebook writers tend to err on the side of caution. Every travel writer dreads the day they get an email, perhaps months or years after the publication of a book they've worked on, telling the ghastly story of a reader who's been hurt (or worse) doing something that the writer had ostensibly suggested was 'safe.' For that reason, this guide – and most others – contains a boilerplate warning against hitchhiking. That said, it would be remiss of this book to not mention the fact that hitchhiking is a common mode of transportation, especially down south, where buses between villages and towns are few and far between.

During the course of researching this edition, I was lucky to have both pickup truck and driver (the amazing Christopher Nesbitt, who, behind the wheel of the green Maya Mountain Research Farm Toyota 4WD, proved nigh unstoppable by even the worst roads), and giving lifts to hitchhikers was a regular part of our trip. During the journey – which ranged from the furthest southern villages and back roads of Toledo to the Mexican border with Corozal – the pan of the truck served as ad hoc public transit for more people than I can recall, with us stopping to drop off when they rapped on the back window. We gave rides to dozens of teenagers, university-aged students, Maya farmers, tourists, Mennonites, young mothers with babes in arms, and one rather gruff police constable (him we let ride up front; the baby-toting mothers, too).

'In rural Belize, if you're driving a pickup truck with room in the pan and you don't offer people lifts, its considered very antisocial,' Christopher told me early on, and judging by the number of pickup trucks we saw with fully peopled pans, this seemed to be the case. There was only one time when we did we not stop to offer a lift (to a group of three teenagers with an air of trouble about them).

Does this mean that hitchhiking in Belize is 100% safe? No. Hitchhiking carries an even greater element of risk than most activities that entail trusting complete strangers. But the fact remains that hitchhiking is a common way for Belizeans themselves to get around. If you do hitchhike in Belize, the best ways to minimize the risks are to travel in pairs if possible, ride in the backs of pickup trucks where possible, and never hitch at night. See also p297.

Pueblo Viejo. One bus a day passes by the Punta Gorda town square at 11:30am and gets to Jalacte two hours later. The return bus leaves Jalacte at 3am, getting to PG at 5:30am. Another bus leaves PG daily at noon, but only goes as far as San Antonio. Periodically, other services emerge to and from the villages, but these tend to be unreliable. For this reason, many Maya villagers tend to get around by hitchhiking.

Tikal & Flores, Guatemala

Just over the border, in the depths of the Guatemalan jungle, the Maya ruins at Tikal are a vast and vivid reminder of the civilization that once spanned Central America.

Tikal covers more area and is more completely restored than any of the Maya sites in Belize. Lodges and campgrounds in the park offer the unique opportunity to spend the night at the ruins and wake up in the jungle; alternatively, the nearby lakeside villages of Flores and El Remate are peaceful and picturesque places to recover from some intensive archaeological exploration. All of this entices Belize-bound travelers to hop over the border to explore the sparsely populated, jungle-shrouded region of El Petén, Guatemala.

Once here, you'll discover that Tikal is only the beginning. There are so many Maya sites in El Petén that only an archaeological extremist could see them all. Many are in the deepest, densest parts of the jungle, largely unexcavated but no less intriguing. Even Tikal – oft visited as it is – is surrounded by rainforest, protecting an abundance of wildlife. The squawk of parrots, the chatter of monkeys and the rustlings of other exotic animals accompany explorers as they roam among the ancient temples.

Tikal is part of the Reserva de Biósfera Maya (Maya Biosphere Reserve), occupying the northern third of El Petén. This Guatemalan reserve adjoins the Calakmul Biosphere Reserve in Mexico and the Rio Bravo Conservation & Management Area (p169) in Belize, forming a huge multinational reserve totaling more than 11,600 sq miles. The amazing array of wildlife is as thrilling as the mysterious Maya – and many sites in El Petén offer a glimpse of both.

HIGHLIGHTS

- Climbing to the top of Tikal's **Templo IV** (p267) for a stupendous view of the tops of temples towering over the canopy
- Watching the sun set over Lago de Petén Itzá from a lakeside café in **Flores** (p276) or **El Remate** (p270)
- Savoring the solitude of the lesser visited Maya sites at **Yaxhá** (p271) or **Uaxactún** (p271)
- Hearing the howler monkeys stake their territory as dawn breaks in the jungles around **Tikal** (see boxed text, p268)
- Zipping across the treetops on the zipline at **Ixpanpajul Nature Park** (p278) or with **Canopy Tours Tikal** (p268)

■ POPULATION: 59,000	■ MONTHLY RAINFALL: Jan 17in, Jun 30in (Tikal)

■ HIGHEST ELEVATION:
984ft

Climate

From December to February, nights and mornings are cool. March and April are the hottest and driest months of the year, followed by rains – and mosquitoes – in May or June. July to November is humid, though by October the rains taper off and the temperature begins to cool down.

Culture

If you are coming from Belize, you may notice that Guatemalans are more conservative than their neighbors to the east. This pertains to their beliefs and behavior, as well as the way they view foreigners.

Guatemalans are a religious bunch. People will often ask what religion you are quite early in a conversation. Unless you really want to get into it, saying 'Christian' generally satisfies. As throughout Latin America, Orthodox Catholicism is gradually giving way to evangelical Protestantism, with the animist-Catholic syncretism of the traditional Maya always present. People's faiths give them hope, not only for better things in the afterlife but also for improvements in the here and now.

Guatemalans are easy to get along with, as long as you follow a few simple guidelines. The pace of life here is slower, and people rarely launch into whatever they're doing – even in such routine situations as entering a store or taking a bus seat – without a simple greeting: *buenos días* (good morning) or *buenas tardes* (good afternoon) and a smile will get conversations off to a positive start. When leaving a restaurant, it is common to wish the other diners *buen provecho* (bon appétit). Handshakes are another friendly gesture and are used frequently.

Pay attention to your appearance. It's difficult for Guatemalans to understand why a foreign traveler, who is naturally assumed to be rich, would go around looking scruffy,

when even poor Guatemalans do their best to look neat. When dealing with officialdom (police, border officials, immigration officers), it's a good idea to appear as conservative and respectable as possible. Shorts are usually worn, by men or women, only at the beach and in coastal towns. Dress modestly when entering churches. Also think about safety in connection with your appearance: don't flaunt expensive jewelry or watches.

Some Maya, especially in villages, speak only their indigenous language. Many Maya are *very* touchy about having their photo taken. Always ask permission before taking pictures. Sometimes your request will be denied, often you'll be asked for a quetzal or two, and maybe in a few special instances you'll make new friends. Many Maya women prefer to avoid contact with foreign men; in their culture, talking with strange men is not something that a virtuous woman does. Male travelers in need of directions or information should find another man to ask. On the language front, using the term *indio* (Indian) to refer to a Maya person carries racist undertones; the preferred term is *indígena*.

Language

Spanish is the main language of Guatemala. Most Tikal tour guides speak English, as do the staff of some upscale hotels. But most hotel and restaurant employees, bus drivers, taxi drivers and other people on the street are unlikely to speak English, so brush up on your Spanish before arriving (see p262).

Money

The unit of currency in Guatemala is the quetzal (Q). Money changers hang around the border, but there are no ATMs or banks on either side of the border. The nearest ATM is in Santa Elena. US dollars are widely accepted.

Dangers & Annoyances

The official but uneasy peace that exists between Belize and Guatemala is manifested in local people's personal opinions about their neighbors. It was only in 1991 that Guatemala officially recognized Belize as an independent nation (a full decade after the rest of the world). To this day Guatemala still maintains its territorial claim over parts of its more prosperous neighbor – which leaves most Belizeans feeling a little uneasy about the relationship. This animosity toward Guatemala

---

GUATEMALAN VISAS

Citizens of the USA, Canada, EU countries, Norway, Switzerland, Australia, New Zealand, Israel, Iceland, South Africa and Japan are among those who do not currently need visas to visit Guatemala. Regulations can change: check with your travel agent or a Guatemalan embassy or consulate well before travel.

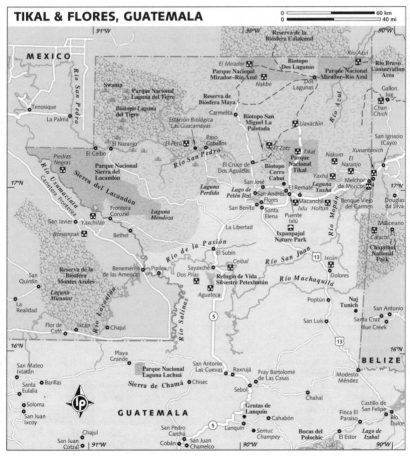

TIKAL & FLORES, GUATEMALA

is heightened by the steady stream of migrants that comes from Guatemala to work in relatively prosperous Belize. As a result of these issues, Belizeans are quick to exaggerate the dangers of traveling to Guatemala and the shadiness of the national character. Travelers should keep a close watch over their belongings, especially when crossing the border. But this part of El Petén is a safe and relatively easy place to travel, so don't be put off by the excessive warnings you might hear in Belize.

Getting There & Away

At the time of research, the flights between Belize City and Flores had been discontinued. The simplest way to visit Tikal is to sign up for one of many day and overnight trips organized by various Belizean agencies. See p198 for tours from San Ignacio.

Independent adventurers can take a direct express bus to Flores from Belize City (p105) or San Ignacio (p201). Alternatively, local buses go from these cities to Benque Viejo del Carmen, where you can get a taxi for the 2 miles to the border (see the boxed text, p210).

Melchor de Mencos is the village on the Guatemalan side of the border. From here, there are onward buses to Flores and Santa Elena. On the Guatemalan side of the border, the road is unpaved for the first 15 to 20 miles.

To go to El Remate or Tikal, get off the bus at Puente Ixlú (El Cruce), and take a taxi

SPANISH 101

Here are a few useful words and phrases to help you get by in Guatemala In the pronunciation guides, the stressed syllables are shown in italics.

Greetings

Hello.	Hola.	o·la
Good morning.	Buenos días.	bwe·nos dee·as
Good afternoon.	Buenas tardes.	bwe·nas tar·des
Good evening/night.	Buenas noches.	bwe·nas no·ches
Goodbye. (rarely used)	Adiós.	a·dyos
See you soon.	Hasta luego.	as·ta lwe·go
Yes.	Sí.	see
No.	No.	no
Please.	Por favor.	por fa·vor
Thank you.	Gracias.	gra·syas
Many thanks.	Muchas gracias.	moo·chas gra·syas
You're welcome.	De nada.	de na·da
Pardon me.	Perdón.	per·don
Excuse me. (used when asking permission)	Permiso.	per·mee·so
Forgive me. (used when apologizing)	Disculpe.	dees·kool·pe
How are things?	¿Qué tal?	ke tal

Introductions

What's your name? (polite)	¿Cómo se llama?	ko·mo se ya·ma
(informal)	¿Cómo te llamas?	ko·mo te ya·mas
My name is ...	Me llamo ...	me ya·mo ...
It's a pleasure to meet you.	Mucho gusto.	moo·cho goos·to
Where are you from? (polite/informal)	¿De dónde es/eres?	de don·de es/er·es
I'm from ...	Soy de ...	soy de ...
Where are you staying? (polite)	¿Dónde está alojado?	don·de es·ta a·lo·kha·do
(informal)	¿Dónde estás alojado?	don·de es·tas a·lo·kha·do
May I take a photo?	¿Puedo sacar una foto?	pwe·do sa·kar oo·na fo·to

Emergencies

Help!	¡Socorro!	so·ko·ro
Fire!	¡Incendio!	een·sen·dyo
I've been robbed.	Me robaron.	me ro·ba·ron
Go away!	¡Déjeme!	de·khe·me
Get lost!	¡Váyase!	va·ya·se
Call ...!	¡Llame a ...!	ya·me a
an ambulance	una ambulancia	oo·na am·boo·lan·sya
a doctor	un médico	oon me·dee·ko
the police	la policía	la po·lee·see·a

or bus the remaining 22 miles to Tikal. For further details, see p269.

There is a BZ$30 departure tax when you leave Belize, even if you are only going to Tikal for the day. Both Belizean and US dollars are accepted, but you must pay in cash (no credit cards). There is a Q250 departure tax when you fly out of Guatemala, but no departure tax when you leave the country by ground transportation.

It's an emergency.	*Es una emergencia.*	es *oo*·na e·mer·*khen*·sya
Could you help me,	*¿Me puede ayudar,*	me *pwe*·de a·yoo·*dar*
please?	*por favor?*	por fa·*vor*
I'm lost. (m/f)	*Estoy perdido/a.*	es·*toy* per·*dee*·do/a
Where are the toilets?	*¿Dónde están los baños?*	*don*·de es·*tan* los ba·nyos

Accommodations

Are there any rooms available?	*¿Hay habitaciones libres?*	ai a·bee·ta·*syon*·es *lee*·bres
I'd like a	*Quisiera una*	kee·*sye*·ra oo·na
room ...	*habitación ...*	a·bee·ta·*syon* ...
double	*doble*	*do*·ble
single	*individual*	een·dee·vee·*dwal*
twin	*con dos camas*	kon dos *ka*·mas
How much is it per ...?	*¿Cuánto cuesta por ...?*	*kwan*·to *kwes*·ta por ...
night	*noche*	*no*·che
person	*persona*	per·*so*·na
week	*semana*	se·*ma*·na
Does it include breakfast?	*¿Incluye el desayuno?*	een·*kloo*·ye el de·sa·*yoo*·no
May I see the	*¿Puedo ver la*	*pwe*·do ver la
room?	*habitación?*	a·bee·ta·*syon*
I don't like it.	*No me gusta.*	no me *goos*·ta
It's fine. I'll take it.	*OK. La alquilo.*	o·*kay* la al·*kee*·lo
I'm leaving now.	*Me voy ahora.*	me voy a·*o*·ra

Directions

How do I get to ...?	*¿Cómo puedo llegar a ...?*	*ko*·mo *pwe*·do ye·*gar* a ...
Is it far?	*¿Está lejos?*	es·*ta* le·khos
Go straight ahead.	*Siga/Vaya derecho.*	*see*·ga/va·ya de·*re*·cho
Turn left.	*Voltée a la izquierda.*	vol·*te*·e a la ees·*kyer*·da
Turn right.	*Voltée a la derecha.*	vol·*te*·e a la de·*re*·cha
Can you show me	*¿Me lo podría indicar*	me lo po·*dree*·a een·dee·*kar*
(on the map)?	*(en el mapa)?*	(en el *ma*·pa)

Public Transportation

What time does ... leave/arrive?	*¿A qué hora ... sale/llega?*	a ke *o*·ra ... *sa*·le/ye·ga
the bus	*el autobus/*	el *ow*·to·boos/
	la camioneta	la ka·myo·*ne*·ta
the pickup	*el picop/la camioneta*	el *pee*·kop/la ka·myo·*ne*·ta
the bus (long distance)	*el autobus/la flota*	el *ow*·to·boos/la *flo*·ta
the plane	*el avión*	el a·*vyon*
the ship	*el barco/buque*	el *bar*·ko/*boo*·ke
I'd like a ticket to ...	*Quiero un boleto a ...*	*kye*·ro oon bo·*le*·to a ...
What's the fare to ...?	*¿Cuánto cuesta hasta ...?*	*kwan*·to *kwes*·ta *a*·sta ...

TIKAL

Towering pyramids pierce the jungle's green canopy and catch the sun. Howler monkeys swing noisily through the branches of trees, as brightly colored birds dart from perch to perch amid a cacophony of squawks. The region's most significant Maya site – both historically and spatially – is contained within the jungles of **Tikal National Park** (☎ 2367-2837; www.tikalpark.com; admission Q150; ☼ 6am-6pm), a

CALLING GUATEMALA

Guatemala has no regional, area or city telephone codes. To call Guatemala from another country, dial the international access code (☎ 00 in most countries), followed by Guatemala's country code, ☎ 502, then the eight-digit local number. To call a Guatemalan number from anywhere within Guatemala, just dial the eight-digit local number.

Unesco World Heritage site. The park's 222 sq miles contain thousands of structures, only a tiny proportion of which have been excavated. Plazas have been cleared of trees and vines. Six majestic temples – some reaching heights over 200ft (61m) – have been partially restored. Hundreds of other ruined structures lie in various states of deterioration, giving visitors an impression of the grand civilization that existed here over a thousand years ago.

History

The Maya began settling at present-day Tikal around 700 BC, with building beginning as early as 400 BC. By 200 BC a complex of buildings stood on the site of the Acrópolis del Norte (North Acropolis).

EARLY CLASSIC

Tikal really reached its zenith as a political power and cultural creator during the early Classic Period, generally starting from AD 200. It was under King Jaguar Paw, in the middle of the 4th century, that Tikal became the dominant kingdom in the region. He was killed by invaders from Teotihuacan, although his temple was supposedly maintained and revered by successive generations.

Records show that the state was constantly warring and allying with neighboring states, in an attempt to keep its dominance in the region. By the mid-6th century, Tikal sprawled across 11.5 sq miles, with a population reaching 100,000. In 562, the kingdom of Tikal was conquered by Lord Water, ruler of Caracol (see p213). The Tikal king Double Bird was captured and sacrificed; Tikal entered a period of decline.

It suffered under Caracol's rule until the late 7th century. This era is often called the 'hiatus,' due to the lapse in construction and inscriptions at Tikal.

LATE CLASSIC

The hiatus ended with the ascension of Ah Cacau, or Lord Chocolate (AD 682–734). Sometimes called King Moon Double Comb for his elaborate headdress, Lord Chocolate defeated neighboring Calakmul in AD 711 and restored Tikal's primacy in the Central Maya region. In the following years, he and his successors were responsible for building most of the temples around the Gran Plaza that survive today. Lord Chocolate is entombed in Temple I, while his wife, Lady Twelve Macaw, is across the plaza in Temple II. The ascension of Lord Chocolate and the resurrection of Tikal mark the beginning of the late Classic Period, which generally starts around AD 700.

Starting in AD 900, which marks the end of the late Classic Period, the power of Tikal waned. There is no evidence of new construction and the population gradually declined, until the site was finally abandoned by the end of the 10th century – another part of the mysterious general collapse of lowland Maya civilization.

EXCAVATION

There were always local legends about an abandoned Maya city in Petén. But it was not until 1848 that the site was discovered by a local *chiclero* (gum collector), Ambrosio Tut. Petén Governor Modesto Mendez and Ambrosio Tut organized the first expedition, which was followed by a publication by the Berlin Academy of Sciences in 1853.

The majority of the excavations have taken place since 1956, led by archaeologists and historians from the University of Pennsylvania and the Guatemalan Instituto de Antropología e Historia. Tikal was declared a Unesco World Heritage site in 1979. Excavation and restoration are ongoing.

Orientation & Information

Although Tikal National Park is spread over 222 sq miles, the area that has been excavated occupies only about 10 sq miles. This central area is located about 12 miles (19km) north of the park entrance.

Your bus will bring you all the way to the parking lot near the central excavated site, which is where you pay the entrance fee. If you enter after 3pm your ticket will be stamped with the following day's date, meaning that it will be valid for the next day, too. Multilingual guides are available at the nearby visitors center (Q390 per half day for up to five people). Also in the visitors center is a museum.

Near the visitors center are Tikal's hotels, a camping area, a **tourist information center** (☉ 8am-4pm), a few small *comedores* (eateries) and another museum. From the visitors center, a network of trails leads around the ruins, past the massive ceiba tree, the national tree of Guatemala. It's about a 1-mile walk southwest to the Gran Plaza. To visit all the major building complexes, you must walk at least 6 miles, so wear comfortable shoes with good rubber treads, as the ruins can be very slick. Bring plenty of water, sun block and insect repellent.

For more complete information on the monuments at Tikal, pick up a copy of *Tikal – A Handbook of the Ancient Maya Ruins,* by William R Coe, available at Tikal and in Flores.

Sights & Activities
GRAN PLAZA
The path leading to the plaza goes around **Templo I**, the Templo del Gran Jaguar (Temple of the Great Jaguar), built to honor – and bury – Lord Chocolate, or King Moon Double Comb. The king's rich burial goods included 16lb of jewelry, 180 jade objects and 90 bits of bone carved with hieroglyphs. Archaeologists also found stingray spines, which were used for ritual bloodletting.

At the top of the 144ft temple is a small enclosure of three rooms that is covered by a corbeled arch. The lofty roof comb (ornamental structure) that crowned the temple was originally adorned with reliefs and bright paint, and may have symbolized the 13 realms of the Maya heaven.

Since at least two people tumbled to their deaths, the stairs up Templo I have been closed. But the views from **Templo II** just across the way are nearly as awe-inspiring. Templo II was once almost as high as Templo I, but now measures 124ft without its roof comb.

The **Acrópolis del Norte** (North Acropolis), while not as impressive as the two temples, is of great significance. Archaeologists have uncovered about 100 structures, with evidence of occupation as far back as 400 BC. The Maya rebuilt on top of older structures, and the many layers, combined with the elaborate burials, added sanctity and power to their temples. Look for the two huge, powerful wall masks. The final version of the acropolis, as it stood around AD 800, had more than 12 temples atop a vast platform.

ACRÓPOLIS CENTRAL
On the southeast side of the Gran Plaza, this maze of courtyards, little rooms and small temples is thought by some to have been a residential palace for Tikal's nobility. Others believe the tiny rooms may have been used for sacred rites.

PLAZA OESTE
North of Templo II is **Plaza Oeste** (West Plaza). To its north is a late Classic temple. To the south, across the Calzada Tozzer (Tozzer Causeway), is **Templo III**, which is 181ft high and yet to be uncovered. Calzada Tozzer, the causeway leading to Templo IV, was one of several sacred ways built among the complexes for astronomical and aesthetic reasons.

ACRÓPOLIS DEL SUR & TEMPLO V
Due south of the Gran Plaza is **Acrópolis del Sur** (South Acropolis). Excavation is ongoing at this 2-hectare mass of masonry. The palaces on top are from late Classic times, but earlier constructions probably go back a thousand years.

Templo V, east of the Acrópolis del Sur, is 190ft high and was built around AD 700. Unlike the other great temples, it has rounded corners and one tiny room at the top, less than 3ft deep, but with walls up to 14ft thick. Restoration of this temple took from 1991 to 2004, and you can climb a wooden stairway to the top.

PLAZA DE LOS SIETE TEMPLOS
Located on the other side of the Acrópolis del Sur is the **Plaza de los Siete Templos** (Plaza of the Seven Temples). The little temples, which are clustered together, were built in late Classic times. Note the skull and crossbones on the central temple. On the plaza's northern side is an unusual triple ball court; another, larger version in the same design stands just south of Templo I.

EL MUNDO PERDIDO
About a quarter-mile southwest of the Gran Plaza is **El Mundo Perdido** (The Lost World), a complex of 38 structures surrounding a huge pyramid. Unlike the rest of Tikal, where late Classic construction overlays earlier work, El Mundo Perdido holds buildings of many

TIKAL

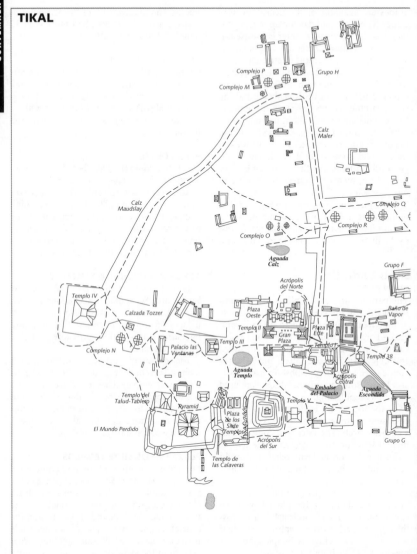

different periods. The **large pyramid** is thought to be Preclassic with some later repairs and renovations, the **Templo del Talud-Tablero** (Temple of the Three Rooms) is an early Classic structure, and the **Templo de las Calaveras** (Temple of the Skulls) is late Classic.

The pyramid, 105ft high and 262ft along its base, had huge masks that flanked each stairway but no temple structure at the top. Each side of the pyramid displays a slightly different architectural style. Tunnels dug by archaeologists reveal four similar pyramids beneath the outer face; the earliest (Structure 5C-54 Sub 2B) dates from around 700 BC, making the pyramid the oldest Maya structure in Tikal.

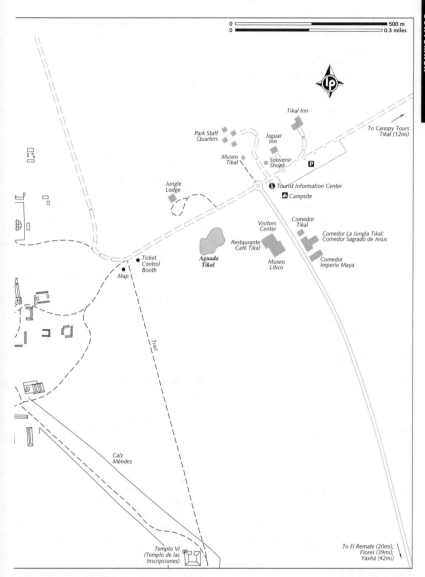

TEMPLO IV & COMPLEJO N

Standing at 210ft, **Templo IV** is the highest building at Tikal. It was completed by about 741, in the reign of King Moon Double Comb's son. From the base it looks like a precipitous little hill. A series of steep wooden steps and ladders takes you to the top for a panoramic view across the jungle canopy. If you stay up

here for the sunset, climb down immediately, as it gets dark quickly.

Complejo N (Complex N), near Templo IV, is an example of the 'twin-temple' complexes popular in the late Classic Period. These complexes are thought to have commemorated the completion of a *katun* (20-year cycle) in the Maya calendar. This one was

---

IT'S ANOTHER TIKAL SUNRISE

Many agencies tout a 'sunrise tour,' which leaves around 4am in order to arrive in time to watch the sunrise from Temple IV. Taking a tour is in fact the only way to do this, as the park does not open early enough for the general public to get there in time.

Keep in mind that it's usually misty at dawn, so your chances of seeing the sun actually rise are minimal. Furthermore, the temple is crowded at this time.

It is absolutely worthwhile to arrive early at Tikal – to hear the jungle awaken and to avoid the crowds. You don't have to join a tour to do this, as public transportation starts at 5am and the park opens at 6am.

---

built in 711 by King Moon Double Comb to mark the 14th *katun* of Baktun 9. (A *baktun* – 144,000 days, about 394 years – consisted of 20 *katun*.) The king is portrayed on Stela 16, one of Tikal's finest.

TEMPLO VI (TEMPLO DE LAS INSCRIPCIONES)

Tikal sports relatively few inscriptions. The exception is **Templo VI**, less than a mile southeast of the Gran Plaza. On the rear of the 39ft-high roof comb is a long inscription; the sides and cornice of the roof comb bear glyphs as well. The inscriptions give the date 766.

MUSEUMS

Museo Lítico (admission Q10; ✦ 9am-noon & 1-4:30pm), located at the visitors center, houses a number of stelae and carved stones excavated from the ruins. Photographs of the jungle-covered temples in various stages of discovery in the late 19th century are intriguing.

Museo Tikal (free with ticket from Museo Lítico; ✦ 9am-5pm Mon-Fri, to 4pm Sat & Sun) has some fascinating exhibits, including artifacts from the tomb of Lord Chocolate (see p265).

CANOPY TOURS

Just outside the entrance to Tikal National Park, **Canopy Tours Tikal** (☎ 5819-7766; www.canopy tikal.com; admission Q240; ✦ 8am-5pm) offers two different zip-lines, as well as a network of hanging bridges. The longer zip-line has 10 platforms, traversing a total of a half-mile. The other option – for those who are short on time – is closer to the road and has nine plat-

forms. If want to explore the canopy at a more leisurely pace, you can opt for the network of hanging bridges, 400m in length, which tours the treetops. Transportation from Tikal or El Remate is included in the price. Add Q40 if you are coming from Flores or Santa Elena.

Tours

One-day tours to Tikal from Flores cost between Q400 and Q560. Taking an overnight tour is one of the easiest ways to get a reservation at a hotel in the park. Recommended tour operators include the following:

Martsam Travel (Map p273; ☎ 7867-5377; www .martsam.com; Calle 30 de Junio, Flores) This highly regarded tour company offers the standard one-day trip to Tikal (per person Q345), as well as trips to Yaxhá (per person Q690, two-person minimum) and other archaeological sites in Petén.

Tikal Travel (☎ 7926-4796; www.tikaltravel.com; Melchor de Mencos) Standard tours include a one-day trip (Q508) or overnight trip (Q900 to Q1200). Leaves at 6:30am daily.

Turismo Aventura (☎ 7926-0398; www.tours guatemala.com; 6a Ave, Santa Elena) Located just over the bridge. Offers one- and two-day trips to Tikal, as well as a boat trip around Lake Petén Itzá. Single-day tours start at Q350. Prices for overnight trips range from Q2100 to Q2800 including hotel and transfer.

Sleeping & Eating

The three hotels at Tikal are often booked in advance by groups, but staying here allows you to savor the dawn and dusk, when the jungle fauna is most active. Book ahead, especially in summer and between Christmas and Easter. All three hotels have their own restaurants. The hotels and campsites all depend on generators for electricity and hot water, which are available at set hours.

Jaguar Inn (☎ 7926-0002; www.jaguartikal.com; camping own/rented tent Q25/60; s/d/tr/q Q312/468/586/703; restaurant mains Q60-80; P ▯) Besides being an excellent option for budget accommodations, Jaguar Inn also offers the most satisfying meals in the park. Freshly ground Guatemalan coffee complements the extensive breakfast menu. Travelers can pop a tent or settle into cozy bungalows, all equipped with ceiling fans and hammocks.

Tikal Inn (☎ 7926-1917, 7926-0065; hoteltikalinn@ itelgua.com; s/d Q412/460, s/d with breakfast & dinner Q535/610, bungalow s/d Q543/665, bungalow s/d with breakfast & dinner Q650/880, breakfast & lunch items Q15-25, dinner mains Q60; P ☎) Spacious and attractive, the thatched-roof bungalows are clustered around a cooling swimming pool, while the smaller rooms are in the main building. Accommodations are simple but comfortable, while bellowing birds and blooming flowers adorn the surrounding grounds.

By the entrance road an official **campsite** (tent space per person Q1, tents for rent Q60) is set in a large, open lawn with some shady trees. You can hang your hammock under a *palapa* (thatched-roof shelter) here, too.

As you arrive at Tikal, you'll see the little **comedores** (meals Q40-60; ☿ breakfast, lunch & dinner) on the right-hand side of the road. These places offer rustic and agreeable surroundings and huge plates of tasty food, including burgers, pasta and hot chicken and meat dishes. At **Restaurante Café Tikal** (visitors center; mains Q60-80), enjoy table service amid the hum of the generator. Picnic tables beneath shelters are located just off Tikal's Gran Plaza, with soft drink and water peddlers standing by.

Getting There & Away

For details of transportation to Tikal from the Belize border, see p210. Heading from Tikal to Belize, start early in the morning and get off at Puente Ixlú to catch a bus or minibus eastward. Shuttles to Belize advertised at Tikal may detour to Flores to pick up passengers. The Jaguar Inn (opposite) has a collective bus going to the Belize border at 7am daily (Q275).

San Juan Travel (Map p273; ☏ 7926-0042, 7926-2146; 2a Calle, Santa Elena; Calle Sur, Flores) operates shuttle minibuses between Flores, Santa Elena and Tikal (Q50 round-trip, 1¼ hours each way), picking up passengers in front of their hotels on the hour from 5am to 10am, then at 2pm. Return minibuses to Flores and Santa Elena depart Tikal at 12:30pm, then every hour from 2pm to 6pm. Outside the normal timetable, you can rent a whole minibus for Q470. A taxi from Flores airport to Tikal costs about Q390.

EL REMATE

pop 2000

On the eastern shore of Lago de Petén Itzá, the small village of El Remate is a quaint and quiet alternative to Flores. It is 18 miles south of Tikal, which makes for easy access to the ruins, while the lakeside location is ideal for riding horses, renting bikes, canoeing and kayaking.

El Remate begins about half a mile beyond Puente Ixlú (also called El Cruce), which is the village where the road to the Tikal road diverges from the Tikal road. El Remate is strung along the Tikal road for a half mile to another junction, where an unpaved road branches west along the north shore of Lago de Petén Itzá to the Biotopo Cerro Cahuí and beyond. Several more places to stay and eat can be found dotted along here. The road continues all the way to the villages of San José and San Andrés near the west end of the lake, making it possible to go all the way around the lake by road.

Sights & Activities

Almost 2 miles west of El Remate, the **Biotopo Cerro Cahuí** (admission Q20; ☿ 7am-4pm) protects 2.5 sq miles of subtropical forest. The vegetation here ranges from *guamil* (regenerating slash-and-burn land) to rainforest. Trees include mahogany, cedar, ramón, broom, sapodilla and cohune palm. There are many species of liana, as well as epiphytes such as bromeliads, ferns and orchids. The hard wood of the sapodilla was used in Maya temple door lintels, some of which have survived from the Classic Period. This is also the tree from which chicle is sapped.

More than 20 mammal species roam the reserve, including spider and howler monkeys, ocelots, white-tailed deer, raccoons and armadillos. The bird life is rich and varied; some 179 species have been identified. Depending upon the season and migration patterns, you might see kingfishers, ducks, herons, hawks, parrots, toucans, woodpeckers and the famous ocellated (or Petén) turkey, which resembles a peacock.

A network of loop trails starts at the road and goes up the hill, affording a view of the whole lake and of Laguna Salpetén to the east and Laguna Petenchel to the south. The one called Los Escobos (3.7 miles long; it takes about 2¼ hours) is good if you want to see monkeys. The guards at the entrance can give you directions.

The dock opposite the entrance is one of the best places to swim along the generally muddy shore of the lake.

Sleeping

Accommodations are strung along the main road and along the road around the lake's north side.

BUDGET

Sak Luk Tikal (☎ 5494-5925; tikalsakluk@hotmail.com; Main Rd; dm Q25, r Q40-50) Look for the massive, multicolored Maya mask at the side of the road for affable and ultra-affordable accommodations in El Remate. Climb the steep stone stairs to find a place to pitch your tent, hang your hammock or take your choice of beds. The most inviting options are the loft-like, open-air dorm rooms, which offer inspiring views of the sunset over the lake. There are communal cooking and other activities for social people.

ourpick Hotel Mon Ami (☎ 7928-8413; www .hotelmonami.com; North Rd; dm Q55, casas per person Q55-75, bungalows s/d/tr/q Q116/195/235/312) You will forgive the minimalism of the rooms at this hotel for the warmth of its atmosphere and (more importantly) the lowness of its prices! This place has a good balance of jungly wildness and French sophistication. Rustic huts have plenty of space between them, porches are equipped with hammocks and chairs, pebbled paths snake through a lush garden of local native plants, and the open-air restaurant serves good French and Guatemalan food.

Hostel Hermano Pedro (☎ 5719-7394; www.hhpedro .com; dm/s/d Q94/133/156; ⚑) Accommodations are simple at this wood-paneled place, but you'll not want for space. An open-air lounge and shady porch are furnished with hammocks and rocking chairs, while the communal kitchen is well stocked for self-caterers. Only four people share each dorm room, each of which has its own bathroom and TV. Rates include a ride to Tikal. Located 20m from the main road: look for the sign.

MIDRANGE

ourpick La Casa de Don David (☎ 7928-8469, 5306-2190; www.lacasadedondavid.com; North Rd; s/d from Q195/281; ⌚ restaurant 6:30am-9pm; P ✗ ✗ ▢) A ramshackle grey house with a tin roof, La Casa de Don David is an inviting place, owned and operated by an American-Guatemalan couple. Modern rooms have wide verandahs overlooking the well-manicured gardens, which stretch down to the lakeshore. English-speaking staff are always at your service. Turn west off the main road to Tikal and this place will be on your left almost immediately. A friendly restaurant opens early for breakfast (Q15 to Q30) and serves American and European food (lunch and dinner Q30 to Q60), as well as

fresh fruit juice, milk shakes and delicious homemade desserts.

El Muelle (☎ 5514-9785, 5581-8087; elmuelle _reservaciones@hotmail.com; Main Rd; r without/with view Q195/300; P ✗ ✗ ⚑) Short on charm but long on value, El Muelle is the preferred hotel of Guatemalan families who appreciate practicalities such as the huge on-site restaurant and the well-stocked gift shop. The rooms are pretty plain, but there is no need for decoration if you opt for one with a lovely lake view.

ourpick Gringo Perdido Ecological Inn (☎ 5804-8639; www.hotelgringoperdido.com; North Rd; r without/with private bathroom per person Q234/312, camping Q40; ⚑) Waking up here is like waking up in paradise, hearing nothing but the lake lapping at the shore a few steps from your door. The rooms have stone walls and floors and full-wall, canvas, roll-up blinds that make you feel like you're sleeping in the open air. Prices include a four-course dinner and a hearty breakfast. Located within the Biotopo Cerro Cahuí.

La Mansión del Pájaro Serpiente (☎ 5702-9434; Main Rd; s/d/ste from Q234/352/586; ✗ ⚑) Dotted along a steep hillside and connected by winding stone paths, cabins here have black-and-white tile floors, sitting areas draped in colorful textiles and screened windows to catch the breeze off the lake. The gorgeous pool area is hung with plenty of hammocks. While you can't quite catch any lake views from the rooms, the breezes and tranquility make for a sublime setting.

TOP END

La Lancha (☎ 7928-8331; www.blancaneaux.com; Aldea Jobompiche, San José; s/d/tr casitas with lake views Q1562/2422/2828, with rainforest views Q1094/1562/1960; P ⚑) Featuring his signature blend of exclusivity and adventure, Francis Ford Coppola has created a lodge of rustic luxury about 8 miles west of El Remate. Secluded casitas have exquisite furniture from native woods, and wide verandahs with amazing views of the surrounding rainforest or the blue-green waters. The grounds are alive with howling monkeys and squawking birds. All room prices include breakfast, use of mountain bikes and hiking trails, as well as a 10% service charge.

Eating

In addition to the eating options listed following, there are excellent restaurants at La

Mansión del Pájaro Serpiente and La Casa de Don David (see opposite).

Las Orquideas (Main Rd; pastas Q40-60, fish & pizzas Q60-90) This semi-swanky spot has a genial Italian owner-chef cooking up genuine Italian fare. It's located on the north shore road, about 450m from the main road to Tikal.

Restaurante Cahui (Main Rd; meals Q60-90) At any time of day or night, the big wooden deck overlooking the lake at this local eatery is a great place to be. The food is simple and filling, the views superb and the healthy selection of beers on the menu won't go astray either. Just before the north shore turn-off, this is also a good stop for information and souvenirs from the gift shop out front.

Getting There & Away

Any bus or minibus going north from Santa Elena to Tikal can drop you at El Remate. For direct buses, see p277.

To get to the Belize border, catch a lift to Puente Ixlú, from where you can flag a bus en route from Flores. A taxi to/from Puente Ixlú is about Q2. Alternatively, you can hail any passing bus or minibus on the Flores–Tikal, but traffic is light after midmorning. Taxis from Flores to El Remate cost around Q170.

YAXHÁ

High upon a hill, overlooking the twin lakes of Laguna Yaxhá and Laguna Sacnab, this late Classic **Maya site** (admission Q80; ☼ 7am-5pm) is the third-largest in Guatemala. Yaxhá translates as 'green water,' likely in reference to its lakeside location. (By the way, don't be tempted to swim in the lakes, as the crocs will get you!) During its heyday in the 8th century, Yaxhá was home to a population of 20,000. Its 400-plus structures included five acropolises, two astronomical observatories and three ball courts.

These days, excavations are ongoing, but it takes at least a couple of hours to look around the main groups of ruins. The high point (literally), towering above all else, is **Templo 216** in the Acrópolis Este (Eastern Acropolis), which affords magnificent views in every direction.

On an island near the south shore of Laguna Yaxhá is a separate, Postclassic archaeological site, **Topoxté**. The dense covering of ruined temples and dwellings may date back to the Itzá, the pre-Columbian civilization that occupied Flores island.

About 10 miles north of Yaxhá, **Nakum** is an old river port on the Holmul River. You'll need a 4WD, but once you get there you can observe the ongoing archaeological excavation. The admission price to Yaxhá includes all three sites.

If you have a hankering to stay near the lesser explored, more mysterious site at Yaxhá, book a room at **El Sombrero Eco Camp** (☎ 7861-1688; www.ecosombrero.com; s/d with shared bathroom Q136/234, s/d with private bathroom Q234/312; Ⓟ). It is on the southern shore of the pristine Laguna Yaxhá, 273yd (250m) off the approach road. Thatched-roof bungalows stand up on stilts, offering breezy views from the shaded porches (fully equipped with hammocks). The on-site restaurant is excellent – important information if you are coming on a day trip. El Sombrero offers boat tours to Topoxté and horseback riding trips to Nakum.

Halfway between Puente Ixlú and Melchor de Mencos, Yaxhá is 7 miles north of the main road. The access road is unpaved. It is difficult to reach without your own vehicle. Your options include taking a taxi (Q500 from Flores) or signing up for an organized tour. **Café Arqueológico Yax-ha** (Map p273; ☎ 5830-2060; Calle 15 de Septiembre, Flores; per person Q275, minimum 5 people) specializes in trips to Yaxhá. Unfortunately, they do not run every day, so contact the agency in advance if you are keen to go.

UAXACTÚN

Uaxactún (wah-shahk-*toon*), 23km north of Tikal along an unpaved road through the jungle, was Tikal's political and military rival in Late Preclassic times. It was conquered by Tikal's Chak Toh Ich'ak I (King Great Jaguar Paw) in the 4th century, and was subservient to its great sister to the south for centuries thereafter. Uaxactún village lies either side of an unused airstrip, which now serves as pasture and a football field.

The pyramids at Uaxactún were uncovered and stabilized so that no further deterioration would result, but they were not restored. White mortar is the mark of the repair crews, who patched cracks in the stone to prevent water and roots from entering. Head south from the airstrip to reach **Grupo E**, a 10- to 15-minute walk. Perhaps the most significant temple here is E-VII-Sub, among the earliest intact temples excavated, with foundations going back perhaps to 2000 BC. On its flat top are holes, or sockets, for the poles that

MORE MAYA SITES FOR DIE-HARDS

If you were tickled by Tikal and excited by Yaxhá, you may be in the market for a few more Maya ruins. Most of the other sites in the Petén are smaller than these two top attractions. Furthermore, some of them require serious effort to reach. But think of it this way: when you finally do get there, you might have the place completely to yourself. And what is more enticing than wandering around alone amongst the ruins of an abandoned civilization? (If that prospect does not entice, perhaps these sites are not for you…) Inquire about organized trips at tour operators in Flores.

- **Sayaxché** On the south bank of the Río de la Pasión, 38 miles southwest of Flores, this is the closest town to nine or 10 scattered Maya archaeological sites, including Ceibal, Aguateca, Dos Pilas, Tamarindito and Altar de Sacrificios.

- **El Péru** In the Parque Nacional Laguna del Tigre, 39 miles northwest of Flores. These trips are termed La Ruta Guacamaya (the Scarlet Macaw Trail), because the chances of seeing these magnificent birds are high, chiefly during their February-to-June nesting season.

- **El Zotz** Completely unrestored and barely excavated, this large site (meaning 'bat' in many Mayan languages) occupies its own *biotopo* (uniform ecological habitat) abutting the Tikal National Park. The three major temples here are all covered in soil and moss, but you can scramble to the top of the tallest, the Pirámide del Diablo, for views of Tikal's temples, 15 miles to the east.

There are also small ruins at **Ixlú**, near Puente Ixlú, and **Holtun**, on the road between Melchor de Mencos and Flores.

would have supported a wood-and-thatch temple. The pyramid is part of a group with astronomical significance: seen from it, the sun rises behind Templo E-I on the longest day of the year and behind Templo E-III on the shortest day. Also look for the somewhat deteriorated jaguar and serpent masks on this pyramid's sides.

About a 20-minute walk to the northwest of the runway are **Grupo B** and **Grupo A**. Some unfortunate early excavation work at Grupo A destroyed many of the temples, which are now in the process of being reconstructed.

If you are visiting Uaxactún from Tikal, there is no fee. But if you are going to Uaxactún without stopping to visit Tikal, you still have to pass through the Parque Nacional Tikal and will have to pay a Q10 fee at the park entrance. Tours to Uaxactún can be arranged in Flores or at the hotels in Tikal.

You can spend the night near Uaxactún at **Aldana's Lodge** (campsites per person Q20, r per person Q35) or **Campamento, Hotel & Restaurante El Chiclero** (☎ 7926-1095; campsites Q40, s/d Q112/136), both of which are very simple.

A bus supposedly leaves Santa Elena for Uaxactún (Q25) at 1pm daily, passing through Tikal about 3pm to 3:30pm, and starting back for Santa Elena from Uaxactún at 6am the following day. But its schedule is rubbery and it

can arrive in Tikal any time up to about 5pm and in Uaxactún up to about 6:30pm. During the rainy season (from May to October, sometimes extending into November), the road from Tikal to Uaxactún can become pretty muddy: locals say it is always passable but a 4WD vehicle might be needed.

FLORES & SANTA ELENA

Perched on an island in the middle of lovely Lago de Petén Itzá, Flores (population 2000) is a tranquil town of red-roofed houses and cool lake breezes. It's really a traveler's town: pastel-painted hotels line the lakeshore, providing easy access to the water and sunset views, and travel agencies, internet cafés and souvenir stands are in no short supply. But it's free of hassle and hustle, which makes it easy to stick around longer than anticipated.

Across the causeway is its sister city, Santa Elena (population 25,000), a rumpled place of dusty streets and honking horns, with a hot, chaotic market. The main street is strung with bus depots, which is the main reason travelers make their way here (there is no bus station in Flores).

History

Flores was founded on a *petén* (island) by a Maya people named the Itzáes, sometime

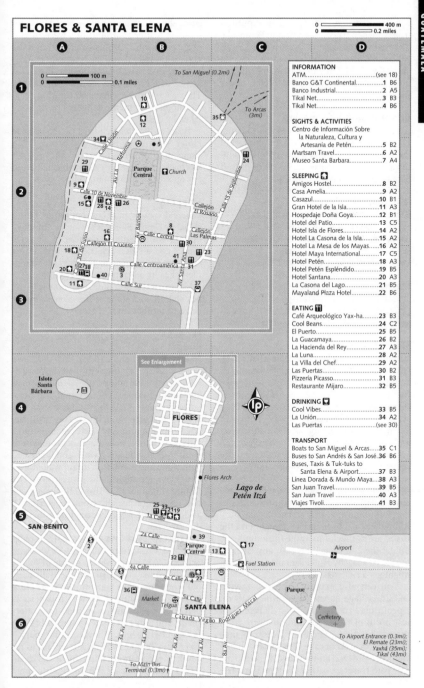

FLORES & SANTA ELENA

between 1200 and 1500, after their expulsion from Chichén Itzá on the Yucatán Peninsula. They named the place Tayasal. Hernán Cortés peaceably dropped in on King Canek of Tayasal in 1524. Only in March 1697 did the Spaniards finally bring Tayasal forcibly under their control.

Orientation & Information

A 1600ft causeway connects Flores to Santa Elena. The airport is located 1.2 miles east of the causeway in Santa Elena. Arriving long-distance buses drop passengers on or just off Santa Elena's main drag, 4a Calle.

ATM (Calle 30 de Junio, Flores; ☾ 24hr) The only ATM in Flores is next door to Hotel Petén.

Banco G&T Continental (4a Calle, Santa Elena; ☾ 9am-7pm Mon-Fri, to 1pm Sat) Has a Visa ATM.

Banco Industrial (4a Calle, Santa Elena; ☾ 9am-4pm Mon-Fri, 10am-2pm Sat) Has a Visa ATM.

Inguat Tourist Office (☎ 7926-0533; Santa Elena Airport; ☾ 7am-noon & 3-5pm)

Tikal Net Flores (Calle Centroamérica; per hr Q10; ☾ 8am-9pm); Santa Elena (4a Calle; per hr Q$10; ☾ 8am-8pm Mon-Sat, 9am-5pm Sun) Internet access, as well as domestic and international phone calls.

Sights & Activities

Visit the **Centro de Información Sobre la Naturaleza, Cultura y Artesanía de Petén** (Cincap; Petén Nature, Culture & Handicrafts Information Center; ☎ 7926-0718; Parque Central, Flores; ☾ 9am-noon & 2-9pm) for some interesting displays on archaeological sites, conservation areas and the local way of life in El Petén. It also sells handicrafts from the region and has an information desk, where you can ask about visits to some of the region's more remote natural and archaeological sites.

On a little island just west of Flores, the small **Museo Santa Bárbara** (admission Q12; ☾ 8am-noon & 2-5pm) shows a collection of ceramics that was found at nearby archaeological sites. Riding the boat over and hanging out on the island are as much fun as the museum itself. To get there, try haggling with any lakeside *lanchero* (boat) by Hotel Santana (where you might get a ride for Q100).

You can also explore the slow-moving lakeside village of **San Miguel**, which sits on a peninsula that juts into Lago de Petén Itzá just north of Flores. Catch a *lanchero* from the northeast side. There is a pleasant 1 mile walk up to a lookout called **El Mirador** with fine views of Flores and around Lago de Petén Itzá. The path traverses part of the **Tayazal archaeo-logical site**, which is a set of chiefly Classic-era mounds scattered around this western end of the peninsula. (Confusingly, this is not the same as Tayasal – the original name for Flores – as these overgrown ruins predate the Itzáes arrival in the area and founding of Flores.) The walk is best done in the morning, to avoid afternoon heat and the danger of being over-taken by dusk.

Boats at the *embarcaderos* (docks) beside Hotel Santana in Flores and Hotel Petén Espléndido in Santa Elena can be hired for **lake tours**. Prices are very negotiable. Expect to pay about Q200 for about an hour on board.

Sleeping

Where do you want to lay your head – Flores or Santa Elena? Flores is the more attractive option, with plenty of choices in all price ranges and a better selection of restaurants and services catering to travelers. But Santa Elena has its advantages, those being that it is less expensive and more convenient to the bus station, and some of the lakeside hotels boast beautiful views (of Flores).

FLORES
Budget

Amigos Hostel (☎ 5584-8795, 5716-7702; www .amigoshostel.com; Calle Central; hammocks Q20, dm Q25-35, d/tr/q with shared bathroom Q70/90/120, with private bathroom Q140/150/160) The original travelers' hostel in Flores is still the most convivial and colorful budget option. It looks tiny from the street, but the property stretches back into a jungly paradise, decked with a profusion of palm trees and hanging vines and furnished with wood and bamboo. Vibrant wall murals and Maya tapestries add some color. The restaurant (meals Q20 to Q40) gets posi-tive reviews (especially from vegetarians!), as does the nightly barbecue that is held in the garden.

Hospedaje Doña Goya (☎ 7867-5513; hospedaje donagoy@yahoo.com; Calle Unión; dm Q25, s/d with shared bathroom Q60/80, d with private bathroom Q100; 🖳) The linens may be worn and the walls bare, but when you make your way to the rooftop terrace, you'll understand why this place is perennially popular. A thatched roof offers shade, and hammocks are strategically hung for optimal lake breezes. If you outdid yourself ascending Temple IV, this is the place to re-cover. Friendly family management and cheap prices mean this place is hard to beat. There is a second Doña Goya up the street – be sure to inquire if this place is full.

Hotel La Mesa de los Mayas (☎ 7867-5268; mesamayas@hotmail.com; Av La Reforma; s/d Q126/200, with aircon Q200/240; 🗙) Despite the lack of lake view, this longstanding hotel is still an excellent option for comfort and hospitality. All rooms are equipped with cable TV and spacious, spotless bathrooms. On the upper floors, wide balconies with wrought-iron railing provide a perfect perch to watch the activity on the street below.

Midrange

Hotel Santana (☎ 7926-0262; www.santanapeten.com; Calle 30 de Junio; s/d/tr Q240/320/400; 🗙 🗩) It's hard to choose the most appealing feature of Hotel Santana. It could be the waterside restaurant, offering a prime vantage point to watch the sun drop behind Isla Santa Bárbara. Or, if you are a private person, you might prefer the view from your sweet little balcony (in which case, be sure to request a room at the back). Of course, those are features of many Flores hotels. But the Santana is the only hotel we know that has all that, plus an ice cream parlor in its lobby (the coconut ice cream is highly recommended).

ourpick Casazul (☎ 7867-5451, 7926-1138; www.hotelesdepeten.com; Calle Unión; s/d/tr Q296/350/456; 🗙) They're not kidding when they call this place the 'blue house' – there are shades of it everywhere, from the pleasing plantation-style balconies to the spacious, comfortable, unique rooms. The highlight of the whole place is the 3rd-floor terrace, where the blue wicker furniture enhances the beauty of the blue-green water and blue-gray sky on display. Despite the exuberance around a certain color, the decor is unquestionably tasteful and the staff incessantly helpful, so this place won't give you the blues.

Casa Amelia (☎ 5462-7269, 7867-5430; www.hotelcasamelia.com; Calle Unión; d/tr Q300/400; 🗙 🖳) Amelia has an eye for aesthetics, and her artistic touches are evident throughout the 12 guest rooms and lobby of this inviting inn. The walls are hung with interesting exotic art; rooms are furnished in rosewood and mahogany. The restaurant is definitely one of the perks of this place.

Hotel Petén (☎ 7926-0692; www.hotelesdepeten.com; Calle 30 de Junio; s/d/tr Q336/400/496; 🗙 🖳 🗩) Lakeview rooms are bright, airy and inviting, with colorful bedspreads and small balconies. But if

you're booked into a dark interior room, you'll probably want to spend your time hanging out on the outdoor deck and dining area. The swimming pool, oddly, winds its way through the lobby, which is rather exotic, but makes it awkward if you actually want to take a dip.

Hotel La Casona de la Isla (☎ 7926-0593; www.hotelesdepeten.com; Calle 30 de Junio; s/d/tr Q360/424/520; 🗙 🖳 🗩) With waterfalls flowing into the swimming pool and superb sunset views from the top-floor terrace, this is a romantic retreat. The lobby is painted in warm tones of orange and blue, with a polished wood ceiling. Rooms are stark in contrast, but the cane furniture and utter spotlessness make them appealing.

Hotel Isla de Flores (☎ 2476-8775, 7867-5173; www.hoteisladeflores.com; Av La Reforma; s/d Q388/544; 🗙) This upscale option calls itself 'an island in the jungle,' much like Flores itself, but there is nothing savage about the white wicker furniture and potted plants that provide the ambience here. All rooms are comfortable and fully equipped; the ones on the upper floors have balconies where you can catch a glimpse of the lake over the red rooftops.

Gran Hotel de la Isla (☎ 7926-0686; www.hoteldelaisla.com; Calle Sur; s/d Q542/620; 🅿 🗙 🖳 🗩 ♿) Everything about this place is big. The massive edifice is arguably out of place in cute little Flores. Some people say that size matters: you might appreciate the vast windows overlooking the lake and a pool where you can actually swim laps instead of sit and soak. Take a tour around the building to look at the murals: a huge painting of Tikal is in the lobby, while the hallways are lined with portraits of the Maya gods.

SANTA ELENA

Mayaland Plaza Hotel (☎ 7926-4976; mayalandplaza@yahoo.com; 4a Calle; s/d/tr Q215/275/375; 🅿 🗙 🖳 🗩) One reason to stay in Santa Elena is that you get more for your money; Mayaland is a terrific example of this. The spacious comfortable rooms are set colonial-style around a peaceful courtyard. All services are on hand, including a recommended restaurant and travel agent.

ourpick Hotel Maya International (☎ 2334-1818; www.villasdeguatemala.com; 1a Calle; s/d Q388/544; 🅿 🗙 🖳 🗩) A wooden boardwalk snakes through lush vegetation to bring you to the airy, thatched-roof reception area at the Hotel Maya International. This whole place exudes an atmosphere of rustic chic: the staff wearing flowing white cotton; the gourmet restaurant in a breezy *palapa*; the wide wood deck overlooking the lake. A neutral color scheme complements the gorgeous guest rooms, which are furnished in pine, bamboo and thatch.

La Casona del Lago (☎ 7952-8700; www.hoteles depeten.com; 1a Calle; s/d/tr Q616/760/904; P 🄿 🄺 🄻 🄻 🄻) The horseshoe shape here allows all the rooms to enjoy the vista of Lago de Petén Itzá and Isla de Flores. At the center of the horseshoe is the lovely terrace, complete with swimming pool and hot tub. Rooms are equally appealing, with sparkling white tiles and ocher-colored walls.

Hotel del Patio (☎ 7926-0104; www.caminoreal .com.gt; cnr 8a Av & 2a Calle; r Q780; P 🄺 🄻 🄻 🄻) A corporate hotel with a touch of colonial charm, this is a good choice for travelers who value comfort over authenticity. Shady corridors lined with terracotta floors wind around a stunning courtyard, centered on a gurgling fountain. The rooms do not quite live up to this level of luxury, but they are tasteful.

Hotel Petén Espléndido (☎ 7926-0880; www.peten esplendido.com; 1a Calle 5-01; s/d/tr/q Q784/880/976/1096; P 🄺 🄻 🄻 🄻) If you think that staff speaking perfect English and sporting colorful tropical shirts are signs of a good hotel, the Espléndido is for you. This is the only place in Flores or Santa Elena that might be called 'swanky'. Spacious rooms boast lake views from their private (if small) balconies, as well as conveniences such as cable TV and safes. The poolside bar is recommended for your day off from sightseeing.

Eating

Most restaurants keep long hours and prepare international foods. Local game animals that appear on menus include *tepescuintle* (agouti), *venado* (venison), armadillo, *pavo silvestre* (wild turkey) and *pescado blanco* (white fish).

FLORES

For atmospheric dining, grab a table at one of the shady shacks built over the water north of Calle 10 de Noviembre. By night, these candlelit, waterside spots are the most romantic in town.

Cool Beans (Calle 15 de Septiembre; coffee & snacks Q15-25; 🕑 6am-9pm Wed-Mon) If you are yearning for homemade bread, muffins and cinnamon rolls, as well as dark Guatemalan coffee, stake out a hammock at Cool Beans. The earthy place is tops for breakfast or for an afternoon pick-me-up.

Las Puertas (☎ 7867-5242; cnr Calle Central & Av Santa Ana; breakfast Q15-25, mains Q60-80; 🕑 8am-late Mon-Sat) Las Puertas is an arty bar and café with painted walls, great coffee and creative cooking. Vegetarians will appreciate the many pastas and salads, but there is also seafood, meat and excellent breakfast options.

ourpick La Villa del Chef (Calle Unión; mains Q25-50; 🕑 breakfast, lunch & dinner) This is a warm and festive place with an eclectic menu: dishes range from local seafood specials (white fish caught in local waters) to Arabic-influenced meats and salads. Homemade breads and pastries guarantee an enticing breakfast. The dining room is sweet, but head out back to the lakeside deck to catch a breeze.

Café Arqueológico Yax-ha (☎ 5830-2060; Calle 15 de Septiembre; mains Q30-40; 🕑 breakfast, lunch & dinner Wed-Mon) Wallpapered with photos and archaeological articles, this café-restaurant serves some standard dishes, but the menu also features pre-Hispanic items and Itza dishes – try spicy chicken with yuca.

La Guacamaya (☎ 7867-7255; Av la Reforma; mains Q40-60; 🕑 lunch & dinner) Local artworks adorn the walls, bright colors and wooden furniture enhance the atmosphere. This Maya-themed place verges on gourmet: if you are feeling fancy, try the baked haddock or filet mignon. Otherwise, burgers and burritos will sate your stomach without breaking your bank.

La Luna (☎ 7926-3346; cnr Calle 30 de Junio & Calle 10 de Noviembre; mains Q40-120; 🕑 lunch & dinner Mon-Sat) Potted palms, wood-framed mirrors and a tree growing in the middle of the dining room are only a few of the funky decor details at La Luna. The menu is equally varied, but undeniably delicious. Look for innovative takes on chicken, fish and beef, as well as plenty of pasta and vegetarian options.

La Hacienda del Rey (Calle 30 de Junio; mains Q60-80; 🕑 4am-9pm) This spacious two-story affair is open to the air and invitingly strung with lights. The specialty is meats, including Argentinean and American steaks. Less expensive fare, such as tacos and burritos, is also enticing.

It never hurts to know the best pizza place in town: **Pizzería Picasso** (Calle 15 de Septiembre; pizzas Q30-50; 🕑 lunch & dinner Mon-Sat).

SANTA ELENA

Restaurante Mijaro (☎ 7926-1615; 6a Av; meals Q15-40; 🕑 breakfast, lunch & dinner) Cool off at this friendly *comedor* on the main street up from the causeway. It has fans inside and in its little thatched-roof garden area, and serves long *limonadas* (a drink made from lime juice) and excellent food.

El Puerto (1a Calle 2-15; mains Q40-60; ✆ lunch & dinner) With its prime lakefront position, this open-air beer barn serves up a mean steak. It gets packed at weekends, when Cool Vibes (below) heats up next door.

Drinking

Flores doesn't exactly jive at night, but there are a few places to hang out. Start off with sunset drinks at the hotels and restaurants that have terraces, located on the west side of the island. Head for Hotel La Casona de la Isla (p275) or **La Unión** (Calle Unión) for a Cuba Libre. There is also a strip of bars along Calle Sur.

Other options include the following:

Cool Vibes (1a Calle 2-25; ✆ 7pm–1am) It *is* kind of fun to be out there lakeside, shaking your thang in the open air.

Las Puertas (☎ 7867-5242; cnr Calle Central & Av Santa Ana; ✆ closed Sun) Good for eating *and* drinking.

Getting There & Away
AIR

The international departure tax at Flores airport (FRS) is Q240.

At the time of research, all flights from Belize to Flores had been cancelled indefinitely. Airlines indicated that the issue should be 'resolved shortly.' The Belizean airlines that previously operated this route were **Tropic Air** (☎ 7926-0348; www.tropicair.com) and **Maya Island Air** (☎ 7926-3386; www.mayaairways.com).

Grupo Taca (www.taca.com) has flights to/from Guatemala City (Q878, three daily) and to/from Cancún (Q1974, four weekly).

BUS

For details on bus services from the Belize border, see p210. For information on buses from Belize City, see p105.

The main bus terminal is in Santa Elena, about a mile south of the causeway on 6a Av. Buses to El Remate stop at the bus terminal, as does **Línea Dorada & Mundo Maya** (☎ 5983-1163). Buses and minibuses go to San Andrés and San José from 5a Calle, just west of the market. Buses of **San Juan Travel** (☎ 7926-0041/2, 7926-2146; 2a Calle) leave from its office in Santa Elena.

Bus and minibus departures include the following:

Belize City (four to five hours, 220km) Línea Dorada & Mundo Maya (Q124, 6am); San Juan Travel (Q155, 5am

and 7:30am) Buses connect with boats to Caye Caulker and Ambergris Caye. It's cheaper but slower to take local buses from Flores to the border and go on from there.

Chetumal, Mexico (seven to eight hours, 350km) Línea Dorada & Mundo Maya (Q180, 6am); San Juan Travel (Q180, 5am).

El Remate (Q15, 40 minutes, 29km) Minibuses travel every hour from 6am to 1pm, but less frequently in the afternoon. Alternatively, buses and minibuses to/from Melchor de Mencos will drop you at the Puente Ixlú junction, 2km south of El Remate.

Guatemala City (eight to 10 hours, 500km) Línea Dorada & Mundo Maya has two daily deluxe buses (Q233, 10am and 9pm), as well as an overnight *económico* (Q155, 10pm). Other cheaper buses run frequently throughout the day and night.

Melchor de Mencos, Belize border (Q25, two hours, 100km) Minibuses depart every hour from 5am to 6pm. Alternatively, four buses depart daily at 5am, 11am, 2pm and 4pm.

Tikal See p269.

Getting Around

Flores, Santa Elena and the airport are connected by buses, taxis and *tuk-tuks* (open-air, three-wheeler vans). *Tuk-tuks* will take you anywhere within or between Flores and Santa Elena for about Q10. A taxi from the airport costs about Q25.

Rental-car companies are in the arrivals hall at the airport. Fill your fuel tank in Santa Elena; no fuel is available at Tikal.

AROUND FLORES & SANTA ELENA
Arcas

The **Asociación de Rescate y Conservación de Vida Silvestre** (Wildlife Rescue & Conservation Association; ☎ 5476-6001; www.arcasguatemala.com; Biblioteca Arcas, Barrio La Ermita, San Benito), a Guatemalan NGO, has a rescue and rehabilitation center on the mainland northeast of Flores. It is home to wildlife such as macaws, parrots, jaguars, monkeys, kinkajous and coatis that have been rescued from smugglers and the illegal pet trade. The rehabilitation center itself is closed to visitors, but a **Centro de Educación e Interpretación Ambiental** (CEIA; Environmental Education & Interpretation Center) has been set up, with a 1-mile interpretative trail featuring medicinal plants and animal tracks, an area for viewing animals that cannot be returned to the wild, a beach and a bird observation deck.

A boat leaves from the northeast side of Flores at 4pm daily for tours of the CEIA. It costs Q30 to Q60 per person, depending on how many people are in your party. It's best to call the Arcas office in San Benito beforehand to confirm that the boat is going. You can also reach Arcas by walking 5km (about 45 minutes) east from San Miguel (p274); tours for people who arrive independently between 9am and 3pm cost Q15 each. Arcas also offers opportunities for volunteers, who pay Q854 per week including room and board.

Parque Natural Ixpanpajul

If you are wild about the rainforest, plan to spend a day at the **Ixpanpajul Nature Park** (☎ 5619-0513, 7863-1317; www.ixpanpajul.com; Km468 de Río Dulce a Flores; adult/child Q200/120), a nature preserve and activity center. It's not a huge place, but it packs a lot of fun into its 450 hectares, and it takes place at all levels of the rainforest.

If you are partial to the canopy level, you will enjoy the Tarzan Tour, or **zip-line**, or you can saunter at your own pace along the **Skywalk**, a network of hanging bridges at the same level. You can explore the understory on **horseback** or by **mountain bike**, and arrange **birding tours** and **night safaris**. Simple cabanas and campsites are also available. Ixpanpajul is about 10km from Santa Elena on the road to Río Dulce; call ahead for a **shuttle bus service** (☎ 5897-6766; Q40) from Flores.

San Andrés

This small town on the northwest side of the lake is home to about 4000 residents of mixed descent, including Itzá Maya. It has an attractive lakefront beach and an overgrown central park, as well as two Spanish-language schools. The village is not one of the standard stops on the tourist trail, so it's a great place to test out the immersion method:

Eco-Escuela de Español (☎ 5940-1235; www .ecoescuelaespanol.org) This community-owned school emphasizes ecological and cultural issues and organizes environmentally related trips and volunteer opportunities. The cost is Q750 a week plus Q582 for room and board with a local family.

Nueva Juventud Spanish School (☎ 5711-0040; www.volunteerpeten.com; Restaurant La Troja, San An-

drés) Also environmentally oriented, this school is closely tied to a volunteer program that cares for the ecological park where the school is sited, and encourages volunteers to develop community projects. Classes cost Q1165 a week, with homestay included.

A few kilometers west of San Andrés, **Ni'tun Ecolodge** (☎ 5201-0759; www.nitun.com; s Q750-1165, d Q1320-1825; P 💻) is a beautiful property, set on 35 hectares of grounds where six species of hummingbird nest year-round. The four huts are rustic but spacious; from the little patio areas in front of the rooms you can just see the lake's tinkling reflection. The room rates include airport transfers and breakfast. Bernie and Lore, who built and operate the lodge, are adventurers and conservationists who also operate Monkey Eco Tours, which offers adventure trips with transport in Land Cruisers.

Bio-Itzá

In the Maya Itzá village of San José, what started as a sort of neighborhood association has developed into a force of ecological and cultural preservation. In 1991 a group of families got together to brainstorm ways to preserve their indigenous Itzá language. Almost 20 years later, the **Asociación Bio-Itzá** (☎ 7928-8056; www.ecobioitza.org) has established an ongoing program for community education, and has protected 3600 hectares of rainforest to boot.

Bio-Itzá funds its efforts through ecotourism. The association organizes trips to the **Bio-Itzá Reserve** (per person Q310), which includes a visit to a small unexcavated Maya site. Guides also conduct **tours** (without/with transportation Q116/194) of San José and of the communal medicinal plant garden.

The best bargain in San José is the Bio-Itzá **Spanish school** (7 days Q1165). Students receive four hours of instruction per day, plus meals and lodging with a local family.

Buses to San José (Q9, 45 minutes) leave from the market in Santa Elena, or make arrangements through **Viajes Tivoli** (Map p273; ☎ 5346-6673, 5604-4012; www.tivoli.com.gt) in Flores.

Directory

ACCOMMODATIONS

Accommodations in Belize range from tents to palm-roofed shacks to guesthouses to luxury seaside resorts and jungle lodges. Many of the upscale places maintain a casual, relaxed atmosphere and a rustic (albeit very elegant) style with wood-and-thatch cabanas.

Belize is more costly than other Central American destinations, so the budget bracket in this book goes up to BZ$90 for a double room. Within this range the best value is usually provided by small, often family-run guesthouses. Only the cheapest budget options have shared bathrooms or cold showers; a few places provide dorm accommodations.

Budget and lower midrange travelers will find the website **Toucan Trail** (www.toucantrail.com) useful. Put together by the Belize Tourism Board (BTB), this site details over 160 accommodations that have rooms for BZ$120 or less.

Midrange prices range from BZ$90 to BZ$240 for a double room. This spectrum embraces many hotels, more-comfortable guesthouses and most of the small-scale lodges and resorts. Many places in this range have their own restaurants and bars, and offer arrangements for activities, tours and other services. The range of accommodation and service is wide within this category.

Above BZ$240, top-end accommodations can be seriously sumptuous. (The fanciest rooms are upwards of BZ$500 for a double.) These are resorts, lodges and classy hotels with large, well-appointed rooms and plenty of other facilities, from restaurants and bars to private beaches, spas, pools, horse stables, dive shops and walking trails. Many have their own unique style and atmosphere created with the help of architecture, decor, location and layout.

Peak tourist seasons in Belize are the couple of weeks each side of Christmas and Easter, while the period between these two holidays also sees a steady stream of tourists. Most establishments have high- and low-season prices, often with extra-high prices for the peak weeks. Prices in this book are high-season prices and include the 9% hotel room tax, as well as any obligatory service charges (some top-end places automatically add on 10% for service).

Cabanas & Cabins

These two terms are pretty well interchangeable and can refer to any kind of free-standing, individual accommodation structure. You'll find cabins in every class of accommodations: they can be made of wood, concrete or brick and be roofed with palm

---

BOOK YOUR STAY ONLINE

For more accommodations reviews and recommendations by Lonely Planet authors, check out the online booking service at www.lonelyplanet.com/hotels. You'll find the true, insider lowdown on the best places to stay. Reviews are thorough and independent. Best of all, you can book online.

DIRECTORY

PRACTICALITIES

- The electrical current in Belize is 110V, 60Hz, with plugs of two flat prongs, the same as in the USA and Canada.
- Belize measures distance in miles.
- Gasoline is sold by the (US) gallon.
- Laundry is usually weighed and paid for by the pound.
- Occasionally a metric measurement might pop up – most likely kilometers on the odometers of some rental cars.
- Prerecorded videos normally use the NTSC image registration system, which is incompatible with PAL and Secam systems.

thatch, tin or tiles. They may be small, bare and cheap or super-luxurious and stylish, with Balinese screens, Japanese bathrooms and Maya wall-hangings. Locales vary from beachside, riverside, surrounded by jungle or on the grounds of a hotel along with other types of accommodations.

Camping

Belize does not have many dedicated campsites, but there are some (mainly budget) accommodations that provide camping space on their grounds, and just a few of those have gear for rent.

Guesthouses

Guesthouses are affordable, affable places to stay, with just a few rooms and usually plenty of personal attention from your hosts. Most are simply decorated but clean and comfortable. Rooms usually have a private bathroom with hot water. You'll find guesthouses in towns or on the coast or cayes. Some guesthouses (also called B&Bs) provide breakfast.

Located in the southern Toledo District, the Toledo Ecotourism Association (p255) runs an excellent village guesthouse program that enables travelers to stay in the area's Maya villages.

Hotels

A hotel is, more or less, any accommodation that doesn't give itself another name. A hotel might sit on a gorgeous beach and have lovely rooms, a great restaurant and its own pool, or it may be a more functional place in town. Hotels generally don't offer a vast range of tours and activities to their guests, but every generalization has its exceptions. Some smaller hotels call themselves inns.

Lodges & Resorts

In Belize the term 'lodge' usually means a comfortable hotel in a remote location, be it in the Cayo jungles or the offshore cayes. Most lodges focus on activities such as diving, fishing, horseback riding, or jungle or river adventures, aiming to provide comfortable accommodations and good meals to sustain their guests between outings. Many lodges have gorgeous island, beach or forest settings, and they tend to be on the expensive side due mainly to their high standards, wide range of amenities and (often) remote locations.

Resorts have a great deal in common with lodges – again they tend to be among the more expensive options and can be found both inland and by the sea. If there is any real distinction, it's that the emphasis in resorts tends to be marginally less on activities and slightly more on relaxation.

Rental Accommodations

In main tourist destinations such as San Pedro, Caye Caulker and Placencia, there are houses and apartments for rent for short stays or by the week or month. If you plan a long stay you'll certainly cut costs by renting your own place. Plan ahead: these places can get booked up.

BUSINESS HOURS

Shops in Belize typically open from 9am to 5pm Monday to Saturday, sometimes with a one-hour closure for lunch from noon to 1pm or from 1pm to 2pm. Businesses dealing with the public, such as travel agencies and airline offices, have similar hours but are likely to be closed on Saturday afternoon. Banks have varied hours but most are open from 8am to 2pm or 3pm Monday to Thursday, and till 4pm or 4:30pm on Friday. A few banks also open from 8am or 9am to noon on Saturday.

For typical restaurant hours, see p284. Opening hours of bars are very diverse. Some open from about noon to midnight, others just for a few evening hours, and others from early evening to early morning.

CHILDREN

Children are highly regarded in Belize and can often break down barriers and open doors to local hospitality. Most hotels, lodges and resorts are child-friendly. Some of the more expensive places allow children to stay free, or at a big discount, and also offer discounts on meals. Additionally, there are plenty of self-catering accommodations that can help to keep down the cost of a family holiday. These self-catering options are referred to as condos, suites, villas or casitas, all available for short-term rentals; the main distinction between them being whether they have one or two bedrooms.

Belize has some special ingredients for a family holiday. You won't have to think too hard about entertaining your kids. Most of the attractions in the country – sea life, exploring caves and ruins, watching for birds, wildlife and bugs – are as delightful for kids as they are for grown-ups, and most activities are set up to accommodate children. See p29 for a tailored itinerary for the younger set. See also Top Picks for Kids, p79, for some of our favorite kid-size adventures.

A few places even have holidays set up for families, for example, the **Oceanic Society** (www .oceanic-society.org) has a family education program to help families get to know atoll ecosystems, such as that of Turneffe Atoll (p156), while **International Zoological Expeditions** (www .ize2belize.com) does eco-adventure and study packages for families, combining South Water Caye (p226) and Blue Creek (p254).

You'll find plenty of traveling families all over the country, especially during North American school breaks. Most do the rounds of the wildlife sanctuaries and major ruins, spend a little time on the cayes or in Placencia, and visit a jungle lodge. Ambergris Caye and Caye Caulker are good spots for teenagers as there's a bit of town life to distract as well as the outdoor activities. English is spoken so there's no language barrier to mixing with local kids. Your children will probably experience a touch of culture shock, but they'll soon adapt to Belize's captivating ways.

Local bus journeys will amuse if they're not too long. Bus drivers in Belize often play their favorite music, and reggae and Latin rhythms can make even a tedious journey quite enjoyable. Teenagers whose minds are open to music will get into the variety of music they hear in Belize.

Food is no problem in Belize (see p88).

Traveling with toddlers and young children can be challenging; you need to be organized. Be cautious concerning insect bites, sunburn and, of course, water and sanitation. If you're staying in good accommodations and not moving around too much, you should have no major difficulties. For tried and tested general advice, check out Lonely Planet's *Travel with Children* by Cathy Lanigan and Maureen Wheeler.

CLIMATE CHARTS

Belize is typically hot and humid day and night year-round. Temperatures vary by only about 4°C between the coolest part of the year (December to March) and the hottest (May to September). The daily temperature range is around 10°C from the hottest part of the day to the coolest part of the night. In the uplands (Mountain Pine Ridge and the Maya Mountains) you can expect temperatures to fall by about 3°C for every 1000ft rise in altitude, making things noticeably more comfortable.

Belize has distinct wet and dry seasons. The wet season runs from mid-May to November

---

GREEN ACCOMMODATIONS

Ecotourism means big business in Belize, and sometimes it seems like every hotel, hostel, lodge, resort and guesthouse is a friend and protector of Mother Earth. But attaching 'eco' to the front of a name does not necessarily make it so. This prefix may mean that the enterprise is taking concrete steps to reduce its environmental impact, whether by practicing recycling, implementing alternative energy, participating in conservation programs or educating its guests. On the other hand, it may mean nothing more than a remote location or rustic accommodation. Most likely, the truth is somewhere in between.

Many lodges, resorts, hostels and guesthouses *are* implementing 'ecopolicies' (with varying degrees of effectiveness). These lodgings are included in the GreenDex (p316).

For a list of our favorite ecolodges, in the true sense of the word, see p68.

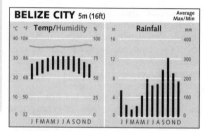

BELIZE CITY 5m (16ft)

in the south and from mid-June to November in the north. November to February is a transitional period, with the year's coolest temperatures and a limited amount of rain. The true dry season is February to April. There's quite a large difference in rainfall between the north of the country (around 1500mm or 60in a year) and the south (about 4000mm or 160in). In the north and center of the country there's a dip in rainfall in August, between peaks in July and September.

For advice on the best times to visit Belize, see p20.

Hurricanes

While hurricane season officially lasts from June to November, Belize has traditionally been struck by its most damaging hurricanes in September and November. The worst hurricanes of the 20th century happened in 1931 (before hurricanes were named) and 1961 (Hurricane Hattie). In 2001 Hurricane Iris, with winds over 150mph, brought severe damage to Placencia, Monkey River and the Maya villages around Toledo, continuing the year-ending-in-1 bogey. Hurricane Dean threatened in 2007, but it made landfall north of the Mexican border thus sparing Belize the worst damage. For more information on Belize's history of hurricanes, see p58.

If you are in Belize when a hurricane threatens, the best advice is to head inland. There is usually plenty of warning as hurricanes are well reported as they make their way across the Caribbean. If it is not possible to get inland, you should shelter in the sturdiest concrete building you can find, as far as possible from the coast and away from windows. Most villages and towns now have official hurricane shelters.

Hurricanes are ranked from category 1 (with winds of at least 74mph) to category 5 (winds exceeding 155mph). A category 3 hurricane will blow down wooden houses and take the tin roofs off concrete houses, and the rains and storm surges that hurricanes bring can do as much damage as the winds. The **Belize National Meteorological Service** (www.hydromet.gov.bz) provides copious information on weather.

CUSTOMS REGULATIONS

Duty-free allowances on entering Belize are 1L of wine or spirits and 200 cigarettes (or 250g of tobacco or 50 cigars). It is illegal to take firearms or ammunition into or out of Belize, and it is illegal to leave the country with fish (unless you have obtained a free export permit from the Fisheries Department), ancient Maya artifacts, turtle shells and unprocessed coral.

DANGERS & ANNOYANCES

Belizeans on the whole are remarkably easygoing and travelers experience little hassle, though extra care should be taken when in Belize City. Local men can be very direct about making advances to women, and ganja peddlers in tourist spots can be over-persistent, but these guys do take 'no' for an answer.

Nationwide emergency numbers for the police are ☎ 90 and ☎ 911.

Belizean police are not always cooperative if you try to report a crime. They may try to discourage you with, for example, stories of how long you'll have to stay in the country to see a matter resolved. If you want to report a crime, be persistent and if necessary seek help from locals (eg your hotel) or from your embassy or consulate.

Some specific areas of concern:

Theft

Occasional incidents of armed robbery and rape of tourists happen in regularly visited but isolated spots; mostly in the west, not far from the Guatemalan border. In 2006 there was a spate of armed robberies against tourist buses on the road to Caracol. The national park service has since implemented a convoy system, whereby all tourist vehicles meet up at Douglas D'Silva (Augustine) ranger station and make the journey on the remote road together, accompanied by armed guards. These precautionary measures seem to be doing the trick. See p214 for more information.

Armed robberies have also been reported against vehicles on the Hummingbird Hwy and on country roads in the west of Belize.

Such incidents are the exception rather than the rule. The vast majority of visitors to Belize have trouble-free trips and it's impossible to tell where the next incident will crop up. What you should do is keep your ear to the ground, talk to other travelers and locals, check bulletin boards such as **Belize Forums** (www.belizeforum .com) and look at the travel advisories issued by your own and other governments (see below). A few foreign embassies in Belize maintain websites with useful information (see right).

The other main trouble spot is Belize City, where some tourists fall victim to muggers and hustlers. You can greatly reduce this risk by a few straightforward steps (see p94).

To avoid becoming a victim of petty theft, take normal travelers' precautions:

- Don't make a big display of obvious signs of wealth (such as an expensive camera, computer equipment or jewelry).
- Don't flash thick wallets or wads of cash.
- Don't leave valuables lying around your room or in a car, especially in plain view.
- Keep an eye on your bags when you're traveling by bus.

Drugs & Alcohol

All drugs are illegal in Belize, including marijuana. Signs bearing the northern cayes' celebrated catchphrase 'No Shirt, No Shoes – No Problem' have recently had a new line added, to read 'No Shirt, No Shoes, No Drugs – No Problem.' Police are enforcing this policy with fines and jailings. Possessing a small amount of marijuana is unlikely to get you into trouble but it is illegal, and getting off your head on drugs or alcohol will make you more vulnerable.

Outdoors Activities

Belize's jungles can be dangerous places. As obvious as this may sound, it's easy to forget in one's enthusiasm for exploring the tropical environment. Apart from the possibility of getting lost, the country has its share of venomous snakes (see p60) and other possibly dangerous wildlife and some poisonous plants. Some parks, reserves and lodges have walking trails where you can wander off on your own (preferably with a map, water, hat, long sleeves and pants, bug spray and all of your common sense), but elsewhere you are better off going with a guide.

At sea, start snorkeling, diving, kayaking or sailing well within your ability limits and get acquainted with local conditions before taking on bigger challenges. See p75 for specific safety hints.

Belize has a system of licensed guides, whose licenses are granted by the Belize Tourism Board only after they have gained certain competencies in safety, first aid as well as other aspects of guiding. Undertake tours and activities only with a licensed guide.

EMBASSIES & CONSULATES

A few countries have embassies in Belize. Many others handle relations with Belize from their embassies in countries such as Mexico or Guatemala, but may have an honorary consul in Belize to whom travelers can turn as a first point of contact.

Australia Embassy (☎ 55-1101-2200; www.mexico .embassy.gov.au) The Australian Embassy in Mexico handles relations with Belize.

Canada Honorary consul (Map p93; ☎ 223-1060; cdn con.bze@btl.net; 80 Princess Margaret Dr, Belize City)

France Honorary consul (Map pp96-7; ☎ 223-2708; 109 New Rd, Belize City)

Germany Honorary consul (Map pp96-7; ☎ 222-4369; seni@cisco.com.bz; 57 Southern Foreshore, Belize City)

Guatemala Embassy (Map p93; ☎ 223-3150; emb belice@minex.gob.gt; 8 A St, Belize City; ⏰ 8:30am-12:30pm Mon-Fri)

GOVERNMENT TRAVEL ADVICE

Official information can make Belize sound more dangerous than it actually is. But for a range of useful travel advice you should consult the travel advisories provided by your home country's foreign affairs department:

Australian Department of Foreign Affairs (☎ 1300-139281; www.smartraveller.gov.au)
British Foreign Office (☎ 0845-850-2829; www.fco.gov.uk)
Canadian Department of Foreign Affairs (☎ 800-267-6788; www.voyage.gc.ca)
German Foreign Office (☎ 03018-17-2000; www.auswaertiges-amt.de)
New Zealand Ministry of Foreign Affairs & Trade (☎ 04-439-8000; www.safetravel.govt.nz)
US State Department (☎ 888-407-4747; www.travel.state.gov)

DIRECTORY

Honduras Embassy (☎ 224-5889; embahonbe@yahoo
.com; 114 Bella Vista, Belize City; ☉ 9am-noon & 1-4pm
Mon-Fri)
Mexico Embassy (Map p189; ☎ 822-0406; www.sre.gob
.mx/belice; Embassy Sq, Belmopan; 9am-12:30pm Mon-
Fri); Consulate (Map pp96-7; ☎ 223-0193; cnr Wilson St &
Newtown Barracks Rd, Belize City)
Netherlands Honorary consul (Map p93; ☎ 223-2953;
mchulseca@btl.net; cnr Baymen Av & Calle Al Mar, Belize City)
UK High commission (Map p189; ☎ 822-2146; www
.britishhighcommission.gov.uk; Embassy Sq, Belmopan;
☉ 8am-noon & 1-4pm Mon-Thu, 8am-2pm Fri)
USA Embassy (Map p189; ☎ 822-4011; usembassy.state
.gov/belize; Floral Park Rd, Belmopan; ☉ 8am-noon &
1-5pm Mon-Fri)

FESTIVALS & EVENTS
January
Krem New Year's Cycling Classic (January 1) Cycle
race from Corozal to Belize City.
Horse Races (January 1) Horse racing at Burrell Boom.

February, March & April
Fiesta de Carnaval (February or March; Sunday to
Tuesday before the beginning of Lent, 49 to 47 days before
Easter Sunday) Celebrated most in northern Belize.
Baron Bliss Day (March 9) Varied celebrations around
the country honoring one of the country's great benefac-
tors (see p98). Festivities include the four-day La Ruta
Maya Belize River Challenge (see p195).
Holy Week (March or April) Various services and proces-
sions are held in the week leading up to Easter Sunday.
Holy Saturday Cycling Classic (Easter Saturday) Cycle
race from Belize City to San Ignacio and back.

May
Labor Day (May 1) Parades.
Sovereign's Day (May 24) Celebrations include horse
races in Belize City and Orange Walk Town.

June & July
Belize International Film Festival (Date varies) See
p99.
Lobster Festivals (Date varies) Caye Caulker and San
Pedro celebrate the opening of lobster season with weekend
festivities featuring plenty of seafood. See p149 and p132.

August
Costa Maya Festival (Date varies) Celebration of Maya
coastal culture at San Pedro, Ambergris Caye, with participants from Belize and the Yucatán. See p131.

September
National Day (September 10) Ceremonies and celebrations around the country.

September Celebrations (September 11 to 20) Festivities in Belize City during the 10 days between National Day
and Independence Day (see p99).
Independence Day (September 21) Ceremonies,
parades and celebrations.

November
Garifuna Settlement Day (November 19) Celebration
of Garifuna culture, with lots of drumming, dancing and
drinking, especially in Dangriga (see p222), Hopkins and
Punta Gorda, where celebrations may last several days.

December
Christmas Day (December 25) Belizeans decorate their
houses weeks ahead with colorful lights and get together
to eat and drink with family and friends; in some places,
festivities continue until January 6, when Garifuna *jonkonu*
dancers (see p222) go from house to house.

FOOD
See the Food & Drink chapter (p83) for an
introduction to what and where to eat in
Belize. Eating sections for each town review
a selection of eateries. Budget restaurants
(often roadside eateries or fast food) include
venues where you can eat for less then BZ$10.
Midrange eateries are usually simple cafés and
restaurants where dishes cost between BZ$10
and BZ$30. Top-end eateries are rare, but
there are some upscale restaurants and lodges
(especially in San Pedro and Placencia) where
dishes cost upwards of BZ$30. Standard res-
taurant hours are 7am to 9:30am for breakfast,
11:30am to 2pm for lunch and 6pm to 8pm
for dinner. In Belize City and main tourist
destinations, many places don't close between
meals and may stay open later at night.

GAY & LESBIAN TRAVELERS
Homosexuality for men and women is legal
(since 1988) and the age of consent is 16.
There isn't much of a gay scene in Belize;
people aren't secretive or closeted, just low-
key. While it's an incredibly tolerant society,
and that Belizean attitude of 'live and let live'
extends to homosexuality, the underlying
Central American machismo and traditional
religious beliefs make Belize a place where
same-sex couples might want to be careful
about displaying affection in public.

San Pedro is the place that has the most
gay- and lesbian-friendly accommodations.
Purple Roofs (www.purpleroofs.com) has some listings in San Pedro and Cayo District. Also
try **Gay-Destinations** (www.gay-destinations.com) or

Gay.com (www.gay.com/travel), although at the time of research neither database included any Belize-specific listings.

Many gays and lesbians visit Belize from the USA, and businesses cater for them. **Maya Travel Services** (www.mayatravelservices.com) is a gay-friendly travel agent that organizes custom-designed itineraries. For dive trips to Belize (and other places), try **Undersea Expeditions** (www.underseax.com), the Gay & Lesbian Scuba Dive Travel Experts.

Further general information on gay and lesbian travel in Latin America can be obtained through the US and Australian offices of the **International Gay & Lesbian Travel Association** (www.iglta.org).

HOLIDAYS

Many of Belize's public holidays are moved to the Monday nearest the given date in order to make a long weekend. You'll find banks and most shops and businesses shut on these days. Belizeans travel most around Christmas, New Year's and Easter and it's worth booking ahead for transportation and accommodation at these times.

New Year's Day January 1
Baron Bliss Day March 9
Good Friday March or April
Holy Saturday March or April
Easter Monday March or April
Labor Day May 1
Sovereign's Day May 24
National Day September 10
Independence Day September 21
Day of the Americas October 12
Garifuna Settlement Day November 19
Christmas Day December 25
Boxing Day December 26

See opposite for information on how some of these holidays are celebrated.

INSURANCE

Cautious travelers may want to take out a travel insurance policy to cover theft, loss and medical problems. Some policies specifically exclude 'dangerous activities,' which can include scuba diving, motorcycling and even trekking. Check that the policy you are considering covers ambulances as well as emergency flights home. Worldwide travel insurance is available at www.lonelyplanet.com/bookings. You can buy, extend and claim online anytime – even if you're already on the road.

You may prefer a policy that pays doctors or hospitals directly rather than requiring you to pay on the spot and claim later. If you have to claim later, make sure you keep all documentation. For further information on medical insurance see the Health chapter (p299). For information on motor insurance see p293 and p297.

INTERNET ACCESS

Belize has plenty of internet cafés with typical rates of around BZ$6 per hour, and high-speed access is widely available. Some internet cafés can burn CDs with your digital photos, usually for around BZ$5. If you have a USB cable for connecting your camera to a computer, you can't lose by taking it along. Many hotels and lodges also provide computers where their guests can access the internet.

For those traveling with a laptop, a growing number of accommodations have wireless access in the rooms or in common areas. This access is fairly reliable, but is easily overburdened if there are several people working simultaneously. For more information on traveling with a portable computer, see www.teleadapt.com. The listings in this book indicate internet or wireless access with the icon 💻 .

LANGUAGE

Travelers in Belize usually don't need to use anything other than English to get by, but the topic of language is an interesting one in Belize. In addition to English, there are three different Mayan languages (Yucatec, Mopan and Kekchi), Garifuna (which has roots in African and Caribbean languages), and Creole/Kriol. The last is the subject of a campaign to get it recognized as a language in its own right, rather than just an English dialect. For more information, see p42, and look for the *Bileez Kriol Glassary an Spellin Gide* in bookstores in Belize, or visit www.kriol.org.bz.

With the influx of immigrants from other Latin American countries, Spanish is also widely spoken in Belize. If you cross the border into Guatemala, Spanish is spoken almost exclusively (with the exception of tour operators and upscale hotels). See the boxed text, p262, for some useful words and phrases.

LEGAL MATTERS

Drug possession and use is officially illegal and, if caught, offenders will generally be

---

PREVENTING CHILD SEX TOURISM IN BELIZE

Tragically, the exploitation of local children by tourists is becoming more prevalent throughout Latin America, including Belize. Various socioeconomic factors make children susceptible to sexual exploitation, and some tourists choose to take advantage of their vulnerable position. Sexual exploitation has serious, lifelong effects on children. It is a crime and a violation of human rights.

Belize has laws against sexual exploitation of children. Many countries have enacted extraterritorial legislation that allows travelers to be charged as though the exploitation happened in their home country.

Responsible travelers can help stop child sex tourism by reporting it. The **CyberTipline** (www .cybertipline.com) is a website where sexual exploitation of children can be reported. You can also report the incident to local authorities and, if you know the nationality of the perpetrator, to their embassy.

Travelers interested in learning more about how to fight against sexual exploitation of children can find information through **ECPAT** International (End Child Prostitution and Trafficking; www.ecpat.org); US (☎ in New York 718-935-9192; www.ecpatusa.org). The Canadian affiliate of ECPAT is **Beyond Borders** (www.beyondborders.org).

---

arrested and prosecuted. In practice, possession of small amounts of marijuana for purely personal use is unlikely to lead to prosecution. You are likely to be arrested and prosecuted for possession of larger amounts of marijuana or possession or use of any other illicit drugs.

Persons found having sex with a minor will be prosecuted – the age of consent for both sexes is 16. For detailed information on the Belize legal code, check out the **Belize Legal Information Network** (www.belizelaw.org).

You are not required to carry ID in Belize but it's advisable to do so. If arrested you have the right to make a phone call. The police force does not have a reputation for corruption as in many countries in Central America, and it is highly unlikely that you will be asked for a bribe. A special **tourist police force** (☎ 227-6082) patrols tourist areas, including central Belize City, San Pedro, Caye Caulker and Placencia. The tourist police wear a special badge on their left shoulder.

MAPS

The maps in this book will enable you to find your way to all of the listed destinations, but if you'd like a larger-scale, more detailed travel map, you cannot beat the 1:350,000 *Belize* map, published by International Travel Maps of Vancouver. It is widely sold in Belize.

You can buy high-class 1:50,000 topographic sheets for BZ$40 each at the Ministry of Natural Resources in Belmopan (see p189). These maps cover the country, including the cayes, in 70 different sheets. Most of them were last updated in the 1990s.

Drivers will find *Emory King's Driver's Guide to Beautiful Belize* useful. Sold in bookstores and gift shops in Belize City, it's a compilation of route diagrams and user-friendly tips about turnoffs you might miss and speed bumps you might hit. A new edition is published annually.

MONEY

Belize's currency, the Belizean dollar (BZ$), has been fixed for many years at US$0.50, although talk of a devaluation is never far beneath the surface. For exchange rates see the Quick Reference page on the inside front cover. The currency bears the portrait of Queen Elizabeth II and the dollar is divided into 100 cents. Coins come in denominations of one, five, 10, 25 and 50 cents and one dollar; bills come in denominations of two, five, 10, 20, 50 and 100 dollars. The 25-cent coin is sometimes called a shilling, and you may hear the 100-dollar bill referred to as a 'bluenote.'

Prices are usually quoted in Belizean dollars, though you will sometimes see prices quoted in US dollars, especially at tour companies and upscale resorts. If in any doubt, ask which type of dollars people are talking about. Many businesses are happy to accept cash payments in US dollars. US dollars are also widely accepted across the border in Guatemala. But the official unit of currency is the Guatemalan Quetzal (Q). For more information, see p260.

For information about costs in Belize, see p21.

ATMs

Atlantic Bank, Belize Bank, Scotia Bank and a few other banks' ATMs are on international networks, accepting Visa, MasterCard, Plus and Cirrus cards. There are internationally compatible ATMs in most major towns, including Belize City, Belmopan, Caye Caulker, Corozal Town, Dangriga, Orange Walk Town, Punta Gorda, San Ignacio and San Pedro. ATMs give only Belizean dollars. They are convenient but the exchange rate you get from ATMs is usually a cent or two under the BZ$2 = US$1 rate used for cash or traveler's-check exchanges. Belize Bank charges a fee for each use of an ATM (BZ$2) and enforces a BZ$500 per day withdrawal limit. Atlantic Bank and Scotia Bank do not charge fees and Scotia Bank has a higher withdrawal limit.

Cash

A few hundred US dollars in cash are handy to have. You can use them to pay for things in most places, and they are also easy to exchange informally, or in most banks, at the rate of BZ$2 = US$1. Canadian dollars, pounds sterling and euros can also be exchanged at many banks but are harder to use as cash than US dollars.

Credit Cards

Visa and MasterCard are accepted by airlines, car-rental companies and at the larger hotels, restaurants and shops; Amex is often accepted at top-end places and is becoming more common among the smaller establishments. Some places levy a surcharge of up to 5% if you pay by card.

You can also use a credit card to obtain an over-the-counter cash advance from most of the banks in Belize. The exchange rate is likely to be the same as the rate for ATM withdrawals, and again you face the commissions and handling charges imposed by your card issuer.

Taxes

Hotel room tax is 9%. Rates given in this guide also include the room tax. Restaurant meals are subject to an 8% sales tax. Prices given in this guide include all taxes to the best of our knowledge.

TOP PICKS – SOUVENIRS

- Marie Sharp's Hot Sauce (p222)
- Primitive-style painting by Debbie Cooper (p155)
- Garifuna drum (p224)
- Striped hardwood cutting board (p190)
- Bamboo furniture (p204)
- Jade jewelry (p140)

Tipping

Tipping is not obligatory but never goes amiss, especially if guides, drivers or waitstaff have provided you with genuinely good service. Rounding up the bill by somewhere between 5% and 10% is usually a suitable tip. Some hotels and restaurants add an obligatory service charge to your bill (usually 10%), in which case you definitely don't need to tip.

Traveler's Checks

You can exchange traveler's checks at most banks, especially if you carry a well-known brand such as Visa or Amex and they are denominated in US dollars. They usually attract the same advantageous exchange rate as cash, though there may be per-check fees to pay.

POST

There are post offices in most towns. By airmail to Canada or the USA, a postcard costs BZ$0.40, a letter BZ$0.70. To Europe it's BZ$0.50 for a postcard and BZ$1 for a letter.

It is possible to receive incoming mail through the post offices of the major towns mentioned in this guide. Mail should be addressed to: your name, c/o General Delivery, town name, district name, Belize, Central America. It will be held for up to two months and must be claimed with a photo ID.

The courier services **DHL Express** (☎ 223-4350) and **Fedex Express** (☎ 224-5221) both have offices in Belize City.

SHOPPING

Belizeans do not trade in handicrafts at the level that Mexicans and Guatemalans do; instead, most gift shops in the country do a booming business in T-shirts, imported sarongs and beach gear, and Belikin beer paraphernalia. Popular regional handicrafts include folding mahogany deck chairs, *zericote* (ironwood) carvings of various sizes, baskets woven by Maya women in southern Belize, carved rosewood bowls, and striped wooden breadboards. These make good souvenirs, but they tend to be expensive when compared with similar items purchased in Guatemala or Mexico. For good handicraft shops see p103, p140, and p190. Drummers should head south to Dangriga if they want to pick up a Garifuna drum (see p117).

Some Belizean-made consumables are popular as souvenirs and are also useful when you're traveling. Among these are Rainforest Remedies, a line of all-natural health products – digestive aids, insect repellents, salves etc – from the **Ix Chel Centre** (www.arvigomassage.com/rainforest_remedies) near San Ignacio (see the boxed text, p209); Marie Sharp's hot sauces (see the boxed text, p84); and Rasta Pasta Rainforest Café spice packets (p154) for creating traditional Belizean dishes at home.

Books by Belizeans and books about Belize can be bought in many bookstores in the country and from **Cubola Productions** (www.cubola.com). **Belizean Perfumes** (☎ 226-0350; belizeperfumes@hotmail.com) creates products that are concocted from natural essences at the Lazy Iguana (p153) on Caye Caulker.

Belize City has a wide range of imported goods. The central shopping district can cater for most of your needs and you'll even find some local art there. Ambergris Caye has some good boutiques with exotic clothing and furnishings imported from Asia, as well as a number of art galleries with paintings by local artists. Local products on Ambergris Caye that are worth buying include handmade jewelry and clothing, fine coconut and wooden serving spoons, notebooks made from handcrafted paper, and brightly painted fish made from sheaths of coconut fronds. Caye Caulker has its share of tourist shops and a few small but excellent craft shops and art galleries (see p155).

TELEPHONE

Belize has no regional, area or city codes. Every number has seven digits and you just dial those seven digits from anywhere in the country. Belize's country code is ☎ 501. When calling Belize from other countries, follow the country code with the full seven-digit local number. The international access code for calling other countries from Belize is ☎ 00.

Public phones are fairly plentiful around the country – there are around 500 in all – and they're operated with cards that you can buy wherever you see the green signs announcing 'BTL's PrePaid Cards Sold Here.' (BTL is Belize Telecommunications Ltd.) The cards come in a range of denominations, from BZ$2 to BZ$50. You scratch the back of the card to reveal its PIN number, then to make a call you dial an access number given on the back of the card. Automated messages will ask you to key in your pin number, tell you how much credit is left on the card, then ask you to dial the number you want, followed by the pound (hash) key. Local calls are usually a flat rate of BZ$0.25. Long-distance calls within Belize can cost between BZ$0.10 and BZ$1 per minute.

Useful numbers (which can all be dialed without phone cards from public phones):

Ambulance ☎ 90
Directory assistance ☎ 113
Fire ☎ 90
Operator assistance ☎ 115
Police ☎ 90, 911

Cell Phones

You can rent cell phones from BTL only at the Philip Goldson International Airport in Belize City. The cost is BZ$12 per day, with a deposit of BZ$300 (credit cards accepted), and you can buy prepaid DigiCell phone cards (available where you see green signs announcing 'BTL's PrePaid Cards Sold Here,' in denominations from BZ$10 to BZ$50) to pay for your calls.

International cell phones can be used in Belize if they are GSM 1900 and unlocked. You can buy a Sim pack for US$25 from DigiCell distributors around the country.

International roaming is provided by T Mobil, Cingular and MexTel, but coverage is patchy – check with your service provider back home about coverage in Belize.

TIME

North American Central Standard Time (GMT/UTC minus six hours) is the basis of time in Belize, as in Guatemala and southern Mexico. Belize and Guatemala do not observe daylight saving, so there is never any time difference between them, but Mexico does observe daylight saving from the first Sunday in April to the last Sunday in October, so Belize is one hour behind Mexico during that period.

When it's noon in Belize, it's 1pm in New York, 6pm in London, 10am in San Francisco and 4am the next day in Sydney (add one hour to those times during daylight saving periods in those cities).

For world time zones, see pp318-9.

TOURIST INFORMATION

The **Belize Tourism Board** (www.travelbelize.org) has tourist information offices in Belize City, Corozal Town and Punta Gorda and there are good local tourist information offices in San Pedro and Placencia.

The **Belize Tourism Industry Association** (www.btia.org) is an independent association of tourism businesses, with an office in Belize City (see p94) that can provide information about what is offered by its many members.

TRAVELERS WITH DISABILITIES

Belize lacks accessibility regulations and many buildings are on stilts or have uneven wooden steps. You won't see many ramps for wheelchair access. More difficulties for wheelchair users come from the lack of footpaths, as well as plentiful rough and sandy ground. With assistance, bus travel is feasible, but small planes and water taxis might be a problem.

Visitors with limited mobility do come to Belize. Accommodations suitable for wheelchair users include the Radisson Fort George Hotel (p100) in Belize City, Corona del Mar (p134) on Ambergris Caye; Mara's Place (p150) and Blue Wave (p150) on Caye Caulker; Orchid Palm Inn (p165) in Orange Walk; Hok'ol K'in Guest House (p175) in Corozal; El-Rey Inn (p189) and the Bull Frog Inn (p190) in Belmopan; Mama Noots Jungle Resort (p229) near the Mayflower Bocawina National Park; Jungle Huts Resort (p223) in Dangriga; and Turtle Inn (p242) in Placencia.

There are a number of useful organizations and websites for disabled travelers, though there's little information that is specific to Belize.

Access-Able Travel Source (www.access-able.com) Has good general information.

Allgohere Airline Directory (www.everybody.co.uk/air index.htm) This site lists, by airline, services available to disabled passengers.

Global Access Disabled Travel Network (www.globalaccessnews.com) Good website with interesting general travel information.

Mobility International (www.miusa.org) US-based website that advises disabled travelers on mobility issues; you can organize a mentor and someone to help you plan your travels.

Royal Association for Disability and Rehabilitation (Radar; www.radar.org.uk) A network of disability organizations and disabled people that lobbies for policy changes.

VISAS

Information on visa requirements is available from Belizean embassies and consulates and the **Belize Tourism Board** (www.travelbelize.org). At the time of writing, visas were not required for citizens of EU or Caricom (Caribbean Community) countries, Australia, Canada, Hong Kong, Mexico, New Zealand, Norway, the USA or Venezuela. A visitor's permit valid for 30 days will be stamped in your passport when you enter the country. This can be extended by further periods of one month (up to a maximum of six months) by applying at an immigration office (there's at least one in each of Belize's six districts). The fee for each extension is BZ$25.

Visas for most other nationalities cost BZ$100 from a Belizean embassy or consulate and are valid for a 90-day stay.

For further information you can contact the **Immigration & Nationality Department** (☎ 822-2423, fax 822-2662), in Belmopan.

VOLUNTEERING

There are a lot of opportunities for volunteer work in Belize, especially on environmental projects. In some cases, you may have to pay to participate (costs vary).

Asociación de Rescate y Conservación de Vida Silvestre (p277) Located in El Petén, Guatemala, ARCAS hosts volunteers to work with rescued and orphaned animals.

Belize Audubon Society (www.belizeaudubon.org) Volunteers assist in the main office or in education and field programs. Volunteer birders are always required for the Christmas bird count.

Cornerstone Foundation (www.peacecorner.org) This NGO based in San Ignacio hosts volunteers to help with AIDS education, community development and other programs. Volunteers commit to a minimum of three weeks and pay a fee to cover food and housing.

Earthwatch (www.earthwatch.org) Paying volunteers are teamed with professional scientific researchers. Most projects are 10 to 14 days.

Eco-Escuela de Español (p278) A Spanish-language school in El Petén, Guatemala, that also organizes educational programs and environmentally related volunteer opportunities.

Elderhostel (www.elderhostel.org) One-week research assistance programs for seniors with Oceanic Society expeditions.

Global Vision International (www.gvi.co.uk) Volunteer placements of over two months in conservation, research and education projects.

Help for Progress (www.helpforprogress.interconnec tion.org) A Belizean NGO working with local community development organizations in fields such as education, gender issues, citizen participation and environment.

International Service Community (www.swarth more.edu/go/isc) Catering to senior travelers, ISC takes volunteers for two weeks to two months, giving them the chance to work at local hospitals, schools, senior centers and other community NGOs.

International Volunteer Programs Association (www.volunteerinternational.org) A source for many volunteer positions such as working in clinics, building schools and helping conserve manatees.

Monkey Bay Wildlife Sanctuary (p114) Monkey Bay's programs provide opportunities in conservation and community service. It also has many links to other conservation organizations in Belize.

Nueva Juventud Spanish School (p278) A Spanish-language school in El Petén, Guatemala that organizes volunteer opportunities in the national parks.

Oceanic Society (p157) Paying participants in the society's expeditions assist scientists in marine research projects at the society's field station on Blackbird Caye and elsewhere.

One World Volunteer (www.volunteertravel.com) This organization places volunteers in wildlife rescue/rehabilitation centers, monkey sanctuaries and ecotourism projects.

Plenty International (www.plenty.org) Opportunities for working with grassroots organizations (such as handicraft cooperatives) and schools, mostly in Toledo District.

Programme for Belize (p169) Volunteer opportunities are sometimes available related to conservation or archaeology.

ProWorld Service Corps (www.proworldsc.org) Like a privately run Peace Corps, ProWorld organizes small-scale, sustainable projects in fields such as health care, education, conservation, technology and construction.

Spanish Creek Rainforest Reserve (p110) For BZ$50 per day, interns/volunteers stay at this organic farm and study medicinal rainforest plants.

Teachers for a Better Belize (www.tfabb.com) US-based organization that sends volunteers to schools in Toledo District to help train local teachers.

Trekforce Worldwide (www.trekforce.org.uk) Offers one- to five-month programs that combine work such as

trail-cutting, visitor-center building in protected areas, rural teaching or archaeological work, with optional jungle treks, diving and Spanish courses.

Volunteer Abroad (www.volunteerabroad.com) Offers scores of volunteer, study-abroad and internship opportunities (listed on the website by country), plus many useful resources. Paid teaching jobs and opportunities for high-school students are also available.

WOMEN TRAVELERS

Women can have a great time in Belize, even traveling solo. You do need to keep your wits about you and be vigilant, as does any solo traveler.

Keep a clear head. Excessive alcohol will make you vulnerable. For support and company, head for places where you're likely to meet people, such as guesthouses that serve breakfast, backpacker lodgings or popular midrange or top-end hotels. Sign up for excursions and if you're using internet cafés you're likely to run into other travelers. Being in an English-speaking country, unlike elsewhere in Central America, can be a confidence booster.

If you don't want attention, try to wear long skirts or trousers and modest tops when you're using public transportation and when on solo explorations. You'll notice other savvy women travelers dressed like this. Some of them will be volunteers or other workers, and they are founts of information about the country and how to safely move about it.

In Belize, especially on the cayes, many men seem to think that unescorted women are on the lookout for a man, and some men in Belize, especially in the heavily touristed areas, can be quite forward with their advances or even aggressive with their comments about your appearance.

In most cases advances are made lightheartedly, although it can be disconcerting if you're from a culture where men are less overt in their attentions. Be direct, say no, then ignore them – they're likely to go away. A bicycle can be an asset in this scenario: you can just scoot. If you're feeling particularly hassled, seek out company. Avoid situations in which you might find yourself alone with unknown men at remote archaeological sites, on empty city streets, or on secluded stretches of beach.

Transportation

GETTING THERE & AWAY

Travelers can get to Belize by land, sea or air. Overland, travelers might enter Belize from Guatemala or Mexico. Boats also bring travelers from Honduras and Guatemala. Air carriers service Belize from the United States and El Salvador. Flights and tours can be booked online at www.lonelyplanet.com/travel_services.

ENTERING THE COUNTRY

Entering Belize is a simple, straightforward process. You must present a passport that will be valid until you leave the country. It's advisable to have at least six months of validity remaining. Officially, visitors are also required to be in possession of an onward or return ticket from Belize and funds worth BZ$120 a day for their stay in the country, but it's rare for tourists to be required to show these.

Tourists are generally given a 30-day stay, extendable once you're in Belize. See p289 for information on visa requirements and extensions.

AIR
Airports & Airlines

Philip Goldson International Airport (BZE; ☎ 225-2014), at Ladyville, 11 miles northwest of Belize City center, handles all international flights. With Belize's short internal flying distances it's often possible to make a same-day connection at Belize City to or from other airports in the country.

Four US airlines, as well as the Central American Grupo TACA, fly direct from the USA; Grupo TACA also flies from San Salvador (El Salvador), with connections from other Central American cities.

AIRLINES FLYING TO & FROM BELIZE

American Airlines (code AA; ☎ 223-2522; www .aa.com) Hubs Dallas Fort Worth & Miami.

Continental Airlines (code CO; ☎ 227-8309; www .continental.com) Hub Houston.

Delta Air Lines (code DL; (☎ 225-3429; www.delta .com) Hub Atlanta.

Grupo TACA (code TA; ☎ 227-7363/4, 225-2163; www .taca.com) Hub San Salvador.

Maya Island Air (code MW; ☎ 223-1140, 225-2219; www.mayaairways.com) Hub Belize City. Although Maya Island Air has long offered twice-daily flights between Belize City and Flores, Guatemala, the airline was forced to suspend its flights to Flores in November 2007, when Guatemala began enforcing new safety regulations. Flights are expected to resume when the Belizean airline is able to meet the new civil aviation standards.

Transportes Aeros Guatemaltecos (code TAG; ☎ 502-2360 3038; www.tag.com.gt) Hub Guatemala City. Regular flights between Guatemala and Flores only.

Tropic Air (code PM; ☎ 226-2012; www.tropicair.com) Hub Belize City. Normally operates twice-daily flights between Belize City and Flores, Guatemala. Like Maya Air, Tropic Air was forced to suspend these flights until it can upgrade its technical requirements.

US Airways (code US; ☎ 225-3589; www.usairways .com) Hub Charlotte, North Carolina.

THINGS CHANGE...

The information in this chapter is particularly vulnerable to change. Check directly with the airline or a travel agent to make sure you understand how a fare (and ticket you buy) works and be aware of the security requirements for international travel. Shop carefully. The details given in this chapter should be regarded as pointers and are not a substitute for your own careful, up-to-date research.

AIR DEPARTURE TAX

Non-Belizeans must pay fees that total US$35 (BZ$70), in cash (US dollars only) or charge, when flying out of Belize City on international flights. Of this, US$3.75 is the PACT (Protected Areas Conservation Trust) fee, which helps to fund Belize's network of protected natural areas. Also included in this total is a US$15 service fee, a US$15 airport development fee and a US$1.25 security fee. Sometimes a portion of the tax is included in the price of the ticket.

Tickets

Airline websites and ticket-booking sites on the internet are the obvious places to start looking for a flight to Belize (see p294), but in the search for a good deal it can also be worth checking out a couple of travel agencies and flight adverts in the press. If you travel outside Belize's main tourist season of December to April, you may find cheaper fares. If you're planning to transfer onto a domestic flight on arrival in Belize City, you may well get a better deal by booking the domestic flight separately.

Australia & New Zealand

The cheapest way to get from Australia or New Zealand to Belize City is usually via the USA (normally Los Angeles). High-season roundtrip fares from Sydney start at around A$3200.

Central America, South America & Cuba

Grupo TACA can fly you from all Central American capitals to Belize City via San Salvador, El Salvador; plus San Pedro Sula, La Ceiba and Roatán in Honduras; Havana, Cuba; and several South American cities. Sample high-season one-way/roundtrip fares are about US$280/350 from Guatemala City, US$300/350 from San Salvador, US$275/295 from San Pedro Sula and US$340/400 from San José, Costa Rica.

Both Grupo TACA and the Guatemalan carrier TAG fly between Guatemala City and Flores for about US$200.

Continental Europe

From Europe, you need to fly to Belize via the USA (high-season roundtrip fares start at €800 to €900 but you may have to pay con-

siderably more), unless you want to fly to Cancún, Mexico, and then travel overland to Belize. Roundtrip fares to Cancún start at €600 to €700, but you're more likely to pay €800 to €900.

Mexico

There are currently no flights to Belize from anywhere in Mexico, but the domestic airport at Chetumal is just 8 miles from the Mexico–Belize border. You can fly from Mexico to Belize City via Guatemala City or San Salvador on a combination of Grupo TACA and Mexican airlines flights. Grupo TACA also flies from Cancún to Flores, Guatemala.

UK & Ireland

To get to Belize from the UK and Ireland, you have to fly via the USA – high-season roundtrip fares from London start at around UK£500 or UK£600. If you want to fly to Cancún, Mexico, and make your way to Belize overland, you can usually get a London–Cancún roundtrip ticket for between UK£400 and UK£500.

USA & Canada

Unless you're starting from a city with direct flights to Belize City (such as Atlanta, Charlotte, Dallas, Houston and Miami), you'll be making a connection in one of those cities. Examples of typical high-season roundtrip fares to Belize City include US$450 to US$600 from Houston, US$600 to US$800 from New York and US$700 to US$900 from Los Angeles. From Canada, sample fares are C$950 from Vancouver and C$700 from Toronto.

LAND
Border Crossings

There are two official crossing points on the Mexico–Belize border. The more frequently used is at Subteniente López–Santa Elena, 9 miles from Corozal Town in Belize and 7 miles from Chetumal in Mexico. The all-paved Northern Hwy runs from the border to Belize City. The other crossing is at La Unión–Blue Creek, 34 miles southwest of Orange Walk Town. If you happened to be driving in from Mexico straight to La Milpa Field Station (p171) or Chan Chich Lodge (p171), you might consider using this crossing, as the road is paved all the way from the border on the Mexican side, whereas you face

---

LAND DEPARTURE TAX

When departing Belize by land, non-Belizeans are required to pay fees that total BZ$37.50 (US$18.75), in cash (Belizean or US dollars). Of this, BZ$7.50 is the PACT (Protected Areas Conservation Trust) fee, which helps to fund Belize's network of protected natural areas.

---

28 unpaved miles on the road to Orange Walk from Blue Creek.

The only land crossing between Belize and Guatemala is a mile west of the Belizean town of Benque Viejo del Carmen at the end of the all-paved Western Hwy from Belize City. The town of Melchor de Mencos is on the Guatemalan side of the crossing. The border is 44 miles from the Puente Ixlú junction (also called El Cruce) in Guatemala, where roads head north for Tikal (22 miles) and southwest to Flores (18 miles). The first 15 to 19 miles west from the border are unpaved.

Bus

Bus passengers crossing Belize's land borders have to disembark and carry their own luggage through immigration and customs. See p179 for further information on the border crossing to Mexico, and p210 for further information on the border crossing to Guatemala.

In Chetumal, Mexico, buses bound for Corozal Town (BZ$2 to BZ$4, one hour), Orange Walk Town (BZ$6 to BZ$8, two hours) and Belize City (BZ$10 to BZ$14, four hours) leave the north side of Nuevo Mercado, about 0.75 miles north of the city center, once or twice an hour from about 4:30am to 6pm. Both Línea Dorada and San Juan Travel run buses from Chetumal via Corozal to Flores, Guatemala (BZ$40 to BZ$50, eight or nine hours).

For details on long-distance buses from Belize City to Flores, see p105. You can also use local services to and from both sides of the border (from San Ignacio, see p201; from Flores, see p277). There are plenty of buses and minibuses that link Flores with Guatemala City and other destinations in Guatemala.

Car & Motorcycle

To bring a vehicle into Belize, you need to obtain a one-month importation permit at the border. This obliges you to take the vehicle

out of Belize again within the validity of the permit. To get the permit you must present proof of ownership (vehicle registration) and purchase Belizean motor insurance (available for a few US dollars per day from agents at the borders). Permit extensions can be obtained by applying to the **Customs Department** (Belize City ☎ 227-7092). In the unlikely event that a Mexican or Guatemalan car-rental agency permits you to take one of their vehicles into Belize, you will also have to show the rental documents at the border.

It's not unusual to see US license plates on cars in Belize, as driving from the USA through Mexico is pretty straightforward and car rental in Belize is expensive. The shortest route through Mexico to the crossing point between Chetumal and Corozal is from the US–Mexico border points at Brownsville–Matamoros (1257 miles from the Belize border) or McAllen–Reynosa (1267 miles), a solid three days' driving. The other main US–Mexico road borders are Laredo (Texas)–Nuevo Laredo (1413 miles); El Paso–Ciudad Juárez (1988 miles) and Nogales (Arizona)–Nogales (2219 miles).

You are required to obtain a temporary import permit for your vehicle at the border when you enter Mexico; as well as the vehicle registration document you'll need to show your driver's license and pay a fee of around BZ$50 with a Visa, MasterCard or American Express credit card. And you'll have to buy Mexican motor insurance, also available at the border.

For information on driving within Belize, see p296.

SEA

The only scheduled boat services into Belize are: from Puerto Cortés, Honduras, to Placencia (p244; BZ$100, three to four hours, weekly) and Dangriga (p225; BZ$100, three to four hours, weekly); from Puerto Barrios, Guatemala, to Punta Gorda (p249; Q114/US$15 to Q147/US$18, one hour, daily); and from Lívingston, Guatemala, to

---

SEA DEPARTURE TAX

The only fee you have to pay when leaving Belize by sea is the BZ$7.50 (US$3.75) PACT (Protected Areas Conservation Trust) fee. It's payable in cash (Belizean or US dollars).

SURFING FOR AIRFARES

You have a choice: talk to a live agent or tap the computer keys. Frankly, your odds are better doing it yourself if you can make the time. The following websites are recommended.

■ **www.kayak.com** Searches hundreds of airline websites and other search-engine sites to give you a cost comparison. It's also possible to do a flexible search to compare dates and routes.

■ **www.expedia.com** One of the original online search engines, this is a reliable stand-by.

■ **www.cheaptickets.com** True to its name, this site often seems to come up with the cheapest fares.

■ **www.statravel.com** Discounts for students and travelers under the age of 26.

■ **www.priceline.com** Name your budget and Priceline will try to find you a ticket. Best for last-minute travel, when airlines are unloading empty seats and hotels are trying to fill empty rooms.

■ **www.bestfares.com** Name your city and this site keeps track of the cheapest flights to destinations worldwide.

Punta Gorda (p249; Q114/US$15, one hour, twice weekly). (Services from Guatemala do not accept Belizean dollars.)

GETTING AROUND

AIR

Belize's two domestic airlines, **Maya Island Air** (code MW; ☎ 223-1140; www.mayaairways.com) and **Tropic Air** (code PM; ☎ 225-2012; www.tropicair.com), provide an efficient and reasonably priced service in small planes on the routes Belize City–Dangriga–Placencia–Punta Gorda, Belize City–Caye Caulker–San Pedro and San Pedro–Sarteneja–Corozal, with plenty of daily flights by both airlines on all three routes.

Many domestic flights departing and arriving in Belize City use the Philip Goldson International Airport; others use the Municipal Airstrip, about 12 miles from the international airport; and some stop at both. Flights using the Municipal Airstrip are usually BZ$20 to BZ$40 cheaper than those using the international airport.

According to the US Federal Aviation Administration, the civil aviation authority of Belize is not in compliance with international aviation safety standards. Belize has been assessed as a Category 2 country (which is why its airlines cannot fly into Category 1 countries such as Guatemala and Mexico). However, both Belizean airlines have decent safety records. There have been about 10 crashes in just as many years; one person has died as a result.

BICYCLE

Most of Belize, including all three of the main highways, is pretty flat, which makes for pleasant cycling, but traffic on the main highways does tend to travel fairly fast; make sure you're visible if riding along these roads. Belizeans use bicycles – often beach cruiser–type bikes on which you brake by pedaling backwards – for getting around locally, but you don't see them doing much long-distance cycling unless they're into racing.

Bikes are available to rent in many of the main tourist destinations for around BZ$20 per day. You don't usually have to give a deposit. See p141 for rental in San Pedro, p155 for rental in Caye Caulker and p244 for rental in Placencia. It may be possible to purchase a used bike from one of these rental companies for longer-term use.

BOAT

The **Caye Caulker Water Taxi Association** (☎ 223-5752, 226-0992; www.cayecaulkerwatertaxi.com) operates speedy water taxis between Belize City, Caye Caulker and San Pedro (Ambergris Caye), with several daily services each way. It's one hour (BZ$15) each way from Belize City to Caye Caulker and 1½ hours (BZ$20) to San Pedro. The Caye Caulker Water Taxi Association also serves three smaller offshore islands: St George's Caye, Long Caye and Caye Chapel. Water taxis are open boats that can hold around 40 people each. Captains usually do their best to avoid traveling during rainstorms; when they can't, passengers huddle together under large tarps to stay dry.

The **Thunderbolt service** (☎ 422-0026, 226-2904), with indoor seating, also operates the Belize City–Caye Caulker–San Pedro route and provides an additional daily service linking Corozal, Sarteneja and San Pedro (BZ$45).

Otherwise, getting to and around Belize's islands and reefs is a matter of taking tours or dive-and-snorkel trips, using boats organized by island accommodations or chartering a launch. As a rough rule of thumb, launch charters cost around BZ$200 per 10 miles. They're easy to arrange almost anywhere on the coast and on the main islands.

Another useful boat service is the **Hokey Pokey Water Taxi** (☎ 601-0271, 523-2376) between Placencia and Mango Creek (BZ$10, 12 minutes) near Independence, which saves a long detour by road for travelers between Placencia and Punta Gorda. See p244 for further information.

BUS

Since the 2004 bankruptcy of Belize's main long-distance bus service, Novelo's, a dozen smaller companies have stepped up to fill the gaps in service. The break-up of the monopoly has caused some confusion, especially in smaller towns where several different companies may run the same route, but depart from different corners at random times throughout the day. But in general, there are still regular buses plying the regular routes, and they are charging – more or less – the same prices.

There are three main bus routes, all of which originate in Belize City:

- **Northern Hwy** From Belize City to Orange Walk and Corozal (and on to Chetumal, Mexico). At last count there were six companies servicing this route and between 25 and 30 buses a day going in each direction.
- **Western Hwy** From Belize City to Belmopan, San Ignacio and Benque Viejo del Carmen. Several companies service this route, resulting in a regular service that runs in both directions every half-hour throughout the day.
- **Hummingbird and Southern Hwys** From Belmopan to Dangriga, Independence and Punta Gorda (buses on this route use the Western Hwy between Belize City and Belmopan; from Dangriga there are separate buses to Hopkins and Placencia). Three main companies ply this route: James, National and Usher. See p250 for more details.

TRANSPORTATION

CLIMATE CHANGE & TRAVEL

Climate change is a serious threat to the ecosystems that humans rely upon, and air travel is the fastest-growing contributor to the problem. Lonely Planet regards travel, overall, as a global benefit, but believes we all have a responsibility to limit our personal impact on global warming.

Flying & Climate Change

Pretty much every form of motor travel generates CO_2 (the main cause of human-induced climate change) but planes are far and away the worst offenders, not just because of the sheer distances they allow us to travel, but because they release greenhouse gases high into the atmosphere. The statistics are frightening: two people taking a return flight between Europe and the US will contribute as much to climate change as an average household's gas and electricity consumption over a whole year.

Carbon Offset Schemes

Climatecare.org and other websites use 'carbon calculators' that allow jetsetters to offset the greenhouse gases they are responsible for with contributions to energy-saving projects and other climate-friendly initiatives in the developing world – including projects in India, Honduras, Kazakhstan and Uganda.

Lonely Planet, together with Rough Guides and other concerned partners in the travel industry, supports the carbon offset scheme run by climatecare.org. Lonely Planet offsets all of its staff and author travel.

For more information check out our website: lonelyplanet.com.

MAIN DRIVING ROUTES

- **Northern Hwy** Belize City to Orange Walk Town (1½ hours, 57 miles), Corozal Town (2¼ hours, 86 miles) and Santa Elena (Mexican border; 95 miles, 2½ hours)

- **Western Hwy** Belize City to Belmopan (1¼ hours, 52 miles), San Ignacio (1¾ hours, 72 miles) and Benque Viejo del Carmen (Guatemalan border; 80 miles, two hours)

- **Hummingbird and Southern Hwys** Belmopan to Dangriga (1½ hours, 55 miles), Hopkins (two hours, 63 miles), Placencia (3½ hours, 98 miles) and Punta Gorda (4½ hours, 148 miles)

Most Belizean buses are old US school buses. Regular-service buses stop anywhere to drop and pick up passengers. Express buses, sometimes air-conditioned, have limited stops and as a result are quicker and usually less crowded. They cost a bit more but it's worth the extra few dollars, especially on longer trips. The 86-mile run from Belize City to Corozal, for example, takes about 2½ hours for BZ$14 on an express, or 3¼ hours for BZ$10 on a regular bus. In general, you pay about BZ$5 per hour on express buses and BZ$3 per hour on regular buses. If you're traveling at a busy time, it's worth buying your ticket a day or two in advance.

A variety of smaller bus companies serve villages around the country. They often run to local work and school schedules, with buses going into a larger town in the morning and returning in the afternoon.

Occasional breakdowns and accidents happen with Belizean buses but their track record is at least as good as those in other Central American countries. Luggage pilfering has been a problem on some buses in the past. Carry valuables with you on the bus and give your stored baggage to the bus driver or conductor only, and watch as it is stored. Be there when the bus is unloaded to retrieve your luggage.

CAR & MOTORCYCLE

Having a vehicle in Belize gives you maximum flexibility and enables you to reach off-the-main-road destinations and attractions (of which there are many) without having to depend on tours and expensive transfers. Though car hire is costly in Belize (you're looking at about BZ$160 per day or BZ$900 per week, plus fuel), it doesn't look so exorbitant when you consider the alternatives, especially if there are three or four people to share the expenses.

Belize has four good, asphalt-paved two-lane roads: the Northern Hwy between Belize City and the Mexican border north of Corozal; the Western Hwy between Belize City and the Guatemalan border near Benque Viejo del Carmen; the Hummingbird Hwy from Belmopan to Dangriga; and the Southern Hwy, which branches off the Hummingbird Hwy a few miles from Dangriga and heads south to Punta Gorda (it's all paved except for a 10-mile stretch around Nim Li Punit).

Most other roads are one- or two-lane unpaved roads. The most oft-used roads are kept in fairly good condition, but heavy rains can make things challenging. Off the main roads you don't always need a 4WD vehicle but you do need one with high clearance, such as a Chevy Geo Tracker.

Driver's License

If you plan to drive in Belize, you'll need to bring a valid driver's license from your home country.

Fuel & Spare Parts

There are plenty of fuel stations in the larger towns and along the major roads. At last report, regualar gasoline was going for just over BZ$10 per US gallon, with prices on the rise. Premium (unleaded) is a few cents more. Spare parts and mechanics are most easily available in Belize City, although San Ignacio, Belmopan and Orange Walk Town also have parts suppliers. Check the Belize **Yellow Pages** (www.yellowpages.bz) under the categories 'Automobile Parts & Supplies' and 'Automobile Repairing & Service'.

Hire

Generally, renters must be at least 25 years old, have a valid driver's license and pay by credit card.

Most car-rental companies have offices at Philip Goldson International Airport as well as in Belize City (see p105 for recommended agencies); they will often also deliver or take return of cars at Belize City's Municipal

Airstrip or in downtown Belize City. Rental possibilities are few outside Belize City, but it is possible to rent cars in San Ignacio (p202) and Punta Gorda (p250).

Rental rates, including taxes, insurance and unlimited mileage, generally start at BZ$160 a day for an economy vehicle with 4WD and air-con. If you keep the car for six days you'll often get the seventh day free.

Most rental agencies will not allow you to take a vehicle out of the country. One agency that allows cars to be taken in to Guatemala is Crystal Auto Rental (p106) in Belize City.

Insurance

Liability insurance is required in Belize, and there are occasional police checkpoints on the main highways, where you may be required to produce proof of it. You face possible arrest if you can't. Rental companies always organize the necessary insurance for you, and you won't be able to bring your own vehicle into Belize without buying Belizean insurance at the border.

Road Conditions & Hazards

Outside Belize City, traffic is wonderfully light throughout the country, but on the main roads you need to watch out for erratic and dangerously fast driving by others. Drive defensively. Also watch for speed bumps (sleeping policemen): these are sometimes well signed, but sometimes not signed at all.

Off the major highways, most roads are unpaved and you need to be careful of potholes, but most of the roads you're likely to travel on are fairly well maintained. After a lot of rain, some roads may become impassable; make inquiries before you set out, and if you're in doubt about whether you'll get through a stretch, don't risk it. Always have water and a spare tire, and always fill your tank before you head off into the back country (and turn back before you've used half of it!).

Note that Belizean signposts give distances in miles.

Road Rules

Driving in Belize is on the right-hand side of the road. Speed limits are 55mph on the open highway, and either 40mph or 25mph in villages and towns. Seat belts are compulsory for drivers and front-seat passengers. If you are caught not wearing one, the fine is BZ$25.

Petty theft can be an issue – keep your vehicle locked at all times and do not leave valuables in it, especially not in plain view.

Mileposts and highway signs record distances in miles and speed limits in miles per hour, although many vehicles have odometers and speedometers that are calibrated in kilometers.

GOLF CARTS

If you're spending some time at the beach and you can't fathom being dependent on your own leg-power, you might consider renting a golf cart. It's relatively inexpensive (compared to a car) but it still gets you to the beach and back without causing you to break a sweat. The golf cart is a popular form of transportation in Placencia (p237), San Pedro (p141) and – to a lesser degree – Caye Caulker (p155). Both gas-powered and battery-powered golf carts are available: gas goes further and faster, but battery is better for the planet. Expect to pay about BZ$130 per day for a four-seater.'

HITCHHIKING

Hitchhiking is never entirely safe in any country and in Belize, like anywhere, it's imperative that you listen to your instincts and travel smart. Travelers who decide to hitchhike should understand that they are taking a small but potentially serious risk. You're far better off traveling with another person, and never hitchhike at night. Also keep in mind that buses in Belize are cheap and fairly efficient; you might decide that a bus is a safer and more comfortable bet.

Hitchhiking is a fairly common way for Belizeans to get around. In a country where vehicle owners are a minority and public transportation is infrequent to places off the main roads, it's common to see people trying to catch a lift at bus stops or at speed bumps, where traffic slows down. If you too are trying to get some place where there's no bus for the next three hours, it's likely that you'll soon get a ride if you hold out your hand and look friendly. Offering to pay a share of the fuel costs at the end of your ride never goes amiss. But always be aware of the potential risks. For more information, see p258.

LOCAL TRANSPORTATION

All of Belize's towns, including the parts of Belize City that most visitors frequent, are small enough to cover on foot, although for safety reasons you should take taxis for some trips within Belize City (see p94). Taxis are plentiful in all mainland towns and are also an option for getting to places out of town. Rates vary depending on where you are: the 7-mile ride from Corozal to Consejo costs BZ$20, but the 6-mile trip from Maya Centre to Cockscomb Basin Wildlife Sanctuary is BZ$36.

Bicycle is an enjoyable way of getting around local areas and bikes can be rented at around BZ$20 per day in many tourist haunts (and are free for guests at some accommodations).

On the cayes, of course, you get around by boat if you're going anywhere offshore. Ambergris Caye and Caye Caulker have a mode of transportation all of their own for land trips: the golf-cart taxi (see p297).

Health Dr David Goldberg

CONTENTS

Travelers to Central America need to be concerned about food- and mosquito-borne infections. While most infections are not life-threatening, they can certainly ruin your trip.

Besides getting the proper vaccinations, it's important that you pack a good insect repellent and exercise great care in what you eat and drink.

BEFORE YOU GO

INSURANCE

If your insurance doesn't cover medical expenses abroad, consider supplemental insurance. See the US State Department website (www.travel.state.gov/travel/tips/brochures/brochures_1215.html) for medical evacuation and travel-insurance companies.

Find out if your insurer will pay providers directly or reimburse you later for expenditures. You may prefer a policy that pays doctors or hospitals directly rather than requiring you to pay up front and claim later. If you have to claim later, keep all documentation. Some policies ask you to call collect to a center in your home country, where an assessment of your problem is made.

Check that the policy covers ambulances and an emergency flight home. Some policies offer lower and higher medical-expense options; the higher ones are for countries such as the USA, which have extremely high medical costs. There is a wide variety of policies available, so check the small print.

RECOMMENDED VACCINATIONS

Since most vaccines don't produce immunity until at least two weeks after they're given, visit a physician four to eight weeks before departure. Ask your doctor for an International Certificate of Vaccination (also known as a yellow booklet), which will list all the vaccinations you've received. This is mandatory for countries that require proof of yellow-fever vaccination upon entry, but it's a good idea to carry it wherever you travel. Note that some of the recommended vaccines are not approved for use by children and pregnant women; check with your physician.

The only required vaccine for Belize is yellow fever, and that's only if you're arriving from a yellow fever–infected country in Africa or South America. However, a number of vaccines are recommended (see the boxed text, p300).

MEDICAL CHECKLIST

It is a very good idea to carry a medical and first-aid kit with you, in the case of minor illness or injury. Following is a list of items you should consider packing.

- antibiotics
- antidiarrheal drugs (eg loperamide)
- acetaminophen/paracetamol (Tylenol) or aspirin
- anti-inflammatory drugs (eg ibuprofen)
- antihistamines (for hay fever and allergic reactions)
- antibacterial ointment (eg Bactroban) for cuts and abrasions
- steroid cream or cortisone (for poison ivy and other allergic rashes)
- bandages, gauze, gauze rolls
- adhesive or paper tape
- scissors, safety pins and tweezers
- thermometer
- pocketknife
- insect repellent containing DEET for the skin

RECOMMENDED VACCINES

Vaccine	Recommended for	Dosage	Side effects
chickenpox	travelers who've never had chickenpox	2 doses 1 month apart	fever; mild case of chickenpox
hepatitis A	all travelers	1 dose before trip with booster 6-12 months later	soreness at injection site; headaches; body aches
hepatitis B	long-term travelers in close contact with the local population	3 doses over a 6-month period	soreness at injection site; low-grade fever
measles	travelers born after 1956 who've had only 1 measles vaccination	1 dose	fever; rash; joint pain; allergic reaction
tetanus-diphtheria	all travelers who haven't had a booster within 10 years	1 dose lasts 10 years	soreness at injection site
typhoid	all travelers	4 capsules by mouth, 1 taken every other day	abdominal pain; nausea; rash
yellow fever	required for travelers arriving from yellow fever-infected areas in Africa or South America	1 dose lasts 10 years	headaches; body aches; severe reactions are rare

- insect spray containing permethrin for clothing, tents and bed nets
- sunblock
- oral rehydration salts
- iodine tablets (for water purification)
- syringes and sterile needles

Bring medications in their original containers, clearly labeled. A signed, dated letter from your physician describing all medical conditions and medications, including generic names, is also a good idea. If carrying syringes or needles, be sure to have a physician's letter documenting their medical necessity.

INTERNET RESOURCES

There is a wealth of travel-health advice on the internet. The Lonely Planet website at lonelyplanet.com is a good place to start. The World Health Organization publishes a superb book, *International Travel and Health,* which is revised annually and is available free online at www.who.int/ith.

It's a good idea to consult your government's travel-health website before you depart:

Australia (www.smarttraveller.gov.au)
Canada (www.hc-sc.gc.ca/hl-vs/travel-voyage/index_e.html)
UK (www.dh.gov.uk)
USA (wwwn.cdc.gov/travel)

FURTHER READING

For more information, see Lonely Planet's *Healthy Travel Central & South America.* If you're traveling with children, Lonely Planet's *Travel with Children* may be useful. *ABC of Healthy Travel,* by Eric Walker et al, and *Medicine for the Outdoors,* by Paul S Auerbach, are other valuable resources.

IN TRANSIT

DEEP VEIN THROMBOSIS (DVT)

Blood clots may form in the legs during plane flights, chiefly because of prolonged immobility. The main symptom of DVT is swelling or pain of the foot, ankle or calf, usually but not always on just one side. When a blood clot travels to the lungs, it may cause chest pain and difficulty breathing. Travelers with any of these symptoms should immediately seek medical attention.

To prevent DVT developing on long flights, you should walk about the cabin, contract your leg muscles while sitting, drink plenty of fluids and avoid alcohol.

JET LAG & MOTION SICKNESS

Jet lag is common when crossing more than five time zones and causes insomnia, fatigue, malaise or nausea. To avoid jet lag, drink plenty of nonalcoholic fluids and eat light meals. Upon arrival, get exposure to natural sunlight and readjust your schedule (for meals, sleep etc) as soon as possible.

Antihistamines such as dimenhydrate (Dramamine) and meclizine (Antivert, Bonine) are usually the first choice for treating motion sickness. The main side effect is drowsiness. A herbal alternative is ginger, which works like a charm for some people.

IN BELIZE

AVAILABILITY & COST OF HEALTH CARE

Most doctors and hospitals in Belize expect payment in cash, regardless of whether you have medical insurance. If you develop a life-threatening medical problem, you'll probably want to be evacuated to a country with state-of-the-art medical care. Since this may cost tens of thousands of dollars, be sure you have insurance to cover this before you depart.

Many pharmacies in Belize are well supplied, but important medications may not be consistently available. Be sure to bring along adequate supplies of all prescription drugs. While most prescription medications are available in Belize, they might be relatively expensive. You can obtain prescriptions from general practitioners, who will provide this service for a small fee. Some pharmacists, especially in smaller pharmacies, will dispense medications without a prescription.

Medical facilities in Belize are extremely limited and the number of doctors is quite small. Routine care is readily obtainable in Belize City and the larger towns, but facilities for complicated problems may be difficult to find. In rural areas, medical care may be unavailable. In Belize City the private hospital **Belize Medical Associates** (Map p93; ☎ 223-0302/3/4; 5791 St Thomas St, Belize City) provides generally good care. In San Ignacio, **La Loma Luz Hospital** (off Map p197; ☎ 804-2985, 824-2087; Western Hwy) offers primary care as well as 24-hour emergency services. For divers, there is a hyperbaric chamber on Ambergris Caye (p125).

In Belize, the phone number for an ambulance is ☎ 90 but this service is not available in many communities. For a private ambulance in Belize City, call ☎ 223-3292.

INFECTIOUS DISEASES
Chagas' Disease

Chagas' disease is a parasitic infection that is transmitted by triatomine insects (reduviid bugs), which inhabit crevices in the walls and roofs of traditional housing in South and Central America. In Belize, Chagas' disease occurs in rural areas. The triatomine insect lays its feces on human skin as it bites, usually at night. A person becomes infected when he or she unknowingly rubs the feces into the bite wound or an open sore. Chagas' disease is extremely rare in travelers. If you sleep in a poorly constructed house, especially one made of mud, adobe or thatch, be sure to protect yourself with a bed net and a good insecticide.

Dengue

Though relatively uncommon in Belize, dengue fever is a viral infection found throughout Central America and transmitted by aedes mosquitoes, which bite mostly during the daytime and are usually found close to human habitations, often indoors. They breed primarily in artificial water containers such as jars, barrels, cans, cisterns, metal drums, plastic containers and discarded tires. As a result, dengue is especially common in densely populated, urban environments.

Dengue usually causes flu-like symptoms, including fever, muscle aches, joint pains, headaches, nausea and vomiting, often followed by a rash. The body aches may be quite uncomfortable, but most cases resolve uneventfully in a few days. Severe cases usually occur in children under the age of 15 who are experiencing their second dengue infection.

There is no treatment available for dengue fever except to take analgesics such as acetaminophen/paracetamol (Tylenol) and drink plenty of fluids. Severe cases may require hospitalization for intravenous fluids and supportive care. There is no vaccine. The cornerstone of prevention is protection against insect bites (see p304).

Hepatitis A

Hepatitis A occurs throughout Belize. It's a viral infection of the liver that is usually acquired by ingestion of contaminated water, food or ice, though it may also be acquired by direct contact with infected persons. The illness occurs all over the world, but the incidence is higher in developing nations. Symptoms may include fever, malaise, jaundice, nausea, vomiting and abdominal pain. Most cases will resolve uneventfully, though hepatitis A occasionally causes severe liver damage. There is no treatment.

The vaccine for hepatitis A is extremely safe and highly effective. If you get a booster six to

12 months later, it lasts for at least 10 years. Vaccination is recommended for travelers visiting Belize. Because the safety of hepatitis A vaccine has not been established for pregnant women or children under age two, they should instead be given a gamma-globulin injection.

Hepatitis B

Like hepatitis A, hepatitis B is a liver infection that occurs worldwide but is more common in developing nations. Unlike hepatitis A, the disease is usually acquired by sexual contact or by exposure to infected blood, generally through blood transfusions or contaminated needles. The vaccine is recommended only for long-term travelers (on the road more than six months) who expect to live in rural areas or have close physical contact with the local population. Additionally, the vaccine is recommended for anyone who anticipates sexual contact with local people or the need for medical, dental or other treatments while abroad, especially transfusions or injections.

Hepatitis B vaccine is safe and highly effective. Three injections are necessary to establish full immunity. Several countries added hepatitis B vaccine to the list of routine childhood immunizations in the 1980s, so many young adults are already protected.

Leishmaniasis

Leishmaniasis occurs in the mountains and jungles of Belize. The infection is transmitted by sand flies. To protect yourself, follow the same precautions for mosquitoes (p304), except that netting must be finer (at least 18 holes to the linear inch) and you should stay indoors during the early evening. There is no vaccine.

In Belize, the disease is generally limited to the skin, causing slow-growing ulcers over exposed parts of the body; less commonly, it may disseminate to the bone marrow, liver and spleen.

Leptospirosis

Leptospirosis is acquired by exposure to water that has been contaminated by the urine of infected animals. Outbreaks may occur as a result of flooding, when sewage overflow contaminates water sources. The initial symptoms, which resemble a mild flu, usually subside uneventfully in a few days, with or without treatment, but a minority of cases are complicated by jaundice or meningitis. There is no vaccine. Minimize your risk by staying

out of bodies of fresh water that may be contaminated by animal urine. If you're engaging in high-risk activities in an area where an outbreak is in progress, you can take 200mg of doxycycline once weekly as a preventative measure. The treatment for leptospirosis is 100mg of doxycycline twice daily.

Malaria

Malaria occurs in every country in Central America. It's transmitted by mosquito bites, which usually occur between dusk and dawn. The main symptom is high, spiking fevers, which may be accompanied by chills, sweats, headache, body aches, weakness, vomiting or diarrhea. Severe cases may affect the central nervous system and lead to seizures, confusion, coma and death.

For Belize, malaria pills are recommended for travel to all areas except Belize City. The risk is highest in the western and southern regions.

The malaria pill of choice is chloroquine, taken once weekly in a dosage of 500mg, starting one to two weeks before arrival and continuing during the trip and for four weeks afterwards. Chloroquine is safe, inexpensive and highly effective. Side effects are typically mild and may include nausea, abdominal discomfort, headache, dizziness, blurred vision or itching. Severe reactions are uncommon.

Since no pills are 100% effective, protecting yourself against mosquito bites (p304) is just as important as taking malaria pills.

You may not have access to medical care while traveling, so you should bring along additional pills for emergency self-treatment, which you should take if you can't reach a doctor and you develop symptoms that suggest malaria, such as high, spiking fevers. One option is to take four tablets of Malarone once daily for three days. If you start self-medication, you should try to see a doctor at the earliest possible opportunity.

If you develop a fever after returning home, see a physician, as malaria symptoms may not occur for months.

Rabies

Rabies is a viral infection of the brain and spinal cord that is almost always fatal. The rabies virus is carried in the saliva of infected animals and is typically transmitted through an animal bite, though contamination of any break in the skin with infected saliva may result in rabies.

Rabies occurs in all Central American countries. The greatest risk is in the triangle where Belize, Guatemala and the Yucatán region meet. Most cases are related to bites from dogs or bats.

Rabies vaccine is safe, but requires three injections and is quite expensive. Those at high risk for rabies, such as spelunkers (cave explorers), should certainly be vaccinated. The treatment for a possibly rabid bite consists of vaccine with immune globulin. It's effective, but must be given promptly. Most travelers don't need to be vaccinated against rabies.

All animal bites and scratches must be promptly and thoroughly cleansed with large amounts of soap and water, and local health authorities should be contacted to determine whether or not further treatment is necessary (see right).

Typhoid

Typhoid fever is caused by the ingestion of contaminated food or water. Outbreaks sometimes occur at times of flooding, when sewage overflow may contaminate water sources. The initial symptoms, which resemble a mild flu, usually subside uneventfully in a few days, with or without treatment, but a minority of cases are complicated by jaundice or meningitis. Fever occurs in virtually all cases. Other symptoms may include headache, malaise, muscle aches, dizziness, loss of appetite, nausea and abdominal pain, and either diarrhea or constipation.

Unless you expect to take all your meals in major hotels and restaurants, vaccination for typhoid is a good idea. It's usually given orally, but is also available as an injection. Neither vaccine is approved for use in children under the age of two.

The drug of choice for typhoid fever is usually a quinolone antibiotic such as ciprofloxacin (Cipro) or levofloxacin (Levaquin), which many travelers carry for treatment of traveler's diarrhea. If you self-treat for typhoid fever, you may also need to self-treat for malaria, since the symptoms of the two diseases may be indistinguishable.

Yellow Fever

Yellow fever no longer occurs in Central America. Belize, Guatemala and Mexico require yellow-fever vaccination before entry *only* if you're arriving from an infected country in Africa or South America. The vaccine is given only in approved yellow-fever vaccination centers, which provide validated International Certificates of Vaccination ('yellow booklets'). The vaccine should be given at least 10 days before leaving and remains effective for about 10 years.

Reactions to the vaccine are generally mild and may include headaches, muscle aches, low-grade fevers or discomfort at the injection site. Severe, life-threatening reactions are extremely rare. Vaccination is not recommended for pregnant women or children less than nine months old.

TRAVELER'S DIARRHEA

To prevent diarrhea, avoid tap water unless it's been boiled, filtered or chemically disinfected (with iodine tablets); only eat fresh fruit or vegetables if cooked or peeled; be wary of dairy products that might contain unpasteurized milk; and be highly selective when eating food from street vendors.

If you develop diarrhea, be sure to drink plenty of fluids, preferably an oral rehydration solution containing salt and sugar. A few loose stools don't require treatment, but if you start having more than four or five stools a day, you should start taking an antibiotic (usually a quinolone drug) and an antidiarrheal agent (such as loperamide). If diarrhea is bloody, persists for more than 72 hours or is accompanied by fever, shaking chills or severe abdominal pain, you should seek medical attention.

ENVIRONMENTAL HAZARDS
Animal Bites

Do not attempt to pet, handle or feed any animal, with the exception of domestic animals known to be free of infectious diseases. Most animal injuries occur when people try to touch or feed animals.

Any bite or scratch by a mammal, including bats, should be promptly and thoroughly cleansed with large amounts of soap and water, and an antiseptic such as iodine or alcohol applied. The local health authorities should be contacted immediately for possible post-exposure rabies treatment, whether or not you've been immunized against rabies. It may also be advisable to take antibiotics, since wounds caused by animal bites and scratches frequently become infected. One of the newer quinolones, such as levofloxacin (Levaquin), which many travelers carry in case of diarrhea, would be an appropriate choice.

HEALTH

Mosquito Bites

To avoid mosquito bites, wear long sleeves, long pants, hats and shoes (rather than sandals). Pack insect repellent, preferably one containing DEET, which should be applied to exposed skin and clothing, but not to eyes, mouth, cuts, wounds or irritated skin. Products containing lower concentrations of DEET are as effective, but for shorter periods of time. In general, adults and children over 12 should use preparations containing 25% to 35% DEET, which last about six hours. Children between two and 12 years of age should use preparations containing no more than 10% DEET, applied sparingly, which will usually last about three hours.

Neurologic toxicity has been reported from using DEET, especially in children, but is extremely uncommon and is generally related to overuse. DEET-containing compounds should not be used on children under age two.

Insect repellents containing certain botanical products, including eucalyptus and soybean oil, are effective but last only 1½ to two hours. DEET-containing repellents are preferable for areas where there is a high risk of malaria or yellow fever. Products based on citronella are not effective.

For additional protection, you can apply permethrin to clothing, shoes, tents and bed nets. Permethrin treatments are safe and remain effective for at least two weeks, even when items are laundered. Permethrin should not be applied directly to skin.

Don't sleep with windows open unless there is a screen. If sleeping outdoors or in accommodations that allow entry of mosquitoes, use a bed net, preferably treated with permethrin, with the edges tucked in under the mattress. The mesh size should be less than 1.5mm. If the sleeping area is not otherwise protected, use a mosquito coil, which will fill the room with insecticide through the night. Repellent-impregnated wristbands are not effective.

Snake Bites

Snakes are a hazard in Belize. The chief concern is *Bothrops asper,* the Central American or common lancehead, usually known in Belize as the yellow-jaw tommygoff and also called the fer-de-lance, *barba amarilla* (yellow beard) or *terciopelo* (velvet skin). This heavy-bodied snake reaches up to 6.5ft in length and is found mostly in the northern region. It is earth-toned and has a broadly triangular head with a pattern of Xs and triangles on its back. Others snakes to watch out for are the brightly striped coral snake and the tropical rattlesnake. All three snakes are deadly, though the coral snake is shyer than the irritable rattlesnake.

In the event of a venomous snake bite, place the victim at rest, keep the bitten area immobilized, and move the victim immediately to the nearest medical facility. Avoid tourniquets, as they are no longer recommended.

Tick Bites

To protect yourself from tick bites, follow the same precautions as for mosquitoes (left), except that boots are preferable to shoes, with pants tucked in. Be sure to perform a thorough tick check at the end of each day. You'll generally need the assistance of a friend or a mirror for a full examination. Remove ticks with tweezers, grasping them firmly by the head. Insect repellents based on botanical products have not been adequately studied for insects other than mosquitoes and cannot be recommended to prevent tick bites.

Sun Exposure

To protect yourself from excessive exposure to the sun, you should stay out of the midday sun, wear sunglasses and a wide-brimmed hat, and apply sunscreen with SPF 15 or higher, with both UVA and UVB protection. Sunscreen should be generously applied to all exposed parts of the body approximately 30 minutes before sun exposure and should be reapplied after swimming or vigorous activities. Travelers should also drink plenty of fluids and avoid strenuous exercise when it is hot. Dehydration and salt deficiency can cause heat exhaustion, which can then progress to heatstroke.

Symptoms of this serious condition include a general feeling of unwellness, not sweating very much (or not at all) and a high body temperature (39°C to 41°C, or 102°F to 106°F). Severe, throbbing headaches and lack of coordination can also occur. Hospitalization is essential, but in the interim get victims out of the sun, remove their clothing, cover them with a wet sheet or towel and fan continually. Give fluids if they are conscious.

Water

Tap water is not safe to drink in Belize. Vigorous boiling for one minute is the most effective means of water purification. At altitudes greater than 3630ft, boil for three minutes.

Another option is to disinfect water with iodine pills. Follow the instructions carefully. Alternatively, you can add 2% tincture of iodine to one quart or liter of water (five drops to clear water, 10 drops to cloudy water) and let stand for 30 minutes. If the water is cold, longer times may be required. The taste of iodinated water may be improved by adding vitamin C (ascorbic acid). Iodinated water should not be consumed for more than a few weeks. Pregnant women, those with a history of thyroid disease and those allergic to iodine should not drink iodinated water.

Water filters with smaller pores (reverse osmosis filters) provide the broadest protection, but they are relatively large and are readily plugged by debris. Those with somewhat larger pores (microstrainer filters) are ineffective against viruses, although they remove other organisms. Follow manufacturers' instructions carefully.

Safe, inexpensive *agua pura* (purified water) is widely available in hotels, shops and restaurants.

CHILDREN & PREGNANT WOMEN

In general, it's safe for children and pregnant women to go to Belize. However, because some of the vaccines listed in this chapter are not approved for use in children and during pregnancy, these travelers should be particularly careful not to drink tap water or consume any questionable food or drink. Also, when traveling with children, make sure they're up to date on all routine immunizations. It's sometimes appropriate to give children some of their vaccines a little early before visiting a developing nation – discuss this with your pediatrician. If pregnant, bear in mind that should a complication, such as premature labor, develop while abroad, the quality of medical care may not be comparable to that in your home country.

Yellow-fever vaccine is not recommended for pregnant women or children less than nine months old. Therefore, these travelers, if arriving from a country with yellow fever, should obtain a waiver letter, preferably written on letterhead and bearing the stamp used by official immunization centers to validate the International Certificate of Vaccination.

HEALTH

The Authors

MARA VORHEES

Coordinating Author, Northern Cayes, Cayo District, Tikal & Flores

Mara first visited Belize as a student of international development, when she traveled the country on a backpacker's budget, researching the outcomes of US-sponsored foreign-aid projects. She fell in love with the reef, the rasta guys and the rice and beans (but not US development policy). The pen-wielding traveler has since taken to seeing and saving the world by other means. Besides this book, she has worked on *Costa Rica* and a slew of other titles for Lonely Planet. Her articles and photographs of Central America have appeared in the *Boston Globe* and the *Miami Herald*, among other US newspapers. Follow Mara's latest adventures at www.maravorhees.com.

JOSHUA SAMUEL BROWN

Belize District, Northern Belize & Southern Belize

Reared in the dreadlock-heavy island of Staten (New York City), Joshua has long been interested in the cultures of both Central America and the Caribbean. A series of strange events brought him first to Taiwan, then to Hong Kong and China before blowing his sails to Belize. There he spent three months living on an organic farm surrounded by Maya villages and ruins, the base from which he explored the country's length and breadth. A prolific traveler and writer, his features have appeared in an eclectic variety of publications around the globe. *Belize* is his second book for Lonely Planet. Read more of his work at www.josambro.com and www.josambro.blogspot.com.

CONTRIBUTING AUTHORS

Dr Allen J Christenson wrote The Ancient Maya World chapter. He earned his MA and PhD in Pre-Columbian Maya Art History at the University of Texas at Austin, and works as an associate professor in the Humanities, Classics and Comparative Literature department of Brigham Young University in Provo, Utah. He is the author of *Art and Society in a Highland Maya Community* (2001; about the Maya community of Antiago Atitlan, Guatemala), and a critical edition and translation of the K'iche'-Maya epic, the *Popol Vuh* (2003).

Dr David Goldberg MD wrote the Health chapter. He completed his training in internal medicine and infectious diseases at Columbia-Presbyterian Medical Center in New York City, where he has also served as voluntary faculty. At present, he is an infectious diseases specialist in Scarsdale, New York State, and the editor-in-chief of the website MDTravelHealth.com.

LONELY PLANET AUTHORS

Why is our travel information the best in the world? It's simple: our authors are passionate, dedicated travelers. They don't take freebies in exchange for positive coverage so you can be sure the advice you're given is impartial. They travel widely to all the popular spots, and off the beaten track. They don't research using just the internet or phone. They discover new places not included in any other guidebook. They personally visit thousands of hotels, restaurants, palaces, trails, galleries, temples and more. They speak with dozens of locals every day to make sure you get the kind of insider knowledge only a local could tell you. They take pride in getting all the details right, and in telling it how it is. Think you can do it? Find out how at **lonelyplanet.com**.

Behind the Scenes

THIS BOOK

This 3rd edition of *Belize* was written by Mara Vorhees, who coordinated the book, and Joshua Samuel Brown, who wrote the Belize District, Northern Belize and Southern Belize chapters. Dr Allen J Christenson wrote The Ancient Maya World chapter. The 2nd edition of *Belize* was written by John Noble and Susan Forsyth. The 1st edition was written by Carolyn Miller Carlstroem and Debra Miller. This guidebook was commissioned in Lonely Planet's Oakland office and produced by the following:

Commissioning Editors Catherine Craddock, Jay Cooke
Coordinating Editor Erin Richards
Coordinating Cartographer Csanad Csutoros
Coordinating Layout Designer Carlos Solarte
Managing Editor Geoff Howard
Managing Cartographer Alison Lyall
Managing Layout Designer Adam McCrow
Assisting Editors Michelle Bennett, Evan Jones, Robyn Loughnane
Assisting Cartographers Corey Hutchison, Joanne Luke, Andy Rojas, Andrew Smith
Cover Designer Pepi Bluck
Color Designer Carlos Solarte
Project Managers Fabrice Rocher, Craig Kilburn
Language Content Coordinator Quentin Frayne

Thanks to Liz Abbott, Yvonne Bischofberger, Lisa Knights, Jelena Milosevic, Katy Murenu

THANKS
MARA VORHEES

Many thanks to my team at LP – to Cat, for sending me to work in the tropics and reminding me why I signed up to be a travel writer, and to Josh, for his endless enthusiasm and constant communication; I owe you both a Belikin beer. Many, many people helped me in Belize, most of whom I don't even know their names. So I'll just say *Aarait* and I owe you a Belikin, too. Finally, to Jerz, for introducing me to Belize almost 15 years ago, for accompanying me this time around, and for sharing my love of the Life Aquatic – no wonder we were meant to be.

JOSHUA SAMUEL BROWN

Many, many thanks to Christopher Nesbitt, his wife, Dawn, and their amazing children at Maya Mountain Research Farm. In addition to acting as both driver and cultural liaison for the research period of Belize 3, Christopher also provided my wife, Laurie, and I with a most amazing and (mostly) scorpion-free place to stay for the duration. Thanks also to the folks who helped me out along the way, especially Vitalino Reyes in Corozal, Bart Harmsen in Cockscomb and David Gobeil in Dangriga. Special

---

THE LONELY PLANET STORY

Fresh from an epic journey across Europe, Asia and Australia in 1972, Tony and Maureen Wheeler sat at their kitchen table stapling together notes. The first Lonely Planet guidebook, *Across Asia on the Cheap,* was born.

Travellers snapped up the guides. Inspired by their success, the Wheelers began publishing books to Southeast Asia, India and beyond. Demand was prodigious, and the Wheelers expanded the business rapidly to keep up. Over the years, Lonely Planet extended its coverage to every country and into the virtual world via lonelyplanet.com and the Thorn Tree message board.

As Lonely Planet became a globally loved brand, Tony and Maureen received several offers for the company. But it wasn't until 2007 that they found a partner whom they trusted to remain true to the company's principles of travelling widely, treading lightly and giving sustainably. In October of that year, BBC Worldwide acquired a 75% share in the company, pledging to uphold Lonely Planet's commitment to independent travel, trustworthy advice and editorial independence.

Today, Lonely Planet has offices in Melbourne, London and Oakland, with over 500 staff members and 300 authors. Tony and Maureen are still actively involved with Lonely Planet. They're travelling more often than ever, and they're devoting their spare time to charitable projects. And the company is still driven by the philosophy of *Across Asia on the Cheap*: 'All you've got to do is decide to go and the hardest part is over. So go!'

shout-out to Rocky Racoon on Thatch Caye; sorry I never came back with the eggs, Rock.

OUR READERS

Many thanks to the travelers who used the last edition and wrote to us with helpful hints, useful advice and interesting anecdotes:

Janel August, Vicky Beauregard, L'Vannah Bielsker, Paul Boehlen, Rody Boonchouy, Scott Burrell, Alana Campbell, Sharon Collins, Susan Crawford, Rori Deleon, Renita Dellacca, Nathan Dhillon, Anne Dills, Sarah Dow, Brian Dunne, Mark Elbert, Wendy English, Roberto Ferrari, Dean & Kay Gardner, Sally Gilham, Ted Goulet, Rebecca Grant, Mirjam Grave, Phil Gross, Thilo Hackenberg, Michael Harn, Layton Holsinger, Kenneth Hoyt, Dieneke Huis in 't Veld, Sunny Hwang, Sam Jackson, Michelle Juneau, Brian Kemsley, Joanna Kirkpatrick, Pete Kolbenschlag, Nicole Lampsa, Todd Lang, Amaury Laporte, Martha Lee, Naara Leuenberger, Ann Llewellyn, James MacDonald, Pete MacDonald, Gabriella Malnati, Mark Manning, Greg McCullough, Jessica McGrath, Juliana Minak, Anna Monnelly, Steven Neuse, Nathalie Nguyen, Claudia Oliveira, Chris Pegan, Merl Peters, Therese Picado, Dora Rafael, Linda Reynolds, Andrew Reynolds, Gene Richards, Helwa Hassan Rosado, Garret Ryan, Heather Sceles, Joshua Sharman, Karen Snyder, Paul Soerensen, Tim Stevens, Sara Tamling, Brandon Tanguay, Jeff Tribbett, Danielle van 't Hooft, Cara Waters, Gabriele Webe, Martin Weinhold, Shona Welch, Ken Westmoreland, Andrea Williams, Paul Wilson, Helen Woolston, Shmuel Yablonsky, Sybille Zitzmann.

ACKNOWLEDGMENTS

Many thanks to the following for the use of their content:

Globe on title page ©Mountain High Maps 1993 Digital Wisdom, Inc.

Plant remedies on p63 reproduced with permission from *Rainforest Remedies: One Hundred Healing Herbs of Belize*, by Rosita Arvigo and Michael Balick, Lotus Press, a division of Lotus Brands, Inc., PO Box 325, Twin Lakes, WI 53181, USA, www.lotuspress .com ©1998 All Rights Reserved.

Internal photographs p5, p6 (#3) Mark Webster; p6 (# 5), p13 (#5) Luke Hunter; p7 (#1), p12 (#6), p13 (#3), pp14-15 (#6) Greg Johnston; p8 (#5) John Sones; p9 (#4) Tom Boyden; p10 (#7) David Sanger/ Alamy; p11 (#5) Danita Delimont/Alamy; p11 (#6), p15 (#5) John Elk III; p14 (#1) Tony Wheeler; p16 (#3) Robert Harding Picture Library Ltd/Alamy.

Index

GreenDex

It's not easy being green. But in Belize, an encouraging number of organizations, individuals and companies are making an effort. We define 'sustainability' in three ways:

■ Environmental: minimizes negative environmental impacts and, where possible, makes positive contributions.

■ Social/cultural: respects culture and traditions and fosters authentic interaction and greater understanding between travelers and hosts.

■ Economic: has financial benefits for the host community and operates on the principles of fair trade.

These are tall orders. The most important criterion for inclusion in the Lonely Planet GreenDex is recognizing one's environmental, social and economic impacts, ideally with a clearly stated eco-policy. Other criteria include involvement in the local community and culture; participation in local conservation efforts; production and/or utilization of local, organic foods; use of renewable energy sources; and effective recycling and waste management programs. Very few enterprises are environmentally perfect; but taking some steps – any steps – is crucial.

Belize does not have any sort of ecological certification program. In Guatemala, we have used the Green Deal *Certificación de Turismo Sostenible* as one indicator to guide our selection.

Our goal at Lonely Planet is to provide sustainable content, but this too is a continuous process. We know we don't yet have it 100% right. You can help by sending us feedback on our selection and by suggesting other enterprises for inclusion at www.lonelyplanet.com/feedback. For more information on traveling responsibly, see www.lonelyplanet.com/responsibletravel.

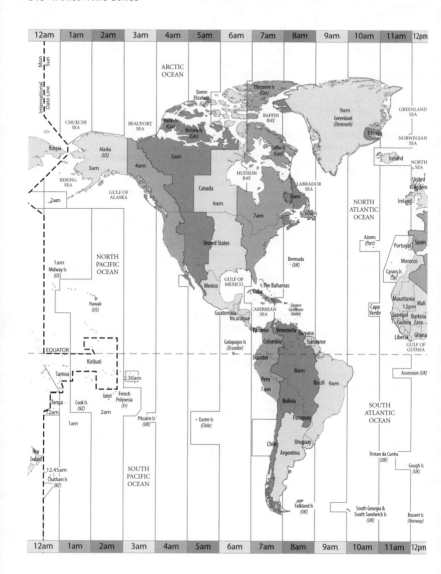

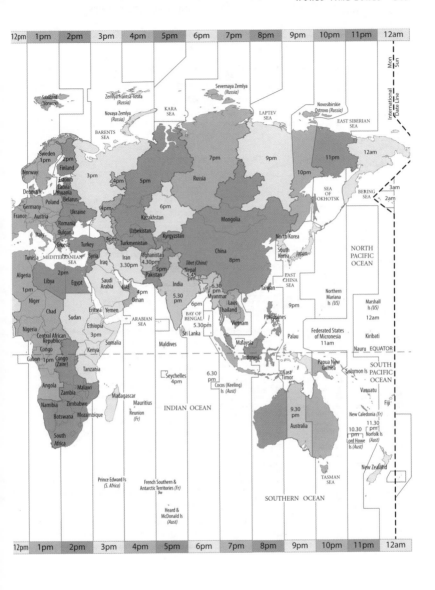

12pm 1pm 2pm 3pm 4pm 5pm 6pm 7pm 8pm 9pm 10pm 11pm 12am

Mon
Sun

International Date Line

Svalbard
(Norway)

Zemlya Frantsa-Iosifa
(Russia)

Severnaya Zemlya
(Russia)

Novaya Zemlya
(Russia)

KARA
SEA

LAPTEV
SEA

EAST SIBERIAN
SEA

Novosibirskie
Ostrova (Russia)

BARENTS
SEA

Sweden
1pm
2pm
Norway   Finland
3pm
Denmark Estonia
Germany Latvia
France   Lithuania
Austria   Belarus
Italy   Poland   Ukraine
Romania
Greece   Bulgaria
Tunisia   Turkey
MEDITERRANEAN
SEA
Algeria   Syria
Libya   Iraq   Iran   Afghanistan
Egypt   3.30pm   4.30pm
Niger   Pakistan   5pm
Chad   Saudi   5.45
Sudan   Arabia   pm
UAE   India
Oman

4pm
5pm
Russia
7pm
9pm
11pm
12am
10pm

3am
2am

SEA
OF
OKHOTSK

BERING
SEA

Kazakhstan
6pm
4pm
Uzbekistan
Turkmenistan
Kyrgyzstan
Mongolia

China
8pm

North Korea
South   Japan
Korea

NORTH
PACIFIC
OCEAN

EAST
CHINA
SEA

Taiwan

Northern
Mariana
Is (US)

Marshall
Is (US)
12am

Nepal
5.30pm
6pm
Myanmar   6.30
Laos   pm
Thailand

9pm

Federated States
of Micronesia
11am

Kiribati

Eritrea Yemen
ARABIAN
SEA
Ethiopia
3pm
Somalia

Nigeria
Central African
Republic
Congo
Gabon 1pm
Congo
(Zaire)
Kenya

Tanzania

Maldives

Sri Lanka
5.30pm
Vietnam
Malaysia

Palau

Nauru EQUATOR

SOUTH
PACIFIC
OCEAN

Indonesia

Philippines

Papua New
Guinea

Solomon Is

Angola   Malawi
Zambia
Namibia   Zimbabwe
Botswana Mozambique
South
Africa

Madagascar

Mauritius
Réunion
(Fr)

Seychelles
4pm

6.30
pm
Cocos (Keeling)
Is (Aust)

East
Timor

INDIAN OCEAN

9.30
pm
Australia

Vanuatu
Fiji

New Caledonia (Fr)
11.30
pm
10.30   Norfolk Is
pm   (Aust)
Lord Howe
Is (Aust)

New Zealand

Prince Edward Is
(S. Africa)

French Southern &
Antarctic Territories (Fr)

Heard &
McDonald Is
(Aust)

TASMAN
SEA

SOUTHERN OCEAN

12pm 1pm 2pm 3pm 4pm 5pm 6pm 7pm 8pm 9pm 10pm 11pm 12am

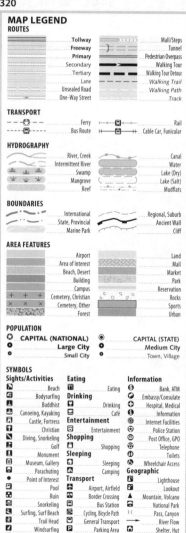

MAP LEGEND

ROUTES

Tollway			Mall/Steps
Freeway			Tunnel
Primary			Pedestrian Overpass
Secondary			Walking Tour
Tertiary			Walking Tour Detour
Lane			Walking Trail
Unsealed Road			Walking Path
One-Way Street			Track

TRANSPORT

Ferry			Rail
Bus Route			Cable Car, Funicular

HYDROGRAPHY

River, Creek			Canal
Intermittent River			Water
Swamp			Lake (Dry)
Mangrove			Lake (Salt)
Reef			Mudflats

BOUNDARIES

International			Regional, Suburb
State, Provincial			Ancient Wall
Marine Park			Cliff

AREA FEATURES

Airport			Land
Area of Interest			Mall
Beach, Desert			Market
Building			Park
Campus			Reservation
Cemetery, Christian			Rocks
Cemetery, Other			Sports
Forest			Urban

POPULATION

○ CAPITAL (NATIONAL)		◉	CAPITAL (STATE)
● Large City		●	Medium City
○ Small City		○	Town, Village

SYMBOLS

Sights/Activities	Eating	Information
Beach	Eating	Bank, ATM
Bodysurfing	**Drinking**	Embassy/Consulate
Buddhist	Drinking	Hospital, Medical
Canoeing, Kayaking	Café	Information
Castle, Fortress	**Entertainment**	Internet Facilities
Christian	Entertainment	Police Station
Diving, Snorkeling	**Shopping**	Post Office, GPO
Golf	Shopping	Telephone
Monument	**Sleeping**	Toilets
Museum, Gallery	Sleeping	Wheelchair Access
Parachuting	Camping	**Geographic**
Point of Interest	**Transport**	Lighthouse
Pool	Airport, Airfield	Lookout
Ruin	Border Crossing	Mountain, Volcano
Snorkeling	Bus Station	National Park
Surfing, Surf Beach	Cycling, Bicycle Path	Pass, Canyon
Trail Head	General Transport	River Flow
Windsurfing	Parking Area	Shelter, Hut
Winery, Vineyard	Petrol Station	Spot Height
Zoo, Wildlife Sanctuary	Taxi Rank	Waterfall

LONELY PLANET OFFICES

Australia
Head Office
Locked Bag 1, Footscray, Victoria 3011
☎ 03 8379 8000, fax 03 8379 8111
talk2us@lonelyplanet.com.au

USA
150 Linden St, Oakland, CA 94607
☎ 510 250 6400, toll free 800 275 8555
fax 510 893 8572
info@lonelyplanet.com

UK
2nd fl, 186 City Rd,
London EC1V 2NT
☎ 020 7106 2100, fax 020 7106 2101
go@lonelyplanet.co.uk

Published by Lonely Planet Publications Pty Ltd
ABN 36 005 607 983

© Lonely Planet Publications Pty Ltd 2008

© photographers as indicated 2008

Cover photograph: Statue of Christ on reef underwater, Ambergris Caye, Belize, Belize, Central America & the Caribbean, Mark Webster/ Lonely Planet Images. Many of the images in this guide are available for licensing from Lonely Planet Images: www.lonelyplanet images.com.

Printed by Hang Tai Printing Company.
Printed in China.